THE BUILT ENVIRONMENT

Creative Inquiry Into Design and Planning

Tom J. Bartuska
Gerald L. Young

CRISP PUBLICATIONS, INC.
Menlo Park, California

THE BUILT ENVIRONMENT
Creative Inquiry Into Design and Planning

Tom J. Bartuska
Gerald L. Young

CREDITS:
Editor: **Tom J. Bartuska/Gerald L. Young**
Typesetter: **ExecuStaff**
Cover Design: **Barbara Ravizza**

Printed in the United States of America by Bawden Printing Company.

Library of Congress Cataloging-in-Publication Data

Bartuska, Tom J.
The built environment / Tom J. Bartuska, Gerald L. Young.
p. cm.
Includes bibliographical references and index.
ISBN 1-56052-187-2
1. Architectural design. 2. Design I. Young, Gerald L.
II. Title.
NA2750.B35 1994
720′.47—dc20

93-43047
CIP

Preface

The "built environment" is a challenging subject. It is pervasive and relevant to all that live in the human-made or arranged world—to all who live on this planet. A healthy built environment makes significant contributions to human life—it fulfills human needs and values, extends and increases comfort and enjoyment. A quality environment can foster a sense of involvement and pride. An environment created without supportive qualities can have a very negative effect on people, causing decreased abilities to learn and perform work. An unhealthy built environment breeds high levels of apathy, crime, vandalism and mental disease. The character and quality of the built environment is dependent on everyone. It is important for all members to be aware, involved and responsible. All of us are an influential part of the on-going story of the built environment.

The use of the term "built environment" is relatively new, but has become increasingly more accepted in contemporary society. In reality, the built environment is as old as the beginning of time, dating back to when humans first fashioned stone tools, created fire for warmth, and modified caves for shelter. The term embodies all human creation.

The primary purpose of this book is to explore and clarify the many interrelated aspects of the built environment and to recognize that design (and other) problems overlap many fields of interest and study. This need to integrate across traditional specialized boundaries is expressed not only in student and faculty interest, but also in professional and societal concerns found in contemporary literature and mandated by state and federal policies. This work is dedicated to the elimination of apathy and, conversely, is intended to encourage people to become aware and involved in the life supportive qualities of the built environment. Awareness and involvement are important prerequisites for all responsible citizens. The book attempts to develop an interdisciplinary forum for collaborative study of the built environment. It encourages involvement from people of all disciplines to enter into study of the built world in which we all live, work and play. It demonstrates the importance of collaborative effort in dealing with complex subjects in a unified and holistic framework.

The genesis of this particular collaborative investigation began at Washington State University in 1973. A graduate-level, special topics course in Environmental Science was first offered in 1974 to explore and develop the related interdisciplinary aspects of the built environment. The course met with considerable enthusiasm from a diverse group of students and faculty. This effort evolved into the development of another experimental and temporary course for undergraduate students in 1977. The same positive results occurred and in 1979 the course achieved permanent status as an interdisciplinary, team-taught course in Architecture/Interior Design/Landscape Architecture. In 1984, it was approved as a class which fulfills General University Requirements for graduation.

Early on, our collaborative group carried out an exhaustive search for appropriate books for this new study. We determined that libraries were full of definitive references on each component of the built environment, but few addressed the important overlapping aspects of the humanly created world. None existed which were appropriate in scope and integrative enough in concept to be useful to our work. Consequently, we decided to create this integrative inquiry into the design and planning of the built environment. The extensive work of all participating authors, their integrative chapters and their searches through the literature to find the best resources are deeply appreciated and have made a significant contribution to this on-going work.

We, the editors, would like to personally express our sincere appreciation to the many past participants, who have collaborated to evolve the book into its present form. The editors, Gerald Young and Tom Bartuska are the only remaining participants from the 1973 initiating endeavor. The collaboration between Ecology (Environmental Science) and environmental design has been an important interdisciplinary thread with a unifying influence on this work. A challenging, but compatible, relationship exists between Environmental Science, which deals primarily with the "Natural" but human impacted environment, and this study, which focuses on the "Built" or human created world.

A special thanks is extended to the years of "202" students—who have provided constant feedback through their interest and encouragement, and their concerns and complaints—challenging us to do a better job.

The hidden, but extensive work of Sandra Tyacke, Sharon Ledeman, and Phyllis Klapwyk needs recognition. They, with others, have been most helpful in typing and retyping a seemingly endless array of written drafts, outlines, references, letters and memos. Sandra Tyacke's remarkable patience and word processing skills have made this whole process run smoothly. We would also like to acknowledge Noel Moffett, Catherine Bicknell and Sarah Recken for their graphics and format design. Helen Bartuska and Bev Young have both patiently seen this volume through many drafts—and many hours and days "away." We thank them for that patience and for so many years of caring and help.

The graphics and illustrations are the responsibility of the authors of each chapter, unless otherwise noted. David Lim, Peter Wolfe, Karl Heitman, Janet Archer and Zulqaisar Hamidin, students of Architecture at Washington State University, have developed many of the diagrams and sketches. Their work is noted by their initials.

To all above contributors, we are deeply thankful.

Tom J. Bartuska and Gerald L. Young, Co-Editors,
Washington State University

Cover: Graphic design is by Sarah Recken and Jon Singleton, School of Architecture, Washington State University.

Contents

Introduction

Ian McHarg

Environments which bear no visible human marks are rare—the realms of ocean, the poles, deserts, mountain summits. There, human works are absent, but nonetheless, these environments have all relinquished the magic qualities of the term primeval. That most pervasive sphere, the envelope of gases that protects and sustains us, is now disturbed, tainted, and has corrupted the innocence of the last natural refugia.

The world is now the human created environment—a built environment.

As long as humans were puny in an implacable, all powerful nature, their works mattered little. They were only another predator limited by their prey, their works trivial, ephemeral incidents in the biosphere. Today, human works have global effect, often accomplished without thought or knowledge. It would be reasonable to assume them to be random, some harmful, some neutral, others beneficial, but not so, they seem to be selectively destructive. Who would have imagined global effects from aerosols, abandoned refrigerators? Who would have assumed that human acts could cause serious transformations to world climate, induced warming, sea level rise, disruption of the protective ozone layer? Can the mind adjust to the transformation of benign rain into a toxin threatening forests in North America and Europe?

Humans have, knowingly or not, accumulated powers to control and modify the environment, and, at last come to the realization that our impact is destructive to ourselves and to the systems upon which we depend. We have no recourse but to come to understand the way the world works and initiate behavior which will maintain the biosphere, enhance human health and well being. The built environment must reflect the intelligence of humans, not their ignorance—a belated conclusion, not widely understood, it awaits application and realization.

The view of the earth from the moon was a profound transformation. After centuries of observing the lunar procession from earth, the subject and object were reversed and we looked from moon to earth to perceive the lonely orb, the earth our home, blue-green from oceans, maritime algae, and terrestrial vegetation. The astronauts view this green layer, this celestial fruit and observe blemishes and lesions pocking the tissue. They and we must ask, are humans but a planetary disease? The answer is blunt, there is disease upon the earth, the lesions are the works of human beings. There are humans and institutions whose fulfillment involves the continuous infliction of disease and death on the world life body. It is intolerable.

Yet, can we possibly contemplate the role of world steward, understanding the operation of this vast system, planning human affairs in such a way as to perpetuate and enrich the biosphere including the human created built environment?

We can take heart from the realization of the past accomplishments and the current operations of simpler organisms. It is now widely accepted that the atmosphere, oceans and lands are the creation of life. The transformation of the lethal primeval atmosphere into the benign envelope that encompasses us was the work of simple microorganisms. Its regulation is largely their work today. It is believed that the evolution of the oceans, their salinity, temperature, pH, are a product of life. Without doubt, microorganisms, plants, later animals, colonized the earth, producing soils, modifying climate, the hydrologic cycle, creating habitats, successively making environments more fit for life.

There is one further analogue to give heart. One simple animal has accomplished greater environmental transformations, uniformly benign, than the sum of all human works in all of human time. The coral polyp with its photosynthetic associates, has transformed vast oceanic deserts, incorporating calcium carbonate and silicate into their beings to create among the richest environments of the world, habitat for incredibly diverse and stable ecosystems.

So, modifying environments is not unnatural. Indeed, it seems to be critical to evolution. Nor were these transformations trivial. So we can accept that modifying the environment and creating a built environment to accommodate human life is perfectly natural and appropriate. But, there is a caveat. The transformations described enhanced the environment for its inhabitants. But there were and will be costs and benefits.

So we can assume that people have reason to undertake the role of consciously manipulating the environment, to make it more fitting for all life, including humans. We have already demonstrated that we can dispose great powers of destruction, why not reverse this power for better creation?

Darwin stated that the surviving organism is fit for the environment. Lawrence J. Henderson augmented this proposition. The world includes a multiplicity of organisms and environments. It is necessary for all organisms to find the fittest available environment, adapt it, and oneself to accomplish better fitness. Implied, but not explicit, was the definition of a fit environment as one in which the consumer found the maximum requirements on any given site, where the least work of adaptation need be undertaken.

In the beginnings of the century, Henderson observed that the oceans exhibited self regulation and thus a responsiveness, a term usually reserved for life. In 1969, moved by Henderson's arguments on "The Fitness of the Environment," I wrote that if Henderson's description of organic fitted the oceans, why not then the atmosphere.

This inquiry was developed brilliantly by the English chemist, James Lovelock, who advanced the Gaia Hypothesis, which, simply stated, suggested that we best consider the earth, its inert and living systems, as a single superorganism. As humans are comprised of many organs, tissues, billions of cells, and include water, sundry gases, calcium, acting as a single integrated organism, so too the earth, rocks, oceans, soils, microorganisms, plants, animals seem to interact coherently as a unitary system.

Lovelock then investigated the matter of the regulating system—did this require a god-like creator? His conclusions were to the contrary, thermostatic devices widely used by living systems would be perfectly adequate. To establish this point, Lovelock invented Daisyworld with light and dark flowers, higher and lower reflectance. Preponderance of the former reduced temperature, the latter increased it. If each has a selective temperature range, increasing or decreasing in numbers would create a natural thermostatic device which would regulate temperatures.

Evidence to support the hypothesis is only preliminary but quite positive, and certainly provocative. I can imagine no greater challenge to science than to investigate the Gaia Hypothesis. Should it be proven conclusively the results could be dramatic. The most immediate would be the necessity for a holistic view and the relegation of reductionism to contributor rather than final product. All parts must be seen as agents in the whole. I suspect that economics would be the next arena of change. If the Gaia Hypothesis is true, and the bulk of the world's work in regulating atmosphere, oceans, temperature and terrestrial ecosystems is performed by microorganisms it becomes necessary to identify them, their roles and to give them value. Perversely, natural areas may well assume inordinate value, highly urbanized areas may well incur significant global costs.

Philosophy and theology would also be subject to revision. How many prayers have been issued from people asking for interventions, prevention of flood, drought, earthquakes, volcanos, hurricanes, pestilence, pleas for good harvests of livestock, game, grains, and fish. What effect they have had we will never know. What change will occur when it becomes clear that many of these matters have been and are regulated by Gaia? Apparently, the rapid increase of carbon dioxide by humans may not only induce world warming, but also exacerbate violent climatic, hydrological and terrestrial events. We are bringing violence upon ourselves. Can we reduce it? So the agents who could respond to prayers will be creatures and processes among us. How do we view these powerful god-like creatures, how do we negotiate, collaborate? We may remain ignorant of cosmic God but encounter a more modest planetary god. This requires a new stewardship—a new theology and philosophy advancing sustainability. Clearly, biology will be affected, no longer plants and animals categorized into taxonomic lists, even ecosystems or biosphere are too limiting. Thc Gaia hypothesis integrates inert and living systems into a biological whole. The challenge to biology is not traditional geochemical cycles but the geobiological processes which comprise Gaia.

In my own realm of planning and design—that which leads directly to a human created built environment—a transformation is necessary. Given a world system with elaborate self-regulating processes, the human role is first to understand these and thereafter engage in conscious modifications for human use which are not destructive of the critical processes. We must evaluate our creations in terms of their contribution to world processes which must be maintained. These environments can then be evaluated to ascertain their tolerance or intolerance to prospective modification. Planning and design must then include responses to global and regional contributions to Gaia, be responsive and expressive to world, region, place and people.

This brings us back to the astronauts' view of the earth, a blue-green celestial fruit on which lesions are visible. The fundamental role for humanity is to contribute to the health of the planet, the earth, our home, to heal disease, to engage in modifications to enhance the global environment, among which none may be more important than the built environment.

Until the advent of the Industrial Revolution the built environment world wide instituted small scale and local interventions into the natural environment of little damage to world ecology. Since then the scale has changed dramatically. Megacities including Calcutta, San Paolo, Mexico City exceed all world urbanism prior to the 19th century. The human capability of environmental transformations has moved from little consequence to global threat.

While the prospect is frightening, history is reassuring. For most of human history, modifying the environment, including city building, has been appropriate to natural systems, responsive in materials and forms, of limited scale, and generally humane. One should not overlook epidemics, floods, earthquakes or oppression, slavery, feudalism, war, but these events are not necessarily a direct consequence of built form. It appears that there are human and technological factors which are identified with successful societal accomplishments. There have been vernacular adaptations in the built environment which are exemplary. In addition there has developed an extensive body of knowledge on the environment which is fundamental to human health and understanding that permits planning and design based upon objective principles—it is challenges such as these that are addressed in this book on the built environment.

PART I

Definition, Design and Development of the Built Environment

CHAPTER

1

The Built Environment: Definition and Scope

Tom J. Bartuska and Gerald L. Young

We all build. We design and build our lives from one experience to another. In a similar way, components of the built environment are created from human needs, thoughts and actions. Sometimes, the substance of human action is grand, and we build quality life experiences for ourselves and others. Other times, human actions are short-sighted, creating uncomfortable situations that are less fit for healthy human activities.

There are as many reasons to design and build as there are objects constructed. Each aspect of the built environment is constructed to fulfill human purpose. Where you are sitting reading this page, you are surrounded by hundreds of constructed objects. These are all contributing components of your "built environment." The words on this page, this book, your chair or desk, the nearby stereo, the phone that connects you to many others throughout the world, even the walls, floor and ceiling of the space that forms your enclosure, are humanly made or arranged, and therefore part of the built environment. Look further afield and observe the environment out of the windows. The buildings, automobiles, roads, bridges, your landscaped garden or yard, and the surrounding city are also part of a human-made or arranged built environment. The environments beyond the city, the parcels of agricultural land, the highways and other transport and utility systems, can also be included. Even state, national, and global organizations are created by people and are an important part of this extensive built environment.

The components of the artificially created world surround us in abundance. It might be harder to find environments that are "natural"—not made or arranged, maintained or controlled by people or society. The sky, weather, free-flowing rivers and streams, wilderness areas seem, for the most part, not "built," but "natural." But, even these are not totally free from human intervention and pollution.

The accumulative results of the changes people have made on the environment are extensive. A large percentage of humanity lives in urban metropolitan areas. These massive urban and suburban developments are the largest, most complex human systems ever created. Equally extensive are the modifications that have occurred in the rural areas of the world: farmlands, domestication of animals, forest and wildlife management programs, damming of major rivers for power, navigation, and flood control.

The built environment fills every nook and cranny of your everyday world. It strongly influences human lifestyles and those lifestyles influence it.

In the most basic sense, people first constructed tools, fire and shelter to survive in the wilderness. Once survival needs were satisfied, people continued to mediate the environment to make life safer, more comfortable and productive.

Although times have changed and populations have grown, the basic reasons for creating a built environment remain essentially the same. We construct tools and products, modify and manipulate space, build structures and cities, and manage regions to make life safe and comfortable, more enjoyable and productive for ourselves as well as for future generations.

When studying interrelated aspects of the built environment we must ask ourselves important questions. Humans have made extensive changes in the environment to satisfy needs and wants, but how often do we consider the consequences of these

1. The built environment: A pervasive and evasive, double-exposure of a city—Chicago, Illinois.

actions—especially the total and long-term consequences? Do we take an equally extensive responsibility for the actions or changes involved? Are we concerned about the overall effect these actions have upon neighbors or upon the earth, its finite resources and delicate ecological systems?

The primary purpose of this book is to develop an understanding of the things we build, how they are created and how they affect human lives. Through an increased involvement and awareness of the design of the built environment, more of those designs may influence our lives in a positive, contributing way. Quality tends to encourage more quality, more personal enjoyment, enrichment and involvement. Poor quality creates apathy and has negative impacts on human health and well-being. Personal interest, sensitivity and understanding are needed to fully appreciate its positive and negative characteristics.

Since the built environment is manifested in physical things, it is relatively easy to observe and study. It is critical for the reader to participate, to visualize and to experience real environments. This involvement can easily be achieved by experiencing and analyzing the many examples that exist in your local environment, home and community, as well as throughout the surrounding region, country and world. The text will encourage your participation and try to increase your interest, sensitivity and ability to analyze various aspects of the built environment. Get involved! Your active participation is necessary and will increase your learning experience, enjoyment and success.

A working knowledge of the built environment is vital for all responsible citizens. Such knowledge allows a citizen—the reader of this book—to be aware of and search out positive aspects of the built environment. Better understanding enables citizens to be more effective in taking corrective measures to eliminate or change the negative aspects. The best environments are created when we all work together in a cooperative way. All the pieces of the built puzzle are better if they are designed to fit together. We all insist upon quality in individual private environments, yet we tend to fall short of collectively insisting on comparable quality in the public realm. Individual and collective actions will greatly affect our lives and the lives of our children (and their children). It is urgent to realize that we are all interdependent participants in the building process; we all can effect positive change. Citizens and politicians, bankers and lawyers, engineers and planners, scientists and humanists are all indispensable and influential parts in the design and management of a quality environment for all.

DEFINITION AND SCOPE OF THE BUILT ENVIRONMENT

In order to become effective in our pursuit of knowledge, we need to first establish the essential elements of a working definition of this evasive and pervasive term—"The Built Environment." In its simplest terms, the built environment is defined by the following four interrelated characteristics: First, it is extensive; it is everywhere; it provides the context for all human endeavors. More specifically, it is everything humanly created, modified or constructed; humanly made, arranged or maintained. Second, it is developed to fulfill human purpose—to satisfy human needs, wants and values. Third, it is developed to protect us from the overall environment, to mediate or change this environment for our comfort and well being. Last, an obvious but often forgotten characteristic is that human actions affect their surroundings; changes in turn change the context, and either contribute to or impact the environmental setting or context.

The simple, but inclusive, diagram below is intended to help visualize and define the built environment and describe the interrelationships of these characteristics:

The Built Environment

The Built Environment is everything humanly made, arranged or maintained;

to fulfill human purpose (needs, wants and values);

to mediate the overall environment;

with results that affect the environmental context.

The built environment has been commonly referred to as the man-made and woman-arranged environment (or vice versa). Although these terms are used in past literature, the authors of this book attempt to use inclusive language (gender-neutral terms), asserting the obvious, that both men and women have made substantial contributions to the creative process. The term "Built Environment" is considered more inclusive, and it is becoming a more accepted term in contemporary literature.

COMPONENTS OF THE BUILT ENVIRONMENT

Understanding of any subject is increased if it can be subdivided and organized into its related parts. To aid comprehension of the variety and scope of the built environment, its diverse content needs to be organized into component parts. The sum of all the interrelated components defines the "scope" of the total built environment. The components selected for this investigation are listed and described below.

1. Products

Materials and products; generally created to extend human capacity to perform specific tasks: tools (pen and pencil, hammer and saw, peace pipe or weapon); graphic symbols (signs; letters form words, then sentences combine into books); materials (bricks and mortar, wood, concrete and steel, etc.); machines (radios and stereos, televisions and telecommunication systems, calculators and computers, combs and hair dryers, roller skates and automobiles, buses and spaceships, etc.).

2. Interiors

A space defined by an arranged grouping of products and within the walls of a structure; generally created to enhance activities and mediate external factors (living room, work rooms, private rooms, public assembly halls, stadiums, etc.).

3. Structures

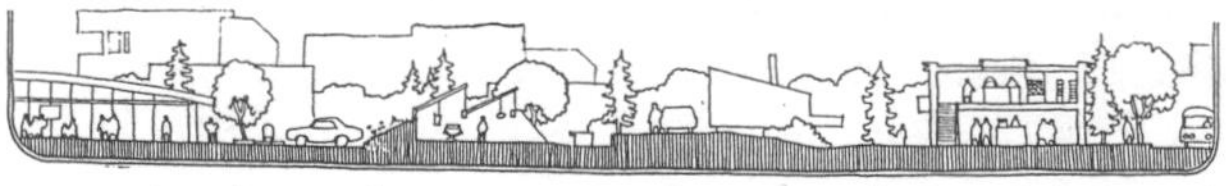

A planned grouping of spaces defined by and constructed of products; generally combining related activities into composite structures (housing, schools, office buildings, churches, factories, etc.; highways, tunnels, bridges, dams, etc.). Generally, structures have a dual internal space and external form characteristic.

4. Landscapes

Exterior spaces and/or settings for planned groupings of structures and spaces (courtyards, malls, parks; landscapes, sites for homes or other structures; farms, countryside, national forests, etc.). Landscapes generally combine both natural and built environments.

5. Cities

Grouping of structures and landscapes of varying sizes and complexities; generally clustered together to define a community for economic, social, cultural and/or environmental reasons (subdivisions, neighborhoods, villages or towns and cities of varying sizes, etc.).

6. Regions

Groupings of cities and landscapes of various sizes and complexities; generally defined by common political, social, economic and/or environmental characteristics (the surrounding region of a city, a county or multicounty area, a state or multistate area, a country, continent, etc.).

7. Earth

All of the above, the groupings of regions consisting of cities, landscapes, etc.—our beautiful planet earth.

These components can be better understood as connected "layers" or "levels" of varying scales interwoven together to form the built environment. This layering concept is illustrated in the following diagram or logo.

These layers or components provide the organizing categories for this book. They will be expanded upon and illustrated in the seven component sections (see Table of Contents). The listing and description of the seven components illustrate a significant overall theme—the interrelationships of each component to each of the others. The content of each component is made from a combination of smaller components. In turn, each component is a part of more complex components. This content-component-context hierarchy is the tool used in this book for organizing and studying the parts and wholes of complex subjects—the complexity and interrelatedness of the built environment.

The interrelationships are also an important aspect to the formulation of the built environment and require a great deal of understanding, forethought and planning. In our age of specialization, we have lost sight of the interrelationships among the components of the built environment as well as among people who participate in the building processes. More times than not, product designers only talk to their own colleagues, engineers only talk to engineers, planners only talk to planners,

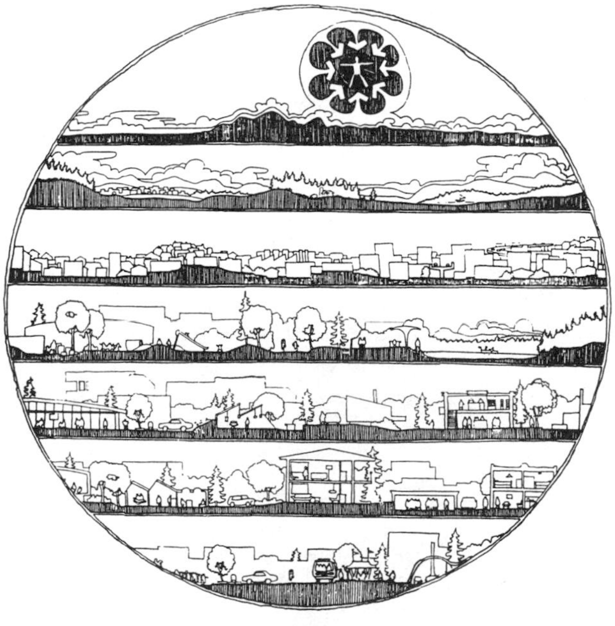

2. The layers of the built environment. *("The Built Environment," composite symbol design by S. Recken; linear graphic formats by J. Singleton).*

etc. In this situation, activities become fragmented; we do not establish common ties that bind us together and integrate the content of the built environment. This lack of integration can result in a fragmented and chaotic environment. We all suffer the consequences.

The term "Built Environment" is an interrelated concept formed from the designed integration of many components. It refers to the totality of all that humans have changed or rearranged within the natural environment. Understanding this is the first step towards recognizing the interdependencies, not only between the many artificially created objects, but also between people, their professions and many individual areas of study. Bringing the design and planning disciplines closer together is another primary objective of this book.

Only you can judge your prior knowledge of the term "Built Environment." In general, it is a comparatively new term describing, in one holistic and integrated concept, the by-products of all human activities throughout history. In fact, most of society's knowledge of past civilizations is derived from remnants of the built environment. Similarly, our civilization can or will be judged by what we have created.

Two general reasons can be identified as to why the term "Built Environment" has been slow to come into general use. First, integrated information on the environment (natural and built) is a relatively new societal interest. Literature on the natural environment and on the science of ecology, although a relatively old discipline, has only been popularized since the late 1960s and early 1970s. Through the "Environmental Movement," ecology and the natural environment have become household words, and an abundance of information has emerged to increase environmental awareness. Much of this literature includes the argument that the natural environment is holistic and integrated, that one cannot understand the whole by studying only isolated components. Similarly, the term "Built Environment" has also emerged from increased understanding of the total environment. It is also based on a holistic and integrated concept and on the premise that one must understand the whole as well as the component parts. Significant problems occur when a part is isolated without understanding its interrelationships to other parts and the parts to the whole. Second, like the natural environment, the built environment is a vast subject. Libraries are full of information on each component (products, interiors, structures, landscapes, cities, regions, Earth). Although the word is becoming more accepted, only a scant literature deals with the totality or the integrative characteristics of the built environment.

In the present era of specialization, vast subjects are subdivided into categories and then subcategories to make them easier to study, comprehend and manage. The divisions are artificially created for convenience and, as models, do not represent environmental reality. Within these convenient subdivisions, disciplines of study are formed, library resources are organized, monetary budgets are programmed and separate academic departments and buildings are created. From this pattern, vocations and professions are formed (product and interior designers, artists, architects, landscape architects, city and regional planners, etc.), which work within a limited sphere, perpetuate fragmented actions and result in a chaotic built environment.

Fortunately, there is more and more evidence of the need for collaboration; increased numbers of people in various fields are combining talents and forming interdisciplinary teams. There is, however, significant room for continued improvement. Societal and governmental pressures are encouraging more integration. National, state and many local environmental policy acts mandate interdisciplinary analysis of complex problems. These changes have emerged from the heightened environmental consciousness of the 1970s, and are re-emerging in the 1990s.

The sciences, traditionally organized in a taxonomy of separate disciplines, are sharing their understanding of the environment through renewed awareness of ecology and its study of the interactions of organisms and their environments. Concurrently, the applied disciplines (i.e., the design and planning fields)—which have also traditionally organized into separate disciplines—are combining into a general field of **environmental design** and increasingly carrying out collaborative studies on the built environment. R. F. Reekie (1972), an English planner, architect, educator and author of one of the first books on the built environment, emphasizes this need for interdisciplinary collaboration:

> [We all should] intelligently participate in the urgent task of abolishing ugliness, dreariness, squalor and also offensiveness from towns, villages and countryside, and in restoring and producing visual pleasure in the environment, so that life can be lived therein more healthily and happily. . . .

> One of the points made in this book is that environmental design, now and in the future, is and will be a matter of expert team-work supported by public appreciation and participation.

Reekie concludes that "integration" is a key word in the creation of a quality-built environment:

> Integration may well be the key-word in good design. Not only does it mean the correct combining of parts into a whole, but it implies, by association with integrity, soundness and honesty.

WHY HUMANS BUILD

The definition of the built environment can also provide some initial steps toward understanding "why humans build." We build to mediate the overall environment in order to fulfill human purpose—to satisfy human needs, wants and values. An eloquent English Prime Minister, Sir Winston Churchill, expressed this relationship very forcefully: "We shape our buildings and then they shape us." Another noted historian, A. Cortell, conveys this same interdependency by claiming, "tell me the landscape you grew up in and I will tell you about yourself." There is a clear "cause and effect" relationship between human purpose and the things we create. To aid in understanding this relationship, it is useful to explore more specifically the nature of human needs, wants and values.

3. Why do humans build? Czechoslovakian Exhibition at the World Expo, Montreal, Canada.

Human Needs and Wants as Manifested in the Built Environment

To survive, all organisms must satisfy certain basic needs. *Homo sapiens*, human beings, are no exception. All humans have the same **basic needs**. Abraham Maslow (1971), a psychologist, postulated a now well known "hierarchy of human needs." At the base of the hierarchy are those needs that are most fundamental, those needs that must be satisfied before any human being can focus attention on the next level. The most basic set of needs Maslow calls physiological—those needed for proper functioning of the body and mind. His theory is that we humans will begin to be concerned about the next level only after first essentials are somewhat assured. Then, and only then, will we turn attention to those "needs" not strictly essential to body function and survival. The same transition is theorized at each level of the hierarchy: humans will (according to Maslow) only be concerned with security needs after physiological needs have been satisfied. If security is assured, then we turn attention to higher needs, such as that for belonging to a group or the need for self-actualization. These are generally referred to as psychological needs. Figure 4 identifies the general types of physical or psychological/social needs (on the left), the hierarchy of six levels of human needs (in the center) and (on the right) the way these needs are expressed in the built environment. Many of the examples extend into more than one category.

Beyond the realm of needs is that of wants—things that are not really needed at any level, but that emerge from personal or psychological desires for self-gratification. For example, we biologically "need" food and water, but instead of beans and rice we want gourmet foods. We need efficient transportation systems, but we "want" a car; we may even need a car in the context in which we live, but we want a newer, bigger or faster car. Needs and wants both, when satisfied, result in the use of material and energy resources in the creation and use of the design components of the built environment. Fulfilling needs is generally more basic than wants. Recognizing the differences will help to establish or reorder priorities in order to minimize costs, to reduce the use of finite resources and to mediate impacts on the environment. The hierarchy is somewhat abstract, the theory even more so; but we do tend to organize and prioritize our desires in such a fashion. And, we

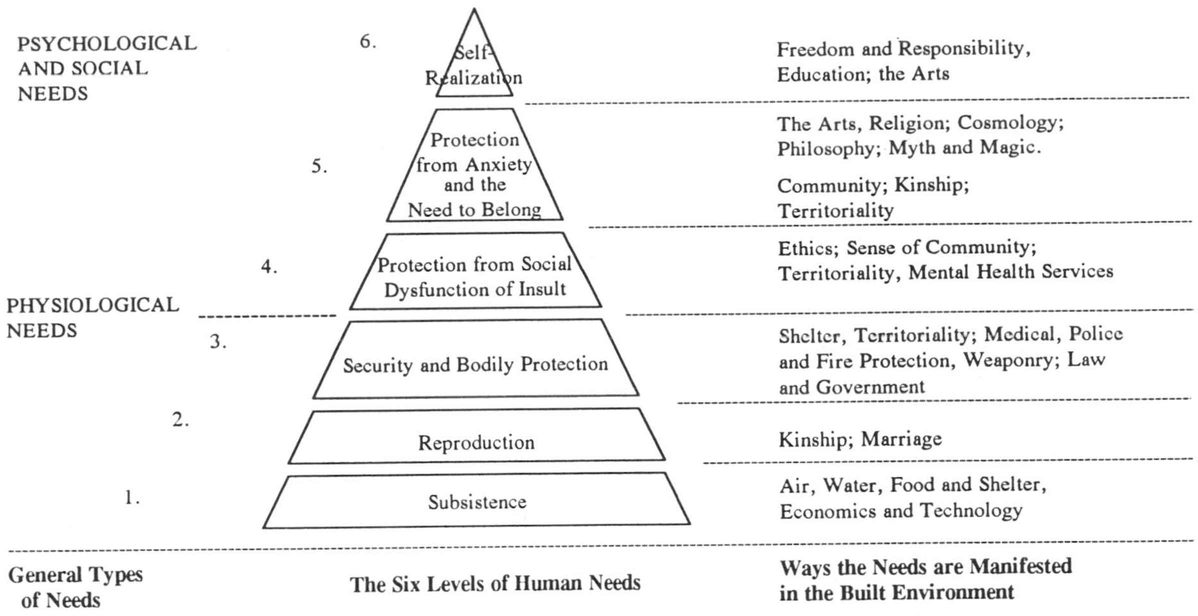

4. Human needs and various ways they are manifested in the built environment.

should also know that many societal differences throughout the world are based upon the needs hierarchy. We would be naive to believe that the millions suffering from malnutrition (or actual starvation) in the world are very much concerned with the ego-gratification gained from a louder stereo or bigger car.

For every need, there must be an adaptive response, an adaptive design strategy. For every want, we adopt a response. The need is satisfied (by every organism) through exploitation of the environment. Humans do this collectively and, since needs are similar and recur, they are quite predictable through every life span, every culture and in each succeeding generation. In humans, this adaptive response is institutionalized; it is organized, formalized and regularized. For subsistence needs, every culture develops an economic response, an institutionalized economic system of some kind to provide healthy air, water, food and other survival needs. It seems obvious, but often forgotten, that the most fundamental needs are air, water and food. One can only live a few minutes without air, a few days without water and a few weeks without food. These are the fundamental building blocks of life on earth and they must be protected from harmful substances throughout the world. To satisfy reproductive needs, every culture develops kinship systems, including (in our culture and many others) the institution of marriage. For bodily protection, we have developed various systems of micro-environmental control: clothing and shelter, the medical professions, even weaponry. To protect ourselves from social dysfunction, we have developed law and politics, and for protection against anxiety, we have developed the varied institutions that deal with science, technology, religion and various systems of cosmology (myth, philosophy, etc.). Every society has such institutions in some form; it is the way societies have elaborated these institutions that make them different. Much of that elaboration is expressed in the various created forms in the "built environment." Subsistence/physiological needs are a general way of saying we have to eat, drink, and breathe and that we must provide ourselves with shelter and clothing. Food is gained through agriculture, and a field of corn or wheat is an artifact created, at least in part, by human endeavor. The field of grain is an artifact of the built environment, as is the grain itself, usually a highly developed hybrid far removed from its origins in a wild plant. And all the other elaborations necessary to modern agriculture (implements, fertilizers, pesticides, machines, etc.) are also created by humans and are artifacts in the built environment. Subsistence and the agricultural response serve as an example, but the same could be said for all other responses to needs and wants; each is reflected (in various and subtle ways) in the artifacts, objects, structures and patterns that we create to satisfy human desires, and that collectively adapts or changes nature into the now pervasive built environment.

Human Values as Manifested in the Built Environment

The built environment emerges not only from attempts to fulfill personal and societal needs and wants, but also reflects personal and collective values. Human values are a bit more abstract than "needs," but a general understanding of their relationship to human activities can aid our understanding of the many attitudes people have about the built environment. These value-formed attitudes manifest themselves in the way we relate to the environment, the way people solve problems and consequently are expressed in the intrinsic characteristics of the built environment. Human values are subjective—they deal with beliefs, opinions and attitudes. They influence the setting of priorities. They are analogous to the "value" or price we are willing to pay for something. In objective terms, one can deal in a monetary measure, but many things are difficult or impossible to measure in economic terms. For example, how can beauty, quality, freedom or equality, really be "measured"? These are things of subjective value.

Values affect subjective attitudes and many of these are expressed in the built environment. For example, people from the United States are very individualistic. The individual house on its own site is an important value. The same is true of transportation: We have developed the world's most extensive auto-oriented systems. Individual values tend to blind us to other alternatives. So far, we have been willing to pay the high costs in taxes and energy of the sprawling land-use patterns that result from such individualistic values. Other countries judge such patterns as wasteful and antisocial. In general, people in the United States have beautiful homes but ugly cities, both the result of setting more individualized priorities. Cities express private corporations and commercial interests—the most expensive and tallest buildings dominating contemporary skylines are banks, insurance companies and large investment firms. Some cities in other countries are dominated by public places and spaces, some by government structures, others by cathedrals.

Human values fundamentally affect one's perception of the built environment. Values color our awareness of problems and the way we approach potential solutions. Values are like an overriding screen, an invisible determinant that directly affects the character and quality of the built environment. Despite this, there is little conscious effort to deal with human values openly and directly.

Many suggest that they should not be addressed, that they are too subjective, that a person's values are private. Others suggest that they are at the heart of the design professions' contribution to society: "In architectural education, any judgment without human values is meaningless. . . . If we want

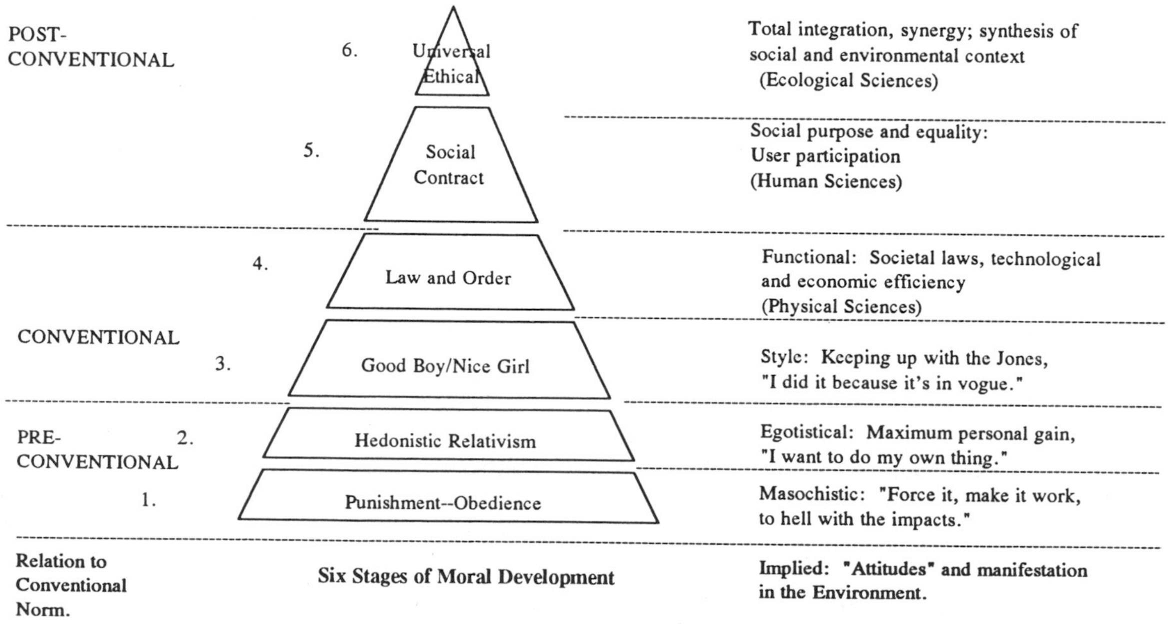

5. Human values/levels of moral development and the various ways they are manifested in the built environment.

a better place for all people, we are going to have to develop a clear philosophy of life, which recognizes the relationship of human values" (Peters, 1981). Regardless of the view adopted, study of personal and collective values can help develop a fuller understanding of the world.

Social workers and psychologists are finding personal values an effective key to communication. They have come to understand that they must relate to human value systems to fully understand human concerns and problems, to really communicate and find effective solutions. They find it equally important not to make "value" judgments about people. A defensive position generally causes hard feelings, gaps in understanding and breakdowns in communication. "Many of the communication difficulties between persons are the by-products of communication barriers within the person. . . . For this reason, the study of the innards of the personality is one necessary base for the understanding of what a person can communicate to the world, and what the world is able to communicate" to him/her (Maslow, 1971). E. F. Schumacher (1973), author of *Small is Beautiful,* also suggests a much more central role for the study of human values: "The task of education would be, first and foremost, the transmission of ideas of value, of what to do with our lives. There is no doubt also the need to transmit know-how, but this must take a second place. . . . More education can help us only if it produces more wisdom. . . . The essence of education, I suggest, is the transmission of values."

Lawrence Kohlberg, extending the work of Jean Piaget, gives clarity and utility to the understanding of various human values. Through his research, Kohlberg has constructed a useful scale of six levels of moral development based upon a cognitive development theory (Lickona, 1972; Wrightsman, 1972; Lazer, 1975). The value scale is illustrated in Figure 12. Each level is referenced to what are considered conventional norms (on the left). The Piaget/Kohlberg model is one way to begin to understand the implications of human values and the varying attitudes they form. The Kohlberg/Piaget "human value hierarchy" (in the middle) is similar to the human needs scale. The implied attitudes formed are also included (on the right).

In very general terms, human values affect philosophy and how we set priorities or solve problems, be it individualistic or based upon a popular style, functional or based upon humanistic and/or total integration of all concerns. It should be noted and emphasized that the "conventional" area is the general operational level of society. It is an arena of societal interaction, of checks and balances, of law and economics. To be successful, everybody needs to understand this level well and operate in it effectively. But, it is not the only value system, nor is it the most inclusive. It must not (as it can) limit our full exploration of theoretical and applied work. Through the understanding of this value scale, we can more effectively understand different sides on issues or arguments among people. More times than not, they are based upon different value-formed attitudes. Knowing this allows us to interpret the many differences in the way humans interact with the built environment.

ORGANIZATION OF THE BOOK

The built environment is a complex and challenging subject. The study of any topic is enriched by the quality of its presentation and the clarity of its organization. As the preface indicates, a great deal of collaborative experience and interdisciplinary thought has gone into the development of this book. It is useful to understand the book's overall structure before the reader gets immersed (and hopefully not lost) in the more detailed content of each component part. The basic organization ties the subject together as it holds the book together. The book is organized in the following four basic sections.

I. Introduction, Definition, Design and Development of the Built Environment: The first chapter in this section discusses the purpose, definition and scope of the topic. The second chapter explores its evasive and pervasive developments and its symbolic meaning. It establishes four general traditions that are expressed in the evolution of the built environment.

II. Central Design Issues: Human-Environmental Relationships: In the most basic sense, the book deals with the integration of what is usually considered a dual topic—people and environment. All people are immersed in both natural and built environments. This section explores essential aspects of this human-environmental relationship. The human part is the people who are involved as citizens, users and creators of the built environment.

The environmental part has two dimensions—natural and built. The hyphen between "human" and "environment" emphasizes interrelationship developed by humans. They are adaptive design strategies that provide the substance for human life, which, in turn, is the substance for this book.

The first chapter of this section explores the complexity, definition and organization of the word environment. The second more fully addresses quantitative and qualitative dimensions of the built environment. The next two chapters study the human part of this dual relation. How people perceive and participate in the built environment is discussed in the third chapter. How people attempt to order its diverse and multidimensional qualities is addressed in the final chapter.

III. Design Components in the Built Environment: The third section, the largest, unravels the built environment into seven selected components. Each component is considered as a separate topic or level which needs to be integrated with the others to form the overall content of the built environment.

This section explores in greater detail the dual human and environmental aspects of each component. More specifically, it defines each component, explores its precedent (its historic developments) and progress by including a study of contemporary design issues and challenges. Although these seven components must be considered as integrated together, individual readers may elect to concentrate on one or more of the following dual human and environmental topics:

1. Products .... & .... Product/Graphic/Industrial Designers
2. Interiors......... & .... Interior Designers
3. Structures...... & ...... Architects and Engineers
4. Landscapes.... & .... Landscape Architects and Planners
5. Cities............ & .... Urban Designers and Planners
6. Regions .... & ....Regional Planners
7. Earth .... & ..... Environmental Scientists, National and Global Planners and Policymakers

IV. A Conspectus on the Built Environment: The fourth section offers the reader a brief concluding perspective—one which hopefully will foster further insight and increase involvement toward resolving the challenges raised by the authors of the book—challenges for a quality built environment for all, for a better future for all.

The intent of this book is to construct an interest in and awareness of the built environment. Its purpose is to open a series of doors that invite a more thorough understanding of this complex, yet fascinating subject. The reader is continually encouraged to further investigate the concepts and components of the built environment. Newspapers, magazines and libraries are full of interesting reading material. Most chapters conclude with a list of references to encourage further investigation and study. The everyday local environment offers an abundance of opportunities to observe and experience built ideas in reality.

REFERENCES

Akbar, J. 1988. *Crisis in the Built Environment: The Case of the Muslim City*, Concept Media.

Bartuska, T. J. 1981. "Values, Architecture and Context: The Emergence of an Ecological Approach to Architecture and the Built Environment." ACSA Proceedings.

Jakle, J. A., and Wilson, D. 1992. *Derelict Landscapes: The Wasting of America's Built Environment*, Rowman & Littlefield.

Knox, P., (Editor), 1988. *The Design Professions and the Built Environment*, Croom Helm.

Lazer, A. (Publisher/Editor) 1975. *Psychology Today:* An Introduction, 3rd Edition. CRM Random House.

Lickona, T., Editor. 1972. *Moral Development and Behavior: Theory, Research and Social Issues*. Holt, Rinehart and Winston.

Maslow, A. 1971. *The Farther Reaches of Human Nature*. Viking.

Peters, R., "The Call for Papers" for the 1981 Meetings, ACSA News.

Reekie, R. F. 1972. *Design in the Built Environment*. Edward Arnold.

Short, J. R., Fleming, S., and Witt, S. J. G., 1986. *Housebuilding, Planning, and Community Action: The Production and Negotiation of the Built Environment*. Routledge & Kegan Paul.

Wrightsman, L. S. 1972. *Social Psychology in the Seventies*. Brooks/Cole.

CHAPTER

2

Four Traditions in the Built Environment

Henry Matthews

A close examination of the surface of the planet earth will reveal very few places that have not been radically changed by human intervention. Only a few remote areas of wilderness have escaped such modification. In densely populated or intensively farmed regions, the landscape is essentially human made.

City dwellers may go out into the countryside and feel that they are experiencing nature; what they see however, is a natural world under human control, very different from the landscape that would have developed if *Homo-sapiens* had never emerged to take charge. We have harnessed natural processes for our own advantage and suppressed others that do not suit us. We have used backbreaking labor for countless generations to reshape the land for our use and more recently employed vast machines to speed up such tasks. When we talk about the built environment, we are referring to something a great deal broader than the environment defined by buildings, for we have built around us a world controlled by our own systems. We have transformed it with systems of irrigation and flood control, systems of communication and transportation, systems of land management, of agriculture and human settlement, and systems of defense. Although many animals build complex and wonderful shelters for themselves, the human race has distinguished itself by building on a vast scale and by building more than is necessary for survival.

The beaver may dam streams and build lodges on artificial islands; the weaverbird may construct its elaborate nest of leaves, grasses and hair actually woven together; ants may engineer fantastic vertical structures, teeming with highly organized life, but the human animal has created an endless variety of products, structures, and settlements which adapt to widely different circumstances, indulging (often wildly) in original expression and unique design ideas. Centuries after they were made, we can study human artifacts and buildings and see in them evidence of the beliefs, fears and obsessions of their makers. They not only provide shelter and tools for survival, but also act as symbols of ideals and aspirations.

1. Systems of water supply and defense dominate a landscape. Arghyrokastro, Albania (*E. Lear, 1848*).

Human endeavors in the built environment have been governed by two distinct traditions, which have existed side by side since the beginnings of civilization. Each tradition can be identified and understood by its own unique priorities and design principles. The two historic ones will be called the **vernacular** and the **high style** traditions. The first has served ordinary people in their daily lives; the second has belonged to the elite, to governments, religious cults and institutions. Its purpose is often ceremonial rather than practical. In recent times, two other traditions have developed—the **speculative** and **participatory** traditions.

THE VERNACULAR TRADITION

The first artifacts and human shelters were made of materials found close at hand. Through a long process of trial and experimentation, designs were developed to serve the users as efficiently as possible. They were shaped according to their purpose, and their form changed only if a refinement in design or a new approach made a significant improvement in their performance. They followed the principles of a vernacular tradition, which links the present with a distant past. Early forms of tools and shelter provide excellent examples of human ingenuity and resourcefulness within this tradition. They show how locally available materials could be exploited to make sound dwellings, well adapted to site and climate and pleasing to the eye.

For example, in the fertile river valleys of the Tigris and Euphrates in Mesopotamia, considered by western historians as the cradle of civilization, two materials proved outstandingly successful and are still used today much as they were six thousand years ago. Mud was moulded into blocks, dried in the sun as bricks and used as a strong and stable walling material. Reeds were bound together into bundles to make columns and woven into mats of varying density as wall panels or roofs. Where light was to be admitted, the reeds were formed into decorative openwork screens. Using local mud or reeds, there was no need to buy or "import" materials or to deplete nonrenewable resources. From our Western standpoint, we might feel that dwellings of mud or reeds are bound to be inferior to our own homes, which are the product of a highly industrialized society. Yet, we would be astonished by the quality of space, the care taken in construction, the strong simplicity of form often found in such houses proudly built by their own inhabitants. We might also be impressed by their natural methods of adaptation to climate. The mud bricks are ideal for a desert climate. The heavy walls have high thermal capacity and absorb heat during the day and cool off by slowly transferring solar heat to the interior at night. The lighter reed dwellings allow the necessary ventilation in humid marsh areas and provide comfortable living conditions.

Another determinant of vernacular traditions is the way of life of the people. Obviously, fisherfolk have different needs from farmers, and animal herders have different patterns of settlement from those who raise crops. Nomadic peoples have developed highly specialized portable buildings which they can carry with them. An example is the yurts of the nomads living in the area between Eastern Turkey and Mongolia, which collapse for transportation on horseback. It is also interesting to note that some of the finest carpets are made by nomadic people who cannot carry much furniture. Easily unrolled and laid out on the ground, they bring immeasurable richness to otherwise simple homes. In a desert environment, a woven rug can even symbolize a garden of richly colored flowers.

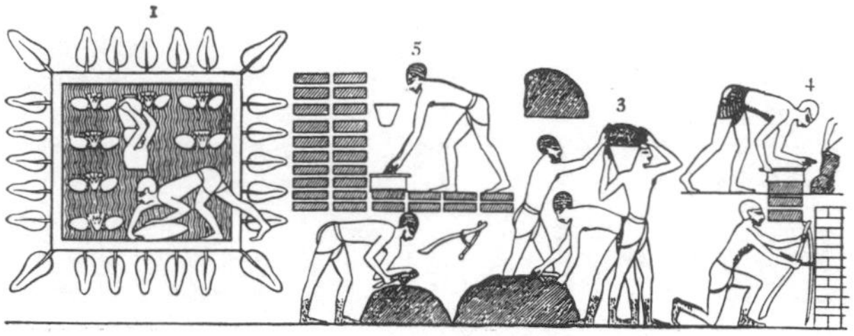

2. Ancient Egyptians making bricks. The same method is used in many places today.

3. A dwelling of the Marsh Arabs of Iraq. Such buildings consume no nonrenewable resources, yet serve their purpose well (*W. Thesinger*).

4. The yurt is ideally adapted to the way of life of nomads in Mongolia. It collapses for easy transportation, yet provides good protection in a harsh climate.

Similarly, throughout the world, building types have emerged that solve the particular housing problems of different cultures in a wide range of climatic zones. The longhouses of the Northwest Coast Indians, the Tipis of nomadic plains Indians, the stone cottages of Cotswold villages in England, log houses in Finland, adobe houses in the southwest of the United States, all belong to strong vernacular traditions in domestic building which have lasted into the twentieth century.

5. Cliff dwellings of the Anasazi Indians at Mesa Verde, Colorado.

The availability of materials has also governed the manufacture of common artifacts. A container for storage fashioned by its owner for daily use may be made in the Arctic of whale bone and sealskin; in Europe of hardwood; in Southeast Asia of woven palm leaves. In Africa, a calabash will serve the same purpose and elsewhere it may be made of pottery or wrought iron. In each place, a traditional method of manufacture is passed down from generation to generation.

Throughout the regions of the world, the exploitation and conservation of the land is controlled by conventional wisdom, often superior to modern methods. What people attempt depends on the opportunities they have and the problems they must solve. Holland was formed out of uninhabitable salt marshes by the building of dikes and the pumping away of water by windmills. Ancient Egypt was made fertile by the digging of irrigation canals to distribute the waters of the Nile at its annual flooding. Vast areas of Asia retain the waters of the monsoon rains in their rice paddies, while in more arid places, whole hillsides are terraced to contain

6. African women carrying calabashes, the dried skins of gourd-like plants (*D. Hill*).

precious soil behind stone walls. In Provence in southern France, carefully planted windbreaks protect spring vegetables destined for the Parisian markets from the icy winds that might spoil them. In England, hedges divide up the fields, prevent wind erosion and create an aesthetic patchwork pattern

7. Terraced fields in Nuristan, a northeastern region of Afghanistan. Generations of hard labor have made a mountainside productive (*T. Bartuska*).

in the landscape. Within the vernacular tradition, farmers have generally worked in harmony with nature and paid attention to the conservation of vital resources. They have known only too well that quick ways of obtaining higher yields make little sense in the long run.

Often agriculture and buildings go hand in hand. In Southern Italy, in and around the town of Alberobello, dwellings known as trulli are built of the stones cleared from previously infertile fields. In this limestone region, the upper layers of stone have been broken up by centuries of changing weather. The farmers have used the largest blocks of stone to build the walls of their houses and the thin, naturally split stones to form their roofs. Rougher stones have sufficed for boundary walls and the remaining rubble and gravel has been put back over the solid beds of impervious limestone. Then the topsoil is replaced over the gravel beds. The result is that the winter rain is stored among the small stones and with such a reservoir below it, the sparse topsoil nourishes good crops. Among the fields stand amazing clusters of trulli, conical structures unique to the area, a testament to human creativity.

8. Trulli near Alberobello, southern Italy. Built of stone quarried on the land where they stand.

Although vernacular traditions can be explained in terms of their response to material needs and practical opportunities, these factors alone cannot explain the rich variety of form. Many types of artifacts and dwellings and their details can only be understood as symbols of diverse cultures. Ritual and ceremony have been of great importance in determining the organization and design of buildings. The value systems and social hierarchies of the owners are often clearly expressed. For example, in many African villages, the design of a family compound will clearly show how many wives the head of the family has, the status of children, and whether cattle are more important than grain.

Sometimes the forms of dwellings can only be explained by tracing them to an earlier phase in the history of the group now inhabiting them. House types can survive even though prevailing conditions change. An outstanding example of such survival is the kiva, the ceremonial space of the Anasazi Indians of Colorado and New Mexico. The origin of this subterranean space is to be found in the ancient dwellings of Siberia. There, the sunken pit with central hearth, covered with a thick insulated layer of turf over a wooden roof, was a response to a hostile climate. The original inhabitants of the North American continent migrated from that region over the Bering Straits, bringing building traditions with them. As they moved south and found ways to build appropriate to new conditions,

9. The kiva, the ceremonial space, of the Anasazi Indians, Mesa Verde, Colorado. Originally covered and provided with a central fire pit, it closely resembled the Siberian pit dwelling.

they might well have abandoned their former type of dwelling. However, at such places as Mesa Verde and Chaco Canyon in the southwest of the United States, where they built with stone walls above ground, the subterranean space still survives. But it is no longer a dwelling. It is a purely ceremonial space, still centered around the fire. The fire is provided with an elaborate air intake and draft deflector system, surely a reminder of the time when fire was the key to survival.

The brief examples given provide an insight into the workings of vernacular traditions. Further study will probably demonstrate that they conform to certain general rules or design strategies, which distinguish them from the high style tradition:

1. Vernacular building and crafts are the province of ordinary people. The builders or makers are generally the owners, or specialists within the immediate community.
2. Materials used are found close at hand and therefore designs have strong local or regional character.
3. Designs are utilitarian. They are made for their purpose, fitting to proven functional patterns.
4. Building and village design is well adapted to climate, solving problems by the use of natural systems.
5. Changes in design are slow to develop. Craftspeople are conservative and prefer to make use of the experience of previous generations. The quality of work is sound and capable but often rough and unrefined.
6. Cultural symbolism, ceremony, and ritual also play a part as influences in design. Sometimes practical needs are overruled by the desire for symbolic elements.

HIGH STYLE TRADITION

From the beginnings of civilization, certain individuals have emerged as leaders and have exerted power over others. Whether they excelled in hunting and battle or gained power through wisdom or magic and ritual, they have sought to distinguish themselves from the ordinary people. To do so, they have needed to wear rich and unique clothing, to create luxurious palaces, forbidding citadels, and awe-inspiring temples, furnished with rare and precious objects. They have summoned the best artisans, imported the finest materials they could obtain anywhere, resulting in many rich designs in the high style tradition.

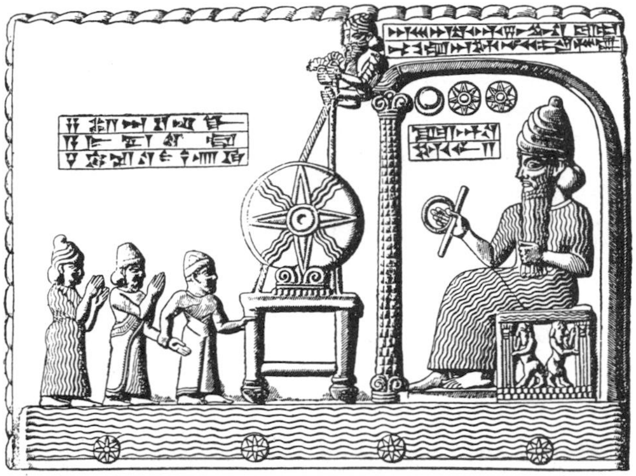

10. Worship of the Babylonian Sun God in a richly designed temple (*From a stone tablet, 900 B.C.*).

At least five thousand years ago, in many parts of the world, tribal leaders demanded unique structures that rose above the local vernacular dwellings in scale, in strength and in artistic richness. Their expert builders experimented with new materials and new engineering skills. They created forms never seen before with lavish decorative interiors. Their aim was to invoke awe in those who saw them and to give protection and pleasure to those who owned them. The human desire for high-style design has continued ever since. While vernacular traditions provided buildings suitable for villages and the edges of towns, the growth of cities promoted the development of high style. Both despotic rulers and democratic governments have employed skilled designers to create urban spaces that express civic pride and convey a sense of order.

As in vernacular design, change in high-style design was often slow. A successful form might survive for many generations. The forms that lasted often arose originally from vernacular designs, but in refined ways and were perceived as powerful symbols. However, a radical change might take place, not for any utilitarian reason but as the result of a new religious philosophy or a new aesthetic impulse. In the vernacular tradition, it is rare for foreign ideas to be imported; for conservatism will turn people against rapid change. But, in the high style, originality is admired. It seems to be a mark of superiority to reject the style of the last generation and adopt a new style or one borrowed from elsewhere. The following examples may give an insight into the workings of the high-style tradition.

The Pharaoh Zoser, who ruled over a united Egypt early in the third millennium B.C., built a great temple tomb for himself, to preserve his body and soul for eternity. It was first constructed in the conventional way as a low structure in which material goods were stored over the grave. However, the architect, Imhotep, breaking with tradition, conceived a radically new design of unprecedented splendor. He enlarged it into a stepped pyramid 200 feet high, perhaps symbolizing a stairway to the heavens. Around this, in a 35-acre enclosure, he built a necropolis, or city of the dead, made up of stone replicas of palaces, shrines, government buildings and store-houses to serve the dead king to eternity. Such buildings for the living had normally been of mud bricks and reeds; so Imhotep imitated the texture of reeds in stone. The columns of the entrance hall symbolized bundles of reeds; other columns were adorned with capitals based on the flower heads of lotus and papyrus that once decorated reed houses. Deep underground by the tomb chamber, stone panels faced with lapis lazuli, a rich blue stone, were carved with the texture of reed matting. Such ornament, carved with the utmost confidence and precision, celebrated traditional building techniques in a totally original way.

11. The temple tomb of the Pharaoh Zoser c. 2750 B.C. A symbolic structure designed for the eternal afterlife of the powerful ruler (*J. Lauer*).

12. Stone columns designed to resemble the bundles of reeds used in traditional Egyptian structures (*J. Lauer*).

Stonehenge, in southwest England, follows none of the normal rules for vernacular building. Far from being useful for human shelter or agriculture, the monument appears to have had symbolic meaning as a great astronomical computer. The materials were imported at the cost of enormous human labor. Eighty-two of the stone blocks, weighing up to four tons each, were brought 240 miles from Wales and it has been argued that those in charge of the building may have come from the Mediterranean. Similar feats of art and engineering have been achieved in many places around the world.

Nothing could exemplify better the human search for architectural excellence than the Greek temple. This building type evolved gradually from the simple hut constructed of wooden posts and beams to the high point reached in the fifth century B.C., when the Parthenon was built in Athens. For the sake of permanence, the material used was

13. Stonehenge, Salisbury Plain, England. This structure demonstrates the human will to overcome obstacles to build religious or symbolic structures (*T. Bartuska*).

changed from wood to stone; but in the same way that Zoser's tomb contained details of reed buildings, the Parthenon retains symbols of wood construction in solid stone. Each part of the temple seems to express its purpose through the refinement of its form. Columns clearly carry loads, beams span between supports, the pediment proclaims the function of the roof. Decoration subtly emphasizes form as in the fluting of the columns or is kept to nonstructural elements, such as the panels of the frieze which were carved with scenes from mythology. Like the Parthenon, Greek temples were often built in dominant positions high above cities. Their beautyand permanence demonstrated their importance and they were often revered by people from far beyond their own regions.

15. The First Temple of Hera (sixth century B.C.), Paestum, Italy and in the background the Second Temple of Hera (early fifth century B.C.). The proportions were refined as the style developed.

14. The Parthenon, Athens (mid-fifth century B.C.). The Doric temple perfected (*T. Bartuska*).

Although almost all Greek temples follow the same traditional design scheme, each one has its own personality. Their designers responded subtly to the character of each site and constantly strove to refine the details. The Parthenon of Athens can be compared with the earlier Temples of Hera at Paestum in which the proportions are cruder. In the earlier temples, the columns seem to taper too sharply and the capitals spread too far. We are able to make this kind of judgment because we are familiar with the perfected version and can appreciate its refinement.

The Greek temple was also adopted by the Romans, with certain alterations, as the model for their temples. Through their imperialist efforts, the Romans spread this essentially Greek design throughout the civilized world of their time. So potent was the Greek temple as a symbol of beauty, order and permanence that its use has been revived many times. For example, in the late eighteenth century, Thomas Jefferson, one of the signatories of the Declaration of Independence and the third president of the United States, proposed a design for the new state Capitol at Richmond, Virginia. Jefferson was a practical man, an ingenious inventor, and a fine amateur architect. He had travelled widely and while serving as American Ambassador in France, he had seen the Roman Temple at Nimes, known as the 'Maison Carree.' He admired this building ardently. In his own words, he "gazed on it as a lover gazes upon his mistress." So perfect was the design in his eyes that he built the Virginia State Capitol as a close copy of it. Although the purpose of his building was to be a democratic place of assembly, not a temple, the form appealed to Jefferson as an example to show the people of the United States what architecture should be. Many generations since have endorsed Jefferson's ideas by building residences, banks, churches, and several other building types to similar designs.

The Romans also discovered the potential of vaulting in stone and built many large-scale vaulted interior spaces. They had plenty of slaves to carry heavy materials and were able to solve structural problems by sheer mass. To ensure that the importance of their structures was perceived, they decorated their surfaces with columns like those of the temple. Thus, the column became something other than a support. It was now a symbol expressing power and beauty.

16. The Virginia State Capitol designed by Thomas Jefferson in 1748, based on the Maison Carree, a Roman temple in France.

17. A Roman vaulted structure. Massive walls support the vault which spans a broad interior space.

Roman vaulted spaces were the direct ancestors of another amazing architectural type, the Gothic cathedral. The medieval masons took over the principles of vaulting practiced by the Romans, but redefined structural design to the point where a minimum amount of stone was used. A gradual evolution had taken place in the Romanesque period, but in the twelfth century, master masons responded to a visionary idea. They set their sights on the almost unattainable objective of producing an image of heaven on earth made of stone and glass. Amiens Cathedral, which represents the high point of French Gothic, is made of no other materials. Looking up into the vaults, one cannot believe that thousands of tons of stone can be made to appear so weightless. This astonishing achievement was only made possible by the daring ingenuity of the masons. Using the flying buttress, the pointed arch, and the ribbed vault, the weight of stone was carried clear of the building and huge areas of wall could be opened up to stained glass windows. The purely decorative columns of Roman architecture had disappeared and structure was honestly expressed. The design through which a dream was realized became a celebration of structure and space.

The middle ages, which produced the Gothic Cathedral, has been described as an age of faith. In the fifteenth and sixteenth centuries, a more secular

18. Amiens Cathedral, France, 1220. The dynamic structure of pointed arches, ribbed vaults and flying buttresses makes it possible to open up the walls to huge stained glass windows (*Viollet-le-Duc*).

19. Amiens Cathedral. The vault consisting of thousands of tons of stone appears almost weightless. The interior is flooded with light.

age followed—known as the Renaissance—in which artists, architects and their patrons tried to revive the architecture of ancient Rome. Of course, they adapted their borrowed forms to suit their own society, but their theorists developed strict rules governing the correct use of the "orders" of Roman architecture.

Since artists rarely accept rules for long, the Renaissance style was challenged in the seventeenth century by the baroque with its more expressive and dynamic approach to painting, architecture, interior design and landscape. Other styles followed: the sober Georgian of the eighteenth century, the Greek and Gothic revivals in the nineteenth, and a variety of experimental movements at the turn of the century. Styles, like fashions, followed so fast, one upon the other, that it seemed as if style was more important than purpose.

In the early twentieth century, a modern movement developed in which designers of all disciplines rebelled against the continued revival of historic styles and the excessive use of "period" decoration. They honestly believed that, by using new technology, they could rise above the concept of style to solve human problems with truly functional buildings and products.

Modern office towers and multifamily housing as well as government and community buildings were built worldwide on an unprecedented scale. But the users of such buildings were often alienated by them. Lacking the human scale and the texture of local materials and details, such buildings tended to ignore local traditions and ways of life.

20. Crown Hall, Illinois Institute of Technology, Mies van der Rohe, Architect, 1950–1956. Although radically modern, the architect's preoccupation with structure, space, proportion and detail is similar to that of the Greek temple or Gothic cathedral.

The most prestigious examples of modern architecture can be seen as works of art, or as brilliant essays in the use of new technology to enclose space with clearly articulated structural systems. However, many ambitious housing projects have now been condemned as utopian failures because they were built with insufficient understanding of how families want to live. Corporate headquarters of shining glass have brought excitement to city skylines, but the plazas at their feet are often unappealing empty spaces or car parks. And it has often been found that the modern environment is not particularly functional. Glass walls, for example, proved wasteful of energy, gaining excessive heat from the sun in summer and losing unnecessary heat in the winter.

During the 1970s and 1980s, architects began to react against the principles of the modernists and returned to a richer architectural vocabulary. Many have tried to evoke the character of historic styles or regional types. They have attempted to be more

21. High-rise housing at Roehampton, near London, built in the 1950s.

responsive to the users and some have ascribed symbolic value to their work. At best, "Post Modern" buildings are sensitive to human needs, appropriate to their context and environmentally efficient. However, too many are simply modern structures dressed up in a decorative exterior with details borrowed arbitrarily from historic sources.

One aspect of high style design in the twentieth century has been the quest for originality. This has perhaps reached its peak in the Post-Modern era. The same phenomenon has also occurred in clothing, vehicles, advertising signs and many products designed to fulfill a seemingly insatiable desire for novelty. Unfortunately, the premium placed on originality is often a source of confusion and ugliness.

The high-style tradition applies equally in small objects and in treatment of the landscape. King Zoser and President Jefferson were both very particular about the objects they had around them;

22. Kimbell Art Museum, Fort Worth, Texas, 1968–72, Louis Kahn, Architect.

23. Office building, Boston, 1989, Philip Johnson, Architect. The Palladian windows, based crudely on the designs of the Italian architect Andrea Palladio, have little relationship to the context of twentieth century Boston.

their furnishings were in the latest style. The objects found in Egyptian tombs such as Zoser's have given us an idea of the superb quality achieved by ancient craftsmen and women. The modern world has also given scope to furniture and product designers who have made use of modern manufacturing processes to produce goods in innovative ways. For example, chairs, instead of being made out of jointed and glued wood, have been made of tubular steel. Although Jefferson was not a lover of extravagance and opulence, the contents of his house were elegantly designed and subtly decorated beyond necessity.

In ancient Egypt, the landscape around temples was carefully ordered for ritual purposes. Long causeways lined by sphinxes linked one temple with another. This was a sacred landscape separate from the surrounding fields. Centuries later Louis XIV, the absolute monarch who ruled France in the

24. A traditional wooden chair and a modern tubular steel chair serve the same purpose using different means.

seventeenth century, laid out the pleasure gardens of his palace at Versailles with ruthless axial symmetry. His design has been interpreted as a symbol of the Divine Right of Kings. In contrast, the English in the eighteenth century developed gardens

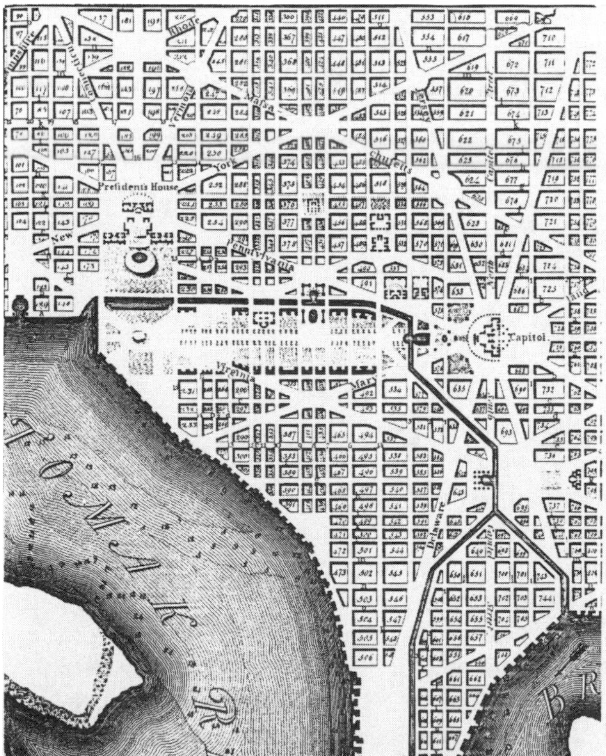

25. The Ellicott Plan for Washington, D.C., 1792. Formal, axial landscape design.

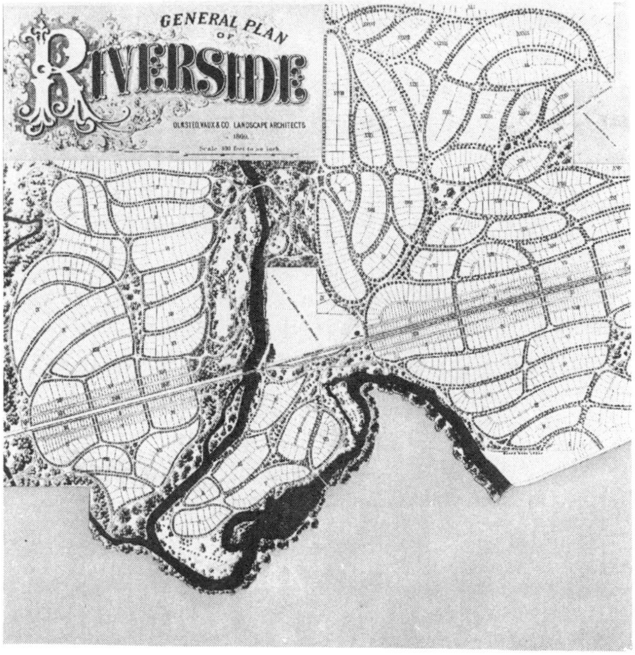

26. Riverside, Illinois. Plan by Olmsted, Vaux and Co., 1869. Planning in the picturesque manner.

that responded to the natural features of the landscape, and made a virtue of irregularity and organic curves, and exploited picturesque qualities.

The people of the United States have also gone to great efforts to control the landscape around important buildings. The Washington Mall linking the Capitol with the White House is an example of formal, axial planning in the classical tradition. The suburban community of Riverside, Illinois is also consciously planned, but it belongs to a romantic movement in landscape design. Frederick Law Olmstead, its designer, consciously avoided symmetry and formality and gave the neighborhoods a picturesque character. He made use of surprise as the forms of the landscape are gradually revealed on curving roads. Riverside is intended to simulate certain qualities of a "natural" rural landscape. Yet, it is a humanly-made landscape contrived in the high-style tradition, the creation of an artist who used trees, grass and water as the expressive materials.

In contrast to the vernacular tradition, the high-style tradition generally conforms to the following design strategies:

1. It is the property of the elite.
2. Designs are conceived and executed by skilled and artistic specialists, who are often brought a long way to carry out the work. The designer is

usually not the maker or builder, but the overseer of the work. The makers or builders are highly skilled artisans.
3. Materials are of high quality; if necessary, they are imported from far away. Rare and precious materials are frequently used.
4. Symbolism, decoration and refinement are often put before simple usefulness.
5. Designs often do not evolve primarily as a response to climate and site, but they may be adapted to suit the conditions.
6. National and regional character is developed, but designs from other cultures are often adopted to satisfy the desire for change or prestige.
7. Changes in design style occur regularly. Great importance is attached to originality.
8. The quality of work is of the highest standard.

27. Houses built in London during the Industrial Revolution (*G. Dore*).

THE SPECULATIVE TRADITION

In the eighteenth and nineteenth centuries, there was a large-scale migration of rural people to the cities. Population in the urban areas exploded. The old-fashioned ways by which people provided themselves with housing were no longer feasible, and speculative builders moved in to fill the gap. Their motive was financial profit rather than social advantage. Many fine residential districts were built by such developers, but throughout the industrializing world, housing units of minimum standard were built on street after street, block after block. In the country, the poor had undoubtedly suffered in appalling hovels. But in the city, they were no better off concentrated in horrifying slums. Even in the wealthier nations, the conditions generated during the industrial revolution have never been fully alleviated, and in some developing countries, the process of industrialization has only just begun. Since the mid-nineteenth century, many of the more affuent people have fled from the cities to the suburbs, giving further speculative scope to developers.

While the profit motive has often encouraged speculative builders to adopt high standards of design, they have generally put up what was easiest to build and have concentrated more on marketing housing units than on creating viable communities. Speculators have drawn something from vernacular and high-style traditions. There is often a simple logic and appropriateness in the houses they built, but they have also sought the superfluous trappings of elite architecture. In many cities, there are hundreds of small houses attempting to imitate the mansions of the wealthy without any regard to regional identity.

28. Speculatively built houses, Daly City, California, 1960s. The backs of another row of houses, behind, are absolutely plain.

As long as life was not too complex, vernacular traditions were always ready to guide the building endeavors of the human race. The high-style tradition has endowed cities and countryside with splendid monuments to wealth, power and creativity. But the speculative tradition has not very successfully fulfilled the remaining requirements. Uncontrolled private enterprise has not demonstrated sufficient thought for the needs of society or care of environmental resources.

Housing has sprawled over the countryside, often without proper provision of community services. Commercial strip developments have spread out along highways, providing easy access and parking for those with automobiles and cheap land for the developers, but at considerable cost in terms of social amenities. The result has been the wastage of agricultural land and the decline of city centers as well as the loss of regional identity and of the unique character of individual cities. Suburban sprawl has made excessive demands on water supplies and dramatically increased the use of gasoline.

Similarly, products of all kinds have proliferated in today's enterprising economy. In earlier times, a family would have few household objects, but those they possessed were useful and solidly made by hand to last a lifetime. Today factories around the world turn out countless products, many of them unnecessary, few of them very durable, and millions of dollars are spent on advertising to persuade people that they are needed. While industrialization has given us possessions that might have caused envy among our ancestors, it has also turned us into a wasteful society. We think nothing of throwing away things we have only had a short time. We are also discovering that the manufacture of certain goods we depend on produces dangerous by-products which poison the environment and endanger life on earth.

Modern agriculture is transforming the world in many ways. While miracles have been performed in bringing fertility to unproductive regions by irrigation and other means, there are also grave causes of concern. Where traditional farming techniques tended to maintain the productivity of the land by rotation of crops and the use of organic fertilizers, today's intensive "agribusiness" is often too concerned with short-term profits to think of long-term effects. For example, in the Amazon Basin, vast rain forests, essential to the production of oxygen for human survival, are being cut to make way for beef production even though the land will only be viable for pasture for a few years. In England, where fields were divided by hedges for centuries, their removal to make way for larger machinery has caused unprecedented soil erosion.

29. Urban sprawl, Alburquerque, New Mexico. While land lies vacant nearer the center of the city, new suburbs requiring an extended urban infrastructure proliferate.

The general characteristics of the speculative tradition, which has been a mixed blessing, are as follows:

1. The profit motive is the guiding force and marketability is the key.
2. Designs are rationalized to be cost effective and mass produced.
3. Instant appeal to the buyer is more important than durability.
4. There is a loss of local and regional character.
5. Social amenity and environmental effects are often not considered.

PARTICIPATION: THE FOURTH TRADITION AND THE FUTURE OF THE BUILT ENVIRONMENT

The building of sound communities has always needed the participation of their members. The most primitive tribes have made group decisions and built together for mutual benefit. Idealistic early settlers in Ancient Greece, South and North America and other regions of the world planned their towns democratically and worked together to realize them. But, as populations have grown and societies have become more complex, people have lost touch with the planning process. Democracy can provide mechanisms for public participation in planning and design, but most of us play no part in the massive building schemes that do so much to change our lives. Elected representatives and public officials have often failed to make the best decisions. In the last four decades, many cities in the United States have been subjected to more construction than ever before. Whole downtown areas have been demolished and rebuilt. New suburbs have proliferated; thousands of acres of good agricultural land have perished under asphalt and concrete. The largest single building program ever undertaken has been the construction of freeways in the United States since the 1956 planning act. Broad ribbons of concrete, sometimes meeting in complex intersections, have run across the countryside and through every major city in the nation. To

30. Interstate Freeway, Seattle. A broad ribbon of concrete dividing neighborhoods of a city.

31. Urban revitalization. A historic district in Denver, Colorado.

make way for these roadways, thousands of buildings and their neighborhood districts have been destroyed. Much of the finest building of the past is gone forever. Individuals, corporations, city, state and federal governments contrive to make decisions without fully understanding the implications.

The boom years between the 1950s and the 1980s were a period of unshakable belief in the future and in the need to sweep away familiar surroundings to make a more modern world. Through this process, we have discovered just how important our familiar environment is to us. Communities are made of human beings, and they thrive on ordinary social activity. The disruption of human groups and their activities, even to make way for dazzling new developments, has often been disastrous.

Today, as we approach the end of the century, we seem to appreciate once more the value of old traditions. Urban renewal is now often a much gentler process. The conservation of historic buildings, the careful insertion of appropriate new structures, and the renovation of entire neighborhoods is a goal in many cities where only a decade ago the bulldozer and the wrecking ball rampaged. The conservation movement has sprung from the grass roots of society to become a potent force reviving lost qualities in the built environment. While it began with the preservation of mansions and places associated with important figures from history, preservationists today are equally concerned with ordinary neighborhoods, the main streets of small towns and vernacular buildings.

An example of participatory planning on a large scale can be found in the city of Boston, where a vast elevated freeway divided the downtown commercial core from the water-front and other city neighborhoods. In 1992, the city, after a lengthy process of consultation, finalized a plan to relocate the freeway underground and to use the land, thus reclaimed, for parks, community facilities and appropriately designed commercial structures. When the project is fully realized, it will be equivalent to the healing of a dangerous and ugly wound on a human body.

Today we can still admire the grand and beautiful high-style designs commissioned by great leaders of the past. We can also appreciate the simplicity and appropriateness of vernacular builders. We are capable of rivaling their works with what we build ourselves, but often we accept mediocrity, leaving it to others to build for their own profit. If we are to attain a built environment which fulfills the aspirations and ideals of a democratic society,

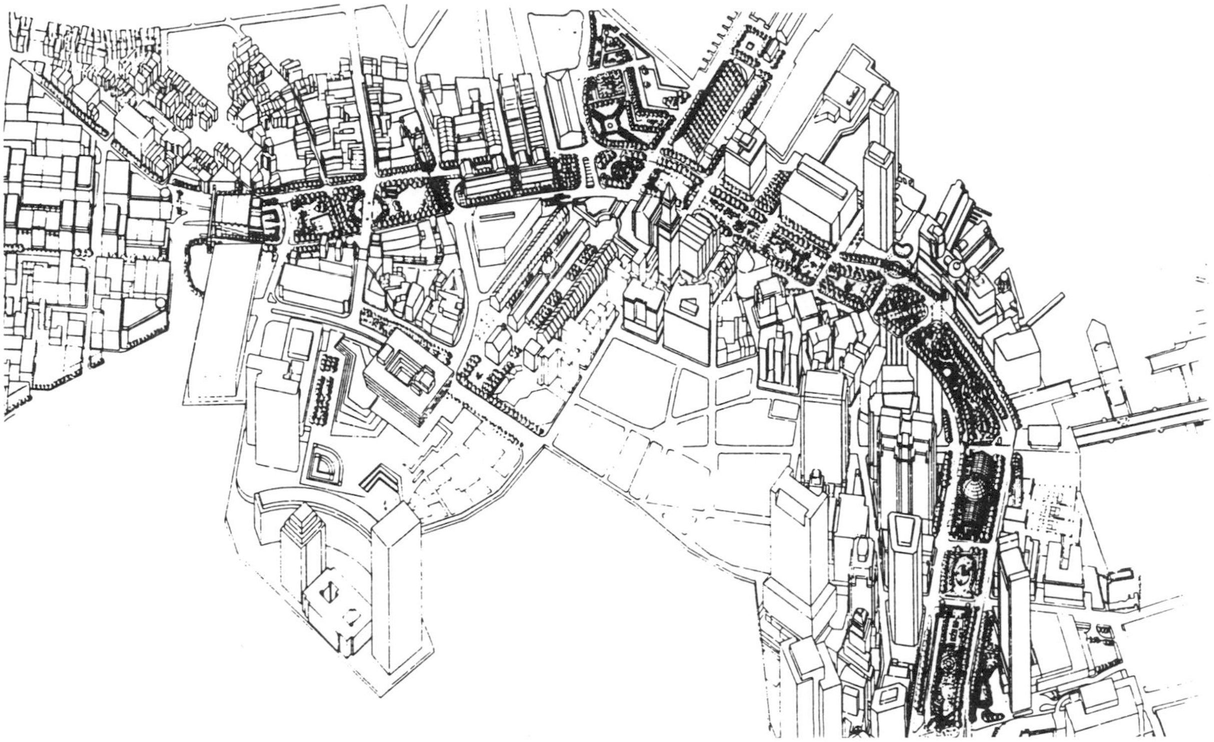

32. Boston, Massachussetts. Plan to relocate Interstate 1 underground and give the land back to the city for parks and community buildings (*Boston Redevelopment Authority*).

we need to play a greater role in its creation. A truly participatory tradition in the built environment can only be attained when the following conditions are met.

1. The public is well educated in environmental design and ready to take a part in the decision-making process.
2. Designers are better trained in responding to human needs and desires than they have often been in the past.
3. Our society gives a higher priority to concern for the environment and the long-term effects of our design decisions.

CONCLUSION

This essay has stressed that human beings strive for expression and meaning in their creations. From small artifacts to great urban designs and gardens, the built environment is full of symbolic objects, structures and spaces. The many styles of design have arisen from the ideals and preoccupations of the societies that produced them.

By examining the built environment today, we may well ask whether it adequately reflects our democratic society and cultural values. If it fails to do so, only we, the citizens, can bring about the necessary change through collaborative effort.

CHAPTER
3

A Historic Timeline

The historic timeline may be a useful outline and reference for those interested in correlating the historic development of various components of the built environment. It may seem complex at first glance, but as you read through the book, various authors will introduce many of the topics listed. The timeline outlines, in a very general way, historic patterns in order to unify readers' overall understanding of past and present events that have shaped the built environment. You are encouraged to personalize it—use it as a reference as well as write down the projects, people or developments which interest you. You may want to note on this outline important events in your own life, your birthday, the oldest object you own, etc.

In the vertical columns, the chart lists various aspects covered in the book. On the left is time. The next two columns list general historic periods and events. The four general traditions introduced by Matthews in Chapter 2 are noted in the next set of columns. A fifth tradition "Conservation," is added, which emerges from many of the chapters in this text. The next vertical columns outline general historic events which have influenced each of the seven selected components of the built environment. More specific detail is contained in the chapters dealing with each component.

Horizontally, the chart or matrix attempts to correlate historic events across the seven components. Collectively, the chart represents a skeleton for the general historic developments that have collectively influenced all of us and which are woven into the complex fabric of the built environment.

	HISTORIC UNITS AND PERIODS: GENERAL / SUBUNITS	MAJOR HISTORY EVENTS	GENERAL TRADITIONS (Chapter 2)	GENERAL DESIGN THEMES	COMPONENTS OF THE BUILT ENVIRONMENT: PRODUCTS (Chapters 8-9)	INTERIORS (Chapters 10-12)	STRUCTURES (Chapters 13-16)	LANDSCAPES (Chapters 17-20)	CITIES (Chapters 21-26)	REGIONS (Chapters 27-29)	EARTH (Chapters 30-32)
			VERNACULAR TRADITION; HIGH STYLE TRADITION; SPECULATIVE TRADITION; PARTICIPATION; CONSERVATION								
BC 10000	I. PRE-HISTORIC Mesopotamia Egyptian	AGRICULTURAL TRANSFORMATION				Mesopotamia Egyptian	Egyptian	AGRICULTURE TRANSITION THE RISE OF CIVILIZATION	PRE-URBAN SETTLEMENT		
5000	II. HISTORIC (3000 BC - 1900 AD)	URBAN TRANSFORMATION							PRE-INDUSTRIAL CITY		
BC 0 AD	CLASSICS Greeks Romans					Greeks Romans	Classic Development Greeks Romans	Greeks Romans			
500				INFORMAL Organic, Design with Nature, Ecological							
1000	GOTHIC Medieval Middle Ages				Medieval Guilds	Gothic	Medieval & Gothic	Medieval Islamic			
1500	RENAISSANCE BAROQUE Revival Periods	INDUSTRIAL REVOLUTION, c 1760		FORMAL Geometric, Symmetrical	Industrial-ization and Mass Production Arts & Crafts	Renaissance Art Nouveau Arts & Crafts	Renaissance & Baroque Art Nouveau Arts & Crafts	Renaissance Dutch Eastern English Landscape INDUSTRIAL TRANSITION	U.S. Constitution & Planning Enabling Laws Garden Cities & New Town Movement		
1900	III. MODERN (1900-present) The Arts The Arts + Crafts The Arts + Crafts + Sciences	WORLD WAR I WORLD WAR II			Bauhaus Industrial Designer Today	Bauhaus International Style Contemporary Design	Modernism International Style Contemporary Trends Mod. Mod. Mod. Hist. Mod. Tech. Environmentalism Fun Participation Deconstruction	ECOLOGICAL CONCERNS NEPA	Urban Renewal and/or Reanimation POST-INDUSTRIAL CITY NEPA Urban Design Stategies	Social Vision Economic Equity Ecological Parity Ecological Planning NEPA Carrying Capacity	World View Global Community NEPA Global 2000 Sustainable Development
TODAY							The Future				GAIA
FUTURE											

PART II

Central Design Issues: Human-Environmental Interrelationships

Central Issues: Human-Environmental Interrelationships

Introduction

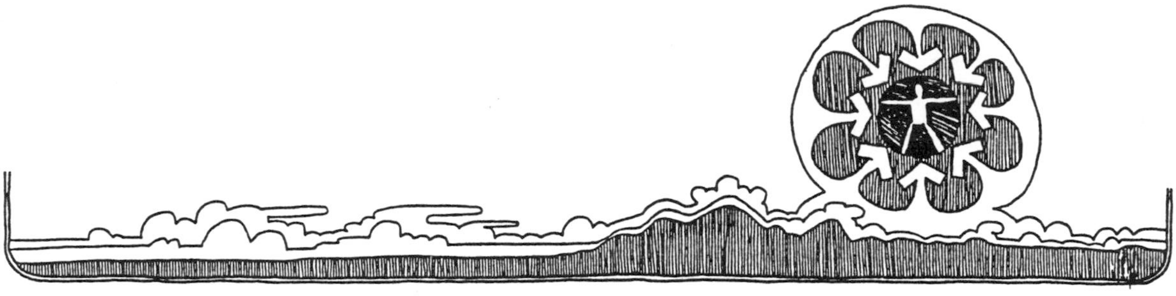

First of all, study of the built environment involves a closer analysis of three essential related parts or variables, which emerge from human-environmental investigation. It is not only important to understand these parts individually, but study of the built environment is greatly enhanced by studying how elements individually are organized and how they interrelate and interact with each other. These three variables are obvious, introduced in the definition of the built environment (reference Chapter 1) and they will recur throughout the text.

The three essential variables are:

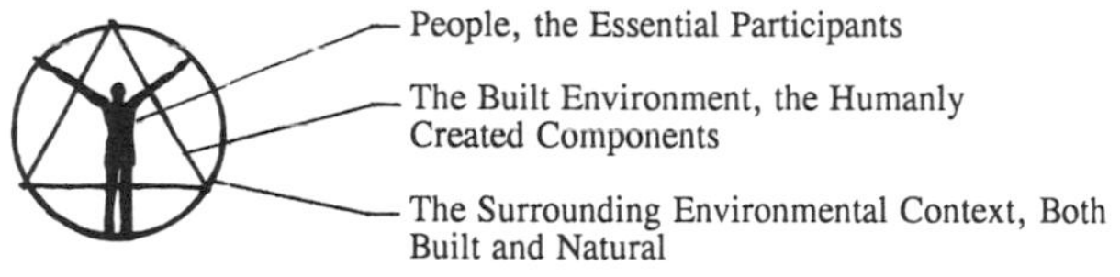

Studying these human and environmental variables and how they interact will provide a better understanding of the purpose and quality of the built environment. These central concerns will help develop a fuller understanding of people, society and their culture; the components of the built environments (created to satisfy human needs and desires), and the resultant built and natural environment.

It is useful to realize that a more general concept is formed by the interaction of the three factors. This general concept is central to the study of almost all subjects; it is particularly important to the study of the design and planning disciplines that participate in the process of shaping the built world. This general concept is commonly referred to as **human-environmental relationships** (in this case "environment" includes both descriptive adjectives "natural" and "built"). The built environment diagram conveys this general concept. (Diagram changed to emphasize interaction or interrelationship between people and environment).

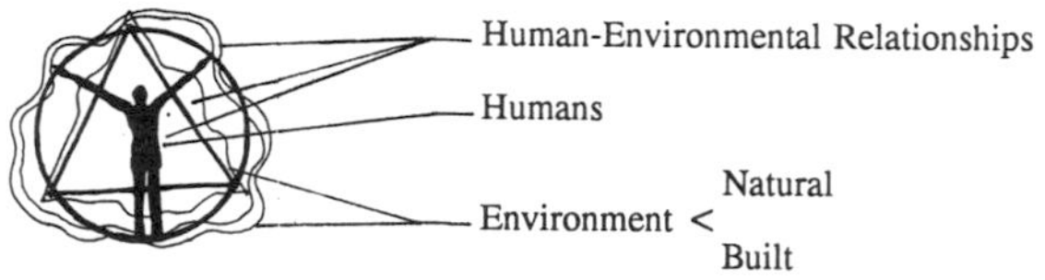

This human-environmental relationship theme is a four-part concept: (1) people, (2) the natural environment, (3) the built environment, and (4) the dynamic interrelationship between parts. This interplay between the parts is emphasized by the hyphen ("-") between the two terms human-environment and re-emphasized by the word relationships (sometimes stated as inter-relationships).

This interplay is also an important adaptive **design** strategy. Design is like a two-way street: humans adapt the environment to fit their needs and humans have to adapt their needs to fit the environment. Ideally, a mutual harmony and balance emerges—one adapting to the other and vice versa. Serious consequences can occur when people overbuild and cause environmental deterioration (polluted air and water, urban sprawl destroying prime farm land, traffic congestion, etc.). Serious consequences also occur when the natural environment destroys human habitat (floods, earthquakes, volcanic eruptions, tornados, etc.). By understanding these central variables as a two-way adaptive-design strategy, people will be able to do a better job in celebrating life and its creative processes, while living in harmony with the best qualities of the natural environment.

The following chapters will investigate the three main elements of this human-environmental concept:

1. **Environment**: Chapter 4, **"Environment: Definition and Organization,"** by Gerald L. Young, explores the complex meaning of the word "environment." It clarifies the definition and explores various popular and professional uses of the word. It introduces a simple theoretical concept "levels of integration," useful in further defining component parts of the environment and for that matter, the structure and linkages of any complex subject.
2. **Built Environment**: Chapter 5, **"Designing with the Intrinsic Organization of the Built Environment,"** by Tom J. Bartuska, examines the built environment, unfolding an organizational structure which helps give clarity to the content, components and context of the humanly-created world. This approach provides a model for analysis and synthesis—the basic thought processes in a design process. The chapter explores qualitative dimensions of the built environment useful in evaluating various components of the built environment.
3. **People**: Chapters 6 and 7 study people and the way they perceive and participate in these human-environmental interrelationships.

   - **"Individual and Group Perception and Participation,"** by Victoria Kolmodin and Tom J. Bartuska: this chapter explores how human sensitivity and understanding affects the built environment. It is an intriguing area of study and the essay should foster a better understanding of ourselves and others by encouraging readers to be more aware and active participants in the creation of a quality built environment for all. Poor understanding and apathy breeds disruptive characteristics. It is important to understand and continually encourage supportive characteristics.
   - **"The Role of Visual Principles in Ordering the Environment"** by Robert J. Patton: The last chapter of this section analyzes how human visual perception can be used to order the components of the built environment. The first two chapters discussed how humans try to create, clarify, organize and compose ideas into ordering concepts. In a similar way, this chapter emphasizes the role of human visual perception in establishing visual principles to clarify, compose and order the physical component parts of the built environment.

A deeper understanding of the variables of human-environmental interrelationships will help evaluate the purpose and function of the built environment, help determine its supportive and disruptive characteristics. Knowledge of these central issues can direct time and talents toward corrective measures to improve the design quality in the things humans create, the things they build.

CHAPTER

4

Environment: Definitions and Organization

Gerald L. Young

"There's glory for you!"

"I don't know what you mean by 'glory,'" Alice said.

Humpty Dumpty smiled contemptuously. "Of course you don't—till I tell you. I mean 'there's a nice knock-down argument for you!'"

"But 'glory' doesn't mean 'a nice knock-down argument,'" Alice objected.

"When I use a word," Humpty Dumpty said, in rather a scornful tone, "it means just what I choose it to mean—neither more nor less."

"The question is," said Alice, "whether you can make words mean so many different things."

The question is," said Humpty Dumpty, "which is to be master—that's all."

—Lewis Carroll

When most of us use the word **environment**, it means just what we choose it to mean, neither more nor less. It is a Humpty Dumpty sort of word and it, not us, remains the master.

Words are building blocks to communication. When people do not use words correctly or choose personal meanings for words, communication becomes difficult. But some common patterns do exist and this chapter attempts to clarify some of them.

Usage of the word environment can be arranged along a continuum; at one end is a simple, **reductionist** definition of the word. Mason and Langenheim (1957), writing in the foremost U.S. journal in ecology, describe environment as a "key concept in the structure of ecological knowledge," but restrict it to refer only to those phenomena that have a direct or functional relation with an organism. Similarly, people in general exclude from the definition the larger meaning implicit in the etymology or historic meaning of the word. To many, thc "reduced" word is more useful with qualifiers, adjectives such as natural or artificial or built that lend specificity.

On the other end of a continuum is the **holistic** definition. Environment, defined holistically, includes everything that surrounds a person or other organism—dwelling, neighborhoods, landscape, city, region and earth. Environment is an essential term, and scientists and ecologists would argue that clarity in its use enhances communication and understanding (Dubos, 1973).

The lack of edges to a holistic concept of environment is certainly a problem. Thinking about environment in the comprehensive sense is a challenge. The implication that everything is environment, extending to infinity, may cause a sense of helplessness condemning a person to a sort of wallowing in an incomprehensible complexity. Setting limits aids in analysis and in doing experiments, so this is the reason some scientists fall back on the reductionist definition.

But such problems, difficult as they are to resolve, don't eliminate the very real need for a holistic perspective. The assumption seems valid that human consciousness needs to be raised not restricted; humans need to comprehend, make connections to, and care about what happens to people and places outside their immediate surroundings. They need to know that conditions and activities in faraway places affect them, their immediate environment and their individual well-being. And they need to incorporate the reciprocal idea that their actions impact people and environments outside the immediate place and time.

ENVIRONMENT: ETYMOLOGY

One key to a clarification of the definition of environment may lie in examination of the etymology (origins and historic development) of the word. Original meanings can provide a foundation for agreement. Environment is derived from the French words *environ* or *environner*, meaning "around, round about, to surround, to encompass." These in turn originated from the Old French *viron* (together with the prefix *en*), which means "a circle, a round, the country around, or circuit." In English usage, environment is the total of the things or circumstances around an organism (including humans) and environs are the "surrounding neighborhood of a specific place—the neighborhood or vicinity."

This brief etymological discussion of the word environment provokes two suggestions for possible restructuring of the word to create a usable contemporary definition. First, the word refers to totality, to "everything" that encompasses each and all of us. This supports a holistic, integrated perspective. Second, the phrase "to environ" infers that the encompassing is active. It indicates process, an interaction between elements found or placed in the environment. This action is reciprocal; the environment is not simply an inert or static phenomenon to be impacted without response. It is interactive: actions impact and change the environment and these changes in return affect the organism.

ENVIRONMENT: ADJECTIVES AND AMENDMENTS

Using the word environment clearly and without ambiguity is a challenge. Descriptive adjectives can help give greater preciseness to the word and, therefore, increased understanding. Commonly used adjectives are numerous: physical, natural, cultural, built, artificial, functional, effective, operational, perceptual, conceptual, total, social, human, geographical, ecological, psychological, behavioral, institutional and so on. Such modifiers can aid in refining the word, allowing more specific reference to the world that surrounds us.

If clarity and understanding is the goal, then we should be aware of the following problems. First, a problem exists when the word is not qualified at all, just simply used in isolation and with few or no hints as to the meaning intended; this is the way it is most commonly used, but it would be foolhardy to assume that the definition intended is always clear. If the word is used without qualification of any kind, it should take on an open or inclusive meaning—the totality of surroundings with no explicit bounds intended. It can then incorporate all

1. Physical environment: mountain and forest.

2. Physical environment: tables, chairs and other furniture.

possible adjective forms. Second, a problem is created by "implied" qualifiers, adjectives implicit in one discipline employing the term, but not apparent to readers from other fields. For example, many people using the word environment mean to imply a "physical" or "natural" context, meaning such phenomena as topography, climate and vegetation. The third problem has to do with the explicit use of adjectives, but ones that have different meanings in different disciplines. "Physical" can again provide an example: To most people, its explicit use refers to physical features of the earth's surface, again, vegetation, soils, climate and topography. But, in environmental psychology and in several of the environmental design disciplines (such as architecture), the physical environment often refers to "physical" objects, such as tables and chairs, objects in the built environment. This leads to unnecessary confusion and difficulty in communication across disciplinary boundaries.

Despite the problems, modifiers will be used and can be helpful and positive, enriching the language with many different descriptive meanings. Certain of these have more potential than the others; selected adjectives that help give greater utility and clarity to the word environment are discussed briefly.

Natural/Artificial/Built

William Blake once observed that where humans are absent, "nature is barren." These days, humans seem to be everywhere on the globe, scurrying about trying to alleviate or blot out that barrenness and producing an environment so transformed that it is often described as a human-created world. The result is an interpenetration, an overlapping, a confusion between the natural world and that created by humans. That dichotomy is of special concern in this book. It arises in the design disciplines because of the use of **artificial** to differentiate human-modified environments from the natural environment. This raises the question of human uniqueness: why isn't the term **natural** as fitting a designation for a human habitation as it is for that of beaver or wasp?

This human modified world, as some view it, a world marked by what many have called a new ecology, has been tagged with assorted labels. These include "artificial environment," "synthetic environment" and even such attachments as the prefabricated, the imitation, or the constructed environment. The phrase **built environment** used in this book is another variation. The latter does seem to be emerging slowly as the dominant form in the literature, particularly in environmental psychology, in the design disciplines, and even in the more general ecological literature. This dominance is marked by such books as R. F. Reekie's *Design in the Built Environment* (1972) or the Hutchinson series on "The Built Environment" edited by Bruton and Ratcliffe. And built environment may indeed be the most appropriate label. It does avoid the negative connotations of other terms, connotations at least implicit in such words as artificial and synthetic. "Built" as a modifier avoids the implication that this kind of human creation is unnatural, somehow counterfeit, even unreal. The built environment is not unnatural or false. It is conceived by the human mind and built by the human hand, and humans are "natural" organisms. And all artifacts are fabricated from the stuff of nature.

The term built environment can be used holistically and/or reductionistically. The built environment to some may be furniture or a room. To others it can mean everything humanly made or arranged—products, interiors, structures, cities, regions, even the heavily modified earth. The holistic use is, of course, the premise for this book.

Operational/Effective/Functional

One of the reasons that many contemporary people feel the need to distinguish between the natural environment and that which they have created with their own hands and tools is that many (if not yet most) people today interact so much more closely with the built environment. Humans now live with the realities of smog much more than sky, in concrete instead of stone, more in contemplation of a flowerbox than natural biota.

The chief interest of every individual is that part of the environment that most directly affects him or her. One version of this, used in biological ecology, is the **operational environment**—meaning that portion of the environment that physically impinges on an organism. The operational environment is defined as things that affect us physically even though we might not directly perceive them. This can also be called the **effective environment**, a term defined in a similar operational sense. These designations focus on the environment that most of us accept as personal, the environment in which we operate or function as living beings and to which we form a functional attachment. A third applicable term, the **functional environment**, is also used to refer to the places where we live, work and play (our habitat to some writers).

These are modifications of the word environment that derive from the realities of the day-to-day process of personal and community interaction. They are expressions of the limitations that humans have as organisms, identifying the real world that we actually occupy as opposed to that larger world of which we must be increasingly aware.

Perceptual/Conceptual

Every organism lives in a different perceptual world: a dog, sniffing the air, lives in a particular sort of perceptual world all its own, one that we humans can only vaguely appreciate. The **perceptual environment** is that part of the effective or functional environment intercepted by senses. We often confuse this with total reality. We cannot hope to understand behavior without knowing the stimuli to which humans react, both favorable and unfavorable.

An interesting example is human life on some of the Micronesian atolls. Inhabitants on some of these islands have coped with their environment very effectively. They are efficient fisherfolk and gardeners, having lived in equilibrium with scant resources for 2,000 years. But, for them the environment of the atoll includes not only the fish and vegetables, the water and the land, but a host of spirits as well. These are a very real part of the Micronesian environment and directly affect their behavior patterns. This has been called the supernatural environment, but a better term might be the **conceptual environment**. This refers to a society's cultural world, including the built environment, a world shaped by ideas and human thought.

Aristotle denoted the differences between the "real" or functional environment and the conceptual one. He introduced the terms "ens reale," real being, as opposed to "ens rationis," conceptual or rational being. What is real and what is unreal? What is relevant to a growing understanding of human relationships to the built environment?

Human experience is enriched by abstractions that form the conceptual world. But, even in this conceptual environment, the subject-object or human-environmental relationship remains the fundamental structure of experience. We name our concepts and abstractions, attaching symbolic reality, and can then interact with them as a "real" part of our environment. So, even abstractions, such as spirits of human myth or legend, are part of the built environment.

VULGATE AND VARIANTS

Environment is the vulgate term, in common use in everyday conversation and in every kind of literature (Young, 1986). That is its strength and its weakness. And that is why it becomes essential to deal with it. The term "environment" is not going to be eradicated from everyone's vocabulary. It requires a careful and thoughtful usage. Many alternatives exist and their use often results from boredom with a too-frequent use of the term environment. Interesting writing demands synonyms, so a variety of words are called upon and simply inserted into a text. But, their careless use as direct synonyms can cause real confusion. The most common of these is the word habitat, but others are used often, including such terms as milieu and mise-en-scène.

Habitat

The word **habitat** is frequently included in the same articles or essays as the word environment. It is employed for variety and interest and intended as an exact synonym. Habitat has two limitations that compromise its use as a direct synonym for environment: the first in etymology and the second in general contemporary usage. Etymologically, habitat derives from the Latin *habitare*, which means to inhabit, to dwell, to reside. This specifically limits the locale, giving it a much more specific meaning than the word environment.

Most contemporary use of the word habitat is based on this specific original meaning, focused on the idea of the place of habitation of an animal, person or plant. It has been used this way most often in natural history and game management. This has led to repeated use of the adjective "natural," so that it is most frequently employed or implied as "natural habitat," that local place where a specific organism is to be found naturally.

Anthropologists employ the term more commonly than other disciplines concerned with humans to designate the natural locale of a particular tribe, rather than as a straight-across synonym for environment. Architects sometimes use the word habitat as a synonym for housing, which is more limited and somewhat misleading. The urban dweller's habitat is the city, not the house. Certainly the city, or the locality of a neighborhood or small town, could be described as a distinctive human habitat, in the correct sense of the word.

Habitat is a useful word, particularly if used with the intended meaning, but it is a poor choice as a direct substitute for environment.

From Milieu to Mise-en-Scène

The French word **milieu** is another commonly used variant, if less so than habitat. This also has a number of limitations that make it less than satisfactory as a direct substitute or synonym for environment. For one thing, the word is too closely associated with social class, with artistic, aesthetic and cultural considerations, connotations evident in a common dictionary example: "Gallery openings tend to be part of a snobbish milieu." When one thinks of milieu, one imagines something quite elegant—whereas we humans must deal with quite the worst as well as the best and the in-between. Milieu has a very definite spatial limitation as well—it derives from the Old French *mi* (middle) plus *lieu* (place) meaning literally that one is in the middle of a place. Milieu is useful in certain contexts, especially for describing the built environment—e.g., when discussing social settings or the mood and character of a limited and heavily modified human habitat. Environment remains the more holistic and comprehensive of the two—and will continue to be so used.

Mise-en-scène, though normally limited to its theatrical sense, does have two connotations of particular interest to the built environment: first, as the physical setting of an action and not just action in a play; second, as the surroundings in which anything is seen. Both of these have obvious utility, but care must again be taken regarding context and shadings of meaning. Mise-en-scène is not an adequate, straight-across synonym for environment but it can be very useful in trying to describe the richness of the built environment.

THE PROBLEM OF JARGON

Jabberwocky is a word in Humpty Dumpty's poem: any unintelligible speech or writing. Uses of the word environment (with or without adjectives) and its synonyms are complicated and seldom clear across disciplinary boundaries. But, reading about human-environment relationships is even more complicated because writers pile on the jargon. Just scan a few book titles on human-environment subjects during the past few years: Ecocide, Ecotopia, Eco-Catastrophe, Ecoscience, Eco-Crisis, Ecosuicide, and Ecocide. Where is the clarity in these, the creativity or imagination? Does such jargon serve any real purpose or does it simply confuse?

The most extreme example of unnecessary coined words is the development of "environic studies" in the architecture department at the University of Notre Dame. A vocabulary rich in usable forms from both ecology and architecture is apparently insufficient for graduate work in environics—whatever that really means. Instead, the environic program seeks to define (among others): dendrotecture, psammotecture, synecopolis, recreology and recreography, poietic encyclement, and tourist and historic enviria. (Environics is dangerously similar to moronics, and understandably so.) According to the brochure, "the foregoing concepts and factors imply the emergence of a new environmental design science/art, that of envirology." Even Paolo Soleri's attempts to combine architecture and ecology into **arcology** is preferable to these.

These are bad, but the jabberwocky doesn't end there. Constantine Doxiadis, a world-renowned Greek planner, felt he had to redefine the study of human settlements in terms of **ekistics** (the human environment?) and the ecumenopolis and ecumenokepos. The Exxon Company titles its annual report Ecolibrium. Add to these, if you will, the recent "ecologism" as a label for the ecological approach in sociology and "ecography" as a new scientific discipline. Most of these are attempts to deal with various aspects of natural or built environments, but they confuse rather than clarify—and most should be discarded.

If we are to ever communicate effectively across disciplinary boundaries, we have to come to some kind of agreement on terminology, especially for the word environment and its modifiers (Young, 1986). When environment is used by itself, without qualifiers, it should be understood in its most holistic, inclusive sense. The word environment should be used as often as possible with a carefully considered and cautiously selected qualifier. For that reason, this book was titled *The Built Environment*, that environment we humans create and build for ourselves to fit our peculiar needs.

DEFINING ENVIRONMENT BY ITS ORGANIZATION

As noted, the word environment serves best as a holistic term. The modifiers only help develop subcategories or parts of the whole topic. Techniques are available to help further organize the complexities of environment as a subject into its component parts and wholes. Dissecting a subject into its intrinsic parts, and then, not focusing on one individual part, but shifting to how those parts are organized into a whole, allows access to content, as well as to the way parts connect and, therefore, to a full definition. Connections between the parts are too often forgotten. Soren Kierkegaard, a philosopher, emphasized this: "All burrowing into existence consists in establishing connections."

Contemporary critics of the reductionist methods of science, engineering and design have become increasingly vocal in recent years. They claim that reductionistic methods, necessary (and successful) as they certainly are, tend to isolate entities and de-emphasize connections. These commentators worry that, in the process of analysis, a great deal of information about relationships between people and environment, if not lost, is often disregarded or misplaced. This fragments our conception of the environment. Regardless of the validity of such a charge, scientists and designers have responded with attempts to insure that connections are restored by climbing back up the ladder, connecting parts to their functional wholes (Molnar, 1966). For scientists and designers, as philosopher Paul Weiss (1971) suggests, "the task arises to look at the total . . . [the task of] synthesis." Consequently, a device for integration is needed—an organizing framework for environment—one that will allow a relating of numerous "parts" to the whole.

Hierarchy or Levels-of-Integration: A Systems Framework

The concept of **hierarchy** has been used for centuries in attempts to illustrate part-whole relationships, to outline sequence and progression and to characterize connections (Salthe, 1988). The philosopher, Leibniz, in the eighteenth century, claimed that "the whole of matter is connected [a connection], of all created things with each, and of each with all the rest." C. A. Patrides (1973), modernized this with his comment that "in effect, the history of hierarchy is the history of Occidental thought."

Three terms are commonly used to help define and link the parts and wholes of complex subjects: "hierarchy," "levels-of-organization," and "levels of integration." All three are useful in study of the built environment. The three have a slightly different meaning but form a single general concept. At different times in this book, different authors introduce various aspects of this general concept. All should be taken as an enrichment of the concept and as a reaffirmation of the breadth of this approach and its utility—in analysis and in the ultimate synthesis of components of the built environment.

Use of the term hierarchy can create negative connotations. The word may raise images of a social order in which human relationships are determined by the degree of authority exercised by one group of people over another. However, hierarchy can be used as a simplifying organizational tool to order and relate the parts of a subject in range—large to small, most important to least, etc. It should—and can—be used in a neutral sense where all parts are unique and important.

Greater utility may be found in the parallel terms **levels-of-organization**, or **levels-of-integration**. These are also hierarchical, a connecting of parts to whole. The first is a reminder of the degree or extent of organization; the second, a declaration of the importance of connections, of levels integrated together to form wholes of increasingly complex systems. Both emphasize the parts (the content)-whole (the context) relationship in an integrated framework.

Scientists are increasingly accepting the hierarchical perspective, especially as an approach to systems analysis. Ludwig von Bertalanffy (1950, 1955), widely recognized as the father of general systems theory, described what he called reality in terms of a "tremendous hierarchical order of organized entities," the higher the level-of-integration, the more complex the organizational structure. Barry Commoner (1972) summarized the extent and comprehensiveness intended by hierarchical linkages through his widely quoted contemporary advice that "everything is connected to everything else."

More fundamental to comprehension of the built environment is the fact that hierarchies make complex subjects more understandable and "more meaningful" (Reeves, 1991). A reductionist view of the world confines and limits capable minds. Hierarchy theory (Young, 1992) frees scholars from the shackles of the analytical mode without requiring them to reject it and provides, as well, glimpses of a wider, more diverse and interesting world.

Most **systems** used in the life sciences are hierarchical in nature (cf., Bradbury, 1991). Any species can be related to any other species in the world by locating it taxonomically in the Linneaen hierarchy (see Figure 5). Another common organizational structure is to place life itself in the matrix of the universe (see Figure 6). Begin perhaps, as J. S. Rowe (1961) did, with the cell: cells form organs, then organisms, then groups or families or populations, then a community, ecosystem, the ecosphere,

Kingdom	Animalia
Phylum	Chordata
Subphylum	Vertebrata
Superclass	Tetrapoda
Class	Mammalia
Subclass	Theria
Infraclass	Eutheria
Order	Primates
Suborder	Anthropoidea
Superfamily	Hominoidea
Family	Homininae
Subfamily	Homininae
Genus	Homo
Species	Homo sapiens

3. Taxonomic placement of the human species (*Homo sapiens*) in the Linnaean hierarchy.

Universe
Galaxies
Stars
Planets
Earth
Ecosphere
Ecosystems
Communities
Populations
Organisms
Organ Systems
Organs
Tissues
Cells
Protoplasm
Molecules
Atoms
Subatomic Particles

4. Hierarchy of the natural world, from cells to universe.

and finally, the universe. Jacob Bronowski (1965) speaks of similar hierarchies in the physical sciences, noting that even matter evolves, through a series of steps, from simple elements to complex wholes (see Chapter 5).

Hierarchy theory, or levels-of-organization or integration, is being used by an increasing number of scholars representing a multitude of disciplines. In Nobel Laureate Francois Jacob's (1970) *Logic of Life*, the single dominant thread is the idea of "integration," levels-of-integration: "There is not one single organization of the living, but a series of organizations fitted into one another like nests of boxes."

5. Nested hierarchical order in Chinese boxes and sets within sets of subdivided triangles.

The physicist L. L. Whyte (1969) concluded that the most widely accepted fact about the universe is that "large portions of it are highly ordered as a system of subsystems each of which can in some respect be treated as an ordered unit." Bronowski (1965) illustrates this beautifully with a conception of stratified stability, his term for evolution "not only of life but of matter," as a slow climbing of a ladder of increasing complexity, from simple to complex by slow but constant steps.

Fitness: The Integration of Parts and Wholes

Understanding environment as a series of integrated levels is an important beginning point. Designing any single part is only one aspect of concern. As with a puzzle, designers must also make sure the parts or pieces fit together. A concept of **fitness** is, therefore, an important aspect of appropriate human-environmental design strategies. Fitness deals with how an entity has adapted, or been adapted, to fit its context as identified by a series of integrated levels. For designers, this should be a constant reminder that context is always there, that any object—the brick, the box, the house or the human—is always placed in a setting or context. Relationships to context should be anticipated in the design process.

Several additional terms and concepts, e.g., holism, holon, functionalism—all derivatives of hierarchy theory, can help in this process of recognizing and creating fitness. **Holism** is a term which emphasizes the existence of an ever-widening totality, a comprehensiveness in dealing with human environments. The writer, Arthur Koestler (1972) refined holism by introducing a new term, **holon**, which he defined as any (and every) entity that is in one sense a whole and in another sense a part. Holon reminds us of a double identity, that every object or entity we work with, placed in such a series of levels, is both a whole (by itself) and a part (of a larger system or levels). We can talk of the human eye as a specific entity, but to understand how it works or functions, we must place it back into the whole human body. Each of us considers ourselves whole individuals, but to understand how we relate as human beings, it is necessary to look beyond the individual to the aggregate—the family, the neighborhood, the community. Working with one level to the exclusion of others is simplistic and incomplete.

Functionalism is a common theme in the design disciplines, especially the old dialectic that interrelates form and function. Functionalism has a dual theoretical meaning, however; first it addresses how the parts of an object function internally, and second, how objects interrelate with each other to

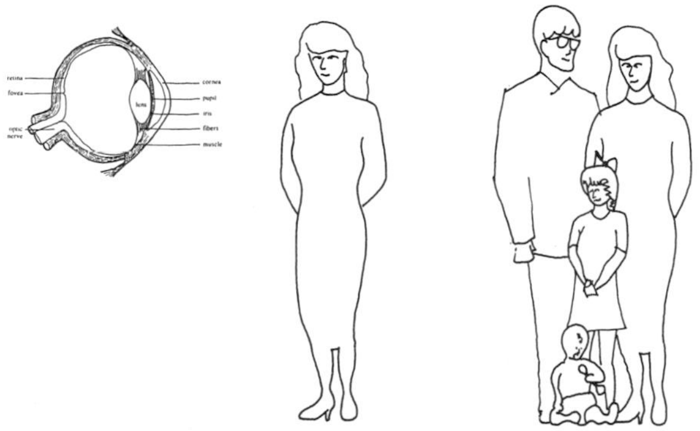

6. The whole human organism (in center); a part of a human organism, the human eye, and its parts (on the left); the human organism as part of a larger aggregate, the family (on the right).

make up a larger functional whole or system. Functionalism is a reminder to creators of the built environment that systems work because each part "fits" together, each is a holon and each fits into its context. Fitness can only be achieved, in individual, structure or city, if the isolated object is connected to its context. Fitness cannot be achieved by attention only to an isolated object or only to a total system. Creation of a healthy, functioning individual in a healthy functioning environment demands both perspectives.

What all this really means is a shift in mindset, in perspective, from a view that traditionally focuses on the isolated object or entity to a focus on objects as content and in context, both defined by levels-of-integration. Placement in a series of integrated levels clarifies the parts from which an object or entity is made. Such placement also reveals more clearly the setting of which the object is itself a part.

Optimization in the built environment can then be more closely approximated by defining optimum as "fitness in context," fit to a larger pattern. Adapting this levels-of-integration perspective as a conceptual and theoretical tool can aid designers in achieving this integrative process, in making more adequate assessments of context in their search for optimum solutions of human-environmental design problems.

ENVIRONMENT: A CHALLENGING FRAMEWORK FOR LIFE

William Wurster, former dean of environmental design at the University of California in Berkeley, is said to have repeatedly emphasized that "the building is not the picture, the building is the frame for the picture; the picture **is** life." That idea needs to be extended to an ever wider audience. The picture is life, human life, that exists not just in a building, but in an integrated built environment that can be best understood as an integrated series of human-environmental frames, both smaller and larger than Wurster's building. Human life, then, can be described as existing and functioning in a sequence of such frames, encompassing frames that connect humans to the natural environment and enrich our creation of the built environment.

We use hierarchical systems to organize the environment, to make sense of the world in which we live. This book is organized into a hierarchical set of seven levels, products . . . to earth (seven being the number scholars say is easiest to remember). The seven levels metaphorically define the limits of a world we can all perceive. Each level is linked to all the others, though the connections are subtle and complex. The listing is not perfect, exhibiting overlaps and discontinuities. But, it does illustrate general categories and relationships. It can serve as a useful approximation, a series of picture frames that will help to expand understanding and awareness of a complex subject—the built environment.

REFERENCES

Bertalanffy, L. von. 1952. "Levels of Organization," *Problems of Life*. Wiley.

Bradbury, I. K. 1991. "Levels of Organization," *The Biosphere*. Belhaven Press.

Bronowski, J. 1965. "The Discovery of Form," *Structure in Art and in Science*, edited by Gyorgy Kepes. George Braziller.

Commoner, B. 1972. *The Closing Circle: Nature, Man and Technology*. Alfred A. Knopf.

Dubos, R. 1973. "Environment," *Dictionary of the History of Ideas*, Vol. 2, ed. by Phillip P. Wiener. Charles Scribner's Sons.

Feibleman, J. K. 1954. "Theory of Integrative Levels," *The British Journal for the Philosophy of Science*, Vol. 5, No. 17, May.

Jacob, F. 1973. *The Logic of Life—A History of Heredity*. Translated by Betty E. Spillman. Pantheon Books.

Koestler, A. 1972. "The Hierarchy and the Game," Chapter 5, *Information Theory and the Living System*, edited by Lila L. Gatlin. Columbia University Press.

Mason, H. L. and J. H. Langenheim. "Language Analysis and the Concept of Environment." *Ecology*, 1957.

Molnar, F. 1966. "The Unit and the Whole: Fundamental Problem of the Plastic Arts," *Module, Proportion, Symmetry, Rhythm*, edited by Gyorgy Kepes. George Braziller.

Patrides, C. A. 1973. "Hierarchy and Order," *Dictionary of the History of Ideas: Studies of Selected Pivotal Ideas*, Vol. II, edited by Philip P. Wiener. Charles Scribner's Sons.

Reeves, H. 1991. "The Pyramid of Complexity," *The Hour of Our Delight: Cosmic Evolution, Order and Complexity*. Freeman.

Rowe, J. S. 1961. "The Level-of-Integration Concept and Ecology." *Ecology*, April.

Salthe, S. N. 1988. "Notes Toward a Formal History of the Levels Concept," *Evolution of Social Behavior and Integrative Levels*, ed. by G. Greenberg and E. Tobach. Erlbaum Associates.

Weiss, P. A. 1971. "The Basic Concept of Hierarchic Systems," *Hierarchically Organized Systems in Theory & Practice*, edited by Paul A. Weiss. Hafner Publishing Co.

Whyte, L. L. 1969. "On the Frontiers of Science: This Hierarchical Universe." *General Semantics Bulletin*.

Young, G. L. 1992. "Between the Atom and the Void: Hierarchy in Human Ecology." *Advances in Human Ecology*.

Young, G. L. 1986. "Environment: Term and Concept in the Social Sciences." *Social Science Information*.

CHAPTER

5

Designing with the Intrinsic Organization of the Built Environment

Tom J. Bartuska

Organizing one's thoughts is a necessary prerequisite to achieving greater levels of understanding. This chapter explores the design implications of the organizational concepts discussed in the previous chapter. The implied characteristics can help us begin to understand complex issues and evolve a basic strategy for designing with the integrative characteristics and qualities of the environment.

A close relationship exists between the "natural" and "built" environments. In the most generic way, built and natural are descriptive adjectives of the same basic term "environment." As discussed in the previous chapter, the two environments have many commonalities and a great deal can be learned from a close comparative study of both.

An examination of the common properties of the natural and built environments can provide an appreciation of their design potential and qualities, their supportive and disruptive characteristics. Probably most important, an awareness of the underlying organization of subject areas helps people analyze and understand complex issues and enables people to make integrative design decisions. It allows designers to take things apart, examine the parts and show the way parts can be put together again, often in better ways. Understanding the sometimes hidden, but essential, working arrangements of parts and wholes allows people to build "new arrangements," which creatively fit into existing patterns within the environment, be it natural or built. Jacob Bronowski (1973), a great contemporary scientist and educator, states this relationship clearly:

> The notion of discovering an underlying order in matter is [the] basic concept for exploring nature [The "nature" of the built and the natural environment]. The architecture of things reveals a structure below the surface, a hidden grain which, when it is laid bare, makes it possible to take natural formations apart and assemble them in new arrangements. For me, this is the step in the ascent of [humanity] at which theoretical sciences begin. And it is as native to the way [people conceive their] own communities as it is to [their] conception of nature.

Bronowski goes on to "lay bare" the similarities in the intrinsic organizational structure of things—natural, built and even human organizational patterns.

> **Natural**: The fundamental particles make nuclei, the nuclei join in atoms, the atoms join in molecules, the molecules join in bases, the bases direct the assembly of amino acids, the amino acids join in proteins. We find again in nature something which seems profoundly to correspond to the way in which our own social relations join us. . . .
>
> **Built**: Stones make a wall, walls make a house, houses make streets, and streets make a city. A city is stones and a city is people; but it is not a heap of stones, and it is not just a jostle of people. In the step from the village to the city, a new community organization is built . . . in that skeleton of a city lies the structure of every civilization, in every age, everywhere in the world.
>
> **Human**: We human beings are joined in families, the families are joined in kinship groups, the kinship groups in clans, the clans in tribes, the tribes in nations. And that sense of hierarchy, of a pyramid in which layer is imposed on layer, runs through all the ways that we look at nature.

This hidden grain, these three comparable hierarchies or levels to be integrated are listed in figure one. The ideas and terms are changed to fit the terms and symbols used throughout this text.

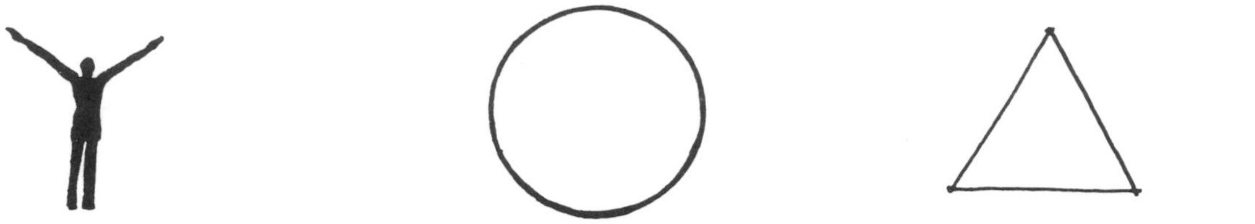

People and Society	The Natural Environment	The Built Environment
Individual	Subatomic Particles	Products
Families	Atoms/Molecules	Interiors
Neighbors/Neighborhoods	Cells	Structures
Communities/Cities	Organisms	Landscapes
County/Regions	Communities	Cities
States/Nations	Ecosystems	Regions
Earth	Ecosphere/Earth	Earth

Solar System Universe

1. The Intrinsic Organization of the Parts and Wholes of Human-Environmental Relationships.

Clarifying the "hidden grain," the intrinsic organizational structure provides a powerful conceptual tool for understanding design. It also develops a basis for designing creative arrangements that fit together and make a healthy contribution to the built environment. As conceptual design tools, the characteristics and qualities of these implied relationships were described in detail in the previous chapter and are listed again here for emphasis.

Organizational Structure. An organizational hierarchy gives a clarity and order to complex subjects. It provides a conceptual tool to aid in thinking about the hidden properties of the way things should fit together. The organization of the remainder of this book is in a hierarchy of levels: products, interiors, structures, landscapes, cities, regions and earth.

Levels of Integration. This organizational hierarchy is similar to the above, except it emphasizes integration. It is also a conceptual tool for understanding how one level merges into or integrates with other levels; how one level becomes the parts or content of the next level; and how that level becomes the parts of the next—an integrated parts-to-whole progression. These interrelationships or hidden connections, when linked together, become the basis of a more complete system. "Integration" is a key word to good design (Reekie, 1972).

Health, Fitness and Creativity. Understanding intrinsic organizational structure enables designers to create new arrangements that are compatible with healthy human relationships and fit the natural and/or built environment. The key qualities suggested in these relationships are as follows:

A. **Health**—achieve a "healthy" compatibility with human needs, values, and relationships.
B. **Fitness**—achieve a close "fitness" or integration between the natural and built environments.
C. **Creativity**—develop new, "creative" arrangements that achieve a high degree of fitness and health.

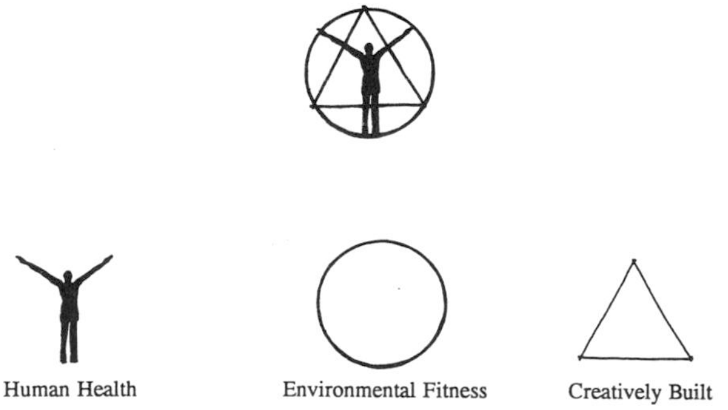

2. Human health + environmental fitness + creatively built: qualitative characteristics within the composite built environment diagram.

These three qualitative characteristics can be applied to the definition diagram used in the introductory section of the book.

The design implications of these important concepts and characteristics are explored in greater depth in the following sections.

LEVELS OF INTEGRATION IN THE BUILT ENVIRONMENT

When confronted with the challenge to understand a complex subject like the built environment, most people take individualized, value-related alternative actions. Because of the subject's inherent complexity, too many people take a reductionist attitude and develop awareness of only one aspect of the topic. This can cause a partial, and at times, distorted understanding of the full subject. Other people may be frustrated by what they consider a chaotic situation and ignore the subject's importance and its more comprehensive characteristics. More times than not, such views will be accompanied by a negative attitude toward those who find the larger topic important and meaningful. These kinds of perspectives and attitudes are far too common, and are a negative rather than a positive contributing factor toward understanding and resolving environmental problems.

Conscientious people have developed simple conceptual tools to aid their understanding of complexity. Although simple devices, they are a bit difficult to explain in normal linear language patterns. Narrative descriptions are not as effective as outlines, charts, matrices, system diagrams and layering techniques. Examples of these graphic conceptual tools (matrices, layering and system networks) are used throughout this text to illustrate integrative ideas. They are also used throughout the planning, design and construction of the built environment to clarify complex and interrelated issues. It is important to grasp the overall concept as a dynamic working tool, and not be overcome by isolated definitions or detail. As Bronowski (1973) states, "The notion of discovering an underlying order . . . is the first step in the ascent of [humanity] at which theoretical science begins."

As suggested throughout the introductory chapter, it is important to understand each part of the built environment as an interrelated level or component of a larger whole. This suggests a simple, but effective, organizational tool—a parts-to-whole or whole-to-parts organizational structure. Any hierarchical organization, once developed, has a part-whole linkage that can aid understanding of complex subjects. Hierarchies suggest an interplay between parts and wholes and between the two basic modes of thinking: **analysis** of parts and **synthesis** of parts into wholes. These two terms are defined more specifically below:

Analysis: The separation of a whole into its component parts, the examination and study of each part.

Synthesis: The composition or combination of parts or elements so as to form a whole.

This organizational structure provides a way to study and design complex issues—a way to analyze the parts and a way to synthesize the parts together to form a complete, whole design. With regard to the built environment diagram, we are analyzing the parts—human, built and natural environments separately and then synthesizing the parts together to form a composite definition.

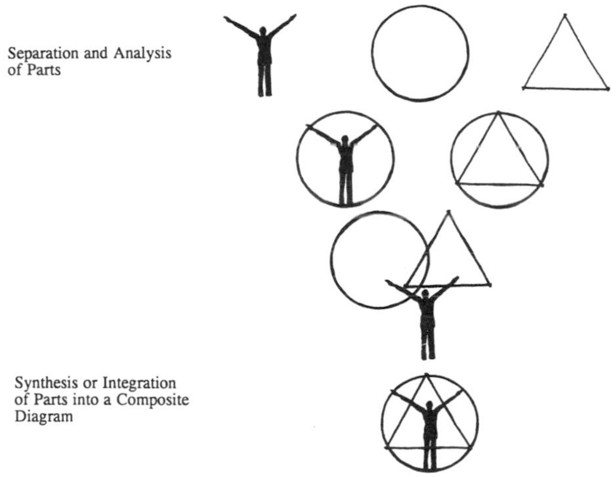

3. Analysis and synthesis within the built environment.

In the built environment, this organizational hierarchy conveys the parts-to-whole structure and the analysis and synthesis modes of thinking about design. Some ways of utilizing a hierarchy are summarized in Figure 4. Selected organizational structures are listed on the left. The middle and right columns summarize the parts-to-whole continuum and the mode of thinking. In other words, if one reads upward, one **analyzes** the content or parts of the system (i.e., structures are made up of interiors

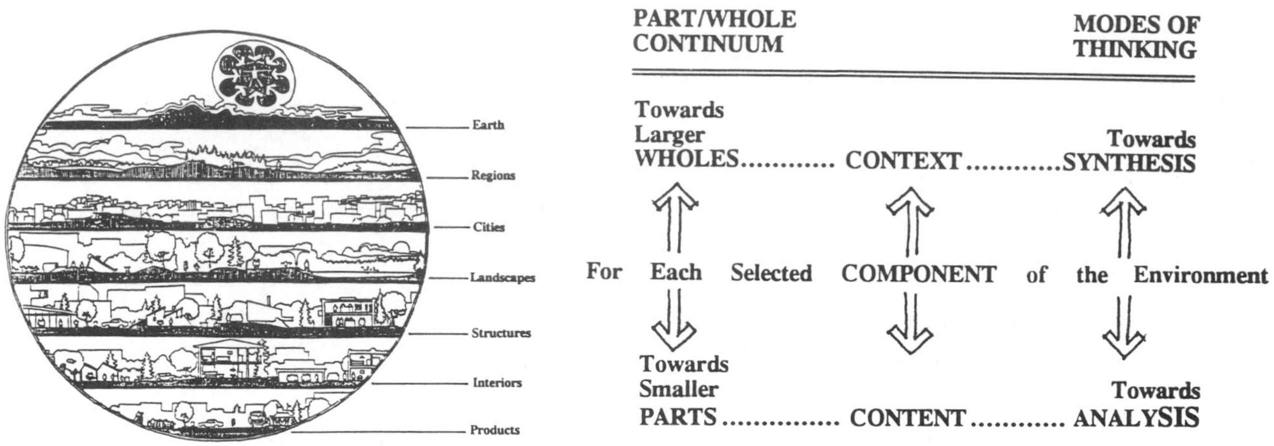

4. Analysis of parts and synthesis into wholes.

and products). Reading down the hierarchy, one **synthesizes** the parts into larger wholes (i.e., products need to be designed to form interiors, products and interiors form structures, etc.).

Numerous hierarchical organizational systems can be identified in the built environment. They are pervasive, fascinating and useful. As these sentences are written, one example of such a design emerges. Any written text evolves through the creation of a hierarchy: Letters form words, a word by itself conveys a minimum of information, but a word integrated into a phrase, then a sentence, has more meaning. Sentences set into a paragraph and the paragraph as part of a chapter and a larger text can convey all the richness of human thought. Similarly, in the theatre where tradition has it "the play's the thing"; but the play again begins with the word. Individual words are strung into a line of dialogue, which (together with the action) build as units to create a scene; scenes integrate to form an act, and acts cohere to form the play. And, as Bronowski (1973) tells us, the play itself, though obviously a whole, is in turn just a unit of the human condition.

An outline of a book or a play is like a comprehensive plan of construction. It is in effect a process of integrating levels, of creating and building by putting pieces together into larger wholes. Letters are combined into words, words into stanzas (as lines of verse), and then stanzas into a poem. The Italian word stanza also means "room"—and rooms are grouped into an 'apparte'ment,' a suite of rooms or house. This latter process is too often seen, by architects and builders in general, as ending at the shell of the structure or at the edges of the development. Too little understanding occurs of how this process of integration should (and in reality does) continue beyond the walls into the neighborhood or city, then into the region and earth. Building stones, instead of barriers, should be stepping stones into neighborhood and nation, and eventually to earth.

It is interesting to note that the hierarchical word "stratify" comes from the Latin *strata*, which means literally a system of roads. Notice the hierarchical system you are on next time you back out of your driveway and maneuver your car down the immediate residential street. You continue to a traffic arterial and eventually onto a major thoroughfare or freeway. You are negotiating an artifact of human design constructed with hierarchical levels and integrated linkages.

This system is similar to the human nerve system and to built electrical and sanitation systems. Some hierarchical patterns can be much more subtle. For example: across much of the central United States, the road and street pattern corresponds to grids imposed by the land survey system. The township-and-range survey system is a hierarchical system, ranging from the "forty" to the quarter-section of 160 acres, through the standard 640-acre section to the six-square mile township. The latter is then integrated into a system of townships and ranges tied into the latitude and longitudinal lines which encircle the earth. In the midwest region of the United States and Canada, aerial photographs frequently reveal a precise correspondence between township lines and transportation patterns. Other human systems are tied even more subtly into this same pattern of regularity, notably gridded land ownership and settlement patterns.

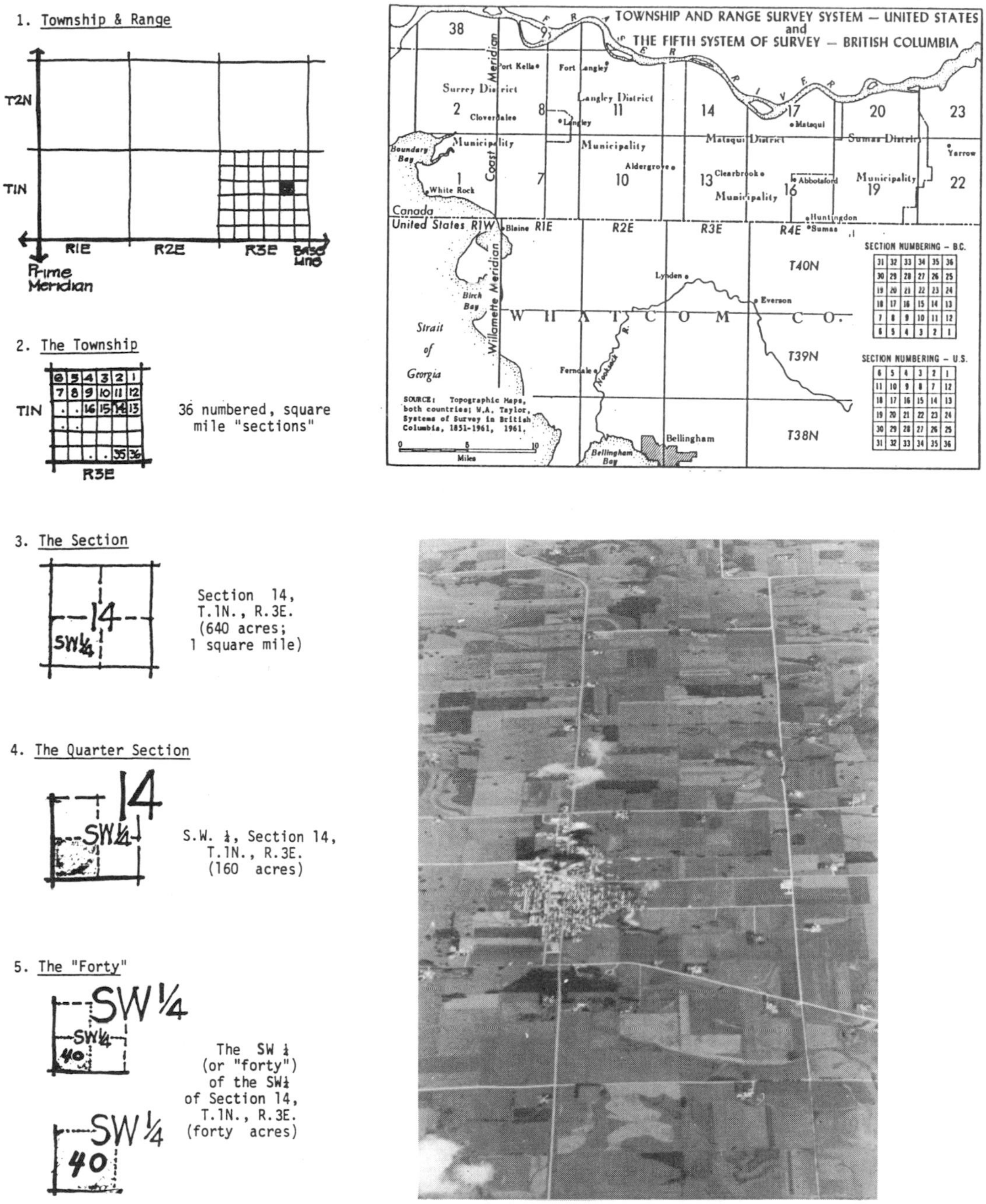

5. Jefferson Grid System. Organizes land from the acre to the prime latitude and longitude to lines which encircle the earth.

Compare these kinds of units to the metric system increasingly coming into use for various kinds of measurement—metrics are simple, integrated, hierarchical systems. Humans have also invented a system of hierarchical units to measure time. The time system interrelates with natural systems of sun-earth relationships and seasons: seconds, minutes, hours, days, weeks, months, seasons, years, centuries, etc. Like so many of the hierarchical systems discussed in these pages, "time-scales" provide context and dimension for human affairs—levels of organization and meaning to lifestyle and livelihood.

Implicit in levels-of-integration theory is the idea asserted by John Donne over 300 years ago that "the roote of all is order." Thinking in terms of integrative levels helps define and clarify the organization and integration of complex subjects like the built environment. Apparent in the notion of hierarchies, especially as expressed as levels-of-integration, is the problem of integrating parts into wholes. Molnar (1966), an artist, has called this the fundamental problem of the plastic arts. He emphasizes the need for designers and builders to seek an understanding of the whole as well as the parts and to recognize that the two are intimately connected. Connection implies relationship and the processes that connect must then be taken into consideration as well. All of this implies a systematic framework for analysis and synthesis, of fitting all human creations together into the built environment.

Organization systems are an important tool for clarifying thoughts and design relationships. It is a first step in understanding how parts organize in "quantitative" hierarchical arrangements. It is also useful in clarifying how each part interrelates to form each level, then each level to the next—a whole to parts or parts to whole continuum. The emphasis here is again on interrelationships and integration. It is useful to increase the meaning of this levels of organization tool in a "qualitative" sense by stressing "integration"—changing the terms to "levels of integration." The emphasis would then be quantitative as well as qualitative. The phrase suggests not only the components, but emphasizes how each part integrates or fits together to form a total meaningful system. The example of letter, word, sentence, book, knowledge deals with the quantity of the levels of organization. The integration of the material in the book, the effectiveness and meaning of the words composed together in the context of chapters and the total book, and the contribution this integrated material makes to the collective body of knowledge, deals with the qualitative dimension—the levels of integrationwithin the book, the book to libraries of knowledge.

In the built environment, as in all of nature, smaller levels or parts become integrated to form each larger component. These smaller levels are the "**content**" or the parts that need to be integrated to form the next level, the larger systems form the "**context**" for the smaller levels. R. Trancik and C. Alexander, contemporary designers and architects, emphasize the importance of creating integrative patterns and wholeness. Trancik (1986) states that in the analysis of historic precedent, various approaches to design theory can be identified, but the optimum brings all together into an integrative layering of these theories. Considered as layers or levels, "they provide potential strategies for integrated urban design." Alexander's (1987) concept of a new theory of urban design is also based upon this concern for "wholeness," on a concept of integrated levels. Alexander states that "every building increment (large or small) must help form at least one larger whole" within the continuum of design levels.

This relationship between content and context may seem simplistic, but the implications are important to fully grasp. Products (furniture, walls, floor and ceiling, etc.) form interiors. Interior spaces are collectively arranged to form structures. Structures, along with exterior spaces (both natural and built), form landscapes. Extended further, this content-component relationship forms cities, regions and finally, the content of Earth. The fundamental quest is not in the simple connection, one forming the other, but in the quality of the interrelationship—how well do the parts integrate and contribute to creation of the whole.

The same relationship can be expressed in a different way to emphasize "context." Products are composed to fit their context-interiors. Generally, the context of interiors are structures, the context for a structure is its landscape and urban setting, and so on throughout the hierarchy. Again, the qualitative quest would emphasize integration—how well each component of the built environment fits its context.

Any hierarchical structure has this three part level-of-integration relationship: that each component is formed by its content and must fit into its context. The chart in Figure 6 summarizes this **content-component-context** relationship.

CONTENT	COMPONENTS OF THE BUILT ENVIRONMENT	CONTEXT
	(ANALYSIS) (CONTENT) PRODUCTS	I+S+L+C+R+E
P	INTERIORS	S+L+C+R+E
P+I	STRUCTURES	L+C+R+E
P+I+S	LANDSCAPES	C+R+E
P+I+S+L	CITIES	R+E
P+I+S+L+C	REGIONS	E
P+I+S+L+C+R	EARTH (SYNTHESIS) (CONTEXT)	

(P represents Products, I - Interiors, S - Structures, etc.)

6. The Content-Component-Context relations within the built environment.

Environmental Design Disciplines

The "levels of integration" concept of the built environment also conveys the differences between various design and planning fields of study. For example, interior design, in a very general sense, deals with a comparatively simple content problem—that being the arranging of numerous products (materials, furniture, lighting, etc.) to create an integrated interior space. However, it also has a larger contextual problem of how the interior design fits into the context of its structure, and then the structure relates to its landscape and city, etc. Landscape architecture deals with a more equal number of content and contextual variables and regional planning deals with a large number of content variables and only a few contextual concerns, though one, the Earth, is most formidable. These issues, of course, overlap various designers—architects, landscape architects, etc., and suggest the need for teamwork or collaboration between all the environmental design disciplines.

In a general sense, these overlapping content-component-context relationships for each discipline are expressed in Figure 7.

HEALTH, FITNESS AND CREATIVITY: A QUALITATIVE MODEL

The content-component-context integrative conceptual framework needs an additional qualitative dimension to assess the effectiveness of planning and design decisions. Three terms were suggested from Bronowski's statements earlier in this

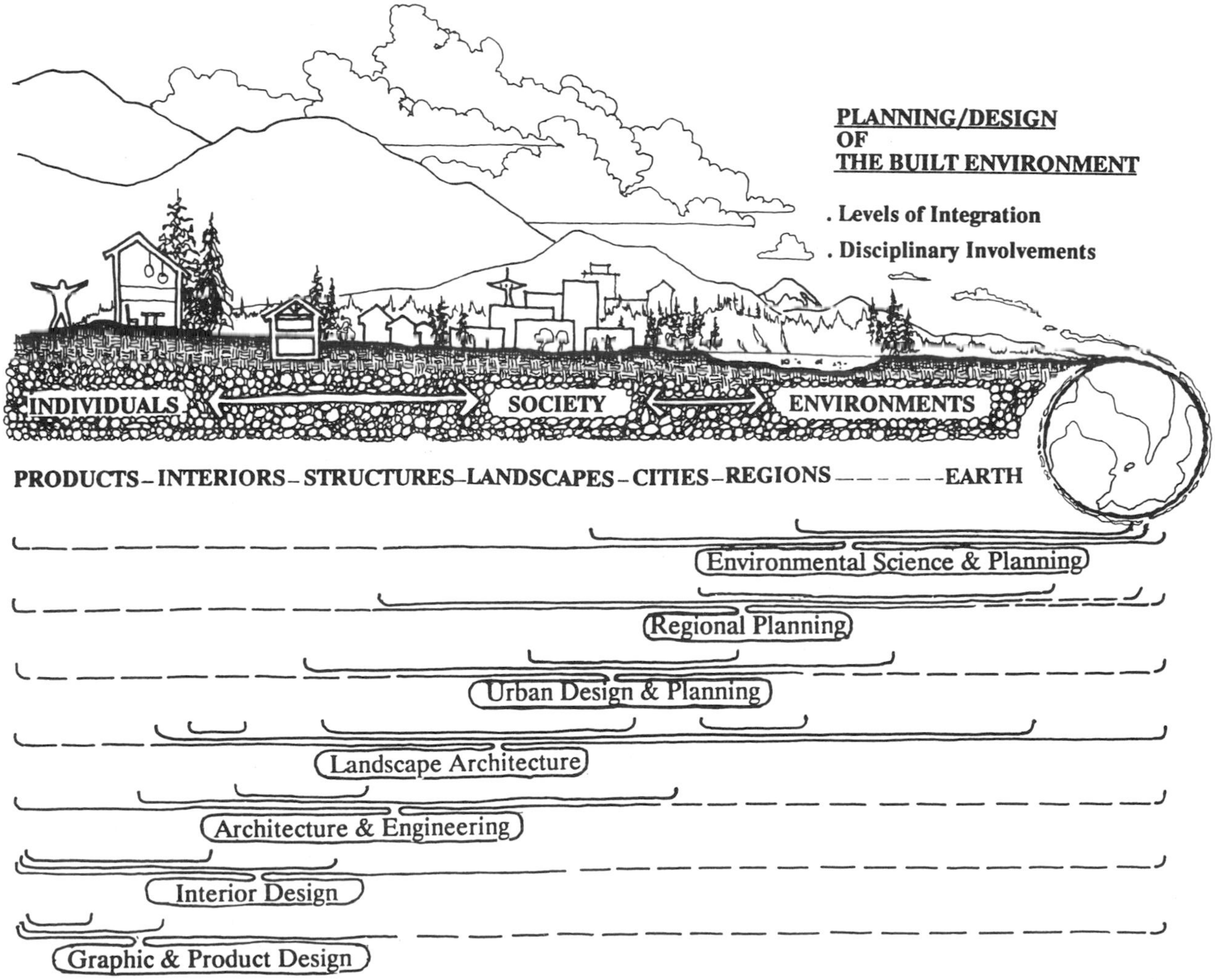

7. The overlapping relationships and responsibilities within the environmental design disciplines.

chapter: health, fitness and creativity. These terms have been in use for a long time and parallel Vitruvius's guidelines for successful built environments: commodity, firmness and delight. (Vitruvius was a Roman architect, engineer and scholar who lived in the first century B.C.) The terms have been adapted very effectively by Ian McHarg (1978) to discuss the utilization of qualitative dimensions in the decision-making process. McHarg is a world renowned, contemporary landscape architect and planner, ecologist, author and educator. He emphasizes that health, fitness and creativity describe ecological qualities of successful, life-sustaining environments. It is essential to understand these terms as an interlocking single triad concept: fitness requires health and creativity; health emerges from creative fitness; creativity is measured by an optimum degree of health and fitness. Each term deserves definition in greater detail.

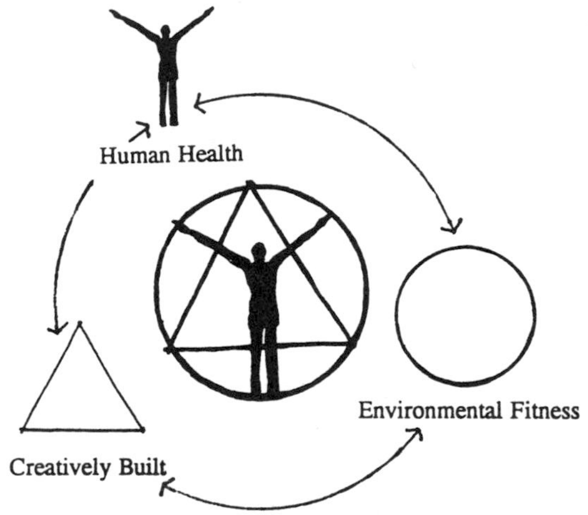

8. Health + Fitness + Creativity relationships within the Built Environment diagram.

Health is expressed in the search for creative fitness (a measure is how well any component functions within its context as established by the levels of integration conceptual framework). Dictionaries define health as of sound body, mind and soul. McHarg (1978) emphasizes the importance of health in the development of ecological design and planning. He builds on the work of Patrick Geddes, an early twentieth century Scottish planner and scholar, who stated a "healthy life is completeness of relation of organism, function and environment, and all at their best." This reinforces an emphasis on healthy human-environmental relationships. McHarg also uses a definition of health from the World Health Organization: "the ability to seek and solve problems," inferring that the most important demonstration of health is finding creative fitness. Health is also emphasized in state and federal laws and professional license requirements enacted to protect the "Health, Safety and Welfare" of society.

Fitness can be defined as an optimum condition for creativity and health (a measure of fitness is how well an entity is integrated into the context provided by the conceptual framework). The dictionary emphasizes the interrelationship of fitness with health by defining it as "adapted, proper, right, in fine physical condition, in good health, right in respect to nature of circumstance, use, etc.; fitness stresses adaptability, suitability by nature." McHarg notes that "the surviving organism is fit for the environment." The act of finding fitness must be a very important creative human activity. Henderson (1913) stressed the importance of this type of creativity by stating, "the quest of the surviving organism is to find the fittest possible environment and adapt that environment and itself." This statement emphasizes the importance of appropriate adaptive strategies—finding the fittest environment and then mutually adapting human needs and the environment to achieve a balance. Fitness also stresses "integration," fitting the components into their context and the idea of healthy human-environmentally fit relationships.

Creativity is the process of finding fitness and health. Webster defines creativity as "the act of bringing into being, the act of creating, to cause to happen, to bring about, to arrange as by intent or design." McHarg (1978) defines creativity in more challenging ecological terms as "the employment of energy and matter to reach higher levels of order," and that successful evolution is a "maximum success/minimum work" solution. Creativity, then, integrates important energy concerns into the central theme of this discussion.

Creativity is important to design and planning. In measuring creativity, some will emphasize newness and uniqueness. The above qualitative terms and definitions more appropriately emphasize effectiveness and appropriateness in achieving human health and environmental fitness.

In practical design and planning decisions, the terms quality and creativity need to be clearly defined and need to be measured. Quality and creativity are challenging and relative terms—some design decisions are considered of higher quality and more creative than others. The qualitative definitions suggest a method to measure and compare the relative creativity of one design to another by measuring the benefits and costs of each alternative. The most effective decisions would maximize the benefits and minimize the costs. This **Benefit/Cost Ratio** is an effective method used throughout governmental, engineering and planning segments of society. A method inclusive of the above qualitative terms would require maximizing benefits in terms of human health and environmental fitness and minimizing costs in terms of energy, long and short term monetary measures and/or environmental impacts. This general benefit/cost ratio is summarized below:

$$\text{Quality} :: \text{Creativity} :: \frac{\text{Benefits}}{\text{Costs}} = \frac{\text{Human Health \& Environmental Fitness}}{\text{\$, Energy and/or Impacts}}$$

Quality is a comparative term and the diversity of factors make it difficult to measure. Health, fitness and related costs can be measured in descriptive terms (listing and describing in verbal and written form the positive and negative characteristics of each alternative), in quantifiable or numerical terms (number of quantities, years of service, quantity of energy and costs in dollars) or relative terms (probably the most used because of the diversity of factors and information). Regardless of the method, the exploration of a Benefit/Cost ratio approach to decision making helps individuals and society make more effective and knowledgeable decisions. The following example will illustrate the use of the Benefit/Cost ratio in relative terms.

Example: A design firm proposed the following three design alternatives for your evaluation and selection. The firm has determined the following relative "benefits and costs." Which is the most effective design?

Design Alternative A. Has 46 Units of Benefits and 23 Units of Costs

Design Alternative B. Has 54 Units of Benefits and 32 Units of Costs

Design Alternative C. Has 44 Units of Benefits and 20 Units of Costs

The Benefit/Cost ratios are as follows (thehigher the B/C ratio, the more effective the design).

Design Alternative A—Comparative Quality ::

$$\frac{B}{C} \text{ Ratio} = \frac{46}{23} = 2.0$$

Design Alternative B—Comparative Quality ::

$$\frac{B}{C} \text{ Ratio} = \frac{54}{32} = 1.7$$

Design Alternative C—Comparative Quality ::

$$\frac{B}{C} \text{ Ratio} = \frac{44}{20} = 2.2$$

The most effective design is Alternative C.

In summary, understanding the intrinsic organization of the built and natural environment offers a challenging perspective on the quantitative

9 and 10. A comparison of quality: two adjacent streets in San Francisco, one exhibits a high degree of fitness & health, the other far less.

11. A predominantly "natural" environment illustrating the beautiful characteristics of a highly integrated natural system (a pathway from Zermat, Switzerland to the distant Matterhorn Mountain).

13. A harmonious design—integrating the diverse elements of the natural and built environment—urban plaza and landscape park adjoining the Provincial Law Court Building, Vancouver, British Columbia, Canada. The building and plaza were designed by Arthur Erickson, a prominent northwest architect. The creatively designed complex integrates products with interiors (reference Figure 15), interiors with the structure, and the structure with the urban landscape of the city.

12. A predominantly "built" environment illustrating the chaotic characteristics of a primarily disintegrated, segmented, competitive system (Chicago from Sear's Tower).

14 and 15. Exterior and interior of the Provincial Law Courts, Vancouver, British Columbia.

and qualitative dimensions of design. A close examination of the components and how they interrelate is aided by a simple conceptual tool, levels-of-integration. Integration is a key to quality environments. Integration requires an understanding of the content-component-context relationships found in the environment. Integration fosters quality—a creative search for healthy human developments that achieve a high level of fitness with the built and natural environment. The health, fitness and creativity characteristics and relationships can help us understand, measure and compare the qualitative dimensions of the built environment.

REFERENCES

Alexander, C., et al. 1987. *A New Theory of Urban Design*. Oxford University Press.

Bronowski, J. 1973. *The Ascent of Man*. Little, Brown and Company.

Henderson, L. J. 1913. *The Fitness of the Environment: An Inquiry into the Biological Significance of the Properties of Matter*. Beacon Press.

McHarg, I. 1970. "Values, Process and Form" *The Ecological Conscience—Values for Survival*, R. Disch (ed.), Prentice Hall.

McHarg, I. 1978. "Energy and The Built Environment: A Conceptual Framework." Lecture given to the Summer Institute on Energy Conscious Design, American Institute of Architects Research Corporation, Harvard.

Molnar, F. 1966 "The Unit and the Whole: Fundamental Problem of the Plastic Arts," *Module, Proportion, Symmetry, Rhythm*, ed. by G. Kepes. George Braziller.

Reekie, R. F. 1972. *Design in the Built Environment*. Edward Arnold.

Trancik, R. 1986. *Finding Lost Space: Theories of Urban Design*. Van Nostrand, Reinhold.

CHAPTER

6

People: Their Perception and Participation

Victoria Kolmodin and Tom J. Bartuska

Human-environmental relationships are a central theme in this study of the built environment. Three basic elements form this interrelationship: people, the natural environment and the built environment. The two environments (natural and built) have been discussed in the previous two chapters. The way people perceive and interact with the two environmental elements is further explored in this and the next chapter.

People are the primary participants in and benefactors of the built environment. People shape and build its contents and these built components then affect their behavior and life activities. We all profit personally, economically, socially, even culturally from the built environment's supportive qualities. We are also disturbed and limited by its disruptive characteristics. A quality environment nurtures public awareness, support and pride. Quality requires public appreciation, participation and support. A disruptive environment fosters alienation and apathy.

To achieve quality, we need first to better understand ourselves and others. We need to understand how people perceive the environment and how they can more actively participate in developing a quality environment.

INDIVIDUAL AND GROUP PERCEPTION

Human perception is complex. Perception is enhanced by increased understanding of three interrelated factors: the **individual** receiving the information, the **media** conveying the information, and the **objects** being perceived. Each factor has important characteristics which can enhance perception and increase understanding. These factors are outlined in Figure 1 and each is further examined in this chapter.

The availability and clarity of the object being perceived is an important aspect of perception. It is important to be able to experience objects firsthand, to be able to see them, to touch and appreciate their characteristics and qualities. Direct contact is an important aspect of perception.

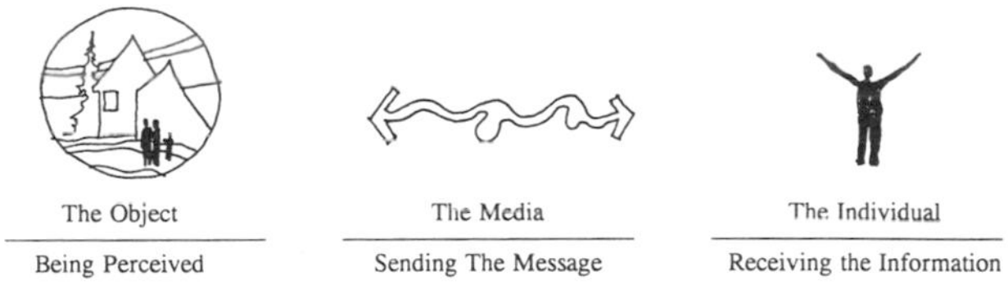

1. Symbols for the interrelated factors which influence human perception.

The Objects Being Perceived

Understanding of the object, its definition, organization and hidden dimensions can greatly

2. The Object: being perceived

The Objects Perceived	The Media Sending the Message	The Individual Receiving Information
* Natural Environment	* Direct Observation	* Attitudes & Values
* Built Environment	* Photography	* Awareness & Interests
• Products • Interiors • Structures • Landscapes • Cities • Regions • Earth	• Video & Motion Pictures • Still Photographs	* Sensitivity (Senses)
	* Scale Models	• Seeing • Hearing • Feeling • Smelling • Tasting
	* Drawings	
* People	* Diagram or Sketches	* Human Brain
• Individual • Groups • Societies • Global Communities	* Narrative Methods	• Right Sphere • Left Sphere
	• Written • Verbal	* Intelligence
		* Intuition & Wisdom

enhance perception. A full discussion of objects, in this case elements of the natural and built environments, has been developed in the previous two chapters. Components of the built environment are further developed throughout the remaining segments of the book. As knowledge of a subject grows, the ability to perceive and understand increases. We are more able to critically evaluate and appreciate the design qualities of the objects in the built environment.

The Media: Sending the Message

3. The Media: sending the message.

The media has numerous characteristics and qualities which can affect perception. Selection of the best type of media is an important aspect which can increase perception of ideas and objects. Since most of the built environment is three-dimensional, the media that best conveys the message should also have height, width and depth. Directly experiencing products, landscapes, cities, etc., conveys the clearest 3-D message about qualities of the built environment. Walking through a designed spatial sequence or landscape garden also develops an additional dimension—time. Dynamic sequences, changing effects of the sun, the speed of travel, etc., are all important aspects of time (commonly referred to as the 4th-dimension). Direct observation also provides multisensory experiences: One can see the object, touch its textures, smell its fragrance, hear any acoustical response, and at times, even enjoy the tastes of a well-designed assemblage of foods and flavors. Although most of us are visually dominant, multisensory experiences can produce greater combined effects on our perceptions, even heighten synergetic or climatic reactions.

Although perceiving real objects in space and time is the best way to appreciate components of the built environment, verbal or graphic techniques are useful and necessary supplements to communication media. The graphic image and the written word are convenient and central to educational experiences. We cannot all travel to Paris to study the beautiful qualities of the medieval cathedral of Notre Dame. For convenience, photographs, diagrammatic plans and sections, possibly a series of images, film or televised sequences (enhanced by verbal commentary) become useful and economical substitutes for the time, cost and energy required to experience the real thing.

Throughout the design and planning process, numerous verbal and graphic techniques are used to help develop and communicate ideas. Drawings and models are valuable tools in the creative process and can convey design ideas before they are built. These tools save enormous amounts of time, energy and material resources by communicating and evaluating ideas in a "real sense" without having to actually construct the product, space, structure, etc. Consequently, graphic and verbal skills are extremely important, not only to the designer and design process, but also to the client and to society. They provide an opportunity to see the design, evaluate and select the best ideas to be built. Scale models, drawings or perspective sketches can convey on paper or cardboard what could take millions of dollars to build in real materials and resources.

4. Designers using a model to replicate and study the qualities of an urban space surrounded by new and existing high-rise office buildings (Seattle, Washington).

Drawings are also powerful tools to aid an overall understanding of the built environment. The old statement that "a good picture is worth a 1,000 words" expresses the utility of graphic tools. In the design process, we constantly draw our ideas. The more we draw, the more we clarify and understand our creative thoughts, images and ideas. A plan, sketch or section drawn through a building or landscape design can convey relationships which are not apparent to a person observing the finished product. A diagram of the structural, mechanical and circulation networks can convey information that is hidden from direct observation. These are powerful tools, like observing the skeleton beneath the skin with x-ray vision. Graphics can be analyzed to foresee problems. They can be overlaid or layered one factor over another to facilitate coordination and integration. Analysis of the parts separately and synthesis of the parts together are important aspects of the ability to understand design.

The appropriateness and clarity of the sketched media can enhance perception of the components within the built environment. They help in numerous and creative ways to communicate human-environmental relationships.

The Individual: Receiver of the Information

5. The individual: receiving the information.

If we assume the environmental information and media are clear, then it is up to the person, the final factor of this three-way interactive-communication process, to receive and interpret the information. This final element is very complex and the most difficult to analyze in objective terms.

Human attitudes and values become a primary screen to perception. Is the person interested or apathetic? The simple mental attitude 'I am bored' can be self-fulfilling and make the best information boring. An open, positive attitude is a basic prerequisite to increased perception, awareness and understanding. Attitudes are like a self-fulfilling prophecy.

If they are positive, the information will tend to be positive ("I will" and probably you will). If they are tired or closed-minded, the information may be lost ("I can't" and probably you will not be able to achieve the objective).

An individual's personal background has a major influence upon the formation of attitudes and values. This is commonly referred to as one's *psycho-history*. For example, the perception of privacy can vary a great deal between a city-apartment dweller, a suburbanite, or a farmer. The concept of open space might vary considerably between a New York city person and one who lives in the mountains of the Pacific Northwest. [It is very useful—at this stage in reading this book—to write a brief psycho-history of yourself, including your background, where you grew up, details of your family and surrounding environment. This statement will help you understand your own unique attitudes and values about the environment.]

Values (discussed in the first chapter) are also a primary screen to personal interpretations of anything. In general, if the information is not valued by the receiver, it will not have very much impact. For example, consider debates where one person is arguing in social or ethical terms, while the other is arguing in economic terms. The values of the two people are different and the information does not have a common "language" or comparative basis. These kinds of discussions generally cannot be resolved, other than calling one person too practical, the other too idealistic and philosophical. Reviewing the value structure discussed in Chapter One may help put in perspective how values can limit or extend individual and group perception and appreciation of information.

Assuming human attitudes and values are positive, a person's sensitivity to information is the next perceptive screen. Individual sensitivity is based upon five perceptive senses: seeing, hearing, feeling, smelling and tasting. Again, various people, even various cultures, have different inbred levels of sensitivity. In general, most human perception is dominated by visual senses, with audio-sensitivity next. Limitations in one sense heighten the remaining senses. A blind person visualizes space by sound and reads by feeling texture. A deaf person hears language by visualizing word formation from the lips or fingers. It is useful to increase sensitivity by personal participation and experimentation. This is like exercises for an athlete. For example, what dominates your perception when in a dark room? Can you hear music better by closing your eyes? Do you enjoy the taste of food more by candlelight? Can you visualize things more by drawing them? All these are experiences which limit one sense and therefore heighten others.

Multiple sensory experiences also enrich perception. A room with the right combination of colors, textures, fragrances, music, etc., is more "experiential" than one which is visually (too much light) or acoustically (too much noise) dominated. A dinner with a delightful sequence of colors, textures, aromas, tastes, music and friends is a richer experience than a standard fast-chain burger-in-a-bun, everywhere, anywhere menu.

Multiple sensory experiences are also important in education. People retain more information if it is perceived by more than one sense. The following is a listing of the approximate percentages of retained information for each type of sensory experience (Kulda, 1975). People retain approximately:

- 10% of what they read .... read carefully
- 20% of what they hear .... listen carefully
- 30% of what they see .... examples are important
- 50% of what they see & hear .... illustrate lectures, take notes
- 70% of what they say .... discuss the issues
- 90% of what they do .... get directly involved.

Individual levels of interest, awareness, experience and intelligence are also important factors in a person's ability to understand and perceive the built environment. Personal understanding of the three basic factors (the object, the media and the individual) greatly enhance comprehension. The primary objective of this book is to make people more aware of the built environment. Various organizational concepts, examples, principles and criteria are intended to help the reader achieve this objective and, hopefully, become more sensitive to and aware of the various dimensions of this complex subject. Prior knowledge and experience help the individual process the information.

THE HUMAN BRAIN: THE PROCESSOR OF INFORMATION

The human brain is the single most important integrator of information. Its ability to receive information from the senses, compare and integrate each new message with past experiences and knowledge, and initiate a response is truly amazing. Understanding the basic brain functions can also give additional understanding of how humans receive and process information.

The human brain is made up of two major sides, or hemispheres, resembling the halves of a walnut. The nervous system is connected to the brain in a crossover fashion; the right hemisphere controlling most functions of the left side and the left hemisphere in charge of most functions on the right side (Edwards, 1979).

The two hemispheres are connected by the corpus callosum, a thick cable containing millions of nerve fibers. The main function of this cord appears to be the transmission of memory and learning between the two hemispheres (Blakemore, 1977). The two sides interact with each other; each one attempting to do what it "knows" it can do better. Sometimes, the sides cooperate, each contributing its special abilities. Other times, a hemisphere can work independently, with one half "on" and the other half "off."

Each hemisphere may be involved in perceptive functions, but each hemisphere appears specialized for different modes of learning (Edwards, 1979). The left hemisphere almost always "does the talking," being specialized for the language function. Understanding the spoken and written word are left hemisphere functions and it is considered "dominant," partially because of its ability to speak out. The right hemisphere has a limited speech function with the vocabulary and syntactical ability of a young child. However, the right excels over the left in recognizing patterns and shapes, especially in perceiving complicated solid objects and spatial or three-dimensional objects. The left hemisphere seems incapable of organizing three-dimensional forms (Blakemore, 1977). The abilities of the right side are important when studying the three-dimensional qualities of the built environment. The left side of the brain is also more capable of methodically analyzing the parts of a problem. The right side is better at synthesizing or integrating the parts into a unified whole. As emphasized before, both analysis (the left side) and synthesis (the right side) are critical to the design process.

Comparisons of the right and left side functional characteristics of the brain are listed in Figures 6 and 7 (Edwards, 1979).

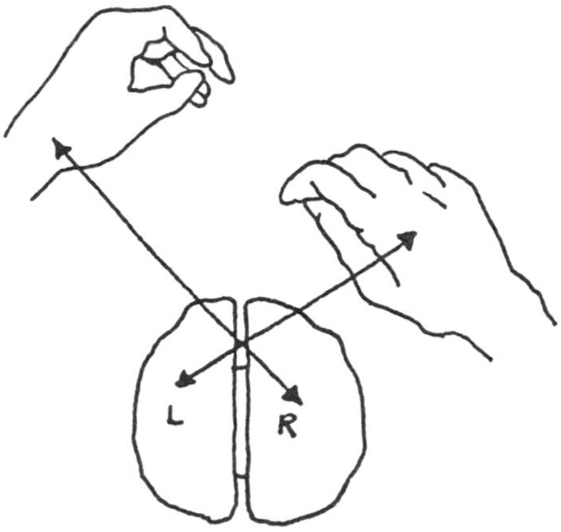

LEFT SIDE/MODE	RIGHT SIDE/MODE
ANALYSIS: Figures things out step-by-step and part-by-part.	**SYNTHESIS**: Integrates things together to form wholes.
VERBAL: Uses words to name, describe, define.	**NONVERBAL**: Awareness of things, shapes and objects, but minimal connection with words.
SYMBOLIC: Uses symbols to stand for something (letters, words, numbers, etc.)	**SPATIAL**: Visualizes shapes and 3-d qualities, see where things are in relation to others and how parts go together to form a whole.
RATIONAL/LOGICAL: Draws conclusions based on logic; one thing follows order--for example, a mathematical theorem or a well stated argument.	**INTUITIVE**: Makes leaps of insight, often based on hunches, feelings, or visual images.
LINEAR: Thinks in terms of linked ideas, one thought directly following another, often leading to a convergent conclusion.	**HOLISTIC**: Sees whole things all at once; perceiving the overall patterns and metaphoric relationships, often leading to divergent conclusions.
TEMPORAL: Keeps track of time, sequencing one thing after another: does first things first, second things second, etc.	**NONTEMPORAL**: Without a sense of time.

6. and 7. The crossover connections of left-hand to right hemisphere, right-hand to left hemisphere of the brain. The mental characteristics of the left and right hemispheres of the brain.

The hemispheres of an infant's brain do not seem to be specialized for separate functions (Edwards 1979). A young child can apparently develop speech mechanisms in the right hemisphere if the left side is damaged. There is, however, a critical period during which an infant's brain is able to develop the skill of talking. If a child has no contact with speaking people before the age of about seven years old, he or she will have a greater difficulty in learning speech later in life (Blakemore, 1977).

Drawing Human Perceptions of Three-Dimensional Objects

Drawing is an important integrative process. It helps the individual study three-dimensional aspects of the built environment. What helps or limits a person in visualizing and drawing 3-D forms?

Many children love working with drawing paper and crayons. But as children mature, their drawing skills seem to remain behind. Children draw like children and do not mind drawing like children. Most adults also draw like children, so many do not like drawing and feel embarrassed or inadequate when confronted with the need to draw. Why and when does this change take place? Tracing the evolution of drawing in the child gives some clues.

The first scribbled lines, "involve the exciting experience of bringing about something visible that was not there before" (Arnheim, 1964). This is a fundamental step in the development of the creative design process. The circle, the simplest possible shape, is drawn very early. Until shape becomes differentiated, the circle does not stand for roundness, but for any shape at all, and for none in particular (Arnheim, 1964).

Next, children enter into "symbols." They realize a drawn symbol can stand for something out in the environment. The child will draw from a collection of symbols and the fact that these symbols exist on paper is enough to satisfy some children.

Children invent symbols for the environment. They enjoy representing layers of ground and sky and use stylized symbols for the sun, a house, and smoke from a chimney. According to Rudolf Armheim (1964), "children and primitives draw generalities and distorted shapes." Some say they may be drawing what they see. Arnheim feels they see more than they draw; they have learned the process of representation. We teach children to accept a flat picture for a round body. Line drawings on blackboards and road maps creatively deviate from the objects they are representing. The child discovers and accepts the fact that a visual object on paper or modelled in clay can represent something that looks quite different in nature.

By age nine or ten, children try to express realism. The drawings become more complex. By age eleven, the specialization of the right and left modes of the brain is complete. The left brain becomes dominant and few know how to access the right brain. Children become unhappy with their sudden inability to achieve this heightened realism through drawings. At this age, many say, "I don't like to draw anyway."

A solution may be in education, developing more emphasis on the right mode, less on the rote left mode memorization process. Society tends to emphasize the language arts at the cost of graphic arts. School programs need more well-trained art and design teachers. People, especially educators, need to understand adolescents' desire for detail and their frustration about correct drawing. Such teachers need to have drawing skills so they can demonstrate principles that seem so obvious to those of us who can draw, such as the fact that we must draw unsquare shapes to draw a square cube three-dimensionally.

Edwards (1979) advocates more emphasis on the abilities of the right brain, but Blakemore

8. A child's drawing of the home environment.

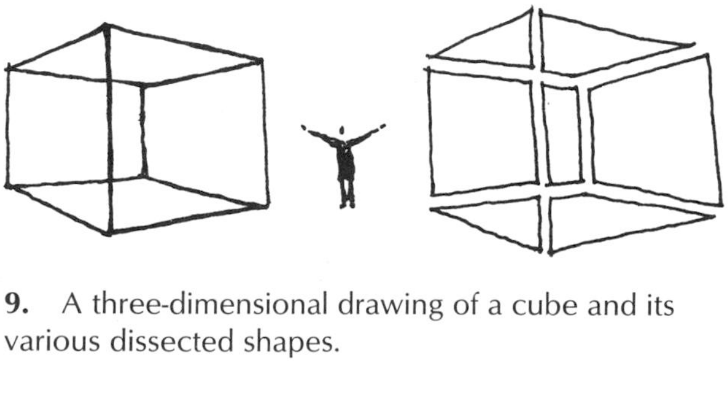

9. A three-dimensional drawing of a cube and its various dissected shapes.

(1977) urges caution. He feels that right hemisphere qualities, those of spatial perception, pictorial recognition and intuitive thought, are not easily taught by conventional education, nor is it clear that such qualities would benefit from years of formal education. Furthermore, according to Blakemore, the ripening of cerebral dominance is one of the important processes in the maturation of the brain. To encourage the minor (right) side to take charge could cause speech or emotional disorders, especially stuttering (disorders that are found in naturally left-handed children forced to use the right hand). It is apparent that more research is needed on how to best develop both sides of the human brain.

Drawing, as well as understanding, requires that the individual look critically at something for a long time. Edwards (1977) thinks that the dominant left hemisphere does not want to process too much information at one time. Since the two sides of the brain process the same information in two different ways, the left brain may dominate in analyzing the information and inhibit the right hemisphere from visualizing three-dimensional form. An individual's ability to draw may be controlled by the ability to shift ways of processing visual information from verbal and logical to spatial and intuitive so that the right brain is in control. Frederick Franck in *The Zen of Seeing* (1973), calls this shift SEEING/DRAWING and explains it like this:

> . . . awareness and attention become constant and undivided, become contemplation. SEEING/DRAWING is not a self-indulgence, a "pleasant hobby," but a discipline of awareness, of UNWAVERING ATTENTION to a world that is fully alive.

This consciousness shift has been felt by others as the different state entered when jogging, meditating, listening to music, or chanting. Feelings from this consciousness shift, into what Edwards calls the R-Mode, may include being unaware of the passage of time; either not hearing background noise or having no desire to hear it; a feeling of being alert, but relaxed; being excited while calm, confident, interested, absorbed and clear-minded. Artists working in the R-Mode may feel a sense of closeness with their work, a sense of timelessness and even difficulty in using words. At the same time, some pleasurable feelings may come just from resting the left hemisphere.

Regardless of one's point of view, drawing is a creative, integrative process which connects the object, the media and the individual together. Collier (1967) writes:

> Drawing should be used by beginning students to record their personal reactions to all kinds of stimuli; . . . in so doing the senses will be sharpened and the mental life quickened, through the exercising of intellect, intuition and feeling.

And Edwards (1979) states:

> Drawing is a teachable, learnable skill. . . . Drawing can expand awareness of the mind, increase creativity and imagination . . . seeing better and seeing more.

Mental Mapping: Drawing Human Perceptions of the Built Environment

Frequently, people are asked to give directions to a particular street or place in a city. The provider of the information generally pauses for a moment to visualize a mental map of the most direct route before beginning: "You need to continue on Main Street until the second, no, the third stop sign. You will know it because there is a grocery shop on the right. At that corner, take a left onto Paradise Street and. . . . " After two or three turns in direction, the receiver becomes overly saturated with information. After an additional turn or two, the receiver is sent off with the encouraging statement, "You can't miss it." It may be necessary, when traveling, to try to remember just the first two or three bits of information, politely ignoring the rest with a pleasant smile and thank you, then try to carry out the initial directives and ask again (hopefully, the new directions will not require back-tracking before finding the ultimate destination).

It is helpful to use a notepad to draw a mental map of the directions. A simple diagram achieves many of the following interesting and helpful things:

1. Drawing can help clarify the director's mental map, listing only the essential landmarks and directions.
2. Mental mapping techniques encourage direct participation. The director usually enjoys clarifying the directions by drawing a diagram.
3. Drawing integrates complex directions which would be difficult, if not impossible, to follow

without a diagram. This reinforces the notion that a picture is worth a thousand words—probably more because few people are able to remember the essential directions within the first few hundred words.

4. Graphic tools, commonly called mental mapping techniques, can be effective in foreign lands. In these situations, graphic symbols can replace language as a communication media.

Mental mapping techniques can be extended far beyond the simple example given above. They can be used throughout the design fields to encourageuser participation in the creative process. This graphic tool can help develop an understanding of how people, individually and collectively, perceive their environment. By analyzing such maps, prominent perceived characteristics and ways of improving the readability of the built environment can be determined. Drawing or diagramming becomes a useful and enjoyable technique for recording human-environmental perceptions of the built environment.

Human Perceptions in Space and Time: Seven x Seven

As noted earlier, individual perception is generally based upon personal values, background, interests, awareness and education. Perceptions generally deal with two dimensions—space and time. Most people are concerned with the immediate environment—their personal space, possessions, and home. Their concerns center around an immediate time-frame: today, tomorrow, possibly extending a week or two into the future. These are immediate concerns in which most people directly participate and which they try to or can control.

Although everybody is part of larger space/time dimensions ("Today is the first day of the rest of your life"), few people are deeply concerned with or involved in larger scale concerns. Too few are involved beyond their families, in their community or in planning for the next 10 years or for a whole lifetime. Most built environments reflect this limited perspective. In general, people take pride in personal possessions, their food and shelter, their stereo and car. They take better care of their own interior space and home than their neighborhood or city. They assume that others will participate at larger scales and take care of city spaces and services. People also resist paying taxes to support public services. Larger scale environments are not part of the general public's space/time perspective and, unfortunately suffer the consequences. Too often, people tend to insist on and attain beautiful homes, gracious private spaces set in sprawling, ugly cities.

Even fewer people are concerned with larger space/time dimensions—the global community and even their own entire lifetime, let alone the life spans of future generations. The chart expands our awareness of space and time. All scales are important, but the long-term ones are critical to the ultimate stability of environment and society. The graph in Figure 10 illustrates this space/time perspective. The black dots represent the relative number of people who are involved in various space/time categories (Meadows, 1972). Time is on the left and space is represented on the bottom by various components of the built environment.

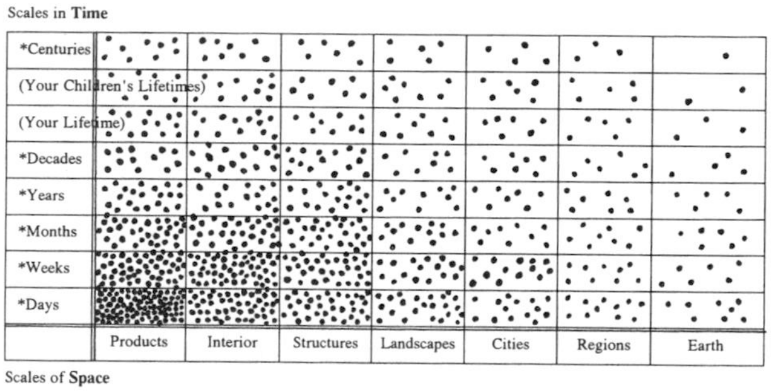

10. Space and Time Perspective (the dots indicate people with various space/time perspectives).

This book is based upon the exploration of seven components of the elusive built environment. In a similar way, we should consider seven components of time. "For guidance, look forward . . . think about the impact of your decisions on seven generations into the future" advises Wilma Mankiller (1991), a contemporary leader of the Cherokee Nation. "While leading her tribe to greater self reliance, [she] draws inner strength from the values passed down to her through generations." This statement directs us also to find wisdom and meaning from the influences of past culture(s), considering at least seven generations into the past.

INDIVIDUAL AND GROUP PARTICIPATION: A CRITICAL PART OF THE CREATIVE PROCESS

Human-environmental relationships are interactive and dynamic processes. Citizen participation is an active part of this basic relationship. Individual and group awareness and involvement are the foundation stones of an effective, participatory tradition and, for that matter, a democratic society. Participation has two rewards. First, knowing how people feel about important issues benefits society as a whole. A great deal of time, money and energy can be saved if decision makers know what their constituents really need and want. Surveys and opinion polls are popular and useful in assessing public attitudes and concerns.

Second, individual people benefit. They generally become more aware of issues and usually the interaction creates more appropriate decisions. It is fun to become more aware of and involved in human-environmental issues. A great deal of personal satisfaction and learning occurs (the highest percentage of learning occurs when people participate in the process, reference previous section of this chapter: people retain 10% of the information they read, 30% of what they see, and 50% of what they see and hear and 90% of the issues which involve direct participation). It is easy to participate. Newspapers and magazines, radio and television are a good place to start. If motivated to investigate the issues, public libraries are full of helpful, related reference material.

An enjoyable way to test ideas and concerns is through an open discussion with a close friend. Sharing ideas enriches true friendships and will help clarify and challenge concerns. (People will retain 70% of the information they convey by a discussion process.) An open discussion or debate is a useful question-feedback process which clarifies and enriches human perception and participation. (People retain 90% of the information relating to things which directly involve them.) Letters to the editor of news media are read or heard by thousands; letters to governmental officials are appreciated by most. All of these informal activities begin the process of citizen participation.

Civic organizations are another good avenue for increased dialogue on issues. Community Civic Trusts, Environmental Quality Commissions, Leagues of Citizen Voters, etc., are useful and enjoyable forums to explore ideas and concerns. Governmental and professional people are honored to speak at civic meetings and generally willing to donate their time and talents to sponsored activities. They are usually open to comments, suggestions and even a diverse point of view. Opinions and resolutions from organized groups have a greater influence on the decision-making process. If an organization does not exist, consider starting a discussion group with a few friends. All organizations have modest beginnings; the Friends of ____________ (you fill in the blank) can be an enjoyable and effective way to meet friends and influence people.

Governmental meetings in the United States are generally open to the public (except when in executive session). Public comments are encouraged (or at least they should be)—especially at formal hearings. Interest in serving on governmental committees and commissions is an enjoyable and fruitful commitment.

* Local (City	* Individual	* Individual Employee
* County (Regions)	* Groups	* Manager(s)
* State	* Committees/Organizations	* Department Head(s)
* Nation	* Councils	* Board of Directors
* Global (Earth)	* Mayors	* President
Geographical	Governmental	Companies, Corporations and Institutions

11. General organizational hierarchy of various public or private organizations.

The process of individual and group participation is like climbing the ladder of an organizational hierarchy. It begins with the individual; individuals form groups, committees or commission; individuals vote for elected representatives for local, state and national governmental offices. It may be tiring for some to climb such a complex hierarchy, but it is exciting to others and both the individual and society benefit from the participation process.

An alternate approach can be used—climb right to the top of the organization. Write a letter or schedule a meeting with the chair of the board, the president of the organization, the mayor of the city, the governor of the state, even the president of the country. They generally have a protected, but open door policy. If they do not, they should. Bring a friend for support. They will be polite if you are and both will be enriched by the interchange of ideas.

CONSPECTUS

Human-environmental relationships are complex, interactive processes—central to understanding the built environment. Human perception is a key to understanding the interplay between people and the environment. Human perception deals with three essential ingredients: the object being perceived, the media sending the message, and the person receiving the information. Awareness of these three factors enhances participation as well as the ability to understand, analyze and improve the intrinsic and supportive qualities of the natural and built environments. People have a variety of perceptions about the world in which they live. Many of these perceptions can be more clearly understood by analyzing our own values and background through a "psychohistory," a "space/time perspective" and perceived "mental maps" of the built environment. Individual and societal participation is important to the ongoing development of a quality built environment in a democratic society.

REFERENCES

Arnheim, R. 1964. *Art and Visual Perception*. University of California Press.

Blakemore, C. 1977. *Mechanics of the Mind*. Cambridge University Press.

Calvin, W. H. 1990. *The Ascent of Mind—Ice Age Climates and the Evolution of Intelligence*. Bantam Books.

Ching, F. 1990. *Drawing: A Creative Process*. Van Nostrand Reinhold.

Collier, G. 1967. *Form, Space and Vision*. Prentice-Hall.

Dulbecco, R. 1991. "The Design of the Brain," *The Design of Life*. Yale University Press.

Edwards, B. 1979. *Drawing on the Right Side of the Brain*. J. P. Tarcher.

Franck, F. 1973. *The Zen of Seeing*. Vintage Books/Random House.

Hall, E. T. 1966. *The Hidden Dimension*. Doubleday and Company.

Jaynes, J. 1976. *The Origin of Consciousness in the Breakdown of the Bicameral Mind*. Houghton Mifflin Company.

Jubak, J. 1992. "The Rules of the Brain," *In the Image of the Brain: Breaking the Barrier Between the Human Mind and Intelligent Machines*. Little, Brown & Co.

Kulda, R. 1975. "Management Workshop Notes," Professional Eloquence Workshop.

Laseau, P. 1989. *Graphic Thinking for Architects & Designers*. Van Nostrand Reinhold.

Mankiller, W. 1991. "She Leads a Nation," *Parade Magazine*, 18 August 1991.

Meadows, D. et al. 1972. *The Limits to Growth*. Universe Books.

Prochiantz, A. 1991. *How the Brain Evolved*. McGraw-Hill.

CHAPTER

7

The Role of Visual Principles in Ordering the Built Environment

Robert J. Patton

Humans not only try to order information by organizational concepts discussed in the previous chapters (hierarchies, levels or systems), but they also order the built environment by visual design principles. Visual principles are based upon human perception—visual response to human-environmental relationships. It is especially important to emphasize that human visual responses are intellectually-based and the resultant design principles help compose or order the diversity of elements in the built environment. This ordering or organizing helps one comprehend and enjoy an environmental setting, finding cohesive qualities and higher levels of comfort.

This chapter is based on a literal translation of the title and will emphasize "visual principles." In spite of their importance in human relationships with the physical environment, considerations such as survival, efficiency, technology, etc., will not be discussed. Another extract from the title which must be explained is the term "environment" (see Chapter 4). Although environment is all-inclusive relative to human perception, this section emphasizes that portion of the built environment composed of individual objects, buildings, groups of buildings and their surrounding landscape and urban design features. These visual principles can be and are applied to other environmental settings, from art and graphic design to urban and regional planning.

THE COMPLEXITY OF ASSESSING VISUAL VALUE: PRINCIPLES AND CULTURAL TENETS

When experiencing the environment, a natural human tendency is to attempt to do so within a visual value system developed as a result of experience or education. The value system would direct a response to a design as favorable or not. A value system developed through education is a learned system which excels in contradiction and complexity. In an attempt to clarify the relationship between perception and a visual value system, the reader should ponder what some might consider an outrageous statement—"there is no such thing as a principle of **good** design." This statement needs clarification and explanation.

The built environment is extremely complex and is composed of many variables. One of the most complex of these variables is the visual perception of physical objects, especially when it is evaluated and categorized as an art form. What makes this composition of elements complex is that throughout its historic evolution, the built environment is constantly being altered in response to changing social, cultural and technological determinants.

When we in the twentieth century study the evolution of the built environment, we find that we are the inheritors of a many-faceted amalgamation of aesthetic notions, some of which evoke positive response and some of which evoke negative response, depending on a particular point of view. The impact of this phenomenon intellectually makes us vulnerable to a broad, opinion-based value system. This can generally lead to confusion, at least in terms of feeling secure about what we have learned.

The most common educational defense against perpetuating this kind of insecurity is to limit the complex variability of opinion. The broadbase of subjective opinion is simplified by sorting it out into categories of facts or principles, which are the most

1. Informal, dynamic composition of a Medieval fortified town—Mont-Saint-Michel, France, thirteenth century (*T. Bartuska*).

objective concepts that the human intellect can comprehend. And this is where the problem lies in terms of developing a visual-value system. When the term **principle** is used, most of us think of the word in its real sense—a general truth or law. When applied to a visual-value system, it implies that there are governing rules which, if observed, will categorize something as "good" design. This could be true, but it is not necessarily always true because of the inevitable impact of human opinion. Opinion is intellectually dynamic and tends to be elusive. The kind of rules and laws upon which concepts of science and engineering are based are not generally applicable in visual design.

What are often being misinterpreted as principles of good design are actually "cultural tenets." A **cultural tenet** is a notion or an idea generated at a point in time perpetuated by an individual or group. In other words, a tenet is a "philosophy." Unlike principles, tenets are subject to change over either a long or short period of time.

Many of the changes in cultural tenets or beliefs have been introduced in Chapter Two on "The Four Traditions in the Built Environment." Changes are particularly expressed in the high-style tradition. In high-style design, we can find vivid examples of these dynamic changes. For example, during the twelfth, thirteenth and fourteenth centuries, great architectural achievements were developed in what is commonly referred to as the Gothic style—magnificent medieval cathedrals and active market towns where trade guilds refined products and produce. Starting in the fourteenth century, Renaissance architects rejected Medieval design because it did not visually emulate their ideal image of stability, power and grandeur. The Renaissance resurrected the more formal, classic forms developed earlier by Greeks and Romans and perpetuated them for the next three centuries. In the Renaissance, architects studied and reaffirmed classical purity to a depth of precision that required measured drawings of Greek and Roman ruins. Yet,

2. Formal classical forms of the Renaissance—Pazzi Chapel, Florence, Italy by Giullano da Sangallo, fifteenth century (*T. Bartuska*).

barely a century later, the transition to Baroque thinking challenged such accepted cultural tendencies and professed these principles of design as too "static" for the new society. Then, by the eighteenth century, the Baroque in its turn was decried as being a decadent art. Even in the nineteenth century, the writer John Ruskin considered the Medieval informal designs as one of the most dynamic periods in the history of art and proclaimed it as the most appropriate aesthetic for his time.

In the early part of our century, the architect Adolf Loos declared in a manifesto that "ornament is crime," setting the stage for a pristine international style which followed for seventy years. This notion was reaffirmed by Mies van der Rohe, who

3. The simplicity of form expressing the Modern Movement manifestos, "ornament is crime" and "less is more"—International Style residence, Berlin, Germany (*T. Bartuska*).

proclaimed that in architecture "less is more" and thus became known as the great modern classicist. Yet within the last ten years, architectural literature is talking about "the failure of modern architecture" and some young architects all over the world have turned to "Post Modernism," which, in part, reflects a return to historic features, including ornament. This aesthetic is seemingly passing and currently there seems to be a diversity of approaches, including regionalism, high technology, environmentalism, deconstructionism, etc. These will be explored in greater depth in some of the following chapters.

The point of these examples is to demonstrate that if the visual factors which highly influenced the architects of each of these eras had been based on "principles," which are defined as unchangeable truths or laws, there would have been, in fact, no change at all and those rebels who effected change would have become victims of time. Instead, what they were visually reacting against were "cultural tenets"—general themes or ideas that are highly influential, yet subject to change.

VISUAL PERCEPTION

The science of visual perception relates strongly to the art of the built environment and, interestingly enough, is based on "principle" in the sense that it deals with truths and laws. To avoid confusing this issue with what is outlined above, it is necessary to point out that principles of visual perception cannot be considered principles of "good" design. The reason for this is that scientific-based visual-perceptual principles cannot be applied by rote and necessarily guarantee good design results, yet they have existed as organizing tools of design throughout history. They exist today and will continue to exist as long as the built environment is a human, creative achievement.

The science of visual perception is based on the effects of human response to what is seen. The effect stems from a psychobiological condition common to all normal, healthy people, regardless of race or sex. It exists as the relationship between the action of environmental stimuli on the retina of the eye and the neurological reaction to these stimuli as this visual pattern is transmitted to the brain. It, together with the other four senses (touch, smell, hearing, taste), influences how people come to know and interpret their surroundings. Through a knowledge of the principles of visual perception, designers and artists can evoke a specific human psychological response to an environmental setting—static or dynamic, ordered or chaotic, formal or informal, etc.

However, the results can only be defined as good or bad design in terms of the broad, opinion-based tenets of the time. This is because the principles of visual perception cannot be applied indifferently with expectations that successful results will follow. Visual perception is best used by creative individuals for its organizational potential rather than accepting it as a principle of good design.

It is interesting to note that visual-perceptual awareness is evident in design and art throughout history, in spite of the fact that a clear scientific explanation of it did not surface until the research work of the German "Gestalt" psychologists at the turn of the century. An important analysis of the interrelationships between scientific visual perception and art did not emerge until the writings of Rudolph Arnheim in the second half of this century.

The following section attempts to categorize a few examples of the role of visual perception in ordering art and the design of the built environment. This is done to clarify the visual principles. In the real world, visual-perceptual notions applied by artists rarely appear as pure isolated examples. They tend to exist as combinations of principles enriched by artistic license and undefinable nuances of human creativity.

The names assigned to the following four categories are based upon human biological and psychological responses. They are listed by the perception type first along with (—) the related compositional relationship or organizing strategy. Again, they help order a composition and help the designers predict a human response. None of the principles are meant in any way to provide a means by which to distinguish between good or bad design. Also, this chapter explores visual concepts that are difficult to explain in words. Readers are encouraged to study the illustrations and seek out real examples in their own surroundings. They are abundant in all the components of the built environment.

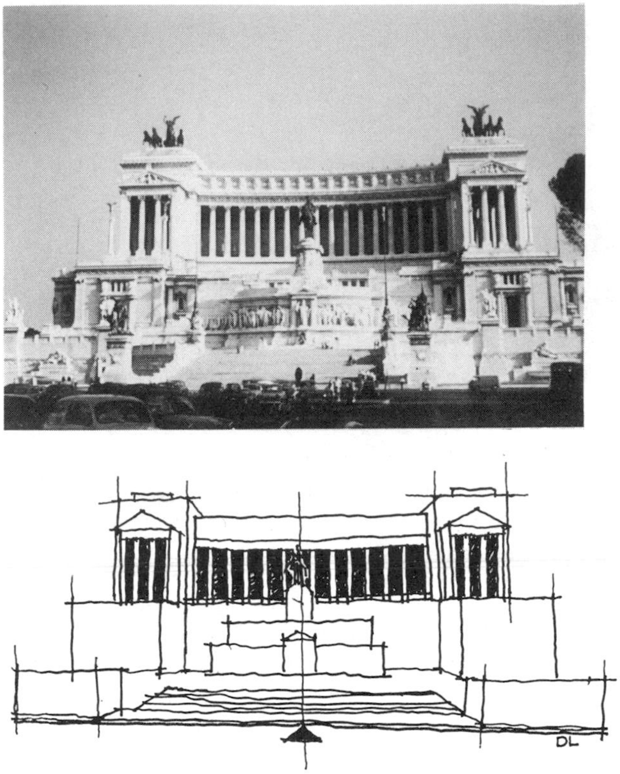

4 and 5. Static balance of a symmetrical composition—Victor Emanuel Monument, Rome, Italy, 1885 (*T. Bartuska*).

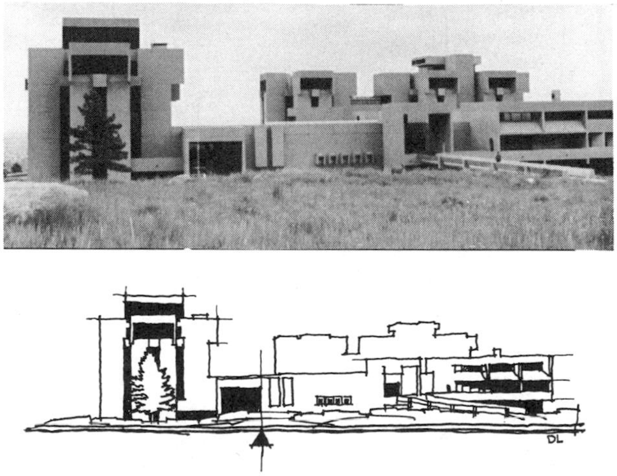

6 and 7. Dynamic balance composition—National Atmospheric Research Center, Boulder, Colorado by I. M. Pei, 1972 (*T. Bartuska*).

Psycho-Association Perception—Balance

Psycho-association is a perceptual experience that results from visually identifying a composition or object in terms of responses familiar or known through the other senses. The most commonly known perceptual relationship is static and dynamic balance. Humans physiologically experience balance. We know when our bodies are stable or falling by means of a message the brain receives from the movement of the fluid mechanism in the middle ear. We can also "feel" our weight, and can sense when it is equally or unequally distributed, particularly in terms of on which side of our center we will fall when we are out of equilibrium.

The translation into visual experience comes early in life through subconscious psycho-association with our known physiology when observing such things as balancing scales or ballet dancers. Likewise, when observing a designed setting or artifact, people relate to the sense of balance as it is expressed in symmetry, axis or focal point when these elements have been used by the designer to evoke stability in the composition.

8 and 9. Proportional relationships of the openings. Creates interest and a sense of organization and unity—Doge's Palace, Venice, Italy, constructed about 1485 (*T. Bartuska*).

Relationship Perception—Proportional Relationships

Relationship perception is a response that results from the identification of a visual element in terms of familiar or known information acquired through intellectual activity. This is generally achieved by establishing proportional relationships of objects by similarities in size and/or shape. Also, unified relationships are achieved by composing similar colors and textures.

For example, the visual-perceptual response to physical proportion has an intellectual relationship to mathematics in terms of equal or relative dimensional characteristics that cannot only be measured, but can also be sensed. Humans can sense when there is an identical or equal relationship between objects of the same size and shape. We can also perceive the relationship between objects that are of a similar shape, but a different size.

Relationship perception has a role in the design of the built environment where the designer wants to achieve a sense of relationship between the different physical elements of form and between those elements and the whole of the composition.

10. Contrast between sizes of openings. Creates multiple points of focus and interest—The Chapel at Ronchamp, France by Le Corbusier, 1950 (*T. Bartuska*).

Contrast Perception—Dominance and Subordinance

Contrast perception is the most acute of all the visual responses. It is based on the human ability to visually differentiate what is dominant and what is subordinate. It is one of the most important

11. The dominance of the Medieval cathedral contrasts with the subordinate scale of the secular buildings—Chartres, France; cathedral rebuilt in the thirteenth century (*T. Bartuska*).

12. The cantilevered forms create a dynamic visual experience—Falling Water Residence, Mill Run, Pennsylvania by Frank Lloyd Wright, 1936 (*T. Bartuska*).

factors that allows people to orient themselves in a complex environment. When the ability to perceive contrasts is cut off by things like darkness or fog, we tend to become disoriented.

Contrast perception is often used by designers to attract the eye to single or multiple points of focus. By organizing elements of contrasting attention, specific eye movement can be predetermined. This can be achieved by contrasting sizes, shapes, colors or textures of various objects composed.

The contrast between dominant and subordinate sized elements is common in both historic and contemporary settings. It is a device used to reinforce the prominence of the most meaningful institutional and/or cultural symbols of a society—religious, political and economic. Often the physical dominance of these elements provides a means of orientation for people in the complex environment of a compact and dense city.

Anticipation Perception—Rhythm

Anticipation perception is the human ability to predict what is going to happen next in a sequence of visual events. It is one of the most dynamic visual situations that can be set up by a designer. Inherently stable elements can be organized to cause the eye to be directed in such a way that it will anticipate movement that actually never happens.

One definition of this phenomenon is illusion. For example, physical elements can be organized in a regular, recurring rhythm that will cause the eye to follow them through the composition. If the regular recurrence is not terminated by a contrasting element, the eye will continue off into space because it becomes conditioned to anticipate the recurrence to continue (even though it does not).

Another form of anticipation perception takes us back to the psycho-associated sense of weight and balance. Modern engineering has provided the means to create structures which have no visible means of support. As human observers, our perceptual senses have conditioned us to expect heavy physical masses to be visibly supported in equilib-

13. The repetitious rhythms of the colonnade and window pattern directs the eye across the composition—Crescent, Regents Park, London, England by Robert Nash, 1821 (*T. Bartuska*).

rium, or they will fall or collapse. A cantilevered or suspended building properly engineered will never fail, but it raises a perceptual question which results in a dynamic visual experience.

SUMMARY

"There is no such thing as a principle of good design." "Goodness" or "badness" is not achieved through the unconditional use of any principles, including visual-perceptual principles. The visual principles described in this essay may or may not have visual value in themselves. They are best accepted as "tools" to help organize the elements of the built environment. Good design is dependent upon how these tools are manipulated by the designer and the cultural value system of those who perceive the result. The true reality of good design is based upon that elusive and indefinable human quality known as creative intuition.

PART III

Design Components in the Built Environment

Design Components in the Built Environment

Introduction

This section marks a transitional point in study of the built environment.

The previous sections explored various definitions and concepts intended to clarify the vast scope, purpose and interrelated complexity of the built environment. It is necessary to comprehend the integrating concepts in order to more fully address the contributions each component can make to the humanly created world. In general, the definitions and concepts emphasized are outlined below:

- Definition of the Built Environment and Its Four Characteristics
- The Seven Selected Components of the Built Environment
- Why Humans Build—Human Needs and Values
- Four Traditions
- Levels-of-Integration, Analysis and Synthesis
- Human-Environmental Relationships and Adaptive Strategies
- Quality Requires Integration; Creativity is Comparatively Measured by Maximizing Health and Fitness while Minimizing Costs and Impacts
- Individual and Group Perception and Participation
- Visual Principles for Ordering the Environment

The seven sections in this part of the text explore, in greater detail, the characteristics and qualities of seven selected components within the built environment: products-interiors-structures-landscapes-cities-regions-earth. Each section also addresses in greater depth the human creative contribution, the people and professions who individually and collectively participate in the design and planning of this elusive continuum, each component adding to the others to form the overall built environment. The active human elements of the design and planning professions are better understood as cooperative, instead of competitive, agents in the creative process. It is through participation or collaborative teamwork that a more fitting and appropriate design is developed, thereby integrating quality components into the total environment. These professions, linked together, are commonly referred to as the **Environmental Design Disciplines**. The following general list shows the seven selected components (environments—on the left) and the related environmental design discipline team (human participants—on the right).

- Products .... Graphic Designers & Artists, Product or Industrial Designers
- Interiors .... Interior Designers
- Structures .... Architects & Engineers
- Landscapes .... Landscape Architects & Planners
- Cities .... Urban Designers & Planners
- Regions .... Regional Planners & Ecologists
- Earth .... Environmental Scientists & Global Planners

Fundamental to the study of this pervasive though still evasive subject, is the integration of previous "conceptual" ideas into the chapters that remain to apply the overall definitions and concepts to the study of each component. The reader will be continually challenged to put all the pieces of the puzzle together, to ask whether issues and design ideas are isolated or integrated, and to fully address each component in context with the others. The sections in this part of the book, each with several chapters, peel back and examine the "layers" that reveal the primary components interwoven into the intricate and beautiful tapestry of the built world. These interrelated layers are emphasized in the book's graphic logo. (See Figure 1.) This symbol abstracts the separate layers or components which must creatively fit together—emphasizing that one level builds upon the next, and then the next, etc., to form a unified and interrelated whole.

The seven selected components or "layers" are organized and tabulated into sections as illustrated in Figure 2.

The reader will find a great deal of overlap between each section, between each design and planning professional role. In general, each professional specializes in one level, but extends some distance into the margins of others. Quality emerges if each professional is aware of overlapping responsibilities, mutual respect and teamwork. Integration is a key word to good design. Environmental designers, to be successful in a larger or holistic sense, must comprehend these interrelationships while fully identifying with the specific characteristics and requirements of each area of specialization. In other words, designers need to be generalists with an area of specialization or, as the great inventor, architect and futurist R. Buckminister Fuller stated, they should be able to respond to the need for "macro comprehension and micro incisive solutions" (1970).

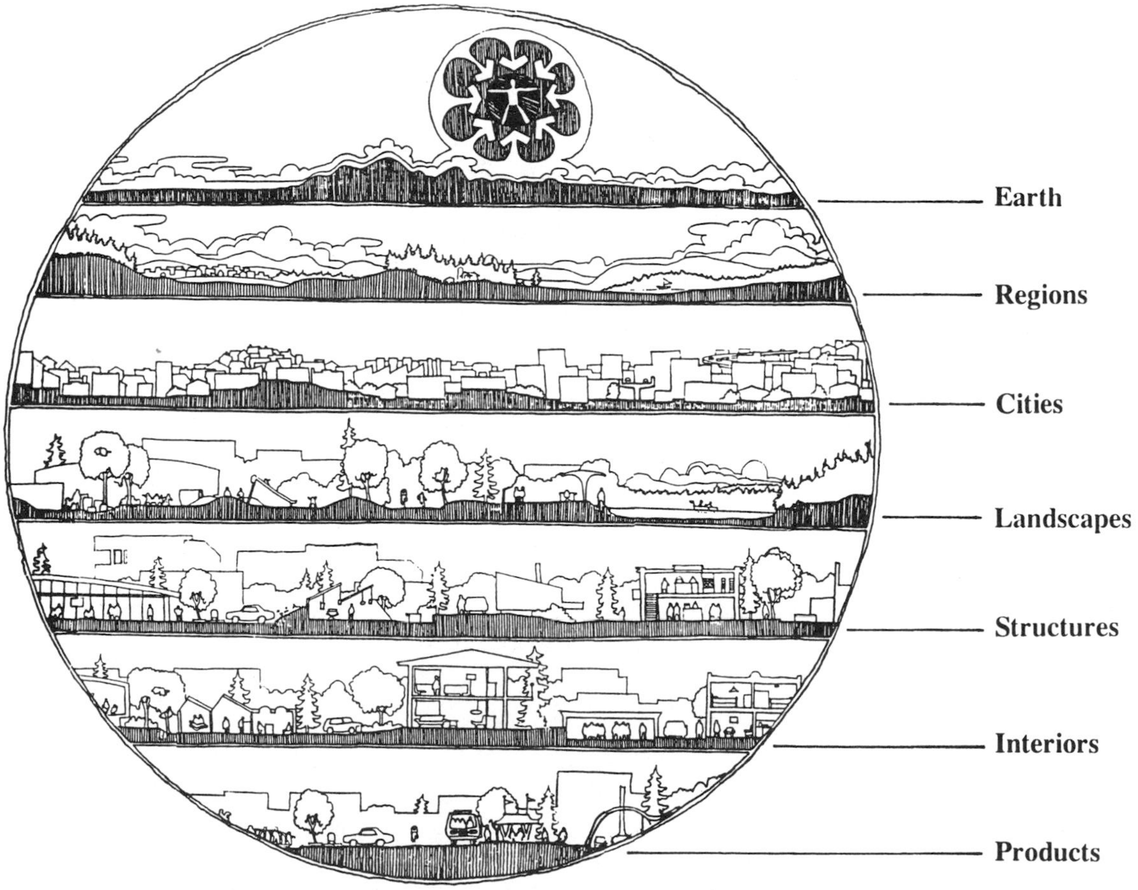

1. Graphic logo illustrating levels-of-integration in the Built Environment (*S. Recken and J. Singleton*).

1. PRODUCTS

Reference pages 77–103 →

2. INTERIORS

Reference pages 105–136 →

3. STRUCTURES

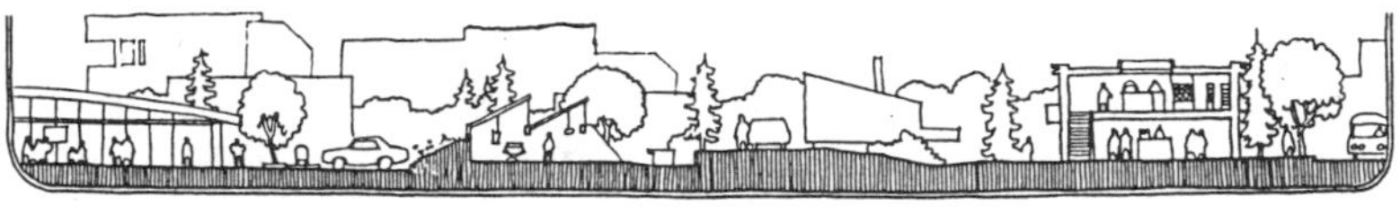

Reference pages 137–189 →

4. LANDSCAPES

Reference pages 191–242 →

5. CITIES

Reference pages 243–302 →

6. REGIONS

Reference pages 303–340 →

7. EARTH

Reference pages 341–368 →

2. The seven levels of the Built Environment (*J. Singleton*).

The special aspects of each component or professional role can be defined by differing "space/time" characteristics. For example, a product or interior designer deals with a smaller scale than a landscape architect or urban planner. The human-environmental variables are similar in kind, but different in scale. Also, the time required to investigate each type of problem is different. The interior designer may take a week or months to achieve a completed design product whereas the urban planner may need years, even decades, to achieve changes in the design of a city or region. These differences should be understood and appreciated. They should also be matched with each individual's personal traits, talents, and interests. If peoples' space/time perspective is compatible with the task at hand, their potential involvement and success will be greater. A compatible, integrated space/time fit is necessary for each professional role, but just as important or more important is that the public realize and appreciate the differences in space/time dimensions, so that society arrives at a collective, integrated understanding of the built environment. The chart below summarizes these space/time characteristics.

In addition to space/time perspectives, the type of client each design discipline works with is very different. Even though all environmental design disciplines are confronted with somewhat similar human/environmental relationships, interior designers and architects may work with an individual or family in the design of a home, while urban, regional or global planners are required to deal with the collective hopes and aspirations of people in large political or geographical regions. Landscape architects can deal with clients directly around a conference table, whereas urban/regional planners may have to deal with political representatives, take public surveys and use public media to approach projects, programs, and policies at larger scales.

All the environmental design fields have a common professional mission—to develop a "quality" built environment for their clients, users and

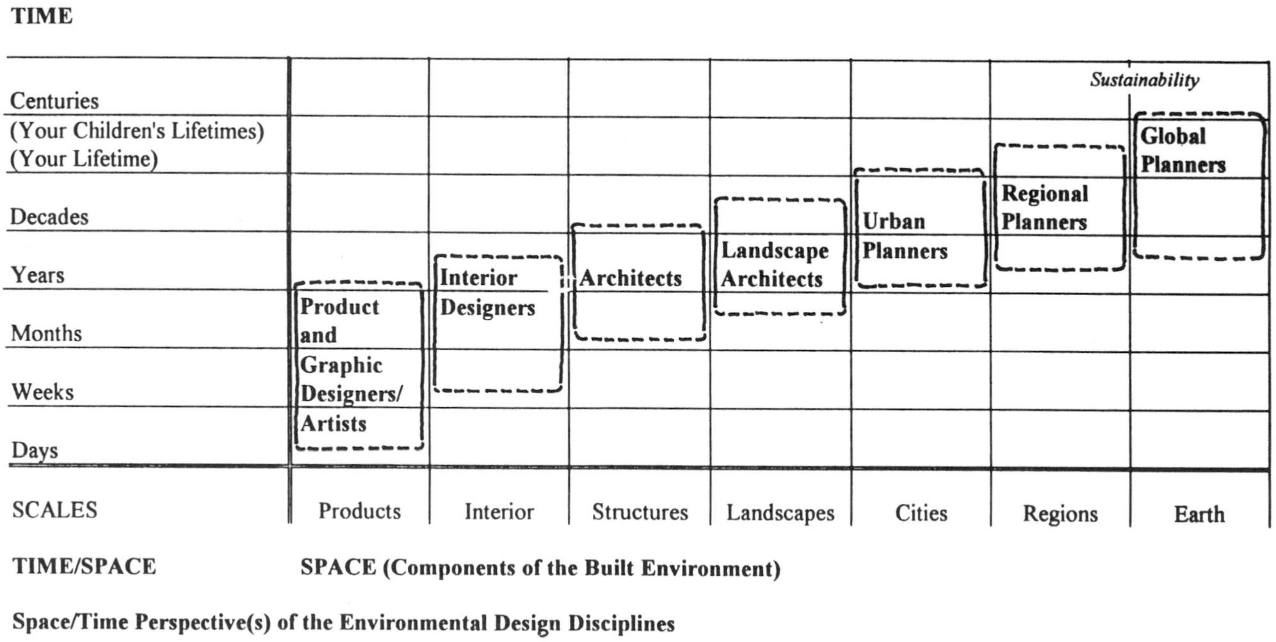

3. Various space/time perspectives of the environmental design disciplines.

the public. There are, of course, many differences in scale (from products to regions to earth) and a great variety in the variables each discipline deals with in design. Design or the **design process** is a common theme throughout the pages of this book as well as throughout all the environmental design fields. These commonalities enable them to understand each other and collaborate more effectively together on complex problems.

Also emerging from the following sections are working definitions of each design profession. By comparing the evolution of these definitions, one discovers additional similarities. In general, all the design professions deal with the "art and science" of solving their particular component of the built environment. This dual charge evolves from the Arts and Crafts Movement and the scientific, technological and engineering discoveries of an advancing global society. Therefore, the design **professions** deal with the **Art, Craft and Sciences** of the built environment. These four terms also imply quality by the inclusion of the following definitions and related characteristics.

1. **Art:** Skill in performance, acquired by experience, study or observation, ingenuity.
2. **Craft:** An art trade or occupation (referencing profession) requiring special skills; to make or manufacture (an object, objects, products, etc.) with skill and careful attention to detail.
3. **Science:** Knowledge, obtained by studying and experiments; accumulated knowledge, discovery of general truths or operation of general laws (engineering, inclusive of physical science, biological sciences, human/social/psychological sciences, and environmental sciences).
4. **Profession:** A public declaration of an occupation to which one devotes oneself.

Robert Pirsig (1974), a popular yet probing author of the late twentieth century, writes about quality. He agrees that quality combines the arts and sciences: it is "a kind of harmony . . . to produce a complete structure of thought [and design] capable of uniting the separate languages of science and art into one."

For the reader's reference, the following chart summarizes the type of variables dealt with at each component level in attempts to solve built environment problems. The reference chart also lists the various types of environmental design disciplines and consultants who are participants in this collaborative

THE ENVIRONMENTAL DESIGN DISCIPLINES

Built Environment Components	Design Profession (Generalized Title)	Disciplines Working at this Scale	Some Support Specialists
PRODUCTS	PRODUCT OR INDUSTRIAL DESIGNER	**Industrial Designer** Designer Interior Designer Architect Furniture Designer Engineer	Graphic Artists and Illustrators Textile Designers Lighting Designers Costume Designers Manufacturer Representatives • Materials • Furniture • Appliances/equipment • Lighting • Computers • etc. Engineers Production Specialists Material Scientists Context: see below

THE ENVIRONMENTAL DESIGN DISCIPLINES (continued)

Built Environment Components	Design Profession (Generalized Title)	Disciplines Working at this Scale	Some Support Specialists
INTERIORS	INTERIOR DESIGNER	**Interior Designer** Architect (Interiors) Interior Decorator Exhibit Designer Stage Designer Space Programmer	Content: see above Manufacturer Representatives • Furniture • Carpets, textiles, paints, stains • Kitchen, Bathroom, etc. • Lighting Engineer or Designer • Maintenance Specialists • Industrial Scientists, etc., etc. Space Programmer Behavior Scientist Architects & Engineers Functional Specialist • Hospital • Airport • Factory, etc. Context: see below
STRUCTURES	ENGINEERS (Professional)	**Engineers** Agricultural Chemical Civil Electrical Environmental Material Mechanical, etc. Technician Scientist	Content: see above Numerous Specialists relating to materials, processes and production.
		Architects Environmental Designer Building Designer Engineer Drafts Person Interior Designer Designer Developer Builder/Contractor	Material Representatives Financial Real Estate Surveyor Programmer Space Planner Engineers • Soils • Structural • Mechanical • Electrical • Acoustical Maintenance/Life Cycle Cost Consultants Landscape Architect

THE ENVIRONMENTAL DESIGN DISCIPLINES (continued)

Built Environment Components	Design Profession (Generalized Title)	Disciplines Working at this Scale	Some Support Specialists
			Interior Designer Construction Managerer Developer Urban Designer & Planners City Planner & Engineers Context: see below
LANDSCAPE	LANDSCAPE ARCHITECT	**Landscape Architect** Gardener Horticulturalist Ecologists Planner/City and Regional	Content: see above Attorney Real Estate Broker Developer Builder Contractor Nurserykeeper Economist Marketing Analyst Sociologist Psychologist Horticulturalist Botanist Geographer Soil Scientist Geologist Forester Context: see below
CITIES	URBAN DESIGNER	**Urban Designer** Architect Landscape Architect Urban Planner Urban Historian	Content: see above All Human-Environmental Disciplines –Natural Environment –Built Environment Political
	CITY PLANNER	**Planners** Urban Designer Architect Landscape Architect Civil Engineers	Economic Transportation and Urban Infrastructure Engineering Social, Cultural, Recreational Educational, etc. disciplines Context: see below

THE ENVIRONMENTAL DESIGN DISCIPLINES (continued)

Built Environment Components	Design Profession (Generalized Title)	Disciplines Working at this Scale	Some Support Specialists
REGION	REGIONAL PLANNER	**Regional Planner** Environmental Scientist Economists and Geographers (In Regional Science) Ecologists Systems Analyst	Content: see above All Human-Environmental Disciplines Geologists Meteorologists Botanists Hydrologists Soils Scientists Behavioral and Social Scientists Biologists, etc. Context: see below
EARTH	GLOBAL PLANNERS	**Global Planner** Environmental Scientist Ecologist Systems Analyst Politicians and Diplomat International Organization (U.N., AID, World Bank, etc.) Futurist	Content: see above All Human-Environmental Disciplines

study. The chart is a useful guide to relate employment and business opportunities in these environmental design, planning and management fields.

As noted, this part of the book is grouped into seven sections which explore various aspects of the seven selected components of the built environment. These seven components interlock and form the **content-components-context** of the study of the built environment. Each section contains several chapters and starts with an introduction to help remind the reader of the unifying definitions and concepts.

REFERENCES

Fuller, R. Buckminster, 1970. *Operating Manual for Spaceship Earth*. Pocket Books.

Pirsig, R. M. 1974. *Zen and the Art of Motorcycle Maintenance*. Bantam.

Introduction

1. PRODUCTS

Products are the first and most basic building block of the built environment. Products are so numerous—ubiquitous—that they are oftentimes overlooked and taken for granted, yet they are of fundamental importance to everyone.

The human ability to develop and use "tools" has extended the somewhat limited natural capacities of the species to accomplish life's ongoing activities. Although humans are not as physically capable as say a lion or tiger, humans have created tools, weapons, etc., to not only survive but to attain the capacity to dominate all other creatures on earth. In the most basic sense, the ability to create products distinguishes humans from other species of the animal kingdom and provides extensive capacities to do many of the things we want to do in the world.

Products not only extend human capacities, but also extend responsibilities. With a stone axe or spear, one may have dominance over a few; but a red button connected to a nuclear arsenal provides the capacity to control or destroy the world—and generates an accompanying responsibility. Consequently, when dealing with products, it is important to connect human intellectual capacities to create with responsibility and social conscience. The simplest of products are "processed" many times, consume large amounts of resources, and cause considerable environmental impacts if they are not reused or recycled.

Definition of the built environment can be adapted to help us define the content and context of "products." The definition can be broken down into a four-part set of subrelationships and implications:

a. Products are objects which are humanly made or arranged;
b. to fufill human purpose, to satisfy human needs, wants and values; and
c. to mediate the overall environment (to extend our capacities);
d. with results that affect the overall environmental context. (The context for products includes interiors, structures . . . to earth. It is important to note from the prior discussion that products such as our nuclear weapon system can affect the ultimate context, can destroy all life on earth.)

Products begin the layering of the components which form the built environment. In general, these layers are as follows:

- **products** build interiors
- interiors combine into structures
- structures and external spaces are combined into landscapes
- landscapes combine with structures and form cities
- cities grow within regions
- regions are subunits of the earth
- Earth . . . the ultimate context for all the above is even referred to by some as a type of product, a "spaceship" earth

This layering, one building upon another, can be placed into the following levels-of-integration continuum:

PRODUCTS-INTERIORS-STRUCTURES-LANDSCAPES-CITIES-REGIONS-EARTH

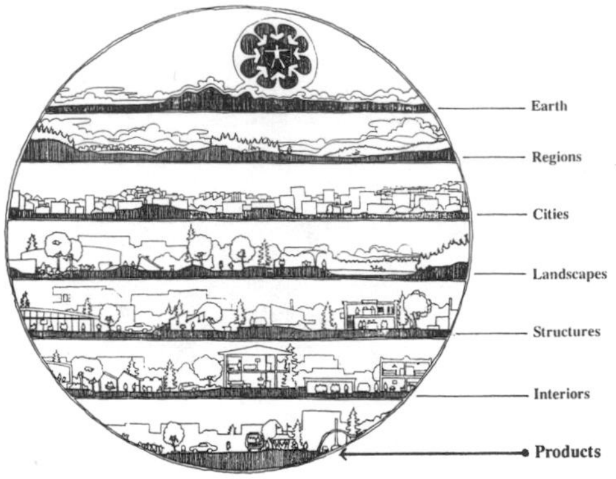

Readers will find it enjoyable—and challenging—to observe the products which surround them, that help them with life activities:

- This book conveys the authors' ideas and concerns, through humanly created letters, arranged in words, sentences, paragraphs, chapters, etc.—the created language of civilizations.
- Eyeglasses may extend human capacity to see, while microscopes and telescopes study the seemingly invisible worlds smaller and larger in scale than normal vision can perceive.
- Clothing keeps us comfortable and warm, helps convey moods, expresses informal or formal values, etc.
- Machines and appliances help people cook, wash clothes, create; envelop human life with music and electronic communication from distant places.
- Walls are made of numerous fascinating products, which help mediate the external climate. They are designed to define quality spaces for almost all life activities.

The products that surround us are extensive. They are humanly created as extensions of human life activities. The chapters in this section explore various aspects of products and their design:

- **"The Humanly Made Object as Part of the Built Environment"** by Catherine Bicknell: The first chapter explores the human impulse to create objects or products and discusses the functional and cognitive meaning they have upon human life. The chapter analyzes various traditions in product development. The author concludes with a discussion of how products have caused a shift in society from natural to human dominance and with the premise that products are part of and dependent on larger systems in the built environment.

- **"From Craft Tradition to Industrial Design"** by Catherine Bicknell: The second and last chapter in the product section examines the historic roots of product development from that of a handcraft art to industrial design today. The author concludes with a discussion about the impact of products on twentieth century society and how this creates important responsibilities for the users and designers of contemporary products today.

CHAPTER

8

The Humanly Made Object as Part of the Built Environment

Catherine Bicknell

Human beings cannot survive in isolation. In order to live, they need air, water, food and light and are, therefore, dependent on their surroundings. They are just a part of a much larger whole. Beyond the bare necessities, the human race impulsively modifies the environment to create objects and to provide shelter and protection.

THE PRIMARY IMPULSE TO CREATE OBJECTS

People from the most ancient and prehistoric times to the present have deliberately shaped utensils, tools, clothes, weapons and ritual or decorative artifacts as extensions of themselves. For example, clothes are created to improve thermal protection, and tools and weapons are developed to extend the use of hands and enable them to perform tasks beyond their original capabilities. These objects are found in a variety of forms in different parts of the world. They are made for the same use, but in different places, so may vary considerably according to local materials and traditions and to different levels of ingenuity and skill.

THE FIRST ARTIFACTS

Archaeological evidence indicates that from earliest times, humans have exhibited the skill to fashion artifacts; the skill to sharpen flint, for example, has appeared in the form of arrowheads, knives and axe heads found all over the world. The original axe, as an object and a tool, was conceived through the selection of an appropriate material and discovery of the functional form.

The first stages in development of the axe were obviously practical. The toolmaker had to select the right material for the axe head and then concentrate on perfecting its cutting power. This involved the gradual smoothing, polishing and refining of the blade until it reached its optimum point of efficiency. The shaping and attachment of

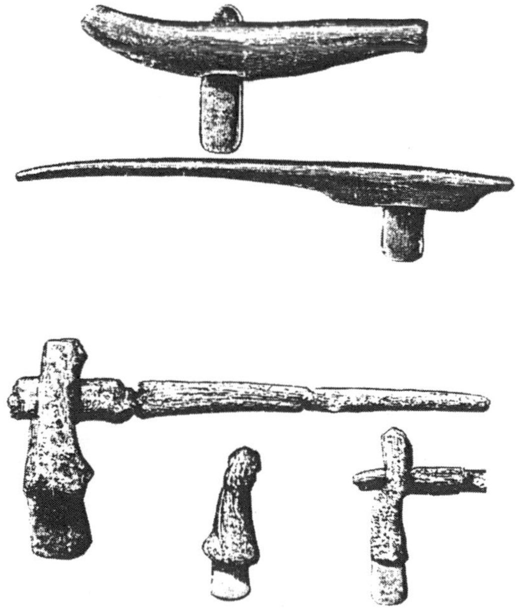

1. Primitive Axes: Shaping and refining the functional form and searching for the most effective materials.

the handle posed a difficult problem, for it needed to be comfortable in the hand, easy to grip and well balanced. By a long process of trial and experimentation, the flint axe developed the characteristic form not very different from the axe we use today. But though its general appearance may have remained the same, the cutting material has been changed and refined way beyond its original concept in stone. The search for the best materials and the most effective functional form emerges even today as an important aspect of contemporary product design.

THE COGNITIVE ASPECTS OF OBJECTS

An axe can be seen as something familiar with a known purpose, like a spade, a fork, a cup or bowl. This familiarity is visible in the external shape of the object. It communicates its purpose without words. What is this visual language? Certain objects communicate what they are by the familiarity of what they do: their **function**. We observe them performing their function and, therefore, we know what they are. Others communicate through their appearance: their **form**. We recognize their form and know what their function is. Some objects do not possess a practical function, but have qualities that are purely **aesthetic** or **symbolic**. They were made to be looked at and enjoyed or to convey ideas or meanings. Their significance or even beauty may not be immediately understood by the uninitiated observer; the growth of an aesthetic sense or the comprehension of complex symbolism may require a process of learning. For this learning process, we need the help of our perceptive abilities. Perception of an object is how we tell whether things are near to us or far away, whether they are large or small, flat or curved. This overall knowledge and related meaning of objects has been developed over time from human experience with nature and with the built environment. Perception is the action of a person's mind to identify objects from external sensations.

Recognition of an object through perception is a communication that transcends the spoken language. For example, most people will recognize the distinct image of a San Francisco cable car or a double-decker London bus; the image alone will communicate a sense of place much faster than the spoken word.

2. Products: Their form expressing the functional purpose and symbol meaning.

The Universal, the National and the Regional Object

Today, as never before, certain common objects can be seen anywhere. For instance, the transistor radio can be seen in places all over the world and is universally recognized. The bicycle has become an object of universal human culture.

Other articles are universally used, but have distinct differences from country to country. For instance, brooms in Britain and the United States are made of different materials and are of contrasting shape. The availability of materials is the same in both countries, the job they have to do is the same, but the common broom looks different, and one in a typical English home can be distinguished from one in the United States. Although the broom may be universally known, such differences in materials and use emerge from and contribute to a national identity.

Some unique cultural or symbolic objects can also be identified with a particular region. Like the

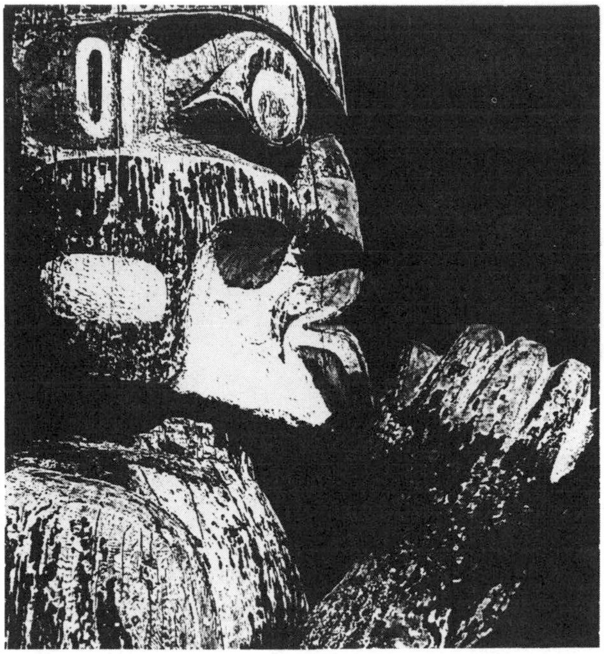

3. A totem pole: A unique regional artifact from the Pacific Northwest.

cable car or London bus, the totem pole is recognizable and representative of the Pacific Northwest region of Canada and the United States.

The Object as Symbol

The axe as an object is at times endowed with unique qualities not connected with its function. In such cases, the axe has reached a satisfactory shape as a working tool and the toolmakers have taken their craft a step further. The handle may have a carved or painted pattern or the head may be decorated in some way, perhaps by an engraved design. Then it is no longer a mere tool; it is also an example of the maker's attempt to create a unique symbol which may endow its owner with special symbolic qualities. After such alterations, a simple tool can become a ceremonial axe, an object for purely ritual purposes. For instance, the ancient Chinese had a ritual axe, a highly elaborate cult object for ceremonial use. To enhance its special nonutilitarian qualities, it was beautifully carved out of the rare and precious Jadite.

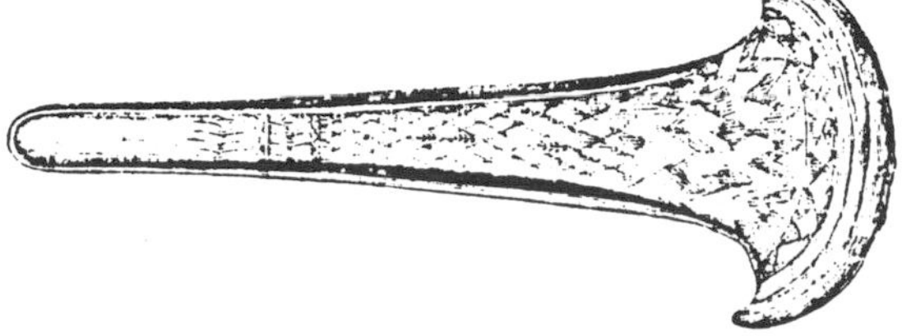

4. A cermonial axe.

THE SHIFT FROM NATURAL TO HUMAN DOMINANCE

Until very recently, most human life was dominated by the larger setting—the earth itself, the solar system, the universe. The natural environment was used and understood by hunters, sailors, and fishermen and women with little significant modification. These people needed what the environment could offer and used what they could obtain from it to create their artifacts—their shelters, huts and tents, their implements and their boats. But, however great their efforts, their creations had little impact on the natural environment. Only in the last four to five thousand years—with the coming of agriculture, towns and cities—has the domination of nature over people gradually diminished. Only in the last two hundred years has this change accelerated to a degree that has made human experience primarily one of humanly made **places** and **things**—the built environment.

The Growth of Materialism

We have gone a long way beyond people's first necessities, so the word materialistic can be used freely when describing the modern world. We work to produce things and then work to earn what we can to acquire more things. For example: houses, cars, televisions, washers, freezers, books, furniture, ornaments, souvenirs, etc., are produced in abundance and are very much a part of the everyday built environment. We are now a population dependent, not only on our natural surroundings, but interdependent with humanly-made objects and the complex systems that produce them. To our detriment in recent years, we have tended to lose sight of our original interdependency with the natural environment.

We do not typically live close anymore to where we can hunt and fish. In order to enjoy naturally fresh food, we rely on fast, motorized transport, and on electricity and other modern systems. We have moved an immense distance from the directness and immediacy of early, uncomplicated ways of living. Most of us probably cannot think of examples of people who still live with a minimum of means and material goods. A lack of modern conveniences may seem empty and inconvenient to many, perhaps most, of us.

5. Candle Holders: Expressing the vernacular and high-style traditions.

The Vernacular Tradition

In the biological process of natural selection, the least fit members of the species die and the strongest members survive. A parallel can be seen in the development of certain objects, a survival of the fittest in which the appropriate object survives over the inappropriate.

The survivor could be a domestic utensil that has been made over and over again; tiny improvements have accrued to the objects, and faults and problems have been gradually eliminated or at least minimized. A modern example familiar to us is the copper, tin and brass saucepan for cooking. The combination of the copper for good heat conduction, tin to protect the food, and brass as a stronger metal for the handle make a functionally superior article respected by all who enjoy traditional quality.

Experiments in nonstick and easy-to-clean surfaces for saucepans have produced many new approaches and finishes, but it is interesting to note that for quality cooking, many modern users are going back to the older, "tried and true" materials and are using traditional heavy cast-iron pots again, not for convenience, but for performance.

Selection by gradual elimination and refinement is common to objects for everyday use; they are developed unselfconsciously by a cultural group rather than a single individual. This gradual and anonymous process is known as the **Vernacular Tradition**. Drastic innovation or radical improvements are not typical of vernacular products. Consistency and continuity are intrinsic to their development.

The vernacular tradition is exemplified by the hand implements commonly found even on today's farms, and by the common tools that many of us still use, such as the hammer and saw. The household dishes, glassware and flatware of today reflect strong vernacular traditions, customs that have long provided for the needs of ordinary people in the form of functional everyday wares.

High Style and the Ceremonial Object

On the other hand, the richness and elaboration of household artifacts serving the sophisticated needs of wealthy people emphasize ceremonial occasions rather than ordinary everyday needs. Such elaborations constitute the parts of another tradition, commonly referred to as **High Style**. The adornments and embellishments of this tradition often show an enjoyment of form for its own sake and a pleasure in decoration. Many cult and ceremonial objects are beautifully made and hand decorated from elegant materials that have particular meaning for selective groups of people.

For many, the high-style object can be exemplified by the luxuries that those of us fortunate enough choose to possess because we admire their beauty. For example, compare an elaborate candelabra to a simple candle holder; both have the same function, but contrasting decorative qualities mark one as vernacular, the other as high style.

The difference between the vernacular and the high style can easily be seen in common household objects, in the chair or the candle holder. The differences also reveal a wide variety of values among the elite. An ordinary chair in the vernacular tradition is solid, well made, comfortable, but unpretentious. Its upper-class counterpart may be richly decorated with carving, upholstered with tapestry or satin, and embellishments may be more important than comfort. Some expensive chairs may conform to the latest style, but not be ideal to sit on. Equally, a high-style chair may be based on a vernacular design, but refined by the use of a more precious material, perhaps rosewood instead of the traditional oak or beech. Rarity has always had value in high style tradition. However, the beauty of simplicity is also enjoyed by high-style makers

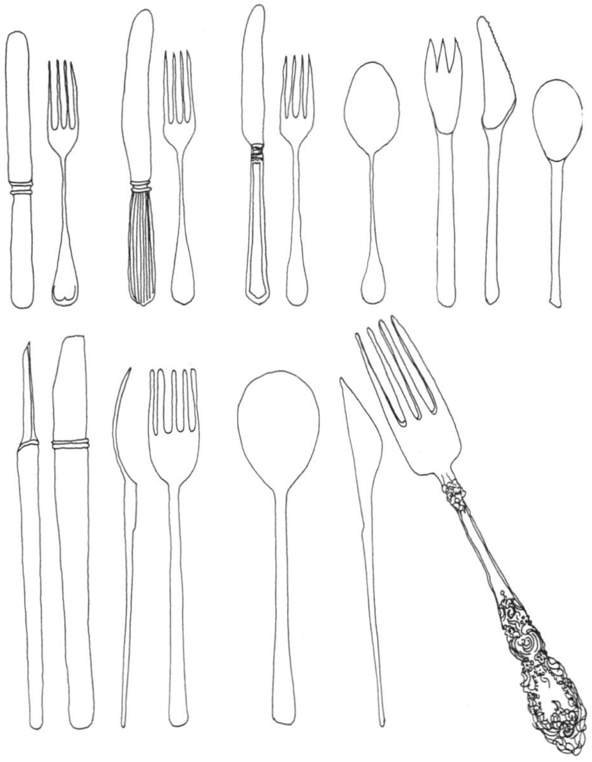

6. The variety of personalities expressed in the many forms of tableware.

and consumers. Eighteenth century furniture makers often produced chairs of utmost simplicity, but with perfect proportions, so that their beauty came from inherent qualities of form, not from applied decoration. Many modern furniture designers have followed this approach, attempting to achieve a high standard through simplicity.

The Development of Mass Production: A Speculative Tradition

Production in recent times has allowed the cheapest of industrially made household utensils to imitate the wares of the wealthy of previous ages. Easily obtained dishes, silverware and glasses are often imitations of high-style objects, reproduced in great numbers in cheap materials, and often of poor quality. Quick and easy reproduction, created by the industrial age, has led to a widespread **speculative tradition**, developed for profit through mass production.

To the uninformed person, a new version of an object that deviates from high-style or vernacular forms might well be an attractive and preferable buy. A plastic bucket can look bright and colorful and be more enticing than the solid and more expensive traditional product. But often, vernacular products are still surprisingly successful, both in practical and visual ways, with an excellence built to last. For instance, when a traditional metal spoon and certain new kinds of plastic spoon are both put in a mug of hot coffee, each shows a totally different performance: the metal spoon remains rigid, but some plastic spoons soften and bend or even melt. Likewise, plastic knives simply do not approach the same cutting performance as metal knives. The cutting edge of stainless steel knives is not as sharp as the earlier carbon steel. Many cooks are still prepared to sacrifice the convenience of stainless steel for the keen edge of carbon steel blades.

The Artificial Need for More Objects

Today, manufacturers are also producing objects that never before existed and have no traditional uses; through advertising and exposure, a public demand is created. No longer content with necessities alone, consumers and manufacturers have created an **Artificial Need**. We can all think of examples of objects for the person who has everything. Our acquisitive society falls for such odd articles as an electric fingernail-polish dryer or mink-covered toilet seats. Victor Papanek, an international design expert, found a distributor who was selling 20,000 diapers a month—for parakeets!

You may not own any of the above, but if you shut your eyes for a moment and imagine all your possessions, from your toothbrush to the pictures on your wall, you will probably find that the list is very long. If you left the room in a panic, could you possibly carry it all?

Yet, a household possessing the bare necessities need not be thought of as impoverished. The ordinary sixteenth century household, for instance, enjoyed good food and fine living. The following inventory from one such household has nothing in it that is superfluous or unnecessary.

> 1 brass pot, a frying pan, a kettle, a gridiron, a skillet and spit, 5 pieces of pewter and a candlestick, 3 pairs of sheets, a cover, 12 pieces of linen, 2 coffers, 2 pillows, a cupboard, a table and some chairs.

This list is in striking contrast to the modern equivalent. Can you imagine listing all the contents of your home in one short paragraph? Two aspects of this medieval list should be remembered: All these objects were expertly and carefully handmade, and all the articles were cherished and valued. Most of these items could be presented proudly today as quality, historical exhibits in any museum. Can we predict the same admiration for the quality of our possessions?

THE OBJECT AS PART OF A SYSTEM

Many of the objects in the medieval house can be thought of as independent, self-sufficient and long-lasting, without the need for external sources of energy or for external connections to support their continued existence.

Our homes today still contain such objects, e.g., tables and chairs, but in addition, televisions, telephones, lights, washers, dryers, sinks, toilets and many other products must be connected beyond the limits of the house to a complex of roads, sewers, electric lines and other external systems. The home, as we know it, has become divorced from its natural surroundings and turned into a small part of a much larger network of support systems, all of which can fail on short notice, or without notice.

In its simplest form, the shelter itself can exist without connections to an external support system (though its inhabitants cannot). It only has to survive the surrounding elements. The simple shelter was originally for people's protection, but it has changed, has become a place to display our many possessions and to display ourselves. As early as 1851, the English designer William Morris spoke of our houses being filled with "tons and tons of unutterable rubbish." Since Morris's time, our houses contain more, more, and still more. The house itself has become a very complex, modern appliance; it has become a machine for living in with all the problems that a machine has to keep running smoothly. Earlier houses may have had inconveniences, but their simplicity also had advantages.

How many of us are ready to look at the social responsibility that we owe to one another and to ourselves, responsibility to reduce this excessive demand for more products, for more and more complex objects?

As noted, the natural world has its own process of survival of the fittest, and people first

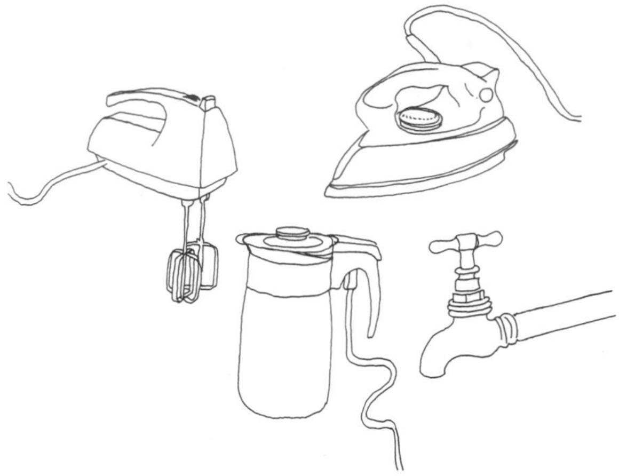

7. Many of the products today are dependent upon various support systems.

created objects that did not interfere with the natural dominance. The long line of humanly made objects (especially those in the vernacular tradition) can gradually show us which objects are of real value, which are most appropriate—if we care to carefully study their qualities. Meanwhile, the built environment has overtaken the natural dominance and our surroundings are inundated with products. Do we have to wait until we are buried under our own possessions before we are able to see the need to slow down? Again, if we had to abandon our households in a hurry, perhaps to avoid the flood by taking to the Ark again, would we know what few things to take with us?

Products are also connected to natural resources and to the natural systems of the earth. Often, in highly industrialized societies, especially in the United States, a single design is manufactured into many thousands, sometimes millions, even billions of individual products, an explosion that can cause significant loss of resources and corresponding environmental impacts. For example, the design of an aluminum soda pop can may seem quite simple. It is a relatively small product, but it is reproduced billions of times and consumes huge amounts of resources. The smallest incremental change in efficiency can make a significant savings in total resources. "In 1985, more than 70 billion beverage cans were used . . . If you throw away two aluminum cans, you waste more energy than is used daily by each of a billion individual human beings in less developed nations" (The Earth Works Group, 1989). Reuse and recycling is a critical design issue.

"In 1988 alone, aluminum can recycling saved more than 11 billion kilowatt hours of electricity, enough to supply the residential electrical needs of New York City for six months. Recycling aluminum cuts related air pollution by 95% . . . [and] uses 90% less energy than making aluminum from scratch" (The Earth Works Group, 1989). Reduction of consumption, reuse, and recycling of the simplest products can often save huge amounts of energy and resources, as well as minimize the air and water pollution associated with its manufacturing and distribution systems.

Designers especially, but all humans (and particularly those in industrialized, consumer societies) must continue to think about such connections between human needs and wants, must consider seriously the level of satisfaction obtained through creation of products and objects in the built environment, and must increasingly understand the implications of such creations and consumption for human-environmental relations, not only in households but multiplied throughout the world.

REFERENCES

The Earth Works Group. 1989. *50 Simple Things You Can Do to Save the Earth.* Earthworks Press.

CHAPTER 9

From Craft Tradition to Industrial Design

Catherine Bicknell

The design of ordinary objects affects us all. Objects that we use every day can give us pleasure or cause real frustration. A tea kettle that does not pour or a door handle with a rough surface that hurts your hand are in direct contrast to the kettle that pours beautifully or the handle whose silky smooth finish caresses your hand. This chapter is concerned with ordinary everyday objects and with the design processes and professions that make their realization possible. The transition from the traditional craftsperson to the contemporary industrial designer is explored in its historical context.

HISTORICAL ROOTS

Medieval Design

In the middle ages, most people had few possessions. In the great medieval halls of the time, the king or the lord would be provided with a throne or chair on which he could sit in state and be able to survey the fine silver or gold plates on the table, the stained glass in the windows, the tapestries on the walls and the costly table linens. So important were all these objects that when the lord moved from house to house, everything was taken by horse and wagon to furnish the next house he was visiting. Even the glass in the windows would be moved and everything was designed, from the glass to the lord's chair, to withstand these rough journeys.

1. The medieval board and chair (*M. Girouard*).

We have inherited the term "chair" as a Western title to designate success as a leader in a position of authority. It is not only the lord who has the chair, it can now be the Chairperson of the Board, a term which comes to us directly from the elevated status of that one chair at a medieval table. The table at which the king sat was known as the board and that is exactly what it was, a board on trestles. Such historic roots are still symbols of contemporary society—we still refer to "chair" as one who sits above the "board" of directors. In the words of Ralph Caplan (1983), "a chair is the first thing you need when you don't need anything and is, therefore, a peculiarly compelling symbol of civilization. For it is civilization, not survival, that requires design."

The making of the king's chair in medieval times required an expert craftsperson whose skill had been passed down from generation to generation, but who might add individual artistry. The table was even an object of pride, for in those early days, cutting a thin board by hand from a great tree was no easy task.

In the past, the availability of materials and technology was severely limited. Obtainment of most materials was restricted to those close at hand, like wood, clay or bone, and artisans had to learn to make the most of them. But limitations have often inspired human creativity; many objects of beauty and utility have been made from the simplest of materials. Certainly, there were fewer colors to choose from, and all were made from natural substances, but the pigments and dyes made from local plants and minerals were in many ways superior to those we make today through complex chemical processes.

The Traditional Craftsperson

Throughout the world and through most of history, craftspersons or artisans working at skilled trades—pottery, cabinetmaking, weaving or metal work—have learned the skills from their own parents who in turn had been taught by theirs. Or they were apprenticed to experienced artisans at a young age, first paying for the privilege of learning, later receiving modest pay, and finally themselves becoming masters, perhaps with apprentices of their own. This system insured proper training and an understanding of the work—from selecting the raw materials to manufacturing, finishing and selling whatever was produced. Originality has rarely been important to such workers. Their role was to make what was needed according to traditional standards, and perhaps to refine or modify standard designs to suit particular needs. Occasionally, outstanding artisans produced new designs which were greatly admired and thus they initiated new traditions or styles. Most of these people worked anonymously, but some were so skilled at their craft that they have been regarded as artists. For example, Thomas Chippendale, the eighteenth century English cabinetmaker, gave his name to a style still well-known today. Although educated through an apprenticeship, he came to represent the design spirit of his age.

THE INDUSTRIAL REVOLUTION

The age-old traditions of handwork by skilled artisans were challenged and, in some cases, brought to an end by the Industrial Revolution. The improved design of the steam engine by James Watt in 1769, was a catalyst in the development of factory production. The use of coke in iron production made possible the casting of large sections of iron. By the nineteenth century, many articles previously made by craftspersons at home were made in factories. With the coming of the machine, standards in both visual and functional design rapidly declined. Machines could instantly stamp out elaborate effects that would have taken a craftsperson days or weeks to create.

This resulted in an increase in ornamentation on all consumer goods—on furnishings, household objects and artifacts; manufacturers strove constantly to outdo each other in lavish decoration. Craftspeople might help in setting up the model for running the machines, but they were themselves no longer making individual, beautiful objects.

2. English carved oak armchair, c. 1250.

3. Wooden hand-crafted Windsor chair.

In the nineteenth century, the number of objects produced increased rapidly. Between 1790 and 1900, 600,000 patents for new devices were granted in the United States alone. Many of those patents covered designs for machines that would transform the size and character of the farm, the office and the home: locomotives, steam ships and bicycles led to mechanized transportation; the typewriter, the adding machine, the cash register, the dictaphone and the telephone, all introduced between 1875 and 1900, brought about the mechanization of office work and, eventually, development of the computer.

Factory canning, baking, the washing machine and the sewing machine simplified housework, if they did not "mechanize" it. Ralph Waldo Emerson's claim that "things are in the saddle and are riding us" was true then and seems even more true today. The big question of the day was, "what should everything look like?" Should designers clothe their products in historic costume or should they forge new styles for machine-made products?

On the whole, most product designers of the eighteenth and nineteenth centuries turned to past styles or to nature as a source of inspiration for their designs. Instead of finding new designs appropriate for the machine age, factory owners preferred to imitate designs from earlier historical periods. Today, we tend to look back to this period as a time when the means of production was progressive, but designs were regressive.

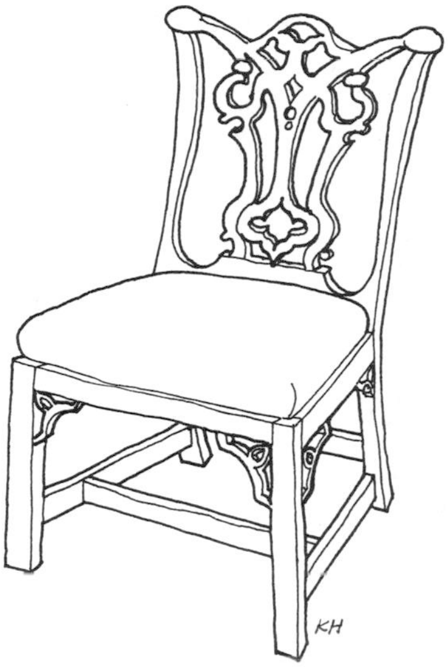

4. A Chippendale chair.

5. Victorian chair.

6. Victorian taste (Crystal Palace Catalogue).

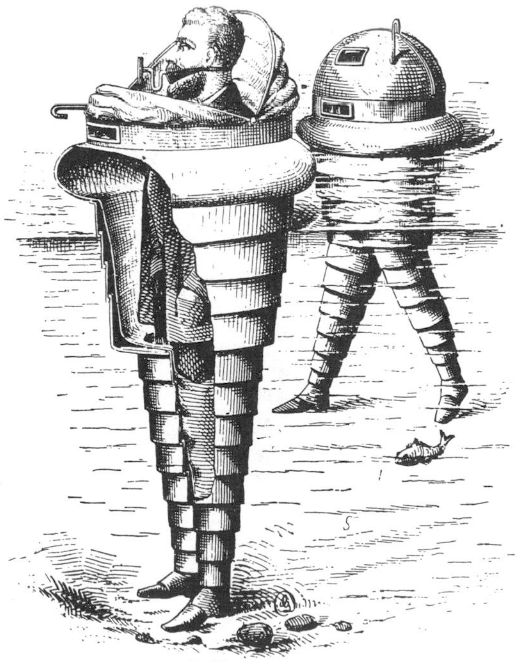

7. A swimming device (*L. De Vries*).

Despite the regressive historicism of the majority of designers, a few responded to the conversion from hand to machine production by adapting to the new technology and by evolving appropriate styles for it. Engineers and inventors were the first to develop "styleless" products and structures, and to introduce the modern look, well before product designers did.

This was particularly well illustrated in the Great Exhibition at the Crystal Palace in London in 1851. Products were exhibited from all over the world. The general impression was that ornament, embellishment and historicism were at their height. From the inside of the palace, with its eclectic pleasures, all the glories of Victorian times were apparent. In direct contrast to the exhibits, the housing of the exhibition itself was in the incredibly modern iron and glass structure by Joseph Paxton, a particularly creative landscape architect. Stripped to its structural necessity, it heralded a whole new era in which simplicity and a functional approach to design were admired. Its clean lines and lack of ornamentation were quite shocking to some of its viewers.

Also shocking were two contributions to the exhibition from the United States. Cyrus McCormick's patent Virginia Reaper and Samuel Colt's revolver were seen as so stark and apparently unstyled that they were a public joke. The London Times reported that the reaper was "a cross between an Astley chariot, a wheelbarrow and a flying machine." But when it cut 20 acres a day, the machine was reported as "the most valuable contribution from abroad to the stock of previous knowledge yet discovered."

The simplicity of the Colt revolver contrasted dramatically with the floridly engraved, handcrafted weapons of France and England. It was the British who were most amazed by its performance, the capability of shooting five or six rounds in succession without reloading. It was mass produced, not handcrafted, and in production each part was duplicated by die-cutting machines. The British Institute of Civil Engineers was so impressed that it invited Colt to set up a factory in England similar to the one that he had set up in the United States.

Not only could Colt's machines stamp out a part many times faster than the human hand could fashion it, but each part was reproduced with sufficient precision to make it interchangeable with the same part from any other unit. This was one of the key elements in the mass production process and an inherent strength of this new system developed in the United States.

A measure of the lack of concern for good design in mass production was that most manufacturers

The 'Remington' typewriter [1891]

8. Remington typewriter, 1891 (*L. De Vries*).

9. The Great Exhibition 1851—showing the simple structure and the over elaborate exhibits.

10. McCormick's patent Virginia reaper (*S. Giedion*).

during the Victorian period failed to record the names of the designers of their products. The names of Thomas Edison and Alexander Graham Bell and others who patented new products are recorded, but names of the designers who decoratively styled the phonograph, telephone and typewriter are not. Neither the Bell Company nor Western Electric has records of any designers in 1877, when Bell introduced the first commercial model of the telephone. But by 1936, times had changed; in that year, Western Electric, the actual manufacturer of later 'phones,' retained Henry Dreyfus as a consultant designer.

11. Victorian inventions (*L. De Vries*).

THE ARTS AND CRAFTS MOVEMENT AND THE BAUHAUS

At the time of the Great Exhibition in London, most designers produced over-elaborate, highly-decorated work. A few were so dismayed by the results of machine production that they attempted to turn back the clock and return to the methods of the Middle Ages. They became part of the **Arts and Crafts Movement** under the leadership of William Morris. Compared to medieval artisans, who were able to take pride in their work and to be directly involved in its final form and finish, Morris saw the factory worker as degraded. Arts and craft designers saw machinists as slaves without any influence on what they were making. The movement also protested against the devaluation of beautiful handmade objects and its members designed objects of great simplicity.

Their aim was to restore the dignity of the craftsperson. Unfortunately, the furniture, fabrics, tapestries and fine handwork they produced were too expensive for the mass market and could only be purchased by rich people. They were also based too firmly on medieval traditions and, therefore, did not meet the challenge of the new age. However, the influence of the Arts and Crafts Movement was tremendous. The origins of modern design are found in its honest, simplified forms.

Not until 1919, when Walter Gropius founded the **Bauhaus** School of Design in Germany, was an attempt made in design education to work with technology. The Bauhaus accepted mechanization and attempted to work with it. Bauhaus designers worked alongside skilled engineers, so that both could make contributions to the overall finished product. Students were taught three kinds of skills—those of an artist, those of a craftsperson, and those of a scientist or technologist.

Shortly before World War II, the Bauhaus School was closed by the Nazis and many of the faculty left Germany. They migrated to England, spread across the United States and took their ideals with them. Design and design education in the Western World became heavily influenced by the Bauhaus. Unlike members of the Arts and Crafts Movement, Bauhaus teachers knew they had to work with the realities of their own age and design for machine production, but they also placed great stress on the development of creativity. In the words of Walter Gropius, only the artist "can breathe life into the dead hand of the machine."

The Artist/Craftsperson Today

In the spirit of the Arts and Crafts Movement, which stressed the satisfaction that individuals can derive from working creatively with their hands, many artistic people chose to work in one of the crafts. Artist/craftspersons today have mostly been educated at a university or art school, but they work like the medieval artisans—from selecting the raw material to finishing and even selling the product. Artist/craftspeople design things through direct contact with the consumer. Their working methods, however, may not be the same as in the days of medieval craft apprenticeships. For one thing, they have emerged from the anonymity of the artisan to become artists known by name, from whom patrons can expect some originality. Exhibitions in contemporary galleries show twentieth century examples of the high standards and refinements that an artist/craftsperson can attain today, from original conception to final completion of the object.

THE INDUSTRIAL DESIGNER OF TODAY

The industrial designer today stands as a bridge between the old world of the craftsperson and the incredibly sophisticated world of mass production.

Industrial designers have seldom been trained in a particular trade, or to work with a specific material. They are very often educated professionals, such as engineers who, through special studies, become qualified to supervise and coordinate the complicated process on which industrial production is based. They stand between the customer and the manufacturer, with the moral duty to protect the customer's interest. They act as coordinators among many different specialists: technicians, artisans and salespeople. Collaboration is the key to success in the design process today.

Design has many influences, but a clear thread of development is discernible, especially the fact that creating the design concept has become progressively integrated with the making or manufacture of an artifact. The designer's professional status has become increasingly sophisticated, but the basic role is that of a problem solver.

Industrial designers today must still possess the analytical and creative abilities of the artist/craftsperson, but also the manager's will to organize and cooperate. They stand in the midst of an explosive development in new materials and new techniques of manufacturing.

Modern designers have an infinite choice of synthetic, humanly-made substances, as well as natural materials from all over the world. Any color can be selected. New types of malleable materials, such as plastics, can be formed to meet demanding performance criteria.

New materials and technology go hand-in-hand; today a chair can be molded out of a single flexible material, dispensing with the traditional wood joints of the medieval craftsperson. That chair can be made so strong that it could survive a journey not just from house to house, but from earth to moon and back. Or we can make a similar molded chair attractive enough to sell well and make a profit, but not at all durable. Such a chair will soon end up on the junk heap with all the other countless billions of abandoned consumer goods.

Designers of molded plastic chairs are necessarily members of a team of specialists, from chemists to marketing experts and manufacturers. They have studied ergonomics, anthropometrics, structural principles, visual design and many other complex subjects. Modern industrial designers will not—perhaps cannot—make the chair by hand, but delegate the task of manufacture to others.

Design at whatever scale, whether it be a small pot or a high speed train, is not only a matter of aesthetic judgment. The designer is expected to make the creative leap, the synthesis and to bring all the conflicting design factors to an optimum visual and functional solution.

THE CHALLENGES OF THE TWENTY-FIRST CENTURY

The potential benefits to society, made possible by advanced technology and improved materials, are obvious. For example, the development of North American bathrooms, kitchens and laundry rooms, with their numerous appliances, has given us improved health, comfort and convenience. We might expect that the entire built environment and all the individual objects which constitute it would show a similar improvement. Unfortunately, this hope has not been fulfilled. We have the means, but it seems that collectively we lack the wisdom and resolution.

People today seem to expect that the individual quality of life should be completely satisfactory, with adequate food, clothing, housing, work, leisure and means of transportation. Satisfaction of all of these is taken for granted by the majority of people in developed countries. Paradoxically, we have not succeeded collectively in designing a coherent and meaningful environment complete with all its constituent parts. The human ability to identify and solve material problems seems inexhaustible, but the ability to anticipate the impact of unlimited production remains comparatively weak. We are only just beginning to realize the collective result of an accelerated multitude of

12. Morris ladder back chair.

13. Barcelona chair, steel construction, cantilevered designed by Mies van der Rohe, 1929.

individual decisions. It is hard for us to absorb the fact that each of us tiny individuals contributes actively to the problems caused by our desire for more and more products.

The common way of thinking about objects is to view them as separate, isolated units unconnected with anything else. The process of making an object, with its needs for materials, tools and power, too often seems remote from the finished product and our immediate convenience.

The automobile is an example of an object that has been invented and designed in the light of a certain ideal vision, a vision of easy, independent mobility and of an attractive, seductive, powerful object that each of us could actually own. Only in recent years have the full consequences of its use begun to catch up with and overtake its advantages. The automobile creates a need for costly and irreplaceable construction materials, a seemingly insatiable demand for increasingly scarce operating fuel, and an extensive landscape of roads and parking lots. It creates extreme problems of safe operation, a distressing output of wastes, and a complicated, multi-ton carcass after it becomes inoperative.

14. The 'Swan' chair, glass-fibre shell, leather- or fabric-covered, designed by Arne Jacobsen, 1958.

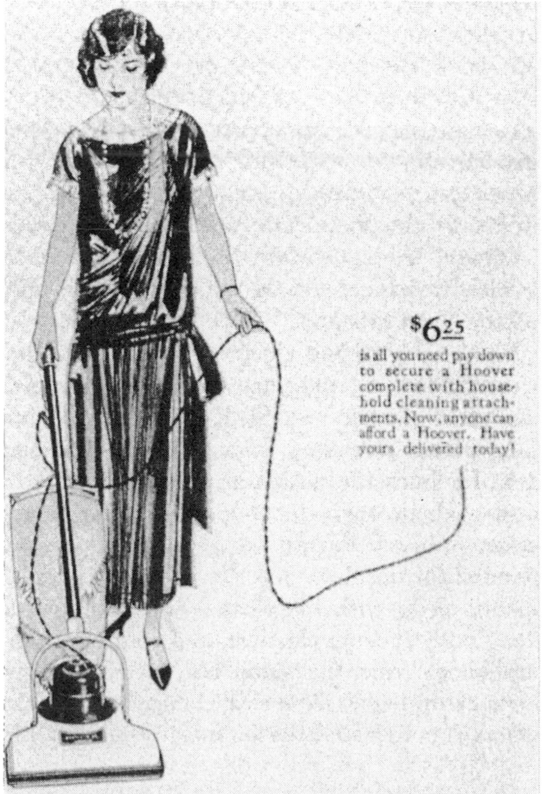
$6.25
is all you need pay down to secure a Hoover complete with household cleaning attachments. Now, anyone can afford a Hoover. Have yours delivered today!

15. Household inventions (*S. Strasser*).

16. Household inventions (*S. Strasser*).

It is an inescapable fact that most of us work at a small scale and feed a large-scale problem. The need to regain a **sense of scale** is not helped by the massive transformation achieved through mechanized industry.

We no longer go to the tailor or cabinetmaker in order to have things "made to measure," to choose the materials, the size and style. We have lost direct contact with the things we enjoyed when handicraft traditions formed a firm basis of design. When clothes and utility wares were made at home, everyone knew about materials and how they should be employed.

In the handcraft tradition, the whole process of design and manufacture could be accomplished by one person. Handicraft skills represent a conscious effort to impose meaningful order and can be applied by a person at any scale, from landscapes and cities down to a tiny bit of jewelry. The making of decisions about finding and producing an appropriate form remains the basic approach of the designer. But, the handicraft tradition allowed the design process and its realization to be experienced by both the practitioner and the observer as a comprehensible unity. In this way, the product could be followed from raw material to finished form.

Now, more often than not, we buy things that are ready-made, out of unknown materials, things in which the contact between practitioner and observer has been eliminated.

A DESIGNER'S RESPONSIBILITY

Industrial designers obviously must have a sense of responsibility to the manufacturer who commissioned a design, but as professionals, they also have a responsibility to society and to future generations. Everyone involved today in creating the complex built environment and its individual components must be willing to confront certain concerns that are all too easy to neglect. A comprehensive approach to product design should consider not only the effective design of the product, but also address the context in which it is to be placed. More specifically, the designer today needs to consider such human-environmental issues as these:

- **The environmental impact of the object.** "Everything is connected to everything else," is a widely quoted statement about the world we live in. But, when keeping a hamburger warm in a Styrofoam container or recharging the air conditioner in a personal automobile can erode the ozone layer, the statement rings true. When choosing exotic woods to enhance a design can contribute to the destruction of tropical forests and ultimately to deterioration in the quality of the atmosphere, neither the design or the resulting object seem so personal or so isolated from the immensity of the earth.

- **How it may affect availability and sustainability of scarce materials.** If designing a more powerful car means a faster drawdown of petroleum supplies, leaving less for future generations, or if invasion of wilderness areas by loggers and mechanized tourists means less appreciation of nature by future generations—or even less nature—then the decision to design, to manufacture (or to buy) that car, transcends the personal, the pocketbook or even the gross national product.

- **Does it produce wastes?** Designers (and consumers) need to be concerned not only with products, but with **by-products**. Is an object designed so that all of it is consumed or used up? Is it designed to be recycled . . . or deliberately designed to be disposable? Is packaging necessary? Is the packaging chosen biodegradable or will it be found in landfills, even inside fish or other creatures, decades after the time of purchase and use?

- **Is it safe?** Do designers think about whether they would want their own children to wear the flammable dress they just created . . . or is caring lessened by the faceless, nameless people who will eventually buy the product? Is protection or profit the bottom line?

- **What is its impact on human health?** Who designs a new cigarette? Or, the seductive packaging for cigarettes? Or, the colorful, attractive advertising? Considering what we know now about tobacco's impacts on human health, what are the ethical considerations for the designers of such things? How far does their responsibility extend?

REFERENCES

Caplan, R. 1983. *Psychology Today*, February.
The Crystal Palace Exhibition Illustrated Catalogue. 1970. Dover.
De Vries, L. 1971. *Victorian Inventions*. John Murray.
Gibbs-Smith, C. H. 1851. *The Great Exhibition of 1851*. Her Majesty's Stationary Office.
Giedion, S. 1947. *Mechanization Takes Command*. Oxford University Press.
Girouard, M. 1978. *Life in the English Country House*. Yale University Press.
Naylor, G. 1968. *The Bauhaus Studio*. Vista.
Naylor, G. 1985. *The Bauhaus Reassessed*. E. P. Dutton.
Oates, P. B. 1981. *The Story of Western Furniture*. Bennett Press.
Papanek, V. 1985. 2nd ed. *Design for the Real World*. Academy Chicago.
Reed, H. 1953. *Art and Industry*. Faber and Faber.
Sexton, R. 1987. *American Style: Classic Product Design from Airstream to Zippo*. Chronicle Books.
Strasser, S. 1982. *Never Done: A History of American Housework*. Pantheon Books.

Introduction

2. INTERIORS

Interiors are the second building block of the built environment. Interiors are commonly referred to as three-dimensional enclosed space, and as the "near environment."

Interiors are a very basic environment created to directly satisfy basic physical and psychological human needs. The ability to design effective interiors has increased human comfort, efficiency and enjoyment. Some spaces fulfill individual and family needs for privacy, others are more public and reinforce social interaction. Interiors protect people from external factors and disturbances such as climate, noise and intruding public eyes. Some specialized spaces, such as space exploration vehicles, are designed to maximize efficiency within limited spatial dimensions. Like the other seven components of the built environment, interiors can be understood as an essential part of the content-component-context continuum. Products are designed together to form interiors, and interiors are integrated into a structural enclosure. The resultant artifact is an interior space.

Once again, the four-part definition of the built environment can be adapted to help define the content and context of "Interiors":

- **a.** **Interiors** are created spaces, which are humanly made or arranged;
- **b.** to fulfill human purpose, to satisfy human needs and values; and
- **c.** to mediate the overall environment;
- **d.** with results that affect the overall environmental context (the context for interiors includes structures, landscapes, cities . . . to earth).

This connected content-component-context relationship can be simply understood by the following levels of integration continuum:

PRODUCTS-***INTERIORS***-STRUCTURES-LANDSCAPES-CITIES-REGIONS-EARTH

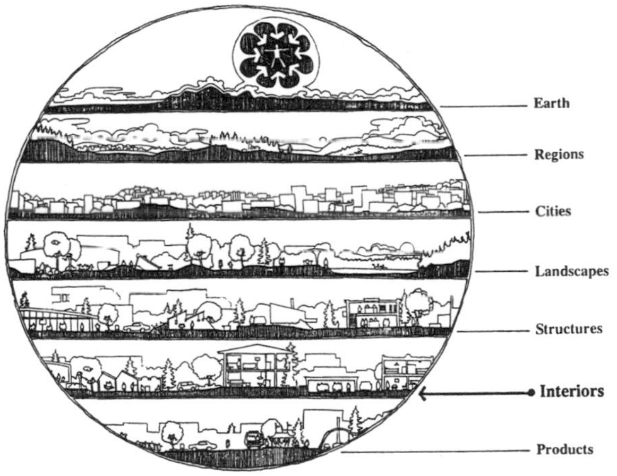

The three chapters in this section encourage the reader to explore more fully the various aspects of interiors and interior design:

- **"Changing Human-Environment Relationships in Interior Design"** by Lorinda K. Silverstein: the first chapter discusses three broad periods of recent design history, especially with reference to interior design. Three factors critical to human-environment relations—nature, human experience, and expression of the relationship in tangible form—are analyzed, and compared in terms of how they have differed from period to period, ending with a look at design today.

- **"Interior Design Today: Contemporary Issues and Challenges"** by Jo Ann Thompson: The second chapter explores the various issues and challenges of interior design today as it responds to the growing needs of the residential and commercial sectors of society. It investigates how interiors are shaped and how interior designers are integrating their understanding of the arts and design with the continuing growth of knowledge in the human behavioral and physical sciences making interiors fulfill human purpose, not only physically, but also socially/culturally and psychologically.

- **"The Quest for Shelter: Squatters and Urbanization Throughout the World"** by Henry Matthews and Bashir Kazimee: this transitional chapter discusses the world-wide quest for shelter—a search for interior space to fulfill basic human needs for security, comfort and fulfillment. It challenges the reader to place human needs and wants in the perspective of a global responsibility to share the earth's finite resources. It exposes the reader to the difficulty of this task, to the world-wide shortage of housing and the breakdown of successful vernacular tradition because of the pressures of industrialization and urbanization. It suggests various ways of recognizing appropriate strategies for fulfilling this most basic need for interior space for the ever-increasing numbers of families who live, work and play in the global community.

CHAPTER

10

Changing Human-Environment Relationships in Interior Design

Lorinda K. Silverstein

Children enjoy creating tree-houses or "forts" in the woods and often like to explore houses under construction. As adults many of us follow the progress of the construction of a new residence in the neighborhood or the renewal of an older building within the urban core. We stop to watch because we appreciate the skill of the workers and the technology of construction. But we also like to think about how it might feel to live or work in these spaces once they are completed.

People have shaped their relationships with the environment, including interior spaces, since the time when those interiors were formed by the walls of caves, but interior design is young as a discipline and as a profession. The profession has emerged into its own during the last half of the twentieth century as a part of that process of diversification that is characteristic of contemporary developments in many fields. Today, as in the distant past, the designer of interior spaces adapts a multitude of resources and products to support individuals and groups of people who inhabit the structures of the built environment.

A BRIEF REVIEW OF A LONG HISTORY

Designers in the ancient civilizations of Mesopotamia, Egypt, Greece and Rome used local and imported resources and craft traditions to give form to ideas and to shape events. A brief examination of the role of light, just one of many factors, can illustrate how the design of structures and interior space mediated external factors of climate and geography and at the same time sustained and nourished the human spirit.

In the hot climate of ancient Egypt, the interiors of temples were cool and dark, but a carefully placed opening would be designed to admit a shaft of light to illuminate a particular place at a time of ritual importance. Many centuries later in the Gothic cathedrals of northern Europe, a new structural system allowed the exterior walls to be composed of large expanses of stained glass that illustrated religious stories. The luminous environment enhanced the awareness of a world beyond the joys and sorrows of everyday life.

During the Italian Renaissance of the fifteenth and early sixteenth centuries, lighting clarified the individual's perception of spatial concepts and classical proportions and details based on ancient Greek and Roman models. By the end of the sixteenth century, lighting created strong contrasts of light and shadow and dramatized the dynamic movement of sculpture and surface. In the "Age of Enlightenment" of the eighteenth century, lighting was less dramatic and was used to encourage a closer examination of the built environment as it played across the major planes of the interior space.

In the early nineteenth century, the source of light was sometimes concealed while surfaces reflected the daylight within the space. By the middle of the century the interiors of homes had become rather dark with heavy window coverings which enhanced a sense of protection and security from the outside world. But in train stations, greenhouses and covered market halls, the new technology of iron and large sheets of plate glass admitted abundant daylight into the interior. Interior design during the 150 years since the Great Exhibition at the Crystal Palace, discussed in the previous chapter, has had a significant influence on contemporary design and will now be examined in greater detail.

It is easier to imagine alternative designs for future interior spaces if we study how people have met the challenge of giving form to their ideas in the past. Three broad periods of recent design history can be identified: (1) Arts and Crafts and Art Nouveau in the late nineteenth century, (2) the Modern Movement from 1910–1965, and (3) Contemporary design since 1965. As the needs, wants and values of people in the industrially developed world have changed, three factors have emerged as critical to human-environment relationships: (a) the concept of nature (the natural environment), (b) the concept of human experience in time and space, and (c) the expression of the relationship in tangible form. Each broad historical period will be examined in relation to each of these factors.

1. Railway Station, York, England. The Corinthian capital of the column contrasts with the iron trusses of the train shed.

ARTS AND CRAFTS AND ART NOUVEAU

In the late nineteenth century people began to react against the effects of the industrial revolution. As discussed in the preceding chapter, ornamental styles were frequently unrelated to the function of the object, what it was made of, or how it was made. The contradiction can be seen in the interior of the railway station in York, England, where columns are molded in the classical Corinthian style.

The standards of health, safety and welfare of industrial workers of the nineteenth century were extremely low by modern standards. William Morris was an English designer who saw the results of the headlong rush to industrialization as destructive and inappropriate. Morris and other designers of the Arts and Crafts movement advocated a return to hand production in order to reinstate the dignity of the worker and to improve the quality of the products available for sale to the rising middle class.

Craft guilds and workshops were founded by Morris and other English designers, who became directly involved in the fabrication of objects and interiors. The architectural details and furnishings of the Arts and Crafts period were relatively simple and rectilinear in comparison to the Art Nouveau (a French term meaning "New Art") period which followed. This period was brief (1890–1910) and found its most visible expression in the interiors designed on the European continent rather than in England.

The Concept of Nature: Particular Places and Details

The natural environment was a source of enjoyment and inspiration to many people at the end of the nineteenth century. The reaction against the industrial revolution and the poor living conditions in the cities led many designers in England to advocate a return to the country and a life in harmony with nature. A typical example was a small cottage designed by Ernest Gimson, which was sturdy and solid, set into a hillside, with an interior that was protected and secure. The view to the informal garden was through small windows, placed in an irregular pattern based on the internal configuration of the house.

Nature was used as a source of symbolic ideas as well as a source of raw materials in designs of the late nineteenth century. Shells of the sea and mushrooms of the forest, thistles of the field and birds

2. Stoneywell Cottage, Leicestershire, England. Designed by Ernest Gimson. Sturdy and solid, with an interior that is protected and secured.

3. Morris chair, pillow cover and carpet at Standen in Kent, England. The elements of nature were stylized into flat, two-dimensional patterns.

of the air were brought into the interior as ornamental motifs. In the textile workshops of Morris and Company, natural dyes rather than chemical dyes were used. Designers stylized the elements of nature into patterns for carpets, wallcoverings and fabrics. Influenced by Japanese woodblock prints, the surface was treated as a flat surface rather than as an opportunity for illusion.

The Concept of Human Experience: Reaction and Transformation

Changes in the way people thought about human experience in time and space were reflected in the approach to design. Initially, designers in the Arts and Crafts movement expressed a desire to return to the simple life as they imagined it might have been 500 years earlier. They developed workshops and guilds based on the medieval model, and the design of houses was based on sturdy, simple, vernacular antecedents. It was a reaction against current conditions in the industrialized countries.

With the development of Art Nouveau around 1890, nostalgia for the past was eclipsed by a desire to focus on a moment in the present. Photographers had been able, since the invention of the camera in the 1830s, to capture a particular moment of everday life. In symbolic sculpture or graphic art, people, especially women, were shown emerging from a flower or a shell, hair tangled in foliage or swept by the wind.

Transformation that takes place during a short span of time was symbolized through motifs such as a butterfly emerging from a cocoon. Ernst Gallé, a French designer, used the theme of "Dawn and Twilight" in the design of a bed—the moment between night and day or day and night—transition times that last a brief moment and are gone. Colors used in the Art Nouveau interior were transitional hues, such as red violet or blue green.

During the Arts and Crafts period more furniture was built in or placed in alcoves to open up interior space. By the turn of the century the aim was a total integration of interior furnishings, materials and architecture into one unified whole. Margaret MacDonald and Charles Rennie Mackintosh, working in Glasgow, Scotland, designed interiors in which the space was conceived as a total work of art. Proportions were elongated; small areas of carefully crafted metal or luminous colored glass played off large expanses of flat surfaces. The work of designers in Scotland and Austria was more geometric and rectilinear than that of Art Nouveau architects such as Victor Horta in Belgium or Hector Guimard in France. By the turn of the century in France, Belgium, Germany and Spain, curvilinear elements tied structure, object and space together in one dynamic and organic whole.

4. "When lilies turned to tiger's blaze/Amid the garden's tangled maze." The representation of transformation and emergence through organic themes.

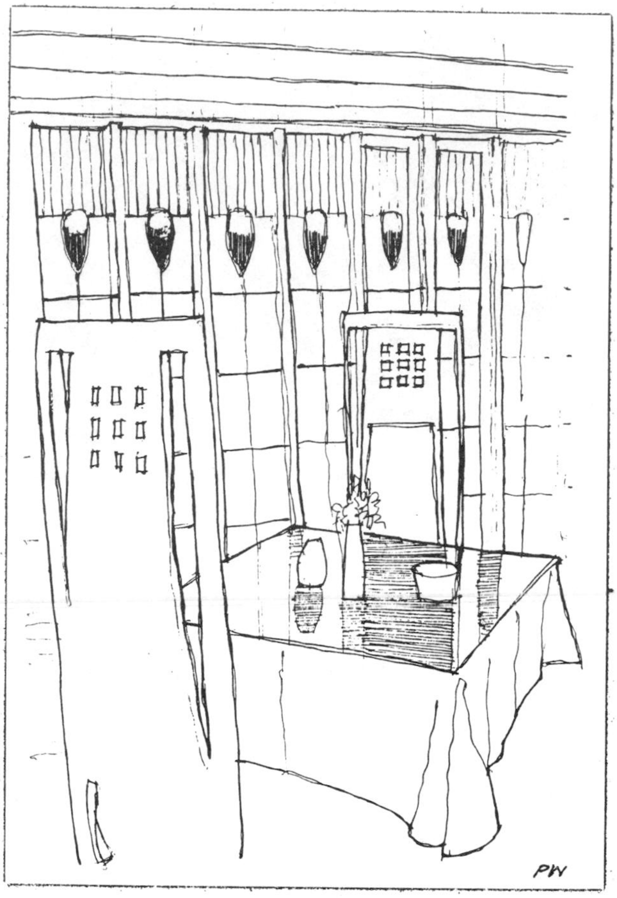

5. Interior by Charles R. Mackintosh and Margaret MacDonald. Willow Tea Rooms, Glasgow, Scotland. Integration of elements into one unified whole.

The Relationship in Tangible Form: The Working of Materials

Designers select materials and processes they think are best suited to give form to their ideas. For Arts and Crafts designers, the honest use of materials and straightforward, simple designs with carefully crafted details expressed the value of the worker's labor. Their cupboards were designed from simple flat planes of wood in which the beauty of the piece derived from the grain of the wood, the joining of the parts and hardware which retained the marks of handforged metal.

In the Art Nouveau period, the materials used were those that could best capture a sense of that fleeting moment of transformation. Molten glass that was suddenly caught and cooled or hot metal that was wrought into shape allowed a flowing quality to be fixed in tangible form. Antonio Gaudi, an architect in Barcelona, Spain, captured the fluidity of water and of life forms that live in water. Railings modeled on the flowing lines of seaweed are part of an organic whole in the La Pedrera apartment building in Barcelona. The forms appear to be undulating before our eyes even though they are in reality static objects.

Light has a special role to play in this illusion of the transitory: translucent glass and iridescent materials shimmer and change with each moment, never appearing twice the same to the viewer's eye. In the United States, Louis Comfort Tiffany demonstrated a high level of invention in glass technology and skill in the creation of glass lampshades, flower vases, and leaded glass windows.

The interiors and related products were fabricated by individuals working in craft studios more akin to the guilds of medieval times than to the factories of modern industrial nations. One notable exception was chairs designed by the Thonet brothers in Austria, manufactured since the 1860s

6. Railing in La Pedrera Apartment Buildings by Antonio Gaudi, Barcelona, Spain. Metal that was wrought into shape allowed a flowing quality to be fixed in tangible form.

in large quantities from standardized steam bent curved components. Most other products by designers required long hours to fabricate and only the rich could afford to buy such unique items or to live in handcrafted interiors.

THE MODERN MOVEMENT

In the first decade of the twentieth century designers began to work toward realization of the idea that well designed objects and housing could become available to a wider population. Although the term "modern" can mean "characteristic of the present or immediate past," in the design fields the term has a more specific application to a movement in design which began about 1910. In attempting to find universal solutions to design problems as well as social problems, artists, architects, designers and psychologists sought to define the objective "scientific" principles underlying natural phenomena, including the behavior of human beings. At the same time there was an emphasis on reason and function in the design of objects and interiors.

One of the most influential schools of architecture and design at this time was the Bauhaus; it was started in Germany in 1919 and was closed by the Nazis in 1933. Its first director, the architect Walter Gropius, believed in an interdisciplinary approach to design, standardization in manufacture and a redefinition of the creative process in design. "The school inherited, reinterpreted and then rejected the craft ideals of the nineteenth century; it attempted to discover 'laws' in art that could be related to design and architecture, and its fundamental aim was to establish a universal language of form that would represent the elimination of social and national barriers" (Naylor, 1985).

The new ideas were disseminated in the United States through a show at the recently founded Museum of Modern Art in New York and through a book (Hitchcock and Johnson, 1932) called *The International Style: Architecture since 1922.* During and after the Second World War, the designers Eero Saarinen and Charles Eames experimented with new molded plywood and molded fiberglass technology that allowed production of comfortable chairs at low cost and in great quantity. The objects and interiors that were created in the 1940s and 1950s exhibited a sculptural quality; they were designed to be in tune with both production processes and human form.

The Concept of Nature: From Essence to Process

Modern artists and designers looked past the particular and transitory qualities of natural phenomena and sought the fundamental principles or essence underlying the diversity of nature. The representation of nature in paintings became more abstract with the development of "analytic cubism" by Pablo Picasso and Georges Braque, painters who worked in Paris during the first decade of the new century. The solid appearance of objects and people was broken up and one object could be seen from multiple viewpoints in the same painting. The interaction of space and the object became more important to the painting or sculpture than a depiction of the object in space. Painters and designers of the De Stijl movement in the Netherlands reduced formal elements to horizontal and vertical (and sometimes diagonal) lines, and to white, black, and primary colors—red, blue, yellow.

Space within structures was opened up horizontally and vertically through the creation of two-story interpenetrating volumes. In many structures designed by the Swiss architect Le Corbusier, load-bearing partitions were replaced by a grid of columns and often the building itself was set up off the ground so that space flowed under and around it. In the United States, Frank Lloyd Wright continued to develop his early ideas of the continuous horizontal flow of space in the house called "Falling Water" at Bear Run, Pennsylvania. The experience of sitting inside such a building, anchored at its core rather than defined by its exterior walls, was almost like being outside. The structure extended out into the landscape and the landscape extended into the interior. By the middle of the century, the walls had been reduced to almost nothing in the Glass House in New Canaan, Connecticut, by Philip Johnson, and the experience of the changing seasons was immediate and direct.

The Concept of Human Experience: The Desire for Universality

Artists and designers at the beginning of the century were fascinated with movement, speed and light. Change took place all the time, and the built

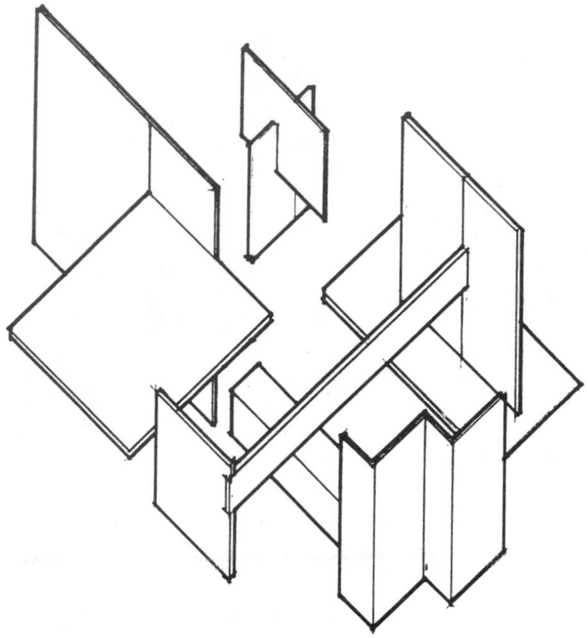

8. Particular planes that defined space could be placed anywhere in this universal grid.

environment was designed to be flexible in the interior in order to accommodate change. Reality at any given time was only one particular manifestation of some underlying universal truth. Space and time were seen to extend indefinitely and to be universal—the same everywhere and at all times.

The visual expression of this idea was articulated in a regularly spaced three dimensional grid. Particular planes that defined space could be placed anywhere in this universal grid. Interior space was not seen to be different in kind from exterior space. Architecture became a rational and humanly-created composition that hovered in the landscape. Mies van der Rohe was a German architect and furniture designer who served as the last director of the Bauhaus and moved to the United States just prior to World War II. Space flowed around and through groups of furniture that "floated" in the middle of the uniform spatial grid of the plan. Careful detailing articulated the expression of structure and the junction of different materials.

The functional program of the human activities to be accommodated in an interior were seen as a major determinant in the design process. In the early years of the Modern Movement, the human face and figure were depicted, like everything else, in geometric terms. The rational and universal

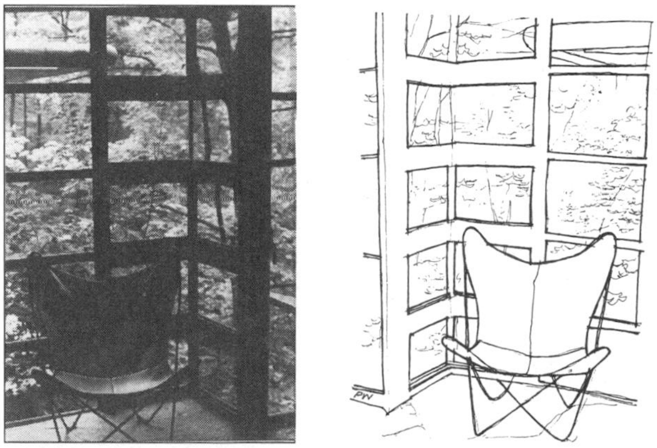

7. Corner detail. Falling Water, Bear Run, Pennsylvania, by Frank Lloyd Wright. The experience of sitting inside such a building is almost like being outside.

9. Sculpture by Henry Moore. Harvard University. By the middle of the century, anthropomorphic forms predominated.

characteristics of people were emphasized, as in the graphic design for a Bauhaus exhibit. But by the middle of the century, anthropomorphic forms predominated, as in the work of the English sculptor Henry Moore. Human dimensions and comfort became of greater concern to the designers of furniture and interiors. Le Corbusier developed a universal "Modular" system of design based on one norm of a human body engaged in various activities. The audience surrounded the state in the theater or the altar in the church to encourage closer interaction with the performance.

The Relationship in Tangible Form: Standardization

Many designers addressed the issues of industrial design and interior design together in order to control all the elements of a rational and functional whole. Production of well designed, low cost furniture and objects to meet functional needs was an aim of the Bauhaus in Germany in the 1920s. In the workshops at the school, students were taught by designers and craft workers who sought to draw out the inherent properties of materials. These properties and the technology of production were expressed in the development of an object's form. Revolutionary products, such as the cantilevered tubular steel frame chair designed by Marcel Breuer, emerged from this context of collaboration. A trademark quality of early modern design is often a smooth plain surface that allowed the attributes of the material, such as the grain of the wood or the polish of the metal or the warp and weft of the woven textile, to function asthe source of aesthetic enjoyment.

By the middle of the century, abstraction of nature became more "expressive" by recording chance events which occurred during creation of a painting or the pouring of concrete to form a wall. Influenced by European artists who had moved to the United States, several New York artists worked in a spontaneous manner that came to be known as Abstract Expressionism. By mid-century, the "machine aesthetic" of forms and interior surfaces had been replaced by a greater emphasis on the textural qualities of materials and the fabrication or construction process itself. The play of light in interiors brought out the irregularities of wood, brick, stone or board-formed concrete and enriched the viewer's perception of the major planes of the space.

The forms of objects and interiors became less geometric and designers became more responsive to human perceptions. Alvar Aalto, the Finnish architect, considered the sense of touch when he used wood in preference to metal where the human hand would come in contact with the component. He designed light fixtures and controlled daylight in his

10. Molded plywood chairs by Charles Eames. Seat and back elements corresponded to the curves of human anatomy.

buildings as a system of indirect "spill light" to reduce discomfort caused by direct glare. In the United States, experiments with materials for seating led to the development by Charles Eames of molded plywood seat and back elements that corresponded to the complex curves of human anatomy.

Interior form also became more sculptural. Eero Saarinen and Felix Candela, a Mexican architect, both utilized the technology of reinforced concrete shells to contain space but meet the ground at minimum points of contact. This relationship to the ground also characterized Saarinen's designs for chairs of molded fiberglass shells attached with rubber gaskets to slender wire legs that met the floor at minimum points. The mass production of many versions of this furniture by the Herman Miller furniture company meant that the goal of widespread distribution of inexpensive furniture had been achieved. George Nelson developed modular storage systems while at Herman Miller, and Robert Probst developed the Action Office system that led to the flexible open office environments of today.

By 1965 it could be said that the ideals of standardization and universality of design were dominant in many parts of the world. A high-rise building in one city looked much like a high-rise building in any other city. Buildings—inside and out—looked pretty much the same regardless of where they were or what activities went on inside them. Objects, interiors and structures were designed to meet the functional needs of a population that was defined in rather impersonal terms.

CONTEMPORARY DESIGN SINCE 1965

Pluralism and diversity characterize developments in all fields since the mid-1960s. The idea of the possibility or even the desirability of universal solutions to problems has been discredited. The diversity of context is important: the design of an interior responds to the structure and larger landscape in which it is located. The diversity of population is important: the design of an interior promotes the opportunity for all people to contribute to society. The diversity of history and culture is important: conservation of historic buildings and inclusion of culture based references, ornament and symbol, allow people to identify with the past while building the future.

It is now possible to create and produce designs that meet human needs without requiring the standardization that was the hallmark of earlier industrial processes. The development of computer technology encourages a high level of participation by the consumer in the definition and development of an array of custom tailored products, much like the proliferation of cable television channels. It is possible to design to fit the diversity of needs and aspirations of the entire range of people within the society. However, political will is required along with the new technology in order to set priorities for design and to include everyone in the global society.

The Concept of Nature: Ecology and the Green Revolution

Designers today consider the ecological implications of the selection of a species of wood from rain forests or the selection of the optimum plants to improve indoor air quality. During the period of industrialization in the eighteenth, nineteenth and early twentieth centuries, there were two sides to the perception of nature: it was regarded as something to be tamed, conquered and exploited for the benefit of human "progress;" and at the same time portions of nature were set aside as picturesque and wild remnants that might refresh the human spirit. Only since the 1960s has the "Green Revolution" brought the entire spectrum of design decisions under scrutiny to assess potential positive or negative consequences for the environment. Examples of issues addressed during the design process include: indoor air quality and toxic emissions of materials, conservation of trees in the rain forests, disposal of waste, toxic byproducts of manufacturing processes, packaging for shipping, design for recycling and energy conservation.

Since the early 1970s, the use of glass in exterior walls has been more carefully designed to help conserve energy. At the same time, designs centered on tall, skylit central atriums filled with plants and water have beome more common. Projects created by SITE (Sculpture in the Environment) are meant to connect plant life and water as an integrated narrative theme in the context of a building or interior. As James Wines (1991) points out, the design professions should "envision landscape

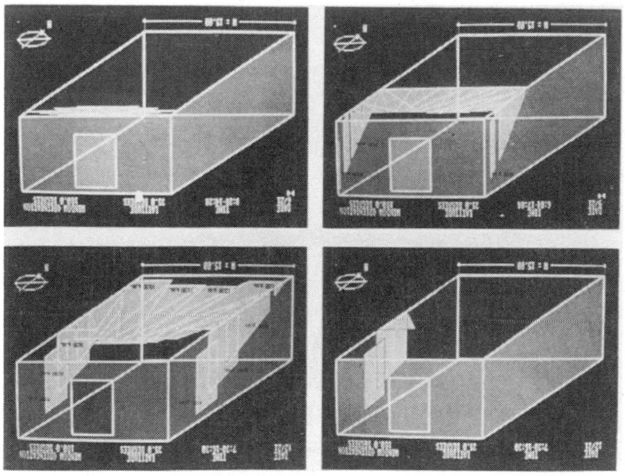

11. Study of sunlight penetration into an interior at 49° North on August 8 (*D. Lord*).

as a microcosm of some larger context, as a philosophical statement, as an intrinsic raw material for interiors—as much so as plaster, wood and metal."

To achieve adequate lighting levels and conserve energy, daylighting is utilized in conjunction with energy saving electric systems. The complex variables of admitting daylight into the structure are studied during the design process. Computer programs can predict the effects of daylighting in an interior on specific days of the year. More efficient sources of light, such as high intensity discharge (H.I.D.) lamps, have been developed. In both commercial and residential applications, compact fluorescent lamps are beginning to replace incandescent lamps that use three to four times as much energy. In today's "intelligent buildings," computer controlled energy management systems regulate the consumption of energy in response to changing conditions of human activity and in the external environment.

The Concept of Human Experience: Human Factors and Diversity

Since 1965, sensitivity to real and diverse human needs, wants and values has become more predominant in the design fields, as described more fully in the following chapter. Today we value diversity more than uniformity. We recognize that people come in all shapes and sizes and degrees of mobility and all have a right to participate in and contribute to society. Tactile signs allow people with vision disabilities to find their way. Toilet rooms are designed to accommodate people in wheelchairs. The Disabilities Act of the U.S.A. mandates improvements in interior arrangements to promote inclusion rather than exclusion. Anthropometrics, or the measurement of humans, has long been applied to design. The difference today lies in the inclusion of a wider spectrum of particular individual cases rather than basing standards on a supposed universal "norm" representative of the whole population.

In the office, the anonymous "bullpen" rows of desks and the isolated private office have both given way to an arrangement that is more personal, with work stations defined by planes of opaque, translucent, or transparent panels. Opportunities for communication within the work group are available and so are opportunities for privacy and concentration. Ergonomic chairs are designed to respond to the comfort and task requirements of the user.

Long term issues of health and psychological well-being and personal control of the environment in the home and workplace are receiving more attention. Careful research into the specification of seating, work surfaces, and lighting can contribute to a good ergonomic fit between humans and computer video display terminals (VDT's), to alleviate symptoms such as eye strain, muscle strain and fatigue. Good acoustical design can contribute to lower levels of noise and disturbance and increase privacy when required.

The fit between humans and the environment at a particular time and place receives more attention today. The demolition of historic structures and entire neighborhoods that was common in the

12. Ethospace Office System by Herman Miller. Work stations defined by planes of opaque, translucent, or transparent panels.

1950s and 1960s has been largely discontinued. In new construction designers frequently use particular figural references, which may be anchored in a particular historic time or geographic place, in a playful way.

The Relationship in Tangible Form: Participation in Events

The definition of interior space is becoming more particular as well. Walls are walls again; windows are placed and framed to call attention to specific views. Inside is inside and outside is outside, although elements of the one may be incorporated in the other as contrast. The thickness of the wall may be emphasized—either by deep recessing or by exposing layers of wall thickness. Particular locations within interior spaces are defined and invite the viewer to take a look from this position or to explore one space in relation to another. Space is no longer conceived as one undifferentiated grid—either between interior and exterior or within the interior itself.

The intent of much contemporary design is to involve all people as participants in the space, to encourage a response. Lighting design has a role to play in the more theatrical interior setting. The distribution of light is much more specific than in the uniformly lit interiors of the 1950s and 1960s. Certain objects or places are highlighted in contrast to their surroundings so that the pattern of light suggests where to look and gives us cues about what to do. With the proliferation of low cost, sophisticated control systems, the user as well as the designer can program variable lighting effects in a random or carefully structured sequence of "events" in the environment.

Formal elements in the interior may derive from high technology. The interiors of Norman Foster, an English architect, celebrate structure, mechanical systems, sun control and electronic displays, as at Stansted Airport north of London. In her designs for the Joseph shops in London, Eva Jiricna incorporated industrial materials and tensioned steel cables to produce an understated setting that enhances the display of the retail merchandise.

Ambivalence and a certain sense of mystery are often the goal. Since the publication of *Complexity and Contradiction in Architecture* by Robert Venturi in 1966, the creation of multiple illusions and a certain playfulness have characterized contemporary environments. Shadow and texture may be merely visual rather than something that can be felt through the sense of touch. There is frequently less emphasis placed on clarity, on the honest expression of materials, or on the flat plane surface which had characterized design since the beginning of the Arts and Crafts movement. The eye can be fooled and false impressions or unexpected relationships can be arranged to surprise the viewer.

Post-modern interiors frequently include deliberate references to historic styles in an attempt to evoke a sense of place and history. Historic references are often used in a way that is more an ironic comment on them than a straight adaptation or revival. Knowing this, people can appreciate the relation of the sculptures on the grand stair to the curved forms of the suspended "arches" at the Seattle Art Museum by Venturi.

In 1981, the Italian designer Ettore Sottsass formed the Memphis Group of designers, who deliberately flouted the notions of "good taste" and "honesty of materials." Their inspiration came from

13. Main stair. Seattle Art Museum by Robert Venturi. The sawtooth details and curved forms of the suspended "arches" echo the forms of the sculptures below.

mass culture and they combined wildly patterned decorative laminates, glowing neon lighting, playful and colorful furniture forms and deliberately "fake" representations of wood grain or flagstones in the same interior. Nigel Coates took this to an extreme in his 1986 design for the Café Gongo in Tokyo. It is a three-dimensional "collage" combining an aircraft wing balcony, Roman statues, soft blue fabric, rusted steel surfaces and 1950s chairs to create a deliberate stage set of internal contradictions.

Frank Gehry, an architect and designer in the United States, uses ordinary materials in inventive ways and lets the results of fabrication processes emerge in the final design. Carved corrugated cardboard building blocks, galvanized metal surfaces, exposed wood studs, trays of electrical conduit and bright colors contribute to a stimulating environment for the Chiat Day Advertising Agency in California.

A number of contemporary architects and designers strive to create a sense of deliberate fragmentation, disjunction and indeterminacy. Buildings, bits of buildings, interior components and artifacts come together at odd angles and in disjointed ways. The architecture and interiors of "Deconstruction" seem to be part of an ongoing flux or change in which a geometry is set up and then at least one other layer is superimposed to clash with it. Connections among what is there and even what is not there are continually reinvented by people who perceive juxtapositions in new ways and participate in the space as actors on a stage.

Contemporary design asks us to abandon our passive habits of acceptance and to participate in spaces as performers in events that are taking place every day. Sometimes it is useful to imagine how future civilizations might view the interior design of today—as an archaeological dig that exposes arrangements of surfaces and products that define spaces. What would they guess about our civilization and the daily lives of people from the material clues we leave them? The layer of interior design is close to us as individuals and easily shaped by each of us. It is a place to start.

REFERENCES

Hitchcock, H. R. & Johnson, P. 1932. *The International Style: Architecture Since 1922*. W. W. Norton.

Lord, D. 1987. "The Computer Department," *Architectural Lighting*. September.

Malnar, J. M. & Vodvarka, F. 1992. *The Interior Dimension: A Theoretical Approach to Enclosed Space*. Van Nostrand Reinhold.

Massey, A. 1990. *Interior Design of the 20th Century*. Thames and Hudson.

Naylor, G. 1971. *The Arts and Crafts Movement: A Study of Its Sources, Ideals, and Influence on Design Theory*. MIT Press.

Naylor, G. 1985. *The Bauhaus Reassessed: Sources and Design Theory*. E. P. Dutton.

Pile, J. F. 1988. *Interior Design*. Abrams.

Smith, F. K. & Bertolone, F. J. 1986. *Bringing Interiors to Light*. Whitney Library of Design.

Tate, A. & Smith, C. R. 1986. *Interior Design in the 20th Century*. Harper and Row.

Venturi, R. 1977. *Complexity and Contradiction in Architecture*. The Museum of Modern Art.

Wines, J. 1991. "Inside Outside: The Aesthetic Implications of Green Design." *Interior Design*, August.

CHAPTER

11

Interiors and Interior Design Today: Contemporary Issues and Challenges

Jo Ann Thompson

Most people spend the majority of their lives in some form of an interior environment. Human beings, throughout their life span, interact with extremely diverse interior spaces. Such spaces range from small, private living spaces to large, public space—with a multitude of variations in between. Not all spaces encountered by individuals throughout their lives are necessarily designed by professionals. Regardless of the origins of the built environment, the fact remains that most spaces in which people must live and work are interior spaces.

1. Spaces should reinforce and reflect the people and their activities.

INTERIORS: CONTEMPORARY ISSUES AND CHALLENGES

Given that interior spaces are a predominant component of each individual's lifetime of experiences, it stands to reason that how to design interior spaces to best fulfill human needs, both functionally and aesthetically, is of primary concern. It is the charge of the interior designer, working in tandem with other design professionals, to meet this challenge.

Concern for human beings and the behavioral, social and cultural needs of the people who interact with an interior space is of primary importance to the success of a design. An interior space, whether it be an office environment, a home environment or a large public environment, is by its very nature a "personal" space in which individuals should be comfortable and properly oriented—not only on a physical level, but psychologically as well.

To accomplish this task, the designer must be sensitive to and cognizant of two primary components that affect all interior design solutions. These are (1) the human issues and (2) the environmental issues. To further complicate the situation, these cannot be dealt with separately. The interrelationships between these issues must be addressed before a successful design solution can be found.

The Human Issues: Functional and Behavioral

The human issues that the designer must address fall essentially into two areas—functional and behavioral. The **functional** component deals with the actual size, shape and form of the human body in relation to the amount of space an individual needs to perform typical tasks effectively and comfortably. The science of measuring the human body—its parts and functional capacities—is called

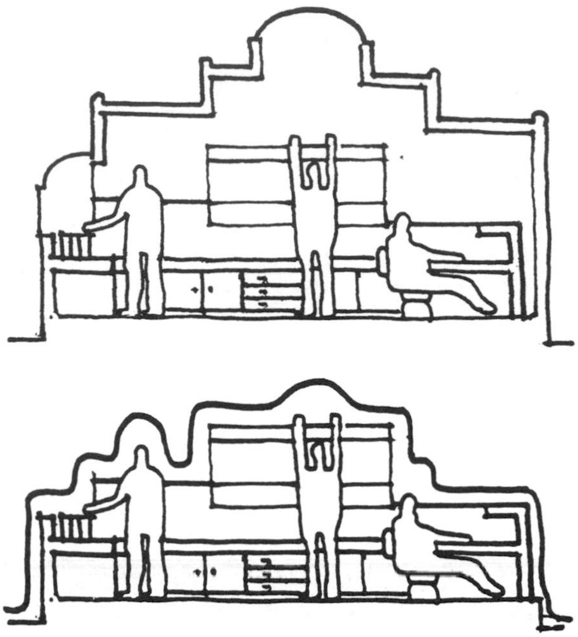

2. The use of anthropometric data to create the scale and size of various furniture and spacial dimensions.

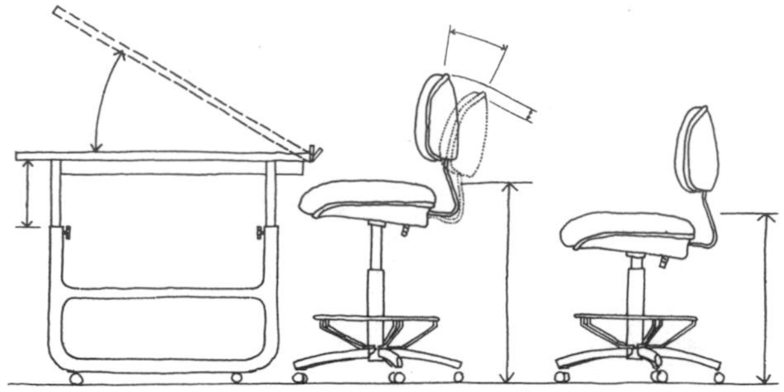

3. The use of ergonomic information to create the scale of various dynamic activities in the work environment.

anthropometrics. This science uses such measurements to determine differences in individuals, groups and cultures. Anthropometric studies address the human body at rest (static), as well as the dimensional characteristics of the human body as it moves (dynamic) through space.

While the measurement of the human body and the identification of basic movements is defined as anthropometry, investigation of the actual performance over various periods of time and the interactions of the human body is known as **ergonomics** or **human factors engineering**. Ergonomics is defined as an interdisciplinary science which integrates the biological sciences with engineering and studies the relationships between people and their environments. This definition is parallel to the definition of human ecology, but ergonomics emphasizes movement and characteristics of the body as a physical entity in a designed environment, rather than the whole organism in relation to a total environment. Anthropometric data is essential to the ergonomist in order to determine the ergonomic fit of the user to various environments. It should be evident that both anthropometric and ergonomic data is critical to the designer, whose major responsibility, after all, is to design spaces which support the activities of human users.

Simply having body measurement data and understanding the amount of space required to perform certain activities is not sufficient. The designer must also address the human issues related to behavior. There are many methods and schools of thought about the proper means of measuring user behavioral patterns, and how to adapt and utilize this information in the design of space. Two significant conceptual models for understanding human behavioral patterns and requirements have emerged in recent years. These warrant a closer look.

Abraham Maslow, a psychologist, developed a comprehensive model of behavioral requirements known as the "**hierarchy of needs**." As emphasized in the first chapter, Maslow (1971) felt that human needs are always changing and, therefore, complete satisfaction of need is not possible. In other words, when one set of needs is satisfied, another set emerges to replace the original set. Maslow's hierarchy begins with the basic physiological requirements that sustain life—air, water, food, clothing, shelter, etc. Once these needs are met, Maslow contends that safety becomes an important need, a concern with avoiding harm and protecting what has been gained, particularly in hostile environments. According to Maslow, these two basic needs have to be achieved before people become concerned about the third step in his hierarchy, acceptance by a peer group—the need to belong. After acceptance is gained, the individual then strives to achieve within the group or organization and ego-status satisfaction becomes an important next step. Moving into a larger office or having carpet in an office may be enough to satisfy this need. The final step in Maslow's hierarchy of needs is the fulfillment of an individual's own highest need or self-actualization.

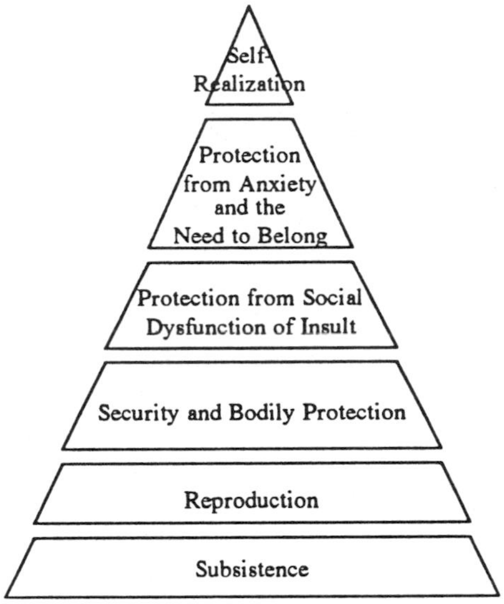

4. The six levels of human needs developed by Maslow (*reference Chapter 1*).

It is important to realize that the model is conceptual. It should be recognized that progression through the various levels will vary with individuals. It should also be recognized that the top of the hierarchy of needs may never be met by some people or some may start over several times in a lifetime.

A second conceptual model for understanding human behavioral patterns and requirements was developed by Edward Hall, an anthropologist, in his studies of people of various cultures and how they relate socially and psychologically to the physical space around them. In his book, *The Hidden Dimension* (1966), Hall developed the concept of **proxemics**.

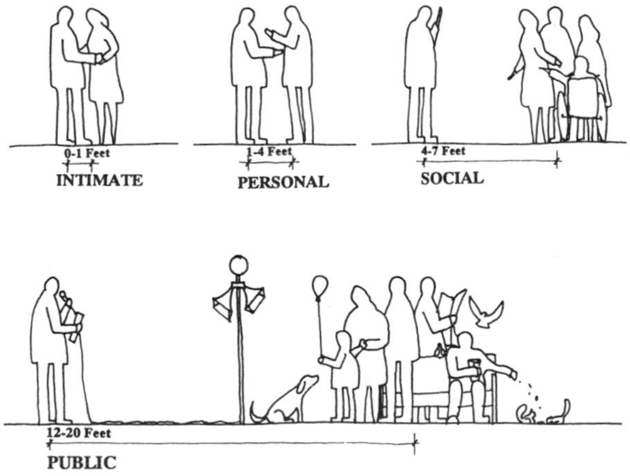

5. The four zones of proxemics developed by Hall—used to develop the appropriate size of private to public spaces.

Hall determined that people function within four "distance" zones—the intimate zone, the personal zone, the social zone and the public zone—each of which has a "near" phase and a "far" phase. Hall maintains that people will select a particular zone for social interaction, depending upon relationships, status and the nature of the activity involved.

The importance of Maslow's and Hall's conceptual models is that they provide the designer with insight into the nature of human beings and how thisrelates to people's perceived satisfaction with the built environment. This understanding helps designers determine the comfortable sizes and definition of spaces, both interior and exterior. Many others have used this concept to study human activities in space, to help clarify human territorial behavior. The better the designer understands the people involved, the more prepared the designer is—and the better the chances are of providing the users with a successful solution to a problem.

Environmental Issues

Human beings do not function in a void. All human behavior occurs within the context of an environment, be it built or natural, interior or exterior. Since this book is concerned with the built environment, and this chapter specifically with the interior environment, we should take a look at some of the environmental components which impact human behavior.

Interior environments and individuals' perceived satisfaction with their environments are affected by several things. Of particular significance are the interior products which give character and definition to the surrounding space. Such things as the furniture style, the color and texture of fabrics utilized in the space and the scale and proportion of the furnishings contribute to the overall satisfaction—or dissatisfaction—of the user with the interior environment. Other aspects deal with interior air quality and control, lighting and other support technologies.

An analysis of user requirements is critical in the determination of appropriate functional relationships for an interior space. Equally critical is an analysis of the psychological requirements of the users. The designer is responsible not only for the physical comfort of the user, but also for the psychological comfort. Most of the time, these two requirements go hand-in-hand. For example, the

6. Public zone of proxemics, observed within the built environment.

development of a lighting scheme that provides not only for efficient task performance and general work conditions, but which also takes into consideration the aesthetics of the space, provides users with both physical and psychological comfort.

The interior designer works with the personal spatial requirements of individuals—whether an office space or a home environment. Even though this is the nature of the job, the designer will many times find that the "legal" client is not the "real" client. The designer may never interact with the actual end users of a large office complex project or a speculative condominium project. Yet, the designer must be sensitive to the needs of these end users on a very personal as well as professional level. The ultimate tools that an interior designer utilizes in fulfilling these needs are products such as furniture, light fixtures, cabinetry, surface treatments and support technologies.

Design Discipline Interactions

It is impossible to separate the human issues of function and behavior from environmental issues of the built environment such as structure, lighting, mechanical/electrical and interior furnishings/products, since these provide the context within which human issues exist. The designer is faced with an extremely complicated and challenging scenario in which the interrelationships between human issues and environmental issues must be dealt with effectively—and in most cases expediently.

The task is not an impossible one to accomplish and the challenge often provides for a very rewarding experience. It is important to realize that any design project encompasses professional expertise from several levels. The most successful design solutions are those that provide an opportunity for designers from various disciplines and areas of expertise to interact and work together as a team toward the completion of the project. The behavioral scientist and ergonomist provide critical data. The architect, the structural engineer, the landscape architect, the interior designer, the electrical engineer and other design professionals integrate this information into the design solution. In the final analysis, all are members of the same environmental design team—working toward the same goal of providing an optimal solution for end users.

7. A well-integrated lighting design (both daylighting controls and electric lighting), Northtown Center, Spokane, Washington (*T. Bartuska*).

INTERIOR DESIGN: A PROFESSIONAL RESPONSE TO THE CHALLENGES

Recognition of the importance of interior spaces in fulfilling human needs has led to the emergence of interior design as a professional discipline. Formal programs of study in interior design at recognized institutions of higher learning began to be developed across the United States around 1950. Initially, interior design programs—along with the profession as a whole—dealt primarily with residential design. As the profession has grown and developed over the years, concern for interior space is no longer limited to the home environment, but rather has widened to include all spaces in which people must live, work and play.

By nature, interior design is interdisciplinary. Because of this fact, interior design programs historically developed under a variety of academic umbrellas, including art, home economics and architecture. Most programs in the United States and Canada still function under one of these academic structures. Each promotes a different philosophical base, while recognizing that dependence upon subject matter from the other areas is critical to the education of a professional interior designer.

As the profession of interior design developed, several insightful individuals working in the profession, along with others from academia, came together to address the future direction of the profession. Through their efforts, three organizations were structured to help monitor and establish quality guidelines for the interior design educational process and for interior design as a profession: the Interior Design Educators Council (IDEC), the Foundation for Interior Design Education Research (FIDER) and the National Council for Interior Design Qualification (NCIDQ).

IDEC membership primarily includes interior design teachers; it was developed to provide a forum for sharing between people involved in the education of interior designers. FIDER is an accrediting agency whose charge is to maintain specific quality standards of interior design educational programs. NCIDQ is charged with the development and administration of a qualifying exam taken by entering interior design professionals before practicing interior design.

Today's interior designer must be a well-trained professional whose charge is to design internal spaces and integrate near environments with the people who interact and function within these environments. The professional interior designer is defined by the National Council for Interior Design Qualification (NCIDQ) as a person qualified by education, experience and examination, who

1. identifies, researches and creatively solves problems pertaining to the function and quality of the interior environment;
2. performs services relative to interior spaces, including programming, design analysis, space planning and aesthetics, using specialized knowledge of interior construction, building codes, equipment, materials and furnishings; and
3. prepares drawings and documents relative to the design of interior spaces in order to enhance and protect the health, safety and welfare of the public.

THE PRACTICE OF INTERIOR DESIGN

The practice of interior design can be divided into roughly four different categories: living spaces, work spaces, public spaces and special-purpose spaces. No matter what category of space, one must remember that the primary guiding principle for every design solution is the creation of a space that optimizes its function and purpose. According to Arnold Friedmann, co-author of the book *Interior Design: An Introduction to Architectural Interiors* (1976) and a pioneer in the development of the Interior Design Educators Council,

> design is above all the solution to a problem. It is not just a matter of combining beautiful forms, textures, colors, and materials. Every interior has some function and purpose, and it is the designer's obligation above all to deal with the required function. An interior that does not "work" might be an attractive stage set or window display, just as a building that does not work might be an interesting piece of sculpture; but if the interior does not work for its stated function, it fails on the most important level of design.

Living Spaces

A **living space** is highly personalized and can even be defined as an intimate environment. Most people spend the major part of their lives in or around a residential environment. A living space must function well for a particular family and/or individuals on a physiological level, while at the same time it must satisfy their psychological needs and values.

These same criteria exist for all categories of interior design. However, when dealing with a

8. The designed relationship of interior finishes and furniture of a lobby in the National Atmospheric Research Center by I. M. Pei in Boulder, Colorado (*T. Bartuska*).

living environment, the intimate nature of the space makes the need for personalization more pronounced. Therefore, in the design of living spaces, it is most important that the interior designer not impose personal preferences onto the client. The designers' expertise should be used to guide clients toward a functional space plan which meets their particular lifestyle. Aesthetic design decisions should be based on sound principles and standards, while enabling clients the flexibility to integrate and personalize the living space to fit their changing needs and values.

The nature of a living space dictates that close communication be maintained between the interior designer, other members of the design team and the client throughout the project. Any breakdown in communication can mean a dissatisfied client. Due to the necessity for close and continual communication with the client, the design of a living space can be difficult for some designers. Because of this, some interior designers choose to work exclusively in commercial space design. Other professional interior designers enjoy this close relationship with the client and work solely in the residential design arena.

Interior design can play a particularly important role in living spaces which are devoid of character. Unfortunately, the United States is dotted with tracts of "builders homes," which have been constructed without the benefit of design expertise. Although, ideally it is best for the interior designer to be a part of the design team from the beginning conceptual stages, this does not always happen—particularly in existing structures or when a design team did not originally exist. The interior designer can provide a client with suggestions that will correct or de-emphasize poor spatial or structural features; ideas can be explored for expanding storage facilities; and furniture arrangements can be planned to better utilize existing space and traffic patterns.

Interior design is not just for the affluent, but addresses issues and needs important to the everyday functioning of all people. Through the design of living spaces, the interior designer offers design solutions that help people function better and feel more comfortable within their living space.

Work Spaces

The importance of comfort and a sense of belonging is self-evident when referring to living spaces. But what about **work spaces**? After all, these are the spaces where the majority of the population spend their lives from eight in the morning to five at night. Placed in this context, it should be apparent that a sense of satisfaction with and safety within the work environment cannot be overestimated.

Many work environments have been put together without any attempt to create a functional and beautiful design. Laboratories, factories and warehouses around the world provide too many examples of such work environments. However, work environments can take on a certain beauty of their own because they effectively solve a problem and, therefore function efficiently.

In today's society, the office environment is designed most explicitly to create both a beautiful and functionally efficient space. This is not to say that other types of work spaces are not being created with this objective. However, with the major

9. A living environment which reflects the lifestyle of its inhabitants.

portion of the United States work force in "white-collar" positions, the office environment has become a major market for interior design services and products. The expressed purpose is to create not only a functional space, but an aesthetically pleasing environment for the employees.

Few other work environments have stressed the integration of function and beauty as much as the office environment. Companies now recognize that a functional space plan is necessary for optimal productivity of their employees. At the same time, they recognize that employee satisfaction with their work environment is also a strong determining factor in their productivity. Thus, the space must not only be functional and efficient, but it must also satisfy and support the emotional and psychological needs of the employees.

Another consideration that impacts upon office design is a concern for the office "image." The aesthetics of the office space are particularly important to many companies that wish to portray a certain progressive image to the public. Therefore, when working with an office space, interior designers, in most cases, are expected to develop a plan that will produce efficient and functional solutions for the work environment; satisfy and support the psychological needs of the employees through personalization and aesthetic treatments of the work space; and, at the same time, project the appropriate company image to the public.

A recent major development in the design of office environments is the concept of the open-office system. Herman Miller, Inc., was one of the first to develop the open office concept. The open office incorporates movable modular panels with work surfaces and storage bins hung from the panels. The concept caught on quickly in the United States and today literally hundreds of manufacturers produce some type of open-office system. The proliferation of open-office systems available on the market has made it possible for the interior designer to offer the client a wide range of options in colors, finishes and textural treatments, along with sophisticated functional solutions for office management.

Public Spaces

The broad scope of the four designated categories of interior design practice have some obvious overlap and similarities. To clarify this, the term "public" is used here to denote those spaces which are open to all people and through which large numbers of people pass in the course of a day or an event. Obvious **public spaces** are gymnasiums, auditoriums, lobbies and airport concourses. The significance is in the fact that large numbers of people routinely interact with these spaces.

10. A functional and flexible furniture system for a working environment (*courtesy of Steel Case Furniture*).

It would be very easy for the designer to depersonalize public spaces, since large masses of people use them. In actuality, personalization is critical to the success of the interior pace—even though the actual users are often faceless masses of people. The space is designed for a purpose. With this as a guide, the interior designer's task is to develop a plan that will provide eventual users with the proper orientation to move throughout the space safely and comfortably, while at the same time allowing them to function efficiently.

Everyone has experienced large public spaces that are uncomfortable, easy to get lost or disoriented in, or which make individuals feel like one of a large herd of animals. Everyone has also experienced public spaces that do the exact opposite, even though the size and number of people moving through the spaces are comparable. What is the difference between these spaces? The difference is usually attributed to a sensitive team of designers who have worked to not only make the space functional, but who have developed a sense of human scale and proportion throughout. This can be accomplished in various ways though most obviously through the space plan. However, to complement the space plan and make the entire package work, the way interior colors, furnishings, textures, artwork, graphics and signage are used is also critical.

Special Purpose Interiors

The category of **special purpose interiors** is very difficult to define since it can include everything from the interiors of churches, restaurants, retail stores and hotels to those of automobiles, ships and airplanes. Obviously, this group of interiors includes highly diversified spaces.

When dealing with special purpose interiors, the development of a strong design program that very clearly establishes the special needs and

11. A very public space, the newly restored internal space of Liverpool Street Station, London, England (*T. Bartuska*).

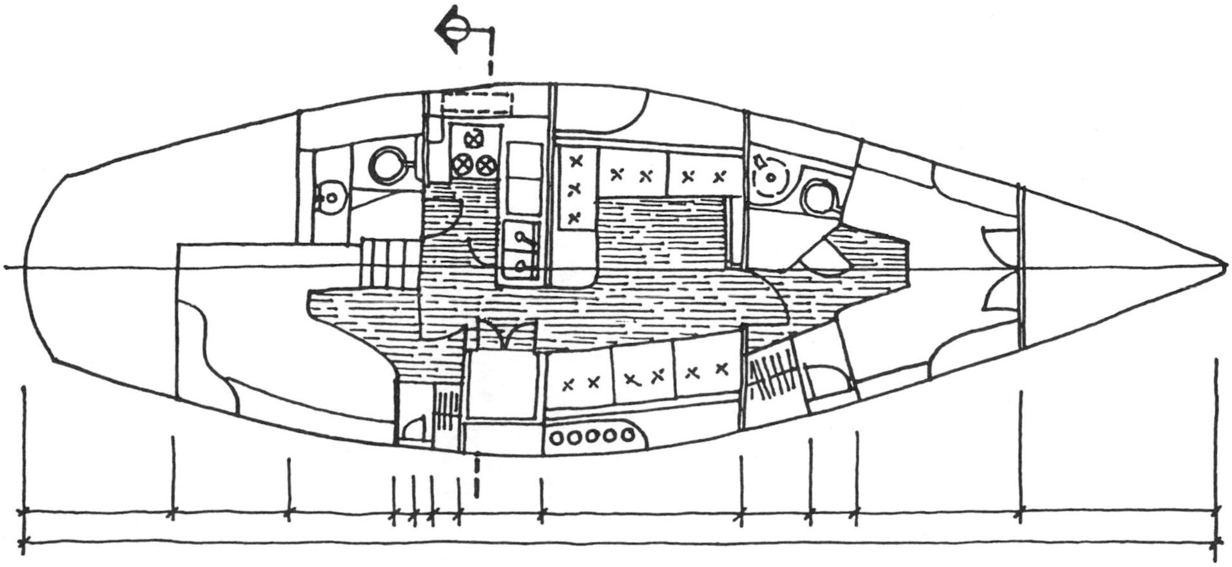

12. Special purpose interiors: an Interior Design student's concept for a sailboat where careful considerations of anthropometric and ergonomic data are critical within the limitations of the space.

requirements of the project is essential. This requires a considerable amount of research on the part of the designer before any design concept and development can begin. In other words, the designer and the design team must first have a complete understanding of the unique and specific nature of the project before a successful solution can be developed. Because of the specialized and confined nature of the problem, understanding of anthropometrics and ergonomics is critical to its effective design. Once a strong and detailed design program has been established, the design process begins and the differences between designing a special purpose interior and other, more typical interior spaces becomes less significant.

SUMMARY

This chapter has looked at some of the contemporary issues and challenges that interior designers must address as professionals in today's society. The reader should especially remember that an interior designer is a member of a professional design team whose primary goal is to provide a built environment which is functional, comfortable, safe and satisfying for human beings. Forest Wilson (1984), a well-known author of several design books, states it this way:

> Many disciplines can contribute toward understanding of these relationships . . . (i.e., physiological, psychological, cultural, and social attributes of the interaction of people and their surroundings). . . . This is an effort to combine the insights of the behavioral researcher, the designer, and that ultimate receiver, the anonymous person who uses the world specified by researcher and designer.

REFERENCES

Altman, I. and Chemers, M. M. 1984. *Culture and Environment*. Brooks/Cole.

Evans, G. W., ed. 1982. *Environmental Stress*. Cambridge University Press.

Friedmann, A., Pile, J. F. and Wilson, F. 1976. *Interior Design: An Introduction to Architectural Interiors*. American Elsevier.

Hall, E. T. 1966. *The Hidden Dimension*. Doubleday.

Maslow, A. 1971. *The Farther Reaches of Human Nature*. Viking.

Michelson, W., ed. 1975. *Behavioral Research Methods in Environmental Design*. Hutchinson Ross.

Panero, J. and Zelnik, M. 1979. *Human Dimension and Interior Space*. Whitney Library of Design.

Thompson, J. A., ed., 1992. *A.S.I.D. Professional Practice Manual*. American Society of Interior Design, Whitney Library of Design.

Wilson, F. 1984. *A Graphic Survey of Perception and Behavior for the Design Professions*. Van Nostrand Reinhold.

Zeisel, J. 1984. *Inquiry By Design: Tools for Environment-Behavior Research*. Cambridge University Press.

CHAPTER 12

The Quest for Shelter: Squatters and Urbanization throughout the World

Henry Matthews and Bashir Kazimee

Most of us, in the industrialized world, take for granted that we live in comfortable houses and apartments; another reality is that an increasing number of people around the world literally live on the streets outdoors. They lack basic shelter and necessary life amenities. A current statistic shows that the number of homeless people in urban areas is increasing more than ever before. Currently, there are 600,000 homeless in the United States and on any given night at least 100,000 children are without homes (Ringheim, 1990).

The disparity in the quest for shelter is even more critical in less developed countries, where significant masses of rural population are moving to the urban centers in search of work and a place to live. Providing adequate space and housing to the growing numbers of people and migrant population offers critical challenges to society and the related design professions. And, this dramatic need for shelter has profound implications for both human and environmental conditions throughout the world. Meeting the need, or not meeting it, will shape almost all aspects and scales of the built environment.

Shelter and Urbanization

The housing crisis in most third world regions is a function of the overall forces of urbanization and the mechanisms within which these forces operate. By nature, the production of housing is an element responsive to many diverse aspects of urban life—population characteristics, employment opportunities and socioeconomic status of the people. The primary force affecting the quest for shelter is the dynamic increase in population of cities, particularly in the less developed countries of Asia, Africa and Latin America (Mc Auslan, 1985).

Contemporary urban growth in and around the cities of the third world is undergoing a dynamic revolution which has no precedent in the history of humankind. By 1985, the total urban population of the world had reached almost 2 billion people (*Prospects*, 1989). More than half of this growth occurred in the metropolitan areas of less developed countries. The United Nations projects that by the turn of the century, the urban population in third world regions alone will increase to almost 2 billion, which duplicates most of the present total urban population. Cities and towns are experiencing a critical transformation from this mushrooming growth in population. For example, Algiers grew from 450 thousand inhabitants to over 2 million between 1950 and 1985 and now is one of Africa's larger cities. During the same period, Lagas grew almost 21 times while populations in Rangoon, Tehran, and Delhi doubled twice over. Between 1950 and 1985, Kinshasa (Zaire) underwent a dramatic transformation, growing from 170 thousand to 2.57 million, a four-fold increase (*Prospects*, 1989).

There are many reasons for the massive growth in third-world cities. Besides the natural internal increase in population caused by improved life expectancy, increased birth rates and advancements in the areas of health and nutrition, a significant share of this growth is attributed to the phenomenon of rural-urban migration. What is more dramatic is that this migration is often directed toward the principal and capital cities of these countries. Because the largest concentration of industries, commercial enterprises, educational and national administrative centers is in the primary cities, they are experiencing the biggest impact from migrant populations. For example, Bangkok, the capitol city of Thailand, with its extensive concentration of resources and urban amenities, has outgrown the second city Chieng Mai by more than 30 times (Drakakis-Smith, 1980).

The causes of migration, however, from rural areas to cities is multiple and complex. Aside from many personal and family motivations, scholars and other experts have identified at least three major factors—rural poverty, natural disasters and political conflicts—as the root causes of rural-urban migration.

Rural Poverty

"Push forces" and "pull forces" are the primary causes of rural-urban migration. **Push forces** are the result of widespread rural poverty and the loss of both economic and social opportunities in rural areas. The **pull forces** are those of urbanization—employment, social and educational opportunities, health and welfare services, and general city amenities and services. The interaction of pull and push forces has created a massive movement of rural population to urban centers. The result is distortion and imbalance in the economic and social order in both the rural village and the city. In contrast, such forces impacted the developed nations in nineteenth and twentieth centuries, where the transformation to industrialization and urbanization has been more complete than in third world regions. The changes have been accommodated and accompanied by a more balanced interaction between economic development and prosperity in industrial and agricultural sectors. Urban transformation took place in the developed world over a period of 200 years, while in the less developed countries it took only 30 years.

The governments of less developed nations often place a high priority on expansion and development of the industrial sector of the economy. As a result of this policy, and a low priority on the agricultural sector, rural areas tend to lack modernization and development. Also, traditional ways of subsistence farming remain predominant in many third-world countries. Over population in the agricultural sector exceeds the productive capacity of the arable land, contributing to significant labor surplus and unemployment in rural areas. Outdated farming techniques, primitive irrigation systems, incidence of drought and pests, all make farming less efficient and less able to support growing populations.

Natural Disasters

Natural disasters, although not limited to rural areas, could be considered the second major cause of rural-urban migration. Natural disasters can also occur in urban areas, but amenities and support services in cities are equipped to provide basic assistance. Clearly defined strategies and precautionary measures to cope with such problems simply do not exist in rural areas. In these areas, both technical and economic means are limited. Upheaval from floods, cyclones and earthquakes often result in phenomenal loss of life and destruction of much of the physical environment. The incidence of flood and cyclone in Bangladesh in 1987 and 1988, for example, was the greatest disaster in the history of that country. The flood affected almost two-thirds of the country with heavy losses in life, property and agricultural land, with at least 1.25 million houses totally destroyed and more than 2.5 million damaged. This destruction caused extreme shortages of housing in a country that could not meet the normal needs of the population (*Habitat News*, 1990). Similarly, in 1988, Pakistan was subjected to major floods that devastated over 4,000 villages and 400,000 acres of fertile agricultural land, wiping out 164,000 rural housing units and rendering 3.3 million people homeless (*Habitat News*, 1990). The effect of massive land slides in Sri Lanka in 1980, earthquakes in the Benquet and Nvera regions of the Philippines in 1990 and the August 1988 earthquake in east and central Nepal, provide other examples of destruction and chaos of monumental proportions, disasters that frustrated already inadequate attempts by the governments of these nations to provide shelter for their citizens.

Political Conflicts

Violent conflicts in a period of post-colonial and cold-war politics, and ethnic or racial unrest, leave tragic footprints in the socio-historical structure of many advanced societies, but their effects have been far more dramatic and unfortunate in poorer countries. The Arab-Israeli conflicts of 1967 and 1973 in the Middle East brought drastic influxes of refugees to the cities. It has been estimated that 250,000 refugees were added to the population of Amman in 1967, while almost half a million people moved into Cairo from the devastated settlements of the Suez Canal Zone following the 1973 war (Abu-Lughod, 1973). The Russian invasion of Afghanistan in 1978 imposed ten years of war on the general population of this country, a war that disrupted and destroyed much of the socio-economic fabric as well as the physical environment on an unprecedented scale. The conflict resulted in the tragic loss of 1.24 million lives and forced almost five million refugees to migrate to the neighboring countries of Pakistan and Iran. The figures represent approximately a 40% displacement of the mostly rural post-war population. Consequently, the number of Afghan refugees in the border cities of Peshawar and Quetta in Pakistan is larger than those of local populations, and many of these desperate people are homeless.

The shift of population from rural areas to urban centers creates a phenomenal impact on the general socioeconomic order of the rural and urban centers of the third world. The capacity of the urban areas to absorb and to cope economically and physically with the influx of migrants creates extreme stress and a tremendous challenge for society. The rate of population growth surpasses the provision of housing, community facilities and services and all the essentials of an urban community. This shortage of shelter has reached crisis proportions and adversely affects many aspects of life.

Many migrants arriving in the cities are not prepared or trained for urban employment. Because of their rural way of life, they face unaccustomed new challenges in the urban labor market, a market that demands new skills, so they must constantly strive for employment and a place to live. Shelter, even of the most humble form, is beyond the financial reach of the majority of these migrants. The inevitable result is that large segments of population in the metropolitan areas attempt to help themselves by building their own shelters in slum areas and **squatter settlements**.

One of the most prominent shelter types that becomes manifest in the urban landscape of the developed countries is the squatter settlement, an almost overnight emergence of spontaneous growth.

1. A view from the older squatter area on the Eastern slope of the Asmaye mountain. The houses are in poor condition and the locality is at the saturated stage of development. Deh-Afghandn, Kabul, Afghanistan (*T. Bartuska*).

Squatters are those who make illegal use of available public, and sometimes even private, urban land for the purpose of building temporary shelters out of the most modest materials they have found discarded.

According to one estimate, many squatter communities are doubling in population every five or six years. This implies an annual increase of 15 to 20%. In comparison, the overall normal growth of such cities is estimated between 5 and 10% annually. Squatters constitute almost 33% of the total population of the city of Karachi, 40% of Caracas, 45% of Lima, 46% of Mexico City, and 50% of Ankara (Mountjoy, 1979). Out of the more than 8 million population of Bombay (India), 54% live in slums and squatter settlements and an additional 2.5% are pavement dwellers (people living on the streets without a shelter of any kind).

Squatter communities throughout the third world exhibit great variation and a wide range of types of physical appearance and socioeconomic structure. They are constructed of any kind of salvageable and rudimentary material available locally—ranging from cardboard cartons, petrol tin cases, straw and matting, to more consolidated structures and permanent materials such as brick, stone, wood and earth. No standards for construction have been established and the settlements lack even minimum conventional amenities. Municipal services such as water supply, sewage system, street lighting or paved roads, and community facilities such as health, education and police protection are virtually nonexistent in many squatter settlements.

2. A view of a comparatively new squatter settlement on the south slopes of Asmaye mountain. The dwellings are built from locally available materials and many dwellings show advanced stages of development. Karti-Sakhi, Kabul, Afghanistan (*T. Bartuska*).

The densities in squatter areas are extremely high, so overcrowding and congestion are common. Poverty contributes to social disorganization, increased unemployment, crime, and delinquency. Rudimentary sanitation and the unhygienic and squalid conditions (especially with open sewage and drainage ditches) expose populations to constant dangers of epidemics of typhoid, malaria and infectious diseases.

Governments have limited resources to provide assistance and community facilities for the poor. Government officials tend to be passive and often indifferent to these complex challenges. Since the biggest portion of the capital for housing the poor would have to be subsidized, investment in this sector of the economy is least favored by many third world countries. The widely accepted economic philosophy that investment in housing will tend to consume available resources rather than produce revenues, makes the provision and improvement of housing the lowest priority in national development policies. The magnitude and scale of the problem is such that any intervention by a developing economy is beyond its means and will consume its scarce resources. A pattern of migration of 5,000 people per week into the city of Rio de Janeiro and a demand of 5 million new homes annually in Brazil convey the magnitude of the problem that developing countries must solve. Housing the homeless is not an easy task, even for an advanced and developed economy, and it is doubtful that the majority of the less developing countries can ever satisfy the needs of their people.

Conversely, the process of building squatter settlements, despite physical ills, poor housing and squalor, has positive aspects and contributes to the socioeconomic life of the city. This participatory, self-help approach to problems is an effective and economical method for providing housing. Communities built in this way are a source of labor and tend to stimulate small commercial and industrial enterprises in the urban area. The people are responsible citizens and their only hope is to overcome poverty and participate in the normal social and economic life of the city. Despite official views that shanty towns only deteriorate, many examples demonstrate that they are often improved, if gradually, by their inhabitants. The inhabitants attempt to provide a decent environment for their families and work very hard over the years to improve their houses. "The root cause of squatting does not lie in the nature of the squatters themselves, but is a response to the lack of access to affordable housing or land. This is caused not only by insufficient production of houses, but also by the limited resources of society" (Drakakis-Smith, 1980).

One of the positive characteristics attributed to squatter settlements is a close sense of community, a sense that reflects the inhabitants' rural values. Tribal and family ties, kinship and extended family structures and village grouping encourage a continuity of custom and culture from their rural village environments. In many cities of Africa, Southeast Asia and the Middle East, squatter settlements follow the patterns of rural villages. Narrow streets and alleyways are designed primarily for pedestrian activity with no vehicular access. These alleys often function as meeting places for people and play areas for children. The continued use in squatter housing of both local materials and traditional construction techniques is very efficient and an obvious connection to the builders' sense of a regional vernacular tradition. Thus, "in third-world cities, we no longer see urbanization of the rural migrants, but rather a growing ruralization of the cities" (Mountjoy, 1979). A study of Egyptian migrant adjustments to the city showed that more than one-third of the Cairo city population is comprised of migrants and the majority are from rural areas within Egypt. When all these migrants come equipped with skills and customs of rural origin, they have a significant impact on shaping the culture of the city as much or more than they adjust to urban qualities (Abu-Lughod, 1961).

What has to be realized is that squatter settlements are a recognizable force in the formation and growth of third-world cities. Reality suggests that this type of settlement is perhaps the only affordable method to provide shelter for the urban poor and will continue to be the way that the majority of urban dwellers in third-world cities use to solve their quest for shelter.

3. Typical vernacular building in rural Thailand. Raised on poles above swampy land the upper story catches breezes and the overhanging roof sheds rain (*H. Matthews*).

KLONG TOEY: A CASE STUDY OF A SQUATTER SETTLEMENT

Next to the port of Bangkok, Thailand, the community of Klong Toey presents a classic example of a third-world squatter settlement. It demonstrates many of the problems and opportunities that arise when thousands of rural migrants to the metropolis attempt to take possession of vacant land and build their own homes. Klong Toey is the home of over 30,000 people who for many years have exercised their own energies and skills to provide for their families. In many respects they have been successful, but they have lacked essential services and met with official opposition and harassment instead of help. The case study is based on observation and study by one of the authors in Thailand in 1971 and on a sociological study made there a year earlier. Although two decades have passed since then, the conditions described have not changed for the better; the world housing crisis has deepened and the suffering in places like Klong Toey has only intensified. In a world dominated by self-interest, apathy and militarism, there is much to learn from the lessons of Klong Toey.

Background

In Bangkok, between 1955 and 1970, the population increased from two to three million. The single greatest factor in this increase was migration from rural areas. Since the city could not absorb such a vast growth in government-built housing or privately financed homes, the inevitable result was that the newcomers attempted to take matters into their own hands by constructing makeshift shelters and gradually improving them. In Bangkok, several squatter settlements developed, mostly on swampy land not serving any other purpose. Of these, Klong Toey is the largest: its location next to one of Asia's major ports where there was plenty of employment made it particularly attractive as a place to live.

Many of the migrants arriving there came from regions with strong traditions of vernacular architecture where it was normal for people to build their own homes. They were generally more skilled at simple building crafts than most long-term city dwellers. The average person from a western country might despair and give up, but those who came to settle on a swamp beside the Port of Thailand chose a site to which they could adapt their building tradition; a resourceful Thai peasant knows how to drive wooden piles into the mud and build a house upon them.

The migrants built their houses mainly of wood and corrugated iron. Most of the dwellings were of a very minimal nature, consisting only of a single room, but they were generally extended by a shaded platform in front, which was used as a living area rather like a front porch. Some of the residents who had been there for several years had managed to improve their homes and reach a higher standard, but some shacks, built entirely over the muddy banks of stagnant waterways with no room for expansion (Figures 2 and 3) seemed to have little potential for improvement. The floors were generally raised up about three feet above the marsh, but on the edges of canals they were higher.

4. Squatters' dwellings connected by boardwalks show the ability of residents to exploit available materials to provide for their families (*H. Matthews*).

5. Minimum dwellings, with no room for expansion, built along polluted waterways (*H. Matthews*).

The houses were connected by raised boardwalks, which were communally maintained.

In 1970, there were about 6,000 families living in Klong Toey, enough to constitute a small city. The average family size was six persons with 50% under twenty years of age. Over 90% of the heads of households were employed, but only at subsistence levels. Many of the residents worked daily recovering and recycling materials from an adjoining garbage dump. A number of small businesses, workshops, cafes and stores were established in the community. In many ways, Klong Toey was as self-contained as any small town, but it was a town in which several vital necessities were missing. The city government did not provide the basic services on which conventional communities depend, so the residents were essentially without clean water, sewage disposal, schools, medical care and easy access to public transit.

The Political Context

The community repeatedly campaigned for the provision of schools, sewers and water supply, but to no avail. It was clear that the city government was afraid of capitulating to these demands and felt that any efforts to improve the quality of life in the settlement would only encourage the squatters in their illegal existence. The only education available was at a few small, unlicensed schools in makeshift buildings. Only a small proportion of the children in the area were able to receive any education at all. The children portrayed in Figure 6 were some of the lucky ones enrolled in a Catholic school run by a small group of nuns.

In 1970, the Port Authority was granted a $12.5 million loan to extend port facilities and Authority officials immediately took steps to clear adjacent land of squatters. These people had no legal tenure to the land on which they lived, but having erected dwellings on it, they had established certain rights and eviction by force was not attempted. Instead, the Port Authority tried a more subtle means to drive the settlers off the land. Dredgers, at work in the vicinity, were ordered to

6. Children in a catholic school, Klong Toey (*H. Matthews*).

discharge their mud into the area where the people lived, swamping the homes and blocking the drainage ditches which ran through it. This action naturally caused great distress in the community but it only served to increase the solidarity of its members. Powerless to resist the flow of mud, the people worked together to rise above it. Many dwellings in the threatened areas were literally raised up overnight on new foundations and life went on as before. Such immediate emergency action showed great engineering skill as well as determination.

That same year, a group of sociologists from Thammasat University in Bangkok carried out a sociological survey in the settlement. They were sympathetic to the plight of the squatters and wished to help them by obtaining factual information about them that could be used to plan better for their future. At first, the sociologists found the people hostile and suspicious. Community leaders believed that they were spies working for those who wanted to destroy the community and they received no help whatever. They were warned that it would be dangerous to enter the area. However, in the course of time, they managed to persuade the people that they wanted to support them in their struggle for a decent environment. Finally, they were able to talk to many families! After several months investigating life at Klong Toey, they formed a surprising picture of the community. Some of their findings were as follows:

1. Most of the inhabitants regarded Klong Toey as a reasonably good place to live. They were satisfied with the environment they had created, except for the lack of normal services.
2. The people did not want to be moved to other parts of the city. They were mostly living close to their work and would not be able to afford long journeys by public transport.
3. The residents vigorously opposed the removal of the nearby garbage dump. Although this appeared to be an environmental nuisance and a health hazard, those who worked at subsistence levels or who had no regular employment at all were glad of the chance to make money by recycling waste. The dump also provided raw materials for a number of local industries.
4. There was no evidence of a higher crime rate in Klong Toey than in the rest of the city.

7. Government built housing in Bangkok (*C. Phisuthikul*).

5. It did not seem to be an unusually dangerous place to live. Two children had been drowned in the last fifteen years, which was not a bad statistic in a city built on so many waterways.
6. The main complaint was the lack of facilities that other communities enjoy. The inhabitants did not feel that Klong Toey was a bad place to bring up children. However, they complained bitterly about the lack of schools. They had high hopes that their own children could do better in the world than they had done, but without schools, there seemed to be little hope.
7. There was clearly a viable community in Klong Toey with a history of self-help and self-reliance. The boardwalks were kept in good repair and people worked together to overcome common problems. It was obvious that the community had leaders and specialist groups of skilled builders. But, the fear of victimization was so great that the leaders were never identified to the university investigators.

At the time of the study, the Thai government was attempting to solve the housing crisis by building low-income apartments. However, on the budget available, only a negligible proportion of the ill-housed people in Bangkok could find places in the new units. The units being constructed, generally five-story, walk-up apartments, were far from ideal for families. They were much in demand from the homeless, but they were also the cause of many complaints, particularly about lack of space and poor ventilation. They were often far from places of employment and lacked community life or spirit. The typical cost of a housing unit for six persons was $3,000 (in 1970 dollars). Shacks in the squatter settlement were built for around $50.

CONCLUSION

The drift from the countryside to the city is a painful process. The vernacular tradition in Southeast Asia works best when family members can cut their own timber and gather bamboo and thatch on their own land. In a hostile urban environment, the speculative tradition has little to offer migrants, for they have too little income to offer any hope of profit to the speculator. The people of Klong Toey came to Bangkok with high hopes and with worthwhile skills. They had the potential to build a community of which they could be proud. However, they met with repeated opposition, much of it based on misconceptions. The government argued, as is typical in such cases, that illegal settlements always deteriorate, and any funds spent on them would be wasted. Klong Toey was seen not as a viable community in the early stages of development, but as a center of crime, vice and disease.

In many developing countries and in wealthy countries too, the tradition of participation in the planning and building process is just beginning to be appreciated and used. Klong Toey and other squatter settlements offer important lessons to society. It is clear that governments must recognize the inevitable results of mass migration to the cities and to take appropriate steps, such as those suggested below:

1. Make land available at low rent and with a possibility of purchase to people who are employed in a given area.
2. Provide an infrastructure of services (sewers, water supply and schools) before or while the settlements are being developed.
3. Assist in the provision of suitable building materials at economic rates, to ensure sound building.
4. Offer encouragement to the self-help labor force and recognize the national resource which already exists in the skill and determination of rural migrants.
5. Set up a self-help building advisory service to encourage higher standards of construction.

The world housing problem, which reached crisis proportions many years ago, will not be improved until the people who need housing the most are invited to participate in its design and construction. Every nation's greatest asset is the ingenuity and hard work of its citizens. Let us use them in a participatory process and all of us regain our sense of human dignity.

REFERENCES

Abrams, 1964. *Man's Struggle for Shelter in an Urbanizing World*. MIT.

Abu-Lughod J., 1961. "Migrant Adjustment to City Life: The Egyptian Case." *American Journal of Sociology*.

Drakakis-Smith, D., 1980. *Urbanization, Housing and the Development Process*. St. Martin's.

Ghosh, K., 1984. *Urban Development in the Third World*. Greenwood.

Habitat 1976. *World Settlements Perspectives, Central Mortgage and Housing Corporation*. Ottawa.

Habitat News, 1990, April (whole issue). United Nations Center for Human Settlements.

Mc Auslan, P. 1985. *Urban Land and Shelter for the Poor*. International Institute for Environment and Development.

Mountjoy, A. B., 1979. *The Third World: Problems and Perspectives*. St. Martins.

Prospects of World Urbanization, 1988. 1989. United Nations (Population Studies, No. 112).

Ringheim, K., 1990. *At Risk of Homelessness: The Roles of Income and Rent*. Praeger.

Introduction

3. STRUCTURES

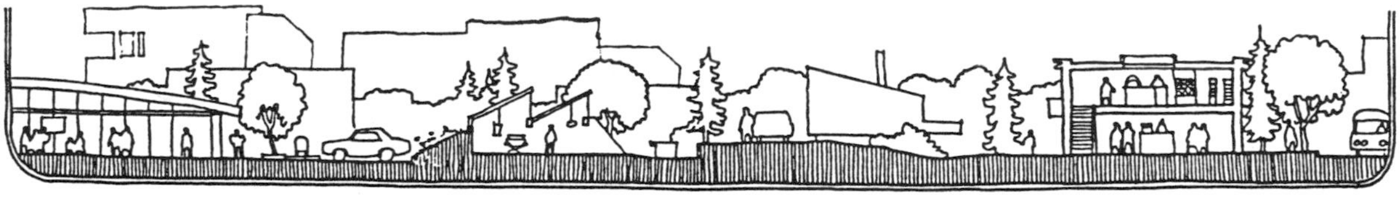

Structures are the third component to this study of the built environment. Building structures to satisfy human needs and desires is a basic creative act, one that has occurred throughout human history. Building is a primary adaptive design strategy for humans, and for that matter, a strategy for many other animals and insects—a strategy developed in order to live more comfortably and more effectively within the natural environment. Buildings symbolically express this permanence and culture.

It is difficult to generalize about structures; they exist in so many different types and sizes. Structures—both old and new—crude and refined, express the numerous reasons to build. The various types of structures possible are limited only by human insights, interests and imagination.

Simply observing the built environment should enable one to list a variety of structures which serve individual and collective needs and desires. Shelter, the most basic structure, has been created in an enormous variety of shapes and sizes. Community structures accommodate commercial, governmental, educational and recreational interests. Even bridges, circulation systems, dams, power plants and energy networks are structures created to interconnect society in various ways.

The cumulative effect of building on land creates larger components of the built environment. For example, a farmstead, a campus, a neighborhood, village or city, even large metropolitan and rural regions are influenced by the way we collectively build and aggregate structures.

Structures, especially buildings, have a dual characteristic and quality: an inside-outside dualism between the spaces for people and the natural environment. This dual quality is unique to the design of structures and does not occur in other design fields. Exploring these two characteristics can expand the appreciation and understanding of structures. Structures express and, therefore, symbolize internal and external human interrelationships with the natural and built environments.

Internally, structures satisfy and symbolize human spatial needs, wants and values. They assemble products and interior spaces in various creative ways. Spaces for human activities are essential ingredients of a structure. This internal characteristic is commonly referred to as the "functional" aspect of structures.

Externally, structures also provide and symbolize a protective envelope, an interrelationship with the outside environment. This external expression is commonly referred to as the "form" of structures. The form becomes, in a sense, an enclosure which mediates the conflict between internal functional needs and the external environment. This enclosure forms the interior environment, which protects humans from the unwanted aspects of the exterior environment, such as uncomfortable temperatures, strong winds, disruptive noises, etc. The enclosure can also open up to beneficial aspects of the outside environment, such as a beautiful garden or landscape, daylight, fresh air and ventilation, even pleasant fragrances and the sounds of water, birds and music.

The external enclosure can be considered closely analogous to the "skin" of the human body, which also welcomes the sun's warmth (clothing provides insulation from the winter cold), its pores open with evaporative cooling in very hot temperatures. Hair screens unwanted contacts while accepting the appreciative touch of a friend or loved one.

Human comfort (light, fresh air, optimum temperatures, etc.) is based upon human senses and either provided for by natural means (windows for light, solar energy for heat, shade for cooling, etc.) or by artificial means (electric lights, heating, air conditioning, etc.). Design without a full understanding of the advantages and disadvantages of natural and built technologies generally causes high operating costs and energy consumption.

The external expression, the characteristics of form, also have a direct effect, even at times a major impact on the overall built environment. Structures can be created to enhance or disrupt the landscapes, cities and regions in which they are built. This impact of how structures "fit" into their context, or adjacent environment, is an important aspect in studying the external form of structures.

The implications of the characteristics of structures, both inside and out, can be effectively summarized by the basic definition of the built environment introduced in the first chapter and by the levels of integration concept (content-component-context) discussed in Chapters Four and Five. In general, the structures component can be defined as follows:

1. **Structures** (the contents of which are products and interiors) are humanly made or arranged;
2. to fulfill human purpose; to satisfy human needs, wants and values;
3. to mediate the overall external environment;
4. with results that affect the overall environmental context (the context for structures includes landscapes, cities, regions and ultimately, the earth upon which they are built).

Structures are part of or in the middle of this interlocking continuum of content-component-context relationships. The levels of integration concept emphasizes that the structures component must integrate content and must fit within its context as represented by the following parts-to-whole continuum:

PRODUCTS-INTERIORS-***STRUCTURES***-LANDSCAPES-CITIES-REGIONS-EARTH

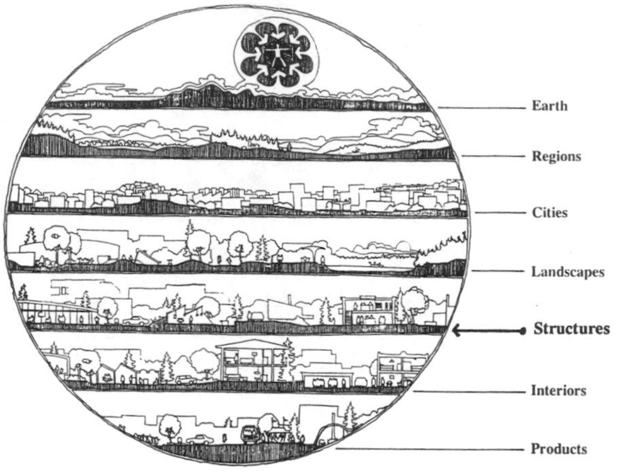

Important quantitative and qualitative differences can be found in the definitions of the related terms: structure, building and architecture:

1. **Structure:** Something constructed or built as a building, a dam, a bridge, and/or to arrange, compose or interrelate all parts to a whole.
2. **Building:** A structure which is built, generally implying human occupancy and/or to construct, the art or work of assembling materials into such structures.
3. **Architecture:** The art and science of building. The art and science of designing and building open areas, communities and other artificial constructions or environments, usually with some regard to aesthetic effects. Furthermore, insights can be learned from the way the word "architecture" itself is structured:

Arch-i-tecture: art + technology (art + craft + science + engineering)

Arch + tecture (tecture referring to "texture," the characteristic of the interwoven or intertwined fabric; the integration of a structure with its internal content and external context).

It seems important to emphasize that there is a quantitative and qualitative dimension implied in the above words. Structure is the most general, all-encompassing word. Buildings are structures in which humans dwell. The definition of architecture combines the noun and the verb. The verb emphasizes the design process, while the noun emphasizes the product.

To "practice" architecture, a person is required to become knowledgeable and skilled in the field before becoming an "architect." National and state laws, which attempt to ensure "public health, safety and welfare," generally require an individual to undertake 5–6 years of university studies achieving a nationally accredited professional degree in architecture, complete 2–3 years of apprenticeship with an architect or engineer, and pass a 3–4 day examination before becoming a licensed professional.

The chapters in this section explore various qualitative dimensions of the art and science of building. They explore the many aspects of function and form in the creative building of healthy human spaces and places which fit environmental contexts. The chapters are organized as follows:

- **"Recent Trends in Architecture: Building as a Response to Human Social and Cultural Factors"** by Noel Moffett: this first chapter discusses the historic development of building and architecture. It emphasizes seven recent trends which emerge from an analysis of contemporary design. It concludes with a synthesis of these diverse trends and suggests important directives for architecture in the future.

- **"The Fitness Test: Building as a Response to Human-Environmental Factors"** by Tom J. Bartuska: this chapter explores various human-environmental factors that shape buildings. It suggests that "Fitness" may be the key to successful building and design in a natural and/or urban context.

- **"Building as a Response to Technological and Creative Processes"** by Ken Carper: the third chapter discusses the purpose of and needs for technology in the creative design process. It defines "appropriate" technology and gives an overview of the scope and complexity of the technologies that are used today. The essay concludes by emphasizing the need for coordination and integration.

- **"Engineering Contributions to the Built Environment"** by Carl W. Hall: the fourth and last chapter of this section analyzes the history and mission of engineering contributions to the built environment. It emphasizes the important interface between science, engineering and the environmental design disciplines and suggests that design synthesis is the common thread which directs their work to meet the challenges of the future.

CHAPTER

13

Recent Trends in Architecture: Building as a Response to Human Social/Cultural Factors

Noel Moffett

"It's a concrete monstrosity." Many a famous (and, by some well-loved) modern building has been contemptuously dismissed in such words. One day in Windsor, an architect was photographing a small office block, which he had designed. As it was close to the castle, he had given it rough, rugged finishes, so that it wouldn't clash with the architecture of the castle. A passerby stopped and asked him: "What do you want to photograph that abortion for?"

MODERN ARCHITECTURE

There can be no doubt that many "modern" architects and their buildings are not popular with the public. Why? Because sometimes their roofs leak, because concrete is a cold, grey, unwelcoming material (architects like it for its plastic qualities), because they have moved too far away from popular taste and created unfamiliar shapes, because they have ignored the lessons of history and because—not their fault perhaps—they have worked from programs written by committees and not by the users of the buildings.

Did we have to have a modern movement anyway? Perhaps not. But, way back in the thirties, the eloquence of the Swiss architect Le Corbusier and the example of the Germans Gropius and Mies convinced us all. We were going to reform the world, clear the slums, let the sun into every room in the house and put a green belt round every city, introduce a new era of light and air and green spaces. But, to bring about these marvelous things, we bulldozed the centers of our cities, destroying many old, beloved buildings in the process, and left them empty and derelict for years. We called it "comprehensive redevelopment," but the people whose homes were destroyed considered it too high a price to pay for the new image of architecture and the city and turned against us. Who can blame them?

THE PAST: OUR ARCHITECTURAL HERITAGE

But it wasn't always like this. Almost everyone today admires the great buildings of the past—the pyramids of Egypt, the fine classic developments of Greek temples and Roman aqueducts, the Mayan temples in Mexico, medieval walled towns and the Gothic cathedrals of Europe the imperial palaces of Japan and China, the Crystal Palace and the Eiffel Tower. This is our heritage designed sometimes by architects, sometimes by master masons, sometimes by dedicated groups of citizens whose names we don't even know. It is useful to briefly trace some of these, emphasizing the achievements of western civilizations.

Egyptian Developments—2000 to 100 BC

The great Egyptian pyramids, ziggurats and temples on the banks of the Nile were the earliest influences on western architecture. The pharaohs, who were god-kings and ruthless rulers, had a fine knowledge of astronomy and mathematics. They used geometry and repetition as symbols of stability and permanence to create monuments to themselves—with multicolumned courts, avenues of sphinxes and walls covered with picture writing—which are as expressive today, in their desert landscape, as they were two or three thousand years ago.

1. Avenue of sphinxes leading from the river Nile to a burial pyramid.

Classic Developments: Greek—1100 to 350 BC and Roman—150 BC to 1000 AD

Today we still marvel at the skill with which Greek masons built their temples and carved their sculpture from marble and limestone. Here the classic orders of architecture (Doric, Ionic and Corinthian) were perfected and used with great sensitivity in their rectangular temples and houses. Greek architects selected the sites for their buildings with care and respect for nature and the result was a striking harmony between buildings and natural materials. Many people believe that the Parthenon in Athens is the finest building of all time.

The Romans were great conquerors and also fine builders. They invented the arch, the vault and the dome, built roads as straight as an arrow and lofty brick viaducts to carry water to the far ends of their empire. They used brick and stone with daring and imagination and erected enormous basilicas, temples, public baths and amphitheaters. Today, the Coliseum and the Pantheon in Rome, and amphitheaters in southern France and northern Africa are among the world's most imposing monuments.

2 and 3. Today the Colosseum and the Pantheon in Rome are among the most imposing monuments the world possesses.

Medieval and Gothic Developments: 800 to 1520 AD

In the so-called medieval "dark ages," civilization was kept alive by monks in fortified monasteries. Towns were designed for defense against

4. Europe's great Gothic cathedrals today testify to the strength of religious belief which grew out of the Dark Ages.

attack, with double walls and moats; narrow, winding streets; towering churches and fortified castles. Merchants formed themselves into guilds and gradually became rich and powerful—challenging the totalitarian rule of the feudal lords. Carcassonne is one of the best preserved examples of medieval fortified towns in southern Europe.

Europe's great Gothic cathedrals today testify to the strength of religious beliefs, which grew out of the Dark Ages. Some of these are structural miracles in stone and glass, with pointed arches, flying buttresses and large windows illustrating Bible stories with brightly-colored stained glass.

Renaissance and Baroque Developments: 1420 to 1860 AD

The great rebirth of the arts began in Florence and soon spread throughout Italy and later to France, Spain, Holland and England. Italian designers Brunelleschi, Leonardo da Vinci, Michelangelo and Bernini reinterpreted the classic lessons of Greece and Rome for their own age and created impressive churches, palaces and public buildings, using the old orders of architecture in interesting new ways. The Italian love of order, vista, axial planning and classical ornament was soon copied in France and England (where Inigo Jones and Christopher Wren introduced order and harmony into medieval London—most impressively at Greenwich and St. Paul's Cathedral).

5. Order and harmony at Greenwich.

Art Nouveau, Arts and Craft Developments: 1890 to 1910 AD

The Art Nouveau movement began in France in the late 19th Century. The Arts and Crafts movement began in England with William Morris and his collaborators, and in Scotland with the architect Charles Rennie Macintosh. They were a reaction against copying the past, against the rigidity and formality of Renaissance attitudes to design. Nature was studied and its organic forms inspired new patterns in design. Plant-like curves, parabolas and hyperbolas were preferred to straight lines and right angles, squares and rectangles.

6. Nature was studied and its organic forms inspired new patterns in design. A Paris nightclub.

Modern Architecture and the International Style: 1920 to Present

Because its principles and precepts ignored regional oddities and local climatic conditions, modern architecture became known as "the international style." Certainly today one finds the same little box-like buildings, with smooth concrete walls and flat roofs, in San Francisco and San Jose, in Toronto and Tipperary.

But, in the later years of the movement, some architects rebelled against this nonrecognition of regional and climatic conditions and architecture began slowly to acquire a more human, more acceptable face. This can perhaps best be seen in the work of the Finn Alvar Aalto and the Japanese Kenzo Tange. Aalto's buildings are unmistakably Scandinavian; he designed sensitively for a northern climate and used his country's ubiquitous timber imaginatively and brilliantly to create an architecture of warmth and charm, qualities too often absent from the work of many of his contemporaries. Tange's early buildings have a strong likeness to those of Le Corbusier, but, as he matured as an artist, he became more and more influenced by his country's traditional architecture and his later buildings are unmistakably Japanese. The work of these two architects heralded the beginning of the end of internationalism and created a vacuum which is only now being slowly and hesitantly filled.

7. Because its principles and precepts ignored local climatic conditions, modern architecture became known as 'the international style.' Blocks of flats almost anywhere.

CONTEMPORARY ARCHITECTURE OF TODAY

Actually it was Le Corbusier who anticipated, although unknowingly and paradoxically, the contemporary attitudes of architecture today. Some call this challenging time "The Post-Modern Movement"—if it can be called a movement. First, Corbu closed down the series of international conferences, because, as he said at the time, "the battle for modern architecture has now been won." Then he built Ronchamp, the little pilgrimage chapel sitting like a sculpted jewel on its hill in eastern France. Ronchamp burst, like a bomb shell, on the architectural world of the day (1955)—dynamically challenging Mies' classical steel-and-glass prism, Gropius' machine aesthetic and mass-production technology and Corbu's own unites d'habitations. It was the first modern building to challenge some of the more static and overly technological principles of the modern movement. It seemed to have been carved, rather than built. It was also rich and mysterious, in a medieval way, with thick walls, a floating roof and tiny windows filled with hand-painted colored glass.

The Spaniard, Antonio Gaudi, although generally classified as an Art Nouveau architect, was probably the first post-modern architect. The winding, twisting road, which Gaudi followed, led away from the international style towards an exciting world of fantasy, emotion and irrationality. His work filled the vacuum created by Le Corbusier's past formal logic and Mies' cold classicism. He satisfied people's yearning for richness, decoration and mystery. And he appealed to their sense of excitement. After Gaudi—in a world of supermarkets and television commercials, where people had dull, monotonous jobs and life was often boring—it was once again possible to enjoy architecture and find that it enriched one's life in not too serious a way.

With Corbu's Ronchamp and Gaudi's playful Art Nouveau buildings, a new, richer attitude towards architecture was born. It had many influences: pop

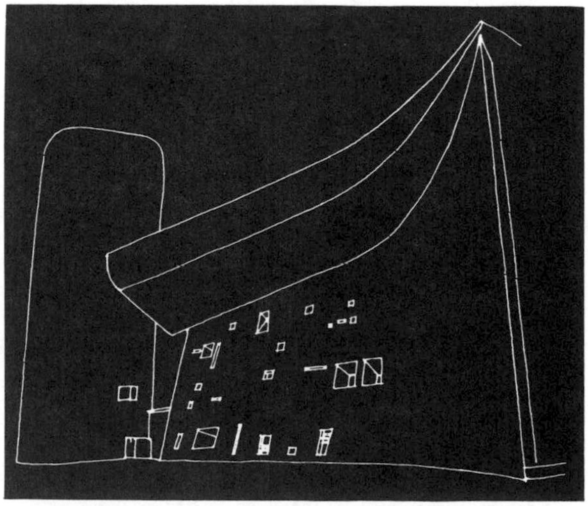

8. It was also rich and mysterious with thick walls, a floating roof and tiny windows. Le Corbusier's chapel at Ronchamp, France (*courtesy of G. Baker, An Analysis of Form*).

9. Gaudi satisfied people's yearning for decoration, richness and mystery. Housing—a block of flats in Barcelona, Spain (*A. Moffett*).

art and pop music, Disneyland, the environmental and anti-pollution movements, solar energy and energy conservation, self-build and do-it-yourself, adaptation of old buildings to new uses, public participation in planning, philosophical statements like "small is beautiful," renewed interest in human scale and anthropology and a growing disenchantment with the motor car. It is difficult to say whether these new "post-modern" attitudes will last. Some believe they are just an architectural fashion, soon to be followed by another fashion or by a return to the principles of the modern movement. There seems to be a new spirit stalking the world, and there is recent evidence that a few architects, notably in the U.S. and in Britain, seem determined to re-examine the modern movement and to express their ideas in a more humane, more acceptable way, with the inclusion of decoration and rich color and with a strong emphasis on context and scale.

It is interesting and worthwhile to glance quickly round the world to see what adventurous architects are doing today. The current era essentially exhibits a diversity of approaches to architecture—there is no clear direction. Like Victorian architecture, it is multidirectional. Like the Victorians, we are studying the history books and reinterpreting lessons in many ways. But the Victorian architects and their clients were guided by a generally-accepted doctrine, which told them which style to choose for each building type. We have, today, no such doctrine—but that may be a good thing. It could result in variety, richness and exuberance, just the qualities society and its architecture need.

It is, perhaps, possible to identify seven directions in contemporary architecture. They are:

1. **Mod Mod**—modification of the principles of the Modern Movement to suit today's needs and demands;
2. **Mod Hist**—a reuse of historical, traditionalist and "modern classical" ideas;
3. **Mod Tech**—modern technology "serving the people";
4. **Environmental**—a responsiveness to nature and natural systems;
5. **Fun**, including pop and a whimsical approach to design;
6. **Participation**—do-it-yourself or pluralism in architecture; and
7. **Deconstruction**—oddness and unpredictability.

You probably know one or two others you could add; it's a guessing game that we play.

These trends—the directions in which contemporary architecture seems to be moving—are discussed briefly here and their design characteristics illustrated through the citing of relevant examples.

1. Mod Mod

Many architects have played the "modified modern" game with varying degrees of success. As realization of the unpopularity of architects with the public began to hurt, some designers (including the author) tried to give architecture a more human face, particularly in the design of low-cost housing.

They called this approach "designing for the user" or "giving the people what they want," but they noticed that sometimes the strongly-modelled faces of the buildings were not human enough. They are still wondering if it was the architect's fault or the fault of the program requirements (medium-rise, high-density apartments at minimum cost).

Perhaps it is easier with a private client and with more money to spend? Certainly Peter Eisenman and the "New York Five" (now disbanded) did some interesting things with the design of private houses. Most of them are full of references back to Palladio and the Renaissance, but these are not obvious and are sometimes difficult to understand without some form of accompanying explanation. Always flat-roofed and severe in concept, usually with plain, brightly-painted walls and exposed structure, they contain subtleties of interpenetrating space, overlapping planes and conflicting, opposing axes.

The exceedingly difficult problem of giving human scale to a huge, multi-story, high-density housing block was solved brilliantly in 1974 by Ralph Erskine. His office moved to the site in Newcastle, England, and worked in close collaboration with the local community. He used different materials to break down the sheer size and massiveness of a long curving block of apartments designed to cut out the noise from an adjacent motorway. Bricks of various colors and textures, corrugated iron, concrete panels and stained and painted timber

10. They did not find the strongly-modelled face of our buildings human enough. High density apartments in London.

11. Ralph Erskine's Byker Housing Estate, New Castle, England (*T. Bartuska*).

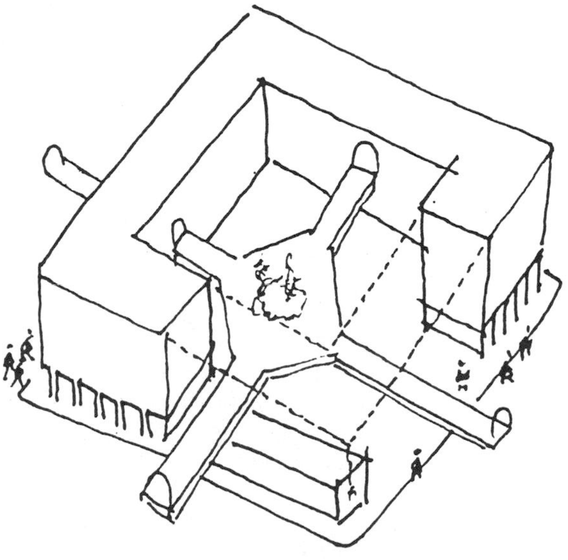

12. New ways of treating downtown city blocks—an alternative to the office skyscraper. (*Students' project from Iowa State University*).

are all used skillfully to form semi-private spaces, to create interest and even visual excitement.

In the United States, it is good to see students experimenting with new ways of treating downtown city blocks as alternatives to the office skyscraper. Even in far-off Iowa, graduate students recently suggested a medium-rise, multi-use treatment, with a glass-enclosed, landscaped internal atrium and pedestrian "skyways" connecting each block to its neighbors across the street.

Michael Graves' new office building, on a typical downtown city block in Portland, Oregon, created a storm of protest when it was built, from the profession and the public alike. Nevertheless, in spite of its too-small windows inadequately lighting continuous perimeter office space, to many people it offers a colorful, welcome alternative to the ubiquitous, glass-clad office building of the international style.

2. Mod Hist

The "modified historical" approach to architecture is still too fragmented, pushing in too many directions, to be able yet to claim it as a classical movement. But today many architects are studying Greek and Roman architecture intently and getting inspiration from them. In England, the work of James Stirling is beginning to have a strong classical flavor, both in the articulation of his planning, the juxtapositioning of the elements which compose the plan and the incorporation into his design of a clearly-recognizable classical facade. This is elitist classicism, appreciated and praised by other architects and sophisticated people generally. But it has none of the popular appeal of say Erskine's Byker housing or Rogers' Centre Pompidou. Here is post-modernism at its most serious.

Another British architect, Quinlan Terry, has actually been a classicist for a long time now. Refusing to accept the precepts of the Athens Charter of modern architecture, he has been ploughing a lonely, maverick furrow and continuing the classical tradition in a quiet, gentle, but convincing manner.

Charles Moore is, of course, also a modern classicist. He gets some of his inspiration from Italy and its Renaissance architecture, but he adds a strong spicy pinch of California humor to his classical pudding-bowl. The result is both delightful and very popular, as can be seen at the Piazza d'Italia in New Orleans. Here he has created, with great wit and vigor, a powerful reincarnation of the Italy which New Orleans citizens of Italian origin dream about. The spirit of classical Italy lives in the use of Roman column, entablature and pediment. It is clothed in bright paint and polished aluminum and lit by neon, prancing about its curious, twisting piazza like a drunken Roman teenager.

In Britain, the reaction against the purism and inhumanity of prefabrication, mass production and the machine aesthetic has been steadily gaining momentum for the last decade. Britain's younger architects have declared: "The Puritan Revolution is over; Cromwell is dead." They have abandoned the flat roof and the undecorated concrete wall and are studying their own vernacular housing with deep concern and dedication. A kind of modern traditionalist style is now emerging which is refreshingly naive and sometimes subtle in detail and which stands a better chance of being accepted by the people for whom it is designed than Britain's earlier bleak square boxes.

Ted Cullinan's recent housing for the London Borough of Hillingdon demonstrates the new mood. It embraces the architect's determination "to find a new expression of the suburban setting, freed from the constraints of the narrow-fronted, cross-wall house" and is an example of what good planning and sensitive detailing can do and what a commitment

13. A powerful reincarnation of the Italy which New Orleans citizens . . . dream about. Charles Moore's Piazza d'Italia in New Orleans.

14. The Georges Pompidou Center of Art in Paris, designed by Piano and Rogers in 1976.

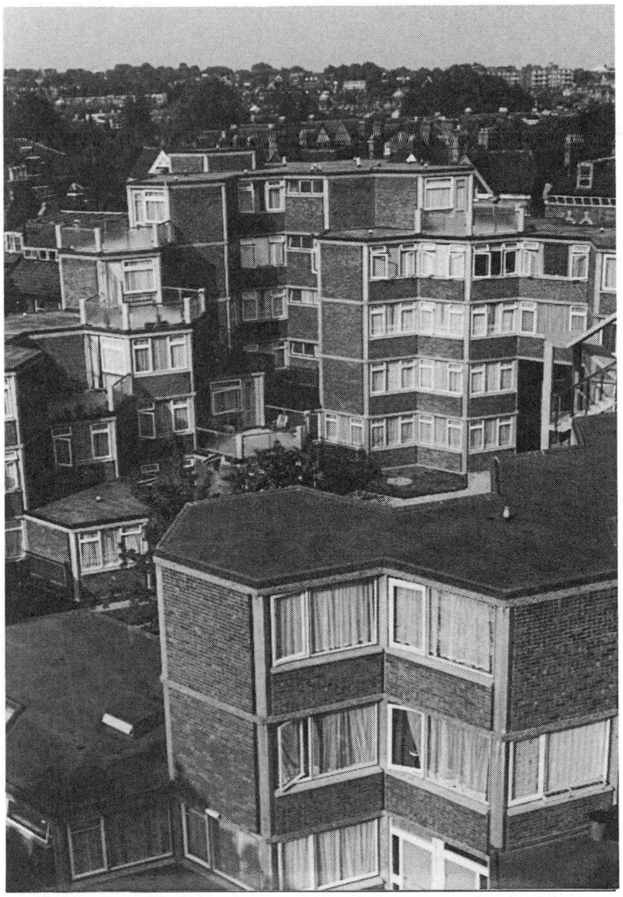

15. Modern concrete technology has been harnessed to serve the needs of senior citizens, at low cost. Flats in north London.

to the ideals of the welfare state can produce in terms of quality, even within the most stringent economic limitations.

In the nineteenth century in Britain, the Queen Anne style was, in fact, a mixture of many different styles in stone and brick, which gave it a wonderful richness and exuberance. Toward the end of the century, architects in some of the big cities of the United States, particularly Boston, Los Angeles and San Francisco, reinterpreted Queen Anne to suit a pluralist, more pragmatic society, and in timber and plaster instead of brick and stone. These houses are fast disappearing now, but they have a charm, richness and vitality which anticipated the Mod Hist trend.

It was to be expected that Japan would show the way forward today. Kenzo Tange followed Le Corbusier, but gave his Calvinism a Taoist flavor; he expressed his country's fine traditional timber construction in new contemporary ways through the use of reinforced concrete. Now younger architects, like Kurokawa, Isozaki and Kikutake, have followed his lead and have gone much further. Some of their recent buildings are an extraordinary mixture of styles, old and new, native and foreign. In a curious, almost mystical way, these buildings have a striking vitality and a dynamism unknown to even the best that the modern movement produced.

3. Mod Tech

The French Government of Georges Pompidou wanted to bring art to the public in such a way that they would really enjoy it. The architects Piano and Rogers certainly enabled that to happen by designing a very modern building, the Pompidou Center in Paris. The building is exciting in itself and uses all kinds of "modified technological" devices (also referred to as "High Tech") to enable the visitor to share that excitement: huge steel trusses creating uncluttered space for multiple use; glass walls through which everything can be seen from outside; covered escalators snaking up the outside of the building; all services exposed; disappearing walls; ever-changing light effects; and maximum flexibility. And the public loves it. A really modern building for once which is popular with everyone.

In designing a cluster of "sheltered homes" for elderly people in north London, the architects used a reinforced-concrete, prefabricated system of construction to create an informal grouping of hexagons, all identical in size, supported by hexagonal columns of equal length. Modern concrete technology has been harnessed to serve the special needs of senior citizens, at low cost.

Sydney Opera House is a technological tour de force. Jorn Utzon's great soaring roofs are a dramatic mixture of romantic semantics and advanced structural engineering technology. Originally conceived

16. Sydney Opera House is a technological tour de force.

17. Sir Norman Foster's bank in Hong Kong used steel structurally and decoratively with dramatic conviction (*courtesy of Foster & Associates*).

as thin concrete shells, the consulting engineer Ove Arup tried for two years to design them as shells and failed. So they are, in fact, heavy beams and pre-cast concrete segments assembled on site, each one an exact slice of a sphere. Dramatically perched on a narrow peninsula jutting out into Sydney Harbor, they remind one of the weekend sails of the harbor yachts or of giant fish leaping out of the sea. Some Australians say it reminds them of other, less flattering things, but nevertheless, the building is a great popular success and, like France's Eiffel Tower or England's Big Ben, has now become a national symbol of Australia.

Sir Norman Foster's new bank in Hong Kong uses steel structurally and decoratively with dramatic conviction. Banking floors overlook a 120 foot-high atrium, naturally lit from the roof by a series of mirrors. A pedestrian plaza extends under the building, from which four escalators take visitors up to the lowest banking floor. A helicopter landing pad and four cranes atop the roof make this exciting building one of the tallest in the Far East.

4. Environmentalism

The oil crisis has combined with the ever-increasing but wasteful use of the motorcar to intensify research into alternative ways of heating and cooling buildings. New ways of trapping and using the sun's rays are giving architecture new, strange shapes, some of which seem destined to become as familiar as the television aerial. Side-by-side with the development of large-scale, automatic, mechanically-dependent solar systems, there is a demand for a return to the study of centuries-old traditional ways of heating and cooling buildings in all climates. Just as tall air shafts trapped the breeze and cooled the rooms below in many a desert town,

18. New solar-heating walls and roofs are making their presence felt in the modern world, Milton Keynes, England (*M. Owen*).

new solar-heating walls and roofs are making their presence felt in the modern world. Many of these "passive" systems have successfully used solar energy for heating and for cooling.

As an ever-more-complex technological age advances, many people are realizing that the richest, most rewarding form of life is one spent close to nature. More and more architects are joining environmental groups and their work is beginning to reflect these more environmental attitudes and philosophies.

Frank Lloyd Wright advocated, for a long time, an "organic" architecture and has designed numerous buildings in the mid-West and Arizona from materials and forms found on or near the site. They exist as important examples of a more environmentally sensitive approach to architecture.

At the time when Le Corbusier was formulating design principles for the Athens Charter—with rational, logical clarity and conviction—and was proclaiming to the world that "a house is a machine for living in," Antonio Gaudi had quietly and almost unnoticed completed in Barcelona some of the most eloquently irrational, emotional structures in the history of architecture. With hindsight, it can now be seen that Gaudi's work was a strong force in bringing about the downfall of the International Style.

His little unfinished Colonial Guell chapel outside Barcelona is a miracle in brick and stone.

Its porch columns lean at extraordinary angles (generally-accepted mathematical calculation would say they couldn't exist) and merge organically into the vaulted ceiling, like tree trunks into their foliage. His casa Batllo and casa Mila, highly ornate Art Nouveau apartment blocks in the center of the city, are full of subjective symbolism; they disturb the senses and at the same time uplift the spirit and stimulate the imagination.

Arcosanti is a new city, at present under construction in desert terrain in Arizona. It was designed by Paolo Soleri in accordance with his arcology (architecture plus ecology) philosophy. Soleri and his working community, who are actually building the city, believe that the sun is the source of both physical and spiritual energy, and Arcosanti is, therefore, designed to take maximum advantage of solar energy. It is, in fact, a tight concentration of accommodation, including enormous greenhouses surrounded by vegetable gardens. This could be considered a precedent for Biosphere II, an experimental community (also in the Arizona desert), which is trying to produce all its own food and recycle its air, water and waste products. Environmentalism in design is currently being popularized by the inclusive term "Green Architecture", which is discussed in more detail in the next chapter.

19. Frank Lloyd Wright advocated, for a long time, an 'organic' architecture.

20. Gaudi's little unfinished chapel outside Barcelona is a miracle in brick and stone.

21. Paolo Soleri's new city at Arcosanti, Arizona—presently under construction.

5. Fun

The great fun building of the nineteenth century was, of course, the Brighton Pavilion designed by John Nash for the Prince Regent as a seaside escape from boring London society and affairs of state. Here many styles are thrown together in an Eastern extravaganza: Hindu, Chinese, Japanese, Moorish, Gothic and several others invented by Nash himself. It started an era of bad taste which has remained with us ever since, but it showed the world's architects that bad taste has a place in our lives and that architecture can be fun.

Walt Disney brought the British sense of fun and fantasy across the Atlantic and blew it up to new proportions in sunny California and Florida. These humanly created worlds give enormous pleasure to countless numbers of children and their parents and, at the same time, make a lot of money. Disneyland and Disney World have been a great success on a huge scale—cities of fantasy and fun.

22. The great fun building of the nineteenth century was of course the Brighton Pavilion designed by John Nash.

New Disney fun cities have been exported and recently opened in Japan and France.

The architect Charles Moore, now teaching in California, has a sophisticated sense of fun. His intriguing piazza d'Italia in New Orleans has already been mentioned in this chapter as a work of Mod Hist. It is also, of course, great fun. People enjoy it because Moore and his colleagues enjoyed creating it—there is even a portrait bust of Moore looking out over the piazza—and somehow managed to transmit something of their enjoyment to their architecture.

Architects don't know what to make of Las Vegas. Is it pop art or just vulgarity on a big scale? Technological artistry or social degradation? The symbolism is there, and also the popularity. If we want the public to approve of us again, shouldn't designers find out what it is they really like and try to express it in their work? Maybe. Las Vegas is good, healthy vulgarity of the Piccadilly Circus kind, but it is more impressive, more scintillating and without any good architecture. The modern world is often too serious, too dull, too depressing. Let's have some tinsel and flashing neon tonight, so we can tackle the daily round again tomorrow.

Actually, one architect wrote a whole book about the city (*Learning from Las Vegas*, by Robert Venturi) in which he praised its vitality and the appeal of its "decorated sheds." To Venturi "Main Street is almost all right." Las Vegas is, whether we like it or not, the pop city of the western world, a kind of kitsch writ large. And the pop city surely has a role to play in our present-day world. And so, perhaps, there is some fun in a hot-dog stand which looks like a hot dog and the donut drive-in which looks like a doughnut, and even the curio shop which is, in fact, a plaster-and-wire dinosaur, with its entrance cut into the animal's huge tail. Like pop

23. Disneyland has been a great success on a huge scale–a city of fantasy and fun.

24. The pop city has surely a role to play in our modern world, Las Vegas.

music, the louder and more vulgar they are, the better some of us like it. It's a pop world. People have to shout loud or no one will hear.

It is rather strange that Philip Johnson, one of the accepted leaders of the modern movement in the United States, should, in his seventies, suddenly embrace some of the ambivalent tenets of post-modernism. But that's what happened. Signs of his whimsicality appeared some years ago in Houston when he engineered a witty conversation between two skyscraper office blocks, with a rakish glass lobby 11 stories high subtly insinuating itself into the conversation. Now his whimsicality has won the day and, in his design for the AT&T Tower in New York, he hides the top few stories behind a huge broken pediment reminiscent of Chippendale's furniture, and sits the rectangular block firmly on a classical arcade four stories high, with a huge, dominating, arched entrance worthy of Bernini.

In his book *Complexity and Contradiction in Architecture*, published in 1966, Robert Venturi roundly condemned the International Style and explored this new, uncharted country of delight and whimsicality. With his wife, Denise Scott-Brown, Venturi combines fitness for purpose with witty, whimsical understatement and a sophisticated assurance of expression. His memorial to Benjamin Franklin in Philadelphia echoes the main lines of Franklin's old house in a subtle, elegant tribute to a great and well-loved historical figure.

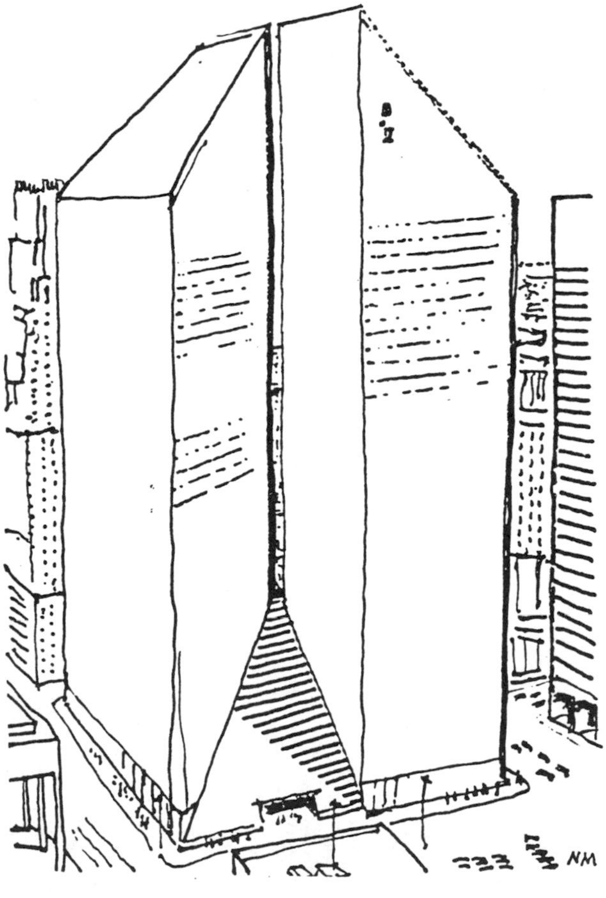

Figure 25. A witty conversation between two skyscraper office blocks, Philip Johnson's Pennzoil Place in Houston Texas.

6. Participation

On the outskirts of some of the world's great cities, extensive unplanned communities have grown up. As discussed in the two previous chapters, these have come into being spontaneously, and often illegally, simply because people wanted somewhere to live near their place of work and could not find anything else. Taking the law into their own hands, they simply moved onto empty sites and built their own houses in their own way, using any materials they could find. These "barriadas" usually have no services provided and are often a serious health hazard, but many of them have a rich vitality and a warm humanity which is impressive. Thousands of families prefer them to the dreary sterility of much official, low-cost housing.

In tropical Africa, of course, and in other parts of the world, the self-build tradition has been very strong for centuries. As people move into the cities from rural areas, they tend to take their traditions with them, and this has created planning problems—often unforeseen by city authorities. In

26. In tropical Africa, the self-build tradition has been very strong for centuries.

Zambia, for instance, John Turner has estimated that between one-third and one-half of the population of the capital city Lusaka are living in squatter compounds on the city's outskirts. Many Nigerians are hoping that in at least some of the large housing areas, which form part of the new federal capital city at Abuja, financial help will be given to people who want to build their own communities.

In Britain, the participation, self-build, do-it-yourself movement has been growing steadily for the past decade. There are now a considerable number of housing associations and co-op societies dedicated to helping people build their own houses themselves. Some architects act as professional advisors to these groups, sometimes representing them at public inquiries and at negotiations with local authorities and central government. Rod Hackney has been pioneering this work in the Midlands of England and some London boroughs are now working closely with such groups, using a simple, easily-understood method of timber construction designed by architect Walter Segal.

7. Deconstruction

Zaha Hadid's prize-winning design for Hong Kong's Peak Club, on a steeply-sloping site overlooking the city (unhappily not built), is a good example of deconstructivist thinking. Described as "a horizontal skyscraper," it is a layering of superimposed groups of accommodation set at different angles and creating positive spaces and voids between. For me, Bernard Tschumi's layout for

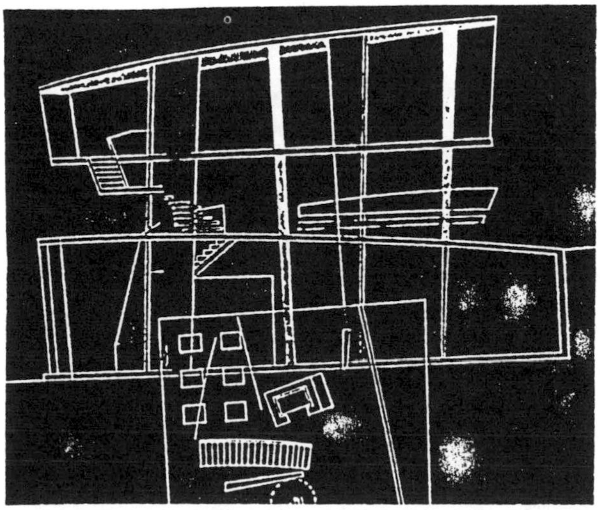

27. A layering of superimposed groups of accommodation set at different angles. (*S. Doari*).

28. Each of Bernard Tschumi's 'follies' offers the visitor a different set of experiences.

Paris' new park at La Villette is a convincing illustration of deconstructivist theory. Each of his "follies"—located at the intersection of a grid of upper-level walkways—offers the visitor a different set of experiences. Here is architecture almost without a purpose—except to fascinate; and the visitor responds by being fascinated. Here function follows form and the form is a steel one, first and foremost abstract and painted bright red.

Frank Gehry's buildings are a series of geometric volumes loosely related to one another and leaning at odd angles. In his *Visual History of Twentieth-Century Architecture*, Dennis Sharp describes Gehry's 1988 furniture design museum at Weil-am-Rhein in Germany: "It looks as if it has been hit by a tornado and its parts transposed and rapidly reassembled bit by bit."

29. Frank Gehry's 1988 furniture design museum at Weil-am-Rhein in Germany (*courtesy of D. Sharp*).

The Future

In this essay, I have been trying to paint, on a wide canvas and with very broad, sweeping brush strokes, a picture of the contemporary world which followed the disenchantment of many architects with so-called "Modernism." It can be seen that architecture, stylistically speaking, is in turmoil; but it is on the whole a positive, constructive turmoil, out of which may come interesting things. Many recent buildings have qualities of richness, fitness of purpose, flexibility and fun rarely found in the work of the International Style.

A new spirit is stalking the world. The principles of the Modern Movement are being re-examined and today's architects are, at the same time, studying our historical heritage and learning from it. The result of this is that many of the recent buildings in the United States and in Europe have a richness and an exuberance that the Modern Movement buildings lacked. Decoration and color have returned to architecture and with them an acceptance by people at large.

The new spirit stalking the world is ensuring that the public and the architectural profession are once again talking the same language. Recent trends throughout the world, outlined in this chapter, seem to show this. The Pompidou Center in Paris has more visitors every year than the Eiffel Tower and Vancouver's Expo 1986 that attracted over 22 million visitors.

What of the future? Where is the contemporary world heading? I suppose crystal gazing is always a bit dangerous, but it is an interesting exercise and may also, perhaps, be helpful. This chapter, gazing into a crystal ball, suggests the present eclecticism continuing; foresees a multidirectional push, prompted by energy conservation and concern about pollution and the quality of the environment; implies new forms emerging and new building technologies developing; predicts regional rather than international styles evolving; and glimpses a humbler profession learning quietly and, perhaps, developing new ways to give three-dimensional expression to the wishes, hopes and expectations of ordinary people everywhere.

The future of architecture is, indeed, challenging. There are no easy answers, no styles to copy. Contemporary architecture, now and in the future, may well be a synthesis of the above trends—a modern architecture which is responsive to the past and challenging to present attitudes, while at the same time anticipating society's future needs.

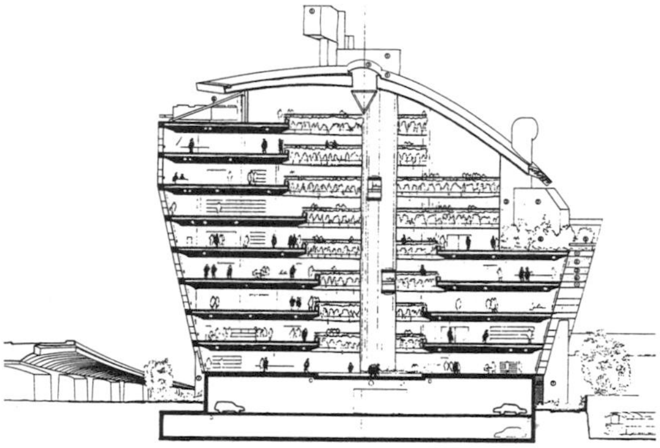

31. Ralph Erskine's 1992 office building at Hammersmith, London (*courtesy of Ralph Erskine*).

30. Vancouver's Expo 1986 attracted more than 22 million visitors (*T. Bartuska*).

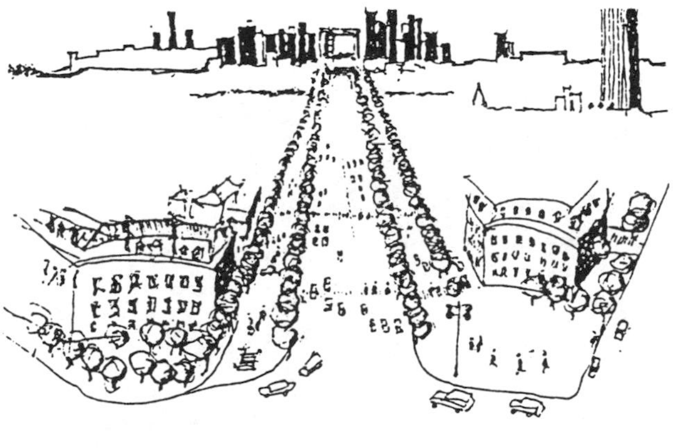

32. Paris' Grande Arche successfully related an unfamiliar Manhattan-like complex of buildings to the old Paris.

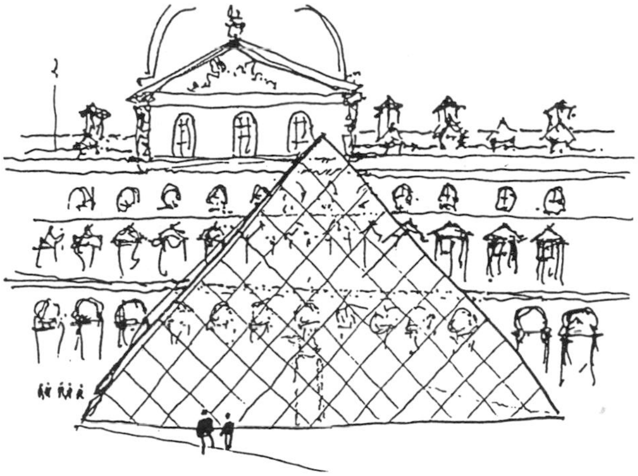

33. Pei's Paris pyramid's simple geometric form strongly complements the strongly-modelled geometric form of the existing buildings.

CHAPTER

14

The Fitness Test: Building as a Response to Human-Environmental Factors

Tom J. Bartuska

As suggested in the introduction to this structures section, buildings have a unique, dual character—an **external** form and **internal** functional and spatial development. This dual human-environmental relationship has many diverse dimensions and challenges.

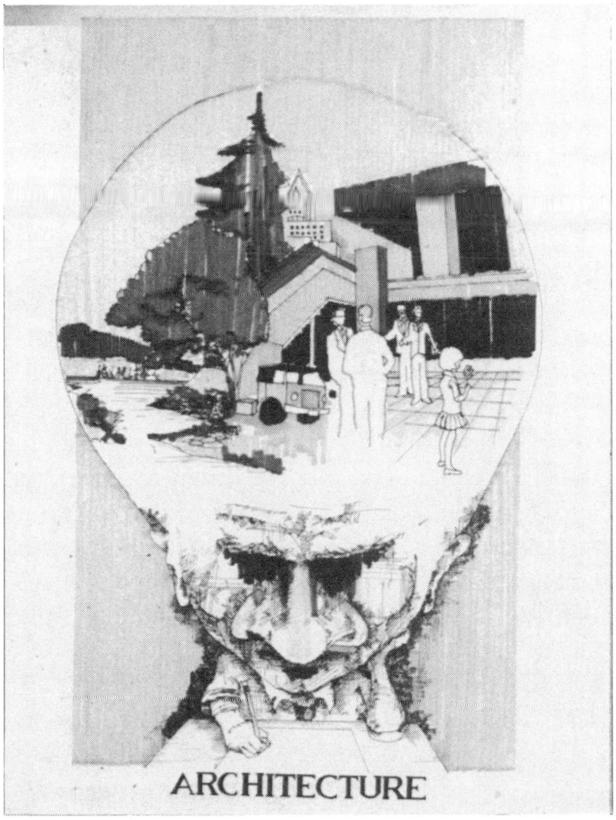

1. What is Architecture? A student response, sitting at a drawing board and thinking about this three part human-built/natural environmental relationship.

Human functional aspects are an important component of architecture and a deep understanding of them is a fundamental prerequisite to building design. Internally, fine buildings provide appropriate functional spaces for healthy human needs, values and activities. Externally, the form of architecture is prominent, expressing the symbolic qualities of a structure, be it an office building, civic center, church or home. This symbolic meaning is a unique cognitive aspect of culture and provides orientation and enjoyment for the public. The external form also interrelates in a positive or negative way with its neighbors and surrounding environment. The reader is reminded again of the levels of integration concept—products form interiors, interiors combine into buildings, and even building functions relate to landscapes, cities, regions, and finally the earth. This internal-external or form-function dualism creates the basis for an interesting dialectic, which is explored in this chapter. Understanding this dialectic and designing with people and the environment, both built and natural, is the only way we can pass "The Fitness Test."

HUMAN FACTORS: THE FUNCTIONAL DETERMINANTS TO ARCHITECTURE

First, the **internal** spaces within buildings directly express the **human** aspects of human-environmental relationships. Buildings fulfill human functional needs and values through physical dimensions (anthropometrics, ergonomics and proxemics: Reference Chapter 11), functional activities, and their spatial organization and relationships (rooms, spatial sequences, circulations and related support services such as lighting and mechanical systems). These spatial requirements must be carefully studied and organized to effectively fulfill the needs of the client and users. These functional-spatial aspects are primary expressive and experiential qualities of buildings. Louis Kahn, a world renowned United States architect and educator, expressed these human-internal environmental relationships by stating that a building "plan is a society of rooms in agreement" (Lobell, 1979). The agreement requires fitness between spatial relationships. This is achieved through grouping of needs and spaces to maximize interaction (combining compatible activities to foster a society) and minimize discord (separating conflicting activities). The concept of **zoning** is often used in design to organize a society or grouping of rooms to create agreement.

The internal aspects of a building also protect the user from unfavorable external influences. Like clothing, a building provides a protective envelope

2. The inter-spatial qualities of the historic arcade, Cleveland, Ohio.

3. The internal atrium lobby of the State of Illinois Center, Chicago, by Helmut Jahn.

which creates a micro climate to help people effectively carry out their activities in a more comfortable, convenient and enjoyable environment.

Human functional requirements are the dual responsibilities of both the interior designer and the architect. This overlapping responsibility can be fulfilled by a single individual for small projects and a team of professionals working closely together for larger developments. (These human functional factors are more fully discussed in the interiors section and are not repeated here.) It must be emphasized that designers not only provide a successful environment for their clients, but also that "clients" should include not only the owner of a project, but also the **users** of the building. The users' needs should never be compromised. Many participatory techniques are available to assess user needs. Users should include workers as well as the general public. The public may need to use the facilities and/or pass by them. They need to accept and enjoy each building as it adds to their environmental context.

4 and 5. The cascading roof forms and spaces (exterior & interior) of the Hult Center for the Performing Arts, Eugene, Oregon.

ENVIRONMENTAL FACTORS: THE NATURAL AND BUILT CONTEXT FOR ARCHITECTURE

The **external** character of a building **form** is shaped not only by internal requirements, but also by fitting a building to its elusive environmental context. Two general categories of "environments" have been identified within which buildings are placed—the natural and built environments. Both settings offer considerable challenges to the creative designer.

Before we investigate the characteristics and qualities of each environmental context, it is necessary to discuss the reasons architecture should or should not relate and contribute to and/or be integrated with its environmental context. Any designer can think of many practical and philosophical reasons to design buildings harmonious with or contrasting with their environmental setting. Do we, should we, place a building **on** its site or should we integrate a building **with** its site?

The easiest path for a designer is probably to just simply place a building upon the site and ignore its context. This strategy allows designers the freedom to be expressive and not limit their design possibilities by having to relate them to the adjacent context. On the other hand, there are practical and economic reasons to design with the environment. Buildings can be more economical, not requiring large excavations and foundations. Creatively responding to similar construction methods and materials within a city can be more cost efficient and allow local builders to participate effectively in the construction process. Also, designing in a way friendly to neighbors develops long-term benefits by creating a sense of community. Designing with local climates and sun orientation can also increase human comfort and reduce energy consumption. This type of respect for others can nurture a fuller, even regional, appreciation of design.

The development of **regionalism** in architecture has evolved within many vernacular traditions. Regionalism or New (Neo) Vernacular design are becoming a popular trend in contemporary architecture. Regionalism in architecture is responsive to regional climates and culture(s), to local materials and construction methods. Many lessons can be learned from studying the vernacular architecture of a specific region. Generally, a design which is sensitive to local cultural and climatic influences, material and construction methods is also energy and resource efficient. Solar energy, natural lighting and ventilation, earth-berming or underground building, etc., are examples of possible regional-environmental stratgies to reduce costs and energy.

The environmental movement has nurtured a greater awareness of our world and of individual and

6. Fitting new with old, infill apartments, San Francisco, California.

societal benefits to be gained by more effectively building with the environmental context. Considerable support has emerged for a more integrated approach, carefully considering needs of users and creating architecture **with** the environment instead of simply placing it **on** the land. This philosophical transition to a more integrated, ecologically sensitive approach to building is an important fitness test for designers now and in the future.

Architecture and the *Built* Environmental Context

Architecture placed in predominantly built areas, not only has to consider and respond to its **natural** environment, but also to its **built** environmental context. Many built environmental influences are very specific and even required (e.g., building codes, zoning ordinances and regulations). Others are less tangible and/or implied. All influences combined require the designer to carefully analyze the surrounding built environmental context. Intangible influences should include society's historic, cultural, social and visual characteristics, though they may be difficult to define in specific terms. Some communities attempt to define such "contextual" issues by establishing **design guidelines**—a set of recommendations which guide the general characteristics of a building to sensitively fit into an urban setting. Some communities require design proposals to be passed by a "design review commission." These review procedures help direct a building's design character to pass a fitness test established by the community. Most communities, however, do not have such guidelines and, consequently, designs are not required or even encouraged to "fit" their surrounding context. In these communities or even regions, contextual issues are responded to or ignored, depending upon the individual values of designers and/or clients (owners and users).

In a legal sense, designers are obligated to consider contextual issues when a community has established design guidelines, identified unique historic conservation areas, or has a design review commission. These communities have established contextual issues as law in order to protect the general societal welfare. If they do not discriminate against people—based upon sex, race, creed or religion—they generally are found legal.

Regardless of what is legal, moral or related to individual creative freedom or rights, designing within the built environmental context is a critical issue in the study of architecture. "Modern" architecture is being strongly criticized by the pubic and by many within the profession because it is too abstract; it either ignores or deliberately contrasts with the environment; it is egocentric and shouts in isolation. Many such criticisms could be minimized by adopting the concept of fitness—carefully designing with both human and environmental aspects of the surrounding built environment.

Fitness can be illustrated by comparing two built environments. One is a city which has achieved a sensitive, cohesive cityscape quality between buildings; the other a city where buildings tend to do their own thing and contrast with each other. In the first example, the city government requires new and old construction to fit-in to the urban design context. The result is a pleasant, cohesive city environment enjoyed by its people. The other illustrates quite the opposite.

Portland, Oregon has established an interesting and provocative set of design guidelines. They were developed through student research, public participation and governmental action. The guidelines help direct the design of new buildings to "fit-in" to the general urban and historic qualities of the city. The guidelines suggest that new projects should reinforce urban organization, emphasize pedestrian spaces and street life (human scale and activities along the walkways of the city), and should encourage harmonious architectural relationships. For example, the "50% guideline," which emerged in the Portland research, recommends that new and old should fit together in a mutual

7 and 8. Exterior and interior of a new building responsive to a historic district–Yamhill Market, Portland, Oregon.

sharing way (Harrison, 1977, 1981). The new should respect and adapt approximately 50% of the old characteristics (materials, colors, heights, proportions, details, etc.) while also contributing 50% new to the city's characteristics and activities. The goal of this guideline is not to insist on a rigid formula for design, but to encourage a flexible way for the city to grow and change—allowing change while still reinforcing existing contextual characteristics. The adaptive reuse of historic buildings is another significant way to build within the existing context.

Such design guidelines can make a substantial contribution to the design of buildings and to the design of cities. Design of structures without considering contextual issues ignores an essential concept of the built environment—levels-of-integration—which suggests one component must be integrated into the next in order to create appropriate designs at the next larger scale. Ignoring contextual issues at the structures scale disrupts, diminishes, or even eliminates overall integration of larger environments such as landscapes, cities and regions. These larger entities are also important design and planning components (just like structures) and require an integration of content (which includes buildings) into an overall design. Buildings designed in contrast to neighbors generally create discord and can disrupt the overall quality.

This "levels-of-integration" concept of the built environment reinforces the idea of "fitness." It becomes an effective tool for understanding how to design not only the internal functional aspects of structures, but also how the external form of structures should fit the built environmental context and contribute to the creative design of landscapes and cities.

Architecture and Its Natural Environmental Context

Besides the built environment, the Fitness Test must also consider the **natural** environment.

9. External integration of building and natural context, Oakland Art Museum, California by Roche and Dinkeloo.

Considering both in every design is a challenge which is creating a profound dilemma for society and the design disciplines. The current debate is reaching global proportions and directs our attention, understanding and renewed commitment to effectively and efficiently deal with natural resources and ecological systems.

Inspirational Achievements

Throughout most of human history, indigenous people have had very deep understandings of how to deal with nature. Native American and Oriental cultural beliefs, for example, exhibited a profound understanding of nature and living in harmony with the environment. This was later celebrated in the western world by the English Landscape Garden Movement.

Vernacular architecture, a product of indigenous cultures, has co-evolved over time with the surrounding environment. It too can be a source of inspiration to designers. In a more contemporary way, the pioneers of the Modern Movement (Frank Lloyd Wright, Alvar Aalto and Walter Gropius) considered site and climate to be prime determinants for architecture. Their seminal work also provides insights and inspiration for contemporary design with nature.

11. The natural environment offers inspirational lessons for designing with nature, Oregon Coast, designed by the wind and waves.

10. An inspirational example of designing with nature—Falling Water by Frank Lloyd Wright.

Many architects practicing today have responded to this long tradition of designing with the natural (and built) environment. The current work of Ralph Erskine (a successful English architect who practices in Sweden) celebrates a deep understanding and commitment to not only the user, but also to climate and context. In North America, the designs of Arthur Erickson (a contemporary Canadian architect who practices in Vancouver, British Columbia) express profound relationships to the magnificent beauty of his building sites in the Pacific Northwest. All the above, and many others, inspire us to see the beauty that can be achieved by designing with nature.

Natural Analogies: More Inspirational Lessons for Designing with Nature

Studying nature itself can also be an inspirational source of design ideas. Like vernacular design, nature demonstrates ecological characteristics and effective form adaptation to environmental factors, such as climate, local materials, or site conditions. In nature, form and function are highly integrated, unified by ecological "processes" or interdependencies. We can more effectively understand function and form relationships by studying natural processes. Successful "designs" in nature require minimal energy budgets. Successful evolution is based upon optimum adaptation with the environment, that requiring the least amount of energy.

Therefore, nature (natural analogies) can help designers understand ecological processes and achieve at least three desirable characteristics:

1. Regionalism: learning to design effectively with local climate, materials and site conditions.
2. Creative integration of form *and* function: discovering how form and function are united by environmental processes.
3. Energy and resource conservation: understanding appropriate technologies which have minimal energy and resource requirements.

An abundance of examples in nature can convey important lessons to those designing and planning the built world. A few examples will illustrate how natural analogies can be used as a creative design tool.

The human eye provides us an effective window to the world. It adapts to environmental factors through appropriate eyebrow and eyelid overhangs. Filtering hair softens the contrast. Overhangs can even be extended by squinting (or by hats) and light intensity is controlled by aperture changes; even dust and dirt are cleansed by automatic washing devices. Can we translate this to effective window design? Do they have appropriate overhangs which shield and soften light and aperture devices to control the desired quantity of light? The window in Figure 13 ignores these environmental factors and develops harsh contrast and glare. The window in Figure 14 begins to develop optical quality by overhangs, filtering by landscape and curtains which control the aperture.

Appropriate design for the thermal environment can be more clearly understood by observing how plants and animals (and some humans) effectively adapt to regional climatic characteristics. Ian McHarg, a landscape architect and planner, author of *Design with Nature* (1969), suggests that a good understanding of a site and regional climate can be developed by observing indigenous plants and animals. These natural analogies can enhance understanding of how to effectively adapt to desert or alpine conditions, to wet river basins or dry

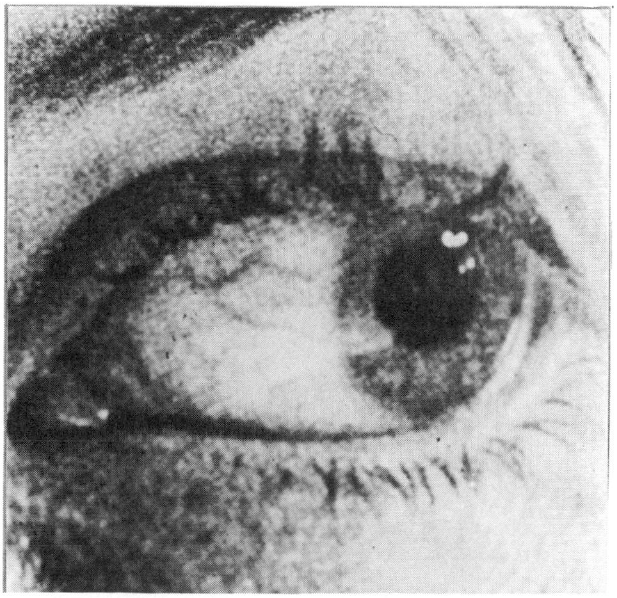

12. The human eye.

13. Windows that cause poor light control and glare.

14. A window that has optical control.

plateaus. Adaptive strategies for use of the sun, both summer and winter, the insulative warmth of clothing, the evaporative cooling of our skin, the efficient wind forms of sand dunes, the structure of a spider web or sea shells, etc., all have inspirational lessons for designing with nature and for developing more appropriate built environments.

Something as basic as rocks on a seashore may convey usable lessons to those trying to design a built environment. The rocks (in Figure 15) illustrate the changing characteristics which occur from different orientations of any object—a rock, a building or a land form. The sun side (the South in the northern hemisphere) is warm, dry and generally more ideal for heating any object with solar energy. The southern orientation of a land form or building, however, needs to be fully understood because it can also cause overheating (even severe sunburn) if not carefully shaded in summer months. The opposite side, generally the north side of a land form or building has the reverse condition. It is cool, shaded and moist. These thermal characteristics are clearly understood in the design of the solar responsive building in Portland, illustrated in Figures 16 and 17. The south side allows a controlled amount of solar energy to be used and stored in collectors, greenhouse and windows. Low windows on the north side allow the cool air to be admitted in the summer (not the warm south air) to cool the building. Double air locks are placed on the north side to prevent this from occurring in winter while solar warmed air from the south side is used to heat the building when needed. The building is also protected from west winter winds by berming and other protective landscaping.

Natural analogies offer numerous inspirational lessons. They not only offer examples of functional design relationships and a conceptual basis for ecological design, but adapting them can facilitate the design of more effective, regionally sensitive and energy-efficient building.

15. Rocks on the seashore—their various surfaces expressing the warm southern side and a frosty cool northern side.

16. The warm southern side of Terra One, a solar demonstration house in Portland, Oregon.

17. The cool northwest side of Terra One, a solar demonstration house in Portland, Oregon.

Comprehensive Approach

The "work-a-day world" of contemporary society is directed to an objective-cost/benefit analysis of design. Few designers have met this challenge while addressing comprehensively the natural environmental issues. The design professions provide a basis for some leadership, though there has been little incentive from U.S. political leaders in the 1980s and early 1990s. Malcolm Wells, Ian McHarg and the National (and state's) Environmental Policy Acts (NEPA and SEPA) have tried to weather this regressive period of deregulation and individual and corporate greed (Phillips, 1990). A close examination of their environmental work provides a basis for a **comprehensive** approach to design with the environment.

Malcolm B. Wells, a practicing architect on the eastern coast of the United States, expresses this comprehensive, environmentally sensitive approach to architecture in an article published in *Progressive Architecture* (1971). The title of the article—"The Absolutely Constant Incontestably Stable Architectural Values Scale"—expresses the strength of his convictions and suggests a way to actually test designs by an array of environmental criteria developed from making an analogy with a natural system.

> Architecture is the outward expression of a way of life and, as such, it must begin to express real reverence for life. More than that, it must actually help support life. We're in far too great a mess to hope that the ecological reprieve can be brought about by cleaning up the skies and the waters, and saving some wilderness. . . . We disagree about degree, about priorities, about directions and goals. . . . Our value criteria are so unstable that nothing can be objectively compared with anything.
>
> But there is a way to evaluate what we do. There's a cold, scientific, stable, constant, absolute and very simple scale on which we can rate one work against another. On it we can measure not only architecture, landscape architecture, engineering and planning, but also zoning laws and everything else that's likely to affect the environment of which we are so visibly a part.
>
> So far as we know, the only fully appropriate structures and the only truly successful communities ever to be established on the North American continent during the geologic epoch were those myriad miracles that we now lump together under the word "wilderness". . . . In that light, then, the kind of wilderness that existed here before the palefaces arrived can be used as an unchanging standard against which we can measure our own solutions. . . .
>
> The . . . forest [for example] must really have been something to see. It actually created pure air. It created pure water. It stored extra water for use during droughts. It created all the food needed for its inhabitants. It created fossil fuels. It created silence. It consumed all its own wastes. It required no detergents, no fertilizers and no insecticides. The forest was supremely in tune with the pace of all creation. And it was host to uncountable species of plants and animals, including more than a few of our own kind. In the...forest, dust was virtually unknown. Wind was something to be heard only far above in the tops of the trees. And the moderating effect of the huge forest kept summers cooler and winters warmer than the ones we have today. . . .
>
> Measuring the city of today against such a standard is so humiliating we usually refuse to do it. We call the comparisons irrelevant or unfair or even silly. But they aren't; the wilderness and the city have exactly the same goal: sustenance of a successful living community on the land. . . .
>
> The shameful cities we've created have only one treasure (to human eyes, anyway), and that treasure is people—human beings and human resources; our culture; the arts, the sciences, and the whole fund of knowledge and wealth that goes with them. The rest of the city is pure failure, for it does what the wilderness long since learned not to do. . . . The city destroys pure air. It destroys pure water. It repels extra water that might have been stored for use during droughts. It creates no food for its inhabitants. It feeds, waters and powers itself by depleting vast areas beyond its own borders. It destroys rich soil. It destroys silence. It consumes none of its own wastes. It creates dust. It requires extensive maintenance and

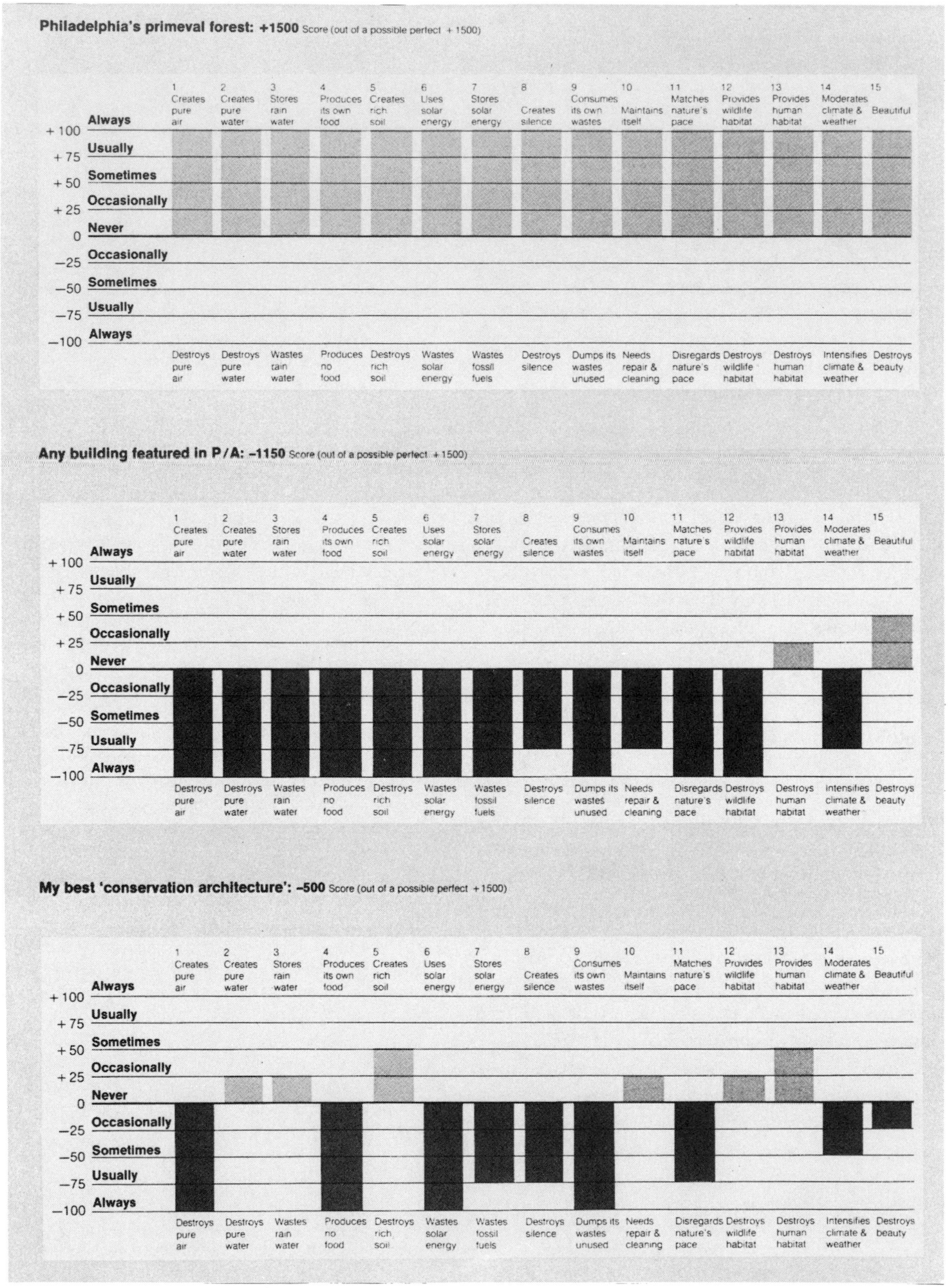

18. Comparative environmental analysis of a forest, a building featured in P/A and Malcolm Wells' best conservation architecture. (Reprinted with permission of *Progressive Architecture*.)

megatons of detergents and poisons. It is utterly out of step with all natural rhythms. It destroys beauty. It makes winters and summers more severe. . . .

That's why it's so important that we recognize the value of the lessons the wilderness offers and the need to apply them right now. We can't get well until we first find out just how sick we are. Which brings me back to the Absolutely Constant Incontestably Stable Architectural Value Scale.

The charts [illustrated] show how the long-lost . . . forest would have scored and, if you don't mind being depressed, how [most contemporary architecture compares] with the miracle of wilderness. Here is my previous rating of any building featured in P/A. I have no idea what it is, but I can rate it, sight unseen, and not be very far off. But, before you think I'm criticizing anyone in particular, let me rate my own best project on the same basis. There is a little factory built on some sound ecologic principles and highly publicized locally as being of real significance. . . .

The best we can say for it is that it's on the green side of the ledger again, and that it points the way to even more hopeful ratings later. Or do you find the comparisons in these graphs unfair? They really aren't, you know. We can't have different sets of rules for different players. Every creature and every community on spaceship Earth must finally be judged by this chart.

No, it's not unfair; not at all, and it hints at some really solid answers to our environmental problems. . . . Wilderness know-how could teach us how to use solar energy and to re-use all our wastes. . . . Some of our food would be grown on rooftop farms where today nothing but housetops stretch to the horizon. All kinds of wilderness-based practices come to mind once we start thinking of wilderness as a . . . guide for cities rather than as an antithesis of them. . . . And our architecture, as it begins to express the new values will become really beautiful again, naturally an earth art. . . .

If we tried hard enough, we could build buildings right now that would rate a few positive scores on the great wilderness scale, but so long as the total score was in the red, we'd still be losing the race. It shows us just how far we've fallen, how we've lost contact with all real values in our temporary love affair with progress. If we worked an architectural miracle, drawing on the finest ecologic knowledge currently available, we might get well up into the green half of the scale. . . .

Considerable progress has been made since the early 1970s, when this article was written. Malcolm Wells has had a very positive effect on creating a "Fitness Test" for design with nature. Over the past decade, Wells' concept has motivated many designers to consider this comprehensive environmental assessment. His designs have achieved very positive ratings from the "absolutely constant incontestably stable architectural value scale" and he has received numerous design awards. His philosophy and work are more fully developed in his landmark book, *Gentle Architecture* (1981).

Malcolm Wells is similar to, and his work probably based on the earlier efforts of Ian McHarg. McHarg is an ecologist, educator and landscape architect/planner, who developed a comprehensive ecological process for assessing the natural environment while making design decisions. McHarg designs by maximizing fitness and human-environmental health and well being (McHarg, 1969 & 1978). His work has made a profound change to the landscape and regional planning professions through increasing use of his ecologically based design process.

A comprehensive approach was also embodied in NEPA and SEPA legislation. The goal in each was to create a balance and harmony between people, the things they build, and the natural environment. This landmark legislation has, unfortunately, been compromised by the lack of governmental leadership in the 1980s and by the United States court system. Short-term profits have remained the controlling yardstick instead of an assessment of long-term costs and a comprehensive approach to design with nature.

Sustainable Systems and Green Movement

McHarg and Wells in reality are using an integrated sustainable systems approach to design—both the **sustainable systems** approach and the comprehensive approach try to adapt to integrated human-environmental ecological processes. The latter emphasizes the importance of dynamic systems and emphasizes complete self-sustainability. Throughout the world, many designers are directing their creativity toward making truly intelligent buildings based upon sustainable systems within the built and natural environment. This is commonly referred to as the **Green Movement** in architecture and planning.

A truly Green architecture is much more than one that is bedecked with plants, conserves energy and minimizes pollution. It recognizes and gently engages

> all of the extraordinarily rich web of forces and relationships that can, and do, exist between architecture, its occupants and its surroundings—both immediate and planet wide. . . . Because it is holistic, Green architecture is concerned with synthesis. It neither ignores nor externalizes any factors or problems. Instead it is alert to and admits all of them in designs that seek a delicate judged equilibrium rather than simplistic statement. . . . Green thinking involves the suprarational. This does not contradict the rational so much as reveal dimensions that it tends to overlook, especially in the crucial emphasis Green thinking must give to the relationship between nature and human nature (Buchanan, 1990).

The fine work of Jørn and Anne Ørum-Nielsen in Denmark demonstrates this commitment to human and environmental systems in design. Anne has just completed Ramshusen, a multiple housing project (Nygaard, 1992), based upon her "integrated ecological systems" approach to design. In the design, she reduced energy use by 50% beyond Denmark's strict national standards (a reduction of approximately 75% of U.S. standards). The project recycles waste water and the normal connection to the local sewage system is unnecessary. Its solar-heated greenhouse/sun space also produces fish and vegetables throughout the year

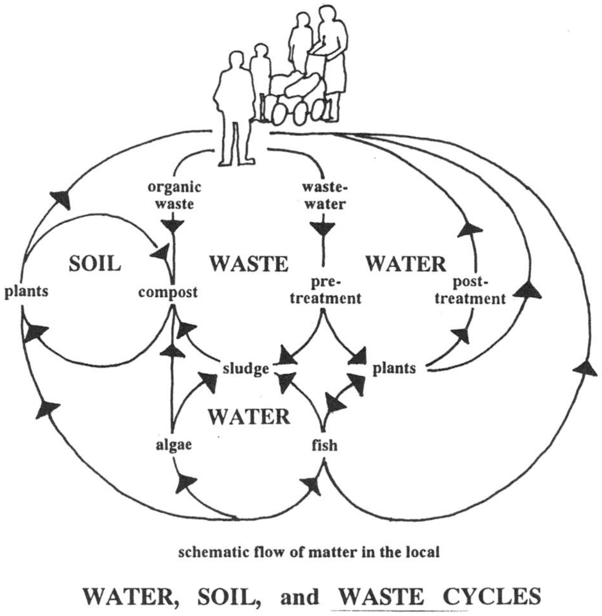

19. Sustainable systems concept by Anne Ørum-Nielsen. Integrating water and wastes systems, growing food and using passive solar energy for heating and cooling.

20. Co-housing, Ramshusene based upon integral environmental systems by Anne Ørum-Nielsen, Denmark (A. Ørum-Nielsen).

21 and 22. Co-housing, Tubberupvaenge, based upon a human-vernacular understanding of housing by Jørn Ørum-Nielsen.

(Nygaard, 1992). Jørn, on the other hand, has based his work on a deep understanding of vernacular traditions—studying how people in the past have designed successful housing environments (Ørum-Nielsen, 1988). He and his colleagues practice separately from Anne and emphasize participatory techniques in their award-winning housing developments. It is interesting to note that both (one from a human perspective and the other from an environmental systems approach) are finding great similarities in their work. Both stand side-by-side in a recent issue of *Arkitektur DK* (Nygaard, 1992).

In England, Brenda and Robert Vale have also been very successful in developing an architectural practice based upon green-ecological principles. Their work and approach is expressed in a recent book, *Green Architecture: Design for a Sustainable Future* (1991). They emphasize the interdependency of human-environmental systems: "Architects and designers must once again realize a shared experience with the users of buildings, and a shared responsibility for Earth's resources."

Besides the pioneering work of Ian McHarg and Malcolm Wells (discussed earlier), numerous firms in the United States base their work on ecological principles (Solomon, 1991). Richard Crowther, an architect practicing in the United States, is a strong proponent of ecological design, arguing in a book titled *Ecologic Architecture* (1992), that there is a "necessity to sustain vital planetary systems for life on Earth and our own well being. . . . The ecologic necessity translates to ecologic coherence in the design of architecture, its products and its systems. Global systems sustainability and ecologic renewal are primary to our planet's habitability. Concept, planning, design and specification of architecture, interiors and all elements of the site and urban infrastructure are critical to ecologic and biologic viability and vitality."

Probably one of the most dramatic developments in the United States is Biosphere II, designed and built in the Arizona desert "as a miniature model of Earth's ecosystem. Biosphere II is an ambitious effort to replicate the planet's complex environmental web within a controlled setting, contained by one of the most remarkable structures ever built" (Crosbie, 1991). Biosphere II, designed by Phil Hawes and many environmental consultants, is in fact a self-contained community, a spaceship on Earth which houses a dozen scientists and tries to recycle its own air and water and produce its own food. The inhabitants are locked within the complete containment of Biosphere II, their health and well-being is as interdependent with their human created ecological systems as the rest of us are contained in Biosphere I, the Earth's envelope.

CREATING A SUSTAINABLE FUTURE: DESIGNING WITH HUMAN-ENVIRONMENT SYSTEMS

What is our vision of the future? What should be emphasized and studied? How can we formulate and design truly "intelligent buildings" to meet the challenges of the Twenty-First Century? The American Institute of Architects (AIA) has just completed a study which attempts to formulate a vision of the future. The study assembled hundreds of professionals throughout the country in a series of far-reaching probes into the future. The study, titled *Vision 2000*, addresses many variables, but focuses on four primary challenges for the profession (AIA, Nov. 1988). They are listed in the chart along with some related design implications (Bartuska and Young, 1989).

Note the emphasis on larger components of the built environment—on creating "livable" cities and dealing with global realities. A major section of the Vision 2000 study deals with "Trends Shaping Architecture's Future." One trend explores the importance of "ecological" design and suggests that "a philosophy [of] ecological design will eventually have a profound impact on architecture and technology." The report goes on to argue that "biological metaphors [natural analogies and bio-technologies] will increasingly supplant mechanical metaphors as the dominant paradigm or pattern of thought. Architecture will aspire to 'go with' natural systems [human and environmental] rather than overriding them, and architectural diversity will increase as buildings are better adapted to the climates and resources of different regions" (AIA, May 1988).

Students of the A.I.A.S. (American Institute of Architecture Students) have expressed a profound concern for environmental education. At the AIAS national meeting in July 1992, they passed a resolution stating "It is vital that AIAS be active and at the forefront of environmental and ecological

HUMAN & ENVIRONMENTAL CHALLENGES	RELATED DESIGN IMPLICATIONS
1. Designing with technological innovation.	• Ecological design • Energy conservation • Computer-aided modeling and design
2. Creating livable cities.	• Urban design and planning (urban & regional) • Cluster development to minimize suburban sprawl. • Balancing transportation systems to minimize infrastructure and auto use.
3. Changing human values.	• General and professional education with social responsibility. • A proactive profession relating to National and Global issues.
4. Dealing with global economic [and ecological] realities	• Global understanding and related design implications (reference Global 2000 Report, Chapter 35). • Creating livable cities with effective regional planning.

issues that are becoming more critical with each passing day." The students charged schools of architecture and their accreditation boards "to require that environmental issues be addressed in all phases of their architectural education" (AIAS, 1992). In 1993, the national AIA assumed some leadership in carrying out a three-part National Telecast Conference on Sustainable Green Architecture and Urban Ecology, Energy Conservation and the Design of "Healthy" Environments (AIA, January 1993). Also, the 1993 national conference theme of the AIA, "A Nation at the Crossroads," was directed at the challenges of designing sustainable environments (AIA, June 1993).

Architecture creates a complex, yet fascinating, internal and external environment which enriches the lives of all who inhabit planet earth. Society is indeed at a crossroads; we collectively must understand life's basic ecological premise and designers must fully respond by creating truly integrated human-environmental systems. "The Fitness Test" challenges the design professions as well as the leadership of our national and global society. We must pass the test, design and manage with people and with the built and natural environments. If we succeed, we will be able to celebrate sustainable life throughout the biosphere. If we fail, it may lead to our demise.

The "levels-of-integration" concept of the built environment reinforces this idea of "fitness." It is a connective tool for understanding how to design the internal functional aspects of structures, and also how the external form of structures should fit the natural and/or built environmental context and contribute to the creative design of landscapes and cities. These larger components are explored in later sections of the book.

23. Housing that destroys its natural context—Daly City, California. (It should be noted that the subdivision saves one mature tree—left of center) (*H. Matthews*).

24. Hill housing, Bern, Switzerland, which is constructed on the warm southern slope to preserve the flat land for agriculture.

REFERENCES

AIA. 1993. *A Nation at the Crossroads*. American Institute of Architects. June.

AIA. 1993. *Building Connections*. American Institute of Architects, January.

AIA. 1988. *Vision 2000: Trends Shaping Architecture's Future*. American Institute of Architects Press.

AIA. 1988. *Architects for a New Century: Findings and Analysis of the AIA Vision 2000 Report*. American Institute of Architects Press.

AIAS. 1992. *Grassroots National Conference: Resolution*. American Institute of Architecture Students.

Alexander, C. 1977. *A Pattern Language: Towns, Buildings, Construction*. Oxford University Press.

Bartuska, T. J., and Young, G. 1989. "In-Between Architecture and Ecology: Addressing a Mandate for the Twenty-First Century." *The Architecture of the In-Between*. Association of Collegiate Schools of Architecture.

Buchanan, P. 1990. "Green Architecture," *Architectural Review*, September.

Crosbie, M. J. 1991. "Desert Shield," *Architecture*, May.

Crowther, R. L. 1992. *Ecologic Architecture*. Butterworth.

Harrison, M. 1981. *Downtown Design Standards, the City of Portland*. Portland Bureau of Planning.

Harrison, M. 1977. *The Identity of Place: Portland*. Portland Bureau of Planning.

Lobell, J. 1979. *Between Silence and Light: The Spirit of the Architecture of Louis L. Kahn*. Shambhala.

McHarg, I. L. 1969. *Design with Nature*. The Natural History Press.

McHarg, I. L. 1978. "Energy and the Built Environment: A Conceptual Framework." Lecture given to the ACSA Summer Institute on Energy Conscious Design, Harvard University.

Nygaard, E. 1992. "Ecologi," *Arkitektur DK*, January/February.

Ørum-Nielsen, A. and Vestergard, B. 1987. *Integrated Systems*. Danish Building Industry Development Board.

Ørum-Nielsen, J. 1988. *Laengeboligen* Kunstakademiets Forlag Arkitektskolen Og Arkitektens Forlag. *Laengeboligen*. Kunsta.

Phillips, K. 1990. *The Politics of Rich and Poor*. Harper Perennial.

Solomon, N. 1991. "Ecological Principles," *Architecture*, May.

Vale, B. & R. 1991. *Green Architecture: Design for A Sustainable Future*. Thames & Hudson.

Wells, M. 1971. "The Absolutely Constant, Incontestably Stable Architectural Value Scale," *Progressive Architecture*, March.

Wells, M. 1981. *Gentle Architecture*. McGraw-Hill.

CHAPTER 15

Building as a Response to Technological and Creative Processes

Kenneth L. Carper

Technology has a profound influence on the design of structures and other components of the built environment. The word "technology" is often misunderstood. This word may carry either positive or negative connotations to many people because of their limited experiences with appropriate or inappropriate applications of technology.

Examination of a few definitions, however, will show that "technology" is a neutral term. It will be seen that an understanding of technological processes is essential to the development of quality design in the built environment. At the "structures" scale, technology is the means whereby conflicts between the natural environment and human needs are resolved. Whether or not the built environment can coexist in harmony with the natural environment depends to a great extent on the designer's ability to understand and creatively integrate the various technologies in an appropriate manner.

DEFINITIONS: CREATIVITY, TECHNOLOGY, DESIGN

Creativity

"Creativity" has been defined by Ian McHarg as the "process of seeking fitness and health." Other aspects of this concept are given in the following definitions:

> . . . the employment of energy and matter to reach higher levels of order...evolution is a least work maximum success solution . . . the surviving organism is an energy-conserver and is successful by finding creative fitness and health . . . (McHarg, 1978)

> . . . the act of bringing into being; the act of creating; to cause to happen; to bring about, to arrange as by intent or design . . . (Webster's, 1977)

As discussed in the previous chapter, the natural environment exhibits many characteristics of these definitions. There is much to be learned about creativity and the creative process from direct observation of the natural environment in its various forms.

Technology

Two definitions of this word are given here; one short definition, and then a more comprehensive definition.

Technology is applied science (Webster's, 1977).

> . . . the totality of the means employed to provide objects necessary for human sustenance and comfort . . . (Webster's, 1977).

The second definition indicates the essential character of technology as related to the design process. It is evident that for quality design in the built environment, the designers must have an understanding of how to apply science, and appropriate technologies (Groak, 1992).

The origin of the word "technology" is found in two Greek words, "techne" and "logos." "Techne" means "art or craft," and "logos" has to do with "creating or making." Thus, the word technology implies "the making of art." Interestingly, this word serves to tie the humanities and the sciences together. Art could have no tangible expression apart from technology. While ideas may certainly exist without technology, the "making" of an idea implies application of technology in some form.

Art and judgment are important aspects in the application of technology, perhaps even more important than mathematical formulas. These aspects, art and judgment, are discussed further in the section on "appropriate technology."

Again, the natural environment is an excellent resource from which to gain an understanding of technology. Natural forms and systems have often served to inspire designers as they pursued efficient, functional and esthetic solutions to built environment problems. Today, we seek to resolve our current problems in the face of energy and material resource limitations. We will continue to find partial solutions by adapting technological examples from nature (natural analogies) to the built environment.

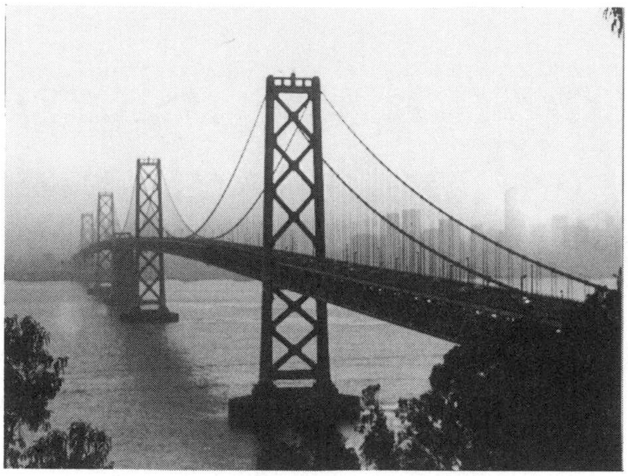

1. A structure that connects two points: San Francisco-Oakland Bay Bridge, San Francisco, California (*T. Bartuska*).

Design

Many definitions for "design" have been attempted, some narrow in scope, and others more comprehensive. Design is an activity that encompasses many scales and many objectives. Perhaps this is why it is so difficult to define. However, for the purpose of this discussion, the following definition is useful:

Design at the "structures" scale is the creative integration of technology.

This definition is sufficiently comprehensive to include all activities present in the design of buildings, bridges and other structures, if the foregoing definitions of "creativity" and "technology" are accepted.

The Need for Technology: Resolution of Conflicts

Technology is the means whereby conflicts between the natural environment and human needs are resolved. Clearly, conflicts do exist at the most basic levels. Indeed, the very reason for the existence of the built environment is the conflict between the unmodified natural environment and human environmental needs.

For example, consider structural engineering, one of the principal built environment technologies. Structural design is a three-dimensional artistic activity, differing from sculpture only in the fact that a structure exists for some utilitarian purpose. The structure may exist for the purpose of connecting two points (a bridge), to withstand natural forces (a dam or retaining wall), or to span and enclose space so that the environment can be made suitable for habitation (a building).

In architectural structures, the structure system provides for the spanning and enclosure of space. Enclosure of space is often an essential first step toward humanization of the natural environment. In one sense, the technology of structural design can be seen as a resolution of a conflict.

The conflict resolved by structural engineering is the conflict between load forces and space requirements. Most load forces are directed vertically. This is because most load forces are the result of gravitational attraction. In architectural structures, these vertically-directed forces must be resisted in such a way that human activity spaces remain unobstructed. Human activity spaces tend to exist on horizontal planes, since we move horizontally more easily than vertically. Thus, a fundamental conflict exists between the vertical direction of most load forces and the human need for unobstructed horizontally-oriented spaces.

Structural design resolves this basic conflict by providing a spanning system which causes the load forces to change direction so that the human activity spaces can remain unobstructed. Therefore, a general definition of structural design is ". . . the art and science of causing forces to change direction" (Engel, 1968).

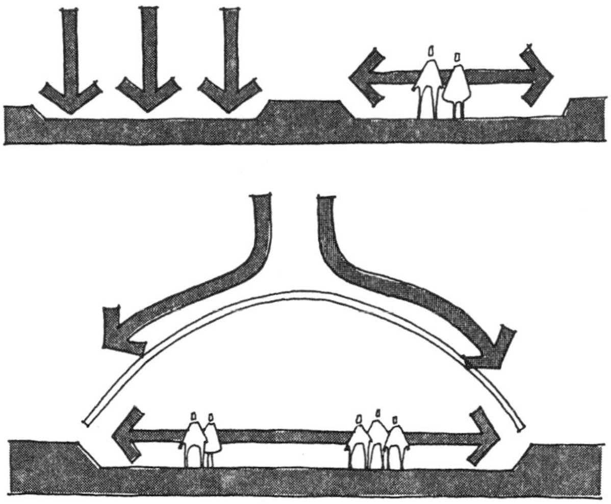

2. A structure system causes vertical load forces to change direction, so that human activity spaces are unobstructed.

3. Enclosing space: the Glass Palm House by Decimus Burton, 1844, Kew Gardens, London, England (*T. Bartuska*).

Similarly, a lighting technology is required because the natural environment provides light only part of the time, and only a very specific type of light. Even when daylight is available, it often must be modified using appropriate technologies. A heating, ventilating and air-conditioning technology is needed because the natural environment does not provide constant thermal conditions which are consistent with human needs or tasks. The other built environment technologies can be described as well in terms of the resolution of conflicts between human needs and what the natural environment provides.

The need for technology is evident. Conflicts exist which must be resolved if human needs are to be satisfied. It is the purpose of technology to resolve these conflicts.

TECHNOLOGY AND THE NATURAL ENVIRONMENT: WHAT IS APPROPRIATE?

The natural environment demonstrates processes which can serve as examples for built environment technologies. Structural forms found in nature often exhibit efficiencies in material utilization beyond the achievements of human technology. Energy is conserved and converted efficiently from one form to another in living organisms and ecosystems. These processes deserve study. Much can be learned from natural analogies as we seek to develop an appropriate response in the built environment.

The natural environment is extremely complex and is constantly changing, involving a multitude of interrelated variables. One of the beauties of natural environment technologies is that they have evolved in a way which produces a dynamic compatibility within the overall system, generally with a minimal use of materials and energy.

The natural environment is not static or stagnant. It is a dynamic system, one in which changes are constantly occurring. These changes can be dramatic, or even cataclysmic. Natural disasters such as earthquakes, floods, tornados and hurricanes are examples of the destructive dynamics of the natural environment. But present within the system is a capacity to restore equilibrium, an ability to replace temporary chaos with order and direction.

The more we develop our understanding of the equilibrium-seeking processes at work in the natural environment, the closer we will come to providing fitness and health in the built environment. The concept of **appropriate technology** deals with the issue of fitness. Appropriate technology can be defined as that which fits with or is compatible with the natural environment. The achievement of successful solutions based in appropriate technology implies an understanding of natural processes and an appreciation for natural systems. An important criteria for fitness and health is compatibility with the natural environment.

It should be understood that technology always responds to requirements placed on it by society.

4. Network of tension structures: Olympic Stadium complex by Frei Otto, 1972, Munich, Germany (*T. Bartuska*).

5. An excellent example of systems integration: Stansted Airport by Norman Foster and Associates, North of London, England (*T. Bartuska*).

What is deemed "appropriate" at one point in history, or in one particular culture, may not be considered at all appropriate in another context. This is discussed later in this chapter.

STATIC OBJECTS IN A DYNAMIC UNIVERSE

Objects built by humans and placed in the environment are temporary. This is because they are static objects with a limited capacity to adapt to changes in the surrounding natural environment.

> The entire physical world is most properly regarded as a great energy system: an enormous marketplace in which one form of energy is forever being traded for another form according to set rules and values. That which is energetically advantageous is that which will sooner or later happen. In one sense, a structure is a device which exists in order to delay some event which is energetically favored. It is energetically advantageous, for instance, for a weight to fall to the ground, for strain energy to be released, and so on. Sooner or later the weight will fall to the ground and the strain energy will be released; but it is the business of a structure to delay such events for a season, for a lifetime, or for thousands of years. All structures will be broken or destroyed in the end, just as all people will die in the end. It is the purpose of medicine and engineering to postpone these occurrences for a decent interval (Gordon, 1978).

In the natural environment, some locations are more susceptible to violent dynamic changes than are others. One extremely useful application of technology is the ability to identify those locations which are most likely to experience the hostile effects of change. Those sites which are most sensitive to the effects of strong winds, flooding or seismic events can be identified, using the tools provided by modern technology. Public policy, land use planning, and design guidelines can be implemented so that these sites are avoided and conflicts between static objects and the dynamic environment are minimized.

Unfortunately, political concerns and economic considerations have often taken precedence in design and land use planning. Coastal regions, susceptible to hurricanes and tsunamis, may be the most dynamic environments of all. Yet, these regions have been developed, even recently, to an extremely dangerous degree. For example, the coastal regions of Florida and the Gulf Coast States have experienced dramatic increases in population and property development, with very little regard for the potential for hurricane activity. Many schools, hospitals and other essential facilities in California have been located in close proximity to clearly defined seismic faults. The prediction capability of modern technology has been largely ignored in these decisions.

As a result of inappropriate land use planning and settlement patterns, many problems and conflicts have arisen. These conflicts add unnecessarily to those already inherent to the design process. Those responsible for unwise land-use development have sometimes belatedly turned to technology, requiring solutions to these conflicts. This, of course, is not appropriate technology. At best, technology can provide only temporary relief from these problems, often with devastating effects on the natural environment.

Judgment is an important component in the application of technology. The natural environment cannot be controlled, or even successfully modified, at the whim of short-sighted politicians or real estate developers. When technology is asked to a ddress problems which should have been avoided by foresight, appropriate planning and enlightened leadership, the results are far from satisfactory. And, when natural disasters do occur, the results are very costly to society.

OVERVIEW OF BUILT ENVIRONMENT TECHNOLOGIES

There are many specialized technologies involved in the creation of the built environment. Professional designers identified with each of the technologies devote their skills and creative energies toward resolving specific conflicts in their areas of expertise. Some of those specialized technologies are listed below. This is not a complete list, but simply a partial listing of some technologies that are making significant contributions to the design of architectural structures.

1. **Structural Engineering:** the design of systems that span and enclose space for human activities. Structural engineers rely on a number of other specialized disciplines, such as geotechnical engineers, foundation engineers, and fracture mechanics specialists.
2. **Heating, Ventilating and Air Conditioning (HVAC):** the technology that provides interior thermal and humidity conditions to support human activities. This field of technology has become more prominent in the last two decades because of concerns for conservation of energy resources, combined with increased demands for environmental comfort. It combines passive (working with nature) and active (mechanical) technologies.
3. **Electrical Engineering:** the development of electrical energy resources and design of systems that utilize this energy in the built environment.
4. **Plumbing Design:** distribution systems for supply and waste products in buildings and communities. Conservation and/or recycling of water resources is becoming an important issue.
5. **Lighting or Illumination Engineering:** the design of systems and products which provide general and task illumination, including artificial systems and daylighting.
6. **Acoustical Engineering:** the control of unwanted noise, and the enhancement of desirable sound in buildings and the environment.
7. **Communications Engineering:** the design of systems that contribute to efficiencies or safety through communication, including computer technologies.
8. **Data Processing:** emerging technologies that help to control building response to changing environmental conditions. This area of specialty is finding applications in each of the specialized technologies.
9. **Conveying Systems Design:** the design of systems that move people or products either horizontally or vertically, e.g., escalators and elevators.
10. **Materials Science:** research in development or application of new materials for the built environment.
11. **Detailing:** construction techniques for combining materials.
12. **Fire Safety Engineering:** a new and rapidly developing profession that specializes in the mitigation of the effects of fire in the built environment.
13. **Construction Equipment and Process Technology:** construction management, the business of constructing buildings and other facilities.

Each of these technologies has evolved rapidly in the past two decades. The process of designing the built environment has become extremely complex, requiring specialists in each of these disciplines. Successful design of constructed facilities must be the result of a team approach, with each of the specialists serving as consultants to the team. It has become impossible for a single individual to maintain the necessary knowledge or skills in all the specialized technologies required for design of any work of significant scale.

THE ROLE OF COORDINATOR

The team approach to design, while necessary, may result in a design solution that lacks coordination or unity. There is a definite need for a single creative individual or small group of individuals to act as design coordinator. Such a coordinator must perform the function of assembling information from each of the specialized consultants and synthesizing that information into a cohesive solution.

Quality design, whether it involves a single building or planning the development of a region, has always exhibited this characteristic of order or overall coordination. The spaces and communities we respond favorably to are those where conscious effort has been expended to select and integrate systems that enhance each other. Those solutions that are not satisfactory contain contradictory or incompatible elements.

The appropriate professional orientation of the coordinator will vary depending upon the scale or level of the project. Sometimes the coordinator is an architect, sometimes an engineer. Often, on large-scale projects, the coordinator is a landscape architect or regional planner. To be successful, the coordinator must be a generalist, having the ability to communicate effectively with each of the specialists and be able to blend many diverse issues and expertises. The coordinator must be able to recognize the implications of individual decisions on the overall design solution.

As knowledge in each of the technologies expands, the design team will include an ever-increasing number of specialized consultants. The role of the coordinator will become ever more important, in order to achieve quality design in the future built environment.

6. The tallest building in the world: 109-story Sears Tower by Skidmore, Owings & Merrill (SOM), 1974, Chicago, Illinois (*T. Bartuska*).

EMERGING DEMANDS ON BUILT ENVIRONMENT TECHNOLOGIES

Societal trends, demands and expectations have always influenced the evolution of technology. Changing settlement patterns and changing functional requirements for buildings have given rise to new technologies and revisions to traditional technologies throughout history. During the past few decades, societal changes have occurred at an unprecedented rate, placing extraordinary demands on technology.

Urbanization and Population Density

The trend toward centralization of the population, that accompanied the industrial revolution, forced the development of new technologies at increasing scales and densities. Building systems and community life-support systems that worked well for small population clusters simply did not work in the urban context with its greater density. Most of the technological developments that occurred as a result of urbanization have focused on the health and safety of large groups of people living in close proximity.

Technology has responded to the demands of urbanization in many ways. The technology to develop extremely dense urban environments is available. Many of the problems associated with urban density, however, are social or political problems, beyond the scope of technological solution. Consider the skyscraper, for example, made possible by the development of technologies responding to urban density requirements. While even taller buildings are now technologically possible, there is need for further research on the social and eco-logical implications.

> The consequences to the urban environment of close grouping of tall buildings are of utmost importance. The impact of scale of some of the super skyscrapers on the city, such as the 109-story Sears Tower in Chicago, more than a quarter-mile high, is apparent. The building's electrical system can serve a city of 147,000 people and its air-conditioning complex can cool 6,000 one-family houses. A total of 102 elevators are needed to distribute about 16,500 daily users to different parts of the building. Visualize the many elevators as equivalent to a dead-end street system and the sky lobbies as plazas where people pass from one part of the building to another either by non-stop, double-deck, express elevators to the next sky lobby or by local low-speed shuttle elevators. Since the building contains all necessary services and amenities, theoretically the people never have to leave it. The support facilities, such as transportation, parking, utilities, waste and sewage services are equivalent to the services needed for a small city. A building of this scale forms a city within a city. The design of such an intricate interaction system requires systematic programming of social, ecological, economical and political implications exerted not just on the surrounding urban context, but also on its own environment (Schueller, 1977).

Historic vs. Contemporary Buildings

As technologies have developed, it has become possible to do things in buildings that were never before possible. Because of this, society has placed greater and greater demands on buildings. Larger, more complex buildings have been made possible, and society has come to expect this complexity, without regard to the cost in energy and material resources. Society has come to expect a greater degree of comfort in buildings, and the ability to modify environments instantly, again without regard to the cost in energy utilization.

Before many of the artificial technologies were developed, planning a building had to respond to environmental criteria, or it could not function as a habitable environment. Dimensions of spaces were limited so that daylighting and natural ventilation potential could be maximized. Many historical buildings rely on the mass of masonry bearing walls to provide constant thermal conditions throughout the daily thermal cycle. Environmental criteria influenced the selection of materials, plan configuration and site orientation.

One of the benefits of adaptive reuse or conservation of historic structures is the minimal external energy which must be supplied to these buildings, as compared to contemporary buildings. Many of these historic buildings are excellent examples of creative response to natural environmental conditions. Compatibility with the natural environment was essential, the only way in which comfort could be achieved. Such buildings provide many lessons in the application of appropriate technologies (those integral with natural systems). Equipment was simply not available to provide comfort "artificially" to the building occupants. Of course, the degree of comfort achievable in these buildings is not comparable to that available in most modern "high technology" buildings. Nor can the environment be modified suddenly, at will, as we have come to expect of our modern buildings.

With the tools and equipment of modern technology, it has become possible to ignore the natural context in the design of structures. Large groups of people are housed in spaces deep within buildings, far from exterior walls. Equipment is available to provide comfort to the occupants, an unprecedented degree of comfort, with very little concern for the natural environment. Building forms have evolved which have no relationship to natural systems and no basis in tradition. In the societal context for which these buildings were developed, they were considered an appropriate response.

However, we now understand that there has been a cost associated with this movement away from compatibility with the natural environment. When energy costs were less, the "high-tech" building, with its limitless complexity and planning freedom, was considered a bargain. Only recently has society begun to realize the significant costs of solving problems without concern for natural systems.

As society has awakened to the fact that energy and material resources are finite in quantity, the current definition of "appropriate technology" has emerged. Traditional forms based on rational natural principles are again appearing in architecture and community settlement patterns.

"Natural" vs. "Artificial" Systems Technologies

At present, new "appropriate technologies" are rapidly developing. Research is underway in many disciplines with the purpose of identifying solutions that are more compatible with the natural environment.

It is important to note that this activity is not a turning away from technology, but rather an evolution in technology. The "natural technologies" require at least as much artistic and scientific creativity as do the "artificial technologies." In many ways, a higher level of intellectual and intuitive skill is required to successfully design appropriate daylighting or non-mechanical ventilation systems than is required to address the same problems with equipment and expenditure of large amounts of energy.

But the rewards of such efforts are already evident. Carefully designed small buildings are now collecting a high percentage of the energy they require from the sun, demonstrating that a reasonable degree of comfort is possible. Larger buildings have illustrated that compatibility with nature can be esthetically and economically desirable. New materials and equipment have been designed to enhance natural processes rather than conflict with them. Along with these developments, society will need to re-evaluate comfort requirements and other demands placed upon the built environment technologies, if significant efficiencies are truly valued.

CONCLUSIONS

Technology is the means employed to resolve conflicts between what the natural environment provides and humans need. Technology is necessary for human sustenance and comfort. Society is a dynamic community, constantly redefining its needs and comfort requirements. Technology, throughout the history of the built environment has responded to the changing demands of society.

"Appropriate technology" has been defined as technology that is compatible with the natural environment, while simultaneously providing for human needs. Within the context of this definition, we can see that technology has often, in the past, been inappropriately applied, or applied to inappropriate problems. All objects in the built environment are temporary, but those based in appropriate technologies have the greatest opportunity for survival.

The application of technology is a creative activity, involving art and judgment as well as rational scientific processes. Design in the built environment has become an extremely complex process, relying on many technical specialists, each employing artistic, judgmental and scientific skills. The team approach to design has become essential, along with the need for a coordinator to provide integration and order in the final solution. Quality design and engineering, now and in the future, require collaboration and creative integration of appropriate technologies.

REFERENCES

Carper, K. L. 1989. *Forensic Engineering*. Elsevier.

Chiles, J. R. 1984. "Engineers Versus the Eons, or How Long Will Our Monuments Last?" *Smithsonian*.

Engel, H. 1968. *Structure Systems*. Praeger.

Gordon, J. E. 1978. *Structures, or Why Things Don't Fall Down*. Penguin Books.

Groak, S. 1992. *The Idea of Building Thought &Action in the Design & Production of Buildings*. E & FN Spon.

Gunts, E. 1991. "Nature's Revenge," *Architecture*.

McHarg, I. 1978. "Energy & The Built Environment: A Conceptual Framework." Lecture given to the ACSA Summer Institute on Energy Conscious Design. Harvard University.

Salvadori, M. 1980. *Why Buildings Stand Up: The Strength of Architecture*. W. W. Norton and McGraw-Hill.

Schueller, W. 1977. *High-Rise Building Structures*. Wiley.

Webster's Seventh New Collegiate Dictionary. 1977. G. C. Merriam.

CHAPTER

16

Engineering Contributions to the Built Environment

Carl W. Hall

We marvel at how the people of 20 centuries ago could build such magnificent structures by hand. They would marvel even more, how we could do it today without hands (Author Unknown).

Engineers work with many others in developing the built environment. Engineers must be aware of the challenges confronting all those designing, constructing, operating and maintaining the built environment. The particular responsibility of engineers deals with energy, materials and information. These are to be used safely and economically to provide appropriate environments for society.

Engineers are characterized by their training and ability to creatively apply scientific principles to design or develop structures, machines, devices and processes. Included in this characterization is the possibility that, in searching for the most appropriate design, several plausible designs are discarded. Often those designs not used result from external influences, often unanticipated in the design process.

The mission of engineering covers a wide spectrum—from designing and building to operating and maintaining human-made devices. In this chapter, attention is focused on the built environment: creating appropriate products, structures and technological systems within all the components of the environment which humans create and in which they live. The spectrum of requirements for providing humans with a built environment may range from fundamental research on the materials to the craftsperson who fashions and assembles the components.

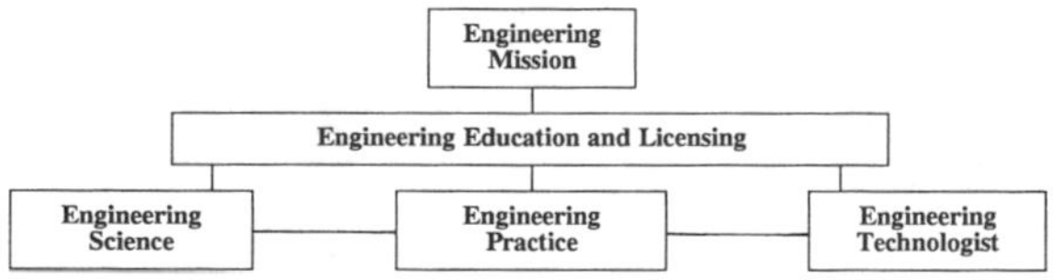

1. The mission of Engineering in society.

The design, planning and construction of the built environment are based on using natural resources to meet the needs, wants and expectations of people in a variety of roles. Government, education, business and industry, along with individuals and families—all make considerably different demands on the built environment. Architects, engineers and planners are often commissioned first to design the built environment for a particular client, whereas manufactured products are designed, built and then sold.

The contributions of engineering to the built environment are largely dependent on external factors, such as

- State of Economy—a vigorous economy not only enhances construction, but also encourages more innovation and new research developments.
- Development of Science—new materials, such as polymers, provide the basis of laminated construction or shapes not otherwise attempted.
- Development of Technology—using conventional materials in new ways, such as fiberboard and particleboard, provides the basis for the use of wood-based products; substitute products for piping, tubing and tile have come from new developments in science and technology.
- Education of Population—the potential for use of new products and ideas is largely dependent

on results of research, codes, craftspeople and public response.

ENGINEERING CONTRIBUTIONS: ANTIQUITY AND CHANGE

Architecture and engineering began as a combined design field. Numerous engineering and architectural works were constructed before the 1500s, by famous engineers (or architects), such as Archimedes and Vitruvius. Many are described and illustrated by de Camp (1963) in his book, *The Ancient Engineers*. However, the Renaissance might appropriately identify the beginning of more organized thinking, writing and engineering design activities. The creativity of the Renaissance formed the foundations and strengthening of the professions of architecture and engineering.

The early work of the Greeks laid the theoretical base for mathematics, measuring and mechanics as represented by the *Mechanics*, the oldest known engineering book, attributed to Aristotle. The developments of the Greeks were followed by the more practical works of the Romans in highways and bridges, irrigation and drainage, canals and locks, mining, and building construction.

Engineers and architects, as well as other scholarly fields, claim Leonardo da Vinci. This is not only an indication of Leonardo's contribution, but of the interrelated activities of many fields at the beginning of the professions. The works of these professions followed the development of various economies throughout all of world history. Originally, agriculture, then mineral, followed by manufacturing and industrial, and now, in the United States, service industries predominate.

The early works of engineers were primarily involved in "engines" of war, thus the name engineer, or military engineer was created. In the 1700 to 1800s, foreseeing the potential for contributing to non-war endeavors, the profession of civil engineering was identified. Civil engineers and architects were primarily responsible for the components of that portion of the built environment used by "civilians" or non-military people. Later, other branches of engineering (electrical and mechanical and their sub-specialties) developed and assisted in the design of environmental control mechanisms. Both architecture and engineering have spawned many sub set and specialty areas. Interestingly, in some institutions, architectural engineering, a recognized field until the mid-1960s, is being reestablished.

* Agricultural	* Electrical
* Architectural	* Environmental
* Chemical	* Materials
* Civil	* Mechanical
	* Transportation

2. The main branches of Engineering.

Developments in materials have an important relationship to advancements in engineering and the built environment. At first stone was used, then wood and timber, brick and masonry, followed by Portland cement and concrete, all of which are still used today. Then came cast and wrought iron, with the first iron bridge constructed in Ironbridge, England in 1779. Iron was followed by steel (the Bessemer process in 1856) and its alloys, some of which withstand high temperature and high radiation levels. Aluminum and light metals development was first used for movable structures, but it now is also widely used in stationary structures. Sheet glass gave way to plate glass. Polymers and plastics are now available for many structural components. Using various combinations of these materials permits a wide variety of structures to serve the built environment. Variations in size, shape, geographical location, weather conditions and uses can be met with composite materials previously not available.

3. The first iron bridge, 1774–79, Ironbridge, England (*T. J. Bartuska*).

Portland cement was developed in England in 1824, followed by reinforced concrete in the 1880s. The use of steel tension bars in concrete construction was developed in 1925 and prestressed concrete in 1945. These cement-concrete developments greatly changed the design parameters; structures previously considered impractical could now be built, a development that dramatically changed the built environment.

The development of materials was followed naturally with major advancements on holding these materials together with fasteners, glue, adhesives and welding. Traditional methods of rivets, bolts, nails and screws are still used today, but have been greatly improved.

New scientific discoveries have been the basis of many new technological developments. Likewise, many technological developments have been based on innovative ideas which themselves became the basis of scientific investigation. Technological developments have many times been improved from the results of scientific developments and analysis. Discovery and innovation in technological development resulted in more efficient use of energy and materials and human labor, and the potential for a better fulfillment of human endeavors.

ENGINEERING: PRESENT AND FUTURE

The development of new materials and their use made possible longer spans for buildings and bridges. In the United States, the longest span for a continuous steel truss bridge is 376 meters (1,232 feet), crossing over the Columbia River at Astoria, Oregon, built in 1966. The longest suspension bridge is 1,299 meters (4,260 feet), the Verrazano-Narrows at New York, completed in 1964. Materials with high tensile strength, low corrosion and light weight were developed to meet design needs. High pressure devices, such as boilers and nuclear reactors would have been impossible without the development of the materials which preceded them. Tall structures which withstand wind and earthquakes would not have occurred without the development of the elevator (1900–1910). The tallest building in the world is the Sears Tower, Chicago, Illinois, at 443 meters (1,454 feet). Improved materials for pavements, foundations and drainage serve the building and transportation industries.

One of the great engineering contributions of the world is the electrical power network. The electric network is used for building structures and for controlling the environment in the structure. Foremost in importance is artificial lighting used inside and outside structures. Air control and flow, temperature and humidity are major domains for engineers contributing to the built environment. The industrial development of the South in the United States is the result not only of resources there, but the availability of air conditioning and energy to provide a desirable physical environment.

As in the recent past, science and technology reinforce each other and will continue to do so into the future. Science is the basis of much of the new technology; and technology assists science in its development and use. In many cases, technology leads science and a creative or innovative idea, such as the transmission of messages by wireless, leads to many scientific studies and findings. Such new findings, whether in science or technology increase design opportunities. Innovative and creative minds are continually at work, at the scientific frontiers and in technological areas.

Recent developments such as artificial intelligence, photonics, lasers, fiber optics and silicon chips are having a tremendous impact on design. The growth in use of the computer not only for manipulating numbers, but also for memory and recall, is greatly influencing engineering and design. Communications networks, within a structure, and connecting to other structures, are adding new design features to the built environment. The concept of the electronic cottage, as described by Toffler (1981), gives additional insights into future possibilities. The electronic cottage is a home equipped with electronic devices to communicate externally for business and to handle transactions. The home would again become the center of society. Only occasionally would employees need go to the office.

New microprocessor controls can drastically reduce energy requirements for the built environment through sensory control of heating, ventilation, cooling, etc. as related to external environmental conditions. The capacity of microprocessors and computers has increased phenomenally. Computer capacity which cost $1 million in 1955, $100 thousand in 1965, $1.00 in 1982, will be $0.01 by the year 2000 A.D.

A major characteristic of recent times is the rapid transfer of scientific information and technological innovations to the marketplace. Photography, which was first discovered in 1727 did not become a reality until 1839, and did not become a common procedure until just prior to the U.S. civil war. The telephone was an idea in 1820, but required over 50 years to become a reality in 1876. The table illustrates the time required for various ideas or discoveries to be developed for societal use. In contrast, the transistor, solar cell and artificial diamonds were in the marketplace within 5 years of conception. Today's world is characterized by rapid, even accelerated flows of knowledge and information to users.

The printing press and communication systems, which are technological rather than scientific developments, have helped spread technology information. This information transfer now takes place throughout an educated society, whereas it previously took place only among peers. The rapid spread of information in some ways makes designing more difficult, though also more effective. First, the designer must be knowledgeable of an incredible array of new developments to avoid criticism of being out-of-date; second, the party considering a design may have unreasonable expectations for a new, but untried or untested material.

The increasing number of people in the world (exceeding 5 billion), longer life expectancy (approaching an average of 80 years), and shift in age distribution (more people at an older age) challenge designers of the built environment. Coupled with these population statistics, designers must recognize that society's knowledge and economic level, along with its needs, wants and expectations, are also continually changing.

Time for an Idea or Discovery to Be Converted to Reality

Item	Dates of Idea to Reality		Time Lag, Years
Photography	1727	1839	112
Electric Motor	1829	1894	65
Telephone	1820	1876	56
Radio	1867	1902	35
Radar	1925	1940	15
Television	1922	1934	12
Atomic Bomb	1939	1945	6
Transistors	1948	1953	5
Artificial Diamonds	1954	1957	3

The exploration and utilization of outer space holds a special fascination for many. The possibility of constructing a built environment in outer space, for whatever reason, challenges the imagination. Almost science-fictional in concept, outer space could provide sites for low-gravity processing and manufacturing, as well as ports for space travel, locations for vacations, and space laboratories. Space colonization is predicted by some to occur within the next fifty to one-hundred years. Within ten years, a space station close to the earth to house about 12 people is a possibility. A space settlement of 10,000 people is predicted within the next 50 years. In a space settlement, the environment would be totally controlled and food would be produced within a wholly contained environment.

New Materials

New materials, developed primarily in the post World War II era, have provided the means of increased flexibility and variety in form and function for the design of structures. Polymers are available that can be shaped to meet unusual forms; mastics are available to seal exterior surfaces; and numerous materials are available to provide vapor barriers and insulation. Water and waste handling systems, formerly of metal, now include a variety of polymers. Each new material must meet rigid evaluation for safety, strength, and economy. Economy includes cost of the fabricated material as well as the cost of installation. Engineered wood materials such as particleboard, panelboard, and composites are now widely used, not only for building itself, but for forms and supports in the construction of buildings. Safety has taken on even greater importance as structures become larger, involve more people, and must perform against earthquakes, floods, fire, wind and water. The strength and durability of materials plays an important role in designing for safety.

Experience has shown that some materials, at first considered safe, are later found undesirable as a result of long-time experience or changed standards of requirements. Asbestos fibers have been found to negatively affect the human respiration system. Formaldehyde fumes given off by some manufactured materials pollute the atmosphere.

Chloroflurocarbons (CFC), chemicals used for refrigerants, are suspected of destroying the ozone layer and thus deteriorating our external environment. New materials are being developed to replace CFCs. The seriousness of these undesirable effects becomes more evident as structures become tighter to conserve energy and as instruments become available to measure smaller concentrations of these harmful chemicals.

A recent development is "smart" materials and structures. One of the objectives of building such structures is to include sensors to measure changes that warn of possible failure. The most obvious use is for bridges, but smart technology is also applicable for other structures and their attachments—such as balconies, canopies, chandeliers, stairways, and internal bridges. Structures can now be designed with internal optical fibers embedded in materials to warn when failure thresholds are being approached. Not only can these sensors warn of impending failure (by a sound, light, or recorded signal), but can also be connected to other devices to correct for, or compensate for destructive factors such as overloading of circuits or other systems.

Manufacturing

Manufacturing has taken on a new role in construction. Traditionally, most construction (manufacturing) took place at the site, particularly for large buildings. For small buildings, virtually the entire structure can now be built in a factory (manufactured) and transported to the site. For larger buildings, subsystems or parts of buildings, such as trusses, walls, floors and arches, can be manufactured and shipped to the site and put in place. Construction at the site itself has also changed drastically. Not only do derricks, cranes, and towers move components into place, and at ever-increasing heights (telescoping towers), but computer-assisted planning and execution are now commonplace. All of these activities depend on engineering contributions, sometimes developed specifically for construction, often adapted from other fields.

Technology Trends

Trends in technological development can be represented by an S-curve, sometimes called a sigma-curve, originally used to represent growth. The S-curve starts out with a flat slope, while basic information and technology are developed. A steeper slope follows in which rapid development takes place. As competitive or new technology is created, further development continues, but increases more slowly. This concept is useful in projecting trends in technology development, diffusion of technology and possible sales patterns for new products.

Predictions of technology developments based on projections usually give a conservative view of trends. One reason is that predictions based on possible new science developments are fraught with uncertainties. For example, predicting the date at which fusion nuclear power will be available is impossible because basic and complex scientific research and extensive development of technology are both needed, and a clear picture of the design is not yet available.

Interface of Engineering with Other Disciplines

Previous to World War II, the technology spectrum consisted of crafts-engineering-sciences. In the immediate post-World War II period, engineers and engineering education were criticized for not staying abreast of advances in the sciences, thereby causing a perceived gap between engineers and scientist. Various studies by members of the profession, assisted by many external to the profession, recommended that engineers should have a stronger base in the sciences to be better prepared to meet future needs. As a result of adoption of these recommendations, the education of the engineer moved closer to that of the scientist. For some educational programs, the curriculum for engineers has been difficult to distinguish from the scientist. These adjustments left another perceived gap between the craftsperson and engineer. To fill this gap, an associate technician degree was developed.

While the scientific base of engineering was increasing, the involvement of engineers with a wide variety of nontechnical people was also increasing and people with broad interests were attracted into the profession. Many engineers were becoming interpreters of science for society. Social sciences and humanities courses took on a new role and importance. One-eighth of all undergraduate

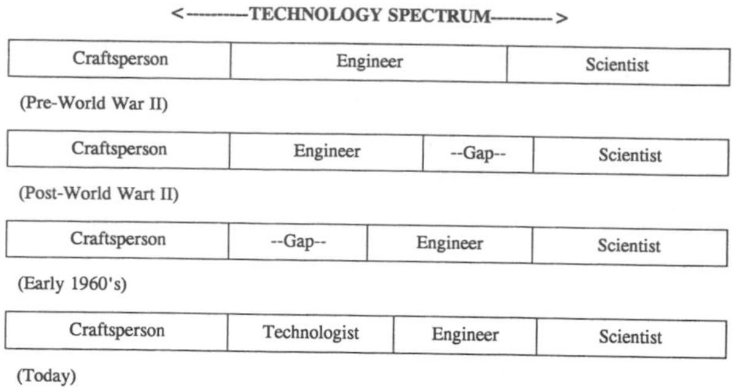

4. Technology spectrum: Crafts—Technologist—Engineering—Sciences.

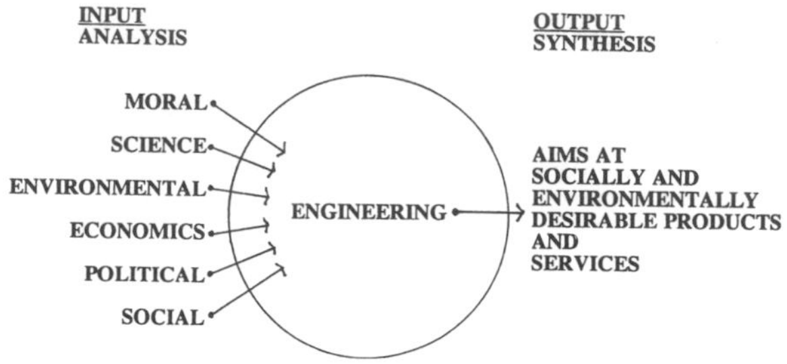

5. Engineering input-output model.

courses taken now by engineering students are in the social sciences and humanities, not including basic skills courses.

The mid-sixties witnessed a concern for what appeared to be a lack of commonality of engineering degree programs and a weakness in preparing highly skilled people to carry out expected problem-solving functions. The various engineering organizations joined efforts through the accrediting agency (ABET) to assure that all programs of study incorporated adequate design instruction.

Engineering education has changed considerably in recent years—by moving from skill to science based courses, by increasing the humanities and social science content, and by strengthening communication skills. Likewise, design instruction itself has changed in emphasis to a new synthesis or integrative approach.

DESIGN: THE COMMON THREAD

Briefly stated, design is the conscious effort to impose meaningful order (Papenek, 1985).

Engineering Design is defined as "the process of devising a system, component, or process to meet desired needs" (ABET, 1981). It is a decision-making process (often interactive), in which the basic sciences, mathematics and engineering sciences are applied to convert resources optimally to meet a stated objective. Central to the process are the essential and complementary roles of synthesis and analysis. Design is the common thread in engineering and the other design/problem-solving professions. Design involves not only analysis, but emphasizes synthesis, not only of internal factors, but also of external conditions. The design question has become more incorporative: no longer just "will the design work," but will it work economically with minimal unfavorable impacts? Not only nature or natural conditions are involved, but also, and primarily, the major thrust is the built environment.

Obviously, science now has a much more important role in the engineering profession. Graduate programs in engineering often focus more now on science and scientific research than in the past. The results of scientific research, however, as far as engineering is concerned, should be considered as information for design parameters. Simon (1981) describes the study of "**what is**" as the task of science disciplines (to research about the nature of things, what they are and how they work). Scientific research focuses on **analysis**—answering inquisitive questions about the nature of things. The scientific method is used to develop information.

Scientific and Engineering Method

Scientific Method (Scientific Curiosity . . . "What Is")	**Engineering Method (Creative Approach . . . "What Can Be")**
Question Identification	Problem Identification
Research and Analysis	Research and Analysis
Hypothesis	Conceptualization
Analysis	**Synthesis**
Proof	Evaluation of Alternatives
Publication	Decision/Implementation/Construction

The task of engineering is to understand about artificial things or "**what can be**." This includes how to make artifacts that meet design requirements and how to design to answer questions dealing with private and public wants or needs, often exemplified in the built environment. The challenge to the engineer is to solve problems, often having many answers, posed by people outside the profession. In contrast, scientists are challenged to a greater extent to answer questions raised by peers. The design method (called by some, with slight variation, the engineering method) is parallel to the scientific method. The similarities and differences are clarified in the chart.

Design consists of translating the knowledge of science and technology into artifacts such as a part, a component, an assembly, a product, a process, or a structure. Design **synthesis** is emphasized. Design can produce a very simple or a very complicated product. Design can result from a very creative, innovative, often unpredictable process or from a highly predictive process. Criteria for design can be established by people within the profession, in government or industry and by the public. Consideration of these criteria is an important part of the design process. As designs are developed, they are tested against the criteria and evaluated for feasibility. Many designs are considered that are never built. Designers, like sculptors and painters, must be prepared for criticism when their designs are placed before the public. When evaluating the impacts of a design through a cost/benefit analysis, the designer should consider not only internal aspects of the problem, but external factors, such as energy, environment, economics and impacts upon society, and must also consider who pays the costs and who gets the benefits. These analyses should not stop with the primary impacts of the design, but should be extended to secondary and tertiary impacts, positive, neutral, or negative.

Engineers, with a basic education in quantification, but necessarily involved in designs and discussions of issues of political and social significance, are often at a loss to understand, let alone resolve, the conflict of these ideas. This conflict might be more easily ascertained and understood if we consider two general kinds of truth—scientific truth and adversary truth. Scientific truth involves scientific uncertainties. Adversary truth, as presented in public debate or in a court of law, usually includes only a selected part of the truth. The presentation of adversary truth includes the uncertainties, which are left to the audience or court. The decisions based on adversary truth are made by those not involved in the subject. People with expertise in the subject under consideration are often rejected from juries considering an issue.

The engineer or scientist questions and delves into uncertainties, attempting to clarify facts, data, procedures or processes. The acceptance of scientific truth requires an overwhelming consensus of the engineering and scientific community. If a consensus is not reached, considerable uncertainty remains about the subject being considered. In a scientific controversy, scientific truth is reached when all the parties involved accept the solution. However, in adversary truth, in which a legal process is involved, there is little, if any, effort toward voluntary disclosure of uncertainties. There may even be a willful withholding of certain information. For adversary truth, only a set of findings is presented and there is no effort to have the two sides agree to what is the truth. The jury or audience decides on the 'truth,' which may actually be counter to the facts. The quality of the truth depends considerably on the ability of the audience to fill in the uncertainties (known by the participants but not known by the audience). Understanding of these relationships is helpful to those who place their designs before the public or adversary groups. An educated public, which can be critical of a design, can also be helpful in understanding the many variables within a complicated situation.

Many examples can illustrate the effect of new scientific and engineering discoveries on the design of the built environment. For example, Henry Bessemer and George A. Fuller studied engineering and contributed to the idea that engineering is an agent of change. In the process of improving guns, Henry Bessemer noted that some barrels burst because the cast iron from which they were made contained an excess of carbon. He reasoned that blowing air through the iron ore during the smelting would help burn up and remove the carbon. This process to improve one product actually greatly improved many. After several experiments, his method provided a new way of making better steel at nearly half of its previous cost, and the process was quickly adopted in almost all industries. The availability of steel at a reasonable price made possible tall buildings. George Fuller was a leader in designing and building tall buildings, calculating weight and strength, and in using steel as a construction material. The Flat Iron Building in New York City was built in 1902 of steel instead of cast iron. The building was 20 stories, 87 meters (286 ft) high, three times as high as the usual buildings at the time. A new material was developed to serve a rather specific need, but was soon used for many applications in construction of the built environment.

CONCLUSION: MOVING TO AN AGE OF SYNTHESIS

In the future, synthesis will become a major thrust in advanced technological societies. The present century is widely recognized as the **Age of Analysis**, both philosophically and technologically. Evidence is now accumulating to demonstrate that the next century will be the **Age of Synthesis**. Synthesis will involve not only the substitution of materials, but the building of new systems, meeting the needs and wants of society. Synthesis will help give direction to analysis by identifying gaps in information. So the trend will be to synthesis in contrast to the present approach based on analysis—synthesis and the deductive—inductive approach by scientists.

Philosophy has focused mainly on the mental domain and the natural domain. Synthesis is a valuable concept for the artificial (built, constructed, or manufactured devices and systems) domain. The arts and design professions utilize a predominance of the synthetic approach; the sciences a predominance of the analytic approach, with the notable exception of physics; and the professions a predominance of the synthetic approach.

Scholars are involved in a search for truth (science) or beauty (art). The approaches and processes used to search for truth have served society in the past, but need to be considered in a new synthesis to more effectively meet the needs of the future. The emphasis has traditionally been primarily on analysis with secondary consideration for synthesis. But, over the past quarter of a century, the use of synthesis has increased rapidly, particularly in the physical world. The stage is now set for major efforts to emerge, efforts based on synthesis.

Thinking synthetically encourages a more global view, considering larger systems that often involve human, natural and physical systems simultaneously. Often synthetic thinking directs one's thought to larger issues, whereas analysis is usually based on precision. The analysis approach does not provide that larger matrix for thinking, but is an important part of the design process. Educators need to accept an enlarged role for synthesis and learn how to guide and teach synthetic thinking. A starting point is provided by some of the theorems developed for systems and hierarchical theory. Systems are characterized by connectivity, interfacing, interactions, complexity, interdependence, and integration—all of which relate to synthesis.

Synthesis is expressed in the patterns of nature. As more is learned about natural systems, that knowledge will be used not only to change those systems, but also to use this knowledge while developing artificial systems (bio-engineering). People in the professions, people who design, in the broad sense—architects, engineers, veterinarians and medical doctors—need a stronger understanding of the role of synthesis in their work.

Most of the disciplines have been built on analysis and reductivism, rather than on synthesis and integration. The growth of interdisciplinary or multidisciplinary fields may be the result of established fields failing to change or to incorporate new integrative fields.

Recent history has witnessed tremendous advances in the science and engineering fields. Designers, indeed all people, now need to integrate these advances within a harmonious system with nature through continued collaboration between the environmental design, engineering and scientific fields.

REFERENCES

ABET. 1981. (*Accreditation Board for Engineering and Technology*) *49th Annual Report*.

Amato, I. 1992. "Animating the Material World," *Science*, January.

Armsby, H. H. 1966. "The Technician and the Engineering Team," *Engineering Education*, December.

de Camp, L. S. 1963. *The Ancient Engineers*. Ballantine Books.

Glorioso, R. M. and Hill, F. S. Jr., eds. 1975. *Introduction to Engineering*. Prentice-Hall.

Koberg, D. & Bagnall, J. 1981. Rev. ed. *The All New Universal Traveler: A Soft-systems Guide to Creativity, Problem-Solving, and the Process of Reaching Goals*. W. Kaufmann.

Lohmann, M. R. 1970. "Engineer's Place in the Technology Spectrum," *Professional Engineer*, November.

Naisbutt, J. and Aburdene, P. 1990. *Megatrends 2000*. Avon Books.

New York Times. 1990. *Information Please Almanac*.

Papanek, V. 1985. 2nd. ed. *Design for the Real World*. Acadamy Chicago.

Parsons, W. B. 1976. *Engineers and Engineering in the Renaissance*. MIT Press.

Pratt, F. 1955. *All About Famous Inventors and Their Inventions*. Random House.

Simon, H. A. 1981. 2nd Edition. *The Sciences of the Artificial*. MIT Press.

Toffler, A. 1981. *The Third Wave*. Bantam Books.

Toffler, A. 1990. *Powershift*. Bantam Books.

Introduction

4. LANDSCAPES

Landscapes are the fourth selected component or level in this study of the built environment. It is an interesting component for it may not be considered by some as built or artificial, yet it does combine the humanly created process of design with or within the natural environment. This component combines the elements of the natural "land" and setting or "scape." Landscapes can be natural or almost totally of human origin: "almost" because to most of us, 'landscape' as an idea includes 'land,' water and vegetation. Plants may be arranged, planted, or manipulated by human hands, and even partly created (genetically) by humans. And, land, of course, is the ultimate natural resource of ancient and earthly origin.

Landscapes also incorporate a variety of shapes and sizes, from a residential landscaping or garden development to an urban courtyard, plaza or park to a large recreational development or regional watershed management plan. Consequently, the people who work with the component landscapes interrelate with almost all levels within the built and natural environments as described by the following content-component-context continuum.

PRODUCTS-INTERIORS-STRUCTURES-*LANDSCAPES*-CITIES-REGIONS-EARTH

The nature and characteristics of landscapes can be further defined by the use of the following:

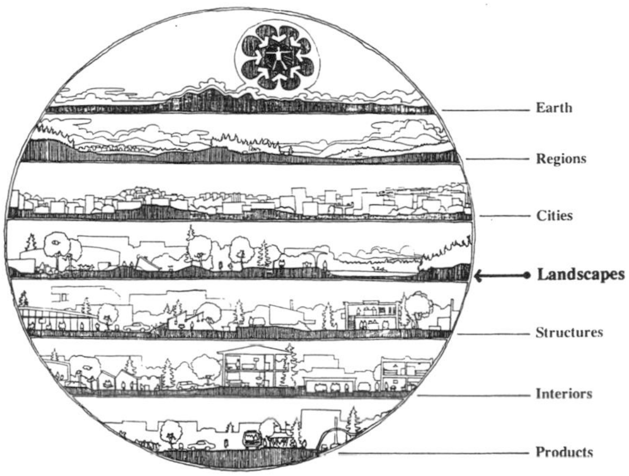

a. **Landscapes** (the contents of which are natural environment and built components of products, interiors and structures) are humanly made, arranged or maintained;
b. in order to fulfill human purpose, to satisfy human needs, wants and values; and
c. to mediate the overall environment;
d. the results affect its context (cities, regions and Earth) in which they are placed.

Members of the design discipline that work at the level(s) of landscapes are usually called landscape architects, but, depending on the scale, might be called landscape planners or (in Europe and recently in the U.S.) landscape ecologists. These are designers that have never fit the stereotype of "backyard gardeners" but have always been intimately involved at the interface between nature and the built environment at a number of different levels. Central Park, for example in New York City, is no one's back yard—it is everyone's. It is the city's front yard and a profound contribution to the quality of urban living.

A clearer understanding of the various dimensions of this component can be gained by thinking about the similarities and differences among three terms: Landscapes, Landscaping and Landscape Architecture.

> **Landscape** (Noun): A portion of land which the eye can comprehend in a single view, especially its pictorial aspects; a picture representing natural scenery; to improve by landscape architecture or gardening.
>
> Other similar words can be formed by changing the first syllable, such as, seascape, townscape, riverscape, etc. They mean, of course, a portion of the environment, both natural or built, which can be perceived in a single view.
>
> As noted, this single view has a variety of scales, from an enclosed yard to the panoramic view from an airplane or mountain top. If we accept the above definition, which links scale to the human view, we can begin to understand the general and specific characteristics of a term that some would argue covers any landscape at any scale, just over the fence or far distant hills. This may be true in a general sense. In a more specific sense, the landscapes beyond our view may have their own unique qualities, so we can conclude that there are interlinked landscapes, perceived by sequential experiences of a mobile observer.
>
> **Landscaping** (Verb): To improve the landscape, to make the land more beautiful, especially by adding trees and plants, etc. This would be synonymous with landscape gardening.
>
> **Landscape Architecture**: A profession focused on arranging the effects of natural scenery over a given tract of land so as to produce the best aesthetic effect, considering the uses to which the tract is to be put.
>
> Profession implies public declaration, a knowledge of the art + craft + science of the design, management and planning of landscapes. This, of course, includes education, apprenticeship and professional licensing.
>
> The professional organization, The American Society of Landscape Architecture (ASLA), incorporates various dimensions and responsibilities within the following defintion (Rosine, 1981): "Landscape Architecture is the art of design, planning, or management of the land, arrangement of natural and [human]-made elements thereon through the application of cultural and scientific knowledge, with concern for resource conservation and stewardship, to the end that the resultant environment serves a useful and enjoyable purpose."

The chapters in this section investigate various characteristics and scales of landscapes:

- **"Landscapes Through Time"** by Frederick Steiner: The first chapter discusses various transitions and the variety of ways people have reshaped the land to their changing needs and values. The author investigates agricultural, industrial and contemporary development of landscapes, including the evolution of the profession.

- **"Landscape Architecture: Definition and Directives"** by Betsy Boehm Hsu: This chapter explores the various dimensions of "landscape architecture" through analysis of contemporary definitions of the profession. The author also explores the various ways landscape architecture serves the private and public sectors of contemporary society.

- **"Landscape Architecture Today: Process and Palette"** by Kenneth R. Brooks: The third chapter examines the specific design and planning process used by the landscape profession. The author also analyzes the design palette used by landscape architects to carry out their work, and the natural and processed materials which express and define the special qualities of landscape design.

- **"Visual Resource Management"** by Kenneth Struckmeyer: This last chapter of the landscape section discusses the importance of managing visual landscape resources within rural areas, cities and regions of the United States. The author analyzes and illustrates various factors and methods of visually assessing landscape types to enhace identification and management for the long-term benefit of society.

REFERENCES

Rosine, R. F. 1981. "Landscape Architecture," Department of Horticulture and Landscape Architecture, Washington State University.

CHAPTER 17

Landscapes Through Time

Frederick Steiner

A landscape is the composite natural and cultural features of a place, including fields, buildings, roadways, hills, forests, deserts and water bodies, that distinguish one part of the earth's surface from another. As noted in the introduction to this section, it is usually that portion of land or territory which the eye can comprehend in a single view. Throughout the ages, people have used the land and changed the landscape to support civilizations. Understanding these changes provides a perspective on the importance of landscapes to humanity as well as the various ways landscapes have been manipulated to fulfill human needs.

Imagine a landscape comprised of wheat fields. An agricultural landscape such as this is not often thought of as part of the built environment, but it is. Farmland requires careful management to reduce erosion and build the fertility of the soil. The structure and form of agricultural crops are determined by careful genetic engineering. Farm machinery and equipment are designed and adapted for each specific crop and terrain. Agricultural landscapes have been an integral part of human settlement through time.

1. The panoramic Palouse region of eastern Washington and northern Idaho. The wheat in this region has been carefully bred to increase productivity. Because of the dry climate and steep slopes, special farm machinery and equipment have been built to manage the landscape (*G. Bedivian*).

THE AGRICULTURAL TRANSITION AND THE RISE OF CIVILIZATION

For most of humans' existence, the species *Homo sapiens* lived without government. In small groups, people lived off the land. Humans depended on hunting, fishing, gathering food, subsistence cultivation and/or pastoralism for survival. The development of governments came with the rise of agriculture. Due to advancing techniques of irrigation and cultivation, the fertile river valleys of the Nile, Tigris, Euphrates, Indus, and Hwang Ho were transformed into nation-states. These nation-states included urban areas with bureaucracies responsible for distributing agricultural surpluses. These new urban areas were dependent, as cities and towns are today, on the capability of land and people to produce food and fiber.

Greek and Roman Landscapes

Civilization spread into the rocky islands of the Aegean Sea and the plains of the Balkan

2. Nabatean tombs built into the landscape. The Nabateans were an ancient people of Arabia who lived between the Euphrates River and the Red Sea. Tombs were a dominant component of early human landscapes. As Lewis Mumford observed, early "civilizations respect for the dead, itself an expression of fascination with...powerful images of daylight fantasy and nightly dream, perhaps had an even greater role than more practical needs in causing [them] to seek a fixed meeting place and eventually continuous settlement." Mumford then concluded, "the city of the dead antedates the city of the living" (1961) (*Courtesy of Ministry of Information, Kingdom of Saudi Arabia*).

3. Agriculture provided the basis for civilization. This ancient grindstone was used for milling grain in the Middle East (*Courtesy of Ministry of Information, Kingdom of Saudi Arabia*).

Peninsula. There in Greece, the hot, dry climate, the folded mountain ranges and rocky coastlines—the whole ecological matrix—determined the health of the people as well as their economic activities and general view of life (Mumford, 1961). In Greece, dark green orchards of olives and figs contrast with sparse, dusty plains and white limestone crags are juxtaposed against cerulean blue seas. In Greek cities (the **polis**), Western ideas about democracy were born.

As the Greek landscape influenced the settlement pattern and political organization of the polis, the relatively open plains and uplands of the Italian peninsula provided the base for the vast Roman Empire. The empire was connected by an elaborate network of roads and aqueducts. As the empire expanded, new towns, known as **castra**, were built.

At the heart of the empire was the city of Rome. The proximity of the sea has influenced the city's climate, resulting in high summer temperatures with little humidity. As the empire grew, the city became a large population center. Because of overcrowding in the city of Rome and the stench of hot summers, many of the wealthy patrician families built villas outside of the town. There were two types of villas: **Villa rustica** were working farms, while **villa urbana** were used primarily for residents (Miller, 1981).

Medieval Landscapes

With the fall of the Roman Empire around the 6th century AD, Europe plunged into the Dark Ages. A semblance of civilization remained through the maintenance of agricultural systems and behind the walls of the religious cloisters. Large regions of France and Italy continued the agricultural systems introduced by the Romans. The order of the Western Roman Empire was replaced by a feudal system. Strongholds were necessary for defense, fortified castles surrounded by fertile agricultural lands. Another form of sanctuary was provided behind the walls of monasteries. In monasteries, monks of the Roman Catholic Church kept gardens of herbs used for medicinal purposes. The monks maintained botanical knowledge in their libraries of Latin and Greek texts. The monasteries acted as nurseries for classical scholarship that would provide the foundation for humanistic thought. Humanism eventually would provide the basis for the rebirth of civilization in western Europe. But, generally, civilization took a backward step in Europe from the 6th to 13th centuries AD.

Islamic Landscapes

Meanwhile, a new religion swept the southern rim of the Mediterranean Sea—Islam. The Islamic

4. Court of the Lions, Alhambra, Granada, Spain. This palace of the Moorish Kings of Spain was completed in the 14th century (*T. Bartuska*).

5. Moorish landscape garden, Alhambra, Granada, Spain. This garden of the Moorish Kings of Spain was also completed in the 14th century (*T. Bartuska*).

world was a striking contrast to the introverted Christian Europe of the Middle Ages. Moors were Islamic people who controlled what is now Spain from the 8th to the 15th centuries. In the regions of Islam, there was an appreciation of the outdoors. This was in part a result of a more favorable climate and the relative safety of the territories under Moslem control. In Islamic cultures, the garden possessed additional significance. The Koran promises supreme bliss in celestial gardens. Moorish gardens in Spain are best known for their use of tile, masonry, and water in geometric design. Water played an important role not only for drinking and irrigation, but also for cooling (Newton, 1971). All are necessary elements for human comfort in the hot, dry Iberian Peninsula.

Landscapes of the Renaissance

Islam, with the new ideas forged by Christian humanism, influenced the rebirth, or Renaissance, of knowledge in western Europe. Moorish garden design was adapted to the Italian hill sides of Tuscany. In Florence, the capital of Tuscany, members of the powerful Medici family were important patrons of the arts, beginning in the 15th century. Renaissance design, that was first evident in the gardens of wealthy Tuscans, influenced other arts, including architecture and later urbanism. Renaissance garden design, borrowing from Islamic traditions, employed the use of symmetry and geometric patterns.

The ideas of the Renaissance then moved northward into France and to the heart of Europe. In France, the Renaissance coincided with the rise of the French monarchy, the Bourbons, and the centralization of administrative power in Paris. The height of this power came during the reign of Louis XIV, who built the spectacular palace and gardens of Versailles. The Versailles gardens were the work of Andre Le Notre (1613–1700).

In addition to Versailles, Le Notre designed the gardens of Vaux-le-Vicomte, Trianon, Saint-Cloud, Chantilly, Clagny, and Meudon. Le Notre

6. Villa Castello, Florence (1540). An example of a hillside villa garden from Tuscany (*H. Abbott*).

7. Villa Capponi, Florence (c. 1570). An example of a hillside villa garden from Tuscany (*H. Abbott*).

8. Main vista from the garden of Versailles to the palace. The palace and gardens were built by the French King Louis XIV in the 17th century. The gardens were designed by Andre Le Notre (*H. Abbott*).

9. Detail from Versailles garden (*H. Abbott*).

was born in Paris and was the son of the head royal gardener. Le Notre studied painting and architecture and traveled (and may have worked) in England and Italy. The French landscape around Paris is relatively flat compared to hilly Tuscany. This difference in terrain made it possible to apply geometric pattems to larger areas. Le Notre's large-scale designs emphasize grandeur. Major focal points are connected by grand tree-lined vistas, with immaculately clipped vegetation. His pupils worked in Germany, Austria, and Spain, and the style he created became dominant throughout Europe. A century after Le Notre's death, the plan for the new federal capital of the United States, Washington, D.C., was developed by Pierre Charles L'Enfant. The layout of the new city was strongly influenced by Versailles.

The Dutch Landscape

To the north of France, another style emerged in the Low Countries (now Belgium and the Netherlands). The Dutch landscape is largely a result of human intervention in natural processes. In the Netherlands, a constant struggle exists between people and the sea. Through the struggle, the Dutch became able sea merchants and hardy farmers. When these talents were combined with a new Protestant capitalist spirit, the Dutch became a world power. Dutch cities expanded into swampy lands by using extensive canals for drainage and transportation. New lands, called **polders**, were made from the sea or lakes by constructing dikes and draining the areas. The polders were used principally for farming.

Polder-building increased in the Dutch Golden Age of the 17th century. Prosperity resulted in a

10. The technology of the windmill was used in the Netherlands to drain land areas below sea level creating polders. Polders are land that has been reclaimed from lakes or the sea. Windmills have had several other historical functions in the Netherlands, such as the milling of grain (*A. Ostrowska-Steiner*).

11. Polder landscape from the North Sea Canal near Amsterdam.

greater demand for food from people in the growing towns. New polder areas were drained through wind power harnessed by windmills. These new polders were financed by the merchants of Amsterdam, Rotterdam, Utreich, Delft and other Dutch cities (Lambert, 1971). In addition to creating new farmland, the building of polders helped control flooding. As a result, the Netherlands is a functional landscape, with a highly productive system of agriculture and with urban settlements situated outside flood-prone areas.

English Garden Movement

The landscapes that took shape in the British Isles in the 18th century were different than the well-ordered farmlands of Holland; the grandiose, French Baroque chateaux; and the Italian Renaissance hillside villas. The English landscape movement was

12. A picturesque English Landscape Garden, Stourhead, England (*T. Bartuska*).

influenced by Romantic poets and writers; French painters, such as Claude Lorraine and Poussin; and new ideas about nature generated by increased contact with the Orient.

The three greatest English landscape gardeners were William Kent (1686–1748), Lancelot "Capability" Brown (1716–1783), and Humphry Repton (1752–1818), with Brown having the greatest impact on the English countryside. His nickname resulted from his habit of saying that he could see "capabilities" in reshaping the estates he designed into a more "natural" or picturesque landscape. More than 140 estates—the property of the wealthy—received Brown's attention. The wealthy class was not limited only to the royalty, as in France, but included those who made wealth through trade and profits from an expanding empire. The major elements in a typical Brown landscape were isolated clumps of trees, undulating grassy areas, and a surrounding belt of woodland. He used artificial lakes and winding water courses, which fit

13. Manor house from Octagon Lake at Stowe, England (18th century). Charles Bridgeman, William Kent, and Lancelot "Capability" Brown were all involved in the design (*H. Abbott*).

14. An avenue of trees, directs ones eye towards a Chinese pagoda, Kew Royal Botanical Garden, London (*T. Bartuska*).

15. The integrated Japanese Landscape, Ninomaru Garden and Palace, Nijo Castle, Kyoto, 1603 (*T. Bartuska*).

well with the damp, misty English countryside (Newton, 1971; Laurie, 1986).

While these landscape developments were occurring in Europe, a different culture became better known to Europe through colonial expansion. The first impact of the ideas from Asia came in the English landscape. "Capability" Brown and his contemporaries often included Chinese pagodas as focal points in their estate landscapes.

Eastern Gardens

In China, Taoism was founded in the 6th century BC by Lao-tse. Tao philosophy is based on simplicity and selflessness. The principles of dualism are expressed in **yin** and **yang**, symbolized by natural opposites such as mountains and water or built objects and nature. In eastern traditions, these diverse elements are integrated into beautiful design compositions. The traditional Chinese design philosophy is known as **feng-shui** (which means wind and water), a philosophy based on the belief that the earth has energy fields flowing through it. People can use this "energy by manipulating landforms, plant locations, water courses and structures in the landscapes" (Mogan, 1991).

In India, the teachings of Buddha were followed from about the 6th century BC. Buddhism teaches that through right thinking and self-denial, the soul will be able to reach Nirvana, a divine state. In Japan, the anti-rational Buddhist sect of Zen became widespread. It differs from other Buddhist sects in seeking enlightenment through introspection and intuition rather than scripture. Taoism, Buddhism, and Zen influenced the landscapes of Asia; many beautiful gardens were developed which express these cultural tenets of the people. These concepts were brought to England and the rest of Europe during the era of mercantilism from the 16th through the 19th centuries.

THE INDUSTRIAL TRANSITION AND THE RISE OF THE LANDSCAPE PROFESSION

While those of the English landscape school were looking back to what was envisioned as a more picturesque era, or were turning toward the Orient for a more natural vision of the land, Europe was changing from an agrarian culture to an industrial one. The Industrial Revolution began in England and quickly moved through Europe and North America. Its impact on people was profound, as deep as the earlier transition to agriculturally based nation-states from hunting and gathering nomadic tribes.

The new products of the industrial revolution made life easier and increased the amount of leisure time for many people. It also increased urbanization, poverty, pollution and urban squalor. Charles Dickens painted an acidic portrait of England during the mid-19th century. In response to these patterns of industrialization and rapid urbanization, the English parks movement was begun. In the 1830s and 1840s, several parks were built in London: St. James Park, Green Park, Hyde Park, Kensington Gardens, and Regent's Park. Although

16. Royal Victoria Park, Botanic Garden, Bath, England (*H. Abbott*).

these parks remained the property of the Crown, they were open to the public.

The industrial revolution moved quickly to the United States, where the agrarian, democratic ideals of Thomas Jefferson had been influential in the establishment of the new nation. Jefferson believed a strong democracy would be based on a nation of small farmers who owned their land. The forces of industrialism challenged this ideal. Partially in reaction to the industrial transition, the transcendental movement grew in popularity in the United States. Transcendentalism is a philosophy that asserts the primacy of the spiritual and the intuitive over the material and empirical. The New England leaders of the movement, Ralph Waldo Emerson and Henry David Thoreau, stressed the presence of the divine within people as a source for truth and a guide to action. This philosophy was based on the writings of the German philosopher Immanuel Kant and influenced by the Society of Friends or Quakers.

Transcendentalism and the English landscape school influenced several American designers. In 1841, the young horticulturist and landscape gardener, Andrew Jackson Downing (1815–1852), published his popular *A Treatise on the Theory and Practice of Landscape Gardening Adapted to North America*. Downing designed country estates along the Hudson River, north of New York City. Like previous estates, these were owned by the wealthy, but this wealth was broader based than that of Europe, a new affluence created by the industrial revolution. The Hudson River valley was transformed from wilderness to farmland, then suburbs, and finally a connected piece in the puzzle of urbanization: a cycle that would reoccur many times through development in the United States and throughout the industrializing world.

Downing was also influenced by English urban parks and urged that such parks be constructed in the United States. Downing was joined in this advocacy by the poet and editor William Cullen Bryant in the New York *Evening Post* (Newton, 1971; Laurie, 1986). The distinction of being the oldest park in the United States probably belongs to Fairmount Park in Philadelphia. The area, originally known as Faire Mount, is shown on maps as old as 1687. It first became a public place in 1812, with a modest five acres set aside for water supply purposes. More lands were continually added to protect the water works, until 1855, when an ordinance was passed making it a public park. Afterwards, it continued to grow in size until the park contained 2,971 acres in 1878. In 1876, it was the site of the United States Centennial Exposition (Hedrick, 1950). A young Austrian immigrant, Hermann Joseph Schwarzmen, was responsible for the centennial's landscape design and much of the park's overall appearance.

17. Frederick Law Olmsted, Sr. (1822–1903) (*Courtesy of National Park Service, Frederick Law Olmsted Historic Site*).

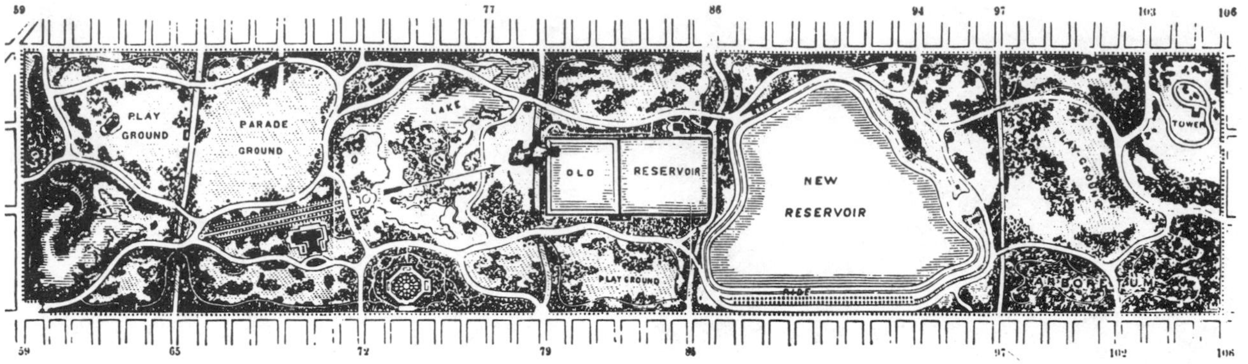

18. The original 1858 plan for Central Park in New York City, developed by the landscape architect Frederick Law Olmsted, Sr. and the English architect Calvert Vaux (*Courtesy of National Park Service, Frederick Law Olmsted National Historic Site*).

The concept of urban parks was developed to a grand scale by Frederick Law Olmsted, Sr. (1822–1903). Born in Connecticut, Olmsted was educated as an apprentice topographic engineer and a part-time student at Yale College. Before becoming a landscape architect, he followed various pursuits and also became a noted writer, experimental farmer, social critic and reformer and publisher. He is often referred to as the father of landscape architecture in the United States.

Olmsted and his partner of many years, Calvert Vaux, an English-born architect, were responsible for the design of New York's Central Park, started in 1857 and completed in 1863. Unlike Fairmount Park, which developed incrementally, Central Park was designed and built as a complete unit. Much capital and labor were required to build it and nearly four thousand people were involved in construction. The results were memorable and popular immediately. Central Park was opened to the public and nearly 25,000 people visited the park each day. The success of the park prompted the building of more parks for city residents in New York and elsewhere, providing much needed open space and recreational opportunities (Fabos, et al., 1968).

Olmsted and Vaux were involved in many other urban parks, including: Morningside, Prospect and Washington Parks (New York); Seneca Park (Rochester, New York); Mt. Royal Park (Montreal); South Park (Buffalo, New York); Charlestown Playground (Boston); Washington Park (Albany, New York); and Jefferson Park (Chicago). Olmsted's other varied works included the planning for Niagara Falls in New York and Ontario (an international park), the design and planning for Riverside, Illinois (new community design), the metropolitan Boston park and park-ways system (regional planning), the plans for Stanford and Washington Universities (campus design), the design of the Biltmore gardens in Asheville, North Carolina (estate design), and his collaboration on the World's Columbian Exposition of 1893 in Chicago (urban design) (Fabos, et al., 1968).

Meanwhile, landscape design continued to develop as an art in Europe. As early as Andre Le Notre in the 17th century, there had been an apprentice system for landscape gardening. This gave way in the 19th century to a more formal

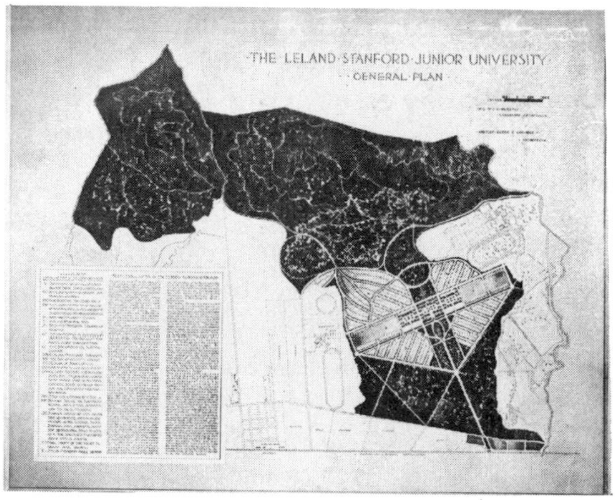

19. Stanford University campus designed by Frederick Law Olmsted, Sr. and his nephew/stepson, John Charles Olmsted, in c. 1886. The Olmsteds collaborated with the Boston architects Shepley, Rutan and Coolidge (*Courtesy of National Park Service, Frederick Law Olmsted National Historic Site*).

approach to education. In 1889, Edouard Andre was named professor of architecture and gardens at the Versailles horticulture school. Before his appointment, he had been responsible for transforming the old fortifications around Paris into public gardens. A contemporary and acquaintance of Olmsted, Andre also wrote *L'Art des Jardins*. The German Society for Garden Arts and Care of the Landscape (Deutschen Gesellschaft fur Gartenkunst and Landscaftspflege), originally the Association of German Garden Designers, was founded in 1887. This society has published its journal, *Garten & Landschaft*, since 1890.

In England, Ebenezer Howard published *Garden Cities for Tomorrow* (originally titled *A Peaceful Path to Real Reform*) in 1898. Howard advocated the development of new towns with a mixed urban-rural character, that would be commonly owned and limited in size. He became involved in the development of two garden cities in the early 20th century—Letchworth and Welwyn. Howard's ideas have continued to influence new-town planning and design in England and internationally.

In the United States, several things happened to influence how landscapes were viewed in the late 19th and early 20th centuries. Land-grant, agriculture colleges were founded; the American Society of Landscape Architects (A.S.L.A.) was established; the Olmsted Brothers firm worked on many projects; and academic programs using the name "landscape architecture" were started.

The idea of agricultural colleges developed during the 19th century, advocated by such influential people as Thomas Clemson, Horace Greeley, Downing, and Olmsted. Justin Morrill, a U.S. representative and later a senator from Vermont, sponsored the Morrill Act. President Abraham Lincoln signed the act into law in 1862 and the nationwide land-grant college system was established. The Morrill Act appropriated certain granted lands "to the endowment, support, and maintenance of at least one college in each state where the leading object shall be to teach such branches of learning as are related to agriculture and the mechanic arts."

Courses in landscape gardening and design were an integral part of the curricula of these schools. Landscape gardening and design were taught from the 1860s on by such men as Adouijah S. Welch at the Iowa Agriculture College (later Iowa State University) and Albert Prentiss and Liberty Hyde Bailey at the Michigan Agricultural College (later Michigan State University). Bailey left Michigan State for Cornell University and became the best known agricultural writer and editor of his time, continuing to write about the importance of art to rural life and landscape design.

Another important individual in the development of landscape architecture at land-grant colleges was Frank Waugh (1865–1949). His 1894 master's thesis at the Kansas State Agricultural College (later Kansas State University) was the campus plan for the Oklahoma Agricultural and Mechanical College and Experiment Station (later Oklahoma State University). He also wrote the book, *Landscape Gardening* (1899), and helped establish, in 1902, the landscape architecture department at the University of Massachusetts (Steiner and Brooks, 1986).

In the 1890s, the aging Frederick Law Olmsted, Sr. became less active in the design firm he had founded, turning it over to his nephew and adopted son, John Charles Olmsted (1852–1920), and Frederick Law Olmsted, Jr. (1870–1957). The firm, the Olmsted Brothers, was involved in design and planning projects throughout the United States into the first half of the 20th century. In 1899, the A.S.L.A. was organized in New York City. Its eleven original members included both of the Olmsted brothers. Women and minorities were active in landscape design through this period. Beatrix Jones Farrand (1872–1959) was one of the founders of A.S.L.A. She carried on an extensive practice in residential and campus design. Princeton, Yale, the University of Chicago, and Oberlin College

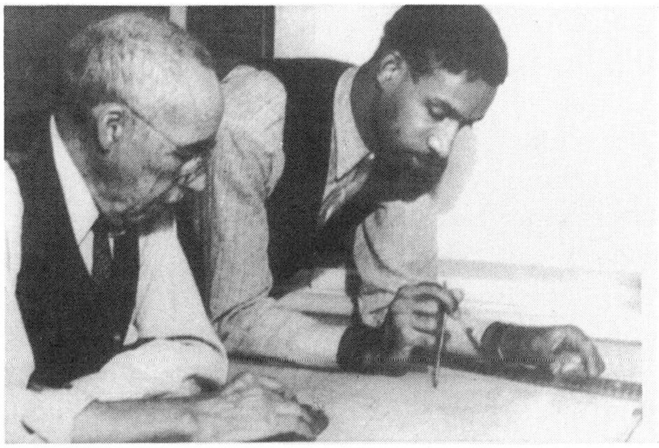

20. David Augustus Williston (1868–1962). He is working with an unidentified landscape professional (*Courtesy of K. Muckle*).

were among the campuses she helped to design (Newton, 1971). David Augustus Williston (1868–1962), a student of Liberty Hyde Bailey at Cornell University was an influential black landscape designer involved in campus design at several colleges (Tuskegee Institute, Howard University, Catholic University of Washington, D.C., and Atlanta University among others) and many projects in Washington, D.C. He also taught horticulture and landscape design at a number of colleges and universities (Muckle and Wilson, 1982).

At the beginning of the 20th century, a number of older, well-established universities formed programs using the term "landscape architecture" instead of the older landscape "gardening" or "design" used at land-grant and European schools. A notable program in landscape architecture was established at Harvard University in 1900. This program received strong backing from Harvard's President Eliot, whose son, Charles, a landscape architect, worked with the Olmsteds (Newton, 1971). Frederick Law Olmsted Jr. became a landscape architecture professor at Harvard, where he also helped to establish the city planning program.

Whereas the older landscape gardening programs had been located in schools of agriculture, Harvard's program, and those that followed, were associated with architecture. From 1900 to 1935, architecture education in the United States was almost entirely under the tutelage of people educated in the system of the French Ecole des Beaux-Arts. As a result, design education, including many landscape architecture programs, was influenced strongly by the Beaux-Arts system of *ateliers* under the direction of eminent educators and of *charrettes* for the review and development of ideas through projects. Some landscape programs resisted this focus and remained associated with agriculture, horticulture, and forestry schools. To some extent, this dichotomy between architecturally-based and plant science-based teaching of landscape architecture still exists.

One proponent of the latter was the Danish-born Jens Jensen (1890–1951). Jensen worked in the Great Lakes region and developed what became known as the "Prairie Style," based on the use of indigenous plant materials and a knowledge of natural systems in design. One of the architects Jensen worked with was Frank Lloyd Wright, who also became known for his "Prairie Style." According to Catherine Howett, "if he could not do the landscape plan himself, Wright preferred that his clients use Jensen, while Jensen often tried to persuade a prospective client that Wright should design the house" (Howett, 1982).

During the first half of the 20th century, landscape architecture grew as a profession in North America and Europe. It prospered in the United States during the New Deal of the Franklin D. Roosevelt administration. The New Deal was the name for the economic and political principles and policies put forth by President Roosevelt in the 1930s to advance economic recovery from the Great Depression. Among the wide variety of projects that landscape architects became involved in during this period were: Greenbelt new towns, state and national parks and parkways (Newton, 1975; Laurie, 1986).

Also during this time, there developed a growing concern about providing good landscape design for the middle class. This movement was especially strong on the west coast of the United States and became known as the "California School." Two prominent members of this school were Thomas Church and Garrett Eckbo, who worked in the San Francisco Bay region. Church was a functionalist who emphasized everyday needs in design and transformed the home garden into a landscape to inhabit, a natural outgrowth of the hospitable California climate. Eckbo was chair of the landscape architecture department at the University of California-Berkeley. Like Church, Eckbo espoused a populist approach to design, believing site planning should be an arrangement of environments for people.

CONTEMPORARY SOCIETY AND ECOLOGICAL CONCERN

Since World War II, the world has undergone rapid change, change thought by many to be as dramatic as the implications for human life of the agricultural or industrial transitions. The change involves new technology that greatly impacts how people relate to environment and society. Automobiles, trucks, airplanes, refrigeration, air conditioners, televisions, radios, FAX machines and computers have dramatically reshaped the urban landscape. Various labels have been applied to this period of dramatic change, including the "post-industrial society" or anthropologist John Bennett's period of "ecological transition." Any period of history is one of ecological transition, but Bennett's observation is particularly apt that the present "transition concerns the tendency to seek ever-larger quantities of energy in order to satisfy the demands of human existence, comfort, and wealth" (Bennett, 1976). What distinguishes the present period of change from previous ones is the speed of acceleration, the extent to which humans can now understand and alter their life-support systems, and the potential to buffer the impacts.

Environmental design, including landscape architecture, has also changed. A number of designers, planners, and ecologists can be identified as pioneers through their work on how humans relate, or should relate to that environment, through their concern for a more holistic approach, and by their emphasis on health, fitness, and creativity as the basis for a substainable adaptive strategy between humans and environment.

Ian L. McHarg, former chair of the Department of Landscape Architecture and Regional Planning at the University of Pennsylvania, has been one of the foremost among these pioneers as an educator, writer, landscape architect, and planner (Thompson, 1991). McHarg has emphasized an approach to design based on thorough study of the ecology of an area to reveal which land uses may be best practiced where. McHarg's method defines areas best suitable for a potential land use by integrating or layering together human and environmental factors deemed favorable for the use, and which are also marked by the absence of all or most detrimental conditions. Such factors include geology, physiography, hydrology, soils, climate, vegetation and wildlife, as well as socio-cultural processes. McHarg revolutionized landscape design and planning by basing design **first** on a thorough analysis of ecological factors from which solutions flow, rather than by a preconceived set of aesthetic principles to determine changes to a place (McHarg, 1969). His vision was holistic. Ecology was to be used to understand how parts interrelate to create whole systems.

21. The Woodlands, Texas is a new town that has been developed since 1971 using ecological principles. The Philadelphia firm, Wallace, McHarg, Roberts and Todd (now Wallace, Roberts and Todd), was responsible for the extensive ecological inventory, the ecological plan, and the guidelines for site planning of the new town. Ian McHarg was the partner responsible for the ecological planning and design (*Courtesy of the Mitchell Energy and Development Corporation*).

McHarg has not, of course, been alone. Table 1 summarizes a few of the important pioneers in the transition to enhanced ecological concern. Landscape architects, foresters, biologists, geographers, community and regional planners and architects have all been active in developing an ecological approach to planning and design.

Zube's research has concentrated on how people perceive their environment (cf., Zube, et al., 1975; Zube, et al., 1982). As a professor, first at the University of Massachusetts and now the University of Arizona, he has worked closely with the U.S. National Park Service. Zube (1986) has traced the advance of ecology within landscape architecture and found that the science has enriched the art.

Meanwhile in Germany, Gerhard Olschowy has been deeply involved in reclamation efforts in the Rhine Brown Coal Region, using extensive ecological information to restore landscapes degraded by strip-mining. Olschowy (1984) has been active internationally in promoting landscape planning and the wise use of land.

John Tilman Lyle received his education in architecture from Tulane University and in landscape architecture from the University of California-Berkeley. A landscape architecture professor at California State Polytechnic University-Pomona, he is the author of *Design for Human Ecosystems* (1985). Lyle has observed that humans have always designed ecosystems and continue to do so, although the issues grow ever more complex. He views such complexity as an opportunity: "Landscape design does not proceed in the abstract, but in the heat

Pioneers in ecological planning and design.

Name	Nation	Profession	Employer	Lifetime
Patrick Geddes	Scotland	Biologist/Ecologist	University of Edinburgh	1854–1932
Aldo Leopold	United States	Wildlife Biologist	University of Wisconsin	1887–1949
Benton MacKaye	United States	Regional Planner/Writer	U.S. Forest Service and other government agencies	1879–1975
Jens Jensen	Denmark/ United States	Landscape Gardener	Private Practice	1890–1951
Lewis Mumford	United States	Urbanist/Writer	Journals, Books; Various Universities	1895–1990
Artur Glikson	Israel	Architect	Private Practice	1911–1966
G. A. Hills	Canada	Forester	Canadian Ministry of Lands and Forests, University of Toronto	1902–1980
Tom McCall	United States	Journalist/Politician	State of Oregon	1913–1983
Eugene Odum	United States	Ecologist	University of Georgia	Current
Ian L. McHarg	Scotland/ United States	Landscape Architect/ Regional Planner	University of Pennsylvania	Current
Gerhard Olschowy	Germany	Landscape Planner	University of Bonn	Current
Ervin Zube	United States	Landscape Architect/ Geographer	University of Arizona University of Massachusetts	Current
John Lyle	United States	Landscape Architect	California State Polytechnic University-Pomona	Current
Malcolm Wells	United States	Architect	Private Practice	Current
Carol Franklin	United States	Landscape Architect	Andropogan Associates	Current
Leslie Sauer	United States	Landscape Architect	Andropogan Associates	Current
Jusuck Koh	Korea/ United States	Architect/ Landscape Architect	Texas Tech University	Current
Gary Coates	United States	Architect	Kansas State University	Current
Carol Smyster	United States	Landscape Architect	Private Practice	Current
Richard T. T. Forman	United States	Landscape Ecologist	Harvard University	Current
Zev Nevah	Israel	Landscape Ecologist	Technion-Israel	Current
J. Glenn Eugster	United States	Landscape Architect	National Park Service	Current
Anne Whiston Spirn	United States	Landscape Architect	University of Pennsylvania	Current

of real issues and the questions, debates, paradoxes, and imbroglios that arise from them" (1985).

Franklin, Sauer, Eugster, Smyster, Koh, and Spirn were all students of McHarg. Eugster, a former director of the Division of Park and Resource Planning in the Mid-Atlantic region of the U.S. National Park Service, has pioneered the use of the "greenline" concept. Greenline planning is the process of establishing and maintaining a greenway, which is a large protected landscape. For further

22. Model of the Institute for Regenerative Studies in Pomona, California. The Institute was conceived and designed by John Lyle and his California State University Polytechnic colleagues to be a laboratory for biotechnical teaching and research. Built on a landfill, the Institute will be an ecological village where student-residents will grow their own food and recycle their own waste (*Courtesy of J. Lyle*).

23. The master plan for the Crosby Arboretum in Picayune, Mississippi, was developed by landscape architect, Edward L. Blake, Jr., director of the Crosby Arboretum. The landscape architecture consultants were Carol Franklin and Leslie Sauer of Andropogon of Philadelphia. This photograph is of the open-air pavilion designed by Jones and Jennings of Fayetteville, Arkansas. It evokes the structure of a southern pine forest. The Crosby Arboretum is comprised of a network of seven natural areas covering 1,700 acres. The goal of the landscape master plan was to create a fully realized ecological garden (*E. L. Blake, Jr*).

information about greenline planning, see Chapter 28 on regional planning.

Carol Franklin and Leslie Sauer teach at the University of Pennsylvania and practice through their Philadelphia-based firm, Andropogon Associates. They established Andropogon with their husbands, Colin Franklin and Rolf Sauer. According to Carol Franklin and Leslie Sauer, ecological design acknowledges the uniqueness of each place and, as a result, can effectively build on the recognized and latent resources of the site.

Carol Franklin and Leslie Sauer are passionate in their views of the role of ecology in landscape design. "The way the whole thing works is the way the thing looks and the way the thing looks is the way the thing works," is how Franklin explains ecological aesthetics. "Our aesthetic comes from the site," declares Sauer. "The style of each place is derived from the natural patterns of vegetation, relief and drainage, and the cultural patterns of past and current land use."

Carol Smyster, a Pennsylvania landscape architect, writes about the application of ecological principles to residential-scale design, an advocacy of indigenous materials reminiscent of Jens Jensen and other practitioners of the "Prairie Style." According to Smyster, "the ecosystem is what determines the arrangement or design of a natural landscape. To landscape with Nature, you must [first] ask Nature where and how to do best what you want to do" (1982).

The Korean born Koh has written provocatively about the need for a sound theoretical basis for ecological design (1982, 1988). He believes traditional environmental design tends to be reductionistic and determinist and like McHarg, argues that "ecological design" presents a more holistic and evolutionary alternative. According to Koh:

> Ecological designers do not in their design process pursue the optimization of the whole in sacrifice of the parts, or vice-versa; rather, they are democratic in that

> they pursue a balance between optimization of the whole and that of its parts. Hence, they do not neglect the parts, just as nature never neglects details. They favor slower, stable, wholesome maturation rather than rapid, stressful, partial growth in the built human ecosystem, because the creative, self-organizing process is necessarily a slow process, and system integrity is a necessity not only for social stability and efficiency but for individual freedom (1982).

Anne Spirn, who succeeded McHarg as chair of landscape architecture at the University of Pennsylvania, is the author of *The Granite Garden* (1984). She urges recognition of the social value of nature and the harnessing of its power so that nature in the city can be cultivated rather than ignored or subdued. According to Spirn (1989), design should respond to the "deep structure" of the place. She defines deep structure as the fundamental geologic, hydrologic and bioclimatic processes that form the landscape. Spirn's design theory is "based upon an understanding of nature and culture as comprising interwoven processes that exhibit a complex, underlying order that holds across vast scales of space and time" (1988).

CONSPECTUS

What distinguishes the current age from the previous ones? And what are the possible impacts on the landscape? People know more about cause and effect of natural forces than in any time in their history. This knowledge can be used to create a more healthy, fitting and productive landscape . . . or, it may be used to destroy the landscape and human life with it.

Marilyn Ferguson, in her book *The Aquarian Conspiracy* (1980), addresses this choice. She speaks of a revolution which is now well underway, a revolution in which "what was" does not equal "what should be." According to Ferguson,

> For the first time in history, humankind has come upon the control panel of change—an understanding of how transformation occurs. We are living in the change of change, the time in which we can intentionally align ourselves with nature for rapid remaking of ourselves and our collapsing institutions.

Ecological design is the appropriate response for this time. Ecology can be a source of design inspirations that are beautiful, productive, and responsive to each place. Ecology offers a threshold to a new way of design that connects people to their environments and that illuminates how landscapes work.

REFERENCES

Bennett, J. W. 1976. *The Ecological Transition.* Pergamon Press.

Fabos, J. G., Milde, G. T. and Weinmayr, M. 1968. *Frederick Law Olmsted, Sr.* University of Massachusetts Press.

Ferguson, M. 1980. *The Aquarian Conspiracy: Personal and Social Transformation in the 1980s.* Houghton Mifflin.

Hedrick, U. P. 1950. *A History of Horticulture in America to 1860.* Oxford University Press.

Howett, C. M. 1981. "Frank Lloyd Wright and American Residential Landscaping." *Landscape*, January.

Johnson, A. H., Berger, J., and McHarg, I. L. 1979. "A Case Study of Ecological Planning: The Woodlands, Texas" in M. T. Beatty, C. W. Petersen, and L. D. Swindale (editors). *Planning the Uses and Management of Land. American Society of Agronomy*, Crop Science Society of America, and Soil Science Society of America.

Koh, J. 1982. "Ecological Design: A Post-Modern Design Paradigm of Holistic Philosophy and Evolutionary Ethic." *Landscape Journal*, February.

Lambert, A. M. 1971. *The Making of the Dutch Landscape.* Seminar Press.

Laurie, M. 1986. *An Introduction to Landscape Architecture.* Elsevier.

McHarg, I. L. 1969. *Design with Nature.* Doubleday/ Natural History Press.

McHarg, I. L. and Sutton, J. 1975. "Ecological Plumbing for the Coastal Plain, the Woodlands New Town Experiment." *Landscape Architecture*, January.

Miller, L. E. 1981. *Landscape Architecture History Handbook.* Crympl Beck Press.

Mogan, E. 1991. "'Wind and Water' The Ancient Chinese Landscape Design Art" in L. Brink (editor). *Selected works: Council of Educators in Landscape Architecture.* 1990 Conference Landscape Architecture Foundation.

Muckle, K. and Wilson, D. 1982. "Douglas Augustus Williston, Pioneering Black Professional." *Landscape Architecture*, January.

Mumford, L. 1961. *The City in History.* Harcourt, Brace and World.

Newton, N. T. 1971. *Design on the Land.* Belknap Press.

Olschowy, G. 1984. "The Large-Scale Surface Mining in the Rhine Brown Coal Area in Connection with Landscape Planning" in F. R. Steiner and H. N. van

Lier (editors). *Land Conservation and Development*. Elsevier.
Spirn, A. W. 1984. *The Granite Garden*. Basic Books.
Spirn, A. W. 1988. "The Poetics of City and Nature: Towards a New Aesthetic for Urban Design." *Landscape Journal*, February.
Spirn, A. W. 1989. "'Deep Structure': On Process, Pattern, Form and Design in the Urban Landscape" in *Linking Landscape Structure to Ecosystem Process*. Colorado State University Press.
Smyster, C. A. 1982. *Nature's Design*. Rodale Press.
Steiner, F. and Brooks, K. 1986. "Agricultural Education and Landscape Architecture." *Landscape Journal*, January.
Thompson, W. 1991. "A Natural Legacy: Ian McHarg and His Followers." *Planning*, November.
Wallace, McHarg, Roberts and Todd. 1971–1974. *Woodlands New Community* (4 volumes). Philadelphia, Pennsylvania.
Zube, E. H., Brush, R. O. and Fabos, J. G., (Editors). 1975. *Landscape Assessment: Values, Perceptions and Resources*. Dowden, Hutchinson and Ross.
Zube, E. H., Sell, J. L., and Taylor, J. G. 1982. "Landscape Perception: Research, Application and Theory." *Landscape Planning*, January.
Zube, E. H. 1986. "The Advance of Ecology." *Landscape Architecture*, February.

CHAPTER

18

Landscape Architecture Today: Definitions and Directives

Betsy Boehm Hsu

Landscapes provide an important role for society: they create universal backdrops where the drama of life is portrayed. However, while landscape settings may provide life-sustaining qualities, and even universal images, they are not everlasting nor are they permanent. Forests, mountains, lakes, rivers, and valleys are dynamic. They alter and change. Today, many landscapes are especially vulnerable to the pressures brought on by growing populations and economic development. The profession of landscape architecture confronts these pressures to create and preserve a quality of life in the built environment.

People enjoy built spaces that are well designed and planned. Just as an ocean shoreline, a spring meadow, or a mountain forest can uplift the soul and give health benefits to the participant who walks in or views the setting (even if for only a few moments), positive benefits are also derived to those who enter and participate in a built space that has brought the forces of nature into play and balanced them with the needs and demands of life. This life-landscape link is vital to the proper planning, design and orchestration of the built environment. Landscape architecture is one of the environmental disciplines to have evolved a working definition which applies design and planning principles that blend the natural landscape forces with life-force needs in the creation of the built environment.

A primary goal of the landscape architect is the creation of exterior spaces which conserve the environment while providing for human needs and enhancing the quality of life. An appreciation for these skills is probably more prevalent today than ever before as human consciousness has finally come to grips with the limitations of the earth's natural resources and has developed a desire for affordable, quality environments where people and nature can live in harmony. How can growth be balanced so that environmental quality is maintained? A look at the evolving definition of landscape architecture yields some enlightenment on this question, but it still remains perhaps the greatest challenge that confronts all the environmental design disciplines. At the heart of this struggle are the concepts of stewardship, resource conservation, and sustainability—the basis for the definition of landscape architecture.

1. Sunset on the Oregon Coast—an inspirational landscape of land and water within one of our nations state park systems which lends peace and harmony to the soul.

STEWARDSHIP AND THE EVOLVING DEFINITION OF LANDSCAPE ARCHITECTURE

Landscape architecture has been concerned with the issues of environmentally sensitive design and planning since its inception as a professional society in 1899, though it took nearly one hundred years for ASLA to clearly state stewardship and resource conservation as part of its constitution. The American Society of Landscape Architects now mandates stewardship and resource conservation as major professional responsibilities. The idea of **stewardship** means that the professional is to be responsible for managing and accounting for the environment so that the earth's resources can be sustained while meeting the demands placed upon them. The definition of landscape architecture evolved from the concept of gardening into a fine art and finally a service profession that incorporates the principles of design, planning and management with resource conservation, stewardship and sustainability. By taking a look at the evolving definition of landscape architecture against the backdrop of history, the changing directives of the profession become apparent.

Landscape Gardening vs. Landscape Architecture

> Landscape gardener or landscape architect: I have come to prefer the latter term, tho I much objected to it when it was first given me. I prefer it because it helps to establish the important idea of the distinction of my profession from that of gardening as that of architecture from building the distinction of an art of design.
>
> Frederick Law Olmsted

By the nineteenth century, landscape design had evolved out of a long tradition of garden design and estate planning for the elite. Landscape gardening had been a viable profession for those who served the wealthy. By mid-century, however, landscape architecture had become, for the first time, a profession that was to be more and more involved in public projects. A social reform movement that grew out of industrialization and congested urban centers began to emphasize the need for green open spaces or parks for the health and benefit of the general public.

The term "landscape architect" was used by Frederick Law Olmsted and Calvert Vaux in the 1860s, while they were engaged in the planning and design of Central Park in New York City. Prior to calling themselves landscape architects, Olmsted and Vaux were the Architect-in-Chief and Consulting Architect, respectively. With the term landscape architect, Olmsted and Vaux wished to preserve a sense of art and a sensitivity to open space preservation. With these perspectives they hoped to preserve a professional code of ethics amidst the heat of political self-interests that pervaded the New York City government during that era.

Landscape architecture would eventually become the title of a new profession with Frederick Law Olmsted as its acknowledged founder. It would distinguish itself as a profession by incorporating design and planning skills infused with a sensitivity towards both natural and cultural landscape forms and systems. Surveying, engineering and construction skills, as well as a knowledge of plant materials and of basic horticultural practices, were

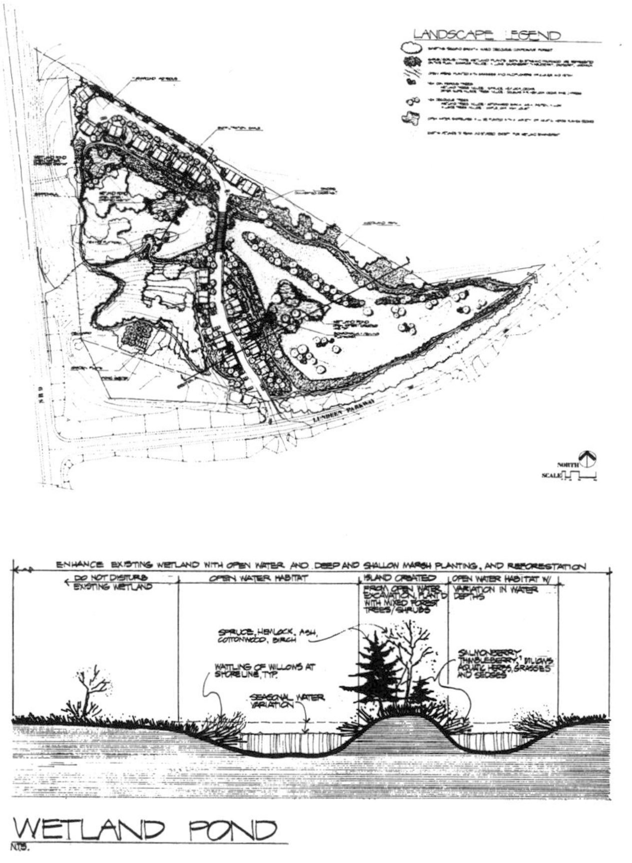

2&3. Landscape architectural stewardship practices by Lee and Associates in a developed landscape and wetland mitigation for a planned residential community. Built elements include boardwalks, viewing decks, jogging loop trail, pedestrian paths, biofiltration swales along access road, and a community park. Headwater Heights PUD Development Plan and Wetland Pond Section, Snohomish County, Washington. (*Lee and Associates*).

additional areas of professional expertise. Landscape architecture was to become a fine art that would be applied, by the late nineteenth and early twentieth centuries, in the development of public parks within increasingly overcrowded urban centers.

Landscape Architecture as a Fine Art

> Landscape architecture is primarily a fine art, and as such its most important function is to create and preserve beauty in the surroundings of human habitations and in the broader natural scenery of the country; but it is also concerned with promoting the comfort, convenience, and health of urban population, which have scanty access to rural scenery, and urgently need to have their hurrying, workaday lives refreshed and calmed by the beautiful and reposeful sights and sounds which nature, aided by the landscape art, can abundantly provide.
>
> Charles Eliot, 1895

The conception of landscape architecture as a fine art derived from a popular nineteenth century design aesthetic based in rural landscape scenery and in the eighteenth century English Landscape Garden Movement. Landscape architecture had become tied to the principles of the fine arts in an attempt to reconcile the forms of nature into three-dimensional art or landscape scenery. At first these natural landscape designs were created only for the pleasure of the wealthy, but as development pressures increased for public parks in congested urban centers, the rural landscape aesthetic became the vogue.

The idea of landscape architecture as a fine art which recreated rural landscape scenery was popularized in reaction to industrialization. Large numbers of the rural population moved into urban centers in search of job opportunities, causing overcrowding and lowering the living standards. Loss of the health-giving benefits of rural open spaces became apparent as more and more of the urbanized people, once accustomed to farming, now suffered from urban blight and disease. However, a new middle class benefitted from their hardships, and with new wealth, power and personal dignity, would adapt the rural landscape aesthetic as part of popular culture. These social forces helped create the nineteenth century public parks movement, which resulted in many of the significant urban open space systems that we still enjoy today. The nineteenth century park movement popularized a rural landscape aesthetic in park layout and design based on picturesque ideas of nature.

4. An example of our earliest parks, the rural cemetery, where rural landscape design accommodated visitors in a parklike setting. 19th Century Rural Cemetery in Norwich, New York (*P. Hsu*).

Landscape architecture as a fine art therefore was at first based on the forms and expressions of the rural landscape aesthetic of the nineteenth century. While landscape design today has taken on a contemporary design expression, the heart of the profession still embodies the concept of preservation and conservation of nature. The popular environmental movement of the past several decades is rooted in the rural land ethic with deep appreciation and desire for open space preservation and the conservation of natural resources (Nash, 1973). Today, landscape architecture applies scientific methodologies in the identification, reconstruction and preservation of natural ecosystems, blending science with art, and promoting itself as a profession that can service the public needs for environmental design and planning.

Landscape Architecture and the Green Industry

> Landscape architecture is involved with servicing some identifiable set of public goods and goals and these are all wrapped up in the quality of the environment; enhancing the capacity of human society to survive and improve; a vision of the world as a better place, a more beautiful place, and a more rewarding place.
>
> Grady Clay, 1970

The profession of landscape architecture has blossomed in the twentieth century. With escalated growth and development, more opportunities for landscape work were created both in the public and private sectors of the job market. Educational programs in landscape architecture also expanded around the nation, training students in aspects of horticulture, physical science, art, architecture, engineering, and management (Lyle, 1985).

During the Great Depression, landscape architects found work in many public projects developed through the Public Works Administration and the Civilian Conservation Corps. After World War II, landscape architects lent their expertise to private and public projects ranging from site planning for suburban expansion to road layout and landscape design for interstate highways. Out of the environmental movement of the late 1960s and 1970s came a public awareness of and an appreciation for the earth and for the limitation of resources. Greater interest in the physical sciences and environmental design was apparent by increased enrollments in these fields in colleges and universities. The "greening" of the United States opened potential markets and turned the "green industry" into a multimillion dollar service industry.

Landscape architects find that their knowledge of the physical and horticultural sciences, their sensitivity towards environmental design and conservation, and their planning, management and construction skills have created a niche in the "green" service sector of society. They plan, design, construct and manage landscapes for the home-owner, the developer and the public. They engage in public policymaking at the local, state and national levels. The landscape architect can also find opportunity in the green industry in home and garden care, nurseries, environmental engineering, ecological design and planning, construction, and leisure and recreation planning (Molnar, 1986; Solomon, 1988).

5. Balled and burlapped trees ready for shipping are inspected by a landscape architect. Landscape architects often work with the nursery industry in the cultivation, selection and maintenance of quality plants for landscape installations.

Landscape Architecture and Stewardship

> Landscape architecture is the art of design, planning, or management of the land, arrangement of natural and [human]-made elements thereon through application of cultural and scientific knowledge, with concern for resource conservation and stewardship, to the end that the resultant environment services a useful and enjoyable purpose.
>
> ASLA Constitution, 1979

In 1979, the ASLA Constitution adopted the terms stewardship and resource conservation for the first time into its by-laws, stating these concepts clearly as significant mandates in the training and practice of landscape architects. Art and science as principles and methodologies in the training of landscape architects combine a broad spectrum of disciplines. Traditionally landscape architecture is based on a working knowledge of geology, soils, horticulture, design theory, graphic communication, site and structural engineering and resource planning. In addition, an appreciation for landscape architecture design and environmental planning history, ecology, government and public policymaking, business management and contract law, and computer applications are emphasized in accredited landscape architecture programs.

Stewardship and resource conservation challenge landscape architects to strike a balance between human demand and sustainability of the natural resource base. Landscape architecture professionals—many times in collaboration with other design professionals—often have to make controversial and complex decisions and trade-offs. For example, in the design and maintenance of a landscape that meets client demands, the landscape architect might offer a choice between a highly manicured design that requires the application of herbicides and a design that is more hand labor intensive in some areas and less manicured in other areas of the site. Landscape architects could develop a community plan that recreates a more prototypical mainstreet design to enhance the sense of place. Alternatives, at varying degrees of cost and benefit, help Main Street merchants find the one best solution. Landscape architects might find success in status quo solutions, but sensitive, ethical choices often place professionals in conflict between their own personal sense of stewardship and current market standards or public opinion.

Nevertheless, landscape architecture today, perhaps more than ever before, is reaching out to all sectors of society—the rich and the poor and the middle-class—under the mandates of stewardship and resource conservation. The definition of landscape architecture has evolved for almost a hundred years from the fine art of landscape gardening into a profession that is rooted in site and structural engineering and environmental design, incorporating resource conservation and stewardship, all working together to create an environment on earth that is sustainable, beneficial, and health-giving to all life.

LANDSCAPE ARCHITECTURE: PRIVATE AND PUBLIC SECTORS

As in other professions, job opportunities in landscape architecture can be found in both the public and private sectors. Each sector offers a range of work options as they relate to the design and planning of the built environment. The private sector provides opportunities in the world of business, while the public sector offers positions in agencies and institutions supported by society at large.

The Private Sector

The landscape architecture design and planning office is the traditional private sector business organization that focuses on the planning and design of quality exterior spaces. A design and planning firm works on projects at varying scales, such as single-family residences, small courtyards, recreational and sports facilities, campus design and planning, urban plazas, park design, watershed conservation, etc.

The services these types of firms offer include data inventory and analysis, recommendations and technical reporting, site design and planning, graphic communication, construction documentation, and post-construction evaluation. A design and planning firm can house under one roof several professionals so that interaction between project phases can move effectively with a minimum requirement for outside consultation. Team professionals might include a landscape architect, architect, environmental planner, engineer, horticulturalist, ecologist, graphic designer, interior designer, accountant and clerical support staff (Booth, 1991).

Sasaki Associates, Inc., is an internationally known design and planning firm which offers services in landscape architecture, planning, urban design, civil engineering and architecture. Its main office is located in Watertown, Massachusetts with branch offices around the nation. The firm is well known for its comprehensive approach to a project and for its outstanding contributions to the design and planning of the built environment. The scope of Sasaki projects include campus planning; community, resort and recreational development; urban design and planning; office, commercial, industrial and institutional planning; etc. This range of project types is demonstrated in Greenacre Park, Constitution Plaza and the Purdue University Open Space Plan.

Greenacre Park is a "vestpocket" park located in mid-Manhattan, New York. It is an example of a small urban park, measuring 60 feet along the street and 120 feet deep, roughly the size of a tennis court. Major park features include a water wall, an arbor, informal seating and shade trees. The park creates a quiet place for visitors to relax and get away from the noise and quick pace of the city.

Charleston's Waterfront Park, located in South Carolina, is an example of a larger-scale park development. Opened in May 1990, the $13.5 million park

6. A delightful urban park, the waterfall masks the sound of urban traffic and the landscape space provides an enjoyable and peaceful retreat from the dynamic urban environment. Greenacre Park, New York. (*Sasaki Associates, Inc.*).

7. Waterfront park & fountain, Charleston, South Carolina (*Sasaki Associates, D. Soliday*).

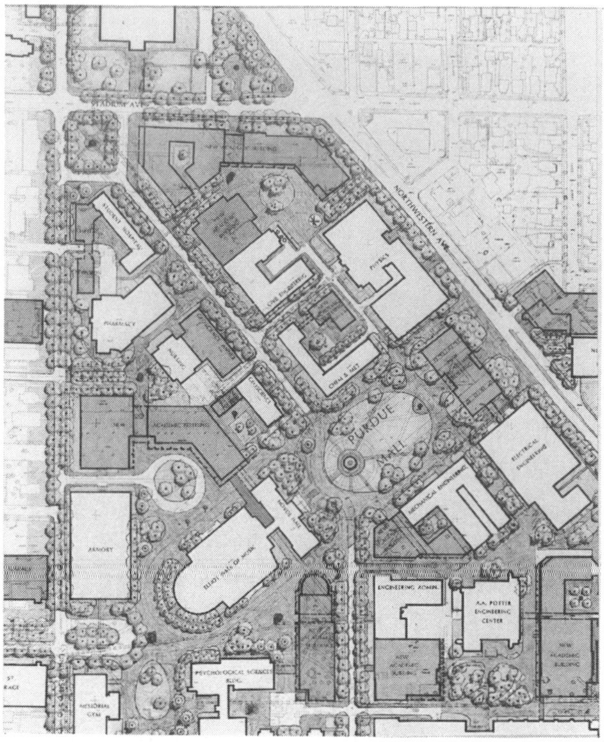

8. The Comprehensive Campus Plan, Purdue University (Sasaki Associates).

extends 800 feet along a waterfront promenade, including a series of outdoor rooms that are linked together by design themes that evoke Charleston's historic past.

The Purdue Open Space Campus Plan demonstrates campus planning and design. This comprehensive plan was developed to build upon Walter Scholer's original 1924 drawings, thus preserving a sense of place and heritage. The new plan calls for park-like settings and eliminates almost all vehicular traffic, providing outdoor rooms for pedestrians and safe circulation for bicycles and handicapped access.

Another private sector landscape architectural business that has become more frequent today is the design-build firm. The design-build firm combines traditional design and planning functions with construction and maintenance to offer the client a full-service organization. Design-build became popular during the late 1970s, when a recession slowed housing starts, causing a lag in the construction industry. At this time, many traditional design and planning firms decided to increase the scope of their services and combined design, planning, contracting and maintenance under one roof. While the singular control of this type of organization opened opportunities, it also challenged the company to orchestrate and integrate additional businesses with which they were often unfamiliar. In general, a design-build firm is composed of divisions in landscape architecture, construction, maintenance, nursery, management, accounting, purchasing and clerical support staff (Hasegawa, 1982).

One of the fastest growing design-build firms in the Northwest is a company called Earth Enterprises, based in Seattle with branch offices in Alaska and California. Over 50 people with degrees in landscape architecture, horticulture, nursery management, construction management, etc., comprise the staff. They offer comprehensive landscape and horticultural services ranging from planning and landscape architecture through construction, irrigation design and implementation, flower programs, interior landscaping and long-term maintenance.

The Koll North Creek Project, developed by Earth Enterprises, demonstrates the range of projects a design-build firm is capable of achieving. The Koll

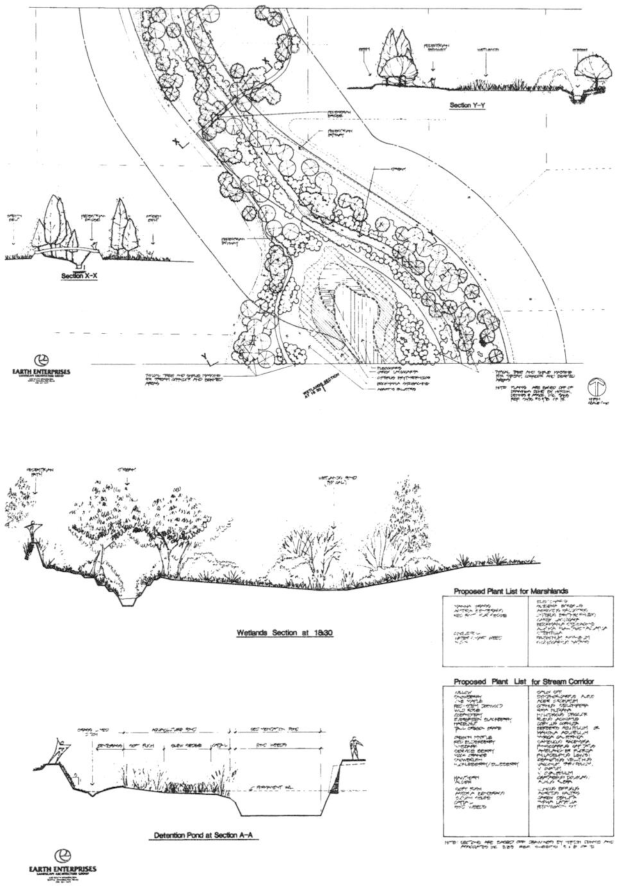

9&10. Landscape design with natural systems, Koll North Creek Project, Bethel, Washington (*Earth Enterprises, M. Davies*).

North Creek Project is a 140-acre industrial park located on an old farm. Site development includes three prominent landscape zones—the streetscape zone, the interior zone, and the 28-acre greenbelt zone. North Creek, which bisects the site, was restored from a farming irrigation ditch into a successful salmon spawning run surrounded by the park-like setting of the greenbelt. Recreational and educational facilities for company employees and nearby towns were also sited in the greenbelt.

Green industry offers other job opportunities for landscape architects in the private sector. Work can be found in retail and wholesale nursery businesses, grounds maintenance and landscape contracting. Landscape architects attracted to these aspects of green industry normally have a greater inclination towards horticulture, construction and mechanics. The nursery trade, grounds maintenance, and landscape contracting can provide viable vocations with national and international marketing potential. Young landscape architects with entrepreneurial inclinations often create their own nursery, maintenance and/or contracting companies shortly after receiving their degrees. As professional experience and reputation matures, some individuals develop their own design-build or traditional design and planning firms and expand their markets.

The Public Sector

Landscape architects in the public sector have typically found work in local, state or federal park and recreational planning offices; natural, community or environmental resource planning agencies; and housing, transportation or engineering departments. While work in the public sector requires a background in traditional design and planning skills, a great part of the daily routine is focused on report preparation, policy decision-making, public meeting organization, public communication and the review of private contract documents prepared for public projects. Therefore, good writing and communication skills are usually required.

In the United States, the National Park Service (NPS), the United States Forest Service (USFS), the Bureau of Land Management (BLM), the Soil Conservation Service (SCS) and the Army Corps of Engineers are some of the federal bureaucracies to commonly employ landscape architects. NPS and state parks departments have at times been the largest employers of landscape architects. When national and state parks were first established in the United States in the early part of the twentieth century, a high demand was created for landscape professionals who could develop and implement plans for recreational facilities and site layouts. These public servants practice their design and planning skills in the preparation of environmentally sensitive plans that function efficiently while protecting and conserving natural and cultural resources.

Being close to urban centers, state parks generally have a higher day use than National Parks, so often include more purely recreational elements, and require more frequent maintenance and upgrading of facilities and grounds. Spring Mill State Park, in the Indiana State Parks system, provides an example of an early state park (established in 1927) on 1,319 acres of land near the Hoosier National Forest in the southern part of the state. This park includes over four miles of heavily used hiking and riding trails with popular facilities for camping, fishing, swimming, boating, horseback riding and educational displays. A reconstructed pioneer village, a grist mill, and an early style sawmill have been built in the park, increasing its popularity—and its maintenance requirements.

A long tradition of park and recreation design and planning exists at the county and city levels too. Most counties and incorporated towns and cities have parks departments which centralize a wide variety of tasks, ranging from facility design and implementation to grounds maintenance and street tree planning. Landscape architects on a parks department staff become involved in many community activities such as the development of community recreational programs; the design, layout and construction of recreational facilities; the creation of a street tree program; the management and development of open space systems and greenbelts; etc. Educational programs for developing proper youth behavior in the parks; promotion of cultural events and fundraisers; user preference surveys and reports are also tasks that landscape architects in a parks department might encounter.

County and/or city planning departments are other municipal units which frequently hire landscape architects. In a planning department, a landscape architect can become involved in a variety of projects that focus on housing, community, and environmental subjects. Members of a planning staff develop and use a site plan review to process development projects. They develop and update community or county-wide comprehensive plans, codes and ordinances, and they sometimes act as enforcement agents to ensure that growth and development stay within the boundaries set by policy. In addition, planners prepare grant proposals to locate additional funds for community-wide programming and development. The educational training required by planning departments emphasizes a knowledge of government organization and procedure, a basic understanding of legal recourse, and good written and oral communication skills.

Another aspect of public sector work for landscape architects can be found in teaching and research at community colleges and universities. Teaching at the community college level usually requires a bachelor's degree from an accredited program, while teaching and research at the university level requires a master's degree with at least one degree in landscape architecture. Some university positions today may also require a Ph.D. in a related field. The master's degree is still considered the terminal degree in landscape architecture, since very few programs offer a Ph.D.

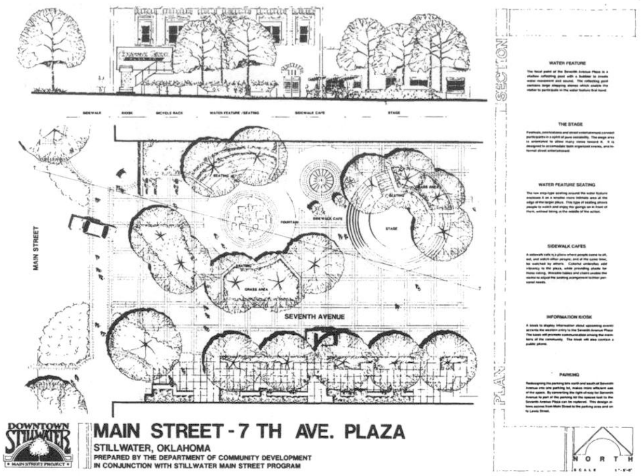

11. Landscape architects often hold public offices in municipal, state and national departments that design, plan and manage the land. *The Downtown Area Plan 2010* for Stillwater, Oklahoma was worked on by several individuals with landscape architectural backgrounds. Main Street—7th Avenue Plaza *Downtown Area Plan 2010*, Stillwater, Oklahoma (*Stillwater Community Development Department and the Downtown Stillwater Main Street Organization*).

Many community colleges offer an associate degree with a landscape component that focuses on horticulture, landscape contracting and landscape design. While community college programs are not accredited by ASLA, they do offer the landscape architect who aspires to teaching an opportunity to contribute to the growth and development of a young professional.

University teaching also requires research and/or creative achievement. University professors are usually specialists in particular facets of landscape architecture, such as construction, design, planning, computer applications, ecology, etc., to build up a strong, balanced faculty team. Besides the specialty, an ability to teach basic design and planning principles and skills is expected. Grant writing, professional development via creative achievement, and/or critically reviewed research and publication are aspects of the work pursued by landscape architects in university positions.

EDUCATIONAL OPPORTUNITIES AND CHALLENGES

As discussed in the previous chapter, most early landscape architecture programs were associated with colleges of agriculture and science in the land grant tradition. Land grant colleges were established in rural areas by an act of Congress to offer higher education opportunities in the agricultural sciences and engineering. In these colleges, landscape gardening was often a component of a horticulture program, emphasizing design, construction, and plant materials.

In 1925, ASLA promoted a change in educational programming for the profession, shifting away from colleges of agriculture and science into colleges of art and architecture. This transition followed the evolving definition of landscape architecture. Landscape programs in art and architecture were focused on design, graphics, architecture and planning with some training in horticulture and the physical sciences. This shift away from science into art and design is still found in many landscape architecture programs today. However, while most programs are located in colleges of art and architecture, educators and administrators in the field work hard to bridge the gap between the sciences and the arts.

Forty-seven programs in landscape architecture in the United States and Canada are accredited. Most of these programs offer degrees at both the undergraduate and graduate levels. The degrees that can be achieved vary according to each program's curricula. Some programs, for example, offer a Bachelor of Science in Landscape Architecture (BSLA) while others offer a Bachelor of Landscape Architecture (BLA). Generally, a BSLA program emphasizes the science and engineering aspects of the profession, while a BLA emphasizes the art, design and planning components. Some undergraduate programs are five years and others are four.

Graduate level programs emphasize research and research methodologies with additional training in an area of concentration, requiring a thesis in order to graduate. There are two- and three-year graduate programs, also called first and second professional degrees. A graduate program can be completed in two years as a second professional degree if the student already has an undergraduate degree in landscape architecture. The three-year graduate program, or first professional degree program, is for students who have an undergraduate degree in a related field, but need to gain basic landscape architectural knowledge and skills.

NEW CHALLENGES IN THE FUTURE

Landscape architects continue to be challenged in their traditional role as stewards and resource managers. Their skills in design, planning and management will always be in demand. But, landscape architecture is a dynamic profession that is changing and expanding to meet the challenges of the twenty-first century. As landscape architects assume more decision-making responsibilities, new opportunities develop. The scope of their professional development is expanding into computer applications, energy conservation, ecology, human resource management and utilization, and public administration and policy formation.

Computers have opened up many avenues of exploration and expression for the design and planning professional. Students now have to be computer literate to be marketable. Traditional design and planning skills are enhanced by computer applications such as computer-aided design and geographic information systems. Other computer applications, such as word processing for business letter and specification writing, and spread sheets for accounting, material list formation, cost estimation and bidding are commonly used and taught (Hsu, 1985).

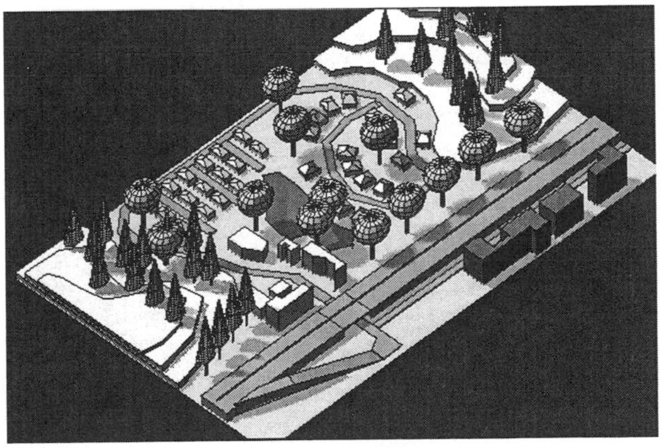

12. Instead of confining clients or critics to an examination of 2D plan drawings, 3D spatial modelling and animation allows users to control a presentation, creating a path through and around its various segments in a virtual reality. Students learn the use of computer 3D modelling and animation as part of their landscape architectural training (*S. Eccelston*).

Energy conservation confronts the profession in numerous design and planning issues. Conservation concerns focus on the shift to alternative energy sources such as solar, wind, or water power, on earth-sheltering and on site planning to mitigate negative energy impacts. Also, open pit and surface mining land reclamation projects offer landscape architects opportunities to demonstrate their expertise in grading sites to recapture their health, beauty and usefulness (Law, 1981).

Ecology, or the study of the complex relationships between an organism and its environment, is becoming a part of the working knowledge of the landscape architect. Issues such as preservation of the habitat of an endangered species are often addressed in land planning and design projects. An understanding of and appreciation for natural, sustainable systems is also fast becoming a part of the landscape architect's working knowledge.

Increased growth of populations with different ethnic and economic backgrounds and increased sensitivity to those with special physical needs mandate a concern for appropriate responses and responsible design and planning in the built environment. The animation and orchestration of the built environment takes on a rainbow hue. New housing will become more densely constructed as land values increase, focusing the need to incorporate sensitive behavioral aspects into open space planning and design.

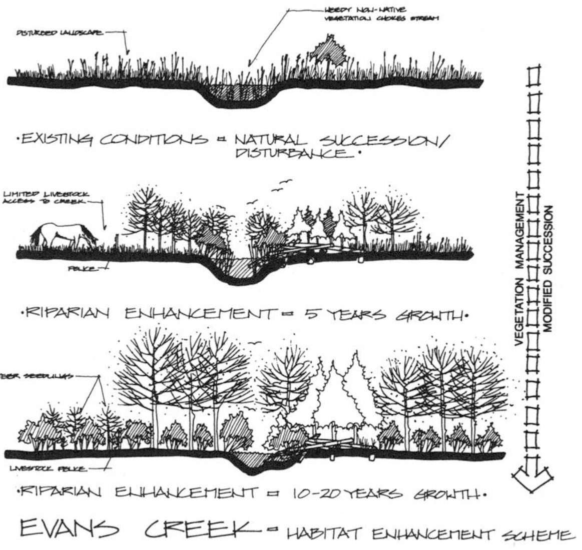

13. This landscape ecological scheme for the enhancement of a riparian habitat is achieved through the planning and design of a stream corridor, analyzing which negative impacts have occurred, and guarding against future like impacts by establishing a management plan that includes vegetation growth succession. Vegetation Management and Modified Succession, Evans Creek Habitat Enhancement Scheme (*Lee & Associates*).

Outdated land use policies, zoning ordinances and other codes need analysis and alteration to be more sensitive toward shifting social, environmental, and economic constraints. Public administration requiring good communication skills, the ability to manage public funds, an understanding of government structure and knowledge of the legal aspects of environmental planning and design will challenge the landscape architect who chooses a public life in the political arena. Landscape architects bring to these public positions a capacity for understanding and compassion that emerges from and is built on the profession's philosophy of stewardship and resource conservation.

Many landscape architects today have already found their niche outside the traditional public or private sectors in areas like mortgage banking, real estate development, computer science, public administration, environmental law and ecological science. As problem solvers and stewards of the land, landscape architects are equipped to work on many of the urgent social and environmental issues that face the world. As the earth and its people enter the twenty-first century, the landscape architect will be there to help shape the future forces of global interaction and help provide leadership toward a more healthy, peaceful, and sustainable world on which to live.

REFERENCES

Booth, N. K. 1991. *Residential Landscape Architecture: Design Process for the Private Residence*. Prentice Hall.

Hardesty Associates. 1984. *Oak Woodland Preservation and Land Planning: Portola Valley Ranch*. Hardesty Associates.

Hasegawa, S., and Eliott, S. 1982. "Design/Build: The Full-Service Option," *Landscape Architecture*, November.

Hsu, P. and Hsu, B. B. 1985. "Microcomputer Education in Landscape Architecture Design/Build Practice," *NACTA Journal*, March.

Law, D., and Linscott, L. 1981. "Ongoing Reclamation: A Procedure for Oil and Gas Fields," *Landscape Architecture*, July.

Lyle, J. T. 1985. *Design For Human Ecosystems: Landscape, Land Use, and Natural Resources*. Van Nostrand Reinhold.

Marshall, L. L. 1979. "A Profession Transformed . . . An Exciting Future for Landscape Architecture," *Landscape Architecture*, February.

Marshall, L. L. 1981. *Landscape Architecture into the 21st Century*. American Society of Landscape Architects.

Molnar, D. J. 1986. *Anatomy of a Park: Essentials of Recreation Area Planning and Design*. McGraw-Hill.

Nash, R. 1973. *Wilderness and the American Mind*. Yale University Press.

Olmsted, F. L., Jr. and Kimball, T., Eds. 1973. *Forty Years of Landscape Architecture: Central Park*. MIT Press.

Solomon, B. S. 1988. *Green Architecture and the Agrarian Garden*. Rizzoli.

Toffler, A. 1981. *The Third Wave*. Bantam Books.

CHAPTER

19

Landscape Architecture: Process and Palette

Kenneth R. Brooks

Careful planning and design of the landscape provides for a more useful and pleasant context for human activities. It improves the natural and built environments and it enhances the human safety, health and enjoyment of that environment. Land planning and design is a conscientious process, done by landscape architects and other environmental designers, to apply and integrate a wide range of science, art and technology to improve the built environment.

GOALS OF LANDSCAPE ARCHITECTURE

The principle goal of landscape architecture is to provide the knowledge, inspiration and experience necessary to bring peoples' interests and aspirations for the use of land together with the opportunities and limitations of the natural environment. When it is done well, this process creates a modified, built environment in which people can live, work and play in a manner that creates the greatest amount of enjoyment, safety and value with the least amount of damage or pollution. Planners and designers try to increase the benefit-to-cost ratio of human-environmental relationships. The level of fitness between environment and human activities is increased when landscape architects are able to provide a design that creates more utility, enjoyment and/or safety in the use of land and decreases the cost of development and environmental damage. As suggested in the definition of Landscape Architecture (see Fig. 1), landscape planners and designers do a variety of planning and design activities in their effort to improve the use of land and management of environmental resources. By law, licensed landscape architects are required to make sure that their designs protect the health, safety and welfare of the public.

Human activities in the landscape (such as housing and neighborhood developments, commercial and shopping areas, recreation, etc.) are usually referred to as land uses. Landscape architects apply their talents in designing these land use activities at a very wide range of scales from projects as small as a sitting area at a bus stop to as large as huge resort developments or whole new cities or regional plans.

"Landscape Architecture is the profession which applies artistic and scientific principles to the research, planning, design and management of both natural and built environments. Practitioners of this profession apply creative and technical skills and scientific, cultural and political knowledge in the planned arrangement of natural and constructed elements on the land with a concern for the stewardship and conservation of natural, constructed and human resources. The resulting environments shall serve useful, aesthetic, safe and enjoyable purposes . . ."

American Society of Landscape Architects
1983

1. Definition of landscape architecture.

THE LAND DESIGN PROCESS

Landscape architects use many methods to plan and design projects. Their efforts are usually referred to as The **Design Process**. This suggests only a single method or process, while in reality, many varieties and types of approaches to the processes of landscape planning and design can be identified. These are usually broken up into several tasks that consider various issues of the project at hand. In spite of the variation in landscape architecture methods, most share several similar characteristics. They are organized to be thorough, systematic, and sensitive to human and environmental issues, characteristics they also share with the other design disciplines. Figure 2 illustrates a general approach in the decision-making process for landscape planning and design projects.

Thoroughness is demonstrated when landscape architects carefully consider all of the possible environmental, cultural, functional, economic and aesthetic factors that might influence the success of a project or its impact on the environment. Such evaluation of all the potential factors is often referred to as a comprehensive, ecological approach to planning and design.

Systematic Approaches in the Design Process

The systematic characteristics of landscape planning and design can be seen in the way that landscape architects evaluate various human and environmental factors by breaking down broad areas of consideration into component parts. Hierarchy theory is often a useful tool in organizing these factors. An example of the orderly way in which the landscape architect considers the whole and its parts is illustrated by the broad area of ecology. An ecological model of a project is created, then broken down into parts—into processes and elements. Ecological processes are further broken down into subparts such as nutrient cycles and energy cycles while ecological elements are subdivided into such subparts as geology, physiography, soils, hydrology, vegetation and animals. Landscape architects often use checklists to make sure that they have systematically considered all of the major components, all the human activities and interests along with the environmental options and constraints that relate to the project at hand. Environmental designers generally analyze these broad human-environmental issues, their subcomponents and the relationships, then synthesize them together to arrive at the best alternatives for the design or plan. This holistic analysis-synthesis process is becoming more common in all design and planning fields.

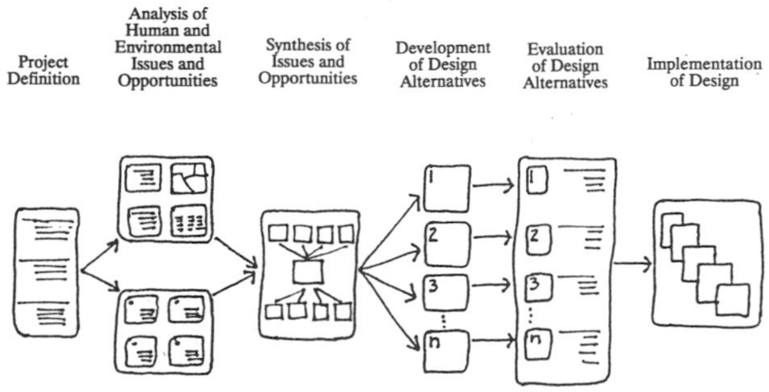

2. Diagram of the design process.

Considering Human Needs and Interests in Land Design

The planning process ideally focuses sensitivity on human uses of and aspirations for the land. This part of the design process seeks to answer questions about client(s), user(s), and the way in which they will use the land. The following are a set of typical questions and issues considered as part of the human aspects of land design.

- Who are the people who will be using this land?
- What are their needs and desires?
- How will they use the land (are there primary and secondary uses)?
- What are the characteristics of the spaces that will be planned to meet the needs of the users (size, function, nature of activities, safety, etc.)?
- What is the relationship of the various land uses or activities within the project to each other?
- Are there related utility or support uses that will enhance the project?
- What will need to be done to celebrate the special aesthetic qualities of the project?
- How will the land use activities within the project be affected by off-site influences and in turn affect off-site areas?
- What are the potential environmental impacts?

This kind of detailed and systematic analysis of user and client needs and desires is often referred to by environmental designers as project programming. In this part of the process, the designer considers all of the possible factors about the projected use of land and probable users and develops recommendations for the best way to organize and accommodate users' interests and human needs.

Environmental Considerations in Land Design

Landscape architects trained ecologically are advocates of environmental quality. As part of the land design process, they evaluate the landscape to determine its suitability for the proposed land use(s) and to assess the potential of the proposed use(s) to cause damage to ecosystems—either on the site or effects which could cause environmental problems somewhere else.

On relatively small projects, most landscape architects conduct what is called a **site analysis**, a study of the environmental conditions of the site, their suitability for the project and potential environmental damage by the project. For larger projects, the landscape architect may conduct an extensive and intensive study of environmental conditions and the suitability and potential impacts of the proposed project on local ecosystems. Large studies may be divided up into several components: an environmental analysis that evaluates existing environmental conditions; a suitability analysis that evaluates the suitability of the site to accommodate the various land uses that are or may be part of the project, or an Environmental Impact Statement that evaluates the potential of a project to cause degradation or pollution of local ecosystems as well as propose means to mediate these environmental impacts. Some of the concerns studied in this type of analysis include:

- What is the ecological structure of this land and what kinds of ecological processes naturally occur within it?
- What are the natural conditions of the land and its features (such as geology, slope, topography, soils, vegetation, animals and climate) and how might these conditions limit the development of the proposed design project?
- What special environmental conditions of the land would be especially suitable for the proposed project? What is the carrying capacity of the ecosystem—what intensities of human use can it absorb without a major disruption to the system?
- How would the development of the proposed project impact the land's present ecosystem? Are there factors or sensitive conditions that could upset the system if they occurred?
- How will development of this project impact other ecosystems on adjoining land?
- Will the development of this project create irreversible changes in the landscape or significant loss of nonrenewable resources?

Design Synthesis: A Search for Fitness

Landscape architects use holistic and comprehensive evaluations of the land, the users and the probable project to prepare a variety of schematic alternative solutions that explore a range of the ways in which the project program and the land could be brought together to accommodate the needs and interests of future users. Designer(s) and client(s) must both evaluate the suitability and potential impacts of the alternatives and then select a design option that will lead to the best fitness of user interests and environmental conditions. The strategy is to adapt both the program (human aspects) and the environment to each other in a manner that provides the greatest user utility, enjoyment and safety with the greatest amount of environmental quality and sustainability.

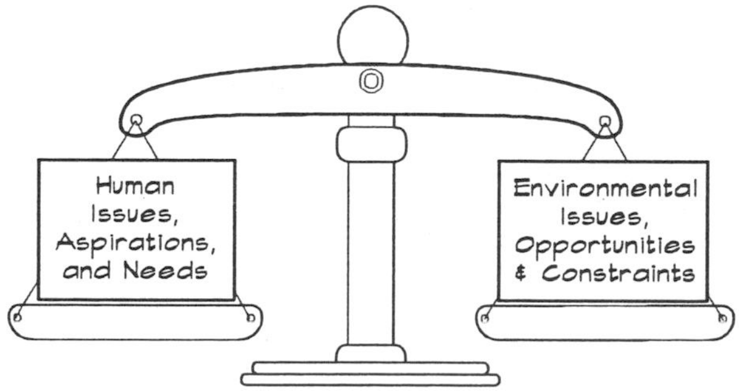

3. The goal of land planning and design is to integrate human interests and land conditions in balance and to create healthy and fit human-environmentland uses.

THE DESIGN PALETTE: THE PRODUCT/MATERIAL COMPONENTS OF LANDSCAPE DESIGN

In the planning and design of the built landscape, the beauty and utility of a site may come as much or more from the selection of materials as from the way they are arranged. Just as fine artists may use clay or ink to create their works, landscape architects have a large palette of materials available for use in design of the landscape.

Other chapters in this book show the built environment to be made up of a large number of component levels (products, interiors, landscapes, structures, cities, regions and earth) that come together to form human-environmental settings. The dynamic relationships between context and content have been used as a means of integrating these various levels. A similar application of this context/content method can be used to describe the design of the built landscape. The landscape is usually perceived as an area where a variety of activities may occur or where one or more structures may be built. To understand the way a landscape is designed, one must take the whole and analyze it as a set of component parts.

The first subdivision partitions the total landscape into individual spaces, much like a whole building is defined by its various rooms and interior spaces. While individual spaces are the components that come together within the context of its total built landscape, each space can be seen simultaneously as the context for its parts. Again, we can use the analogy of the building—each interior space (room) is defined by the structural elements that form it, including walls, floors, ceiling and/or other space dividers. In the exterior space, the "walls, floor and ceiling" are created with hills, masses of plants, walls, paving, lawns and other installments. The interior space is not only formed and defined, but is furnished and decorated with equipment to meet the functional and aesthetic intent of the designer. Exterior spaces can also be furnished and decorated to enhance interest and beauty. Landscape furnishings (called street furniture) may include benches, trash containers, signs, lighting and other equipment. Decorative components are elements that don't materially affect the use or structure of a space, but that can add interest and enhance the character of the space. These elements can be created in a wide variety of ways—such as special patterns in the paving, decorative ironwork or colorful plantings. Structural, furnishing and decorative elements can be further analyzed by examining the materials from which they are formed. As indicated in Figure 4, materials are put together to make up elements, the elements are combined to form spaces and the spaces are organized to make the total built landscape.

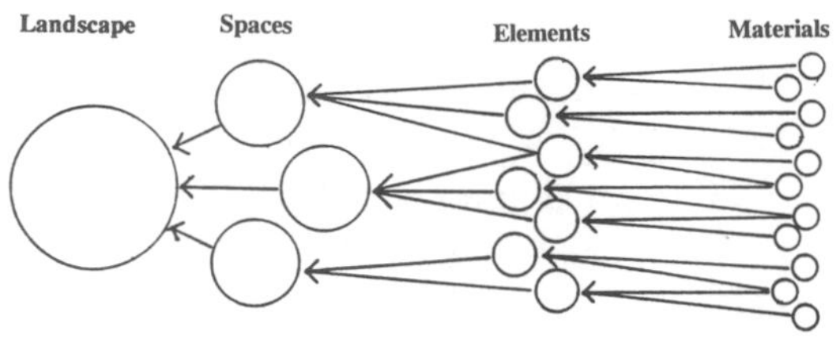

TOTAL BUILT LANDSCAPE (A CITY PARK)

Spaces that Make up the Park	**Elements** that make up the spaces	**Materials** that make up the elements
entry	sign, plant massings, lighting	carved wood, cut stone plants
parking	paving, plant massings, signs, lighting	concrete, plants, wood, metal
ball fields	structure, fences, furniture, plantings	concrete, metals, plants
rose garden	plantings, benches, fountain	plants, stepping stones, water
picnic area	benches, plant massings, trash receptacles, drinking fountain	wood, concrete, plants
tot lot	play equipment, benches, plant massings	wood, steel, sand, plants

4. Diagram and examples of materials, elements, and spaces forming a landscape.

5. A variety of materials (concrete, plants, water, and stone) are used to create elements (paving, seating, fountains, bollards, planting). The elements are combined to make spaces within a plaza (*R. Forsyth*).

Materials of the Built Landscape

To be able to design with the large variety of materials available, landscape architects must know and understand the inherent characteristics and properties of those materials and how they relate to each other. The materials that make up the landscape architect's palette are both natural and built. They include such things as earth (soil), rock, plants, wood, masonry, water, concrete, asphalt and metals. These materials have a variety of properties that determine their utility, beauty and character in the landscape. To understand the design potential of various materials, it is useful to explore the characteristics of building materials as shown in the table.

Landscape architects must consider a large variety of visual (aesthetic), physical and functional properties when selecting materials for the built landscape. The character and setting created within the landscape will strongly reflect the properties of materials that make up that landscape. The fitness, quality and character of the landscape will be significantly influenced by the characteristics of the materials that are used in the design. Designing a landscape with a large proportion of processed, modular, hard or massive materials will give the resulting space a feeling of strong human control, commonly referred to as a "hardscape." By contrast, if the designer creates a space or landscape dominated by natural, irregular and/or soft materials, it will have a feeling of being a more naturally occurring landscape (a "softscape").

Uses of Plant Materials in the Landscape

Many people think of the landscape as made up of primarily plant materials, without thinking of

OUTLINE OF CHARACTERISTICS OF LANDSCAPE MATERIALS

Characteristics	Examples
1. Physical Characteristics	
a. Origin	
• Natural	• plants, drift wood, rough timbers, native stone, flowing water or ponds or lakes
• Processed	• brick, tile, dimensioned lumber, cut stone, processed metals, water in fountains
b. Form (shape)	
• Modular or Regular	• brick, dimensioned lumber, sheared hedges
• Plastic or Irregular	• untrimmed plants, poured concrete, undulating landforms
c. Firmness (rigidity)	
• Hard	• paving, fencing, architectural structures
• Soft	• planting, flowing or languid water, fabric (banners, flags)
2. Visual Characteristics	
a. Color	
• Warm vs. cool colors	• red, yellow & orange colors vs. blue, green & lavender colors
• Bright vs. subdued colors	• bright floral displays & painted surfaces vs. weathered or earth-toned surfaces
b. Texture	
• Coarse vs. fine textures	• large-leaved oaks vs. honeylocusts with very small leaflets
c. Size	
• Large vs. small size	• big oak tree vs. small dogwood tree
d. Mass	
• Heavy vs. light mass	• solid block of granite for a bench vs. light wood for a bench
3. Functional Characteristics	
a. Utility	• material for a specific use, such as concrete used for paving
b. Economic	• high cost granite pavers vs. lower cost asphalt paving
c. Dynamic vs. static	• static materials like stone vs. changing materials like plants

6. A pastoral setting is created with generous use of plant materials. An irregular stone path adds to the casual nature of the space. Even the deliberate use of light and shadow adds to the mystery and interest of the space (*R. Forsyth*).

7. Hard materials are used to create paving and sitting walls. Earth berms and plant materials soften and help subdivide the plaza (*R. Forsyth*).

8. Color in the paving pattern organizes the spaces in this plaza. Firmness and durability create a surface that can suport intensive pedestrian activity. Plant materials help define subspaces within the plaza (*R. Forsyth*).

the many other materials discussed in this chapter. Plants are not the only material, but they are a very important and useful material for landscape development. Trees, shrubs and flowers not only contribute oxygen to the atmosphere (a most basic human need) but also add beauty and make functional contributions to the fitness of the landscape. Designers often think of the uses and values of plant materials in five general ways: (1) architectural uses of plants, (2) engineering uses of plants, (3) plants for climate modification, (4) aesthetic uses of plants, and (5) other uses of landscape plant materials (Robinette 1972). **Architectural uses** of plant materials means arranging plants for the purpose of creating spaces in the landscape. The **engineering** category are those uses where the plants serve to solve technical environmental engineering situations in the landscape. The **climate modification** category is the use of plants to change climatic conditions within the landscape. **Aesthetic** uses of plants are intended to appeal to visual, fragrance and intellectual senses. The fifth category—other uses—refers to additional uses that do not fit easily into one of the other categories. Examples of uses of plants in the designed landscape are outlined in the table.

Elements of the Built Landscape

In applying the context/content model of integrating levels in the built environment, the

EXAMPLES OF PLANT MATERIAL USES IN THE DESIGNED LANDSCAPE

Architectural Uses of Plants

- defining spaces with "walls," "floors," & "ceilings" created by plants
- controlling views, enframing vistas
- creating screening for privacy or to eliminate an undesirable view
- marking the location of an entry or a pathway
- groupings to create linkages or connections between other elements

Environmental Engineering Uses of Plants

- reducing glare and screening unwanted light
- controlling and/or directing traffic
- reducing soil erosion and protecting the soil surface
- intercepting rainfall, slowing runoff and directing drainage
- reducing wind flow
- absorbing and reducing noise
- absorbing and reducing air pollution

Climatological Modification Uses of Plants

- temperature modification by the cooling action of plants
- modification of the relative humidity through evapo-transpiration
- retaining daytime heat from nighttime loss within tree canopy
- channeling air movement for ventilation
- trapping static air around buildings with plants for insulation

Aesthetic Uses of Plants

- visual interest through color, form, texture, movement of plants
- attractive and pleasant fragrances
- creating special interest or attention with highly visible plantings
- influencing the "mood" of the landscape through color and texture

Other Uses of Plants

- wildlife habitat
- food values (for humans and wildlife)
- educational values
- recreational values
- historical and social values
- economic goods such as building materials, fuel

materials described in the table can be combined to form various defining elements used in design of the landscape. A rich variety of elements or products can be used to create the "walls," "floors," "ceilings," and "furniture" of landscape spaces. Some examples of these are listed below:

- Landforms
- Plantings
- Paving
- Decks
- Walls and Fences
- Furniture
- Lighting
- Other Structures

The "floor" or ground plane provides the base for human activities. Ground planes can be made from natural and processed materials such as earth, sod, or paving, etc. "Ceilings," often created by architectural coverings, by tree canopies or trellises, form the cover and protection for landscape spaces. "Walls," made from plants, landforms or architectural materials, create the vertical elements that mark the edges of spaces. They enclose and define spaces and subspaces.

Landforms are created by earth (soil and rock). They may be flat, rolling or steep. Land provides the base for structures and for human activities. Flat and gently sloping areas usually provide the "base plane" for spaces in the landscape and serve the same function as a floor in a building. Steeper areas usually are perceived as boundaries for a space or as the transition between spaces.

Plantings are a very visible part of the landscape. In natural landscapes, plants form communities that interact with each other and the environment. In the built environment, plants may be arranged singly, in groups or in naturalized associations. Plants can serve a variety of uses in the built landscape, some of which are described in the last section of this chapter.

Paving is a very useful product in the built landscape. Paving materials are regularly used in places where there will be intense human activity, such as pedestrian or vehicular circulation. They may be designed as linear elements (like walks or roads) just to accommodate traffic or they may cover larger areas (such as malls, plazas, and terraces). Such materials provide not only the structural support necessary for intense activity, but can also be used to define spaces and subspaces within the landscape. Paving can also direct people through the landscape or provide places where they can

9. Elements making up this space include balustrades, fountains, benches, paving, hedges, tree rows and lighting (*R. Forsyth*).

gather. Detailed changes in paving can help people with direction and orientation and can provide additional visual interest.

Decks are very similar to paving in that they provide a base plane for activity. They are often somewhat different from the harder paving materials in that they are usually suspended above the surface and are usually made of wood or other softer material. Although they may be placed out in the middle of a very public space, they are more likely to be an auxiliary space adjoining a building.

Walls and fences have a very powerful effect in the landscape because of their vertical position and their processed nature. Vertical elements are quite visible because they contrast with the dominant horizontal nature of the landscape and with the base plane. Just as walls in a building are the clear definers of interior space, vertical elements in the landscape signal the edge of one space and the start of another. Walls can be transparent like a series of pillars or trees or they can be very solid and opaque. The exterior wall of a building also can serve as a wall for the exterior space adjacent to it. Besides serving as edges of spaces and as screens, some walls, with land-fill behind them, provide a transition in topography.

Furniture, street furniture to landscape architects, serves several functions in the built landscape. Just as it may enhance the utility of the interior space, furniture can be selected and arranged to meet the needs of people using the landscape. Benches, chairs, tables, trash receptacles, water fountains, signs, lights and other furnishings are intended to provide for such needs as sitting, trash disposal, direction and similar functions to improve the comfort, utility and attractiveness of the site for the user. Furniture can be used to separate two spaces or to subdivide areas within one space. Furniture can add interest and can determine the character of the space through expression of the materials used by the style and placement in the landscape.

Space Components of the Landscape

The next level of context/component integration in the built landscape is the combination of the component pieces—landforms, plantings, paving, decks, walls, fences, furniture and others, to form an important component referred to as space. **Space** is the primary product of the landscape architect. Space is the ultimate component of the media of landscape design, because it is in space that buildings are built and where human activities occur. Space is not the void that is left after all of the materials have been installed. It is the positive commodity created by materials. Materials and elements are designed to define space.

Spaces are usually classified (named) by the uses that are contained within them. People think about landscape spaces in terms of the way that they are used and they usually think of these spaces by the intended use before they think of the qualities that make any one space different from other spaces.

10. Trees serve like columns in a wall to define the principle vertical division of space. Other plantings provide spatial separation and enclosure. The tree canopy provides shading from summer sun and the turf also contributes to cooling and humidification (*R. Forsyth*).

11. A slope next to a tennis court becomes a sitting space. It is designed with hard materials as a series of sitting walls and steps. Tree plantings help to provide vertical elements to separate sitting spaces from the tennis court.

12. The Capital Mall in Madison, Wisconsin is a streetscape project that provides a major urban linkage between the University of Wisconsin campus and the state capital grounds. Vehicular and pedestrian circulation, sitting, gathering and display spaces make up the mall.

It is how the spaces are used that give them their value. Uses may be active (such as circulation or recreation) or they can be passive (such as sitting or viewing).

Common spaces found in the built environment (although not all necessarily in the same landscape) include: entries, playfields, playgrounds, malls, courtyards, plazas, sitting areas, patios, circulation systems, gardens and open space. This isn't intended to be an exhaustive list of possible landscape spaces, but rather to suggest some common ones.

The nature of landscape spaces in the built environment can be explored by looking at their inherent properties in much the same manner as was used to compare the properties of landscape materials. Spatial definition is one of the properties of a built landscape space: where are the boundaries of a space? How strong and definite are they? Is the space easy to perceive as a space or is it rather informally delineated? The form or shape of a space makes a big difference in the character and the use of that space. Spaces with more specific edges give better definition to the activities for which they were designed. The more formal or geometric the shape, the greater the affinity with the built environment; the more picturesque and organic, the greater the affinity with nature.

The firmness of a space, like the firmness of building materials, is a measure of how hard or how soft the materials are that define its character. Hardscape spaces are suited for more intense activity while softer materials enhance a feeling of relaxation and casual activity. Some activities

13. Constitution Plaza in Hartford, CN is made up of refined circulation and sitting spaces and subdivided with mounds and plantings in raised planters (*R. Forsyth*).

require a solid base plane while other activities are better suited to a softer, more relaxed environment.

While landscape architects plan spaces to serve a variety of uses, once the project has been built, the characteristics of landscape spaces influence the kinds of activities or uses that occur in the space. Each activity (whether it be walking, driving, sitting, playing with a frisbee, viewing a concert, playing softball, getting a drink, collecting trash, delivering the mail, etc.) has its own needs of size, form and characteristics. Some spaces require such specialized design that other activities cannot be very well accommodated. Other areas can be designed to accommodate a variety of activities. Landscape activities can be classified as active (such as playgrounds or entrance areas for major public buildings), while others are passive (such as sitting areas or patios). The designer will carefully analyze the various user activities and organize or zone the space to separate incompatible activities and to integrate complementary uses. Integration of similar activities may be done by arranging complementary spaces next to or near each other while separating or buffering incompatible activity spaces. A major part of the design process in such cases is involved with analyzing the relationship of one activity space with each of the others in the landscape design.

The character and organization of the space—the way it feels, the way it influences our senses—is a great part of the art and science of landscape architectural design. The landscape architect is interested in creating a space that not only works well (functionally and ecologically), but also stimulates us physically, psychologically and emotionally. Such properties are the special defining characteristics that landscape architects consider while designing and integrating materials into elements, elements into spaces and spaces into total landscapes.

CONCLUSIONS

A wide variety of ways can be found to evaluate the design of landscapes in the built environment. The total landscape can be subdivided into spaces, the spaces into products and the products into materials. It should be clear that the organizational structure of the landscape, its use and function and its character, beauty and personality, result from the careful consideration and combination of materials, products and spaces. The manner in which landscape architects use materials to create elements that define spaces is systematic and comprehensive. A comprehensive ecological process and design palette can harmoniously bring together human needsand aspirations with natural land opportunities to improve the interrelationships between environment and human life.

14. A variety of landscape/spaces/elements/materials enhance the qualities of urban life: Azalea garden in Richmond Park, London, England (*T. Bartuska*).

REFERENCES

Booth, N. K. 1983. *Basic Elements of Landscape Architectural Design*. Elsevier.

Carpenter, P. L., Walker, T. D. and Lanphear, F. O. 1975. *Plants in the Landscape*. W. H. Freeman.

Laurie, M. 1986. *An Introduction to Landscape Architecture*. Elsevier.

Olgyay, V. 1963. *Design with Climate*. Princeton University Press.

Pierceall, G. M. 1990. *Sitescapes: Outdoor Rooms for Outdoor Living*. Prentice Hall.

Robinette, G. D., Compiler. 1972. "Plants/People and Environmental Quality." U.S. National Park Service in collaboration with the American Society of Landscape Architects Foundation.

Simonds, J. O. 1983. *Landscape Architecture: A Manual of Site Planning and Design*. McGraw-Hill.

CHAPTER

20

Visual Resource Management

Ken Struckmeyer

One of our inalienable rights is the right to an aesthetically pleasing environment. Visual resource management (VRM) is a useful concept and procedure for evaluating environmental resources of visual value and should be included in the design and planning process. Visual resources have been identified by the United States Congress as a resource to be managed, much the same as the forest and the soil have traditionally been. The United States Supreme Court has upheld this concept of aesthetic resources, as it relates to the urban as well as the rural landscape. Therefore, the task before the design and planning professions is one of describing a landscape in terms of visual resources and then placing a value on that landscape in terms of whether it should be conserved or altered to either a minimum or maximum amount.

Identification of the landscape as a visual resource requires an inventory which can take either a **descriptive** or **evaluative** format. Examples of both procedures are reviewed in this chapter.

A further question facing the designer and planner is that of ranking the visual resource as of either national or local value. The state of Washington possesses one of the most diverse landscapes in the United States and yet large sections of the state are viewed as lacking visual stimulation because of the sameness of the landscape.

BASIS FOR VISUAL RESOURCE MANAGEMENT

Aesthetics! Is it a word to be ignored, shunned, cursed or appreciated? How do you spell it and what does it mean? What is its relationship to the common and equally undefinable terms of inalienable rights, quality of life, and nature? (Cf., Berleant, 1992).

In January of 1970, the Congress of the United States passed the National Environmental Policy Act (NEPA). The stated objectives of the act were:

a. To declare a national policy which will encourage productive and enjoyable harmony between people and their environment.
b. To promote efforts which will prevent or eliminate damage to the environment and biosphere, and stimulate human health and welfare.
c. To enrich the understanding of the ecological systems and natural resources important to the Nation (NEPA, 1970).

To achieve these objectives, several goals and policies were established. Two of the six goals pertain to visual resources and aesthetics: "assure for all [citizens] safe, healthful, productive and aesthetically and culturally pleasing surroundings"; and, "preserve important historic, cultural, and natural aspects of our national heritage, and maintain wherever possible, an environment which supports diversity and variety of individual choice" (NEPA, 1970).

Perhaps Supreme Court Justice Brennan, writing in the majority opinion of the Grand Central case, stated it best when he wrote: "Historic conservation is but one aspect of the much larger problem, basically an environmental one, of enhancing—or perhaps developing for the first time—the quality of life for people" (Penn Central Transportation Co. vs. City of New York). The

Supreme Court has also ruled that "the concept of the public welfare is broad and inclusive. The values it represents are spiritual as well as physical, esthetic as well as monetary. It is within the power of the legislature to determine that the community should be beautiful as well as healthy" (Brace, 1980).

The terms inalienable rights, health, quality of life, nature and aesthetics have been used complementarily. Defining each of these terms may identify more clearly why we are dealing with the subject of visual management and why it is being said that visual resources are as important as soils or hydrology in land use planning and site design. These are terms important to all design aspects of the built environment.

Aesthetics has been defined by William G. E. Blair (1980) as the "science or philosophy concerned with the quality of sensory experience. Sensory could mean visual, hearing, smell, taste and touch. However, vision is the primary human sensory mode." This definition assumes that management of aesthetics deals primarily with visual stimulations or sensations which are in themselves either beautiful or artful. Because of the visual connotation, the new term **visual resource management** is used.

Quality of life may be defined as a manner of healthy living, where a degree of excellence is obtained due to the absence of monotony or sameness. Perhaps Thomas Jefferson was right when he introduced the phrase "pursuit of happiness." Quality can be measured in terms of job satisfaction, family and friends, recreation opportunities, visual and climatic stimulation as well as health. However, the key phrase may be the lack of monotony or sameness.

Nature is perhaps even more difficult to define. Many people would say something in the following vein; Nature is the quality or qualities "that make something what it is." Generally, this consists of scenery, including the plants and animals that are part of it, while containing no human or artificially created alterations. Many would contend that humans are part of nature and that some of their efforts do constitute a "natural scene." Writers such as Artur Glikson and Nan Fairbrother have discussed the relation of humans to the landscape and both identify modified landscapes as providing a base for the majority of these interactions with "nature." Fairbrother (1974) claims that "woodland, though it appears to be natural, has generally been human influenced, as in the eastern U.S., where most woodland is regrowth after felling of the original forests." She goes on to claim that "nonetheless, the old methods of farming produced beautiful and harmonious landscapes—created, for instance, the English countryside we still cherish and the old New England landscape [we] still look back to with affection."

Health is easily defined as a person's physical or mental well-being. This is usually interpreted as being free from disease as well as having a positive or uncluttered mental attitude. Aesthetics, in terms of quality environments, may contribute to healthy mental outlooks for individuals. This reinforces earlier discussions (see Chapter 5) in which it was suggested that health is achieved by the measure of creative fitness between humans and environment.

All of these concepts and opportunities generally fall under the umbrella of the inalienable rights of an individual. Such rights may be defined as something belonging to a person by law, nature, or tradition, which cannot (or should not) be taken away, though we can lose them through misuse.

United States citizens, and people throughout the world, have at least the right to enjoy a visually stimulating landscape. The question of property rights, in terms of what can be done developmentally on "our land—we own it," is still somewhat unclear, but overall, nothing should be done which could be interpreted as altering a landscape or structure so as to infringe negatively on others' opportunity to enjoy a view or experience the aesthetics of either the natural or the built environment.

How are we to inventory or evaluate a landscape, before alterations or new projects are begun, to ensure that the results are not negative? Two basic approaches are reviewed: the descriptive approach of R. Burton Litton, and the evaluative approach of the U.S. Bureau of Land Management.

DESCRIPTIVE VISUAL RESOURCE INVENTORY

Perhaps the most influential study dealing with visual analysis is R. Burton Litton's *Forest Landscape Description and Inventories: A Basis for Land Planning and Design* (1968). This work is examined more closely because it generally is the basis for the most current concepts and work being done in visual inventory and mapping. These factors are useful in consideration of all the components of the built environment, because they increase sensitivity to aesthetics and quality. This exploration into composition can also be employed by those who enjoy photography, painting and analyzing what is perceived through the senses.

Factors of Scenic Analysis and Observation

Litton (1968) identified two components of the visual resource: "factors of scenic analysis and observation" and "compositional types." Within the factors of scenic analysis, six elements are identified and described: distance, observer position, form, spatial definition, light and sequence. Each of these elements is important in terms of how people see and are influenced by where they are in the landscape.

Distance, or more explicitly "viewer distance," is defined as the space or interval between the seen landscape and the location of the viewer. This element may be manipulated by the person in the landscape or by conscious or accidental decisions made by others. Three distance zones have been identified: foreground, middle ground and background. Litton's observer, traveling in a car, defined the various zones as foreground, 0 to 1/2 mile; middle ground, 1/4 mile to 3 to 5 miles; and background, 3 to 5 miles to infinity (Litton, 1968). If the person moving through the landscape is walking, the distances and the dimensions should be adjusted, probably towards reducing the scales, since the pedestrian is able to discern greater detail in the foreground.

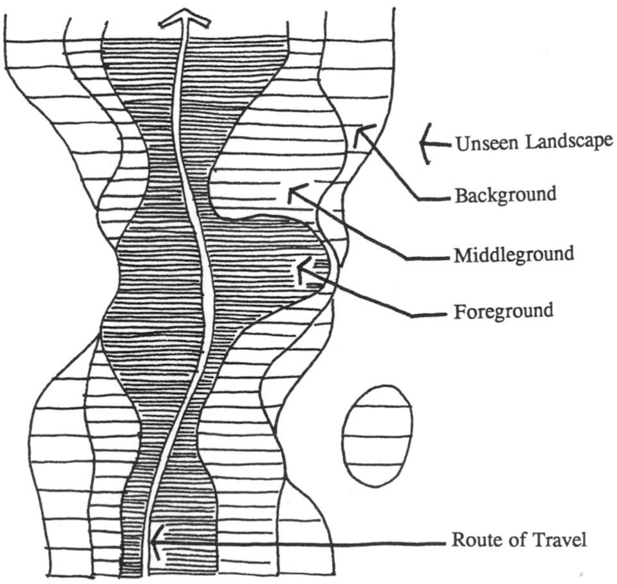

1. Viewer distance.

Observer Position, refers to the position in the landscape which the person is occupying while viewing the landscape. Litton identifies three positions: observer inferior, observer normal and observer superior.

The person in the observer inferior position is basically surrounded by the landscape being viewed, standing in a canyon for example, or looking at or into a grove of trees. The view being limited, more attention may be directed to the nearby landscape or foreground (see Figure 2). In the observer normal position, the viewer is generally on a level plane with the landscape elements being viewed (see Figure 3). The observer superior viewer is generally above the landscape being observed, looking down on it. Observers may be either on a pinnacle with an unobstructed 360-degree view or on a crest with a landscape behind them, while looking out over a 180-degree view.

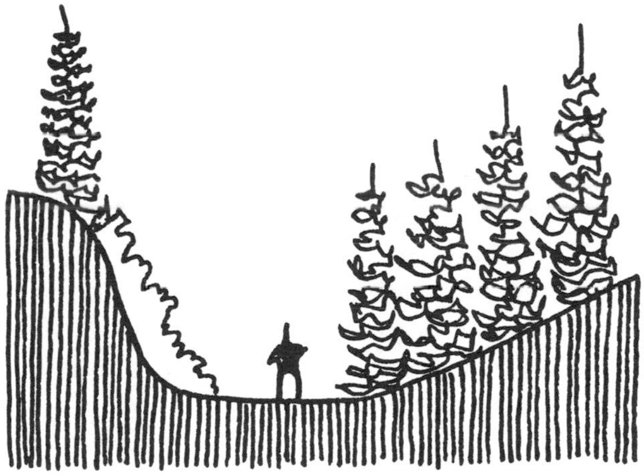

2. Observer inferior: a contained view of a landscape.

3. Observer normal: on a level plane.

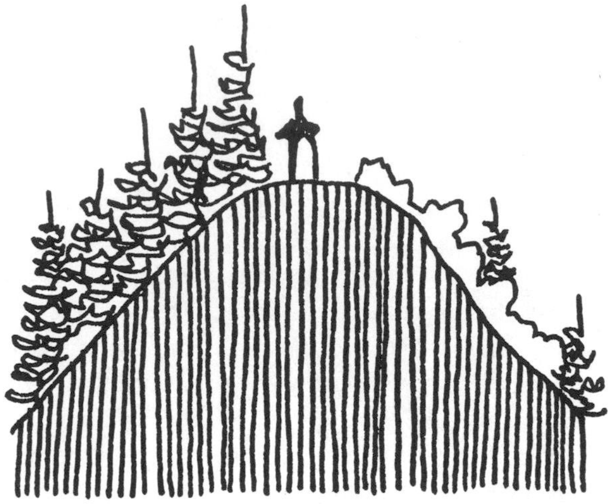

4. Observer superior: elevated with a panoramic view.

5. Form: silhouetted landscape characteristics—shape, size and position.

Form is a very difficult concept to define. Perhaps Robert Gillam Scott, in his book *Design Fundamentals* (1951) defines it best when he says:

> Form refers to the quality of individual thingness that comes out of the contrasts of visual qualities. It is what distinguished each thing and its perceptible parts. It is not a simple idea, but consists in a particular relationship between three factors: shape, size, position.

Litton takes these concepts and interrelates them to the landscape by identifying contour distinction or silhouette and surface variations as primary components of form. Contour distinction or silhouette consists of landscape objects, such as mountains, hillsides, berms, rocks (see Figure 5). Surface variations consist of materials on the earth's surface, particularly variations of plant materials, such as plant species, time of year, type of plant community and type of land management (see Figure 6). Both of these components can be expressed or viewed in terms of shape, size and position.

Spatial Definition refers to "rooms" in the landscape which may be either natural or created. These rooms consist primarily of vertical elements on the base plane or floor and may be created either individually or in combination with depressions in the earth's surface, with plant materials or with water. Litton identified four variations of these components.

1. There is an important correlation between the size of the base and the enclosing vertical material. The designers of the Renaissance identified spaces where, if the vertical is greater than the floor dimension, the space becomes tight and enclosed. When the vertical is less than a quarter higher than the length of the floor, the space becomes less dominant and the person is no longer enclosed. It is important to recognize the difference between a natural and a created space and, in particular, the materials involved. Perhaps the definitions of the Renaissance designers for urban spaces should be altered for natural places.
2. The materials that make up the base and vertical elements influence an individual's response to a place. The materials may possess elements that stimulate all of the senses which would further impact peoples' reaction to a place.

6. Form: surface variation expressing characteristic shape, size and position.

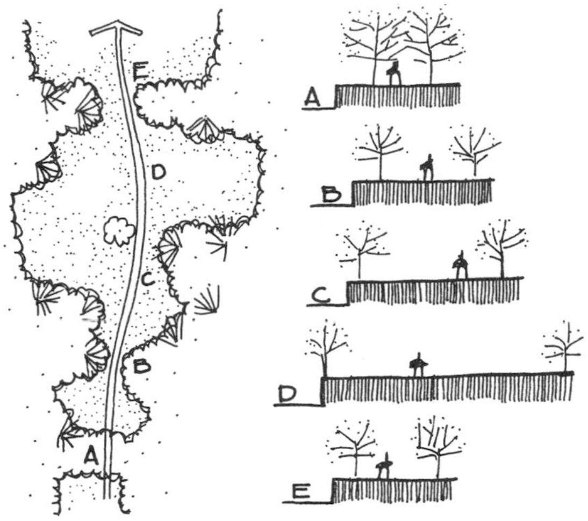

7. Spatial size: enclosure to non-enslosure.

3. The type of base material that meets the vertical spatial definer is important. Is it a natural material versus a humanly made artificial material? Is the material in "good" condition or in a decayed or mismanaged condition?
4. The actual size of the space and the position of the observer in the space are important. When the viewer is above the space, a sense of total understanding about the space is achieved. When the viewer is next to one of the vertical elements, the viewer may have a sense of security and ease within the space. When the viewer is below the space, the person may either have a sense of anticipation or a sense of fear of the unknown.

The important thing to remember is that all of these points are significant aspects of spatial design at any scale and for all components of the built environment.

Light, its color, direction and distance is perhaps as little understood as aesthetics, though it is the major component of visual resources. It is interesting to note, at this point, that Litton lists it fifth in his factors of scenic analysis and observation. But, he also suggests that "an understanding of light and its effects is essential to predict the visual consequences of land-use decisions. We tend to overlook the importance of illumination of the landscape. But the effects of light change profoundly during the course of a single day and during the course of seasons." The subject of light seems to be invisible; it is seldom identified in any course title. For example, "light" appears in only one course description of the total of 88 courses listed for the design disciplines at Washington State University. In this designer's education, light was only dealt with for ten minutes while drawing a light pole detail (But, See Moyer, 1992).

As stated earlier, color, direction and distance are the general components of light. Color has two components, hue and value. Webster (1970) defines hue as "the distinctive characteristics of a given color that enable it to be assigned a position in the spectrum." In turn, spectrum is defined as "the series of colored bands diffracted and arranged in the order of their respective wavelengths by the passage of white light through a prism or other diffracting medium and shading continuously from red (produced by the longest wavelength) to violet (produced by the shortest wavelength)."

Value has been defined by Litton (1968) as "that value of color through which an object is called dark or light." The pure colors of the spectrum are rare in the landscape; they are usually seasonal and last for short periods of time. Pure colors are usually seen against a backdrop of subdued colors of grey and green. This is where the value of color becomes important, both in the composition of the scene and how it is perceived and remembered. Litton (1968) has identified six rough rules dealing with light and color in the landscape:

1. The sky is invariably lighter than earth elements, clouds being infrequent exceptions.
2. Grasslands are lighter than tree or shrub cover.
3. Soil is likely to be lighter than tree or shrub cover, or only infrequently darker.
4. Disturbed soil has distinct value contrast compared to undisturbed soil or plant cover. In the Sierra Nevada, e.g., disturbed soil is generally lighter.
5. Hardwoods are lighter than coniferous trees.
6. Overcast conditions or flat lighting diminish value contrasts; intense or full light increases contrast.

Distance is important in perception of color and light within the landscape. The general rule is that as landscapes recede from the viewer, color value changes to a blue or gray tone, where hues diminish to a uniform tone.

The direction in which light is shining on an object or landscape is crucial in terms of how they are perceived. The source of light can either be backlighting, sidelighting, or frontlighting. Backlighting occurs when the source of light is behind the landscape being viewed—the source of light is in the viewer's eyes. When this occurs, the outline of object or landscape is prominent while details within the landscape are less visible. This condition usually occurs at dawn or dusk.

Sidelighting occurs when the light is to the side of the object or landscape being viewed. Sidelighting usually intensifies the three-dimensionality of landscape or object by showing the roundness of objects and by showing light and dark sides. The concept of sidelighting is especially effective and desirable when preparing drawings or sketches in professional design projects.

In front lighting, the light source is behind the viewer. In this instance, less detail is seen because the viewed surface is in full and direct light. In this position, the view tends to read "flat".

Litton observes: "If extended observations are not possible, then side lighting should be taken as the criterion, for it may contribute to the single

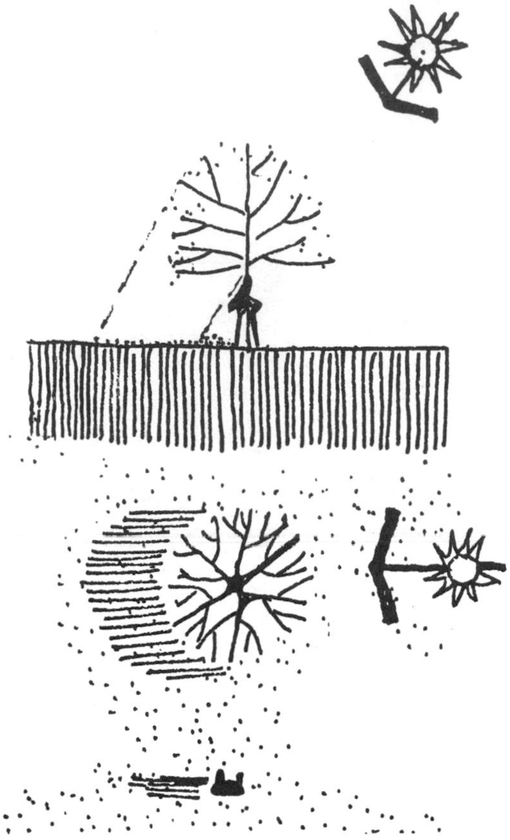

9. Side lighting in plan and section.

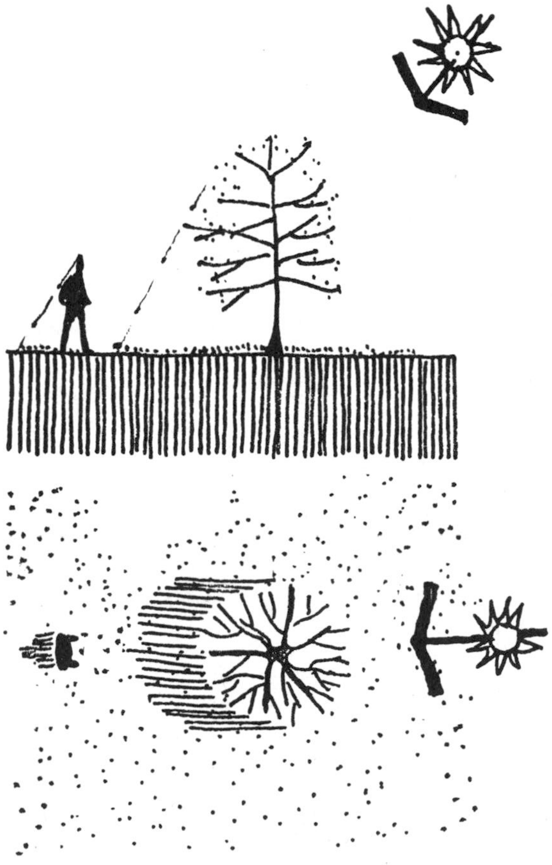

8. Backlighting in plan and section.

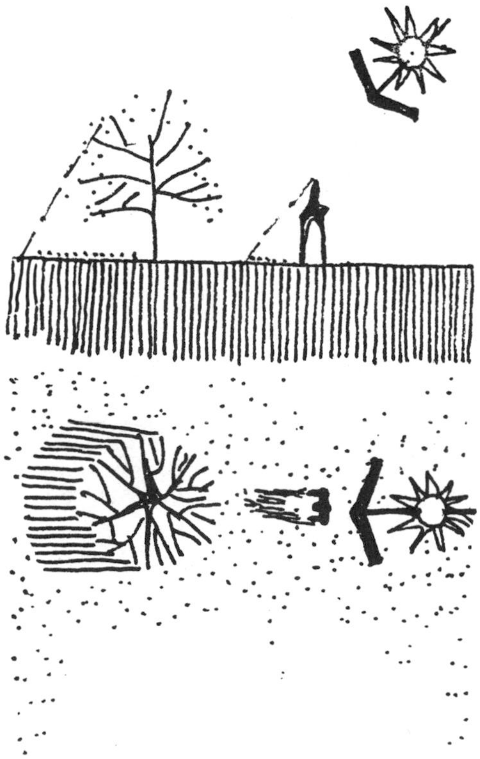

10. Front lighting in plan and section.

clearest impression of landscape." What makes work with light in the landscape difficult is the seasonality, climatic conditions and time of day in which the landscape is being viewed. These conditions can seldom be controlled by the designer or planner.

Sequence, the sixth factor in describing landscape, is the visual order in which the landscape is being seen. Webster defines sequence as "the following of one thing after another in chronological, casual or logical order; succession or continuity. A continuous or related series, often of uniform things." Sequence then, may be interpreted as the impression a person receives while moving through the landscape—or through architecture and other designed environments. Litton points out that factors such as space, lighting, observer position and distance change the character of space. Form, size of the space and scale of the space are important factors in the manipulation of sequence. A look at old traditional gardens as well as "accidental" design of historic cities, best shows the most interesting combinations of sequential manipulation (see Figure 11). This, as well as lighting, is an important aspect of the built environment not stressed as thoroughly as it should be in design education. Certainly landscapes, with their range of scales—small to vast—and their dynamic qualities, offer significant challenges to designers. Design at smaller scales, however, can begin to establish understanding of this important design component.

11. Dynamic sequences of spaces.

Compositional Types

The composition and combinations of the six factors described above form the ingredients of the visual landscape. Litton has identified seven combinations of these factors which create spaces or rooms in the landscape: panoramic, feature, enclosed, focal, canopied, detail and ephemeral landscapes. These may be placed in a sequential path or route in the design of landscapes.

The compositional types are classified into fundamental and secondary categories. Panoramic, feature, enclosed and focal landscapes are considered fundamental. The question arises as to what happens in the vacuum between the identified spaces. Litton suggests that the unspecified areas serve as backdrops for the "nodes" or areas of greater interest. D. W. Meinig (1979), in a collection of essays titled *The Interpretation of Ordinary Landscapes*, hits one of the major problems: What is unique? What is ordinary? Significant examples of compositional landscapes help to answer Meinig's questions.

Panoramic Landscapes may consist of 360-degree views, but more commonly consist of 180-degree views. In this landscape, foreground and middle-ground are usually insignificant compared to the background. A feeling of great distance is usually associated with this landscape.

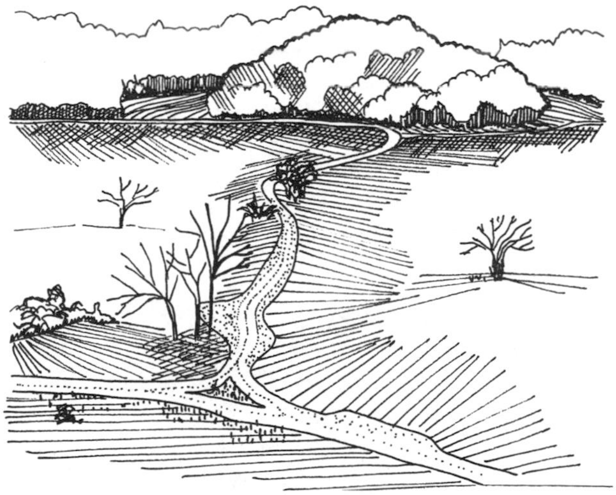

12. A panoramic landscape with fore, middle and background features.

Feature Landscapes are those which are dominated by a contrasting vertical form or a cluster of such forms. The dominance of the vertical is a function of scale and can range from a tree to a mountain. In this landscape, the feature can be an object

13. Feature landscape: dominated by contrasting vertical form.

seen at the end of a sequential route of travel. When the feature or dominant element is being viewed, the surrounding landscape should serve as a backdrop or to frame the view.

Enclosed Landscapes occur when vertical elements surround a space and limit the views outward. The enclosed space can be natural as in a forest meadow, canyon floor, or shoreline, or it can be created as in any of the previously mentioned landscapes. The enclosed landscape is important in terms of scale. The presence of enclosing elements has an important influence on people as they traverse from one landscape to another. For example, a common concern about the Palouse Region of rolling hills in southeastern Washington state is that it has no trees. Could the openness of the Palouse, its long views and vistas, be a factor contributing to the commonly felt sense of no intimate space, especially when compared to the massive tree-enclosed landscapes of western Washington?

14. Enclosed landscape: vertical elements surround and limit one's view.

Focal Landscapes occur where the line of sight is channeled in a particular direction. This direction can either be actual, as cut through a forest, or implied, as on a prairie when traveling a straight road. Litton identifies four such landscapes: the point convergence landscape, where the observer's attention is directed to a point on the horizon line; feature terminus, where the observer's attention is directed to a terminal focal feature, such as a mountain or tower; the portal landscape where vertical sides enclose the view and a vertical curve at the end terminates the view; and self-enclosure landscapes where the view is controlled by vertical sides and is terminated by a horizontal curve to the side. Feature landscapes, with strong visual terminus, are the most dominant and memorable.

15. Focal landscape: channeled sight directed into the distant landscape.

A **canopied landscape** occurs when an overhead plane is present, usually vegetative. A canopied landscape is more noticeable and dominant to a pedestrian, because of the slower speed, than to an automobile passenger. The type of tree, the density of the stand of trees, the maturity of the trees and the number of highway lanes present, all influence the perception of canopied landscapes. This type of

16. Canopied landscape: framing one's view.

landscape may provide the traveler a framed or controlled view and can create a strong foreground for the composition.

A **detail landscape** is another where small pieces of information may contribute to a viewer's overall impression. This landscape is best perceived by walking and is enhanced by a pedestrian's ability to assimilate the impressions received by all of the senses. This information can give one a "sense of place," can communicate the difference between a rain forest or a high desert. This may be compared to fine cooking, where many unidentifiable ingredients, when mixed together, provide a new and delicious entree.

17. Detail landscape focusing on foreground elements.

Ephemeral landscapes are perhaps the most memorable, the most photographed and the least controllable by the designer or planner. According to Litton, such landscapes occur under one or more of five conditions: atmospheric and weather conditions; projected or reflected images; displacements; signs; and animal occupancy.

Atmospheric and weather conditions can include cloud and fog formations, precipitation, vagaries of light and wind-motion effects. Projected or reflected images may consist of shadows on the ground or reflections on water. The sun or moon may be seen as a reflection. Displacement occurs when parts of plants have become detached and are found elsewhere. The value of these displaced elements is perhaps greater for the pedestrian because there is an opportunity to see where elements are not located, their condition and their color.

Ephemeral signs occur where "indications of former life or occupancy by animals or plants occur" (Litton, 1968). Generally, these impressions are only seen by the pedestrian. However, some landscape changes, such as fire or large square clearcuts, are signs on a large scale, visible from afar and at greater speeds. In concluding his statements on ephemeral landscapes, Litton suggests that "even though the ephemeral landscape may be beyond susceptibility—or desirability—to control, it adds so much to appreciation of the environment that land

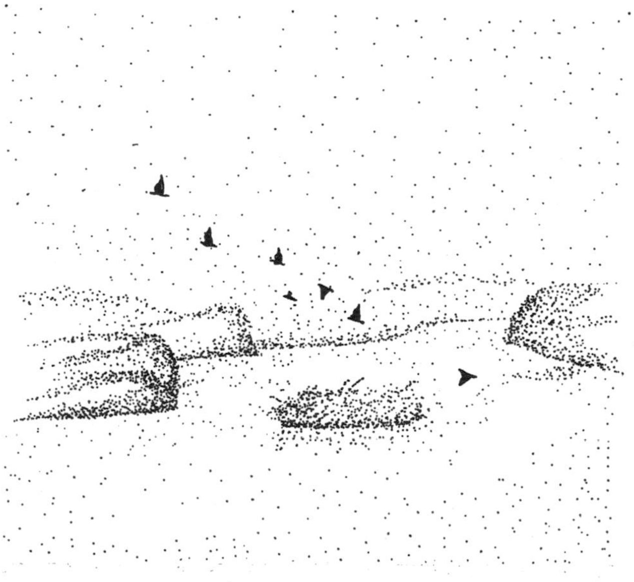

18. Ephemeral landscape: the most dynamic and memorable.

managers and landscape architects should develop a special sensitivity to this compositional type and thus to recognition of the full complexity of the landscape."

EVALUATIVE VISUAL RESOURCE INVENTORY

The study titled *Visual Resource Management* (1980) by the U.S. Bureau of Land Management (BLM) provides an additional concept for analyzing and evaluating landscapes. In this study, seven components of the visual whole are identified: landforms, vegetation, water, color, adjacent scenery, scarcity and cultural modifications. These seven components can be identified as ingredients of Litton's compositional types and as "what is seen by the observer." The seven are ranked on a scale of minus four to ten, with minus four being low and ten being high. The class rankings are established by adding the numerical evaluation of each of the components together. The BLM suggests that if a landscape total is from 19 to 33 points, the landscape is Class A; from 12 to 18 points, Class B; and from 0 to 11 points, Class C. The importance of this rating system is that it identifies a means of ranking a scene or landscape based on the percentage of various components present, and the diversity of each. This system can be used then to identify a series of landscapes. The BLM chart illustrated in

Landform	Vegetation	Water	Color	Adjacent Scenery	Scarcity	Cultural Modifications
High vertical relief such as prominent cliffs, spires or massive rock outcrops; **or** severe surface variation or highly eroded formations including major badlands or dune systems; **or** detail features dominant and exceptionally striking and intriguing such as glaciers. 5	A variety of vegetative types in interesting forms, textures, and patterns 5	Clear and clean appearing, still, or cascading white water, any of which are a dominant factor in the landscape. 5	Rich color combinations, variety or vivid color; **or** pleasing contrasts in the soil, rock, vegetation, water or snow fields. 5	Adjacent scenery greatly enhances visual quality. 5	One of a kind; **or** unusually memorable; **or** very rare within region. Consistent chance for exceptional wildlife or wildflower viewing. 6	Free from esthetically undesirable or discordant sights and influences; **or** modifications add favorably to visual variety. 2
Steep canyons, mesas, buttes, cinder cones and drumlins; **or** interesting erosional patterns or variety in size and shape of landforms; **or** detail features present and interesting though not dominant or exceptional. 3	Some variety of vegetation, but only one or two types. 3	Flowing or still, but not dominant in the landscape. 3	Some intensity or variety in colors and contrast of the soil, rock and vegetation, but not a dominant scenic element. 3	Adjacent scenery moderately enhances overall visual quality. 3	Distinctive, though somewhat similar to others within the region. 2	Scenic quality is somewhat depreciated by inharmonious intrusions, but not so extensively that they are entirely negated; **or** modifications add little or no visual variety to the area. 0
Low, rolling hills, foothills **or** flat valley bottoms. Interesting, detailed landscape features few or lacking. 1	Little or no variety or contrast in vegetation. 1	Absent, or not noticeable. 0	Subtle color variations, contrast or interest; generally muted tones. 1	Adjacent scenery has little or no influence on overall visual quality. 0	Interesting within its setting, but fairly common within the region. 1	Modifications are so extensive that scenic qualities are mostly nullified or substantially reduced. -4

19. BLM Scenic Quality Inventory—evaluation rating criteria and scores.

Figure 19 identifies the rankings and potential number assignments for outstanding examples in each category. The critical number assigned to designate the landscape is a value judgment by an individual or small group of people. The concern with this system, or any other kind of ranking, is that arguments arise over who is best qualified to make these judgments as well as over the resulting ranking system. Obviously, if a person agrees with the decisions made, they will feel the evaluation is correct and the evaluators highly qualified. If there is a disagreement, the evaluator may be accused of being incompetent or at least a representative of a special interest group. Whatever the outcome of this last argument, a more refined map is now available, which can be included with other resource maps in the design and land use decision-making process.

CURRENT PRACTICES

A basic framework is now complete for identifying and analyzing the landscapes we see. What is to be done next? Many agencies, firms and individuals are taking Litton's concepts and redefining them, adapting them and adding new terms to identify and map landscapes which are significant, distinctive, common or ordinary. The key to the discussion is how we evaluate and how we rank landscapes.

Perhaps the most difficult point still emerging from the BLM and other studies is the classification of landscapes into A, B and C categories. In a U.S. Forest Service handbook, *National Forest Landscape Management* (1974), a section on "The Visual Management System" addresses the problem of national versus local importance of visual resources and argues that national concern and value outrank local value. (See also *Landscape Character Types*, 1989). In other words, Mt. Rainier is more important on a national scale than Kamiak Butte, a local feature also in the state of Washington. Others argue that local landscapes are equally or more important for local inhabitants, especially if they lack mobility. Kamiak Butte is, perhaps, the most important landmark in the Palouse region of Whitman County, Washington because it can be seen from afar in an area largely without trees and because, covered with rare stands of fir and cedar, it is a shelter for deer and other animals. Would this mean then that two maps should exist—one of local importance and one of national importance? Should they be overlaid or combined together?

An interesting continuation of this discussion is the Palouse Region itself. To some, it is dull and boring. To others, it is subtle, alive and active. On the basis of such local perceptions, it might rank, on a national scale, perhaps as low as a two. However, there is only one other landscape like it in the world, formed by the same geological processes, in the Ukraine. With this information, does the national ranking then change? (Cf., Hough, 1990).

A second major concern is that visual resource management work is currently concentrating on the rural landscape. Urban work is being done, but both the Litton and the BLM studies deal with rural lands, which are usually controlled by one land owner and seen from one or two circulation routes. The urban landscape compounds the problems of classification and description. Perhaps only computers can take all the bits of information and provide a study map. Perhaps the problem is so complex that people cannot feed enough information into the computer to make a decision. And, information fed into the computer is still the value judgment of one or a few people. However, since most people live in urban areas, visual resource management must be undertaken there as well. And, it was an urban area that served as the test case when the Supreme Court ruled that aesthetics were one of our inalienable rights.

CONSPECTUS

Ephemeral landscapes are those that appear and disappear according to natural or climatic conditions. Visual resources and aesthetics share the same fleeting moment, a resource experience which is exciting, but can quickly be replaced by a fog of complexity and value judgment.

Experts working in the visual resource area must determine if their study will be descriptive or evaluative. Descriptive landscape analysis consists of describing a landscape, both in terms of how the viewer is positioned and what is happening with the view being observed. Evaluative landscape analysis consists of discerning the quality of the landscape and then placing some sort of comparative numerical value on it. Both have validity, each serves different purposes in visual management.

Compounding the complexity of the visual landscape inventory is the question of national versus local importance of the resource. The problem may not be too critical for major landscape features, such as Mt. Rainier or Yellowstone, but on the local landscape scales of Washington's Palouse Region, the Dakota Badlands, the Wisconsin Hill Country, or the Great Plains area, it is more controversial. Their value is their scale and their openness of space, yet their evaluative rating may be quite low nationally.

Visual resource management is a concept which is here to stay. It is important, both in planning and design of the increasingly built environment that we all live in. The goal of the design and planning professions should be to refine the system and incorporate it into the design and planning process.

REFERENCES

Berleant, A. 1992. *The Aesthetics of Environment*. Temple University Press.

Blair, W. G. E. 1980. "Visual Resource Management," *Environmental Comment*. Urban Land Institute.

Brace, P. 1980. "Urban Aesthetics and the Courts: A Review of Current Judicial Opinions on Community Appearance," *Environmental Comment*. Urban Land Institute.

Elsner, G. H. and Smardon, R. C. 1979. *Our National Landscape: A Conference on Applied Techniques for Analysis and Management of the Visual Resource*. Pacific Southwest Forest and Range Experiment Station.

Fairbrother, N. 1974. *The Nature of Landscape Design: An Art Form*, A Craft, A Social Necessity. Knopf.

Glikson, A. 1966. "The Relationship Between Landscape Planning and Regional Planning," *Towards a New Relationship of Man and Nature in Temperate Lands*. Nature and Natural Resources.

Hough, M. 1990. *Out of Place: Restoring Identity to the Regional Landscape*. Yale University Press.

Landscape Character Types of the National Forests in Arizona and New Mexico: The Visual Management System. 1989. U.S. Forest Service.

Litton, R. B. 1968. *Forest Landscape Description and Inventories: A Basis for Land Planning and Design*. US Dept. of Agriculture.

Meinig, D. W. Ed. 1979. *The Interpretation of Ordinary Landscapes: Geographical Essays*. Oxford University Press.

Moyer, J. L. 1992. *The Landscape Lighting Book*. Wiley.

National Forest Landscape Management: Volume 2. 1974. U.S. Forest Service.

National Environmental Policy Act. 1970. U.S. Government Printing Office.

Penn Central Transportation Company v. City of New York. 1978. US-57L Ed 2d 631 98 S Ct. No. 77-444.

Scott, R. G. 1951. *Design Fundamentals*. McGraw-Hill.

Visual Resource Management Program. 1980. Bureau of Land Management..

Webster's New World Dictionary. 1973. The World Publishing Company.

Introduction

5. CITIES

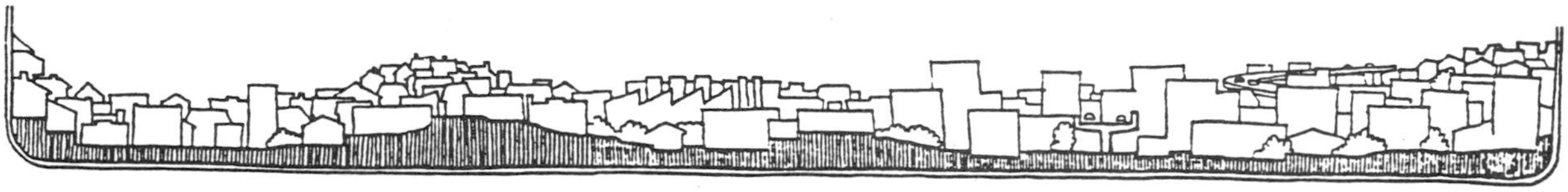

What is a city? One answer might be to describe it as the ultimate artifact. Another might say it is the final expression of human creativity . . . or human folly.

The fifth component of this study, the idea of a city, has always been difficult to delineate. The Dutch architect, Aldo van Eyke, tried by linking two levels of the built environment together: "a house must be like a small city if its to be a real house . . . a city [must be] like a large house if its to be a real city." This gives a hint that the city is a built environment: a city has edges, and myriad components, and that multitude of parts must be tied together into a functioning whole. It is a settlement form, a place where people live, a place that can be described, as the philosopher Berkeley did (in Essential Visions),with the statement that "many houses go to the making of one city," a further hint of the city as an integral part of the built environment. The city is larger, of a higher order, more complex than an individual structure, than a neighborhood, or even a hamlet, village, or town. A city usually connotes organization (and integration—health, fitness, and creativity if you will) of a more complete or higher kind.

A city is a place created or built for people to live: Those houses are occupied houses. Aristotle did not call the city a place "builded with houses, and environed with wals, but (he) saieth that it is a companie. . . ." (Elyot, 1540). Shakespeare much later would agree, in Hamlet, that "what is the Citie, but the People?" And, that is the point: the more people there are, and the more sophisticated their techniques, the more they modify their environment into a "human" creation, an increasingly rich, complex, and varied creation . . . the city.

The city is a human creation, an assemblage of pieces. It has content and a context as recognized by the following continuum:

PRODUCTS-INTERIORS-STRUCTURES-LANDSCAPES-***CITIES***-REGIONS-EARTH

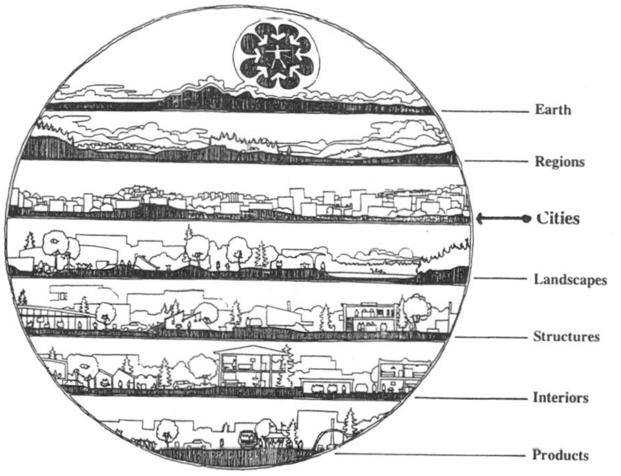

In general, the definition and purpose of cities can again be illustrated by the following four-part statement:

a. cities (which combine products, interiors, structures and landscapes in various ways) are humanly made or arranged;
b. to fulfill human purpose, to satisfy human needs, wants and values; and
c. to mediate the overall environment;
d. while affecting context (regions and earth).

Urban places not only hold a position in the hierarchy formed by their content-component-context continuum, but are also classified and differentiated in a hierarchy according to size: "village notes could ne'er supply that rich and varied melody" the poet Scott (1813) considered so essential to satisfaction with city life. Such satisfaction may well be synonymous with the higher order complexity of urban life. Country and village life have their own satisfactions, of course, but it is in the city that human diversity and civil qualities are found.

People consider a city a higher form of civilization and for a city to even exist, to function, requires a high level of organization. This image of a city as a higher form is widely reflected even in "official" nomenclature. In Canada, a place labeled "city" is generally a municipality of the "highest" class, though urban terms are used variously in different provinces. In Ontario, for example, a village is traditionally an urban place of 2,000 people or less and has a right to be made a town if its population exceeds that number; a town on reaching the magic number of 15,000 can be "erected" into a city, at which time it is separated from the jurisdiction of county government. In the United States, Iowa provides a similar example, in that "cities of the first class" are those of 15,000 or more and cities of the second class are those from 2,000 to 15,000. Ohio originally divided its municipal corporations into cities (urban places over 5,000 inhabitants), villages (200 to 5,000), and hamlets (incorporated places with fewer than 200 people). The two smaller places are more frequently described in built environment terms, especially as clusters of houses or subdivisions, but the city provides the greatest expression of size and complexity.

Dan Fabun (1971) considers the word city still indefinable, describing it as a form that is a "change in dimension of a magnitude for which there is no historical precedent . . . we can no longer look it up in a book." He prefers to describe the entity we call a city as a force field, a field in which transactions take place as exchanges of energy "through the media of various organic systems." The field concept, used in a number of places in this book, is useful in defining an important aspect of cities, that of human interactions, exchanges and circulation. It is useful to understand the city as an interaction field, which allows a necessary humanistic shift in focus, emphasizing the relationships among people as an important settlement feature, of community at all levels.

All this means that the best cities are inclusive, rather than exclusive and segregated; they are integrated rather than disintegrated and fragmented. And, they are part of, rather than apart from, their context, the region within which they are located. In other words, they should be the epitome of health, fitness, and creativity: healthy, pleasant places to live; fit into environment and into context, appropriate to scale and level; the epitome of human culture and creativity. Unfortunately, cities are too often void of these human-environmental qualities. This should not discourage citizens and designers from striving to realize the promise that is inherent in the purpose or idea of a city. The city may be the place where the vision of human life most fully conceptualized is finally realized.

Paul Valery (1977) claimed that the city is "virtually all of civilization and indispensable in this role." Lewis Mumford has suggested (1934, 1968) that the city is "at once a microcosm and a microscope, containing and magnifying the best and worst of humanity." The best, he says, derives from the level attained, "the scale of the city (being) one of its chief sources of enjoyment and edification." The best cities enrich the lives of those (both public and professionals) who understand and/or participate in their creation, a dynamic expression of culture and civilization, an important symbol and contribution to future generations. The worst are plagued by so many problems that it is hard to know how to help, causing too many of us to not care about the quality of our cities or to get involved in their revitalization.

The following chapters examine the city, its problems and potential. They emphasize the best and discuss ways to reanimate the rest, and remind the reader of the importance of this inherited resource of civilization:

- **"The Evolution of Urbanization"** by Robert Patton: this first chapter analyzes the way cities have developed through time and space. The author examines and illustrates the constants of village and urban development. These are common characteristics which have been evolved over the vast history of urban development and are present in the cities of today.

- **"The Inherited City as a Resource"** by Robert Baron: this chapter discusses the importance of cities as a resource which needs to be recognized and conserved. The author suggests that these historic resources of the city need to be constantly reanimated and describes various ways to achieve this desirable goal.
- **"Cities, Climate and Environmental Context"** by Michael Owen: the way cities have been adapted to environmental factors—land and climate—is examined in this chapter. The variables and different types of climatic conditions are analyzed, along with various human-environmental adaptive strategies to design with climate and to celebrate the qualities of more comfortable places to live, work and play.
- **"Cities Today: The Imprint of Human Needs in Urban Patterns and Form"** by Tom J. Bartuska: this chapter examines the human aspects of cities today—how human needs are manifested into institutions, the ways land is used, and infrastructures which define the patterns and form of cities. The author illustrates how these human-environmental patterns can be used to design and plan more effective cities in the future.
- **"Urban Design and Planning"** by Michael Owen: this chapter surveys the various legal and procedural developments which define urban planning and design in the United States. The author illustrates how these developments have shaped the cities of today and presents a planning process which can address the future needs of urban settlement.
- **"Urban and Regional Hierarchies: Central Place Theory"** by Gerald L. Young: the last chapter of this section discusses a theory which clarifies the general patterns of urban and regional development. It discusses the general tendency for small villages to cluster around larger cities, which group around even larger metropolitan areas throughout the world. This hierarchical theory is a useful model for investigating urban and regional patterns and development.

REFERENCES

Elyot, Sir Thomas. 1540. *The Image of Goueraunce Compiled by the Actes and Sentences Notable, of the Most Noble Emperour Alexander Seuerus*. Bertheletter.

Fabun, D. 1971. *Dimensions of Change*. Glencoe Press.

Mumford, L. 1968. "Architecture as a Home for Man," *Architectural Record*, February.

Mumford, L. 1934. *Technics and Civilization*. Harcourt, Brace and Company.

Scott, Sir Walter. 1813. *Rokeby–A Poem*. Ballantyne.

Shakespeare, W. 1923. *The Works of William Shakespeare: "Hamlet"*. Macmillan.

Valery, P. 1977. *An Anthology*. Princeton University Press.

Von Eckardt, W. 1978. *Back to the Drawing Board*. New Republic.

Wordsworth, W. 1904. *The Complete Poetical Works of William Wordsworth*. Houghton Mifflin.

CHAPTER

21

The Evolution of Urbanization

Robert J. Patton

The twentieth century city is the largest, most dynamic manifestation of any living organisms' interaction with its environment. It is not possible to analyze the total complexity of forces which created the city. So, it is necessary to limit the context when dealing with cities and urbanization. This essay discusses the evolution of urbanization as it relates to the changing **wants** and **needs** of humankind through history and defines the characteristics that are common to all aggregations of people whose settlements are considered to be urban.

Throughout history, urban areas have expressed two aspects which help define their characteristics and qualities. On one hand are the **variables**: size, cultural, political and social character, and the resultant built environment. It is difficult to understand urban evolution only in terms of variables, since they change radically from culture to culture.

On the other hand are the **constants** common to all contemporary urban societies: permanence, density, institutionalism, segregation, dominance—and later, decentralization and subcentralization. They have accumulated through the process of urban evolution and reveal themselves in the twentieth century city of today. It is through these constants that the evolution of the city through history can best be understood.

THE VILLAGE

The constants of **permanence** and **density** have their roots in pre-urban or village society dating back more than 10,000 years. During this period (known as pre-history), people were nomadic, existing at the simplest level of material technology, often limited to what could be carried by individuals.

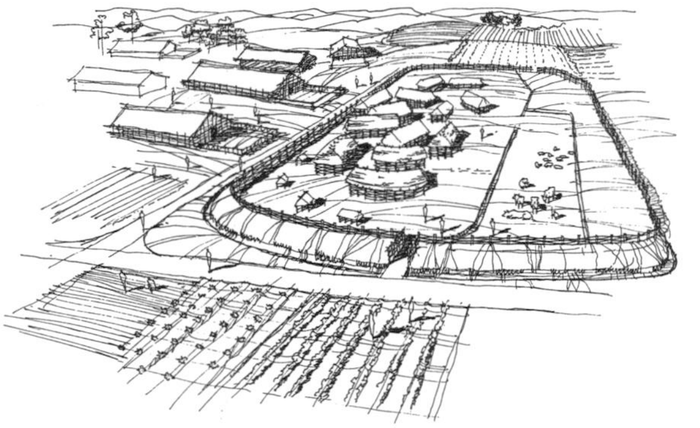

1. Permanence established through the domestication of animals and development of agriculture, as illustrated in an early village settlement.

The precise time in history when pre-urban people altered their nomadic, wandering lifestyle is not clear, but the probable cause is domestication of plants and animals, which led to horticulture and agriculture, to herding, cultivating and harvesting, which allowed a stabilization of the food supply.

Permanence and Density

With the advent of domestication, the first villages appeared as permanent settlements. **Permanence** provided two qualities of life important to ultimate development of the urban unit. It gave people the ability to identify with a **sense of place** within the larger environment, a refuge to which they could return no matter where they roamed. It also provided a sense of community, creating new kinds of relationships not previously experienced between people. This sense of place is an expression of the composite built form of an urbanized area and is still today a memorable quality of successful cities.

The pattern of early villages reveals another characteristic, an image of compactness with built elements clustered in close spatial proximity. Compactness resulted in greater **density** of people. Such clustering provided mutual protection, efficient sharing of the work load, and the opportunity for increased social interaction. The concepts of permanence and compactness (or density) are common to all cities throughout history, including those of today.

If two of the constants of urbanization, permanence and density, were formed in pre-urban society, what then differentiates village settlement from urbanization? The difference is based on a change caused by a revolution in village society occurring somewhere between 10,000 and 5,000 years ago. This change is referred to by historians as the **Urban Transformation**.

Village society was based on a tribal or communal concept oriented toward cooperative action to fulfill the needs of the group at large. The organizing methods of an urban society are something quite different. They are based on a hierarchical division of power, a structure in which the needs for one part of the group are often achieved at the expense of others.

In the late pre-urban village society, one segment of the population appears to have risen to a position of dominance over others. Villages were increasingly producing surpluses beyond sustenance needs, making them ripe for urban transformation. A divisional power structure created an opportunity to make the village even more productive, thereby raising the level of existence for some to that of affluence. As a result, the village was transformed into what is defined as an urban unit, characterized by mobilization of the work force, division of labor, and separation of classes.

2. Density expressed in the compactness of village settlements (*T. Bartuska*).

THE PRE-INDUSTRIAL CITY

As a result of the urban transformation, a new set of constants emerged, creating an urban unit referred to as the **pre-industrial city**. The pre-industrial city spanned the period from approximately 3000 B.C. to 1760 A.D. in Western civilization and included the ancient cities of Mesopotamia and Egypt, the classical cities of Greece and Rome, the medieval guild cities, and the metropolises of the Renaissance.

The urban constants that emerged in pre-industrial cities were **institutionalism**, **segregation** and **dominance**. These constants were not prominent in village settlement, but all of them appeared in the pre-industrial city and are basic to twentieth century urban settlement.

Institutionalism

Archaeologists have determined that the city of UR in Mesopotamia contained a population of 5000 people by 3000 B.C. Records show that the population of Rome had grown to 1,000,000 by the first century B.C. During this growth process, religious, political and economic activity intensified, creating three dominant power structures having a simultaneous impact on this vast new urban society. To assure their individual strengths and identity, each group intensified their organization and structure, institutionalizing their social, economic and religious purposes. The resulting institutions transformed these power groups into the major organs of the urban body.

Segregation and Dominance

Once institutions were structured, a dynamic ordering process took place in the pre-industrial city known as **segregation**. It was partly ecologically based and partly socially based. Ecologically, it

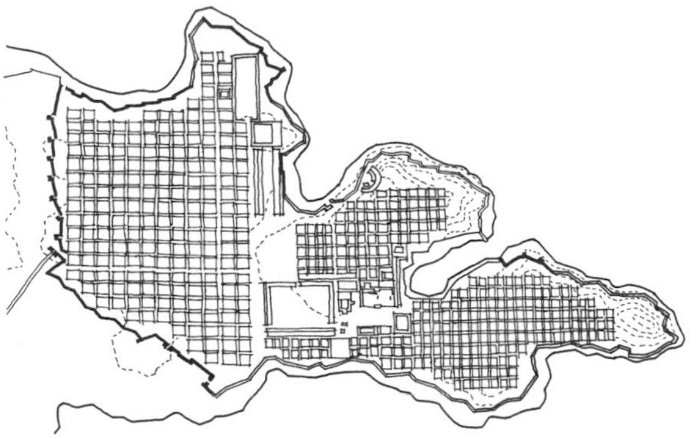

3. Segregation of public and private urban activities, Greek colonial town of Miletus, 5th century B.C.

4. Dominance by physical size of a medieval cathedral over the city, Chartres, France (*T. Bartuska*).

5. Spatial dominance of a public square, Siena, Italy.

resulted from a tendency for people and institutions with similar characteristics and interests to cluster together in aggregation. By doing so, they attained a stronger sense of identity as well as separation from that with which they felt incompatible.

Segregation was also planned. The military, the laboring class, the merchant class and others were forced to live in segregated residential districts. The church, the palace, or the guild hall were often built centrally, depending on which was the dominant institution.

Segregation affected the physical appearance of pre-industrial cities. Patterns were generated which expressed sharp lines of demarcation. The lines established territorial limits to preserve institutional identity. Some boundaries were natural, based on topography, rivers, lakes or vegetation. Others were constructed, the most common being the street system.

Some institutions in the pattern of segregation dominated because of physical size and/or position. This was often planned purposely to exert, by virtue of visual presence (be it religious or autocratic), a controlling influence on the inhabitants.

Interestingly, **dominance** had a positive influence on the pattern of pre-industrial cities. In some cases, it punctuated the otherwise monotonous character of the city. In other cases the center of the city was dominant, providing a feature of orientation and a social place of assembly. The architecture and scale of spaces provided a background for exciting civic life.

Centralized dominance is not unfamiliar to us today. It exists as the manifestation of economic institutionalism in the central business district of almost every major modern city.

THE INDUSTRIAL CITY

Toward the end of the eighteenth century, a second social change occurred in Europe comparable in terms of its impact on pre-industrial cities to the impact on village life of the urban transformation 5,000 years before. The **Industrial Revolution** significantly altered the course of urban development. The industrial city was created, imposing new environmental complications that have left their mark on the development of all major cities throughout the world.

Invention of the steam-powered assembly line and related advances in technology and manufacturing in the 18th century caused the Industrial Revolution. The factory was built around the assembly line, establishing a new and powerful economic institution. It created a powerful demand for products and for people to produce those products.

Factories grew in two places. One was in rural areas near the sources of raw materials. These factories became a catalyst for the disordered development of new towns. Factories were also imposed on large, existing pre-industrial centers, taking advantage of population concentrations to provide a labor force and of location to centralize markets and trade. The advent of the factory system caused one of the greatest immigrations in human history. Rural, agrarian people flooded into the cities hoping to increase their prosperity.

At this point, trouble began for the city as an environment for human habitation. The politics of the new industrialists perpetuated a belief that if economic enterprise was allowed to flourish, free of any governmental control, the system would be self-organizing. The new society believed that an ordered urban environment would also result.

It did not! No period in the evolution of urbanization is more impoverished than that of the late eighteenth and nineteenth centuries. Every detail of urban life became subordinate to the factory. No plan determined its location. It usually claimed the most amenable sites on flat land near water. Mass substandard housing was located near the noxious factory to create proximity of home and work for the laborers.

6. Image of the eighteenthth century industrial city.

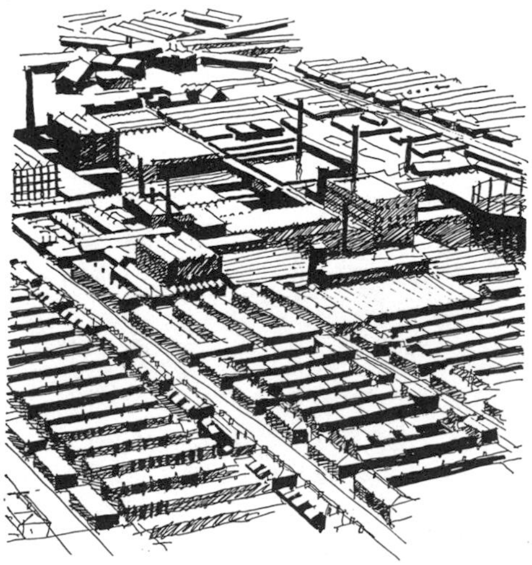

7. Crowded industrial housing developed adjacent to factories caused the outward movement of decentralization.

Decentralization

The urban area as an environment for living continued to deteriorate as a result of the negative impact of the factory. Upper classes began to move out of the city. They settled in rural locations just far enough away to avoid the crowdedness and blight, yet close enough to easily access the city for working, entertainment and access to material commodities.

This outward movement of a segment of the population gained momentum to the point where it began to affect the demography of the urban population pattern. This dynamic movement is referred to by urbanologists as **decentralization** and was a major factor affecting the transition of the industrial city into the post-industrial city, the twentieth century metropolis that we know today.

THE POST-INDUSTRIAL CITY

Prior to the advent of the automobile, de-centralization was accommodated by development of the commuter railroad. Originating at the center of

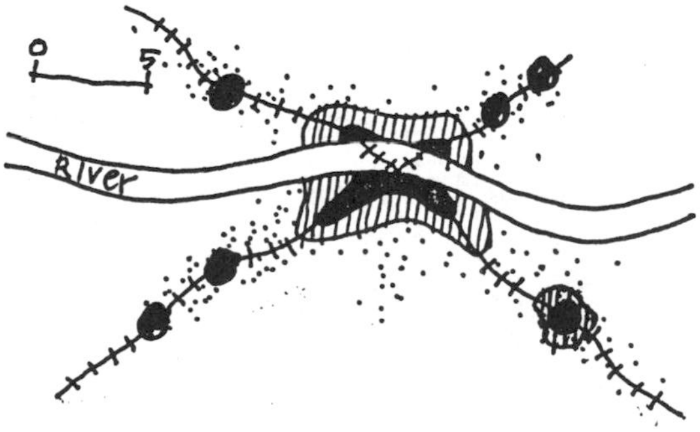

8. Radial patterns of urban development, a central city and surrounding decentralized villages served primarily by rail transit.

the city and projecting outward, the railroad connected a series of planned suburban residential villages. Although built on a speculation basis, these villages had certain amenable environmental qualities. They were spaced evenly along the rail routes and surrounded by greenbelts of agricultural land or forest. Their populations were limited to five to ten thousand people, all of whom could depend on local services.

Subcentralization

In time, however, the inexpensive railroad fares allowed a broader segment of the population to move out of the city. This increased decentralization created a demand for more residential land and speculators began buying, platting and building between the clustered suburban villages. The expanding villages merged and soon ceased to be places with a special identity.

As the decentralization process continued, major urban commercial establishments began to build in the outer areas to take advantage of the suburban economic market. These new commercial centers set up origin-destination routes that ran across the original radial transportation pattern of railroads and roads leading to and from the city. Crossroads were built and subsequent residential construction along these routes filled-in the remaining open space.

The original concept of the commuter railroad came into conflict with this new suburban density. The railroad had to make too many stops to serve the large population and lost its efficiency as a mass transportation system. Concurrent with this event, the automobile arrived on the scene. The car was

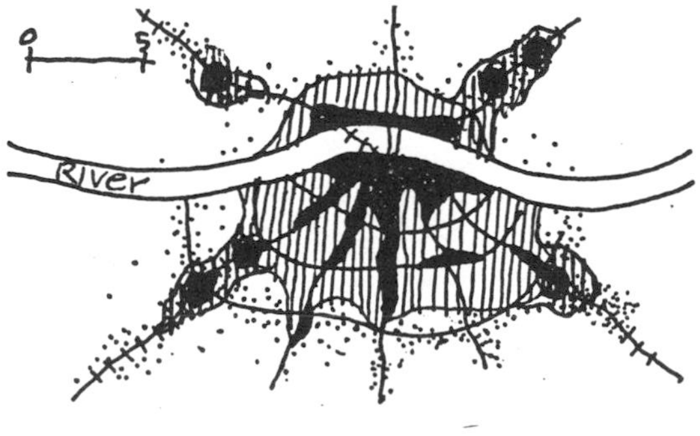

9. Spider web pattern of urban development, illustrating subcentralized growth between villages and the city primarily served by the automobile.

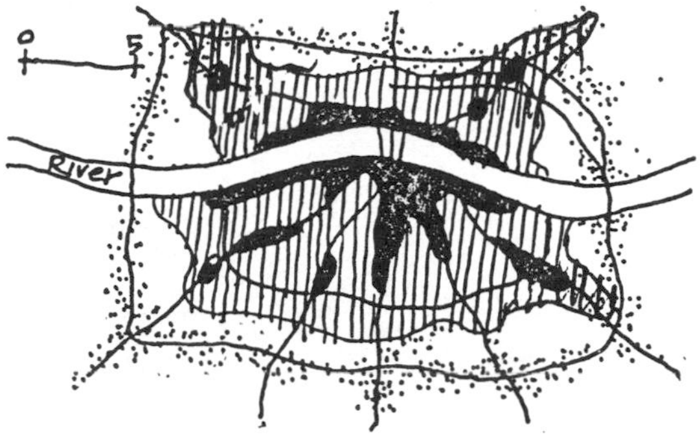

10. Extensive subcentralized development, suburban sprawl and the dominance of the automobile.

individually owned, convenient, and small enough to negotiate a grid-iron street pattern, which was the norm for many rapidly expanding cities. The automobile essentially caused the demise of public mass transportation and perpetuated the creation of the low-density, single family suburban living unit.

11. Deteriorated areas surrounding the city caused by subcentralization, near the north side, Chicago, Illinois (*T. Bartuska*).

12. Dominance and density of a contemporary city core, Seattle, Washington (*T. Bartuska*).

13. The delightful qualities of a livable city—the reanimation of an industrial site into an enjoyable urban environment, Gas Works Park, Seattle, Washington (*T. Bartuska*).

In this way, a continuous settlement was created surrounding cities and extending across the countryside without any clear point of termination. The product of the decentralization dynamic is referred to as **subcentralization** from which the familiar term "suburb" is derived.

The suburb is an environment particularly characteristic of the post-industrial or twentieth century metropolis. Other characteristics are the dominant economic center, massive industrial and transportation complexes and the intricate vehicular freeway system tying it all together.

A saturation of untenable complexity rendered most United States cities nearly unlivable by the end of World War II. Major steps were taken in the 1950s to unravel this condition, but many were unsuccessful. Beginning in the late 1960s and continuing today, a movement that includes inner city renewal, open space planning and new transport systems is slowly bringing a new livability back to the city. It will always be a place people love or hate, but its presence as part of civilization will have an impact on the human condition far into the indefinable future.

REFERENCES

Gallagher, W. 1993. *The Power of Place*. Poseidon Press.

Gallion, A. 1986. *The Urban Pattern*. Van Nostrand.

Hawkes, J. 1963. *Pre-History and the Beginnings of Civilization*. Harper and Row.

Matzerath, H. 1989. "Local History, Urban History, Historical Research in Urbanization," *Geschichte und Gesellschaft*.

Mumford, L. 1961. *The City in History*. Harcourt, Brace and World.

Niehuss, M. 1989. "Aspects of Urbanization: Recent Literature on Urban History," *Historische Zeitschrift*.

Paret, L., Brezzi, P., and Petech, L. 1965. *The Ancient World*. Harper and Row.

Smith, D. 1988. "In Pursuit of the Urban Variable," *Journal of Urban History*.

Spreiregen, P. 1965. *The Architecture of Towns and Cities*. McGraw-Hill.

CHAPTER

22

The Inherited City as a Resource

Robert M. Baron

This chapter is concerned with the significance of the historically formed city as a cultural and material resource. Recent enthusiasm for historic preservation, restoration and urban conservation has made the public more aware of the importance of the existing urban inheritance to further urban development. The particular role played by the built environment in the cultural and social life of contemporary society has not, however, been fully understood nor appreciated. Most geographical and sociological research has viewed the physical resource of the city as relatively inconsequential in the structure of societies and in the process of social change. Reuse and adaptation of historic environments signals a very different perception of its value. Recent experience with historic preservation and renovation, however, has not been fully assimilated into design and planning theory either, nor have its implications been developed (Corboz, 1978). As a result, historic preservation, as popularly understood, seems to be a general notion that can have several meanings: recycling, preservation, adaptive reuse, modernization, renovation or conversion, and rehabilitation.

In the United States, past interest in historic preservation was based on economic imperatives reflecting a convergence of political instincts. The conservatives' regard for a pre-industrial society (with its nostalgic backward glance at Jeffersonian agrarianism and economic liberalism) has merged with liberals' concerns for an ecological consciousness, urban quality and criticism of modern architecture (Corboz, 1978). We have seen the emergence of this trend with the successful development of Ghirardelli Square in San Francisco in 1962.

1. Reanimation of an old chocolate factory into an urban shopping and office center, Ghiradelli Square, San Francisco, California (*W. McCure*).

Before going further in this discussion, however, it is necessary to define terms and premises on which these issues depend.

The aim of **reanimation** is to adapt the physical structure of old buildings and urban areas to accommodate changing functions. **Restoration** is a "historicist" approach in which the objective is to conserve the original formal appearance of the building. The "restorer" is interested in bringing an old building back to its historic origin. As an illustration of these two approaches, consider the difference, in form and intent, between Ghirardelli Square and Colonial Williamsburg, Virginia. Recent experience has shown that restoration and reanimation must work together, however, to produce a balanced design that both preserves the inheritance and carries new uses (Corboz, 1979).

2. Restoration of an historic town, the Governor's Mansion, Williamsburg, Virginia.

The study of urban morphology involves describing and analyzing the *physical form and structure of cities* or any of its parts (Vance, 1977). Such form can be analyzed by classifying its typical parts and understanding the structure which organizes each component into larger contexts. Components could be defined as the urban plan, buildings, monuments, neighborhoods, streets, trees, parks, sidewalks, residential districts and houses. Each of these parts could be further de-constructed into smaller parts and materials, details, colors, proportions, etc. Sir John Summerson (1963) defines **urban morphology** as "the whole physical mass of marble, bricks and mortar, steel and concrete . . . metal conduits and rails—the total artifact." In other words, every material substance, artificial or natural, makes up the urban artifact. We are particularly interested in the ways that urban morphology is formed and adapted through time as it adjusts and affects the changing social and economic conditions of its inhabitants. In many historic cities, for instance, one can clearly see this evolutionary process at work through cycles of growth and adaptation. Few cities have been developed *tabula rasa*—from a clean slate.

In order to understand the ways that cities are formed through physical and social processes, a theory is needed. This chapter uses a theory formulated by urban and historical geographers to understand this process: **urban morphogenesis** (Vance, 1977). The built environment is a continuous historic process formed and transformed through time. Urban morphogenesis is the study of this process of growth and change of urban morphology (the evolutionary changes in the form and patterns of cities).

The built environment is a collectively constructed total environment which manifests itself at different scales—in regions, landscapes, farms, towns, cities, urban domains, streets, squares, parks, avenues, suburbs, neighborhoods and buildings. These parts are considered artifacts of material cultures and can be studied as such. In regard to material cultures (high style or vernacular traditions), components of the built environment, "especially in the case of city sectors, are rarely designed environments, but rather artifacts in the sense mentioned earlier—the products of human action, but not of human design" (Anderson, 1978). Its products are understood as both built environments and symbols of our intention to live, work and play together in communities. Acts of building and design intervention operate collectively to bring intelligibility to the environment.

A BREAK IN URBAN CONTINUITY: MODERN URBANISM

Most urban renewal projects constructed in European and U.S. cities after the Second World War have been destructive to the traditional city. Modernism in design has led to morphological fragmentation and to demolition of historical cities. The net effect of this all-too-prevalent tendency has been to create a condition which prevented the conservation, reuse, or adaptation of the existing building stock and provoked a rupture in social and morphological continuity (Perez de Arce, 1976). The reasons for this disruptive impact are numerous and complex. Most observers, however, would agree that Modernism failed because it was not based on the premise that a city is a continuous production made by periodic adaptations and that continuity, both in morphological and social terms, is an essential condition to be conserved (Krier, 1979; Robertson, 1981).

Modern or avant-garde movements active at the beginning of the twentieth century reacted against the traditional city and its culture, losing sight of the need for continuity. Designers and theorists were reacting to what they thought was a society, culture and city in need of revolutionary change. The most revolutionary of the avant-garde were the Italian Futurists, whose rhetoric was anti-traditional city and who considered the existing city as obsolete, requiring replacement (Grassi, 1978).

Most designers, however, followed the "progressive" urban theories of Robert Owen, Charles Fourier, Soria y Mata, Tony Garnier and Ebenezer Howard, who rejected the city only to propose a new replacement form. Their planning concepts were presented as utopian settings in which open space, landscaping and fresh air became symbols of social progress (Choay, 1969). As a result, many early modernist designs were unrelated to the patterns of existing cities. The Garden-City Movement and Le Corbusier created powerful images of a new type of urbanism. For example, most post-war urban renewal was, in fact, based on ideas present in Le Corbusier's Voisin Plan of 1922, a theoretical study funded by the Voisin Automobile Company. It proposed a total rebuilding of historic Paris. In order to realize his idealized vision of an entirely new society, Le Corbusier proposed that each section of Paris be razed and rebuilt with a new pattern of street grid overlaid with radiating auto connectors, high-rise slabs, and housing blocks set in vast parks (Evenson, 1969). The traditional street space for people to shop, to greet, and to socialize was gone. The new urban morphology was to be strictly zoned to separate urban functions like housing from work places. This theoretical design suggested profound social implications. Not designed for the conventions of Parisians, it proclaimed a new way to live. The zoning indicated in the plan would have resulted in dissolving networks of interaction between related functions. As Jane Jacobs (1961) notes, this kind of zoning leads to disintegration of lively social vitality and diversity. Christopher Alexander (1965) also criticizes this type of "zoning" by pointing out that its rigid hierarchical structure breaks down social contact among individuals.

POSTWAR URBANISM: URBAN RENEWAL

In the United States, Le Corbusier's Voisin Plan was implemented in housing developments like the Alfred E. Smith Project of 1948, the Stuyvesant Middle-Income Project of 1947, and the Polo Grounds Middle-Income Project as late as 1964–67. These developments, inserted into New York City, became emblems of the U.S. interpretation of the Voisin Plan (Scully, 1969). To many architects of the 1950s and 1960s, these designs connoted the image of "social progress" and enlightened urban policy which seemed consistent with national social goals (Stern, 1969). Many up-to-date young architects began thinking about design in these "visionary" terms, causing them to ignore existing physical and social contexts. We cannot underestimate the influence that historians like Giedion and Pevsner had in basing their historiography on something as abstract as the "spirit of the age" (Ackerman, 1980). Under this ideology, the city would seem outdated and would require continual reformulation to embody the Zeitgeist. This kind of history inferred that each age required its own form. Old forms corresponded to past times. For instance, the Middle Ages had its medieval city and the eighteenth century its neoclassical city. Then what is to be the form of the modern city? The continuous historical city was perceived as irrelevant to contemporary life. Here we see the basis of an ideology of discontinuity and a rejection of the past in the present.

Three case studies illustrate the problems discussed as they have appeared in the modern city.

Cataclysmic Urban Renewal: Lincoln Center Redevelopment Area

Complete destruction of a whole inner-city neighborhood is recorded in the history of New York's Lincoln Center Project directed by Robert Moses, a master implementer of modern urbanism. In this project, the existing buildings in the area were totally destroyed. Its poor residents were required to be relocated. After the area was cleared, an expensive Performing Arts Complex (Lincoln Center) and housing towers were built in its place. The existing neighborhood was physically and socially razed. Robert Stern (1969), a U.S. architect and urbanist, calls these developments "cataclysmic urban renewal." A kind of "frontal lobotomy" was performed on the body urban. The logic for this strategy was to revitalize a sagging inner city economy, but for whom? Certainly not for the original residents. The neighborhood, both its morphology and its social life, was not seen by its developers as an important resource to be studied and reanimated.

Antiurban Myths: The Oak Street Connector Project

In his criticism of the Oak Street Connector Project in New Haven, Connecticut, Vincent Scully (1969) identified four persistent anticity myths given expression in the project. "The city is bad." "Tear it down." "Get on the road." "Be a pioneer." These myths, which can be uncovered in U.S. social and cultural history, have joined with modern urbanism to produce a rather potent monster. In New Haven, a "slum" was cleared (the city is bad; tear it down) to provide space for a freeway connector (get on the road), which was built to bring suburbanites (be a pioneer) into the city center to work and shop and return to their suburbs to live. Scully observed that due to the decay of public transportation, over the 1950s, an urgent need existed for the city to encourage the construction of yet more automobile connectors which eventually cut up the block pattern of New Haven, isolating areas and buildings. This development "syndrome" and its side effects worked like a self-fulfilling prophecy. In the end, the old neighborhood was totally replaced by vast open spaces, new commercial buildings and luxury apartment slabs. Regrettably, this seemed to be a reoccurring pattern of development that can be traced across the country.

The Designer as Form Giver vs. Responsive Agent: The Brighton Beach Competition

Modernism, in general, has relied on the designer as a "form giver" rather than as a responsive agent who interpreted and articulated the values of an urban community (Ackerman, 1980). An example of this problem can be seen in the results of the Brighton Beach Competition, in Brooklyn, sponsored by the Housing and Development Administration of New York City. In this competition, the architectural firm of Wells-Koetter won first prize, while the Venturi-Rauch Firm received third. The winning solution seemed to be a modernist design, while the Venturi-Rauch scheme illustrated a more contextual response to existing social and physical conditions. Two competition jurors, Philip Johnson and Donlyn Lyndon, delineated the philosophical differences in the two solutions. Johnson defended the Wells-Koetter submission in this way:

> This jury is indicative of many problems in today's architecture and deserves full discussion and publicity. To the majority, of which I am one (the Venturi-Rauch submission), seemed a pair of **very ugly** buildings. We felt that the buildings looked like most ordinary apartment construction built all over Queens and Brooklyn since the Depression, that the placing of the blocks was ordinary and dull. The forms that the buildings took were, in our eyes, deliberately ugly. There were some obvious merits: the town houses set around the cul-de-sac of the street, and the extension of the boardwalk surrounding the base building. But these minor virtues seem to us overwhelmed by the all-pervading ugliness. . . . The first prize winner, strikes me as a rich and satisfactory solution. . . . The general conception . . . pleased us all (Venturi, 1972).

Lyndon defends the merits of the Venturi-Rauch design in real experimental terms to the user:

> The Venturi-Rauch scheme has a modesty that is appropriate to the scale and location of the project. The competition terms neither called for, nor allowed, a major social or technological reform. The scheme

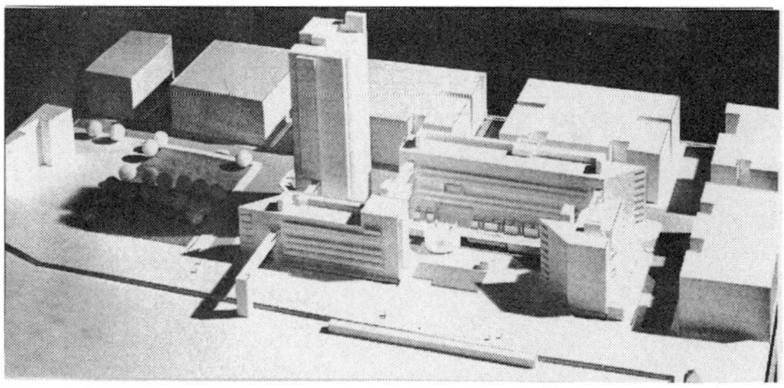

3. First prize submission for the Brighton Beach Housing Competition by Wells and Koetter, 1968 (*courtesy of MIT Press*).

4. Third prize submission, Venturi and Rauch, 1968, in association with Kawasaki, Brown and Clark (*courtesy of MIT Press*).

> does not detract from or demean the surrounding neighborhood. It respects, but is not bound by, the existing order. In our view, it offers real benefits for the people who might occupy it rather than give polemic satisfaction to those who consider it. The method of building (proposed) is intrinsically so simple that it could be built well, not meanly. We think this would contribute to the personal dignity of its occupants. We think that it in no way represents "more of the same," but is instead a thoughtful use of existing possibilities (Venturi, 1972).

If Johnson's comments were representative of the views of most modern designers and planners, then some revealing observations can be made. Modernists have seemed impatient with existing urban conditions. The first prize design seemed to be an "abstract form" inserted without connection to established urban morphology. At least one-half of the residents could not have enjoyed a view of the water from their apartment windows, while the Venturi-Rauch submission gave almost every resident a view. The Venturi-Rauch design also allowed the street pattern to continue to the waterfront without obstruction; the Wells-Koetter design did not. The winning project emphasized expensive exterior concrete work, while Venturi-Rauch placed priority on items which residents used on a day-to-day basis, like quality interior detailing (Venturi, 1972).

Historic preservation has focused attention on the importance of the physical city as a historical **resource**, rather than as a **liability** to be overcome. Too little research has contributed to the development of theories guiding environmental design, however, and most of them have emphasized the behavioral aspects over the morphological. Stanford Anderson (1981) and James Vance (1977) have produced significant research in their studies of the interaction between urban morphology and its social consequences.

URBAN MORPHOGENESIS

James E. Vance, Jr. (1977) asserts that geographers have not accorded enough attention to the implication of physical form and structure on the life of human societies. He postulates that an **ecological** relationship necessarily exists between the physical environment and social processes and has found that the morphologies of various cities were created through such interaction. Urban morphology changes slowly, supporting the notion that political and social institutions may change rapidly, yet do not remake cities. For example, he explains that, after 1945, eastern Europe underwent major political-economic changes which did not affect the historic core of many cities. Sofia, Budapest and Prague have persisted in their pre-War form. Urban morphology seemed to act independently of institutional processes (Vance, 1977). Perhaps this explains how built forms can be adaptable to changing functions. Why does urban morphology behave in a quasi-autonomous way? Vance (1977) gave three reasons:

1. Since biological and psychological qualities of humans persist, then built forms relate to human scale, e.g., the height of doors does not change very much.
2. Properties of the physical world, like geographic characteristics are relatively unchanging. Due to its materiality, urban morphology changes less than human institutions.
3. Physical change is evolutionary. Old buildings slowly are being transformed or replaced by new ones following precedent in materials and in form. This perpetuates the existing form of the city.

Urban morphogenesis is concerned with the *processes* that establish and transform cities over time. It takes into account material form and socio-economic change. Vance was also interested in the constantly changing form/function relationships that can be found in any ancient city. Form has a kind of autonomy. In urban history, building types like Roman basilicas and coliseums have undergone dramatic changes of function, and yet remain in continuous use. For example, the Agora was in the beginning a religious building type, but through time, the social functions changed—it became a school, then a market and finally an urban square. The form or morphology of the Agora remain fundamentally the same (Vance, 1977), even though functions and meanings have changed.

Vance explains that urban morphogenesis occurs in stages. Each stage is synchronized with its patterns of social use. As there are changes in social activities and values, the physical environment will have to be reanimated or adapted. An adaptive process, therefore, is at work mediating between stages. This process works in two ways: (1) adaptation of existing morphology from one stage to another (Vance, 1977), and (2) adaptation from one form/function relationship to another. In both cases, the physical form is a resource to be developed.

Adaptation from One Stage to Another

The urban morphology of Bath, England is very interesting because it reveals six morphological stages, each integrated into the others: (1) Roman settlement, (2) abbey town, (3) medieval market town, (4) society town of eighteenth century, (5) home of the Admiralty during World War Two, and finally (6) the Bath of today (Vance, 1977). Each stage has left its permanent mark. Its Palladian eighteenth century form, however, is still the most dominant.

Rome is a striking example of a layering of old and new form. It has eight stages of growth: classical archaeologists and urban historians can identify (1) a tribal Rome, (2) an early Republican Rome, (3) an Imperial Rome, (4) a medieval Rome of successive sackings and political neglect, (5) a Papal Rome reflecting the planning of Sixtus V at the end of the sixteenth century, (6) a Rome of King Victor Emmanual during the unification of Italy in the mid-nineteenth century, (7) a Rome of Mussolini, and finally (8) a Modern Rome with auto connectors, auto-businesses and suburban tower developments. Rome, as it is today, is an urban collage of all these previous Romes. The sense of historical continuity in the city is remarkable. This kind of continuity was not arrived at by a policy of "urban renewal." Ancient streets and civic buildings have been continuously re-animated. All previous stages of morphogenesis were seen as touchstones for further development.

Adaptation From One Form/Function Relationship to Another

One of the most amazing morphological adaptations of an ancient building has occurred in Split, Yugoslavia. Originally, it was a palace built for a retired Roman Emperor, Diocletian, and later during the early middle ages that one building complex was converted into an entire town (Perez de Arce, 1976). Examples of this kind of reanimation abound in Europe.

The arena of the Roman amphitheater at Lucca was changed into a piazza and the ancient amphitheater at Arles, France was converted into a fortified town (Rossi, 1982). The same restorative and reanimative processes are at work in the United States, with the transformation of a chocolate fac-

5. Plan of Rome, 1873 (*S. Kostof*).

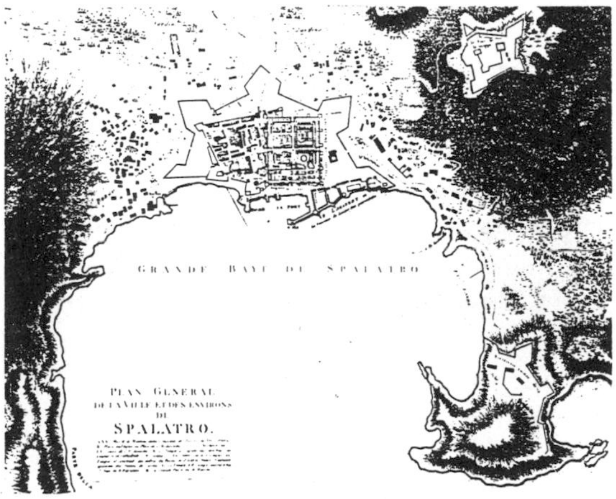

6. Split, Yugoslavia at the end of the eighteenth century (*L. F. Cassas, Voyage Pittoresque et historique de l'Istrie et de Dalmatie, Paris, 1802*).

7. Aerial view of Roman amphitheater adapted into a piazza in Lucca, Italy (*A. Rossi, 1982*).

tory and old warehouses into popular retail centers in San Francisco. There are also many examples of railroad stations converted into city halls or community centers, and of conservation in historic districts.

SOCIAL SPACES AND PHYSICAL RESOURCES

In his study of Savannah, Georgia, Stanford Anderson observes that past historical studies have focused on the origin of environments and not on the ways that such environments adapt to change. He notes that the urban pattern can be studied to identify the permanent adaptable parts and to understand the complex interactions between environmental form and its social context. Anderson (1981) asserts that every built environment can support multiple uses and interpretations. The physical forms have a certain degree of independence. The urban morphology undergoes a pattern of changes due to an interplay of quasi-autonomous physical conditions and social behaviors. In his study of the changes of occupancy in Savannah, Anderson shows that the city plan has been able to adapt and support a series of different patterns of habitations. He concluded his investigation with the observation that all urban environments can be understood through analysis of two systems: (1) social spaces, and (2) environmental resources.

All of the above examples challenge the functionalist doctrine—"form follows function." Given the evidence, function is more adaptable and, therefore, "function also follows form."

DETERMINISM VS. POSSIBILISM: A CRITIQUE OF FUNCTIONALISM

Some form of determinism is behind most notions of the functionalist doctrine (Anderson, 1982). This modernist doctrine, although an ambiguous concepts suggests that the use of a building determines its particular shape (Scruton, 1979). This is a form of social determinism. If true, then what happens to the form when the original functions change? Does this lead to a nonfunctional state? Most urban morphologies, like individual buildings and street patterns, are being used for very different purposes than what was originally intended. This doctrine, a "naive functionalism" (Rossi, 1982), implies that, to be relevant, the form of the city would have to be replaced every time social structures change (i.e., at the end of each morphological stage). This kind of policy, as we have seen in urban renewal, leads to massive destruction of established physical environments.

Equally mistaken is the reverse notion that **function follows form**, based on another determinism (environmental determinism), which states that the physical environment shapes human behaviors (Anderson, 1981). This would suggest that if an original function were changed, then the past form would no longer be relevant in the present. Recent research has shown that designed environments, like rooms or plazas, can *afford* numerous types of uses and visual meanings (Lang, 1980). Anderson, therefore, notes that every physical form will support multiple **uses** and **meanings**, but at the same time impose constraints on its use. He rejects determinism and embraces a concept of **possibilism**, which better explains the relationships between people and their environments. Even design traditions, like the neoclassical (Corboz, 1978) or the urban grid pattern (Groth, 1981), possesses a **transfunctional** quality. When transfunctional possibilities are exhausted, then the built form will become obsolete, abandoned or demolished.

NEGOTIATION AND POSSIBILISM: A RESPONSE TO THE INHERITED BUILT RESOURCE

If the relationship between form and function is "possibilist" and necessarily complex and new projects are inevitably inserted into an existing urban context of irreplaceable quality (like historic buildings or districts with valuable physical characteristics), then programs of development need to be carefully adjusted to inherited urban resources. If not done, developers make building programs that do not take advantage of existing potentials and invariably insist on development plans that require total replacement of urban settings. If the built environment has a possibilist relationship with its social life and is evolved through adaptive use, a process of **negotiation** occurs (Corboz, 1978). This is quite different from the functionalist approach. A possibilist theory enables the designer and user to appreciate the ways to negotiate between the limits and opportunities of both form and function—the ways that **form suggests uses and that uses suggest form**.

Now, having challenged the functionalist doctrine, the various ways that the urban resource can be used can be examined. Through urban history, according to Perez de Arce (1976), urban morphology has been reanimated in three general ways: (1) as **quarries** for building material, (2) as **foundations and founding plans** for new buildings, and (3) as **supports and frameworks** for formal insertions.

Quarries

Using existing built resources as quarries for new construction is a useful form of recycling, one that has occurred throughout history. For example, many Roman constructions were made from the parts of dismantled older buildings (Perez de Arce, 1976). The Roman Forum and Coliseum were used as quarries for new constructions during the Middle Ages. The Aurelian Wall was erected using the debris of destroyed monuments. The composition of inherited parts combined in a contemporary building creates what Kevin Lynch (1972) called "temporal collage." This temporal ensemble can be seen in many of the eighteenth century etchings of Piranesi, who was fascinated by the ancient ruins. His etchings provide an image of a kind of urban recycling operation that was common in the preindustrial city.

8. Bascilica, Pompeii (120 B.C.) used as a resource quarry for building material throughout the ages.

Foundations and Founding Plans

The amphitheater of Domitian became the foundation for the buildings surrounding the Piazza Navona (Perez de Arce, 1976). Piazza Navona was originally a Roman racetrack and now its enclosed form is used for a wonderful urban plaza. This is an

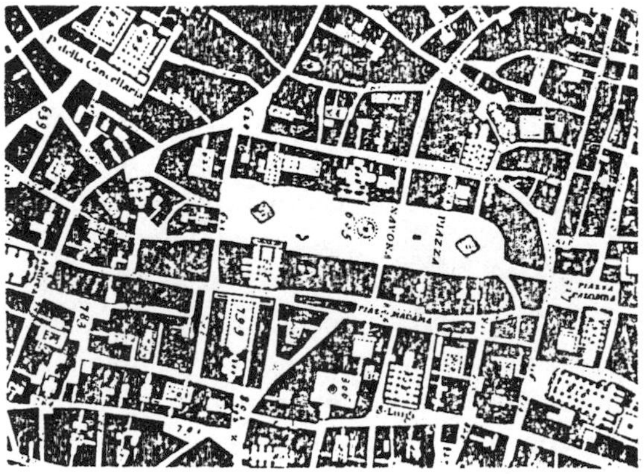

9. Rome, a section of Nolli's plan of 1748. Piazza Navona at center.

archetypal example of how a ruin can be used as foundation and founding plans for new use and urban development.

Another example can be found in Florence, Italy, in the Santa Croce district. Absorbed in the residential textures is the foundation of an ancient amphitheater (Rossi, 1982). The existence of the ancient building is hardly noticeable. As discussed earlier, the urban plan, like the foundation, is a permanent feature. The founding plan offers a fixed context for evolving spatial structure of social territories and boundaries. These relationships, between people and things, become defined and associated with law and custom and are nearly impossible to eliminate.

In Turin, Italy and Regensburg, Germany, both typical examples, the founding plans laid by the colonial Romans are still persistent in the cores of their morphological development (Morris, 1972). Perez de Arce (1976) described how the Spaniards employed the existing plan of Cuzco, Peru, as the Inca left it, for building the colonial town (second stage in its morphogenesis). The Spanish builders subdivided and provided the context for the development of new buildings and urban spaces. The founding plan provided possibilities for changing uses.

Supports and Frameworks

Habraken (1981) defines the "support" concept as a physical form which allows a variety of insertions: "It must-in-itself-be a true piece of architecture, strong enough to hold the variety of forms that will be expressed within it." He cites the Rue de Rivoli in Paris as such a morphological support: "within it you find a rich population of shops, restaurants, cafes and even hotels." Many urban buildings, like the Palazzo della Ragione in Padua, carry an amazing variety of social functions over time (Rossi, 1982). The coliseum in Rome has a

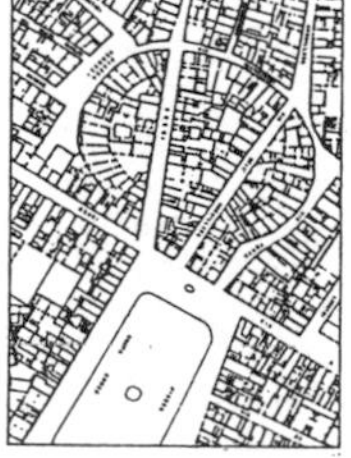

10. Plans of the Santa Croce district of Florence (*P. Fontana, Libro Secondo in cui si ragiona di alcune fabriche fatte in Roma et in Napoli dal Cavaliere Romenico Fontana, Naples, 1603*).

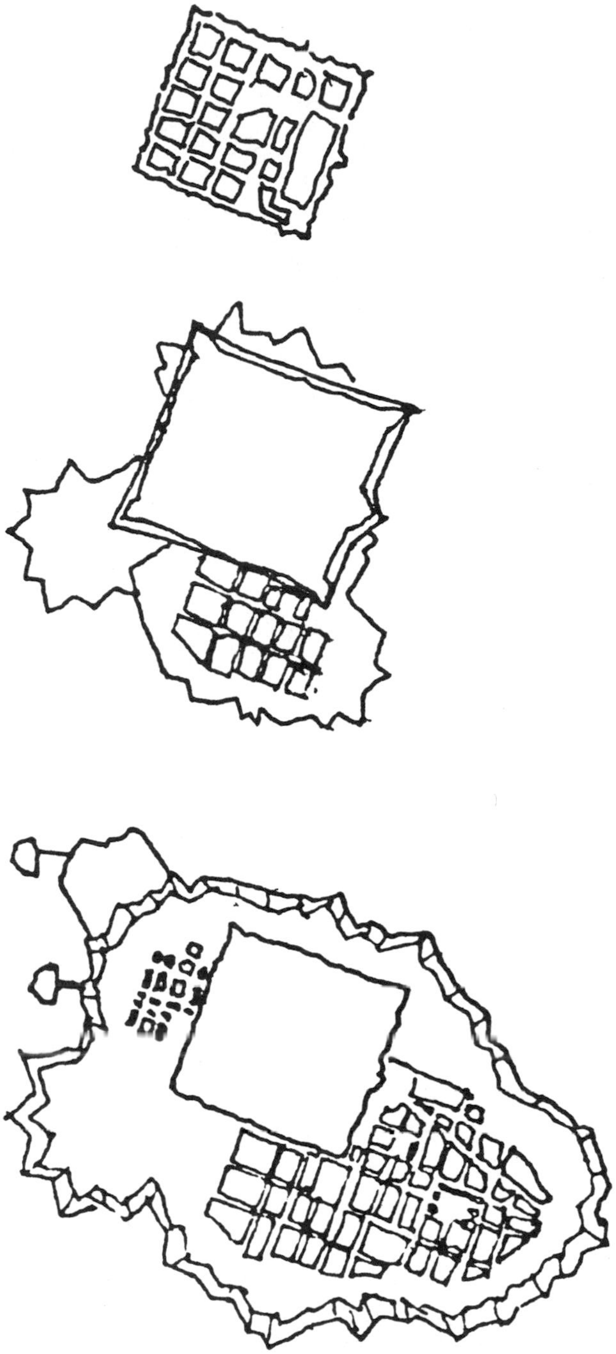

11. Turin, three stages in morphological growth: (a) Roman colony, (b) defensive walls, sixteenth century, and (c) late seventeenth century (*S. Forester*).

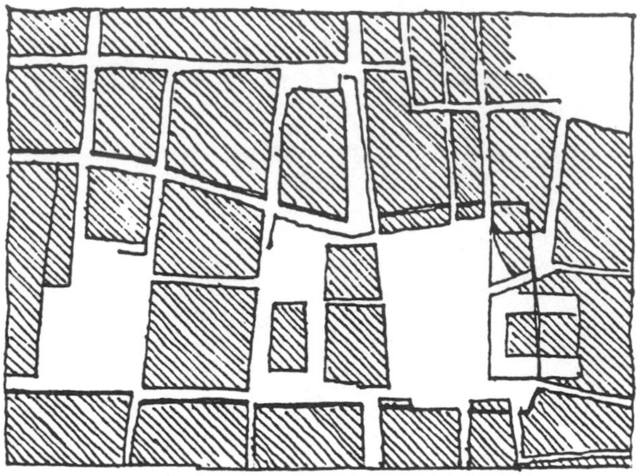

12. Central Square, Cuzco, as developed by the Incas before the conquest (*S. Forester*).

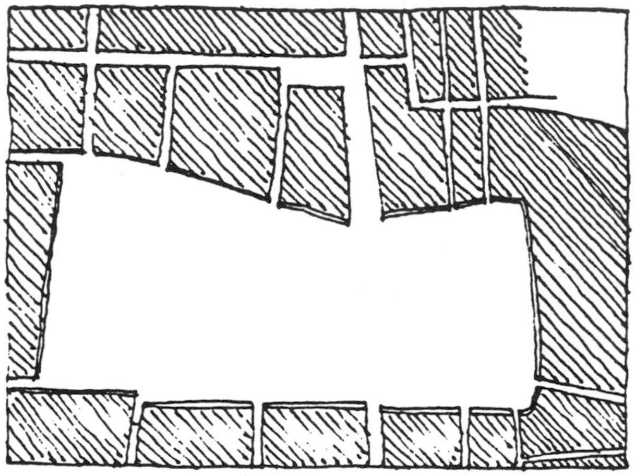

13. Cuzco Central Square transformed by Spaniards after the Conquest (*S. Forester*).

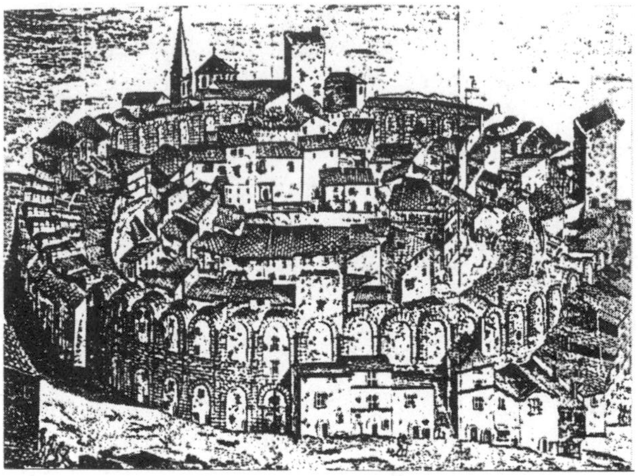

14. Arles, town built within second century Roman Amphitheater (*J. Noble de la Lauziere*).

15. Pirenasi engraving of the Theater of Mancellus. Transformed into an apartment building in Rome.

fantastic transfunctional character. It became the site of two proposed reanimation operations. A drawing dated 1590 presents Pope Sixtus V's proposal for its transformation into a wool factory with worker's apartments (Rossi, 1982). In 1707, Carlo Fontana made a drawing that shows it as a forum for a centralized church.

As morphological parts, streets and squares have provided the support for public functions like strolling, dining, waiting, entertaining, sitting, selling, shopping, horse racing (as in Siena), political rallies, parking and public processions. Amsterdam's old lot pattern, a good case in point, with its brick walls perpendicular to the street, provides a structure for insertions. The lot space is six meters, the distance needed to span the space "with a wooden beam from one brick wall to another" (Habraken, 1981). This kind of supporting system has given the city a remarkable consistency since the Middle Ages.

Whereas the foundation is a horizontal connecting element, the support is the vertical link for insertions or additions to established urban patterns. Charles Moore's extensions to the Citizens Federal Savings and Loan Association Building in San Francisco provide a contemporary example. The existing bank building furnishes support, linking Moore's addition to the street and block pattern. As noted before, the Yugoslavian town of Split presents a dramatic demonstration of the use of an inherited urban framework. As a support for its inhabitants, the ruined Palace of Diocletian was dramatically

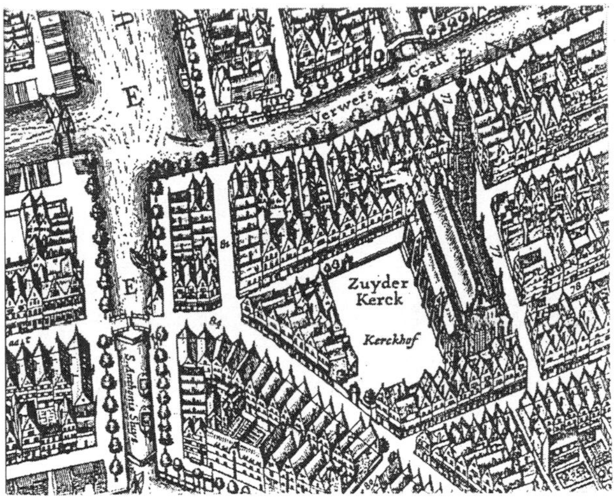

16. A segment of a 1625 map of Amsterdam (*Via Culture and the Social Vision*).

reused to establish social space marking private and public zones. The wealthy, for example, made homes in the larger, palatial apartments, while the poor found accommodations in the basement chambers. The ruined and unroofed basilica became a public square. The palace provided the framework for changed social uses (Perez de Arce, 1976).

The true significance of any inherited urban morphology then, is its value as a cultural resource, with great capacity for being reused as social functions change. This understanding of the physical city, if practiced, leads to the conservation of urban continuity and culture. The next step is to begin searching for the inherited morphological resources in your own communities and asking how they could be creatively reanimated in future development.

REFERENCES

Ackerman, J. 1980. "The History of Design and the Design of History," *VIA: Culture and Social Vision*.

Alexander, C. 1965. "A City Is Not a Tree," *Architectural Forum*, April.

Alexander, C. Ishikawa, S. and Silverstein, M. 1987. *A New Theory of Urban Design*. Oxford University Press.

Anderson, S. 1978. "People in the Physical Environment: The Urban Ecology of Streets," *On Streets*. MIT Press.

Anderson, S. 1981. "The Plan of Savannah and Changes of Occupancy During Its Early Years: City Plan as Resource," *The Harvard Architecture Review*, Spring.

Charles, Prince of Wales. 1989. *A Vision of Britain*. Doubleday.

Choay, F. 1969. *The Modern City: Planning in the 19th Century*, Braziller.

Corboz, A. 1978. "Old Buildings and Modern Functions," *Lotus International*.

Evenson, N. 1969. *Le Corbusier: The Machine and the Grand Design*. Braziller.

Grassi, G. 1978. "Avant-Garde and Continuity," *Oppositions*.

Groth, P. 1981. "Street Grids as Frameworks for Urban Variety," *The Harvard Architecture Review*, Spring.

Habraken, N. 1981. "The Leaves and the Flowers," *VIA: Culture and Social Vision*.

Jacobs, J. 1961. *The Death and Life of Great American Cities*. Vintage Books.

Lang, J. 1980. "The Built Environment and Social Behavior: Architectural Determinism Re-examined," *VIA: Culture and Social Vision*.

Lynch, K. 1972. *What Time is This Place*. MIT Press.

Morris, A. E. J. 1972. *History of Urban Form*. Wiley.

Perez de Arce, R. 1976. "Urban Transformation: The Architecture of Additions," *Architectural Design*.

Robertson, J. 1981. "Only Connect: Recognition of Old and New," *The Harvard Architecture Review*, Spring.

Roe, L. K. and R. E. Rucker. 1991. "Human Ecology and Urban Revitalization: A Case Study of the Minneapolis Warehouse District," *Mid-American Review of Sociology*.

Rossi, A. 1982. *The Architecture of the City*. MIT Press.

Samperi, P. 1991. "Rome: A 1991 Urban Planning Update," *Studi Romani*.

Scruton, R. 1979. *The Aesthetics of Architecture*. Princeton University Press.

Scully, V. 1969. *American Architecture and Urbanism*. Praeger.

Stern, R. 1969. *New Directions in American Architecture*. Braziller.

Summerson, J. 1963. "Urban Forms," *The Historian and the City*. MIT Press.

Trancik, R. 1986. *Finding Lost Space: Theories of Urban Design*. Van Nostrand Reinhold.

Vance, J. 1990. *The Centeneeing City: Urban Morphology in Western Civilization*. John Hopkins.

Venturi, R., Brown, D., Izenour, S. 1972. *Learning From Las Vegas*. MIT Press.

Yelling, J. 1990. "Urban Renewal and Regeneration in Historical Perspective," *Area*.

CHAPTER

23

Cities, Climate and Environmental Context

Michael S. Owen

The fundamental elements of the physical environment are land, water and air. Early villages and cities, based on agricultural economies, located in fertile valleys with abundant water nearby. As urban society became more specialized and complex, waterways became the principal means of transportation. Ease of transportation and agricultural specialization allowed the spread of urban settlements into ever more diverse geographic areas of the globe. Human settlements eventually developed in every climatic condition on earth.

Today, major cities can be found in the weather extremes of the arctic circle and great inland deserts. To settle in such adverse conditions, humans have had to adapt to the airborne physical environment, in other words, to **climate**. Much of the global diversity and variety in city form may be traced to specialized means of adaptation in response to the world's diverse climatic and geographic conditions.

To understand how such diversity has come about, it is first necessary to examine the relationship between climate and geography and to identify the aspects of this relationship to which urban form must respond. Second, it is useful to explore the range of design strategies used in cities to adapt to geographic and climatic factors. Finally, it is instructive to compare purely technological (mechanical) responses to achieve such adaptation with less energy-consumptive, ecologically sound concepts—those of spatial manipulation and conscientious use of materials and landscaping.

CLIMATE AND GEOGRAPHY

Simply stated, climate is a function or consequence of geography. The general climate of a region is determined by its level of insolation (the amount of sunlight which reaches the earth). Insolation is most constant at the equator where there are exactly twelve hours of daylight and twelve hours of darkness, 365 days per year. Temperatures at the equator are typically warm and constant.

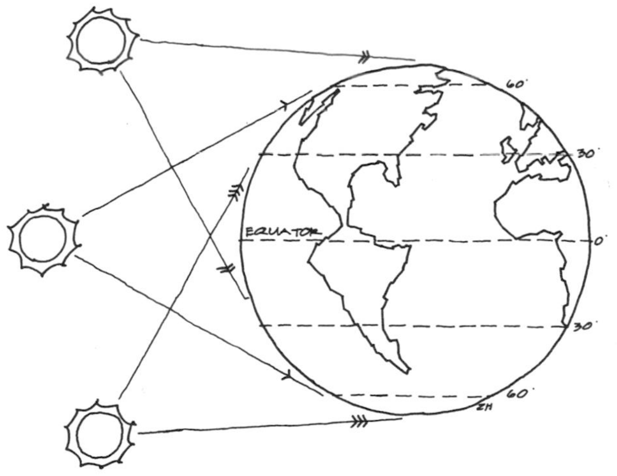

1. Latitude/Insolation of the earth influences weather patterns by the amount of sun reaching the earth. The highest, most consistent insolation occurs at the equator and becomes less and less as one moves north or south. Distances from the equator are measured in degrees of latitude.

Moving north or south of the equator, insolation periods begin to vary (e.g., long summer days, short winter days). The closer to the poles, the greater the variations, hence certain periods in arctic climates are characterized by twenty-four hours of darkness or twenty-four hours of light (the "midnight sun"). Movement away from the equator is measured by lines of latitude: the equator is 0° latitude, Mexico City is 19°, Seattle is 49°, and the Arctic Circle is 67°. Latitude therefore is the primary determinant of general climatic conditions. Longitude, which measures distances east-west around the globe, is not a determinant of climate; it functions as an indicator of location and time.

In addition to latitude, other primary geographic features determining general climatic conditions are large areas of water and land. Large water bodies tend to mediate temperature extremes because of their capacities to absorb and store heat for maintaining a constant temperature and their properties of evaporation. More moisture and land/water temperature difference also tend to cool warm regions and to warm cold areas by creating winds and rain. Large land areas tend to suffer the greatest temperature extremes—the greater the distance from water, the greater the variation. For example, the central plains area of the United States and Canada typically experiences extremely cold winters and hot summers. Large variations in day versus nighttime temperature are also typical.

Latitude and the relationships of land and water masses are geographical features which establish the general or larger **macro**-climatic patterns of a region. Geographic features, particularly elevation (above or below sea level) and vegetation, also influence the local or **micro**-climatic conditions of a specific area. Typically, higher elevations yield relatively lower temperatures and greater quantities of precipitation (rain and snow). In mountainous areas solar orientation plays a major role because exposures facing the sun (southern exposure in the northern hemisphere) can be far warmer than shaded exposures.

Trees and other forms of vegetation are very important as potential wind breakers, heat absorbers, and air cleaners. Like water bodies, forests tend to mediate temperature extremes. The lack of significant vegetation in arctic and desert climates testify to this fact. And the properties of snow and sand tend to amplify temperature extremes in these climates; snow reflects the heat and sand absorbs it.

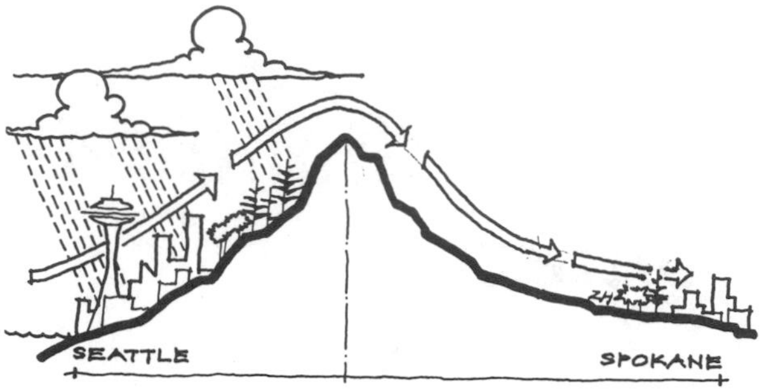

2. Water, mountains and other land masses also determine weather patterns. Areas near or surrounded by water tend to be more temperate with only minor fluctuations in temperature. Inland areas, on the other hand, exhibit severe temperature ranges from icy cold to desert hot. Mountains also modify the weather by creating barriers to the movement of warm air and precipitation.

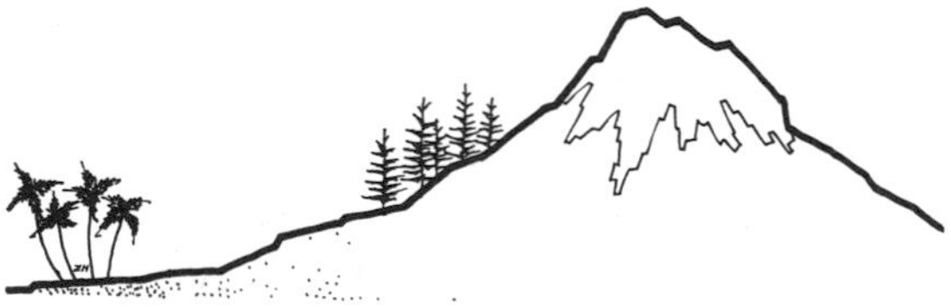

3. The elevation or altitude of an area also modifies temperature. Typically, temperatures lower by 3° for every 1,000 foot rise in altitude.

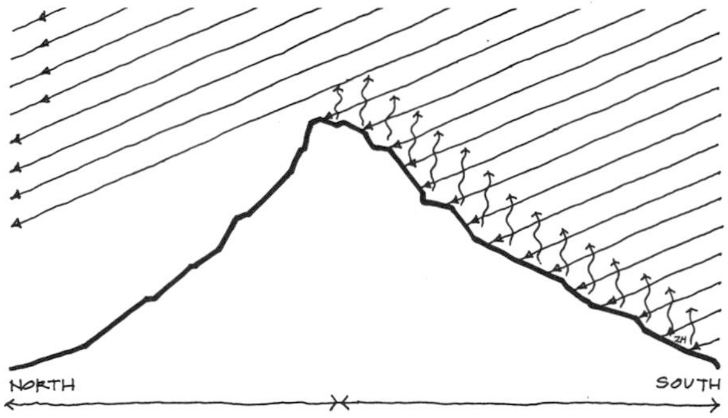

4. Solar exposure is important to building. Especially when building on slopes, it is wise to locate major developments on exposures facing the sun.

What are the design consequences of this range of geographic and climatic zones? What are the weather conditions humans must contend with when developing their settlements? What are the critical geographic and climatic factors that must be taken into account when creating a living environment?

Although the subject of climate and geography appears complex in its diversity and variety, the number of factors which must be taken into account related to building or urban design are really quite simple: temperature, wind, humidity, and precipitation—rain and snow.

The design objectives of adapting the built environment to these factors are two-fold: first, to reduce the extremes of each condition that might cause discomfort and dysfunction in the daily lives of humans. The built environment then should be structured to:

- maintain tolerable indoor temperatures (65°–75 °F)
- protect occupants from freezing winter winds, but allow cooling breezes in the summer
- provide protection from rain and snow

Second, to celebrate the special features of each climatic zone and season. The built environment should be created to enhance such opportunities as:

- the warm feeling of the sun indoors and out
- the beauty of the sound and movement of rain
- the quiet beauty of snow, blanketing the outdoors
- the movement of trees and banners in the wind

5. In desert towns, designing with nature means constructing cities compactly with narrow streets which can be shaded by adjacent buildings. Buildings are often constructed with thick mud walls to "insulate" the inhabitants from the hot sun during the day, and to release radiant warmth during the cool of the evening.

DESIGN FOR CLIMATE AND GEOGRAPHY

How can the dual objective of mediation and celebration be achieved in the city environment? Again, the principles are simple, but the diversity of climatic conditions must be taken into account. Four general climatic categories can illustrate some of the human-environmental adaptive design strategies.

Arid (Hot-Dry) Climates

In arid climates, city design must be structured to minimize insolation on buildings and streets, encourage air movement for ventilation and cooling, and capture and retain precipitation. Even in hot climates, during certain seasons, nights can be quite cool. Often it is necessary to retain the heat of the day to mediate nighttime cold.

Inhabitants of human settlements sited in desert regions have a long history of fine-tuning their city designs to respond to hot-dry conditions. The street systems are structured to minimize building exposure to the rays of the sun. Streets are narrow so they may be shaded by surrounding buildings during most parts of the day. Settlements are built compactly to minimize exposed surface areas and to enhance the effects of thick mud and masonry walls shared among neighbors. Such thick walls absorb the heat and "insulate" inhabitants from the heat of the day, but release the day's heat in the cool of the night.

The compact design of settlements also shields desert people from severe winds, while allowing cooling breezes to ventilate living areas and streets during the day through careful siting of buildings and through the use of such devices as "wind scoops." Such settlements are also designed to capture and retain precious rains through the careful crafting of drainage systems to feed into underground cisterns. Water, and the green growth it creates, is celebrated in desert communities by specially siting protected plazas to serve as spectacular

6. Water and greenery are celebrated in desert cities through the creation of oases, or lush, verdant gardens.

7. Shaded Streets are useful in desert and jungle cities. Awnings and cloth screens provide colorful shade while allowing breezes to cool the city on hot days.

oases for public use. When water is available, it is used to moisten and cool the built environment of the city.

Tropical (Hot-Humid) Climates

People living in tropical climates (e.g., jungle habitats) approach urban design in a way just the opposite of desert cultures. In hot-humid climates, shade and air movement are the most critical factors in assuring human comfort, hence buildings are separated from each other and often set on stilts above the ground. This allows maximum air movement around and through streets and structures. Shade is achieved through long overhangs and by arcades (covered sidewalks along building and street fronts), which provide protection from rains but are open to breezes.

Typically, temperatures in hot-humid climates do not cool off during evening hours. Jungle vegetation retains daytime heat and releases it at night. Structures are therefore designed of lighter materials such as wood, bamboo, and palm leaves—materials which do not appreciably retain heat. Consequently, tropical settlements are not designed compactly, but

8. Jungle towns in hot-wet climates are constructed less compactly than in desert climates to avoid blocking cooling breezes. Construction materials such as bamboo and palm leaves are employed to minimize heat retention in buildings (*T. Bartuska*).

buildings are separated to maximize air flow. Public plazas are designed to be used in the hours of early evening and are surrounded by arcades, where people can sit protected while watching and listening to the cooling afternoon rains.

Temperate (Cool-Wet) Climates

Cooler temperate climates, typically, are characterized by greater seasonal variations of temperature, winds, and precipitation than hot climates. Cool-wet climates are at sea-level or at higher latitudes and are often associated with large water bodies and mountainous terrain, conditions which create cooler temperatures and rain.

In predominantly cooler climates, settlements need to be designed to achieve the greatest exposure of streets and buildings to the warming rays of the sun. In mountainous areas, cities should be located on the sunny side of slopes (on the south side in the northern hemisphere). Although daytime and nighttime temperatures vary, the range is not typically as great as in desert environments—seldom lower than 32°F or greater than 80°F, hence, the characterization as "temperate."

Temperate conditions tend to mediate climatic extremes and consequently most of the world's largest cities are located in these zones. Designers of such settlements need to pay special attention to seasonal variations. They should attempt to locate streets and buildings to protect inhabitants from cold winter winds, but allow cooling summer breezes. This can be accomplished because prevailing winds in the winter and summer generally blow from different directions. Also, designers must pay attention to protection from rain. As in hot-humid regions, arcades and canopies are employed in cool-wet conditions to shelter people from hard-driving rains. Although snow may occasionally fall, it does not typically remain for long periods of time, and therefore is not a primary determinant of settlement design.

Appropriately designed settlements in cool-wet regions allow people to celebrate the special climatic qualities of each season—summer, fall, winter and

9. Arcades are excellent for protecting people from the sun and rain.

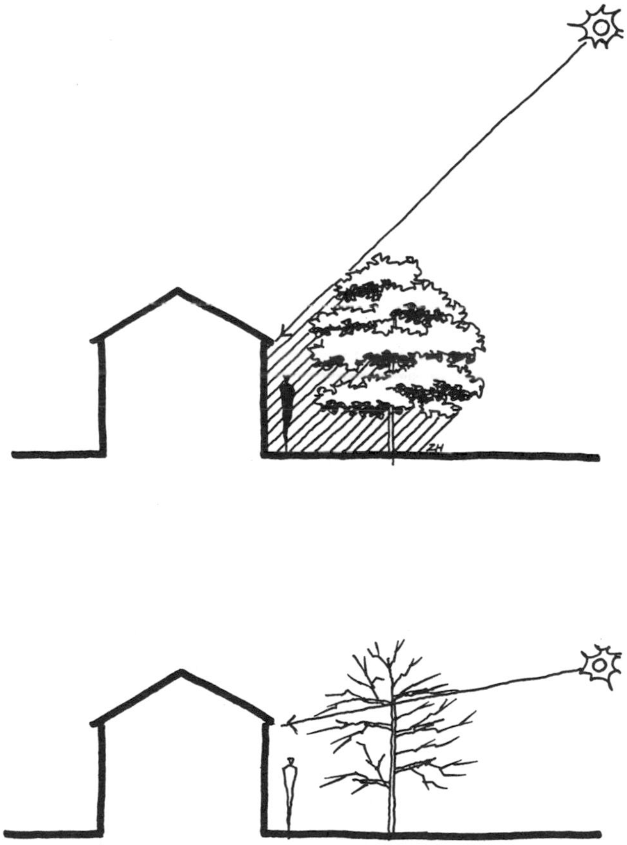

10. Deciduous trees play a special role in cold and temperate cities. During the summer, when their leaves are full, they provide needed shade. During the winter, when their leaves have fallen, the sun's rays are able to penetrate to warm buildings and open spaces.

spring. Summers are spent outdoors; the arcades and canopies which protect against the rain also provide shaded areas for especially hot days. In fall, people celebrate the brightly colored leaves of deciduous trees and the special delight of feeling the warmth of sunshine in the midst of cool, brisk temperatures. Winter is a time for quiet contemplation; the pace slows, dense fog can occur and turns people's thoughts inward, frequent rains keep people inside to be warmed by fires. Spring unleashes the rebirth of greenery and flowers; rain and sunshine alternate and heighten peoples' feelings of being alive.

The use of "landscaping" is an important dimension in the design of settlements to mediate seasonal climatic extremes and also to celebrate climatic variations. Deciduous trees and shrubs planted on the south side of buildings and streets offer shade from the intense summer sun; the loss of foliage in the fall allow the same rays to penetrate and warm the cool surfaces in winter. Dense groves of evergreen trees and shrubs can be strategically planted to reduce the freezing effects of cold winter winds. Trees and ground cover also contribute to visual beauty in human settlements by providing color and texture while absorbing excess heat, dampening excess noise, and filtering airborne dust and particles.

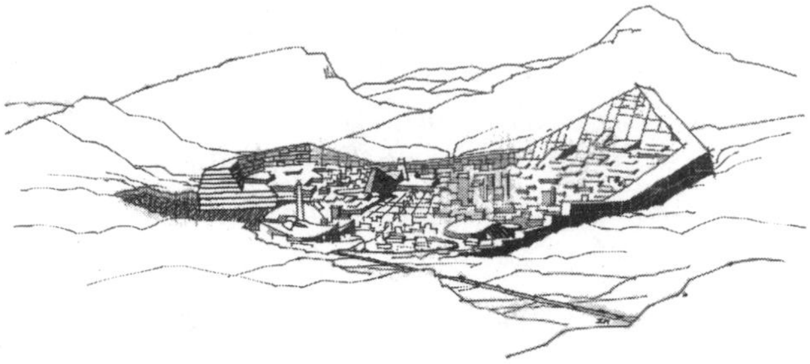

11. Ralph Erskine, an English architect practicing in Sweden, designed an ideal arctic town, developed on the sun-facing slope. Compact buildings share many common walls; large, continuous buildings on the perimeter block the arctic wind; and streets, paths and green spaces are organized for maximum sun exposure and wind protection.

Cold Climates

Cold climates typically are found in inland regions, such as the Great Plains of North America and the Siberian Plains of Russia, or in high latitude areas. These climates also exhibit variations in season but the transitional periods (spring and fall) are less pronounced, and winters are longer and more severe. The extreme cold means that precipitation generally falls in the form of snow and may remain for several months.

In response to these conditions, people living in these areas attempt to expose as much building and street area as possible to the warming rays of the southern sun. As in any cold climate, settlements should be located on the sunny side of slopes to conserve heat, and settlements should be compact. Living areas would ideally have as much insulation as possible to retain the maximum degree of warmth. Whenever possible the sun should be allowed to penetrate into buildings, especially during the short days of the winter months. The sun's warmth should be retained by heat absorbing materials and released during the long cold evenings.

Since people will spend 60%–70% of the winter time indoors, buildings and streets should be connected and enclosed. Settlements should be shaped to protect inhabitants from freezing winds. As in cool-wet climates, outdoor landscaping should be used to shield cold winds, to provide shade in the summer time, and to contribute to the visual quality of the environment. In addition, trees and shrubs should be employed on the inside of buildings to absorb heat, release moisture, and soften the inevitable effects of "cabin fever."

Snow is the special feature of winter cities. It is a natural insulation material; as such, it can aid in retaining heat in buildings and to soften sounds. It provides unusual opportunities for transport such as sleigh rides, snowmobiling, and cross-country skiing, as well as recreational uses such as sledding, skating, and skiing. Aesthetically, snow provides a white background against which rich building and landscape colors may be contrasted.

THE THREAT OF INAPPROPRIATE TECHNOLOGY

The preceding descriptions clarified appropriate urban design responses to various climatic conditions. They focused on approaches or methods which address climatic factors through the manipulation of spaces, structures, materials and vegetation. Note that no mention was made of mechanical environmental controls such as furnaces, air conditioners, ventilating fans, and the like. In fact, advanced technology and the widespread use of such devices has had a major impact on how people living in cities have responded to climatic and regional factors. The overall impact of mechanical environmental controls has been to reduce the use of more traditional or vernacular design responses in shaping cities and urban centers.

In other words, ever since humans have been capable of heating, cooling, dehumidifying and ventilating city buildings by mechanical means, the need and, to some extent, the knowledge, to make city environments more dramatically responsive through urban design to the specifics of climatic variation has declined or been lost. These mechanical methods consume higher levels of energy throughout the world with little regional or climatic responsive design qualities. As a consequence, city forms in very different areas in the twentieth century tend to be increasingly similar. Most contemporary cities, especially suburbs, are not compact: streets sprawl over the land without attention to solar orientation or wind protection; tall buildings shade streets and other buildings from solar access; snow is plowed, not used. Cities have in fact created their own miserable micro-climates: windswept streets and plazas; places that are too hot in the summer and too cold in the winter; places that cannot sustain pedestrian activity and social contact, but instead rely on people going about their business separated from each other in disconnected buildings and isolated vehicles.

12. Banners add color to cities and "celebrate" the wind (*T. Bartuska*).

The consequences of establishing so much reliance on mechanical control of the environment have not only reduced human ability to appreciate the positive benefits of nature and climate, but have contributed in no small way to social decentralization and personal alienation. These results of mechanical "leavening" of human-environmental relationships seriously threaten the benefits of city living which, when responsive (fit and healthy) promote a sense of social well being and advance learning about design that is responsive to varying factors in the natural environment.

With the advent of the world-wide "energy crisis" of the 1970's, urban inhabitants began to reassess their dependence on technology. Recognizing the inherent vulnerability of relying solely on fossil fuels—finite and often imported—for powering environmental control systems, people are seeking new methods to reduce this dependency. Ironically the "new methods" being rediscovered are not new methods at all! They are methods employed for centuries before the invention of steam and the combustion engine. They are the vernacular methods of traditional, indigenous societies who, by necessity and adaptive ingenuity, shaped their cities to respond to climate and region, and, as a consequence, established principles of energy efficiency and effectiveness. Today, contemporary designers and urban inhabitants have begun to come full circle.

REFERENCES

Fitch, J. M. 1972. *American Building: The Environmental Forces That Shape It*. Houghton-Mifflin.

Golany, G. 1982. *Desert Planning*. Nichols.
Guterbock, T. M. 1990. "The Effect of Snow on Urban Density Patterns in the United States," *Environment and Behavior*.
Konya, A. 1980. *Design Primer for Hot Climates*. The Architectural Press.
Pressman, N. 1985. *Reshaping Winter Cities: Concepts, Strategies and Trends*. University of Waterloo Press.

CHAPTER 24

Cities Today: The Imprint of Human Needs in Urban Patterns and Form

Tom J. Bartuska

The city today should be a civil place. Some are and some fall short of this admirable goal. In reality, the cities of today reflect the best and worst aspects of contemporary societies and their cultures. They are exceedingly complex, depressing to some, exciting and challenging to others. They convey a collective story of human-environmental adaptation, evolution and change. Cities express individual and collective human needs in urban patterns and form. The story they tell is expressed in both supportive and disruptive environments.

First the bad news—an unfortunate set of problems that pose some of the greatest challenges confronting contemporary society. Some aspects of cities are void of any positive human-environmental qualities, urban areas that express cycles of degradation and human folly, negative cycles that rob cities of their civil potential. Instead of places to actively live, work and play, some cities have become places to just use and continue to abuse, to rush to for work or profit and to rush away from to live and play in the suburbs. In the worst cases, even work places and shopping centers are moving out into the surrounding countryside, the city centers left for less fortunate people who cannot escape this decay. Many of these people have to rent old, deteriorating buildings generally owned, but not maintained, by people who long ago escaped from these ghettos. They profit while the children of the less fortunate play near alien factories or amidst urban rubble in old neighborhoods dissected by freeways and vacant parking lots. Too many cities are marked by a disintegrated built environment, unhealthy and unfit for human habitation. It fosters polluted human-environmental relationships. It also creates people who are alienated from a society which creates and profits from this residual wasteland.

Decaying inner-city environments cause two basic problems. First of all, blight causes serious environmental and social problems and a disincentive to improve the city. Like tooth decay, these problems can be prevented by daily maintenance or corrected by surgery (painfully).

The second problem may be more serious, more costly and even more difficult to correct. This problem occurs outside the city and is caused by those who escape the city and its problems and choose to live in satellite growth areas. These are commonly called suburbs or sub-urban communities by some, suburban sprawl by others. The costs of suburban growth areas are tremendous. Regardless of the measure, suburban sprawl is costly: in energy (excessive transportation and low efficiency rambling homes), in resources (loss of prime agricultural land and high energy resource use in transportation and construction), and in dollars and cents (very high cost of sprawling community services, high energy expenditures). Unfortunately, few people connect the high cost of living, high tax structure, high energy consumption, even high crime rates, with the double difficulties of urban decay and suburban sprawl.

There exists an abundance of good news too. Many cities are healthy and exciting places to live, work and play. The great cities of the world are as vivid in many peoples' memories as they are in the following popular lyrics:

- Things will be great when you are Downtown, everything is waiting for you . . .
- I left my heart in San Francisco . . .
- Chicago, it's a wonderful town . . .
- If you are tired of London, you are tired of life . . .
- Wonderful, wonderful Copenhagen . . .
- I love Paris . . .

Great cities have many wonderful qualities, services and facilities: great parks and fountains, museums, hospitals, governmental services, fine restaurants and pubs, jobs, markets, theaters and concert halls, penthouse apartments and swank townhouses, sports, zoos and aquariums, art galleries, police and fire safety services, festivals and parades, etc. Cities, great cities, are the dynamic center of the very best aspects of society. They are built to fulfill human needs, celebrate a civil urban life, and express the collective characteristics of the culture which they exemplify.

It is easy to dismiss cities, to focus on their negative aspects. And, the numerous ills must be corrected. But, most cities are resilient places; they can be revitalized with care and concern. This chapter emphasizes the positive and explores the imprint people have made on that special built environment, the City. Emphasis is placed upon the purpose of cities, how they are shaped by human minds and hands to serve individual and societal needs and values. The concluding segment demonstrates important qualities of cities, how these complex issues have been successfully managed and planned to creatively develop healthy and fit human-environmental relationships.

HUMAN NEEDS AND THE CITY

Human lifestyles are intimately interrelated with the support systems of cities and with related components of the built environment. In order to fulfill human needs and desires, almost everyone is dependent upon a seemingly endless array of urban, regional and national support systems such as energy, urban services and institutions. These relatively invisible support systems are commonly referred to as **infrastructure**. It would be a useful exercise for the reader to carefully trace one day's activities and relate them to societal support systems; understanding of the purpose of society and cities and their institutions would be enhanced. The story on the next two pages attempts to analyze these complex human-environmental relationships.

It is really challenging to grasp the complexity of all the support services and institutions that are integrated into a city. It is a difficult, but tremendous accomplishment of society to organize, build, and operate these complete life support systems.

We all have good days and bad days. Similarly, there are good aspects of cities and unfortunate ones. It is important to everyone—environmental design professionals, political leaders, and most of all the general public—to build positive environments in cities. It is also important to analyze, repair and correct the negative aspects of cities, reanimating the inherited city as an important resource of civilization. The following are some

1. Vancouver, British Columbia.

2. Delightful activities of the city, animating its human purpose and spatial qualities.

Human-Environmental Relationships

Examples of Needs and Activities & ....Institutions & Infrastructure

The music from the clock radio comes on at 6:45 a.m. Tuesday morning. It's dark on a cold fall morning and the warm bedroom is a welcome transition to what will be a busy day at the office. To erase the darkness, Chris flicks on the lights on the way to the bathroom and shower. Refreshed, clean and dressed, Chris goes to the kitchen alcove for breakfast. Fresh coffee is on the table, cereal and milk are hastily retrieved from the refrigerator. The 7:30 news comes on as the newspaper headlines are quickly reviewed before cleaning up a bit and leaving for work.

- Radio/Electrical Energy
- Time: Who invented time to organize our lives?
- Heat and Ventilation/Energy
- Products and Interior Space
- Lighting/Electrical Energy
- Water/Sanitation Systems
- Clothes, Commercial Institutions
- Food, Commercial Institutions
- Appliances/Electrical Energy
- Communication Networks: Newspapers, Radio and Telecommunications

The evening rain storm has freshened the air. Workers are busily cleaning the storm drains of debris to ease the ponding before the rush hour traffic intensifies.

- Street Maintenance, City Services
- Garbage Services
- Storm Drain Systems

The pace of activities quickens as the sidewalks and streets fill with people hustling to work. The pedestrians seem a little irritated to have to wait for traffic lights and to have cars, as if in a different world, spray water onto the curb. At 4th and Washington, the lights are not working and a police officer is actively directing traffic. Fortunately, Chris is able to catch the 7:40 transit and it whisks off to the city center. It is a more relaxing time to finish reading the paper and reflect upon the challenges of the work day.

- Walking and Bikeways
- Traffic Control, Public Services
- Auto/Road Systems/Energy
- Public Safety Officers
- Public Transit System/Energy
- Communication Networks

At the city center, Chris leisurely walks to work through the integrated underground and second level pedestrian system. A few people pause to view the urban square and park where workers are busy building a stage for the noon concert. The weather, as predicted, looks promising.

- Structures and Landscape and Urban Design Components
- Pedestrian Priority Circulation Networks
- City Maintenance Staff
- Weather Services and Satellite Systems

On time at work, Chris reviews the computer screen for important messages, responds to two by phone and transfers another to a colleague. The office seems warm and workers become a bit sleepy. By 10 a.m., interoffice, regular and express mails are sorted and reviewed. . . .

- Computer Networks/Energy
- Heat, Ventilation & Lighting Systems/Energy
- Communication Systems (Phone and Mail—Interoffice, Local, National and International Addresses)

At 11:45 a.m., Chris anxiously awaits a luncheon date with some close friends. The once introverted city dramatically changes as its employees discharge

- Time, Scheduling
- Social/Cultural Institutions

onto the outdoor spaces and places of the city. The fine weather and people animate the qualities of the city. Chris and Jean meet on the museum steps and decide to go to the concert instead of the urban waterfall park to have a chat and lunch. The restaurants and outdoor cafes seem busy. They walk to a sandwich vendor as an ambulance, followed by two fire trucks speed by and muffle their conversation. The concert is wonderful and the people and environment animate the city's purpose and finest qualities. The city clock tower strikes 1 p.m., Chris hastily says farewell and returns to the office refreshed and motivated to continue....

- Diversity of Employment
- Cultural Institutions (Art Museums and Galleries, Churches, Entertainment)
- Urban Parks and Services
- Restaurants and Food Distribution Systems
- Public Service (Police, Fire, Health and Safety, Government)
- Time

---

important generalizations to be made from the above analysis:

a. Human-environmental relationships are an important way to understand the purpose and function of cities.
b. Human and societal needs are a reflection of culture and are manifested in the purpose and functions of cities.
c. Human-environmental relationships are manifested in institutions, support systems (infrastructure) and built facilities in the urban environment. This requires careful governance and planning as well as expenditures of energy and resources.

These conceptual relationships are summarized in Figure 3. The city is placed in an environmental context (its climate and natural landscape—outer sphere of influence). Within this context, society works to satisfy human needs by creating institutions (on the left). Institutions build various facilities, services and support systems through the use of energy and resources (in the middle). These services form the built environment of the city (on the right). Within the city are two basic elements: **land use** and **infrastructure**.

Land uses reflect the construction of numerous facilities and institutional support systems. Political institutions of the city are manifested in governmental buildings and services; cultural institutions are accommodated in museums, theaters, and churches. Infrastructure (or interaction field) ties these elements together: streets, walkways and circulation networks; electrical, sanitation and communication systems; even police, fire and health services, etc.

An additional element is expressed in Figure 3, which reflects the dynamics of the city. People and their society continually participate to resolve problems, analyze and improve institutions, and upgrade the resultant environment in which they live. These dynamics hopefully improve the city and are reflected in Figure 3 as a cycle (on the bottom). The cyclic responses to problems and potential improvements in the built environment (right), create new policies and procedures (bottom center), which adjust human expectations and institutions (left).

Human needs and values create a definite imprint upon the city which defines urban land use and infrastructure. The imprint of each and every individual is part of the excitement and complexity

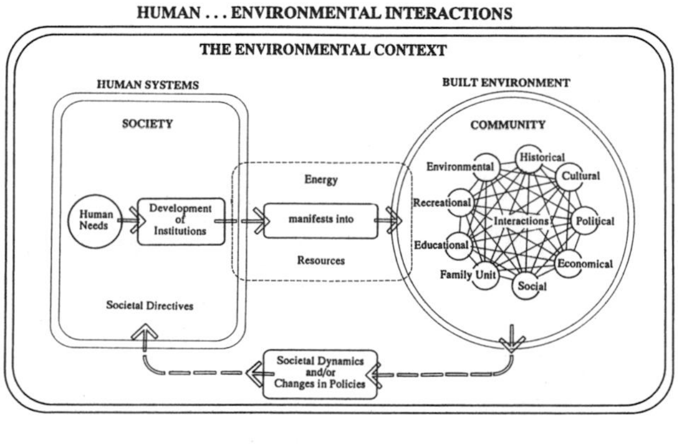

3. Conceptual diagram of society and the city's built environment and interaction systems.

of the city. These patterns, like fingerprints, begin with the individual and radiate outward into the city. This imprint is expressed in human-environment patterns and urban form and can be traced—starting with the individual and his or her doorknob and radiating outward into the neighborhood, city and its region.

HUMAN-ENVIRONMENTAL PATTERNS: THE DOORKNOB AND ITS URBAN CONTEXT

The doorknob may be a good place to begin a tracing of urban patterns and form in the built environment. The knob opens the door to a lot of insights into human-environmental relationships and qualities. Inside the door is, of course, the personal or private domain—the products, interiors and structure of its owner. Outside the door is an exit/entry—leading to a fascinating set of neighboring structures, landscapes and urban patterns, which collectively define the townscape or cityscape.

Like the doorknob, these elements can be considered as a part of related patterns radiating outward into the street—the street defines the neighbors, neighbors form neighborhoods, and so forth to the city and its urban region. The best doorways have clear welcoming expressions. The best patterns throughout the city also have a clarity of purpose and design.

Barrie Greenbie (1981), author of *Space: Dimensions of Human Landscape*, challenges the imagination by depicting these related patterns like an object thrown into a still pond. At impact, the object becomes the center of concentric waves which radiate outward. These patterns intersect other patterns and cause secondary ripples and adjustments. Urban patterns also radiate outward—waves from each person's door, intersecting other patterns from other households throughout the city.

The doorknob is conveniently and proudly placed on the door for visitors, yet it controls access to peoples' private world of the **dwelling unit**. The door is designed to be part of an entryway or porch. This entry porch relates to a front garden or lawn. Where the front garden territory intersects those of neighbors, society has established ways of defining the intersecting relationships—commonly used boundary elements, such as property lines, terraces, gates, hedges and fences, important defining elements of private or semiprivate territories in the built environment.

Like the design of a good doorway, semiprivate aspects are essential to understand and to express in design of the urban environment. Density is a critical factor. In rural or suburban low-density

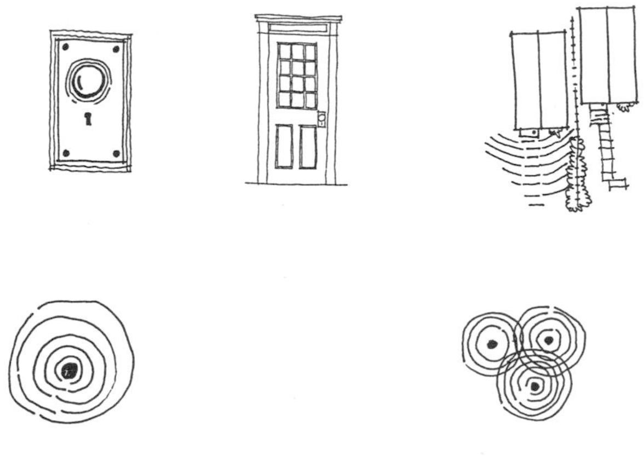

4. Diagrams of humanly-defined territories from the doorknob to the dwelling.

5 and 6. Defining territories of clustered urban townhouses and low-density, suburban development.

developments, these defining elements exist but are not strongly expressed. In medium and higher density developments, the patterns which define and protect one's territory should be more clearly expressed. When they are so expressed, they can be considered signs of a responsive, healthy environment—one which shows personal involvement and pride. When these factors are not expressed, apathy results, which can lead to deterioration of human-environmental patterns. This can cause loss of personal involvement and pride. The people and the city are impacted in negative ways, and crime and vandalism may increase (Newman, 1972).

The semiprivate territories discussed above (doorknob-door-porch-front garden) relate to nearby houses, walkways and streets. Such neighboring elements are commonly referred to as semipublic patterns or activities, "semi" because they are **subdivisions** of the large city—a more public place. The residential walkways and streets collect a cluster of neighbors together and then combine with other residential streets and walkways to form a neighborhood.

The **neighborhood** is an important planning unit in the design and development of cities. Good neighborhoods are well defined and foster community and civic pride. To be effective, they should provide some of the basic needs of society—a small grocery shop, meeting places, a neighborhood park and playground, and an elementary school where young children can walk safely to school and chat and play on the way home.

Many leading urban planners and scholars consider the neighborhood a critical unit to healthy urban environments. Wolf Von Eckardt, author and architectural critic in *Back to the Drawing Board: Planning Livable Cities* (1978), emphasizes the importance of the neighborhood unit:

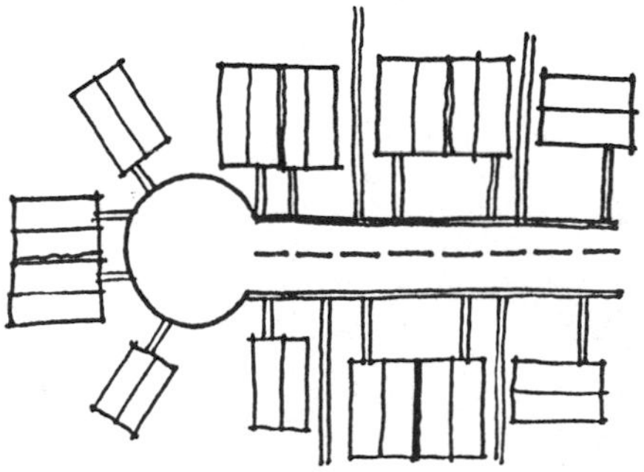

7. Diagram of a component of a subdivision housing clustered along a street.

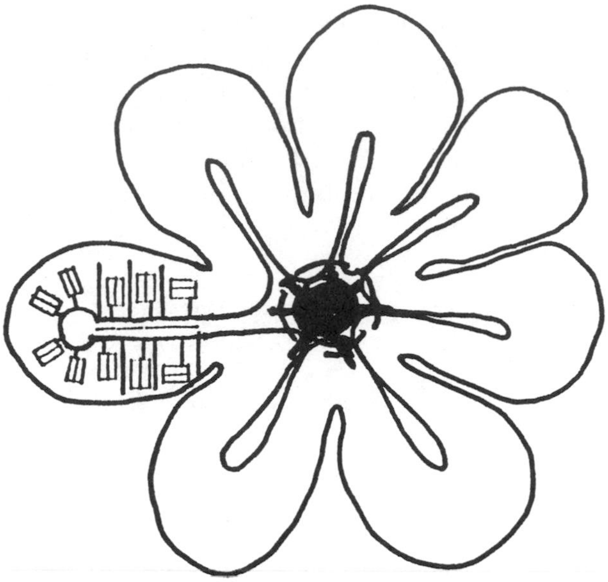

8. Diagram of a neighborhood formed by subdivisions clustered around common facilities.

> Neighborhoods became instruments of civilization . . . the Ebenezer Howard-Lewis Mumford school of urban thought tried to preserve and strengthen it as the basic unit in the urban order, the cell in the urban organism.
>
> The most widely accepted definition of a neighborhood is that which city planner Clarence Arthur Perry set forth in 1929, in his contribution to the "Regional Plan for New York and Its Environs." The neighborhood, Perry wrote, is a residential district of sufficient size to support an elementary school. That would be a population of from 3,000 to 10,000 people. . . .
>
> Neighborhoods . . . are constantly changing. There is just one common denominator: For a neighborhood to be a neighborhood and to form neighborhood ties, the basic necessities of life ought to be within easy walking distance. It is awfully difficult to relate to others and feel neighborly while driving an automobile.
>
> What are the basic necessities of life? Certainly food stores. Certainly an elementary school with a playground. There must be a neighborhood meeting place, either in the school or church, or in a recreation center that also houses community activities. If there is no lake or river, there should be a public swimming pool. There must be laundromats, dry cleaners, a

tavern or two. There ought to be a park. Parks are the lungs of the city.

It is best if the neighborhood coincides with the election precinct and the police precinct. It should also contain a fire station and a post office. In short, ideally the neighborhood should be a clear, complete, and consistent political and administrative entity with some degree of self-determination and representation in city hall. . . .

The virtues of neighborhood were rediscovered by Jane Jacobs in her book . . . , *The Death and Life of Great American Cities*, first published in 1961. Since Jacobs rediscovered old neighborhoods, notably Greenwich Village, she did not notice that Ebenezer Howard, Lewis Mumford, and the Garden City movement urged a way to embody the old neighborhood spirit and old neighborhood values in new, new town neighborhoods. . . .

Throughout the civilized world, people have debated the importance of the urban and suburban neighborhood. In the United States, the threatened disruption of a cohesive neighborhood unit will bring out more people to government meetings than almost any other topic. Such topics as the closure of neighborhood schools, parks or even a public transit stop; the bisecting of a cohesive neighborhood by major street arterials; and disruptions caused by proposed industrial or commercial developments, are hotly contested issues. These disruptions are, in fact, dynamics which can destroy healthy neighborhoods and have negative impacts on property values, the safety of children and the cohesive qualities of this important semipublic unit in the urban environment.

Neighborhood support services and facilities create an important bridge between the individual and society. They create neighborliness—a primary bridge between the family and the purpose and qualities of the urban community. The doorknob has a basic function; it opens the door to the neighboring environment. In a similar way, the neighborhood connects the people behind the door to the basic social, cultural and recreational purposes of a friendly urban unit. Fortunately, people still exhibit a great deal of interest in development of urban neighborhoods. In cities throughout the world, new ones, like False Creek in Vancouver, British Columbia are being built, and old ones are being revitalized with sensitive infill housing and the reanimation of neighborhood facilities.

9 and 10. Clustered housing within cohesive urban neighborhoods, False Creek and Fairview Slopes, Vancouver, British Columbia.

A new, more complex, pattern develops when neighborhood units are combined to form a larger urban **district**, village or small town. These require careful planning and development and should include a middle school, recreational, commercial, medical, governmental and cultural facilities serving a larger population.

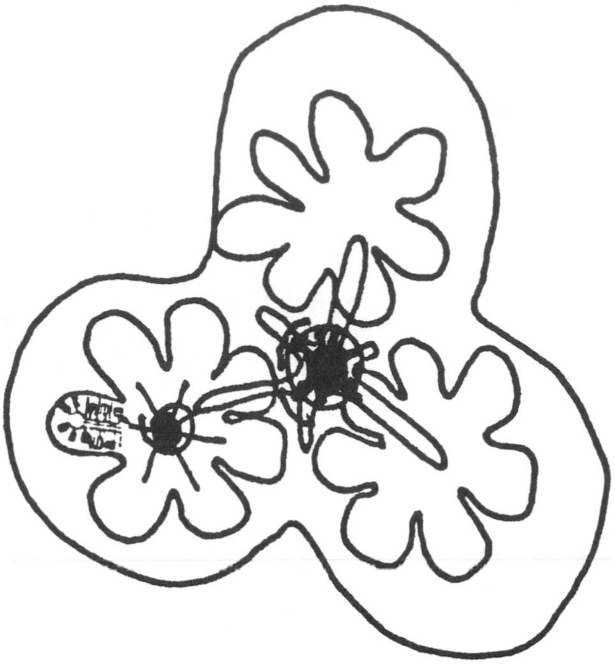

11. Diagram of a district or village formed by a grouping of neighborhoods around community facilities.

Districts or villages combine to form the **city**. The larger the city, the more districts and neighborhoods. Large cities will have a greater diversity of social/cultural, commercial and recreational opportunities. Like the neighborhood unit, the city is an important expression of society and civilization. The focus of the city is the city center. Some are delightful, exciting and dynamic places where all aspects of human needs and values are expressed in the built environment. Other city centers are not so fortunate. Many are in a negative cycle of decay, the facilities less interesting; they are less human and their loneliness brings forth crime and fear—a deathly disease of the city.

Cities need dynamic, healthy centers, full of life and activities. Besides the basic functions of government and a work place, cities need to provide restaurants, concerts, festivals, art galleries and museums, parks and river walkways, open markets, even the friendly clown to celebrate life and make being in the city fun. Labeling city centers "Central Business Districts" (CBDs) is limiting and one-dimensional. Cities need business, lots of it, but also places to live, work and play. Accepting that a city center can be replaced by "shopping malls" is even

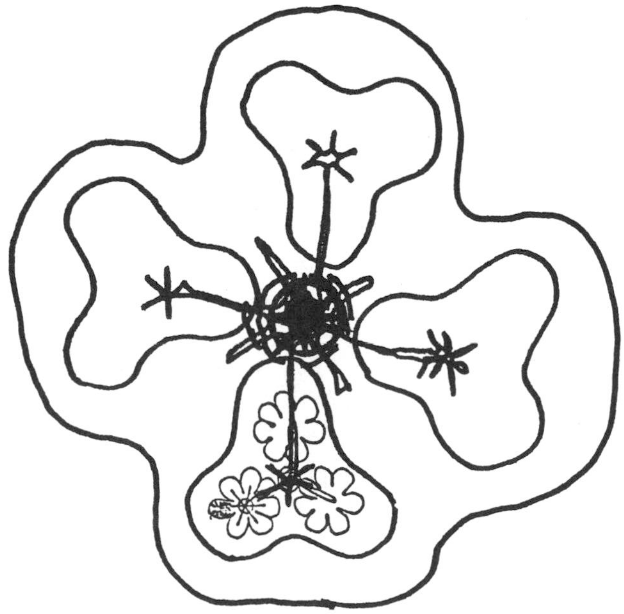

12. Diagram of a city formed by a grouping of districts or villages around a dynamic city center.

13 and 14. Dynamic qualities of the city center or strip commercial development.

worse. New shopping malls built on the edges of cities too often rob the city centers of business, increase transportation problems and costs, and foster suburban sprawl. City center decay—vacant stores and lonely streets—generally follow. But city centers are resilient; like the neighborhood school they can return to serve an important role. This can result from positive leadership, proactive government and concerned citizens who understand and support the city in an involved, holistic way.

Fortunately, in city centers of many urban settlements, these difficult challenges are being met: they are being revitalized, pedestrianized and enjoyed by increasing numbers of people. Natural amenities like waterfronts, landscapes, parks and fountains, and distant views of mountains and forest give city centers an exciting contrast between the very urban/built environments and the natural environment.

In an increasing number of places, cities are combining into even larger combinations of urban units, commonly referred to as **metropolitan regions**. Cities also have a tremendous impact on the surrounding **rural regions**. The requirements of people in urban places (those who live behind the doorknobs), for food, water, energy, and other essentials is huge—and growing ever larger. Such materials largely come from rural regions. The chart in Figure 15 itemizes the daily requirements of food and energy for New York City. Imagine supplying a city with 108,000,000 eggs each and every day—almost 40 billion eggs a year. Fulfilling all the specific requirements of urban dwellers is a very complex task and illustrates the extent of this collective dependency on regional, national, and even international resources, manufacturing and distribution systems. This may seem incredibly complex, but it is far more efficient than each individual person trying separately to fulfill these needs. For eggs alone, that would require at least 2 or 3 chickens behind every doorknob in the city.

Each and Every Day New York City Requires (and Consumes) the Following Resources

Energy and Water Supplies		
Electricity	2,600,000	Kilowatt Hours
Oil and Gasoline	5,500,000	Gallons
Water/Sewage	1,000,000,000	Gallons
(Approximates the amount of incoming supply and outgoing sewage discharge.)		
Food		
Vegetables	5,200,000	Lbs
Meat	2,700,000	Lbs
Poultry	1,300,000	Lbs
Eggs	108,000,000	Eggs

15. Chart of daily urban needs for the city of New York (*Royston, 1985*).

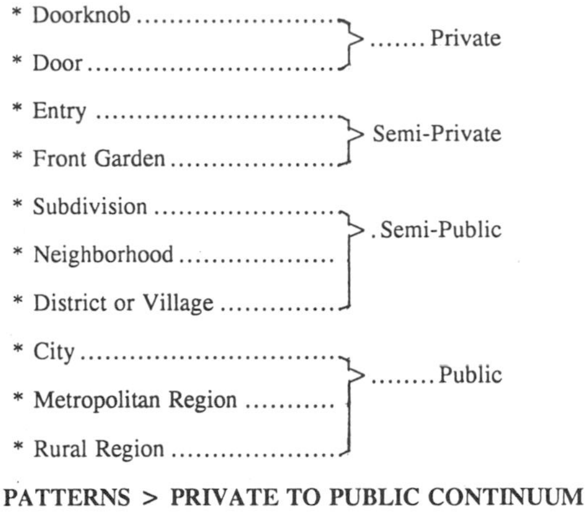

16. Urban patterns: private to public territorial continuum.

The complexities of cities can be better understood by looking at them as a series of patterns radiating outward from the doorknob, private domain of the individual, to the most public aspects of a city and its regional context. These interlocking sets of urban patterns are difficult to observe when walking or traveling through a city. They are more apparent from the air. The problem is analogous to studying the human body. True health and beauty are not just skin deep. External observation can be appreciated, but the health of the person requires X-ray and laboratory studies of its structure (skeleton) and biological systems. An almost X-ray vision of urban patterns and built form is required for the understanding and effective design of cities. The patterns define a continuum: private . . . to . . . public territorial zones of space and facilities.

History has proven that cities are more effective and efficient if they are integrated and the relationships of parts are well defined. This not only requires knowledge of the important defining patterns of cities, but also people who care and who get involved to insure they are created and maintained. "Integration may well be the key word in good design. Not only does it mean the correct combining of parts into a whole, but it implies, by association integrity, soundness and honesty . . . environmental design, now and in the future, is and will be a matter of expert teamwork supported by public appreciation [awareness] and participation" (Reekie, 1972).

URBAN FORM: LAND USE AND INFRASTRUCTURE

As discussed earlier, cities express human-environmental relationships in patterns—from the doorknob to the region—from the most private to the most public. These patterns are manifest in the way land is used (land use) and in the internal structure which ties the city together (infrastructure). These two terms express basic organizing aspects of urban settlements and are implied in human-environment (the way humans use—land or environment) relationships (infrastructure or interaction field).

Land use patterns or zones define the various functions of a city (residential, commercial, governmental and industrial zones of activity). Infrastructure is externally expressed in the circulation patterns (walkways, bike lanes, auto and public transit systems), which allow people and goods to move within and interconnect the land use patterns. Infrastructure also includes other less visible but important systems, such as energy (electric, gas, oil, geothermal hot water, etc.), utilities (water and sanitation, telephone and cable systems), and services (police, fire and street maintenance). **Infrastructure** is complex and costly. Planners and designers try to keep it efficient by minimizing its length and complexity and by maximizing its use by increasing the density of land use. Efficient examples of urban form (land use and infrastructure) can be found by comparing various types of urban developments throughout the world. In general, clustered urban forms are most efficient; sprawling grid forms are least efficient and most costly.

Some of the best examples of land use and infrastructure are found in new town developments. The most direct expressions of these defining aspects of urban form can be observed in Harlow, a New Town in England. Designed in 1946–47 by Sir Frederick Gibberd, Harlow exhibits almost ideal urban patterns of clustered land use and infrastructure:

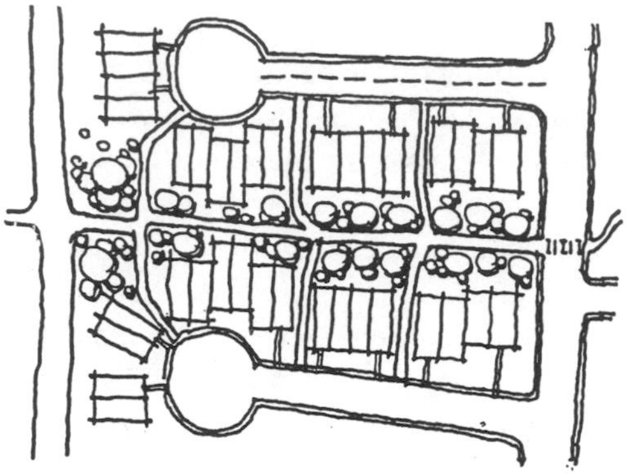

17. A subdivision diagram of housing clustered around a pedestrian circulation system.

- **a.** Housing is clustered in small groups to encourage and define a close sense of neighborliness. Housing clusters are formed by a variety of housing types (medium density) and connected to other parts of the city by convenient walkways. Residential streets and related infrastructure are kept to a minimum—eight times less than the typical sprawling grid common in the United States.
- **b.** Housing clusters or subdivisions are arranged around parks, small shops and a primary school, even a renowned English pub or two to form a cohesive neighborhood. The moderate density of the housing keeps distances relatively short to encourage walking and to increase efficiency. Automobiles and bus transit play a secondary role within these neighborhoods.
- **c.** Three or four neighborhood units are clustered around a larger grouping of shops, parks and a secondary school to form a district or village. Again, the infrastructure provides a balance between walks and bikeways, public transit and auto circulation.
- **d.** Then four villages are clustered around a large center with city-wide facilities, shopping, government offices, a community college, and cultural and recreation facilities of a more public nature. By careful design, it is convenient to walk to the city center. Public transit, auto circulation, and industry are placed in strategic locations to serve the city, but not disrupt the patterns. Rail transit is readily available for transportation ties to other cities in the region. London is just 30 miles or some 30 minutes away.
- **e.** Green space (parkland) separates the parts and defines the above organization. Pedestrian circulation is developed in the green ways to encourage walking and friendly interaction. The whole urban unit is surrounded by a "green belt"—a

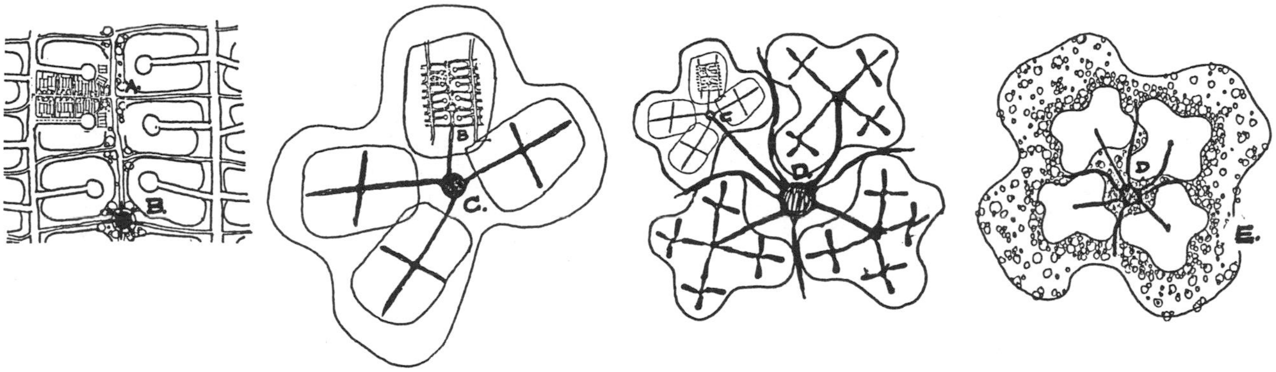

18. Diagrams a + b + c + d + e, cluster housing forming subdivisions and cohesive neighborhoods, neighborhoods forming a cluster of villages around a dynamic city center, all surrounded by a green belt.

preserve of agricultural and open space to contain and define the city. The average amount of parks and green space in most United States cities is between 5 and 10%. Harlow has over 40% of its land use defined in green space.

In order to encourage a walking environment, a great deal of study was undertaken to determine the optimum density of housing. Walking requires short distances (1/4 to 1/2 mile) and pleasant pathways to schools, parks and shops. These neighborhood facilities require a certain population to support them. The population dictates the number of housing units. The walking distance determines the radius and the area in which most of the housing needs to be built. These studies determined that a walking community needs a housing mix designed at a moderate density—primarily clustered townhouses. Neighborhoods of single, detached housing are too spread out to encourage walking or the efficient use of public transit. Harlow has some single detached housing units and duplexes balanced by a few apartment units, but the predominant form is clustered townhouses. This is considered low density by the English, but a density too high for most United States families. The fact remains: to make the neighborhood unit work requires convenient facilities within walking distances and this mandates a moderate range of housing densities.

Harlow planning strategies are effective and efficient. The town has approximately 80,000 people living, working and playing within its green belt. The people enjoy walking and take comfort that their children can walk safely to school. Traffic is not a problem and the energy consumed by the automobile is minimized. The town's overall land area, including the 40% open space, is about half that of a comparably-sized city in the United States, so much more of the surrounding prime agricultural land is saved from suburban sprawl. The infrastructure is efficient, developing and maintaining a network approximately 8–10 times smaller than that which U.S. citizens pay for with their tax dollar.

Planning with patterns makes a lot of sense for existing cities too. This method of defining human-environment relationships was also used in the planning of London during and after World War II. Sir Patrick Abercrombie and a team of environmental designers developed an internationally acclaimed planning strategy for London, at that time equal in size to New York City, the two largest cities in the world. London, like all industrial cities, was experiencing tremendous growth. Urban and suburban growth was spreading outward, eating up the surrounding country and prime agricultural resources at an alarming rate. The infrastructure (transportation network and public services) was being extended to serve these sprawling developments at a very high public cost in Pounds and inefficiency. The uncontrolled growth and extensions were overtaxing the existing systems, (auto, public transit, water and sewage, air pollution, energy, police and fire protection, etc.). The land use patterns and extensive infrastructure were like a cancer—an uncontrolled, unhealthy growth of the urban organism, destroying itself and its regional amenities and resources.

Abercrombie's team, through extensive study, made a number of critical decisions about London's growth and urban form. These are here generalized as land use and infrastructure strategies for balanced urban and regional growth.

a. In order to stop uncontrolled growth, a green belt or "girdle" was placed around London to contain sprawl, preserve the surrounding rural resources and countryside, and stop the inefficient expansion of the urban infrastructure.

Today, when travelling outward from London, one is amazed at the same kind of monotonous sprawl that surrounds most cities. In this case, all the growth occurred before WWII. Then suddenly one explodes out into the green belt, open countryside and rural agricultural farms, villages, open space and beauty. The contrast is remarkable.

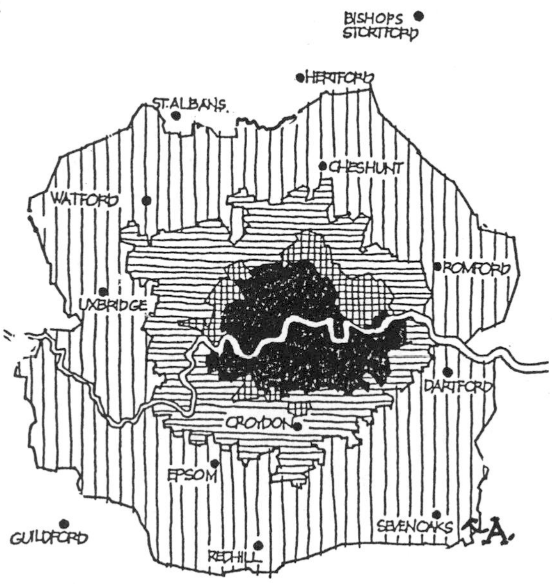

19. Diagram a. Green belt placed around London to contain its subcentralized growth.

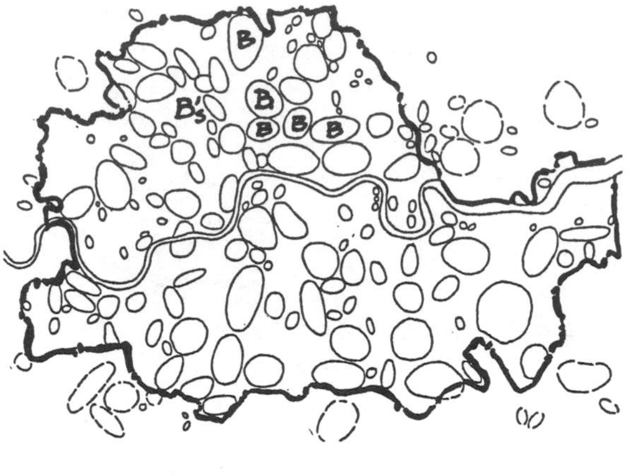

20. Diagram b. Defining London as a city of villages.

b. In order to improve inner London, villages were defined as important planning units. The villages were the focus of further internal development/redevelopment.

Today, London is known as a city of villages. These places may not be completely recognizable by an untrained eye, but the local people strongly identify with clustered urban villages and neighborhood units. Highgate, Hampstead, Camden Town, etc., are all wonderful villages within the fabric of metropolitan London.

c. To allow for normal urban growth to continue, Abercrombie proposed and the government implemented "town and country" growth policies which achieved the following:

- New towns were established and built some 30 miles from London, beyond the green belt. In fact, thirteen new towns were built with an approximate population of 60–80,000 people each. Harlow, discussed earlier, was one of these new towns. Actually, around 40 were built in Britain, others being located around other major cities throughout the country. There is even one called Washington, named after George Washington's ancestral home.
- Existing towns outside of London were carefully planned and, where appropriate, designed expansion occurred.
- London's internal villages were studied and, where appropriate, redevelopment and expansion occurred.

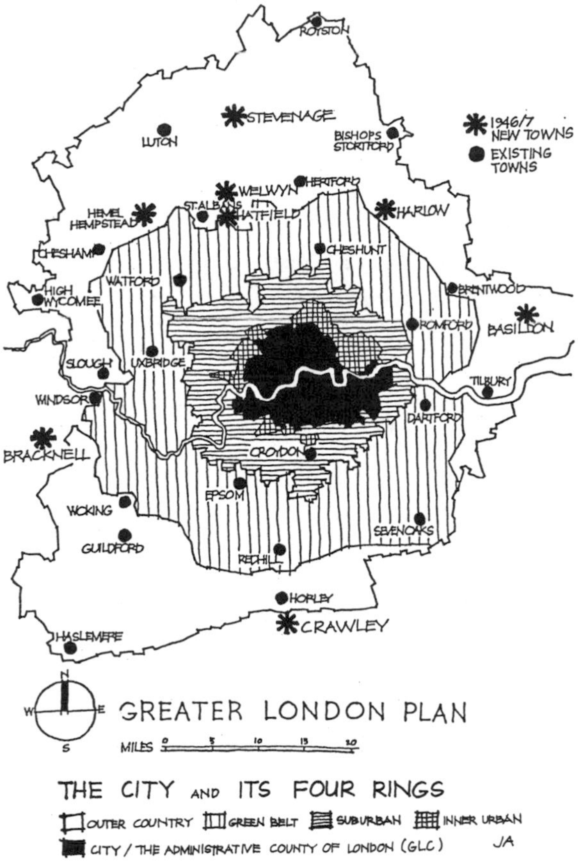

21. Diagram c. Greater London Plan of 1946.

Today, the New Towns are successfully complete and this complex system, although not problem free, is effective in planning for the future. Harlow and London are excellent models for urban and regional growth strategies for contemporary cities and new urban developments.

A CHALLENGING FUTURE FOR URBAN SOCIETY

Cities have an important purpose for contemporary society—and a bright future. Cities are complex built environments and require detailed analyses and multidimensional programs for their continued improvement and development. A civil and constructive attitude about cities is critical for many who foster a less caring point of view. Cities, like all components of the built environment, need enlightened citizen participation and effective governance, guided by expert teamwork from the environmental science, planning and design disciplines. Such analyses and programs require a detailing of the inherent complexities of cities and a summation of the abc's of those critical human-environmental relationships which enhance cities. Strategies for responsible citizen action in order to make a positive imprint on the city are also necessary. Such strategies might include:

a. ***Human Strategies:*** Get involved in a collaborative effort; it is challenging, rewarding and enjoyable.
   - **Active Citizens Participation:** It is fun to become aware and involved in environmental issues. Citizen participation is an important quality of a democratic society. Share your ideas with friends, civic organizations, local news media, governmental representatives and administrative officials. [Chapter 3, "People: Their Perceptions and Participation" more fully addresses the importance of citizen participation and suggests ways a person can be involved in the formation of ideas into action.]
   - **Effective Government:** Democracies welcome citizen awareness and participation (or at least they should). City committees, design and planning commissions, and city councils generally welcome public input. The primary purpose of these governmental organizations is to represent the populous, and it is useful to understand the governmental planning process. [This will be explored in the next chapter.]
   - **Collaborative Environmental Design and Planning:** The design and planning of urban settlements is a complex task. Numerous professionals are trained, licensed and experienced to guide and shape the development of the built environment. Because of the multidimensional aspects of most urban issues, a holistic perspective and a collaborative effort of various design disciplines with the general public is desirable.

b. ***Environmental Strategies:*** Be sensitive to the healthy human-land use patterns—from the doorknob to the dynamics of the urban environment.
   - **Strengthen Neighborhoods:** Friendly and integrated neighborhoods are a key element in making healthy linkages between the individual and community. Encourage and support neighborhood activities and amenities: the use

22. Dynamic qualities of healthy, human-fit environmental interrelationships.

23. Urban neighborhoods and fine clustered housing.

of neighborhood parks and recreational activities, schools, the creation of walking and bike paths, convenience shopping, garage and craft sales, etc. Encourage the city to develop a neighborhood association or planning group to clarify and strengthen its qualities and repair its problems. These neighborhood action plans can be part of the comprehensive planning process. Avoid at all cost the closure of neighborhood support facilities (especially parks and schools). Avoid plans for traffic routes that cut through cohesive neighborhoods. Mixed housing densities can offer young and old a range of dwelling alternatives. Increasing the mix and density of housing can provide a rich diversity of people and more support for neighborhood facilities at reduced cost.

- **Revitalize City Centers:** The traditional focus of a city is its center. It should be a special place, the center of a civil society and a manifestation of all human support institutions and services. Many city centers are revitalizing old buildings into exciting new uses (they are important and irreplaceable parts of our heritage) and are building new structures to fit in with the urban streetscape. Numerous urban spaces are being enhanced by landscaping, water amenities and street furniture. More and more are filling with people instead of cars. Restaurants and cafes, arts and craft shows, outdoor concerts and parades, flower boxes and banners are enriching the diversity and enjoyment of the city center, celebrating that special place called the city. Avoid the single function business districts, strip developments and sprawling shopping centers which rob the city of its diversity, centrality and activities.
- **Protect Regional Resources and Avoid Urban Sprawl:** This dual problem requires effective and coordinated urban and regional planning policy and procedure. This program is not antigrowth, but promeaningful growth and proconservation of finite resources. Careful planning can achieve both objectives.

24 and 25. Revitalization within a city center, Westlake Center, Seattle, Washington.

Designing urban development with natural amenities can enhance both. Refocusing city centers and developing cohesive neighborhoods can help prevent suburban sprawl and minimize costly infrastructure services and extensions.

c. ***Interrelationship Strategies:*** (Infrastructure: circulation, utilities and services.) Through these strategies, more efficient, less costly infrastructure systems can be developed to improve services and reduce societal costs.
   - **Minimize Infrastructure Costs—Cluster, Don't Sprawl:** Clustered community development with a mixture of townhousing densities can create cohesive neighborhoods and achieve efficient infrastructure patterns without compromising residential qualities. An efficient infrastructure can enhance the cost effectiveness of public services and minimize utility and property taxes. Low density sprawl is the most costly and wasteful form of urban growth.
   - **Balance Transportation Systems:** Encourage a balanced coexistence of diverse circulation systems. Because of society's love affair with the private automobile, most United States cities are not in balance; they are almost consumed by the space requirements, noise, gridlock congestion, air pollution and high energy use caused by automobiles. Studies have shown that up to 2/3 of the land use in most cities is given over to auto circulation, parking and related services; 1/3 in suburban areas. That does not leave much space for people, services, buildings, landscaping and open areas. Balance can minimize costly inefficiencies and pollution while providing more options for young and old—who cannot drive a car—and, most importantly, make cities more enjoyable and healthy places to live, work and play. The chart in Figure 26 summarizes the relative efficiencies of various circulation systems in terms of energy per passenger mile and land use: The automobile is hopelessly the most inefficient. The bicycle is approximately 40 times more efficient than the automobile in terms of energy and three times more in terms of land efficiency.

These human-environmental relationships and strategies are complex and highly interrelated.

RELATIVE EFFICIENCIES

Circulation Type Use	Energy	Land
Bike	40	3
Walking	28	2
Pubic Transit Bus	4	17
Public Transit Rail	3	12
Automobile	1	1

26. Relative efficiencies of various urban circulation systems. Energy in passengers per mile, land use in passengers per lane width (*DeBell, 1970*).

Cities were not built in a day. Time and positive human effort can help strengthen urban communities as places which express and celebrate human cultures. Apathy can foster urban decay and higher monetary and human costs. The suggested strategies

27 and 28. The enjoyment of the city, Portland, Oregon.

can help those who want to creatively guide cities to become more healthy human and environmentally fit places to live, work and play.

REFERENCES

Amos, F. J. C. and R. W. Archer. 1992. "Urban Planning Policies, Land, and Institutional Factors," *Regional Development Dialogue*.

DeBell, G. 1970. *The Environmental Handbook*. Ballantine Books.

Gillette, H. J. 1990. "Rethinking American Urban History: New Directions for the Posturban Era," *Social Science History*.

Greenbie, B. 1981. *Space: Dimensions of Human Landscape*. Yale University Press.

Jacobs, J. 1961. *The Death and Life of Great American Cities*. Vintage Books.

May, G. H. 1990. "The Future of the City: Issues for the 21st Century," *Futures*.

McNulty, R. et al. 1986. *The Return of the Livable City: Learning from America's Best*. Acropolis Books.

Newman, O. 1972. *Defensible Space: Crime Prevention Through Urban Design*. Collier.

Reekie, R. F. 1972. *Design in the Built Environment*. Edward Arnold.

Royston, R. 1985. *Cities 2000*. Paulton Books.

Von Eckardt, W. 1978. *Back to the Drawing Board: Planning Livable Cities*. New Republic Books.

CHAPTER 25

Urban Planning and Design

Michael S. Owen

Few people realize that cities are actually planned and designed. Most cities, U.S. cities in particular, appear to be highly complex, complicated and chaotic. It is true that they are complex, but most cities exhibit an underlying order or rationale. This rationale is brought into being by the processes of urban planning and design. This chapter describes some basic concepts related to these processes and the professionals who carry out the work.

THE AUTHORITY TO PLAN

Do private property owners have the right to do whatever they choose with their land? The answer is "not entirely"; the drafters of the U.S. Constitution believed in a balance between private rights and public welfare. Drawing from English law, two primary authorities were granted to the Federal Government under the Constitution: the authority of eminent domain and the authority of police powers. These authorities were intended to provide the Federal Government the legal means for regulating the use of private property on behalf of the general welfare of the community.

Under the authority of **eminent domain**, the federal government has the power to own property and to expropriate property from private landowners. The 10th Amendment of the Constitution (part of the Bill of Rights), however, stipulates that private citizens have the right to be compensated for the compulsory "taking" of their property when the Federal Government has condemned it for public use. In other words, the Federal Government is required to pay private citizens a fair market value for their property.

Among other powers governing the health, security and safety of U.S. citizens, the **police powers** established in the Constitution allow the Federal Government to regulate the use of property by private owners. Similar powers were passed to state governments in 1928 under the Standard State Planning Enabling Act. In turn, each state legislature has passed police powers to local city and county authorities through enabling legislation. Therefore, like the federal government, cities and counties also have the power to expropriate and

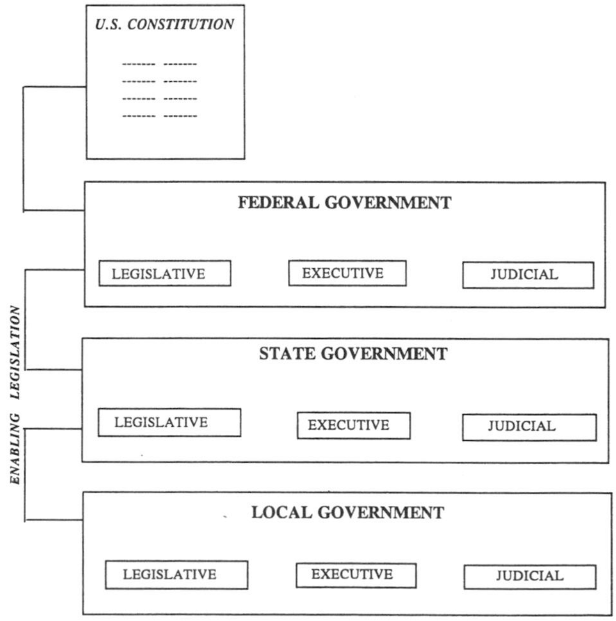

1. Graph showing the transfer of authority via the Constitution to the three levels of government.

regulate private property under authority of the U.S. Constitution. Most property-related issues therefore are argued on constitutional grounds, often to the level of the U.S. Supreme Court.

GENERAL WELFARE OF THE COMMUNITY

Most people intuitively understand what is meant by the general welfare of the community. If tax dollars are traced to government functions, the wide array of structures and services that the government provides is revealed. At the local level, they include:

- Safety: fire protection and emergency procedures.
- Security: police protection.
- Health: adequate provision of light, air, water, sanitation, emergency and hospital services.
- Transportation: walkways, bikeways, streets, highways, public transit and traffic regulations.
- Education and recreation: schools, parks, playgrounds, civic and cultural amenities.

Along with this obvious list is a function which most people would not immediately consider: the preservation and stabilization of property values. This is an inherent part of the government's responsibility for protecting the general welfare of the community. The mechanisms for carrying out this responsibility are called **comprehensive planning** and **zoning**.

ADMINISTRATIVE PLANNING STRUCTURE

By definition, urban planning and zoning are carried out by local governments: cities and counties. Note, in Figure 1, that the organization of government in the U.S. follows a similar structure at each level: a **legislative branch**, which writes and enacts laws, an **executive branch** which "executes" or administers the laws, and a **judicial branch**, which interprets the laws. At the city level of government the legislative body is called the city council and the executive is called the mayor. Local courts typically have jurisdiction over small (damage) claims and traffic violations and do not

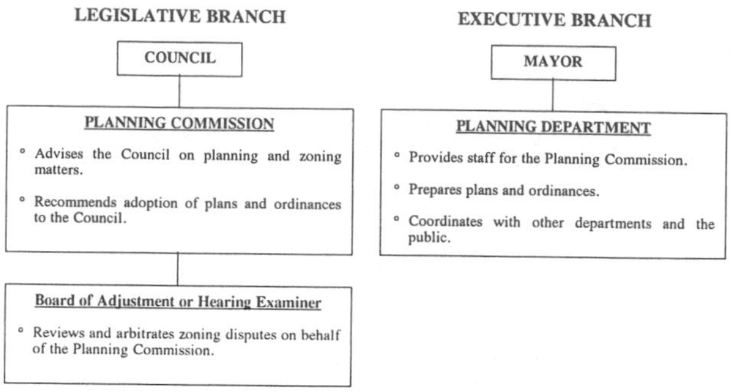

2. Graph showing how local governments are organized to carry out planning and zoning.

play a role in planning or zoning. When the courts do get involved with planning and zoning, it is typically at state and federal levels.

City Council

Members of city councils are elected officials whose role it is to "govern" on behalf of the general welfare of the community within their geographical boundaries—the city limits. In this capacity, councils write and enact laws called ordinances and codes. City councils are the final authorities for regulation of land use within these jurisdictions. All planning and zoning questions and disputes for a particular city are decided by the council. A similar organization occurs at the county level.

Since planning and zoning are only a small part of the total responsibilities of any city council, most cities create an advisory body (to the council) called a planning commission, which is composed of local citizens appointed by the mayor. As an advisor to the council, the planning commission makes recommendations pertaining to the adoption of plans and ordinances and to arbitration of zoning disputes. For planning and zoning issues, it is the city (or county) council which has the final authority. Councils may approve, revise or reject any or all of a planning commission's recommendations.

In larger cities, a subcommittee of the planning commission, called the board of adjustment is also maintained to review and arbitrate specific requests for zone changes, conditional uses, and variances. This function may also be carried out by an individual hearing examiner.

In all instances, the actions of all persons involved with zoning arbitration are strictly governed by regulations in the local zoning ordinance.

Also, and again in all instances, final interpretation of the regulations are made at the city council level.

If property owners want to dispute a finding of the city council, they must proceed with a legal suit in a court of law. Typically, suits will be one of two kinds: first, a question of "due process" or "fairness"—whether the council acted in compliance with its own ordinance, or second, a question of "constitutionality," that is, is the zoning ordinance itself in compliance with the U.S. Constitution? In either case, the city must demonstrate that the decision it made against the property owner was not arbitrary or capricious.

Public Participation

In all of the instances mentioned above, decisions by a city council, a planning commission, a board of adjustment or a hearing examiner are made only after the public has had an opportunity to comment on the issue in a **public hearing**. Public hearings are an inherent part of the process in a democratic society. Notice of such meetings are typically advertised in local "newspapers of record" and often posted within 200'–300' of the location of a proposed action.

The intent of the public hearing is to encourage public participation, to "air" all views; it is part of the fact finding necessary to evaluate a proposal. The final decision is not necessarily based, however, on public sentiment. The final decision affecting a land use is (presumably) based on careful deliberation of all facts and a fair judgment in accordance with the interpretation of accepted planning principles. Sometimes this requires city councils to make unpopular decisions, but hopefully serves the general welfare of the community over the long term.

Planning Department

As mentioned, the city council is part of the legislative branch and the mayor is the head of the executive branch of local government. These are elected positions which change with the political cycles inherent in a democratic form of government.

To execute governance of a city, the mayor relies on an organization of administrative departments. The organization responsible for planning and zoning in city government is the **planning department**. This organization is composed of persons trained in the discipline of urban planning and/or urban design. The planning staff, sometimes with the help of outside professional planning consultants, prepares the planning ordinances of the city. Although the city council has the final approval authority for planning and zoning, the planning department has the technical expertise and professional knowledge of the field.

In addition to preparing plans and ordinances, the planning department has the responsibility of issuing development approvals based on developers' compliance with the zoning ordinance. If planners determine that a development proposal is not in compliance with the zoning ordinance, it will be turned down and/or referred to the board of adjustment for review.

Ultimately, it is the responsibility of the planning department to bring professional knowledge to bear on the preparation and administration of city plans and ordinances. At times, the recommendations of the planning department run counter to the political objectives of the elected officials. Environmental conservation and protection versus economic growth and development is an example of the type of dispute that often arises.

Such tension is an inherent result of the democratic process and the system of checks and balances. Essentially, and ultimately, all land use and development decisions are economic and political in nature. They bear on the fundamental rights of individuals to "life, liberty and the pursuit of happiness" within a context which protects the general welfare of the community. This balance is what citizens charge both elected officials (mayors and councils) and professional staff (planners and administrators) to negotiate on their behalf. Citizens—"the public"—are the third essential ingredient to ensure the process works. To protect the public interest, citizens should insist upon an open process and should be involved enough to gain, and then maintain, the necessary knowledge and understanding of how the system works, to insure that it works for them.

THE COMPREHENSIVE PLAN

A **comprehensive plan** in and of itself is not a strict law; it is a policy document which, through (ideally) rigorous research, analysis and public input, identifies the goals, objectives and methods of providing for the orderly growth and development of a municipality. Comprehensive planning is an on-going activity performed by the planning department. From time to time, dependent on the rate of change a city is experiencing, a comprehensive plan document will be updated, printed to represent the culmination of analysis and recommendations for a certain period, until it is again updated in a subsequent plan. The comprehensive plan for a small town may consist of a single volume, while plans for large cities can run into dozens of volumes and thousands of pages. All governmental decisions regarding land use must be in compliance with the Comprehensive Plan, or such decisions can be challenged as arbitrary and capricious.

Analysis Elements

As noted, the intent of the Comprehensive Plan is to provide policies and general guidelines for the development of the city. As such, it must address the goals and objectives of every aspect of urban life, including:

- Population
- Environmental Quality
- Energy Consumption/Conservation
- Transportation
- Housing, Commerce, Industry/Manufacturing
- Health, Education and Welfare
- Public Safety and Security
- Public Recreation and Culture

Note how these compare to the elements which make up the general welfare of the community. This is because the comprehensive plan is intended to guide government decision making as it relates to both public and private development.

In recent years, planners have attempted to incorporate into the comprehensive planning process an element on urban design or aesthetics. These are often called urban design framework plans and provide design guidelines for visual consideration of specific parts of the city. Often, design commissions are appointed to review developers' compliance with the design guidelines. These are discussed at length later in this chapter.

After comparing the goals and objectives for future development of the city with an inventory of existing conditions, a set of recommendations will be stipulated in the comprehensive plan. This plan of action will indicate what programs and policies must be developed to achieve the goals and objectives. Typically, this will result in plans for each sub-element such as:

- *Capital Improvements Plan* (CIP): This is a listing of projects and associated costs to extend or repair the physical infrastructure of the city. As such, it might include new buildings for schools, fire and police protection; parks; libraries; courthouses; transit facilities, etc.
- *Circulation Plan:* This is a listing of changes and improvements to the system of city streets and highways. It is typically written in conjunction with such items as changes in land use, extending city boundaries through annexation, schedules of repairs and replacements of existing roads, etc.
- *Land Use Plan:* This is of primary concern to urban planning and design because it specifies general categories of the division of land in the city and the policies, guidelines and standards which will govern their development. It also identifies potential land for annexation if the city determines the necessity to grow. As part of the comprehensive plan, an analysis of the new land use plan is performed to bring the zoning ordinance into compliance with the new land use designations.

Implementing Ordinances

The primary "tools" used to regulate the physical development of a city are building codes, subdivision ordinances, environmental impact assessments, and zoning codes. Of these, zoning codes are the most fundamental to implementing the comprehensive plan and therefore receive the most detailed coverage here.

Building codes regulate the safety of individual structures. They are concerned with the structural capability of buildings to stand up under the various conditions they might be subjected to: occupant loads, seismic (earthquake) loads, wind and snow loads, impact loads, and the loads imposed by their own weight. Codes are also concerned with fire safety, both in terms of the fire resistance of construction materials as well as the protection of life and property; for example, adequate exits and sprinkler systems. They are also concerned with plumbing, electrical power and sanitation. Hence, building codes actually reference a variety of specialized regulations published nationally, including the National Building Code or the Uniform Building Code. Most municipalities adopt the national codes and supplement them with local regulations to formulate their own proprietary building ordinances.

Subdivision ordinances regulate the requirements for the subdivision of land for the purpose of sale. The end result of a subdivision proposal is a plat map, which designates the legal boundaries of private property, street right of ways and public easements. The initial layout of street and property sizes, geometries and relationships can significantly impact the density and quality of development of an area.

Environmental impact assessment requirements were enacted nationally in the United States early in the 1970's to assure that all developments, both public and private, have been evaluated prior to implementation as to their adverse impacts on the natural and human environment. All developments larger than a two-family attached dwelling (duplex) must have an environmental checklist identifying potential impacts. A threshold determination of "significance" or "nonsignificance" is then made by a government authority. If the development is considered to have "significant" impacts, then an environmental impact statement must be prepared which identifies all adverse impacts and the measures to be taken by the developer to mitigate them. City-related environment assessment is typically governed by the State Environmental Policy Act (SEPA). Overall federal coordination is regulated by the National Environmental Protection Act (NEPA). Compliance with SEPA is required when state funding is involved in a project and NEPA is required when federal funding is involved.

Zoning codes are the specific laws which regulate land use in accordance with a comprehensive plan. In general, **zoning** refers to the division of land into districts, a description of how the land within each district may be used, and a listing of standards for the land's development. A zoning code consists of a map showing the designated zoning districts and text describing the regulations governing each district.

The primary districts of most cities include residential, commercial, and industrial. The standard notation for designating a district includes a letter

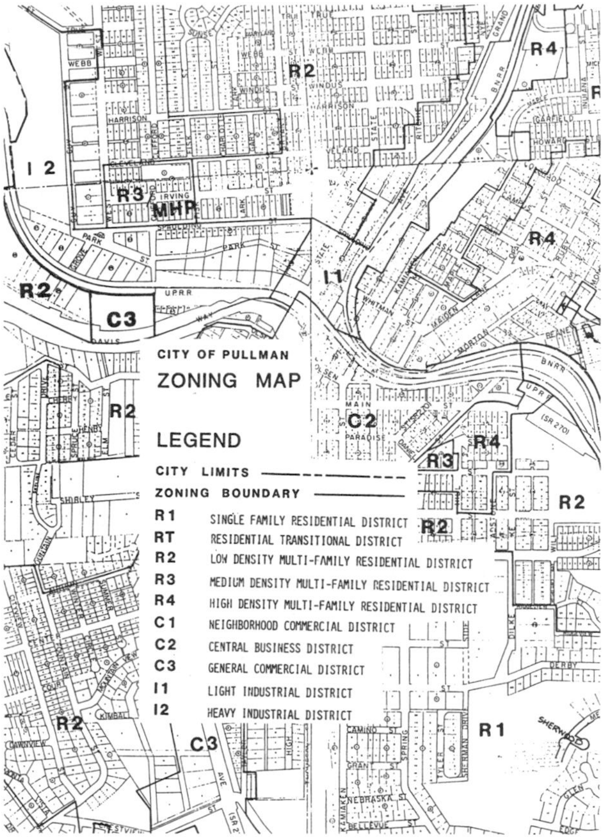

3. A typical zoning map showing districts of a city and their zone designations (*courtesy of the City of Pullman, Washington*).

(for example, "R" = Residential, "C" = Commercial, etc.) and a number designating the allowable intensity of use (for example, "R-1" allows single family detached homes, "R-2" allows single family detached homes and duplexes, "R-3" allows multi-family attached dwellings such as townhouses, "R-6" allows high-rise apartments, etc.). Typically, the lower the number, the more restrictive the use designation.

Each zone designation indicates the types of uses that are permitted. Certain other uses may be permitted if they comply with conditions specified in the ordinance. Uses not stipulated in these categories are banned outright unless a developer can demonstrate that the proposed use can be made to be compatible with the other uses in the designated zone. In this way zoning is a unique law because it provides individual citizens the right to change the law if the change can be demonstrated to benefit the general welfare of the community.

Within the zoning ordinance, each district is governed by a set of development standards (discussed in the next section). Since zoning standards are written to meet general assumptions about land subdivisions and adjacent uses, often unique circumstances arise (such as odd-shaped lots, for example). If property owners can demonstrate that due to unique circumstances they will suffer a hardship by complying with zoning standards, then they may petition for a **variance**. Variances are routine, administrative modifications built into the standard procedures of most zoning ordinances and do not require a change to the comprehensive plan.

Under certain circumstances, city councils have the authority to allow non-conforming uses to occur, if the new use meets special conditions. For example, school districts which have found school buildings surplus to their needs due to demographic shifts have petitioned city councils and planning commissions to allow the buildings to be used for other non-educational functions until such time that the facility may be needed again as a school. Hence, a change of use is allowed under condition that it revert back to a school if circumstances change at some point in the future. **Conditional use permits** may be granted by city councils without a corresponding change to the comprehensive plan.

Citizens may also petition city councils to actually change the zone designation of a district. This is a long process which requires a corresponding change to the comprehensive plan. It may result in a downzone (a change to a more restrictive use category) or an upzone (to a less restrictive use). Again, as long as the petitioners can demonstrate that the change will benefit the general welfare of the community, and that it is consistent with the goals and objectives of the comprehensive plan, then the change may be enacted.

For each designated zone, in addition to permitted uses, specific development standards apply to each property. Keeping in mind that the intent of zoning is to regulate property use for the benefit of the community, it is necessary for the ordinance to set limits of building size, site access, and other elements which impact the environmental qualities of the zone. Accordingly, most zoning ordinances set a variety of standards.

There is, for example, a direct relationship between building height and intensity of land use, quality of views, amount of solar insolation/shading, and access to air and light by the public. Ordinances set building heights by establishing maximum limits. Sometimes heights are set by establishment of overall building envelopes, which also set the volumetric shape or bulk of the building.

A related limitation is that of lot coverage or the relationship between building and open space on a site. Lot coverage can be regulated in several ways, the most common being setbacks from property lines and floor area ratios. Typically, residential zones limit built areas on lots by establishing setback standards for front, side and back property lines. Downtown, city center sites are generally regulated by what is called floor area ratio or F.A.R.

Downtown sites normally require no setbacks of buildings from the property line at the ground level. To ensure greater flexibility in building design, however, the building height and bulk is governed by a ratio of building floor area to lot area. For example, a F.A.R. of 2.0 would allow a two-story building to cover the entire lot (100%) or a four-story building to cover 50% of the lot. The four-story building would allow for 50% of the lot to be used as open space and would result in a taller, slimmer building. Both of these aspects are considered potentially more aesthetically pleasing.

In many districts, developers are required to provide some number of on-site parking spaces to avoid overloading city streets with cars—one parking space for every 300 square feet of building in office structures, for example, or 1.5 spaces for every unit of multi-family residential development.

The zoning ordinance covers many other aspects of site use and development. Auxiliary structures, such as signage, fences, garages and sheds are regulated as well as such uses as home occupations. Often, the latter is recommended for residential areas as part of a city's overall energy strategy—persons working at home do not drive their cars, saving on gasoline and transit demands.

A final set of standards being incorporated into many zoning codes are those governing aesthetics—landscaping, building styles, colors and shape. Such standards are called **design guidelines** and are tied to designated districts. They form the basis for the multidisciplinary field called urban design.

URBAN DESIGN

Most urban planning is concerned with the preparation of two-dimensional plans or maps and related ordinances. **Urban design** considers the city in three-dimensional terms with emphasis on visual spatial quality of the overall built environment.

Urban designers must find ingenious ways to integrate their ideas into the city because they do not always have control over individual building and landscape designs. They are able to influence the shaping of cities by using all of the standard city planning tools like zoning coupled with design guidelines. In this way, they are able to design cities without designing buildings.

For the most part, design guidelines are applied in **special zoning districts**. With the help of planners, urban designers, landscape architects and architects a city will designate certain districts as having a special character and enact ordinances to assure that character is retained.

The Pike Place Market in Seattle, Washington, for example, was designated an historical district and, through public and private investment, was renovated and restored to its original character. In addition to restoring the streets, sidewalks and buildings, the city used **inclusive zoning** to require that all renovated and new housing in the district include a proportion of handicapped and single room occupancy units, and that rents for these be subsidized. This resulted in retaining the handicapped and retired elderly population in the area, thus retaining a range of socio-economic classes,

5. An example of Santa Barbara's mission style architecture.

which many felt contributed to the original charm of the market.

Other cities have designated large areas as architectural zones. Two cities that require all new buildings be designed in accordance with a particular character are Santa Barbara, California (Spanish Mission Style) and Santa Fe, New Mexico (Pueblo Style). As a consequence, these cities have been particularly successful in attracting upscale commercial and tourist activities.

Whereas special zoning districts are useful in maintaining the existing character of an area, **planned unit developments** provide opportunities for creating vibrant new communities. Planned unit developments differ from the typical planning approach by combining both subdivision design and

4. Seattle's Pike Place Market was restored after its designation as a historical district.

6. Downtown Santa Fe; the city has adopted the traditional pueblo style for its buildings.

7. The planned unit development of Seaside, FLA. Note the pedestrian path and variety of overlooking porches (*J.Gehl*).

zoning within the same development. The city provides the developer with a set of performance standards for a piece of property, then the developer subdivides, zones and designs it with a variety of densities, building types, landscaping and amenities. This provides developers, urban designers, landscape architects and architects greater latitude in providing innovative schemes, which often achieve higher qualities of social integration, energy conservation and environmental protection.

An example of this is Seaside, Florida, a highly publicized recreational community which combined traditional patterns of street planning with design guidelines to create a unique residential environment. Large developments such as this can often be financially risky, but Seaside is a commercial success and is considered a model for the effective use of planned unit developments and design guidelines.

Another innovative technique of urban designers is the use of **incentive zoning** to involve private developers in the creation of public amenities. Essentially, the concept is that city planning authorities allow private developers to build rentable floor area beyond that provided in the zoning ordinance, if the developers also agree to construct certain public amenities at their own expense. Public amenities might include: parks, lobbies and atriums, connections to public transit, squares and plazas, second-level walkways and bridges (skywalks), etc. The incentive for the developer is that although there is a higher front end construction expenditure, this cost will be recovered and profits will be made on the long-term rental of additional space. Also, the public amenities often result in the ability to charge higher rents.

An excellent example of incentive zoning is the Calgary, Alberta "Plus-Fifteen" skywalk system in Canada. It is the most extensive system of second (third and fourth) level pedestrian walkways in the world. It incorporates stair connections for every bridge. Bridges are wider than usual—12'–20' in Calgary versus 8'–12' in Spokane, Washington. The system connects over forty atrium buildings in the downtown, many of which include usable indoor and outdoor open space at the ground and second levels. All of the features were put into place as a result of incentive zoning along the principles stated above.

While reading this and the previous chapter, you will have noticed a hierarchy of central places in the built environment; urban places range in scale from small neighborhoods to vast regions. The "theory of central places" is examined in the next chapter.

At the regional scale, cities interact with each other. Design and planning of these regional networks are typically carried out by a consortium of city and county governments. For example, the Puget Sound Council of Governments coordinates regional planning for all of the municipal jurisdictions within a four-county area surrounding the city of Seattle, Washington.

In 1990, the Puget Sound Council initiated a major planning study, Vision 2020, which involved generating and evaluating alternative strategies for the growth of the region. These strategies and their environmental consequences were presented to the public in an extensive series of newspaper supplements, public meetings and phone surveys. The

8. A pedestrian bridge and street in Calgary, Alberta (*T. Bartuska*).

9. One of over forty atrium buildings in Calgary, Alberta. Often these spaces are filled with artistic hangings to celebrate seasonal holidays.

results of the extensive public review were surprising in a country whose past preferences have generated low-density sprawl. By a significant margin, 90% of the public favored two clustered growth alternatives. The Council then created a combination of the two, integrating the best features of both in what is called the "Preferred Alternative." This plan suggests a number of principles to manage urban growth.

- **A hierarchy of central places** to cluster urban growth in compact, well-defined communities framed by a network of open space and connected by public transit.
- **A public transit and ridesharing concept** to support the centers concept with "a heavy investment" in moving people instead of automobiles "during peak periods." It also provides for highway improvements which correct severe traffic problems.
- **An emphasis on density and design strategies** for new residential areas, with higher densities clustering around convenient transit stations.
- **The conservation of sensitive environmental and historic resources and qualities.**
- **The maintenance of a strong regional economy and accommodation of growth.**

These inclusions and conclusions, after being reviewed by the public, and adopted, will result in strategic policies to implement planned growth at a reduced rate for the region. In the words of one proponent, the people have decided to "create the dream and **not** let the nightmare happen."

CONCLUSION

Urban planning and design is an ongoing process which has a major impact on our lives. As important as it is, few people really understand what its intentions are and how it is carried out. Few classes on the subject are offered in schools; civics classes, for example, focus on political, not physical structure. Typically, people become aware of comprehensive planning and zoning only when they want to subdivide, buy or develop a property and when they must obtain city or county permission. Often these encounters are confrontational because the average citizen is not aware of the complex laws which govern land use and development.

Once citizens understand the principles and processes involved with planning and zoning, they can use this knowledge to achieve their own personal goals as well as contribute to the general welfare of the community. The U.S. Constitution and corresponding local ordinances are structured to assure a balance between private interests and public good. This is achieved through comprehensive planning, environmental review and public participation. After nearly a century of planning and zoning test cases, the legal precedents and procedures for controlling the shape of U.S. neighborhoods, towns, cities and regions are in place. It is now up to an informed partnership between government leaders and an active, concerned citizenry to provide the vision, energy and guidance necessary to realize the potential of urban environments.

REFERENCES

Boden, R. 1992. "The Influence of Traditional Values and Historic Symbolism on Urban Design," *Journal of Architectural and Planning Research*.

Branch, M. C. 1985. *Comprehensive City Planning*. Planners Press.

Fowler, E. P. 1992. *Building Cities That Work*. McGill-Queens University Press.

Gallion, A. B. and Eisner, S. 1986. *The Urban Pattern*. Van Nostrand Reinhold.

Knudsen, T. 1988. "Success in Planning," *International Journal of Urban and Regional Research*.

Levy, J. M. 1988. *Contemporary Urban Planning*. Prentice Hall.

Peponis, J. 1989. "Space, Culture, and Urban Design in Late Modernism and After," *Ekistics*.

Puget Sound Council of Governments. 1990. *Vision 2020* publications: "Region at a Crossroads: Time to Choose," "Region at a Crossroads: The Preferred Choice," and "Final Vision 2020 Plan."

Rakodi, C. 1991. "Cities and People: Towards a Gender-Aware Urban Planning Process?" *Public Administration and Development*.

Romaya, S. M. 1990. "Urban Design in Developing Countries: Some Case Studies from Malaysia and Zimbabwe," *Third World Planning Review*.

Shirvani, H. 1985. *The Urban Design Process*. Van Nostrand Reinhold.

Smith, H. H. 1980. *The Citizens Guide to Planning*. Planners Press.

Smith, H. H. 1983. *The Citizens Guide to Zoning*. Planners Press.

Southworth, M. 1989. "Theory and Practice of Contemporary Urban Design: A Review of Urban Design Plans in the United States," *Town Planning Review*.

Whyte, W. H. 1988. *City: Rediscovering the Center*. Doubleday.

CHAPTER

26

Urban and Regional Hierarchies: Central Place Theory

Gerald L. Young

Hierarchy theory has been used in this book as an ordering device, as a way of relating levels of human creativity as diverse as a simple product or a grand city to other levels of artifact and nature. This same device, in the form of hierarchies of urban places, is well established as a way to understand the patterns of urban and regional development. **Central Place Theory**, developed by the German scientist, Walter Christaller (1933), is "a general theory designed to explain the size, number, and distribution of towns" in the belief that some "ordering principles govern their distribution." A regional pattern, such as the theory proposes, is a categorization, a taxonomy, invented to enable us to better handle totalities or wholes, i.e., the complexity of our world. The theory assumes (or imposes) a pattern or order and a set of relationships; it is an organizational device. Central place theory posits a measure of tendency: there is a tendency in human settlements toward centrality.

The features of Christaller's theory, in brief, are as follows, enumerated for clarity and ease of understanding. They are presented in simplified form, and without some of the theoretical convolutions that have been more recently built into the theory. The idea is to present as simply as possible the basic idea of how urban places, and their surrounding regions, relate to each other in a simplified hierarchy. Examples and illustrations follow the listing.

First, the basic function of a city or town is to be a central place, providing goods and services for a surrounding tributary area. The term "central place" is used because to perform such a function efficiently, a city locates at the center of minimum aggregate travel of its tributary area, i.e., central to the maximum market area it can command.

Second, the centrality of a city is a sum measure of the degree to which it is such a service center. Third, the greater the centrality of a place, the higher is its "order." Fourth, higher order places offer more goods, have more establishments and business types, larger populations, tributary areas, and tributary populations, do greater volumes of business and are more widely spaced than lower order places.

Fifth, a minimum population is needed to support a particular function. This is called the **threshold population**. Demand (or need) varies with the good or service. Specialty goods and services are in less demand and therefore require a larger population for support . . . and a larger service area.

Sixth, low order places provide only low order goods to low order tributary areas. These low order goods are generally necessities requiring frequent purchasing with little consumer travel. Seventh, high order places, conversely, offer not only low order goods, but also high order goods sold by high order establishments. These high order goods are generally "shopping goods" for which the consumer is willing to travel longer distances, though less frequently.

Eighth, the higher the order of goods provided, the fewer are the establishments providing them, the greater the trade areas, and the fewer and more widely spaced are the towns or cities in which the establishments are located. And, finally, ninth, because higher order places offer more shopping opportunities, their trade areas for low-order goods are likely to be larger than those of low-order places for the same kind of goods, since consumers have the opportunity to combine purposes on a single trip. This acts like a price reduction.

Central places fall into a **hierarchy** comprising discrete (or separate) groups of centers (Berry, 1970; Young, 1978). Centers of each higher order perform all of the functions of lower order centers plus a group of central functions that differentiate them from and set them above the lower order. A consequence of this is a "nesting pattern" of lower-order trade areas within the trade area of higher order centers, plus a hierarchy of routes joining the centers.

Circles would be the ideal shape for service areas, except that gaps with inefficient service are left. So, Christaller postulated the hexagon as the ideal shape, leaving no gaps in the area served by the central city. The geographer, Brian Berry (1970) has made several studies based on Christaller's scheme. He did his graduate work at the University of Washington and went into the field, measuring the "central tendency" of cities in the Puget Sound region, finding that they "approximately" correlated to Christaller's nested hierarchy in terms of orders and spacing.

Seven levels of hierarchy were postulated by Christaller, from farm hamlet to world city:

- Market town
- Township center or county seat
- District city
- Small state capitol or provincial head city
- Regional center or capitol city
- National city or capitol
- World city

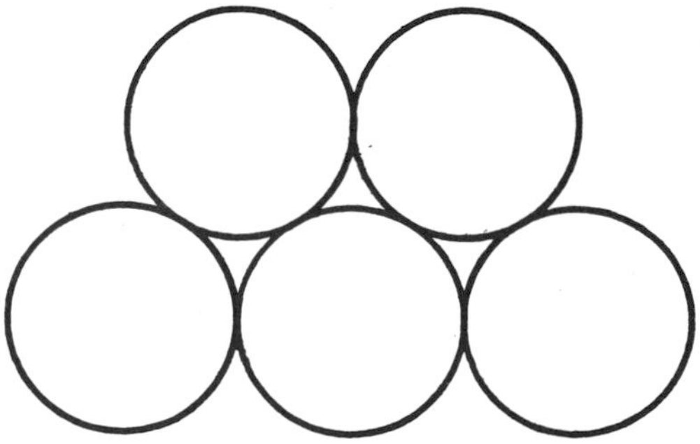

1. Hexagons were used in the nesting pattern because circles left areas unserved by the market structure.

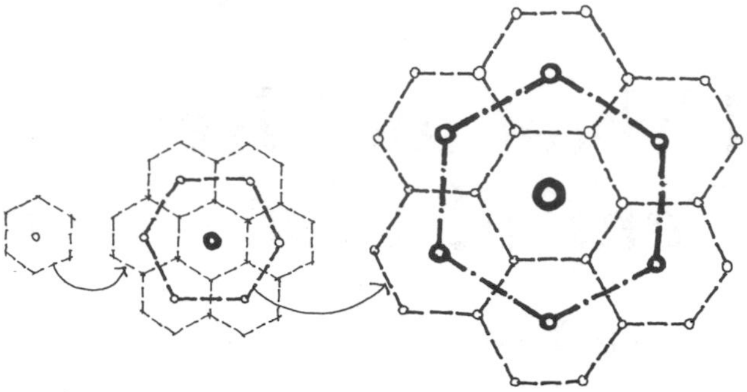

2. A hierarchically nested set of central places.

Remember that this is a general theory, even more simplified here, one that is postulating order and pattern in the spacing and location of cities, and that this chapter is only a brief summary of that theory. In reality, it is much more complex (see King, 1984). The "perfect" shape is, in fact, most often distorted through the incidence of physical features, especially mountains and bodies of water. For example, note the constriction of Seattle by Puget Sound and the Cascade Mountains, though the pattern complies quite closely North and South, with the theorized hierarchy (see Figure 3). Other distortions are caused by transport routes, especially highways, and even by human nature or whim. But, the theory provides more evidence that the systems that comprise the human environment—the built environment—can be organized hierarchically to help make connections, to better comprehend relationships, and in general to aid toward an integrated understanding of the built environment (see Young, 1978).

A theory, yes, but also logical and down-to-earth. If you have lived in a town of, say, 2000 people, you know that it is easy to walk or drive down to the store for a candy bar, or to the bar for a beer. But, you probably can't buy a car there; to purchase a Chevy or a Ford automobile, you have to travel to the nearest town large enough to command the market area for a dealership. If your tastes run to more exotic and expensive vehicles—say a Lamborghini or a Rolls Royce, the local dealerships don't handle them because the market population necessary for such high order goods is not yet satisfied. For such cars, you might have to travel to a "world city," one whose market area for some goods is global in extent. In the Pacific Northwest region of the United States, for example, Seattle could be classified as such a city. If you want a Boeing 727,

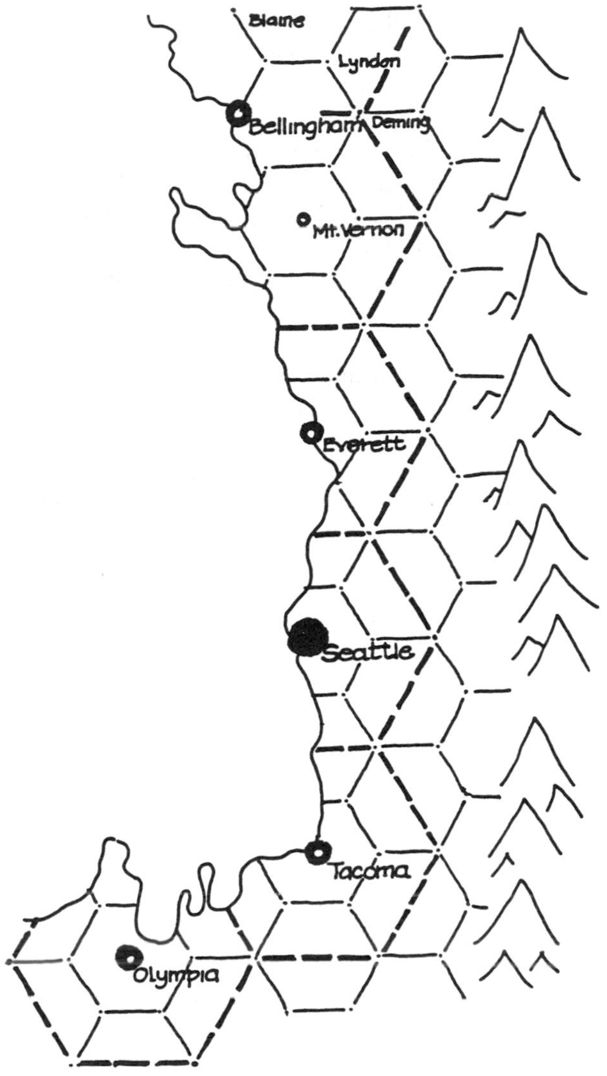

3. Hierarchy of nested central places in Puget Sound, Washington.

you have to buy it in Seattle—and they are sold to customers world-around; but you can also buy toothpaste there, and cheaper than in that small town of 2,000 people. These examples are somewhat exaggerated, but are also true. And they go a long way toward providing a general, yet simple framework for grasping major influences in the distribution, spacing and size relationships of cities and their surrounding regions.

The Seattle area, because of Berry's work, provided an early illustration of the reality of central place patterns on the land, thereby holding a significant place in the early development of the theory. But, thc Scattlc area, or the "Central Puget Sound Region," also provides some recent evidence of the actual applicability of Christaller's vision. In May, 1990, the Puget Sound Council of Governments distributed, in newspaper supplement, tabloid form, five alternatives for "Vision 2020," an attempt to identify strategies to deal with unprecedented—and uncontrolled—growth (see previous chapter). The people of the region were asked to choose between "No action;" "Existing Plans;" "Dispersed Growth;" "Major Centers;" and "Multiple Centers," as alternative ways to plan for growth, and for the development of transportation routes to handle that growth. About 90 percent of the respondents favored some sort of "centers" approach.

The preferred growth strategy that emerged out of the centers approach is a **hierarchy of central places**, with Seattle remaining the most central, the "most significant business, cultural, governmental, recreational and management center." The growth strategy designates four cities, less central to the region than Seattle, as "Metropolitan Centers," places where new employment and residential growth are desirable. Next, "subregional centers" will be developed in suburban locations along rapid transit facilities. Smaller than metropolitan and subregional centers, and not on rapid transit lines, are "activity clusters" which will see limited growth, mostly in service employment to surrounding residential areas. Next in the hierarchy are "small towns," in which growth will be limited in an attempt to preserve their small town atmosphere, and to insure that diversity in choices of places to live is guaranteed.

The centers approach for the central Puget Sound Region takes advantage of the tendency toward centrality in a hierarchy of places as a design strategy to order future development and growth. It is not clear that the planners involved in Vision 2020 knew about the earlier work by Berry in the Puget Sound Region, or about Central Place Theory at all. And, it does not matter. They did utilize the basics of the pattern to good advantage to create a plan to bring order, through a hierarchically integrated regional system, to a place where individualized tendencies, the automobile especially, were creating increasing congestion and potential chaos.

Describing central place theory, Brian Berry claimed that "to understand the system as a whole demands that each of the subsystems be understood, as well as the relationships between them." If the strategy is maintained, the central Puget Sound region will grow, but it will be ordered growth, where cities relate to each other as "cities as systems within systems of cities" and where "*urbi et orbi*"—the city and the world around it—change in relationship to each other rather than in increasing conflict.

REFERENCES

Berry, B. J. L. 1970. "Cities as Systems Within Systems of Cities," *Urban Economics: Theory Development and Planning*. The Free Press.

Christaller, W. 1933. *Die Zentralen Orte in Suddeutschland: Eine Okonomisch-Geographische Untersuchung Uber die Gesetzmassigkeit der Verbreitung und Entwicklung der Siedlungen mit Stadtischen Funktionen*. Verlag.

Fujita, M. H. O. and Thisse, J. F. 1988. "A Spatial Competition Approach to Central Place Theory: Some Basic Principles," *Journal of Regional Science*.

Gober, P. and Behr, M. 1982. "Central Cities and Suburbs as Distinct Place Types: Myth or Fact?" *Economic Geography*, October.

King, L. J. 1984. *Central Place Theory*. Sage.

Ohuallachain, B. and Reid, N. 1993. "The Location of Services in the Urban Hierarchy and the Regions of the United States," *Geographical Analysis*.

Shuper, V. A. 1989. "Deformation of Central Place Systems in the Formation of Large Urban Agglomerations," *Soviet Geography*, January.

West, D. S., Von Hohenbalken, B. and Kroner, K. 1985. "Tests of Intraurban Central Place Theories," *The Economic Journal*, March.

Wheeler, J. O. 1993. "Characteristics and Recent Trends in Urban Geography," *Urban Geography*.

Young, G. L. 1978. "Hierarchy and Central Place: Some Questions of More General Theory," *Geografiska Annaler*.

Introduction

6. REGIONS

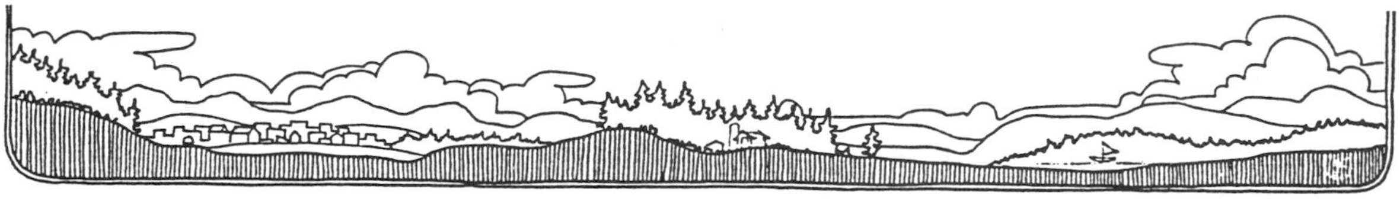

The region, the sixth component of the built environment, is of interest for a number of reasons. One is that the concept of a region is itself an artifact, an invention of the human mind and, though useful in real terms, should be recognized as such. Second, society is becoming increasingly concerned with manipulation of the environment at the regional scale; humans have spilled over the boundaries of their cities causing numerous impacts at the regional level. In the attempt to solve larger problems of pollution, transportation, loss of valuable farm land to suburban sprawl, etc., representative governments have enacted regional planning procedures and comprehensive plans. Third, some of the most impressive and significant artifacts of the built environment have been created as links between regions, more clearly emphasizing the nature of regions while interconnecting them: regional canal networks; national highways and interstate systems; watershed management; pipe and power networks; regional and international airports and air lines, among others.

Region is not easily differentiated from other middle-level expressions of the built environment, from landscape or city. It is possible, for example, to speak of an urban landscape or an urban region. People in eastern Washington talk of the picturesque Palouse landscape, and this means the same thing as the Palouse region.

Perhaps the easiest way to clarify this is to describe regions more specifically in terms of a level of the built environment with specific interest to a set of design disciplines. Again, there is overlap, but the concept of levels-of-integration has been used in this book on the built environment to help deal with overlap, to conceptualize an interrelated, integrated continuum. So, the differentiations made are for the sake of organization and design. Both content and context should always be kept in mind; regions like all other components are holons made up of parts and part of something larger.

Therefore, for the purposes of this book, regions indicate categories as well as relationships. Landscapes are local entities, either rural or urban, more encompassing than a single structure, but less comprehensive than a region. A city can be within a landscape or region, is usually clearly demarcated by the edges of urbanization, is usually made up of numerous landscapes, and is part of a region. A region can be a landscape or a city, but is normally thought to represent the next level of part-whole relationships, as incorporative of many landscapes and of several cities and their environs. This content-component-context relationship can once again be symbolized by the following:

PRODUCTS-INTERIORS-STRUCTURES-LANDSCAPES-CITIES-***REGIONS***-EARTH

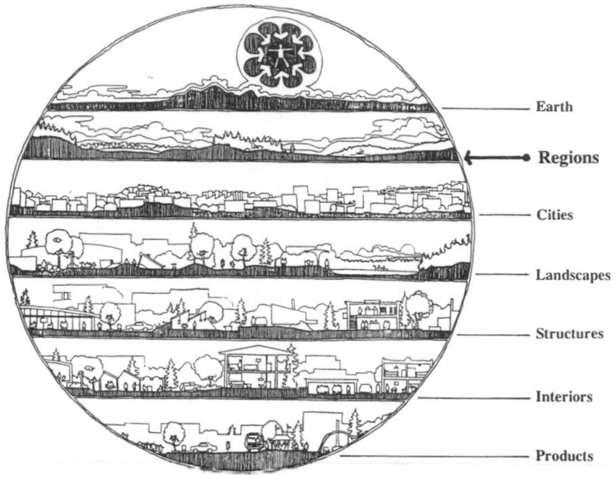

The purpose and definition of regions can also be clarified by the following:

a. regions (contain products, interiors, structures, landscapes, and cities) and are, in part, humanly made, arranged, or maintained;
b. to mediate the overall environment (to manage farm and resource production, to provide a coordinating sub-unit of the globe);
c. to help fulfill human purpose and the need for organization;
d. while affecting their context, Earth.

The previous section helped define, at least in a conceptual way, how cities relate to each other within regions. The chapters in this section explore the various ways regions can be defined, their many factors more clearly understood, managed and planned:

- **"Planning the Built Environments: Determining the Regional Context"** by Gerald Young, et al: this chapter analyzes the various factors that combine to define regions as political, biophysical, social/cultural or economic types. These overlapping dimensions are useful in attempting to manage, plan and coordinate the resources of a region.

- **"Regional Planning in the United States: Contemporary Examples"** by Frederick Steiner: this chapter clarifies and illustrates how regions are planned in the United States in an attempt to manage and coordinate their diverse resources and attributes for the nation.

- **"Connections: Products, Regional Planning, and Policies"** by William W. Budd: this chapter links the levels of the built environment, from products to regions, by tracing the waste materials generated by the manufacture and use of products, as they affect each level.

CHAPTER 27

Planning the Built Environment: Determining the Regional Context

Gerald Young, Frederick Steiner, Kenneth Brooks and Kenneth Struckmeyer

All humans live in a world with an explicit spatial dimension; do now, always have, and always will. Being human, we prefer that the world be as ordered and predictable as possible. So, ordering is an ongoing human endeavor in all environments, those real and those perceived. That is one reason the built environment is so pervasive. Planning, as a process and as a discipline, particularly as one of the ways we manipulate the built environment, has emerged as a result of that need for organization and through the effort to establish it. Part of the planning response has been a search for mechanisms or techniques to make or allow the ordering process to be more accessible, clearer and more useful. One such concept is the human artifact known by the label **region**: we use regions to identify and order spatial patterns. The concept of region, indeed, seems intrinsic to the thought patterns of contemporary humans, especially in western, industrialized nations. Planners, perhaps more than most, have to work within the patterns imposed by this ordering process. However, they also can often take advantage of such patterns, can sometimes manipulate them to help achieve specified goals, and can even occasionally create regions to their own specifications.

What is true for planning in general is also true for each of the more specialized orientations within planning—city and urban planning, regional planning, community planning, landscape planning—by whatever label. All are concerned with, and confined by, regions at some level, of some type or other. Recognition of this is implicit in Artur Glikson's (1967) statement that "to become fully effective, landscape planning has to form part of regional planning." Accepting that, however, creates problems rather than solutions: What is a "region"? What is "regional" planning? At what levels is it appropriate? How do planners deal with such ambiguous concepts? How can planners set and achieve reasonable goals, confronted as they are by a multiplicity of regions at a number of different levels in every place where planning is attempted?

This chapter is an attempt to clarify some of these issues in a way appropriate to planning the built environment. The approach is one of synthesis, first by comparing a variety of specific and then composite regions useful to the planner and, second by identifying theoretical ideas within an ecological perspective, especially that of human ecology, which should prove useful in applying the concept "region" in planning.

DEFINING REGIONS AND REGIONAL TYPES

Regional planning is often undertaken with the presumption that there is an inherent understanding of the meaning of the terms region and regional. In spite of its wide usage, region is a difficult word to apply. Regions have been used by governmental agencies and others to delineate multijurisdictional areas, such as those comprised of more than one town, city, county, state, or nation. Natural scientists use regions in reference to a part of the surface of the earth, such as watersheds, physiographic provinces, climatic zones, or faunal areas. Geographers define a region as an

1. Hunt' s Physiographic Provinces (*Hunt,* 1967).

uninterrupted area possessing some kind of homogeneity in its core, but lacking clearly defined limits. Even standard dictionary definitions are ambiguous: any more or less extensive, contiguous part of a surface of space.

Regions may be political, economic, biophysical, and/or sociocultural. **Political-regulatory regions** are the quickest and easiest to identify. Political regions are simply civil divisions such as state, county, and township boundaries in the United States and similar divisions in other nations. Though such civil divisions bound a number of basic regulatory functions (zoning is a U.S. example), impingement or overlap of other regulatory agencies may be present and must be considered.

Biophysical regions are commonly used by planners and resource managers. Most simply, biophysical regions may be described as the pattern of interacting biological and physical phenomena present in a given area. Purely physical (see Figure 1) and more complex ecological (see Figure 2) regions have both been mapped. **Sociocultural regions** are perhaps the most elusive type. Unlike most of the phenomena that constitute biophysical regions, people with widely varying social characteristics can occupy a single settlement space. Such groups of people can be relatively independent, but the more usual case is some measure of interdependence. Either can be useful in defining a region. Human movement in response to seasons means also that different populations may occupy the same space at different times of the year.

Geographers especially have made repeated attempts to define regional patterns, usually expressed in common, widely accepted terminology. For example, regions commonly known by the public in North America are often identified by popular labels, such as New England, the South, the Midwest, or the Pacific Northwest in the United States and the Maritimes, the Canadian Shield, the Prairies, or the Yukon in Canada. These can be accepted as common cultural regions because they are so deeply implanted in public consciousness.

Wilbur Zelinsky (1980), a geographer, has suggested a wider use of such **vernacular regions** to describe social and cultural components. Basically, a vernacular, or popular, region is the spatial perception of indigenous people. Zelinsky suggests that regional, ethnic and historical questions may be answered by looking at vernacular regions (see Figure 3). While popular regions are well-known in Europe (France is a good example), popular regions in North America are not as widely recognized by U.S. scholars and practitioners.

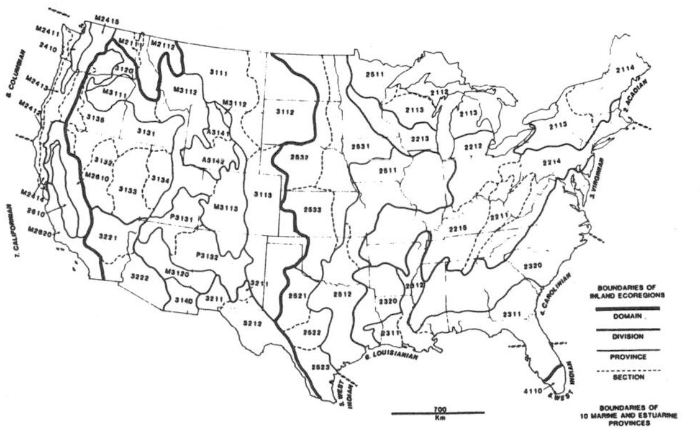

2. Ecoregions of the United States after Bailey (1976) with the addition of 10 marine and estaurine provinces proposed by Cowardin et al. (1979).

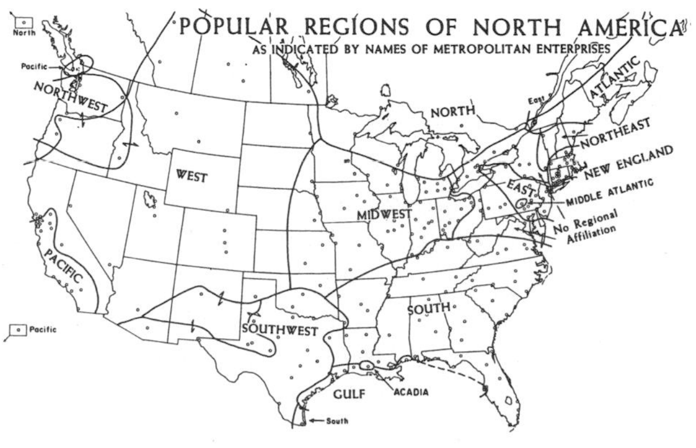

3. Zelinsky's Popular Regions (*Zelinsky,* 1980—Courtesy of the *Annals of the Association of American Geographers*).

Functionally, **economic regions** are a special case of the cultural region, often the dominant one, e.g., when a metropolitan region is defined by such factors as daily trips to work and circulation of newspapers, by shopping trips or as market centers. Agricultural regions are a common delineation of this type (c.f., Eveling, 1979), and are often taken as a synthesis of all regional types, especially in terms of landscape analysis. The basic resources of agriculture are the biophysical factors of soil, water, and plants and the sociocultural factor of people, with climate providing a linkage, a measure of coincidence for the production of food and fiber. It is not uncommon to substitute labels from agriculture as synonyms for more incorporative regional types: Cotton Belt for the southeastern United States, for example, or Corn Belt for the Midwest.

Poets are often far ahead of the rest of us in recognizing and using language forms that help organize the environment; they have long recognized the importance of regions and regionalism. T. S. Eliot (1949), for example, in his attempt to define "culture," found region to be a particularly useful idea by which to examine unity and diversity: "we have not given enough attention to the ecology of culture," a "regional problem" that can best be addressed by giving "our attention to the question of unity and diversity within the limited areas that we know best" though the "regional problem has to be seen in [a] larger context." The Kentucky poet, Wendell Berry (1975), defines region in the following manner:

> The regionalism that I adhere to could be defined simply as local life aware of itself. It would tend to substitute for the myths and stereotypes of a region a particular knowledge of the life of the place one lives in and intends to live in.

Similarly, Gary Snyder (1980), a poet who strongly identifies with the biomes of northern California, especially the Sierran forests, has long urged a return to regionalism for an at least partial cure of the ills that beset humankind: "people have to learn a sense of region, and what is possible within a region . . . we are extremely deficient in regional knowledge . . . it takes a long time to get to know how to live in a region gently and easily and with a maximal annual efficiency." Snyder and many others now advocate **bioregions** as a way of creating a context for reinhabiting the earth (Berry, 1988).

A region is a complex entity that involves many phenomena and processes. To be useful, such information must be ordered. This involves establishing cores and boundaries, hierarchical classifications and interrelationships.

On a map, boundary lines always strike the eye. Boundaries tend to appear more real than the zones they symbolize and to divert attention from actual connections and separations. Boundaries are most often determined for planning purposes through the political process. Goals are established for planning in a variety of ways and these goals result in irregular boundaries, a well-recognized problem of regional planning. A major difficulty in preparing, and especially in effecting regional plans, is that most "real" units rarely coincide with governmental jurisdictions. The boundaries of metropolitan New York, Chicago, London, Tokyo and Paris enclose other municipalities and many units of local government. River basins are seldom included entirely within states or provinces and many of them (the Rhine, Rio Grande, Columbia and Congo, etc.) are international.

Regions, then, are defined in many different ways, with many possibilities, even for one area. An operational definition for region must be uniquely interpreted for each planning effort. For a specific planning project, the region is the area affected by the collective biophysical, political, economic, and sociocultural influences related to the project. Despite this uniqueness, the concept of region can be approached from a perspective that should be useful to planners in whatever context they are confronted with the regional problem.

THE FUNDAMENTAL PROBLEM

Rupert Vance and Howard Odum, in *Regionalism in America*, both emphasize, in Vance's (1965) words, that "region gains its significance only from its relation to a total structure," that "the relation that regionalism presumes to study is that of parts to wholes," and that "no region can be defined except in relation to the total structure of which it is a component part." The fundamental problem in regional planning, then, is in abstract terms, the **relationship between the unit and the whole**. In social terms, the problem is reconciliation of the often conflicting needs and goals of the individual (the unit) and the society (the whole).

A common definition of planning is one which outlines as objectives the attainment of balance and equilibrium between competing factors, which can again be defined as a problem of conflict between unit and whole. In this sense, region is a particularly apt tool because as Howard Odum (1965) describes it, "always, regionalism is a two-way concept. The region, yes, but primarily the region as a composite unit of the whole," a way of saying that regions, once acknowledged, are reminders of the part-whole problem: "we have to distinguish between that which concerns the area primarily and that which pertains to the area in relations to other areas, or to the place of the area in some total structure."

REDEFINING REGIONS: OPTIONS FROM HUMAN ECOLOGY

Because the part-whole problem is fundamental to so many areas of inquiry (perhaps to all), a number of theoretical techniques can be identified (again common to many disciplines) to help deal with such relationships. In planning, the most evident unit is the human-being—as individual human, as individual population, or individual community of some sort; the whole of concern is the landscape, or environment, especially as expressed in spatial or regional terms. In this sense, unit-whole relationships become a problem of classical ecology, especially of human ecology: a study of process and relationships in a regional landscape setting. The techniques then, are expressed in terms of ecological theory, focusing on (a) interaction and field theory; (b) levels-of-organization or hierarchy theory; (c) the ecosystem and general systems theory; (d) functionalism and studies of structure; and (e) holism. These should all be useful in planning, especially as order in the environment is expressed regionally and if the fundamental problem of the region is considered a parts-whole problem.

Interaction and Field Theory

Biological ecologists early asserted that one of the distinguishing features of ecology was its major emphasis on process. Marston Bates (1956) and many others have argued that organism and environment should never be thought of as discrete, definable entities, but rather in terms of "transactions between processes." Reality in human ecology (and then in regional planning) can also be defined as a product of process, or rather, of processes. The most fundamental of the almost innumerable processes in the systems of concern to the planner is the process of **interaction** (Young, 1974). Simply defined, interaction means reciprocal action, the action or influence of persons or things on each other. Even such a simple definition clarifies and emphasizes the significance of a sort of double-ended arrow, underlining the salient nature of reciprocity as a condition in the formulation and emergence of ecological relationships, including those of the natural and built systems of concern to the planner.

Interaction is commonly used in the definition of that basic ecological unit, the ecosystem. Tansley (1935), when he coined the word ecosystem, underscored the importance of interaction, declaring that all parts of such a system may be considered interacting factors and that it is through such interactions that the entire (or whole) system is sustained. A number of ecologists have since reiterated Tansley's notion of the ecosystem as an **interaction system**, as the total sum of organisms and environment and the processes of interaction between and among all parts of the system. Use of the term and concept of interaction has become commonplace in most such unit definitions in ecology.

The same is true in the social sciences, disciplines most strongly identified with an ecological approach to the study of human beings. Interaction is the keystone in many approaches to the study of social systems. Interaction holds a cardinal position as the first-order step beyond the nonreciprocal action concept toward formulation of social system.

A human ecological synthesis relevant to planning should be a synthesis of interaction theory, as it has become known in the social sciences, blended with its latent dimensions in biological ecology. It is the nature and frequency of interaction that most strongly affects relationships and associations, including those with the landscape or environment. Ecology is the essential study of these kinds of connections; process is the essence of ecology; interaction is the quintessential process. Once connections have been established, then some sort of interactional system or field has been created and is maintained through the same process. It seems possible to frame nearly every kind of ecological problem, and by extension planning problem, in terms of subsequent processes that derive their particular forms from the interaction context in which they occur. Interaction provides the medium through which systems, including ecosystems and regional systems, perform functions and, in terms of human systems, carry out intended purposes. Unless interaction takes place, no system can continue to exist.

A **field** is a construct that emerges out of this process. When psychologists use field theory to describe the life-space of an individual or group, that space is defined by the way the individual or group interacts with others and with the environment. The life space of a person or group consists of that person or group and its environment as it exists for the organisms being considered: "all behavior is conceived of as a change of some state of a field in a given unit of time" (Cartwright, 1951).

So, the field motif, notably that of **interactional field**, provides planners with a paradigm through which the part and the whole can be analyzed and regions at various levels derived. Regions so defined are interactional fields relating organisms and environments, in which each initially has common parameters and a common base. Fields can be constructed around individuals or around groups at various levels; they can be inclusive or exclusive of environment; and they can be "real" or simply products of perception, or imagination, or even of convenience. We think of field as a bounded area, e.g., a pasture with a fence, but fields in physics deal with flux and certainly with probabilities and they should as well in ecology and planning. Field, in this sense, is a quicksilver concept, a gestalt concept tying figure and ground; a field sort of flows out from the figure (or figures) in a dynamic way—Venn diagrams with fuzzy edges.

A practical example of the field concept, one directly applicable to planning and the built environment, is provided by Smailes (1966): "modern communications [interaction] have enabled town and city greatly to extend their range . . . [forming an] urban-rural continuum." Smailes goes on to say that as this process develops, the town "becomes the focusing point of a district" or region, the development and acceleration of interaction greatly increasing "the urban integration of life . . . the range and power of the influence of towns." Smailes goes "so far as to suggest that the fundamental unit in the geographical structure of community life . . . is today the town region," an "urban field . . . [that] must be reckoned with the town's own inhabitants in a single community" or region.

Hierarchy Theory

Another key to better understanding of the increased integration of human life into dynamic fields or regions is **hierarchy theory**, the idea of levels-of-intergration or hierarchical systems (see Chapter 4 in this book). The real meaning of integration in a series of levels begins with an understanding of how the integration takes place, of how the levels are connected each to the others. The essential process, the mechanism of integration, is interaction, creating a set of "interacting levels," an all-pervading matrix of forces and interactions (Young, 1992).

Once such a connection is made, between two theretofore isolated entities, once the entities are connected through the process of interaction, then neither, in terms of planning, are ever again understandable in totality without reference to the other. This is going beyond the first, isolated entity or unit to the next step, a higher and more integrated level composed of the first and second entities plus the connective or interactional process.

Thinking in terms of levels formalizes the part-whole relationship, implies synthesis as well as analysis, provides context and implies interdependence in the sense intended by Smailes' discussion of the urban-rural field. Interdependence implies connectivity, which in turn implies communication, the essence of the interaction process. All of these imply order and that leads naturally to an idea of system.

Functionalism and Studies of Structure

One way to deal with parts and wholes in a systems framework is best labeled **functionalism**. Simply defined, functionalism is the study of how the parts of a whole or system are interrelated. One approach, in terms of analysis of the social or ecological systems of interest to planners, is to consider interrelationships as a product of connectivity . . . and, again, interaction is a connective process. Interaction processes, communication, for example, or transportation improvements, provide the cement that holds the parts into an interacting whole—into a system, a field, or a region.

Such systems can be thought of in structural terms—ecological structure as an interactional organization of functions, activities that become dependent on other activities: a system depends on the interaction of its parts for its functional integrity. Functional relationships are the means of integration in social systems, and can be described as the critical relations—mutual interactions—between structure and process, between process and structure.

More explicitly, in terms of regions and planning, how is a region organized, how does it work (or function), and why does it work that way? The form of the region is described as its structure, which can be compared to a scaffolding of parts that come together to make up the whole. In biophysical regions, this scaffolding is the geology, physiography, groundwater, surface water, soils, climate, vegetation, wildlife and land use. Structural components of economic regions include resources, products of labor, markets, capitalization and consumption. Finally, structural components of sociocultural regions are demographic aspects such as population size and density, age, ethnicity, education, occupation, and cultural aspects, such as values, beliefs, attitudes, knowledge, information, technology, literature and aesthetics.

As implied above, the working of a region is dependent upon the interactions of these structural components, on functional connections between the parts. In biophysical regions, these functions include such processes as biochemical cycles and energy flows. The structural/functional relationships of biophysical, economic, political and sociocultural regions may be fairly simple, defined perhaps by the significance of a single factor or small group of factors, or they may be rather complex. Where the complexity is not easily reduced, as is often the case, then regions can still be considered in totality, as wholes or total systems.

Holism

The most evident manifestation or expression of interactions between parts and wholes is the utility of **holism** in the definition of systems, an expression that has already been noted and that will be developed more fully later. Short of that, interaction can still be said to lead inevitably to consideration of a greater whole because it is, in essence, a connective process. This suggests that examination of the process leads naturally from consideration of a part, to its connection to another part, through its interaction with that part to consideration of the next higher level as a greater, more integrated whole.

Arthur Koestler (1967) coined the term **holon** to deal with this notion of an entity that must be considered as *both* part and whole, but also to incorporate its existence or function as part of a larger whole, a context that appreciates through the connections issuing from the interaction process. Koestler's term is a more concise explanation of statements by Odum and Vance: a region as a holon is a composite of its component parts and in turn part of something larger.

Ecosystem and Systems Analysis: The Watershed Example

For a system to exist, including ecosystem or anything organized enough to be called a region, there must be ordered, connecting channels of communication, the essence of the interaction process. Societies are more than the sum of their parts, i.e., **systems**, only to the extent that there is controlled interaction among those parts. As noted earlier, the reality of **ecosystems** can be described in interactional terms: ecosystems function as an interacting whole.

Eugene Odum (1971) suggested the **watershed** as an ecosystem and as a practical unit for management that combines natural and cultural attributes (see Figure 4):

> It is the whole drainage basin, not just the body of water, that must be considered as the minimum ecosystem unit when it comes to [human] interests. The ecosystem unit for practical management must then include for every square meter or acre of water at least 20 times an area of terrestrial watershed.

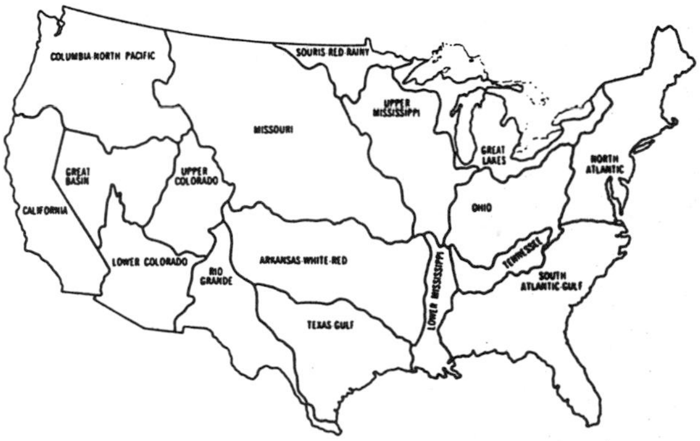

4. Eighteen major river basins of the United States.

Table 1

Region	Area or Subregion	Drainage Area Alaska sq. mi.	Drainage Area Canada sq. mi.	Drainage Area Total sq. mi.
Arctic	1.1 West Arctic	31,000	—	31,000
	1.2 Colville	24,000	—	24,000
	1.3 East Arctic	26,000	—	26,000
	Total For The Region	81,000	—	81,000
Northwest	2.1 Kotzebue Sound	41,000	—	41,000
	2.2 Norton Sound	26,000	—	26,000
	Total For The Region	67,000		67,000
Yukon	3.1 Lower Yukon	38,000	—	38,000
	3.2 Central Yukon	19,000	—	19,000
	3.3 Koyukuk	33,000	—	33,000
	3.4 Upper Yukon-North	60,000	25,000	85,000
	3.5 Tanana	45,000	500	45,500
	3.6 Upper Yukon-Canada	9,000	105,000	114,000
	Total For The Region	204,000	130,500	334,500
Southwest	4.1 Kuskokwim Bay	58,000	—	58,000
	4.2 Bristol Bay	40,000	—	40,000
	4.3 Aleutian	11,000	—	11,000
	Total For The Region	109,000		109,000
Southcentral	5.1 Kodiak Shelikof	11,000	—	11,000
	5.2 Cook Inlet	38,000	—	38,000
	5.3 Cooper River-Gulf of Alaska	34,000	1,000	35,000
	Total For The Region	83,000	1,000	84,000
Southeast		42,000	35,000	77,000
	Total For The Region	42,000	35,000	77,000
	TOTALS	**586,000**	**166,500**	**752,500**

The watershed, then, is one possible unit for determining the regional context for planning. Watersheds have discrete boundaries. Watersheds can vary in scale. These characteristics provide flexibility adaptable to social, economic and political issues.

The use of watersheds for planning is not new. John Wesley Powell essentially suggested the use of watersheds in his 1879 plan for the Western regions of the U.S. The use of watersheds is also consistent with past efforts of river basin commissions, such as the Delaware River Basin Commission, the Columbia River Basin Commission, and the Tennessee Valley Authority. An excellent example of the use of watersheds for regional planning is the Alaska regional profile series (see Table 1). Alaska was divided into six regions for planning: Arctic, Northwest, Yukon, Southwest, Southcentral, and Southeast. These regions and related subregions were determined by the drainage patterns (or watersheds) of major river basins. A detailed inventory and analysis of bio-physical, sociocultural, economical, and political structures and processes was produced for each region (Selkregg, 1974). The watershed is an ideal, but one that offers an exciting framework for planning. Some applications of the concept are discussed in Chapter 28.

Once boundaries have been identified, it is necessary to describe and classify the structure, or internal phenomena, of ecosystem regions. Many hierarchical classifications have been developed to accomplish this. One is the U.S. Fish and Wildlife Service's system for the classification of wetlands and deep-water habitats. Another is the U.S. Geological Survey's system for classifying land use and land cover. An environmentally sensitive areas classification has been developed by Steiner and one of his graduate students, George Newman. Hierarchical structures, even in applied forms such as these, exist primarily as a tool to link parts and wholes in a series of levels.

The U.S. Fish and Wildlife Service system was established for regional inventories of wetlands and deep-water habitats. It is intended to describe ecological taxas (parts), arrange them in a system (whole) useful to resource managers and regional planners, and provide uniformity of concepts and terms. Wetlands are defined by plants, soils, and frequency of flooding. Ecologically related areas of deep water are also included. Systems form the highest holistic level of this classification hierarchy (see Figure 5). Lower levels (parts or units) include subsystems and classes. This scheme is especially helpful in classifying the biophysical components of a region.

A useful system for classifying human land uses of an area has been developed by the U.S. Geological Survey (see Table 2). This system was originally developed for use with remote sensor data, but is applicable to other land-use and land-cover classifications. It is designed for use throughout the United States (Anderson et al., 1976). The hierarchy consists of a number of levels with increasing specificity. For instance, in Table 2, Level I includes urban or built-up land, while Level II includes residential. Carrying the system to Level III would include low-density residential and to Level IV single-family detached houses.

Other systems have been developed for more specific situations. Table 3 is one such system developed for identifying environmentally sensitive areas (Newman and Steiner, 1982).

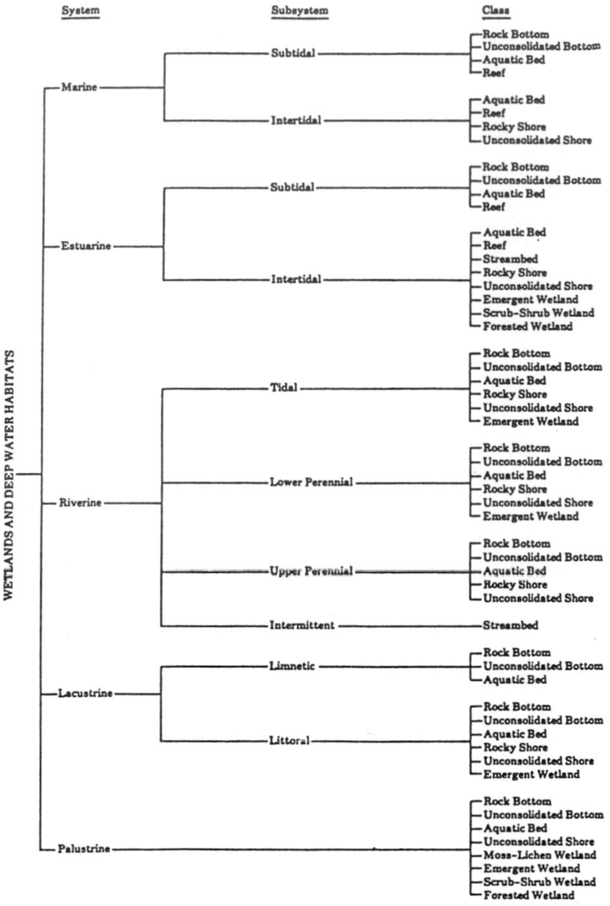

5. Classification hierarchy of wetlands and deep-water habitats (*Cowardin et al.,* 1979).

To show process, it is also necessary to clearly establish interrelationships between the structural components or phenomena of regions. One tool to accomplish this is to identify bivariate relationships. The matrix in Figure 6 is a convenient way to show such relationships. Both spatial and process relationships exist between each numbered pair of elements. For instance, the geology of a region exerts a direct influence on its physiography. Through geologic time, the physical form of the landscape is developed. Likewise, the physiography influences the microclimate. Rainfall and temperature vary from mountainous areas to valleys. Climate, in turn, affects potential habitats for plants and animals and so on. For each number on the chart, the indicated interaction may be described (Steiner and Brooks, 1981). Such a matrix helps to illustrate human functions and processes within a region.

Another tool to show interrelationships is the layer-cake model popularized by Ian McHarg (1969).

Table 2

Level I	Level II
1 Urban or Built-Up Land	11 Residential 12 Commercial and Services 13 Industrial 14 Transportation Communications and Utilities 15 Industrial and Commercial Complexes 16 Mixed Urban or Built-Up Land 17 Other Urban or Built-Up Land
2 Agricultural Land	21 Cropland and Pasture 22 Orchards, Groves, Vineyards, Nurseries and Ornamental Horticultural Areas 23 Confined Feeding Operations 24 Other Agricultural Land
3 Rangeland	31 Herbaceous Rangeland 32 Shrub and Brush Rangeland 33 Mixed Rangeland
4 Forest Land	41 Deciduous Forest Land 42 Evergreen Forest Land 43 Mixed Forest Land
5 Water	51 Streams and Canals 52 Lakes 53 Reservoirs 54 Bays and Estuaries
6 Wetland	61 Forested Wetland 62 Nonforested Wetland
7 Barren Land	71 Dry Salt Flats 72 Beaches 73 Sandy Areas Other Than Beaches 74 Bare Exposed Rock 75 Strip Mines, Quarries and Gravel Pits 76 Transitional Areas 77 Mixed Barren Land
8 Tundra	81 Shrub and Brush Tundra 82 Herbaceous Tundra 83 Bare Ground Tundra 84 Wet Tundra 85 Mixed Tundra
9 Perennial Snow or Ice	91 Perennial Snowfields 92 Glaciers

The four classes in this system have been adapted from Odum and the New Jersey Pinelands Commissions (1980). The thirteen subclasses were adapted from the Center for Natural Areas of the Smithsonian Institute (1974).

Table 3: An Environmentally Sensitive Area Classification System (Newman, 1982)

Class	Subclass
Ecologically Critical Areas	1 Natural Wildlife Habitat Areas 2 Natural Ecological Areas 3 Scientific Areas
Perceptual and Cultural Critical Areas	4 Scenic Areas 5 Wilderness Recreation Areas 6 Historical, Archaeological and Cultural Areas
Resource Production Critical Areas	7 Agricultural Lands 8 Water Quality Areas 9 Mineral Extraction Areas
Natural Hazard Critical Areas	10 Flood Prone Areas 11 Fire Hazard Areas 12 Geologic Hazard Areas 13 Air Pollution Areas

Layer-cake models help to gain a perspective about how various components of the environment interact across the landscape (see Figure 7). A cross-section of an area is drawn and then the components of the bio-physical and social environment stacked like a layer cake (Steiner, 1982). In this manner, elements, notably parts and whole, can be compared and analyzed. McHarg has easily adapted his method for use in computerized Geographic Information Systems (GIS).

	RESIDENTIAL	COMMERCIAL	INDUSTRIAL	TRANSPORTATION	RECREATION	AGRICULTURE	EXTRACTION
CLIMATE							
GEOLOGY							
PHISIOGRAPHY							
HYDROLOGY							
SOILS							
VEGETATION							
WILDLIFE							

6. Bivariate relationships: land uses and biophysical processes.

CONSPECTUS

There should be little argument that some conception of "region" is a given in planning, not only in the United States but around the world, indeed a given in the cultural, social, economic, and political affairs of humanity in all its manifestations —from local levels to a global entity (OECD, 1987; Malecha, et al. 1989). Planners then can never lose sight of this given, must indeed keep it in mind in all of the broad range of considerations that make up the complexity of planning.

Despite this, planning is quite often proto-planning, concerned too exclusively with the lowest or most local, forced into the atomistic mode by parochial politics. Or, planning is centralized, emanating from a national center and imposed on the locality. But, regional planning, if worthy of the name, must account for the local *and* the larger, for transcendent "fields," for regions as holons as Koestler intended the term.

Region is both a discriminatory device and an integrative concept (and reality). Factionalism is a problem in contemporary human relations, as it has always been, and a realistic conception of region can be an integrative factor, can help planners achieve conflict resolution. Identity, likewise, has always been a human problem, but especially so in the mass societies of the modern world, so that a popular or even a mythical formulation of region

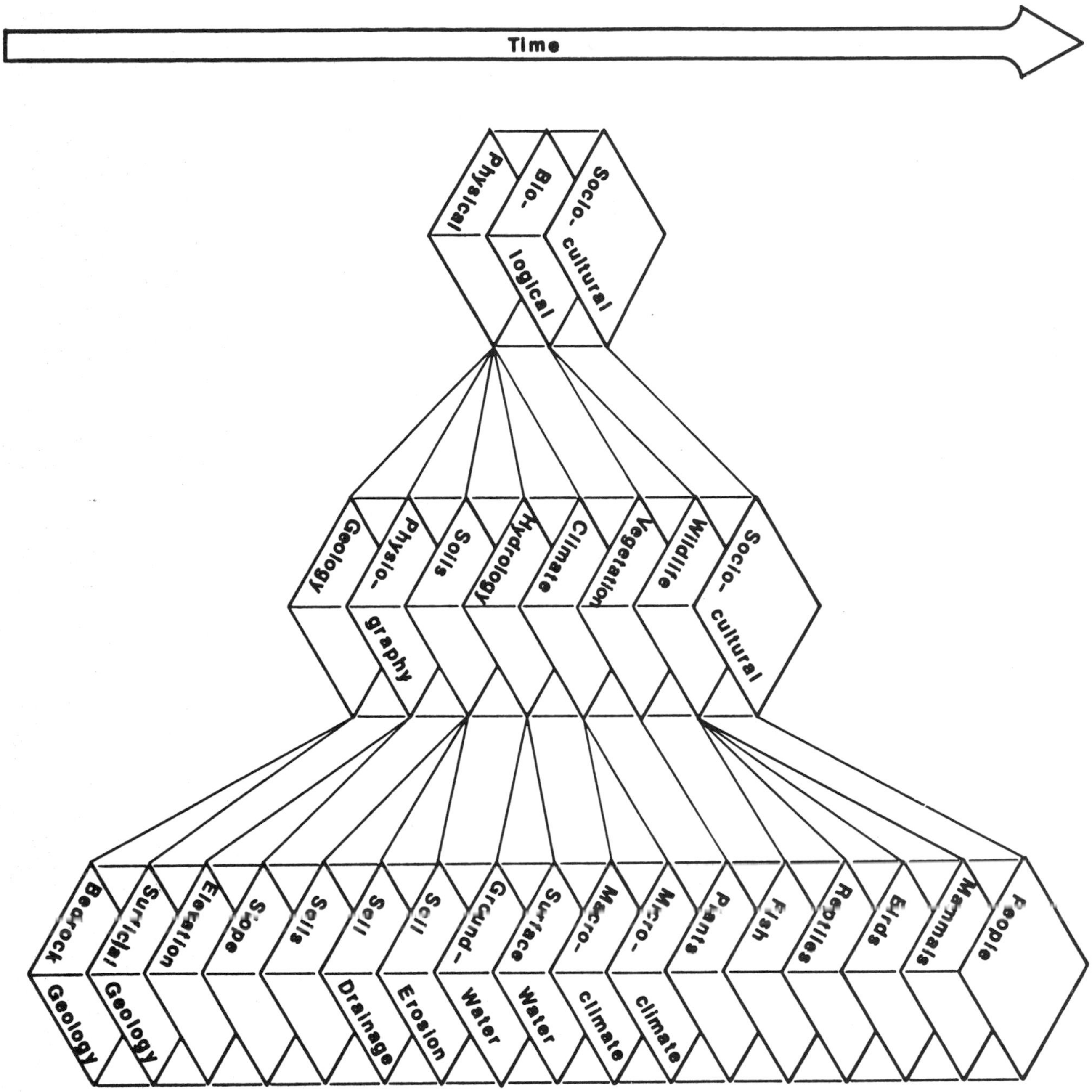

7. Layer-cake simulation model.

can be a factor in group discrimination, thus helping to distinguish and to establish identity (Hough, 1990). "I am a citizen of the United States" is a regional claim to separate the speaker from others in the world, but also to integrate the speaker with other citizens of that country, to establish identity through both separation and integration. On another level, the claim "I am a Southerner" accomplishes the same purpose in the same way, though even more "regionally" defined. Such pronouncements provoke distinction in one direction and provide identity in the other.

Human ecology—as a study of the relationships between parts and wholes—may hold the key to the integration of regional types, structure, and complexity. A region can be viewed as a frame for multidisciplinary research to work toward the synthesis needed in ecological planning. Since humans are living beings, human ecology may be thought of as an expansion of general ecology to how humans interact with each other and with all components of their environments. Interaction then, has been suggested here as both a basic concept and an explanatory device.

> In human ecology, the way people interact with each other and with the environment is definitive of a number of basic relationships. Interaction provides a measure of belonging [of community], it affects identity versus alienation, including alienation from the environment. The system of obligation, responsibility and liability is defined through interaction. The process has become definitive of the public interest as opposed to private interests which prosper in the spirit of independence (Young, 1976).

Planners, then, should be more familiar with human ecology, especially with planning as applied human ecology (Johnson, 1981).

A human ecological approach to planning advocates that regions be considered in terms of sustainable relationships between parts and wholes, using a number of conceptual techniques to gain access to such relationships. Ultimately, the interaction of parts and wholes in a functional regional system is a measure of fitness. Ian McHarg (1981) summarized human ecological planning in terms of such fitness:

> All systems aspire to survival and success. This state can be described as synthropic-fitness-health. Its antithesis is entropic-misfitness-morbidity. To achieve the first state requires systems to find the fittest environment and then adapt it and themselves. Fitness of an environment for a system is defined as that requiring the minimum work of adaptation. Fitness and fitting are indications of health and the process of fitness is health giving. The quest for fitness is entitled adaptation. Of all the instrumentalities available to [humans] for successful adaptation, cultural adaptation in general and planning in particular, appear to be the most direct and efficacious for maintaining and enhancing human health and well being.

REFERENCES

Anderson, J. R., Hardy, E. E., Roach, J. T., and Witmer, R. E. 1976. *A Land Use and Land Cover Classification System for Use with Remote Sensor Data*. U.S. Government Printing Office.

Bailey, R. G. 1976. *Ecoregions of the United States*. U.S. Forest Service.

Berry, T. 1988. "Biogregions: The Context for Reinhabiting the Earth," *The Dream of the Earth*. Sierra Club Books.

Berry, W. 1975. *A Continuous Harmony, Essays Cultural and Agricultural*. A Harvest/HBJ Book.

Cartwright, D. (Ed.). 1951. *Field Theory in Social Science: Selected Theoretical Papers of Kurt Lewin*. Harper and Row.

Center for National Areas, Smithsonian Institute. 1974. *Planning Considerations for Statewide Inventories of Critical Environmental Areas: A Reference Guide*. Smithsonian.

Eliot, T. S. 1949. *Notes Toward the Definition of Culture*. Harcourt, Brace.

Glikson, Artur. 1967. "The Relationship Between Landscape Planning and Regional Planning." *Towards a New Relationship of Man and Nature in Temperate Lands*. Conservation of Nature and Natural Resources.

Hough, M. 1990 *Out of Place: Restoring Identity to the Regional Landscape*. Yale University Press.

Hunt, C. B. 1967. *Physiography of the United States*. W. H. Freeman.

Johnson, A. (Ed.). 1981. "Special Issue: Human Ecological Planning,". *Landscape Planning* .

Koestler, A. 1968. *The Ghost in the Machine*. Macmillan.

McHarg, l. L. 1969. *Design with Nature*. Doubleday/Natural History Press.

McHarg, I. L. 1981. "Human Ecological Planning at Pennsylvania," *Landscape Planning* .

Malecha, M. J., et. al. (Eds.). 1989. *Interchange: A Special Issue on "Critical Regionalism."* College of Environmental Design, California State Polytechnic University.

New Jersey Pinelands Commission. 1980. *Critical Areas Study for the Pinelands*. Rogers, Golden, and Halpern.

Odum, E. P. 1971. *Fundamentals of Ecology*. W. B. Saunders Company.

Odum, H. W. 1965. "The Promise of Regionalism." *Regionalism in America*. University of Wisconsin Press.

OECD. 1987. *Recent Regional Policy Developments in OECD Countries*. Organization for Economic Cooperation and Development.

Selkregg, L. L. (Ed.). 1974. *Alaska Regional Profiles* (6 Volumes). Arctic Environmental Information and Data Center, University of Alaska.

Smailes, A. E. 1953. *The Geography of Towns*. Aldine.

Snyder, G. 1980. *The Real Work*. New Directions Books.

Steiner, F. and Brooks, K. 1981. "Ecological Planning: A Review," *Environmental Management*.

Steiner, F. 1982. *Ecological Planning for Farmlands Preservation*. APA Planners Press.

Tansley, A. G. 1935. "The Use and Abuse of Vegetational Concepts and Terms," *Ecology*.

Vance, R. B. 1965. "The Regional Concept as a Tool for Social Research," *Regionalism in America*. University of Wisconsin Press.

Young, G. L. 1974. "Human Ecology as an Interdisciplinary Concept: A Critical Inquiry," *Advances in Ecological Research*.

Young, G. L. 1976. "Environmental Law: Perspectives from Human Ecology," *Environmental Law*.

Young, G. L. 1992. "Between the Atom and the Void: Hierarchy in Human Ecology," *Advances in Human Ecology*.

Zelinsky, W. 1980. "North America's Vernacular Regions," *Annals of the Association of American Geographers*.

CHAPTER

28

Regional Planning in the United States: Historic and Contemporary Examples

Frederick Steiner

In some areas of the world, the natural environment and culture of the region are closely linked to its government. Many parts of Europe come to mind—France, Italy, Germany, and the Low Countries. In France, for example, one can sit in a village and drink the distinct wine and eat from the distinct cuisine of the region in a structure of distinct architecture or on a terrace with a distinct garden design.

Prior to the sixteenth century, when Europeans began invading the Americas in large numbers, the native people lived in a variety of cultural regions. The U.S. ethnographer and explorer, John Wesley Powell, recognized this and, as a result, proposed a plan for the Southwestern U.S. based on its ecology. According to Carl Frederick Kraenzel, Powell's 1879 report to Congress about the Southwest "stressed the need for new land and water use policies, an adapted land-settlement pattern, and an adapted institutional organization and way of living that was intimately suited to the conditions of the arid and semi-arid lands" (Kraenzel, 1955).

These concepts, and those in the previous chapter, have long been used by planners, often in an eclectic manner. The early origins of regional planning in the United States are relatively easy to trace. Frederick Law Olmsted, Sr. and his protege Charles Eliot developed metropolitan park plans for the Boston region in the late nineteenth century. The concept of **regionalism** flourished as a form of cultural philosophy in the 1920s and 1930s. This activity was encouraged by a small group of intellectuals organized in 1923, the Regional Planning Association of America, which included Benton MacKaye, Lewis Mumford, Clarence Stein, Henry Wright, Catherine Bauer and others. A similar group, called Telesis, was formed later (1939) in the San Francisco Bay area. Telesis had considerable influence in the Bay region and is partially responsible for the beauty of its built environment (Violich, 1978).

Benton MacKaye explicitly linked regional planning to ecology in 1940. He defined regional planning as "a comprehensive ordering or visualization of the possible or potential movement, activity or flow (from sources onward) of water, commodities or population, within a defined area or sphere, for the purpose of laying therein the physical basis for the 'good life' or optimum human living" (1940).

According to MacKaye, a comprehensive ordering referred to "a visualization of nature's permanent comprehensive 'ordering' as distinguished from the interim makeshift orderings of people" (1940). MacKaye quoted Plato to emphasize this thought—"To command nature we must first obey her." MacKaye found the purpose of the "good life" or optimum human living incorporated in what the U.S. Congress has called the "general welfare" and what Thomas Jefferson called the "pursuit of happiness." MacKaye concluded that "regional planning is ecology."

Furthermore, it is, according to MacKaye,

> Human ecology: its concern is the relation of the human organism to its environment. The region is the unit of environment. Planning is the charting of activity therein affecting the good of the human organism; its object is the application or putting into practice of the optimum relation between the human and the region. Regional planning in short is applied human ecology (1940).

Two additional advocates of ecological and conservation ethics for land use were the wildlife biologist Aldo Leopold and the sociologist Howard W. Odum. As early as 1933, Leopold stated: "if our present evolutionary impetus is an upward one, it is ecologically probable that ethics will eventually be extended to the land. . . . If and when it takes place, it may radically modify what now appears as insuperable economic obstacles to better land use" (1933).

SOCIAL VISION AND THE HARNESSING OF HUMAN AND NATURAL RESOURCES

The ideas of MacKaye, Leopold, Odum, and others were used on a broad scale in the New Deal programs of President Franklin D. Roosevelt. These programs were enacted in response to the human suffering of the Great Depression. Examples of such programs include the Tennessee Valley Authority, the Columbia Basin Irrigation Project, and the Greenbelt New Towns. Other nations embarked on similar projects that involved the harnessing of human and natural resources for social purposes. One such example is the Zuiderzee reclamation works in the Netherlands.

The Tennessee Valley Authority (T.V.A.) stands as one of the most successful examples of regional planning in the United States or internationally. The T.V.A. stresses cooperation between levels of government and the provision of multiple benefits for citizens. The jurisdiction of the T.V.A. is generally limited to the drainage basin of the Tennessee River, but some of its activities extend beyond. As a result, the T.V.A. provides a model for Eugene Odum's ideal of the use of river basins as the optimum unit of planning, as stated in the previous chapter (Odum, 1971). The Tennessee River drainage basin, an area of almost 39,000 square miles (99,803 square kilometers) covers parts of seven states: Alabama, Georgia, Kentucky, Mississippi, North Carolina, Tennessee, and Virginia.

Before proceeding with a discussion of the T.V.A., it is appropriate to take note of an instrumental individual and his influence on this project. The first chairman of the T.V.A. was Arthur E. Morgan, a humanist engineer, born in Cincinnati, Ohio. Morgan was previously the chief engineer and organizer of the Miami Conservancy District and later the president of Antioch College. The Miami Conservancy District was organized after the city of Dayton, Ohio was destroyed by flood in 1913. The city's business leaders organized themelves and instituted many municipal reforms. Morgan was retained to develop a scheme to protect the city from future flooding. He developed a system of five earthen dams. Behind each were large open spaces that could act as a catch basin in times of flooding. Development easements were purchased on this land where farming and recreation are permitted, but no homes are allowed (Morgan, 1951, 1971). Today, this system provides an open space network for Dayton and flooding has not caused major damage since 1913. Morgan brought this practical experience and the philosophy of regionalism with him to the T.V.A. But perhaps he was a bit too much of an idealist, because disagreements with President Roosevelt resulted in his removal from office in 1938.

The T.V.A. was established in 1933 by the U.S. Congress as a part of Roosevelt's New Deal. Under this legislation, a broad plan was proposed for the Tennessee River drainage basin. A semi-independent authority was created to promote the economic and social well-being of the people of the entire region. It was a region where rich timber and petroleum resources had been ruthlessly exploited leaving a derelict landscape and an economically depressed people. The people of the region ranked among the poorest in the United States at the height of the Great Depression.

The 1933 act recognized the potential of water as a basic resource that could be used to revitalize the region. The three broad, basic powers granted the T.V.A. included: the control of flooding, the development of navigation, and the production of hydroelectric power. As a result, the Authority was conceived as having multiple purposes. Morgan and his colleagues used a system of dams to accomplish many of these purposes. The multiple-use plan was extended beyond the three basic purposes to include reforestation, soil conservation, outdoor recreation, new community buildings, the retirement of marginal farmland and the manufacture of fertilizers.

A second regional project conceived at the same time, as a part of the New Deal, was the Columbia Basin Irrigation Project, located in

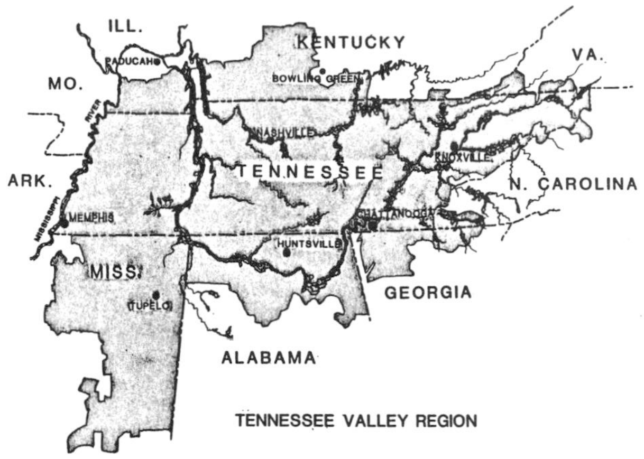

1. Location of the Tennessee Valley Authority.

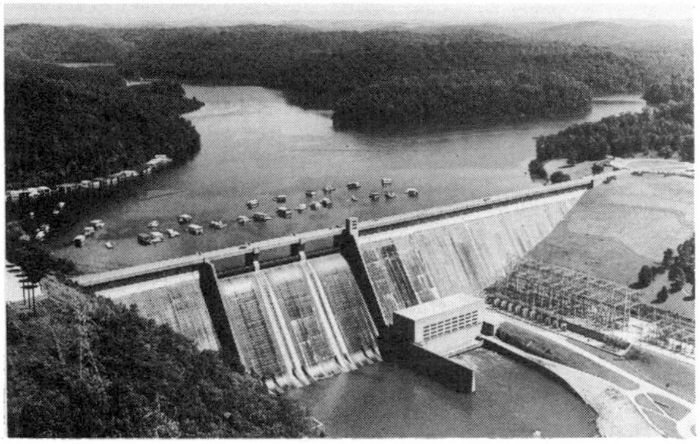

2. Norris Dam was started in 1933 and completed in 1936. It was the first dam built by the Tennessee Valley Authority. Located in Clinch River in east Tennessee, it is 265 feet high, 1,860 feet long. Its reservoir has a storage capacity of two and half million acre-feet of water of which 1,922,000 is useful, controlled storage. The power installation consists of two 50,400-KW units. (*Photograph courtesy of the Tennessee Valley Authority.*)

east-central Washington State. Like T.V.A., the Columbia Basin project involved the harnessing of water resources for social purposes through comprehensive planning. The general authorization for the project came from the National Industrial Recovery Act of 1933, with specific project authorization from the Rivers and Harbors Act of 1937 and the Columbia Basin Act of 1943. The primary purposes of the project, like the T.V.A., were multiple: irrigation, power generation, navigation, regulation of stream flow and recreation.

Before the project, the Columbia Basin was a sparsely populated semi-arid region. Attempts to homestead the area from the late nineteenth century on had been thwarted because of the lack of water and the lack of the appropriate irrigation technology, although lands close to streams were successfully settled. Irrigation became feasible with the construction of the Grand Coulee Dam (another New Deal project begun in 1934). From the 1930s on, much effort was devoted to the planning of the Columbia Basin Project (Doka, 1979).

The planning activities included: extensive resource inventories of the Columbia Basin, land classification, suitability analysis, the establishment of optimum farm sizes, and economic and transportation studies. The planning efforts were coordinated by the U.S. Bureau of Reclamation under Secretary of Interior Harold Ickes, a strong supporter of the project. The coordinated effort of federal, state, regional, and local agencies was called the Columbia Basin Joint Investigations (Doka, 1979).

The Columbia Basin Joint Investigations were started in 1939 and completed in 1942, with various reports that resulted from the studies published between 1941 and 1946. Three hundred people, representing 40 federal, state, local and private agencies, participated. Altogether, 28 separate problems in 16 divisions were studied (Table 1). Through these efforts, a general comprehensive plan for development and settlement was established (U.S. Bureau of Reclamation, 1941). This plan provided the basis for the Columbia Basin Act of 1943. The Grand Coulee Dam was finished in 1941. The Columbia Basin received its first water in 1948 and development continues into the 1990s.

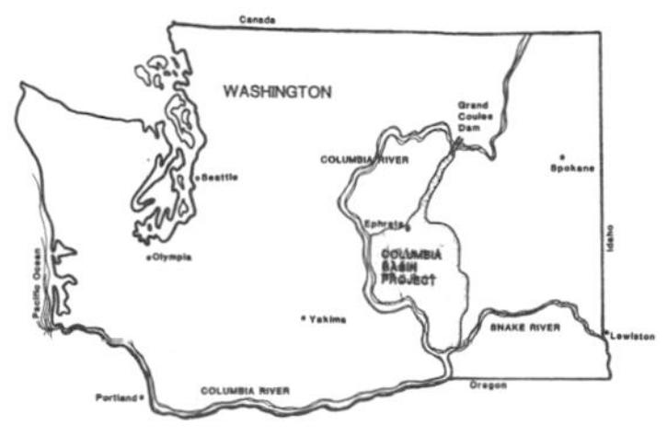

3. Location of the Columbia Basin Project in Washington state.

Table 1
Summary of Divisions and Problems of the Columbia Basin Joint Investigations (U.S. Bureau of Reclamation, 1941).

Division Number	Division Title	Problem Number	Problem Title
I	Basic Surveys	—	Basic Surveys
II	Types of Farm Economy	1	Farm Experience
		2	Types of Farming
		3	Insuring Proper Land Use
III	Water Requirements	4 and 5	Water Requirements
IV	Size of Farm Units	6 and 8	Optimum Farm Size and Adjustment to Topography
		7	Special Land Units
V	Layout and Equipment of Farms	9	Farm Improvement
		10	Patterns of Rural Settlement
		11	Allocation of Costs
VI	Allocations of Costs and Repayments	12	Equitable Payments
		13	Allocations of Repayments
		14	Financial Aid to Settlers
VII	Control of Project Lands	15	Control of Privately Owned Lands
		16	Control of State, County, and Railroad Lands
VIII	Rate of Development	17	Development Rate of Project Land
IX	Villages	18	Optimum Number of New Villages
X	Roads and Other Transportation Facilities	19	Road Network
		20	Railroad Facilities
		21	Columbia River as Commercial Route
XI	Underground Waters	22	Underground Waters
XII	Rural and Village Electrification	23	Rural and Village Electrification
XIII	Manufacturers	24	Manufacturers
XIV	Recreational Resources and Needs	25	Recreational Resources and Needs
		26	Plans for Use of Roosevelt Reservoir
XV	Rural Community Centers	27	Plans for Location of Schools, etc.
XVI	Government Organization, Public Works Programming and Financing	28	Government Organization, Public Works Programming and Financing

A third example of regional planning during the New Deal era was the Greenbelt New Towns. Again, the intellectual impetus came from those involved in the Regional Planning Association, in this case the architect Clarence Stein and the landscape architect Henry Wright. Another influence was the British garden cities of Ebenezer Howard, popularized in the U.S. by those involved in the Regional Planning Association. The idea was simple: a regional approach was needed to overcome urban squalor. A solution offered was the establishment of new communities buffered by gardens or green space.

The person most responsible for the Greenbelt New Towns was the New Deal economist Rexford Guy Tugwell, who received his education from the University of Pennsylvania and taught at Columbia University. Rexford Tugwell was the undersecretary of the U.S. Department of Agriculture and, as such, proposed the Resettlement Administration. This administration was established to develop a comprehensive approach to alleviate the socio-economic problems of rural regions. In less than two years, from 1935 to 1936, Tugwell's agency planned and constructed three new communities and started a fourth (Myhra, 1974).

The three new communities built were Greenbelt, Maryland; Greenhills, Ohio; and Greendale, Wisconsin. (A fourth, Greenbrook, New Jersey was planned but never built.) Tugwell's ideas for these new communities diverged from those of the Regional Planning Association in his unbiased acceptance of the automobile as an element to be affirmatively considered in the planning process. The design of the new communities consisted of low-rise, single and multi-family housing units with a traditional design, clustered commercial and public facilities, a surrounding greenbelt, and a road network linking the communities with their metropolitan region. Each town had its own interdisciplinary design team consisting of architects, planners, and engineers. Through time, these communities have proved quite popular with their residents and remain an outstanding example of new town planning (Myhra, 1974; Steiner, 1981; Miller, 1981).

The New Deal planning programs in the United States had, and continues to have, an international influence. The Zuiderzee reclamation effort was actually begun earlier than those of the New Deal. However, its planning was still influenced by the T.V.A. Like the U.S. projects, this Dutch example involved a comprehensive regional approach to harnessing natural resources to help solve the social problems of the Great Depression.

The Dutch landscape has resulted largely from human intervention in natural processes. It represents an eloquent equilibrium between people and their environment. The Zuiderzee reclamation works is a long-term, large-scale planning effort. The Zuiderzee (Southern Sea) was an extension of the North Sea into the heart of the Netherlands. As early as 1667, the Dutch speculated on damming the Zuiderzee and reclaiming it, but lacked the appropriate technology. However, by the late nineteenth century, serious plans were developed by the engineer Cornelis Lely.

In 1918, the Zuiderzee Act was passed by the Dutch parliament. That legislation established goals for flood protection, water control, the formation of a fresh-water reservoir, transportation and the creation of farmland. These goals were accomplished by damming the Zuiderzee and creating a large lake—the IJsselmeer. New land, **polders**, displaced this lake under the direction of a government agency—the IJsselmeerpolders Development Authority. The planning for several of these polders coincided with the New Deal programs in the U.S., and was influenced by New Deal regional planning. For a comparison between the Dutch Zuiderzee project and the Columbia Basin effort (see Hall, et al. 1989).

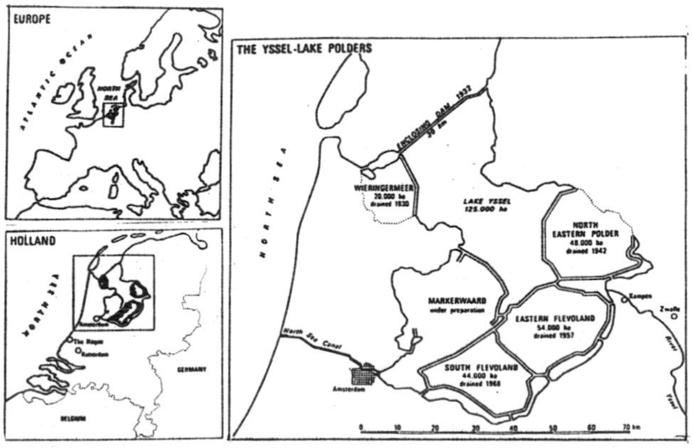

4. Location of the Zuiderzee Reclamation Works in the Netherlands.

ECONOMIC EQUITY AND ECOLOGICAL PARITY

After its noteworthy beginnings, regional planning languished and for years it was considered an oddity in academic circles (Friedmann, 1964). Regional planning was reborn in the 1960s, but its rebirth came in the form of fraternal twins. For the sake of simplicity, one twin is epitomized in the writings of John Friedmann (1973 and 1964 with Alonso), while the other is illustrated in those of Ian McHarg (1969).

Friedmann defined regional planning as "concerned with the ordering of human activities in supra-urban space, that is, in any area which is larger than a single city" (1964). This definition McHarg would no doubt accept, for he describes a metropolitan region in the following way. "A city occupies an area of land and operates a form of government. The metropolitan area also occupies an area of land, but constitutes the sum of many levels of government" (1969).

From here, however, each offers widely different perspectives. According to Friedmann, "regional planning theory has evolved out of special theories in economics (location) and geography (central places); [while] city planning theory is based on human ecology, land economics and the aesthetics of urban form" (1964). This view of regional planning, based on economics and social science, may be contrasted to McHarg's natural-science approach. McHarg has stated repeatedly that "the world, the city and [people] as responsive to physical and biological processes—in a word to ecology—are entirely absent from the operative body of planning knowledge. If the planner is part social scientist, part physical planner, he [she] is in no part natural scientist or ecologist" (Young, 1974).

John Friedmann received his education from the University of Chicago and has taught for many years at U.C.L.A. The Chicago school is famous for its pioneering efforts in the social sciences since the early twentieth century. From the 1940s on, this school has provided the leadership in changing the planning profession in the United States by introducing techniques of sociology and economics. Ian McHarg has also revolutionized planning, but he and his colleagues from the University of Pennsylvania pioneered the use of ecology in the planning process.

5. John Friedmann, University of California—Los Angeles, 1989 (*G. Conner*).

The sociologist Carl F. Kraenzel has proposed an approach to regional planning somewhere between Friedmann and McHarg. According to Kraenzel.

> Regionalism, and regional planning, are a recognition that geographic and natural environment forces still set the broad limits within which culture can function. Culture, in cooperating with nature rather than fighting it, can also, within limits, use natural and geographic forces to its own ends. Regionalism and regional planning assist in defining the natural and physical limits within which culture can operate and aid in pointing the way for a dynamic coordination between culture and natural force (1947).

CONTEMPORARY REGIONAL PLANNING IN THE UNITED STATES

The ideas about economic fairness and ecological relationships discussed in academic circles during the 1960s started to influence legislation for new regional planning programs of the late 1960s

6. Ian L. McHarg, University of Pennsylvania, 1986.

and early 1970s. These programs reflected both social and environmental concerns. A few examples of such programs include: the Appalachian Regional Planning Commission, the New York Adirondack Park Agency, the Tahoe Regional Planning Agency, the New Jersey Pinelands Commission and the U.S. Forest Service system for land and resource management.

The Appalachian Regional Planning Commission resulted from federal legislation: Title V of the 1965 Public Works and Economic Development Act. Under this act, the authority was provided for two or more contiguous states that were related either culturally or geographically, and that were experiencing slower economic growth than the rest of the nation, to join together and request the designation as an economic development region. By 1967, five such regions had been created and a separate regional planning commission provided for Appalachia (Estall, 1982).

The Appalachian Regional Commission covers some 195,000 square miles in parts of thirteen states with a population of 18 million people. The Commission is comprised of representatives from the federal and state governments. The president appoints a co-chairperson with another elected by the governors of the participating states. The Appalachian Regional Commission also reaches local government. It requires multicounty development districts comprised of city and county officials (Estall, 1982).

The focus of the Appalachian Regional Commission is on economic development. Its activities have been in the areas of highway building and community development. Programs have included a regional development highway system, vocational education projects, health projects, child development, community infrastructure development (roads, solid waste disposal, housing, and water and sewer systems), and environmental and natural resource projects.

Robert Estall, a British critic of the Appalachian Regional Commission, has concluded that the impact of these programs on the economic health of the region has been "in the main positive and beneficial" (1982). He notes that the regional commission has assisted local governments. By helping to fund projects, local confidence has grown along with the availability of local funding for projects and risk-taking. Estall concludes that the Appalachian Regional Commission demonstrates that "state governments can cooperate with each other, and jointly with the federal government, in a single forum of the kind represented by the regional commissions, and such cooperative endeavor can aim at goals that could be overlooked or ignored in an approach based solely on state or federal perspectives" (1982). He also observes that this regional commission shows that local areas can be involved effectively in plan production and implementation, especially when they are organized on a multicounty approach.

New York's Adirondack Park Agency is an example of a multicounty region within one state. The focus of the agency is on natural resource management, rather than economic development. The Adirondack Park encompasses some 6 million acres and was created by the New York legislature in 1892, having been set aside as a forest preserve in 1885. The park includes 107 towns and villages in 12 counties and consists of a patchwork of private and state lands. The Adirondack Park Agency was established in 1971 after growing land-use conflicts in the region and discussion about the area being converted to a national park. The agency was directed by the legislature to accomplish two tasks: write a comprehensive plan for the state-owned lands and propose legislation for land use on private lands within the park.

The land-use plan for the state lands was adopted in 1972 with little controversy. Since then, the plan for the private lands has been a source of much debate and court action. The plan for the private lands provides for control by the Adirondack Park Agency over projects with regional impacts. Projects with less regional impact are subject to local government review, but local plans must be approved by the Adirondack Park Agency (Hahn and Dyballa, 1981).

During the 1960s, the Lake Tahoe Basin region grew at a rapid rate. People were attracted by the area's natural beauty and recreational opportunities. Like the Adirondack region and many other parts of the United States, there were many overlapping city, county, and state governments and federal agencies—often with conflicting policies and programs. In 1969, the bi-state Tahoe Regional Planning Agency was created cooperatively between Nevada and California. This agency was the focus of heated controversy and debate between environmental groups and development interests through the 1970s (Widby, 1980; Rubin, 1981).

To help resolve these conflicts, the U.S. Congress passed and President Jimmy Carter signed into law, the Tahoe Regional Planning Compact in 1980. This compact gave federal recognition to the regional agency and gave it the power to establish environmental threshold carrying capacities. These carrying capacities were defined as "an environmental standard necessary to maintain a significant scenic, recreation, educational, scientific or natural value of the region or to maintain public health and safety within the region" (U.S. Congress, 1980). The Congress further directed that these thresholds

8. A mix of forest, stream, wetlands, glacial erratics and distant mountains are all present in this scenic view from an observation deck at the Adirondack Park Visitor Interpretive Center at Paul Smiths. The Center, which contains miles of interpreted trails, indoor exhibits and audio visual presentations, is open to the public year round without charge (*L. Viscome, Adirondack Park Agency*).

7. Location of Adirondack Park in New York state.

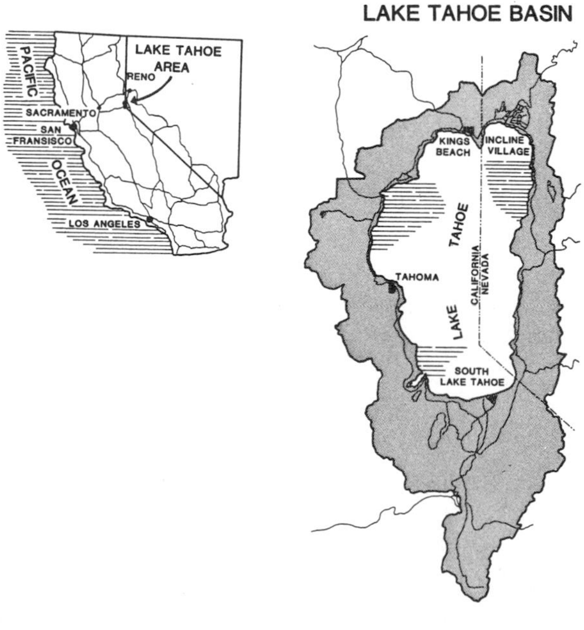

9. Location of Lake Tahoe Basin.

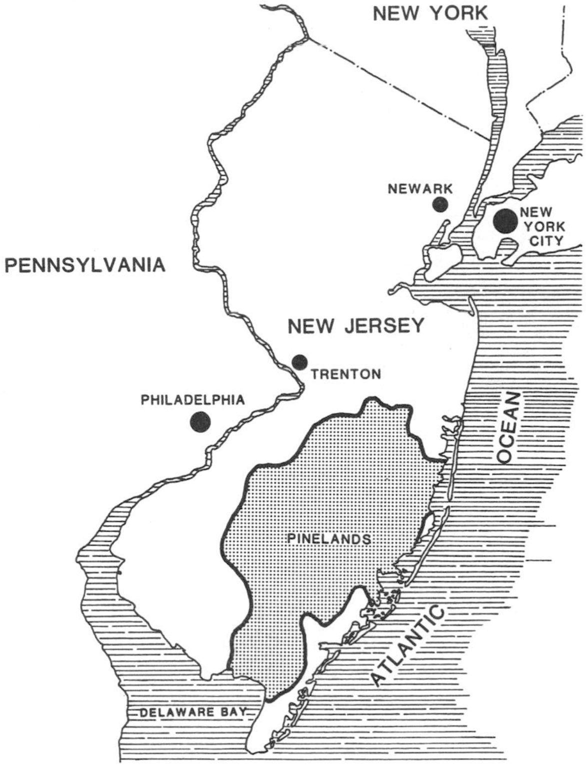

10. Location of the New Jersey Pinelands.

11. Pinelands vista includes restored Ironmasters' Mansion, and outbuildings of the iron-working village of Batsto, one of the thirty bog-iron furnace and forge sites in the Pinelands between 1760 and 1860. To the north is Batsto Lake and Wharton State Forest, now a part of the 337,000 acre preservation area of the million-acre Pinelands National Reserve (*courtesy of Pinelands Commission*).

be incorporated into the basin's regional plan and its implementing ordinances.

The New Jersey Pinelands, called the Pine Barrens by local residents, is a million-acre area with unique landscape qualities in the midst of the most densely populated region of the United States. The plan for the area derives from the designation by the U.S. Congress in 1978 of the Pinelands as the country's first national reserve and the passage in 1979 of the Pinelands Protection Act by the New Jersey legislature. To comply with these laws, the Pinelands Planning Commission was established by then New Jersey Governor Brendan T. Byrne. This commission is responsible for coordinating the planning of the local, state, and national governments (Pinelands Commission, 1980; Berger and Sinton, 1985).

The Comprehensive Management Plan developed by this commission includes a number of strategies for the region. The plan includes: a natural resource assessment; an assessment of scenic, aesthetic, cultural, open space and outdoor recreational resources; a land-use capability map; a comprehensive statement of land-use and management policies; a financial analysis; a program to ensure local government and public participation in the planning process; and a program to put the plan into effect (Pinelands Commission, 1980). The plan is the culmination of an intensive research and planning effort. It received the approval of Governor Byrne for the state government and of former U.S. Secretary of the Interior Cecil D. Andrus of the Carter Administration for the national government.

Regional planning also occurs on the nation's public lands. These activities are important because approximately 42 percent of the land in the United States is in some form of public ownership (Lewis, 1980). One example of this type of planning is the U.S. Forest Service's system for land and resource management planning.

The purpose of this planning process is to meet the requirements of the Forest and Rangeland Renewable Resources Planning Act of 1974 and the National Environmental Policy Act of 1969. These requirements direct each regional forester to develop a regional plan. The development of the plan must follow a specific process that includes: the establishment of planning criteria, inventory of data and collection of information, analysis of the forest's management situation, formulation of options, estimation of the impacts of these options, evaluation of the options, selection of an option, implementation of the plan, and the ongoing monitoring and evaluation of the plan. An interdisciplinary team approach is used to develop these plans. The team is to integrate knowledge of physical, biological, economic and social sciences as well as the environmental design arts (U.S. Government Printing Office, 1979).

The long-term effectiveness of the U.S. Forest Service's regional planning and that of the Pinelands Commission, the Tahoe Regional Planning Agency, the Adirondack Park Agency and the Appalachian Regional Planning Commission cannot be judged at this time. These relatively recent efforts represent a renewed interest in regional planning in the United States. Each is an attempt to coordinate planning at various levels of government in a large region. These endeavors have influenced more recent regional planning such as the growing interest in greenways.

12. The Yakima Greenway in Washington combines open space protection and recreational use (*C. Vogt, Yakima Greenway Foundation*).

GREENWAYS FOR THE FUTURE

A greenway, or greenline park, is a large scenic landscape which is protected by law and regulation from being degraded by unplanned development to the extent that it retains its significant attributes. Often, a greenway is a region that remains in productive use by land-oriented industries, like fishing, farming, ranching, or forestry. The protections for such a region are cooperatively arranged and managed by citizens and agencies on the local, state, and federal levels, usually through a joint commission (Corbett, 1983). Examples of such commissions include the New Jersey Pinelands Commission and the Columbia River Gorge Commission in Oregon and Washington. Greenway planning, or greenlining, is the process of establishing and maintaining such a region. This process includes both citizen and government involvement in analyzing the region's ecology, deciding on priorities for conservation and development, establishing legal protections, and following through by managing the region according to an agreed-upon plan (Corbett, 1983).

Modern greenway planning began in 1970, when a 25-year-old North Carolina State University landscape architecture graduate student named Bill Flournoy developed a greenway plan for his hometown of Raleigh (Little, 1990). Interest in greenway planning gained much momentum during the 1980s when President Ronald Reagan reduced federal funding for park acquisition and environmental protection and encouraged private-public partnerships. U.S. National Park Service employees involved in river planning—led initially by Glenn Eugster in the Philadelphia regional office—saw greenways as an opportunity to address open space development in an era of less federal funding and greater public-private cooperation. From the 1980s to the present, other National Park Service regions have become increasingly active in river conservation through greenway planning.

Greenways from Raleigh, North Carolina to Yakima, Washington have proven to be a popular form of regional planning. Large scenic landscapes and regional water systems have been protected. Regional recreational opportunities have been created. As the quality of life has improved, so have regional economies, as businesses have chosen to stay or have been attracted to areas with open space amenities.

REFERENCES

Berger, J. and Sinton, J. W. 1985. *Water, Earth, and Fire*. Johns Hopkins University Press.

Corbett, M. R. (Ed.). 1984. *Greenline Parks*. National Parks and Conservation Association.

Doka, Y. 1979. *Policy Objectives, Land Tenure, and Settlement Performance: Implications for Equity and Economic Efficiency in the Columbia Basin Irrigation Project* (Unpublished Ph.D. Dissertation). Department of Agricultural Economics, Washington State University.

Estall, R. 1982. "Planning in Appalachia: An Examination of the Appalachian Regional Development

Programme and Its Implications for the Future of American Regional Planning Commissions." *Institute of British Geographers Transactions, New Series.*

Friedmann, J. and Alonso, W. (Eds.). 1964. *Regional Development and Planning.* M.I.T. Press.

Friedmann, J. 1964. "Regional Planning as a Field of Study," *Regional Development and Planning.* M.I.T. Press.

Friedmann, J. 1973. *Retracking America.* Anchor Press/Doubleday.

Hahn, A. J. and Dyballa, C. J. 1981. "State Environmental Planning and Local Influence," *Journal of the American Planning Association.*

Hall, D., van Lier, H., Steiner, F., Duchhart, I., and Budd, W. 1989. "Planning in the IJsselmeerpolders and the Columbia Basin: A Comparison." *Landscapes and Urban Planning.*

Kantor, H. A. 1973. "Howard W. Odum: The Implications of Folk, Planning and Regionalism," *American Journal of Sociology.*

Kraenzel, C. F. 1947. "Principles of Regional Planning: As Applied to the Northwest," *Social Forces.*

Kraenzel, C. F. 1955. *The Great Plains in Transition.* University of Oklahoma Press.

Leopold, A. 1933. "The Conservation Ethic," *Journal of Forestry.*

Lewis, J. A. 1980. *Land Ownership in the United States, 1978.* Economics, Statistics and Cooperatives Service, U.S. Department of Agriculture.

Little, C. E. 1990. *Greenways for America.* Johns Hopkins University Press.

MacKaye, B. 1940. "Regional Planning and Ecology," *Ecological Monographs.*

McHarg, I. L. 1969. *Design with Nature.* Doubleday Natural History Press.

Miller, Z. 1981. *Suburb.* University of Tennessee Press.

Morgan, A. E. 1951. *The Miami Conservancy District.* McGraw-Hill.

Morgan, A. E. 1971. *Dams and Other Disasters.* Porter Sargent.

Myhra, D. 1974. "Rexford Guy Tugwell: Initiator of America's Greenbelt New Towns, 1935 to 1936," *Journal of the American Institute of Planners.*

Odum, E. P. 1971. *Fundamentals of Ecology.* W. B. Saunders Company.

Pinelands Commission. 1980. *New Jersey Pinelands Comprehensive Management Plan.* Pinelands Commission.

Rubin, H. 1981. "Lake Tahoe, A Tail of Two Cities," *Sierra.*

Steiner, F. 1981. *The Politics of New Town Planning.* Ohio University Press.

U.S. Bureau of Reclamation. 1941. *Columbia Basin Joint Investigations, Character and Scope.* U.S. Government Printing Office.

U.S. Congress. 1980. *Tahoe Regional Planning Compact, Public Law 96–551.*

U.S. Government Printing Office. 1979. "National Forest System, Land and Resource Management System," *Federal Register.*

Violich, F. 1978. "The Planning Pioneers," *California Living.*

Widby, T. 1980. "Trouble in Tahoe," *Planning.*

Young, G. L. 1974. "Human Ecology as an Interdisciplinary Domain," *Advances in Ecological Research.*

CHAPTER 29

Connections: Products, Regional Planning and Policies

William W. Budd

> Recognizing the limitations of human nature . . . is a necessary prerequisite to designing a social system that will minimize the effects of those limitations . . . that too . . . is a means of modification of human behavior (Konner, 1982).
>
> An endless feedback loop: Past functioning has produced today's structure; today's structure produces today's functioning; today's functioning will produce future structure (Forman and Godron, 1986).

How individuals perceive their environment and the relationship of those perceptions to values and attitudes is central to the design process. The objects, institutions, and organization of the built environment, which emerge from design and planning processes, develop understanding or vision of human-environment relationships. Under general and ideal conditions, these relationships are seen as ones of balance and harmony. It is not society which interacts with the environment, but rather the collective action of individuals interacting within a dynamic series of social, economic, and ecological dimensions.

As a result, understanding of the relationship between design and the environment must be through the individual. It is through individual expression and creativity that design becomes tangible. But while individual in form and content, "designing with nature," to use the title of Ian McHarg's seminal work, entails and requires a much larger responsibility. It is the designer's charge to understand and become sensitive to the collective interaction of humans, society, and nature. It is vital for the individual to be able to envision design and the resulting built environment as interconnections within a series of integrated levels. To understand these connections, it is essential to know the magnitude and extent to which change in any level may affect another level of integration.

This integrative process has come to be known as **synthesis**. It is a vision, an understanding, a sensitivity to all the components of the built environment which operates from the level of products to that of regions and global systems. This chapter is about that vision. The questions that need to be examined are: To what degree can changes in one level of integration affect other levels? And also, given these relationships, what are the implications and responsibilities for design and planning?

ASSESSING ACTIONS ACROSS LEVELS: THE IMPORTANCE OF CULTURE

How do humans assess the effects of their actions on the environment? What are the "right" set of "things" to measure? How are these measurements made? These are difficult questions. They are questions that continue to challenge decision-makers and professionals because the nature of the problems which societies address is constantly changing. Where do we start?

All too often people lose sight of the fact that in addressing a problem, whether perceived or realized, any design action has human-environmental impacts. Humans alter the environment to provide an improved quality of life, an improved sense of well-being, of purpose, of achievement. There is nothing inherently negative or positive about such efforts, indeed they may well be viewed as noble. However, humans often forget, or ignore, that these interventions are occurring within a dynamic system, a system within which *Homo sapiens* is but one component. It is, however, a system that exists by balance, interaction, change and adjustment. In this sense, culture is inseparable from nature. Human societies exist at the interface between cultural processes and natural processes. Changes in culture do have effects on natural systems. Too often human assessments are rooted in the space and time of social constructions but not of natural processes. As a result human actions on any scale will have ramifications on a variety of other scales.

Societies, in general, and more specifically industrialized societies, have failed to recognize and to incorporate into their behavioral patterns and traditions an understanding of these connections. Even within the fields of planning and design, the very fields in which one would expect such revelations to occur, the incorporation of such a holistic perspective has been slow to develop. At times, tradition and practice have served as obstructions to such a visionary change. People operate under the premise that a new technology can always be developed to treat any problem. As new technologies are created, new problems are also created, which require newer technologies. The cycle appears endless.

The critical questions which must now be asked are: What are the limitations that such a connective vision places on the design fields? How can citizens, planners and designers respond to the challenges presented by a connective, integrated vision of human-environment relationships?

FROM PRODUCTS TO HOUSEHOLDS: THE UNSEEN/UNEXPECTED TOXIC PROBLEM

Perhaps the most fundamental relationship in the built environment is that of the interaction of products which humans consume and their personal lives. In many instances, particularly in developed societies, there is a perceived need for a diversity of products and goods. Unfortunately, there are hidden costs associated with a wide variety of consumer products, and all too often those costs are not assessed or in many instances are not well known. This is most severely felt for products that exhibit some hazardous or toxic characteristics.

Despite what people think or feel, their risk of getting cancer from chemicals in drinking water or from paint strippers and other solvents found in their homes is greater than from the same chemicals found in a hazardous waste site.

The link between individual action and effects on fresh water would seem apparent to most individuals. Fresh water is a fundamental human need. While that connection may indeed be "apparent" and of "vital importance," a cursory review of the ledger of human interactions with this resource suggests a different level of understanding. U.S. Environmental Protection Agency figures show that nearly 2,000 publicly-owned treatment works (POTWs) have recorded organic (e.g., solvent) contaminant levels in excess of those considered to be safe. This translates into an affected population of nearly seventy-five million. Nearly sixty-seven percent of all rural drinking water supplies have some measurable level of organic contamination.

What is even more revealing about this particular problem, and society's lack of understanding about the interconnections between products and, in this case, water quality is that use of ground-water (the major source being contaminated) has been increasing during a period of increased pollution. As a consequence, members of society have been increasingly exposing themselves to many of the most toxic compounds known to humankind—many of which likely came from their own kitchen shelves.

Most people are not aware of it, but those chemicals which are used to clean and beautify their homes may be doing quite a bit more. Some of the same toxic wastes which are contained in hazardous waste sites are used in paints, paint thinners, cleaners and other household goods. More importantly, the amount of material which individuals are exposed to in every-day use of these materials is often significantly higher than if the home were next to an abandoned hazardous waste facility.

Major offenders are the pesticides used so freely in the United States. The most widely used garden pesticides are 2, 4-D, benomyl, chorothalonil, and glyphosphate (read the labels of products on the store shelves to see how common these are). These chemicals are all linked to cancer and reproductive problems. A really serious offender is the compound chlordane, the most

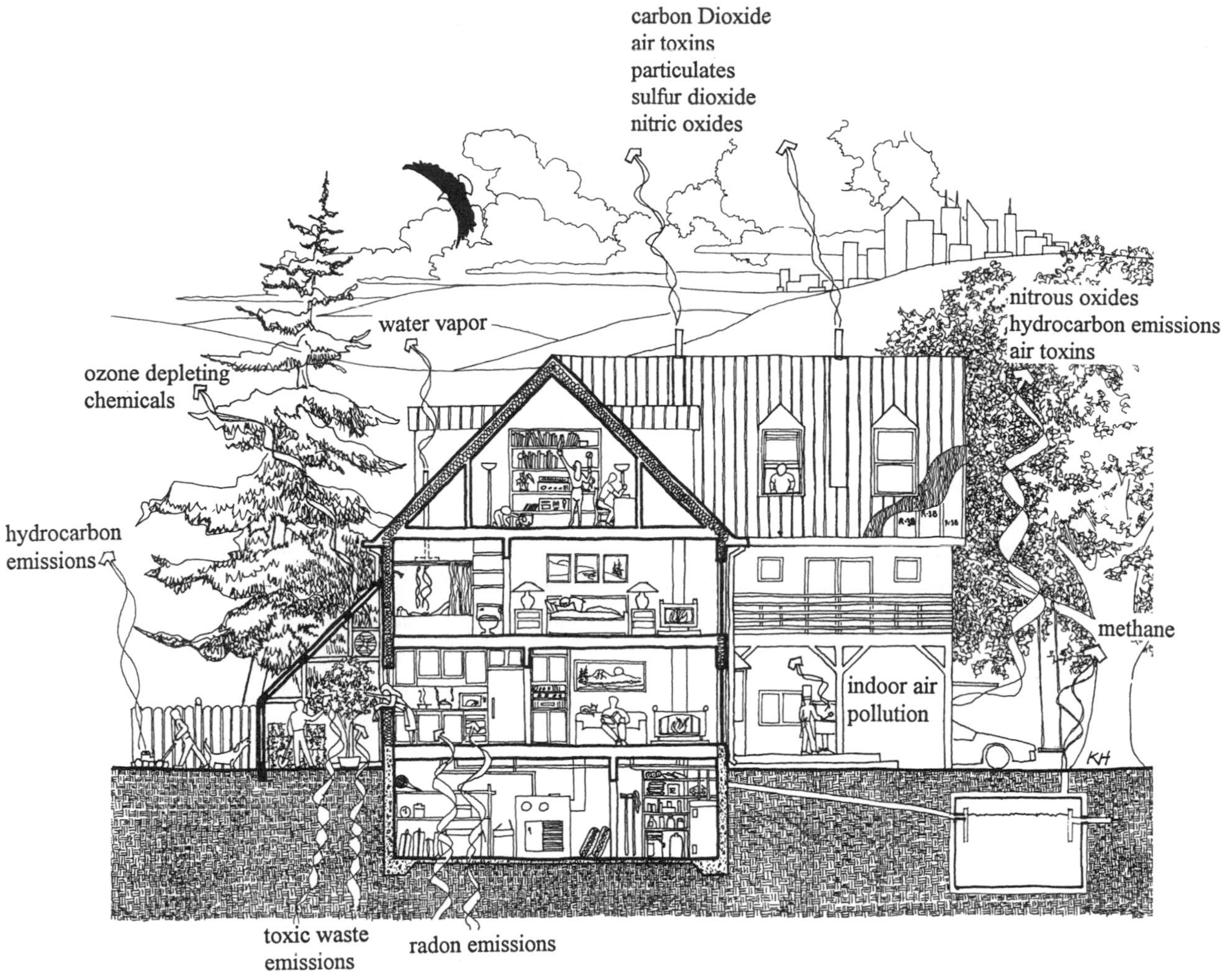

1. Products to Household. Asbestos—in insulation, floor and ceiling tiles, paints and joint compounds. Radon—in rock and soil beneath houses. Combustion Gases—from gas appliances, wood stoves and furnaces. Household Chemicals—in pesticides, paints, paint strippers and cleaning fluids. Water Pollutants—lead in water pipes or pipe solder and chemicals that leach into water supplies. Formaldehyde—in cabinets, bookcases and other furniture constructed with particleboard or plywood, as well as drapes, upholstery, carpets and wallpaper adhesives. Allergens—molds, bacteria, dust and pollen that collect in air-conditioning vents, humidifiers and dehumidifiers.

widely used termite-killing agent in the U.S. It has been linked to cancer, to a host of neurological disorders and to miscarriages. It has been banned because of these effects, but the government has graciously permitted exterminators to use up the supplies of this material stored in their warehouses (Gilbert, 1987).

In fact, approximately 70,000 different chemicals are in everyday use in U.S. society. Monsanto Corporation, a major chemical manufacturer, asks "Where would we be without chemicals?" At least in quantitative terms, this statement seems quite justified. But look a little closer at this claim: Of those 70,000 chemicals, the EPA indicates that thousands are potentially hazardous to human health and the environment. What is even more disturbing is that of these thousands of known toxics, good information concerning exposure, effects and risks has been developed for only a handful. For the overwhelming majority of these compounds, using them is to be exposed to questionable risks.

The Toxic Substance Control Act was passed in 1976 to provide some level of protection and evaluation for the public. But here too, there has been bureaucratic obstinacy. Since 1976, the U.S.

Environmental Protection Agency has received health and environmental results on only 22 chemicals and has assessed the test results for only 13 of these chemicals. Although the agency has determined that three compounds are dangerous, it has taken no regulatory action because it believes the chemicals do not pose "significant or unreasonable risk" (General Accounting Office, 1991a).

But blame cannot be leveled only at agencies and governments in this regard. Just think for a moment about the passion in the United States for a green and well manicured lawn. The U.S. EPA estimates that sale of lawn care pesticides exceeds $700 million annually. Further, about 67 million pounds of active ingredients from these sales are applied to lawns and parks nationwide each year. In addition, approximately 5,000 lawn care firms are doing $1.5 billion in annual business servicing about 12% of the remaining homes in U.S. society (General Accounting Office, 1991b). Central to all of these environmental concerns is the individual and personal choice.

FROM PRODUCTS TO COMMUNITIES: SOLID WASTE

The relationship of culture and the effect of changes in human values on design and planning is nowhere more explicit than in the evolution of cities. Cities represent and are expressions of human-environmental relationships. The demand for shelter and security is fundamental to the species. Urban environments, however, have a history of environmental neglect and distress. The critical questions are why and what was the role of design?

It is important to recognize that human-environment relationships in cities are dynamic. For example, city officials and urban populations have not always viewed refuse, trash and pollution as a social evil. During the early years of the Industrial Revolution, pollution was a sign of progress. Pollution and waste were the "smell of money." During this period, industrialization was the primary social objective, and buildings and cities were constructed to meet specific social and economic needs.

The ideas of free market (laissez-faire) growth coupled with a rapid increase in wealth, which characterized the Industrial Revolution, spawned a wide range of social and environmental concerns. By 1880, New York had moved from a walking "town" to an industrialized city. Along with large numbers of factories, mills and tanneries, some of the largest slums in the world had also been created. Population densities in these slums exceeded 900 people per acre. Cities began to reek of a variety of odors. Ammonia gases, sulfur, offal rendering, bone boiling, animal wastes, manure heaps and unwanted litter were found throughout these environments. The standard practice for dealing with these problems was to find an empty lot or the nearest river and dump the waste there (Petulla, 1988). Epidemics began to occur at alarming frequencies. Typhoid fever, cholera, dysentery and yellow fever were commonplace. Each of these diseases has its root in pollution. To get rid of the mass of wastes, cities began to use rivers and lakes, only to have these environments deteriorate and in some instances die. Ultimately changes were made, but for several decades this legacy of neglect was practiced and tolerated.

In an evaluation of planning or design, clear documentation is now available of the broader interconnections between the city and a wide range of other levels of integration. Individuals, specific products, and regional watersheds are all examples of levels adversely affected by the form and structure of cities. Cities are aggregate representations of human preferences. The design and planning process in today's cities is being forced, or conditioned, by global factors.

Modern cities are concentrations of material wealth. As societies have become wealthier, there is a tendency to want to consume more. For a wide range of reasons, most of which are obvious, increased disposable income leads to increased desires for material goods. To meet this demand, a wide variety of products are created. As populations have grown, the demand for more and more goods has also increased. This demand for greater quantities and diversity in goods has had a tremendous impact on the design and planning disciplines. People in these fields are in great demand because they provide and define the forms of the objects being consumed: From split-level homes to condominiums, from glass bottles to flip-top cans, from the paper wrappings on packages to clean Saran wrappings. The design traditions "read" consumer demand and responded.

The average person in the United States generates 7.7 kilograms of solid waste every day, and projections are that this will nearly double by the year 2000. This means that an average family of four generates more than 3 tons of solid waste each year. Viewed collectively, this is enough solid waste to fill the Superdome in New Orleans twice every day for an entire year. As a result, people in this country

- import more goods
- waste more energy
- suffer increased inflation
- endure more environmental degradation
- expose more individuals to increased health risks.

The costs associated with managing this problem are substantial. Last year over $20 billion were spent on solid waste management in the United States.

These impacts cannot be viewed as attributable exclusively to designers or planners. These are problems which have at their heart a lack of understanding of connections and an unfortunate shared, social belief that the planet is nothing more than an infinite resource base. This attitude fosters careless consumption patterns and demands for goods without any thought as to how these goods are produced, and without any prior assessment of the long-term impacts on the environment and human life. This can be illustrated with a couple of vivid examples, packaging and chemical waste.

EXAMPLES OF THE SOLID WASTE DILEMMA

Packaging

About 50% of all the paper, about 8% of all the steel, about 75% of all the glass, about 40% of all the aluminum, and about 30% of all the plastics produced in the United States are used to wrap and decorate consumer products. This means that one dollar out of every ten dollars spent on a product is for packaging, an item that will ultimately be thrown away.

This increased demand for stylish and fancy packaging is a relatively recent phenomena. The trend was initiated around 1958, often referred to as "the packaging explosion year." If U.S. society was less interested in, and designers did not respond to, the demand for products which contain so much waste, tremendous amounts of energy and money would be saved and not anywhere near the quantity of solid waste would be generated. Some things would have to be sacrificed. Excessive paper wrappers and plastic packaging for fast-food burgers, for example, would fall by the way-side. But look at the net gains. If packaging levels were held to those of 1958, 566 trillion BTUs of energy would have been saved every day—an equivalent of 267,000 barrels of oil every day!

Container packaging is another example of product effects at higher levels of integration in the built environment. Large numbers of people consume milk. In fact, 70 million homes in the U.S. consume at least a half gallon of milk every week. If those households bought that milk in one half-gallon containers rather than two quart containers, there would be a reduction in the amount of paper discarded in this society of approximately 42 million pounds per year. The amount of plastic discarded each year would be reduced by 6 million pounds. In doing so, about 146 million dollars per year in packaging would be saved, along with about 1 trillion BTUs of energy. That is enough energy to heat and cool a community of 7,500 households for an entire year—just from reducing the number of milk cartons!

While solid waste illustrates a direct and visible connection of products to effects at higher levels, the translation of change into energy and resource savings is difficult for the average citizen to envision. Even the cost savings are often muted because when the data are disaggregated to the individual level the perception of the problem changes. It simply does not seem to be a real concern.

What is needed to solve the solid waste problem is the changing of individual behavior. But making these types of changes is often difficult and takes a great deal of time. For attitudes and behavior to change, alternative products must be developed and their use encouraged. Simpler packaging and the use of recyclable materials can have a significant impact, as the illustrations above indicate. Moreover, with such new products planners can begin to develop policies which will encourage society to first **reduce** use of packaging, then **reuse** and finally **recycle**.

Chemical Waste

A far more insidious problem is that of dealing with the use and demands for chemicals in society. To be sure, chemicals are an important part of U.S. society. Tremendous quantities of synthetic fabrics and petroleum products are consumed. The demand for new and different paint products, the desirability of buildings constructed with preserved wood products, and the desire to have that bright clean shine on linoleum floors are a few examples of the use of chemicals in this society.

Prior to 1977, industry in the United States indicated that it was annually generating about 23 MmT (million metric tons) of hazardous waste. In 1977, following a study by the EPA, it was discovered that this figure was slightly off and that U.S. society was now generating about 35 MmT of hazardous waste. But the more alarming finding of the study was that only 10% of the waste was being disposed of in a manner consistent with what then were proposed regulations for managing hazardous wastes.

In fact, 50% of the waste was being placed in open lagoons, 30% was being disposed of in unsecured landfills, and 10% was being dumped directly into sewers. Further studies now show that the demand for chemical products has produced a monster of an environmental problem. It is now estimated that people in the United States are generating approximately 600-750 MmT of hazardous waste each year. What is more, this quantity of waste is increasing at a rate of about 4% per year.

The true tragedy of this problem is that the principal mechanism to dispose of these materials has been the land. Here, as with the quantity of solid waste generated, the figures are staggering. In 1979, industry reported that 3,383 waste sites had been used from 1950–76. But only six months later, EPA revealed that the figure was more like 30,000–50,000, with 2,000 of those sites posing an immediate threat to human health. Now it is generally felt that there are somewhere between 180,000 to 390,000 waste sites, of which 20,000 pose some form of serious threat to human health and/or the environment. What makes this so serious is that these materials include some of the most dangerous compounds on this planet—carcinogens, mutagens, and teratogens—and increasingly they are showing up in the very water that people drink. Products now affect the city and the region.

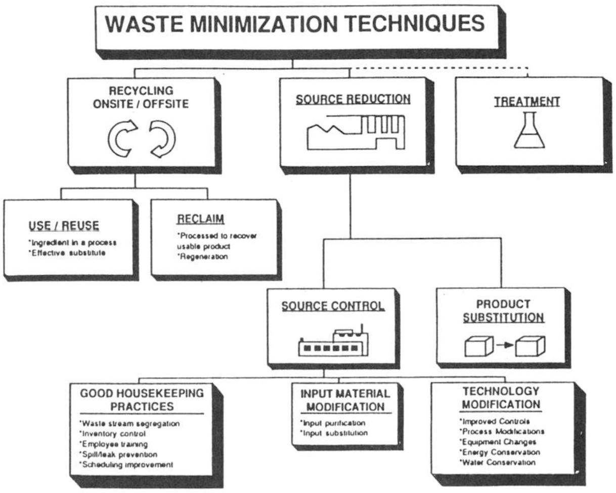

2. Opportunities for future change in hazardous waste management (GAO, 1988).

This circle is now complete. Nature has modified, transported, and returned to a higher level of integration in the built environment the materials people have so carelessly placed into its bowels. From the seeds of convenience, consumer economics and/or design, humans are now reaping cancer, retardation, pain, suffering and death. The most fundamental activity in the built environment, the development of a product, is not immune to interaction with other levels of integration. Indeed, as with the city, products cannot be viewed as end states. The definition and acceptability of products changes with changes in human behavior.

As with solid waste, the roots of the chemical waste problem lie in human behavior. What is needed is not a better "technology", but a better understanding of the connections between what people use and their collective impacts on the world around. To minimize chemical waste generation requires investigation and promotion of waste reduction, reuse and recycling, as well as source reductions and treatment programs. U.S. laws require these changes for major businesses, but they must also apply to households for the chemical waste problem to be resolved. Individuals must recognize their role in the chemical cycle. Without changes at the level of the individual, chemical waste will remain one of the most serious crises facing societies for decades to come.

FROM PRODUCT TO REGION: ACID DEPOSITION

Energy is central to all components of the built environment. At all levels of integration energy is the critical factor in determining what is produced, what is planned and what is constructed. This resource determines in a real way the form of the built environment. More energy is consumed in the United States than anywhere else on this planet. The United States consumes about 22% of the electrical power generated in the world. The principal sources of energy are fossil fuels—coal, oil and natural gas. Coal is used to generate a significant portion of this electrical energy.

One of the by-products of using coal to generate electrical power is pollution. The original pollutant of concern associated with coal combustion was particulate matter. In the mid-1950s, this was viewed as a very serious local issue. In 1952, a climatic inversion settled in over the city of London and the resulting buildup of pollution killed 3,000 people. A similar incident, fortunately with many fewer deaths, affected Johnstown, PA in 1954. Communities near power facilities became concerned about these particulates.

To resolve this problem, industry designed a new technology. Tall stacks were erected to deposit the pollution high into the atmosphere. The rationale: the atmosphere is but another endless resource for human use. Dilution is the solution to pollution! The impacts of the new technological solution to this pollution problem did not manifest themselves for nearly thirty years. Since 1968, however, a noticeable change has been occurring downwind from these stationary sources of pollution. "Downwind" here means thousands of miles, distances which transcend political boundaries and the institutions that humans establish to manage the environment. This has created a new problem, continental in scale, of acid deposition (acid rain).

Acid deposition is a secondary form of pollution. The problem, as the term suggests, is that by-products of fossil fuel combustion lead to large, regional deposits of acids. The acids are not emitted directly, which is why the problem is referred to as secondary pollution. The term "deposition" is used because the acidic inputs can be either wet (i.e., as rain or snow) or dry (i.e., as particulates). The specific acids of most concern are sulfuric and nitric, and the major precursors of these acids are sulfur dioxide and nitrogen oxides.

Acid deposition is a complex phenomenon. At all levels, natural and cultural, the problem requires dealing with transformations and transfers over large regions and time. There is considerable uncertainty about what acid deposition does, how it does it, and who or what is responsible.

Some general known and potential effects of acid deposition have been identified. These effects graphically illustrate the degree to which developments and actions at a low level of integration affect higher levels. More importantly, this particular example illustrates that there may not be any level of control at this higher level.

Scientists know that in certain sensitive aquatic systems, changes in acidity can lead to wide changes in fauna and flora. Some of these acid-sensitive lakes are acidifying in Canada, the northeastern United States and Scandinavia. A second major potential impact of acid deposition is on forest growth. Some forests in regions that have been experiencing acid deposition for several decades are showing signs of decline, a change that may be related to acid deposition. The mechanisms associated with such declines, however, are very complex, involving at a minimum, nutrient flows, plant physiology and plant-soil interactions, all of which are operating across regions and over decades. Scientists cannot tell with certainty whether acid deposition is the cause of these concerns, but it is evident that something is occurring within these systems. Further, it is also clear that increased rainfall acidity occurred during the same period of time that the declines in growth were noted. This may well be coincidental, but it may also be causal.

Finally, evidence exists to indicate that structures of the built environment are being affected by acid rain. Some experts suggest that increased damage to buildings and monuments has been caused by acid deposition, but no one has been directly studying these changes and their relationship to acid deposition. Misinterpretations and false analyses regarding nonliving effects have occurred. The best example is the damage to Cleopatra's Needle in New York City, originally thought to be associated with acid deposition. In 1978, the New York Times commented, "The city's atmosphere has done more damage than three and a half millennia in the desert, and in another dozen years the hieroglyphs will probably disappear." This was proven to be false. The damage was actually due to advanced salt decay and the increased humidity of New York, coupled with some misguided attempts at preservation. Nevertheless, it is clear that acidic deposition does cause significant incremental damage to non-living materials beyond that brought about by natural processes.

Dealing with issues such as acid deposition requires large, far-sighted, trans-boundary institutions which have yet to be created. Costs, benefits and reduced risk have dominated outcome evaluation. These measures have become institutionalized and therefore continue to influence design and planning. New institutions are needed to integrate knowledge about natural processes with knowledge about social and economic processes.

Resolving the problems of acid deposition, like most problems involving human-environment relationships, requires changing the level and degree of interactions and requires changing human behavior. There is a tendency for individuals to throw up their hands when asked to do something about acid deposition. Opportunities for individual action appear difficult. Change, however, can come about through energy conservation programs and political action. Change can come about by individuals voicing concerns with political representatives. Again, the primary determinant for affecting change is individual action.

FROM REGION TO PLANET: INTERNATIONAL MANAGEMENT OF TOXICS

The effects of human actions extend well beyond products to region. The planet is in many ways quickly becoming a global society. Within this context, regions, or more precisely nations or collections of nations (supra-national regions), market their traditions and their culture in interactions with other nations. Here, as in all of the previous illustrations, the costs are not always fully measured or assessed. In this case the damage is particularly profound.

The effect of this type of cultural influence can be shown best in economic development. With the conclusion of World War II, there was a great deal of interest in promoting economic development in the Third World. The societies involved in this effort are commonly referred to as market societies. When reaching out to help a developing nation, developed societies impose their own model, their own perspective of the built environment. This influenced (in many cases "established") the manner in which humans interact with nature. As material in this text has shown, developed societies have changed the nature and degree of human interactions with the natural environment. The results have been dramatic.

In traditional societies the ways in which natural resources are used have developed from an immediate dependency on the natural environment. The very livelihood of individuals, families and small groups in Third World societies depends upon immediate environmental feedbacks. As a result, the use of resources—and the development of a built environment within this context—mandates designing "with" nature and the maintenance of ecological stability. In contrast, developed societies, with the exception of a few professionals and interest groups, have been desensitized to the interrelationships between their well being and the natural environment.

In developed societies, the incentive is to produce as much surplus as one can sell. This type of stockpiling behavior is perceived as necessary because it leads to increases in material power. In this type of system there is no incentive to conserve. While conservation is not precluded from this framework, it is also not a driving force or primary criteria for evaluating the changes being made in the environment.

On a more substantive level, the effects of more developed regions on global processes can have more profound meanings. An increasing number of toxics have become ubiquitous. There is simply nowhere on this planet a person can go without being able to measure some amount of these added chemicals. Examples include radionuclides, poly-chlorinated biphenyls (PCBs) and more recently a number of pesticides.

The pesticide issue is of particular interest. The impacts of pesticides are a growing global concern. The use of these substances is increasing in all areas of the planet, and with this increased use comes increased risks and consequences. The issue is more than simply applying and using a dangerous material; the pesticide case represents adoption of a particular view of human interaction with the environment. Again, it is a short-term production, surplus generation model which developed societies impose on nations that they intend to "help."

But look at the costs. While it is true that over the last twenty years the gross national product of less developed nations has increased by about three percent each year, has there been an analogous change in the quality of life for the people being aided? Between 400,000 and 2 million pesticide poisonings occur worldwide each year. Most of these are happening in those less developed countries; approximately 10,000 to 40,000 result in the deaths of those affected. Compare this figure to the number of deaths which resulted from the chemical plant tragedy at Bhopal, India. That accident was the result of a system failure in the built environment: a valve failed, management was poor and response capabilities were absent. In this case, the resultant release of a toxic gas led to the deaths of over 2,500 individuals. Upon learning of this disaster, the world was outraged! At the same time, U.S. citizens, officials and advertisers ignore the fact that promoting the use of pesticides creates the equivalent of four to sixteen Bhopal-like accidents each year.

Pesticide use in agriculture could likely be cut in half and industrial waste cut by a third within the next decade. For societies to realize the benefits of such change, policies and funding priorities need to be changed to actively promote the use of new agricultural practices and sustainable methods of production. As Wendell Berry (1977) notes, "Food is a cultural product; it cannot be produced by technology alone. . . . A healthy culture is a communal order of memory, insight, value, work, conviviality, reverence, aspiration." To affect change at the level of societies, individuals must change. This can include changing the products consumed to only those that are pesticide free; insisting on increased monitoring for such chemicals in food; and supporting policies which seek to promote alternative agricultural methods.

CONSPECTUS

> The ancient spiritual teachings of the Cheyenne Indians tell us that we meet ourselves in almost everything we confront. . . . When we meet an animal, feel a touch, or take a hike down the street, we see a reflection of ourselves and of humanity (Hazeldon Foundation, 1987).

Can the design and planning fields provide the guidance and foresight needed to improve the built environment? What skills are required? What knowledge is needed?

Problems associated with making decisions about the distribution of scarce resources are critical choices in today's world. In *Tragic Choices*, Calabresi and Babbitt (1978) argue that, "We do not live in the timeless days of a dog or sparrows. As we become aware of what we, as a society, are doing, we bear responsibility for those allocations that will be made as well as for what has already been done in our names."

In dealing with pollution and wastes, United States society can be characterized by the phrase "out-of-sight, out-of-mind." We design our buildings and communities so as to hide waste cans and dumps. We have used air, water and land to dump wastes, and now we are seeing that there is a price.

There are alternatives. They require innovative minds, new designs and new institutions. The design fields are on the cutting edge of this challenge. From the development of new product designs to community planning, individuals in these fields provide both the tools and the procedures with which the future will be managed. To effectively use this information requires learning to foresee the impacts of projects, to incorporate uncertainties and contingencies into plans, and, above all, to view problems and activities within a holistic context. There will always be impacts. There will always be unanticipated consequences. Indeed, tragic choices will always have to be made.

What then, can individuals do? What skills are required? There is no formula, no model for success which will provide greater insight or understanding about the relationships examined in this chapter and this book. A number of key aspects, however, will be of importance for any program of study seeking to strengthen training in this area. First, in the design and planning fields the challenge has been one of attempting to preserve the relationship between the liberal arts tradition and professionalism. To understand the interconnections between levels of integration, individuals must be able to transcend their discipline and acquire a comprehensive world view. For most fields, this relationship has weakened, but students need to become more aware of its importance and work toward developing this level of understanding. Second, it is vital that young scholars develop conceptual skills which have methodological rigor. Conceptual power without analysis is impotent, analytical rigor without synthesis is lethal. Finally, students must learn philosophy as well as politics, ethics as well as technology.

Humans will continue to use natural resources to meet social goals and objectives. What they must learn is how to use those resources in a sustainable way. Planning and design, because they are interdisciplinary, can help meet these goals and can transcend limited levels of interaction. The impact of these fields is tremendous because they affect activities which affect human behavior, and it is human behavior that is the core of all human-environmental problems.

One final note: there is no assurance that humans will be able to avoid the types of problems discussed in these pages. Humans are probably not capable of planning or designing perfect systems. Consequently, there is no certainty that problems will be averted. What emerges, however, from an increased sensitivity to the importance of connections in human-environment relationships, is a new paradigm for interactive, interdisciplinary learning. It is a paradigm that does not seek to provide humans with prescriptions for change, but rather forces humans to recognize the impacts of their decisions across levels.

Environmental problems exist because humans have not taken to heart a multilevel, holistic framework for learning. Most people remain ignorant of the array of connections that immerses them in and binds them to the complex natural and built environments in which they live. To change, we must learn how to learn—and then put that knowledge into action. That is the challenge of design and planning.

REFERENCES

Berry, W. 1977. *The Unsettling of America: Culture and Agriculture*. Sierra Club Books.

Calbresi, G. and Babbitt, P. 1978. *Tragic Choices*. W. W. Norton.

Forman, T. T. R. and Godron, M. 1986. *Landscape Ecology*. Wiley.

General Accounting Office. 1991a. "Toxic Substances: EPA's Chemical Testing Program Has Not Resolved Safety Concerns," GAO/RCED-91-136, June.

General Accounting Office. 1991b. "Lawn Care Pesticides: EPA Needs to Assess State Notification Programs," GAO/RCED-91-208, September.

Hazeldon Foundation. 1986. *Touchstones*. Harper & Row.

Konner, M. 1982. *The Tangled Wing*. Holt, Rinehart and Winston.

Petulla, J. M. 1988. *American Environmental History*. Merrill.

Postel, S. 1987. *Diffusing the Toxics Threat: Controlling Pesticides and Industrial Waste*. Worldwatch Institute.

West, R. 1966. *The Birds Fall Down*. Viking Press.

Earth & Environmental/Global Planning

Introduction

7. EARTH

Earth, the globe itself, is the seventh level, the last selected component of the built environment study in this book. It is the region to contain all regions. It is, of course, possible to take such an organizational series further—to the solar system, then the galaxy, etc., but with respect to the built environment, earth is the ultimate level, a measure of the present limits of human domain. To a degree, the earth itself is an artifact, manipulated, however inadvertently, by human actions.

The earth as artifact is rather a mind-boggling conception. And, it is not an artifact in the exact same sense as those discussed in previous sections: it was not created by human hands. But, it is an artifact in the sense that so many of its complex systems are now impacted and altered by humans, to the farthest reaches of the globe.

This is illustrated most vividly by the fact that the vast complexes of atmosphere and ocean are nowhere on the globe untouched by the effluents of industrial civilization. The by-products of creating a built environment can now be found in Antarctic ice (and in the penguins there) . . . in the jet stream sweeping down from the Arctic cold . . . in the vast reaches of the stratospheric ozone layer . . . in the sediments at the bottom of the deepest oceanic trench. The more immediate realm of life, the level of the biosphere, has been dramatically impacted, irreversibly, on a global scale. Humans have saved themselves from lethal infectious diseases by eradicating the tiny bacterial sources. Similarly, though less deliberately, humans have placed the largest mammals of the ocean, the whales, on the brink of extinction.

Earth's finite resources, the materials and energies required to construct and manage the built environment, are being consumed at an alarming rate. The conservation ethic in design and planning (recycling products, use of renewable resources, and energy conservation, etc.) is helping a great deal to resolve once foolish attitudes and consumptive ways.

The articles in this section, in essence, make the point that every individual—all people, lay people and designers alike—must try to expand their consciousness, become more aware of the interconnections that tie them to other people, to other organisms, to all systems around the world. The point is repeated that the boundaries that humans draw around each discipline, each nation or region, are intended to help organize our world, not limit our view of it.

Having accepted levels-of-integration as the basic organizational structure of this book, we know that one level of the built environment builds upon the next and then the next, etc., as denoted on the next page:

PRODUCTS-INTERIORS-STRUCTURES-LANDSCAPES-CITIES-REGIONS-***EARTH***

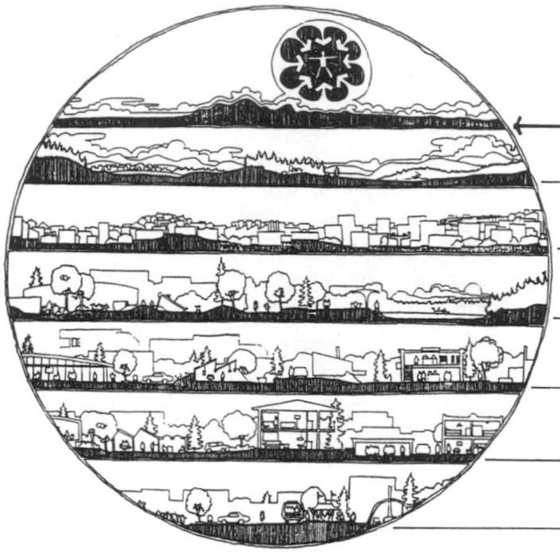

Consequently, the earth is the final component as well as the context and receptacle for all human actions. Some of those actions are considerate, perhaps even profound, and complement earth's systems; others cause immeasurable impacts often negative in consequence. One set of products, those of nuclear fission, could destroy all life-supporting systems, all life on earth. This four-part definition of the built environment is finally concluded:

a. the Earth (containing all humanly made or arranged actions) must be planned and managed, even at this level;
b. it is the environmental context which is mediated;
c. it is used or abused to fulfill human purpose; and
d. it is the ultimate context.

Many people can be considered global thinkers, global planners—deeply concerned about the management of the earth. Many organizations have been formed to try to "unite" the people of earth and coordinate national and global issues (the United Nations; the World Bank; the International Union of Architects, Landscape Architects, etc.).

If readers can internalize an interest in any one level of the built environment, they should be appreciative, at least in part, for those who transcend all levels: those who try to be considerate of collective welfare, the needs and desires of all, in managing the global system, the planet Earth.

The following chapters investigate this last, and most inclusive, component of this book:

- **"Earth/System"** by Eldon H. Franz: this chapter explores the earth as a living system, a process which is continually evolving in space and time. The author illustrates this concept by discussing various national and global issues and suggests that it is fundamental to establish human-environmental adaptive strategies which will be nondestructive to this earth-system.

- **"Taking Action in the Built Environment: A Global Agenda"** by Dianne Armpriest: this chapter surveys various environmental issues at the global scale and then suggests ways that designers especially can take action toward eventual resolutions of global problems.

- **"Earth: World-as-Presence"** by Gerald L. Young: the final chapter on this final component continues to analyze the earth in a holistic way. It emphasizes the importance of understanding both the unit and the whole (the component parts and the whole earth)—suggesting that both need to be integrated into a holistic world view.

CHAPTER

30

Earth/System

Eldon H. Franz

We shall not cease from exploration
And the end of all our exploring
Will be to arrive where we started
And know the place for the first time.

T. S. Eliot, 1943

Late in this, the twentieth, century, we humans are increasingly recognizing the whole Earth as the context of our actions, we have truly started to "think globally." Without thinking globally and without knowledge of the way the planet works, we would otherwise "act locally" without comprehending the potential for global impacts. Earth system processes involving global weather patterns, the amount of carbon dioxide and other trace gases in the atmosphere, stratospheric ozone and the very diversity of species are all subject to influence and modification by "local" activities with the cumulative effects mounting to global scale. It is the purpose of this chapter to introduce the global context of the built environment, in order to facilitate the forging of necessary connections between global processes and their implications for the design and planning processes that shape the built environment.

1. Earthrise as witnessed from the moon by the crew of Apollo 8 (Cortright, 1975).

EARTH/SYSTEM SCIENCES

Knowledge of environmental conditions on the surface of the Moon, Mars, Venus, and other planets in the Solar System, vastly augmented during the explorations of the last 30 years, confirms the uniqueness of the Earth. The Earth is a living system. It is the only one we know.

In some measure, the diversity of living forms must hold the key to Earth's uniqueness. How well yet do we really know the Earth? Not very well it seems. The biological and ecological exploration of our planet has barely begun. The Earth teams with species. But the total number of living species is not known. It has been estimated that there are between 10^7 and 10^8, closer perhaps to the higher number (Ehrlich and Wilson 1991). Order-of-magnitude estimates are appropriate, given the uncertainties involved. Our most certain knowledge is that approximately 1.4 million have been given scientific names. *Homo sapiens* is one of them.

For the vast majority of the Earth's 4.5 billion years, the impact of *Homo sapiens* has been small. Humans are but one species in the biosphere and the conditions of life have been largely determined by other species (Woodwell, 1974). It is those other species, all 10^7 to 10^8 of them, especially the plants and microorganisms, which constitute the life-support system of the planet (Odum and Franz, 1980). It is the other species that have maintained a constant environment capable of supporting the Earth's human population and all its manifest creations, those called the built environment in this text.

Now, however, the human impact has grown, and continues to mount. Just how much of an impact we now have, and how it might change in the future, can be seen in our share of the **net primary production (NPP)** of the globe. NPP is the total amount of food available to feed organisms that are not photosynthetic: *Homo sapiens* and essentially all other organisms except plants, including all animals and fungi, and most microbial species. At present, nearly 40% of terrestrial NPP is consumed directly by humans, co-opted, or forgone because of human activities (Vitousek et al., 1986). At the current rate of increase, estimated to be 1.7% per year, the global human population would double every 41 years. There were 5 billion people in 1986 and, assuming the current rate of growth, there will be 10 billion in 2027, or in 2046 by more conservative estimates.

To further increase the human share of the global NPP is to cut the amount available to support millions of other species. But it is clear that humans must either increase NPP, or further increase their share of it. That is the choice. And the likely consequence of increasing the human share is to accelerate the rate of extinction of other species. That is the apparent dilemma and challenge: increase NPP and the food supply for *Homo sapiens* or increase the human share of NPP and threaten thereby the integrity of the global life-support system.

These considerations suggest just how, within only a few generations, *Homo sapiens* has become an agent of global change and the most polymorphic species on Earth (Catton, 1987). For much of human history, adaptation to environment involved primarily local choices with local effects. Management of local ecosystems has sometimes enriched and sometimes impoverished local populations with disastrous effects, but there were few, if any, truly global effects (Marsh, 1864). As the scale, magnitude, intensity and duration as well as the kinds of human interventions in the environment have changed, so has the potential for global effects. That means that the future course of human interactions with environment will be defined and limited not only in relation to local processes, but also by global change. Humans are now awakening to this new reality and public awareness of the spatial and temporal scales associated with global processes is reflected in concerns about the greenhouse effect, acid deposition, stratospheric ozone depletion, hazardous waste, persistent pesticides, species extinctions, and a host of other environmental problems.

WHAT DOES GLOBAL THINKING IMPLY?

When the first humans in North America reached the Marmes rock cave on the Snake River Canyon, they built fires with wood to heat their dwellings. Such fires can be imagined as the first step toward an ever enlarging impact on the environment. These impacts were only local at first but have expanded and grown to the point that humans are now agents of global change. Wood fires, where used today, add their load of carbon monoxide, acid precursors, and carcinogenic particulates to the already heavy impacts on the atmosphere of automobiles and power plants. Local governments in many U.S. cities have banned wood burning because it is easily identified as a direct source of pollutants and because most urban households have other sources of heat. The burning of wood (like the combustion of all fuels) also generates carbon dioxide which can contribute to climatic change on a global scale. This is not the same perception as that of ten thousand years ago.

Resource use always has a specific historical and social context. Historically, the scale of the social context has been local and human approaches to environment and to the management of natural resources have been dominated by linear thinking. The left side of the human brain is associated with this kind of thinking, thought processes which are linear, sequential and analytical (see Chapter 6 in this book). The most fundamental ecological fact is that the earth and life are an intertwined global system. For this to be recognized, the Earth must be perceived as a dynamic whole, not just in parts. The structure and organization of the ecosphere is relational and simultaneous, not linear and sequential. The right side of the brain should be able to grasp this because it is capable of thought processes which are simultaneous, relational and holistic. To know the Earth and humans' place in it will require careful analysis and synthesis, using both right and left-brain modes of thought.

We now know that favorable conditions for life are maintained by a global system of complex interactions among the biosphere, the oceans, the atmosphere, glaciers and sea ice, and the land surface. This system operates cybernetically, maintaining a constant environment favorable for life through feedback loops which are integrated at the scale of the Earth as a whole. The metaphorical equivalent of this concept has been called "Gaia" after the Greek goddess of the Earth (Lovelock, 1972, 1979, 1986).

Detailed knowledge of the mechanisms of the Earth-System is still a long way in the future. Massive scientific programs are just now being designed to obtain that knowledge (Malone and Roederer, 1984; U.S. Committee for an IGBP, 1986; ICSU, 1986; Earth System Sciences Committee, 1986). Studies of the whole Earth have been slow to develop. People tend to view systems smaller than themselves as distinct objects. Human perception of systems of which they are but a part tends to be of interactions bounded locally, limited by direct or physical experience rather than as a global whole (Laszlo, 1972). The goal of obtaining "a scientific understanding of the entire Earth System on a global scale by describing how its component parts and interactions have evolved, and how they may be expected to continue to evolve on all timescales" is a recent development (Earth System Sciences Committee, 1986).

THE NATURE OF GLOBAL PROCESSES

Identification of global processes begins with a consideration of the cycles of the major chemical elements of life: carbon (C), hydrogen (H), oxygen (O), nitrogen (N), sulfur (S) (Likens, 1981; Bolin and Book, 1983). These are parts of the global whole which must all be understood—each locally and each on a global scale and then understood all together as a global system. A few of the combinations of these elements in the ecosphere are shown in Figure 2.

Natural processes such as nutrient recycling in the oceans, respiration and decomposition, transpiration and nitrogen fixation along with fossil fuel combustion serve to link the various combinations of elements into global biogeochemical cycles—a striking illustration of the need to understand the parts and the whole, both at a global scale. Taken together, at the earth systems level, these processes determine the composition of the atmosphere, including, for example, the amount of carbon dioxide it contains. The energy balance of the atmosphere, which depends on a combination of these processes called **the greenhouse effect**, accounts for

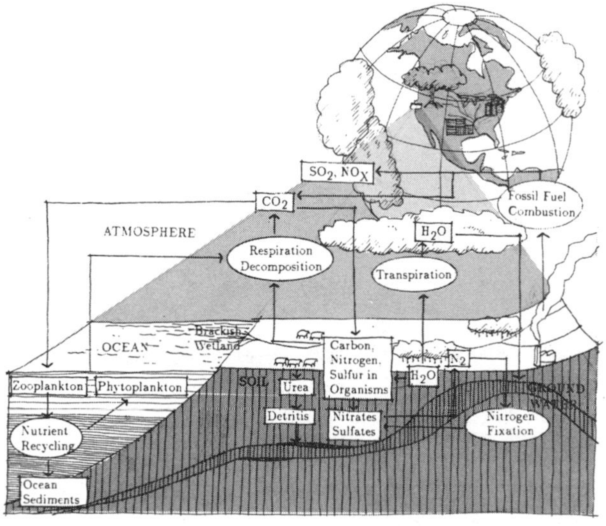

2. Cycles of the major elements in living systems which are integrated at the global scale.

global temperature and climate. The greenhouse effect has been an important news item in recent years and will serve as a clear example of the need to think globally and act locally. The basic physical processes which produce the greenhouse effect are well understood. The earth is continually receiving shortwave radiation from the sun and emitting longwave radiation from its surfaces. The flow of sunlight through the atmosphere to the earth is virtually unimpeded, but much of the longwave re-radiation from the earth is absorbed by the atmosphere. The net effect of differential absorption of shortwave and longwave radiation by the atmosphere is retention of heat energy in the earth-atmosphere system. If the earth had no atmosphere the average temperature of the surface would be close to minus 4 degrees Fahrenheit. The average observed temperature is 59 degrees Fahrenheit. The earth is warmed by the greenhouse effect, an effect that makes it a liveable planet.

Atmospheric gases are responsible for the greenhouse effect. The longwave radiation they absorb determines the global temperature at which the earth's energy budget is balanced. The temperature is influenced by the rate of energy storage in the earth-atmosphere system or the rate of receipt minus the rate of loss. When energy storage increases, temperature goes up and climates are changed on a global scale.

Basic understanding of the greenhouse effect requires knowledge of both the spectrum of longwave radiation emitted by the earth and the absorption spectrum of the atmosphere. The earth's black body radiation is mainly confined to the 5–30 micron region of that spectrum. Radiation is minimal at the upper and lower limits of the region and rises to a peak in the middle. The location of the peak intensity depends upon the earth's surface temperatures. A cold surface, such as a field of snow at a temperature of minus 4 degrees Fahrenheit emits radiation with maximum intensity at 11.5 microns. A hot surface, such as a bare soil, emits maximally at 8.2 microns. Active ecosystems with temperatures between these cold and hot extremes emit maximally at intermediate wavelengths. The maximum radiation at the average surface temperature of the earth is 10 microns. Some of the long-wave radiation is transmitted directly through the atmosphere into outer space. The rest of the long-wave radiation is reflected or absorbed by the atmosphere.

The absorption spectrum of the atmosphere is determined by its constituent gases. Historically, water vapor and carbon dioxide have been the major greenhouse gases. Water vapor has its principal absorption bands at 3, 5–7 and beyond 13 microns. Carbon dioxide absorbs most strongly at 4.3 and 14–15 microns. In an atmosphere composed of these gases, there is a "window" between 8–12 microns where there is no significant absorption. This window lies in that part of the longwave spectrum where the surfaces of the earth are emitting maximally.

Global temperature has always been sensitive to changes in the concentration of carbon dioxide. Water vapor concentration has important effects which can compound the effects of carbon dioxide. These kinds of interactions are discovered, and come to be understood, only through big-picture analysis, through study of phenomena at the global level.

Complicating that picture is the fact that the carbon dioxide concentration of the atmosphere is increasing. The greenhouse effect is a necessity for life as we know it, but numerous questions are raised by increases in the effect. A National Research Council study (1983) suggests that the pre-industrial concentration of carbon dioxide in the atmosphere was between 260 and 290 ppm. Now, the concentration of carbon dioxide in the atmosphere exceeds 350 ppm.

The rise is due principally to the combustion of fossil fuels. A portion of the increase could also be due to deforestation and soil drainage, but despite a substantial amount of detailed work on the carbon cycle, there is still no consensus about the magnitude or even

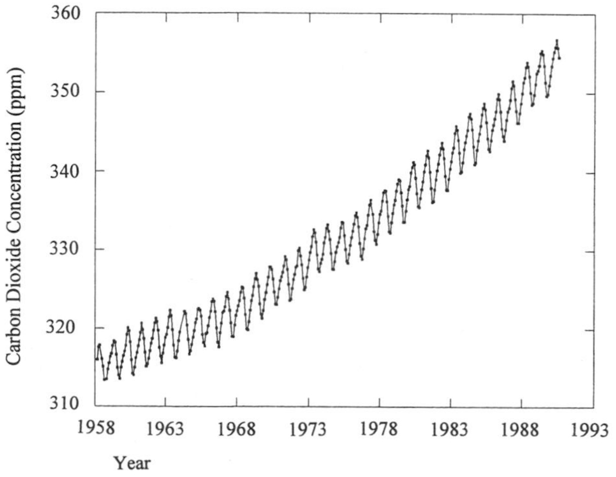

3. Monthly averages of carbon dioxide concentrations in the atmosphere at Mauna Loa, Hawaii (*Keeling, 1990*).

the net direction of movement of carbon between the world's biota and the atmosphere (Kerr, 1983).

Concentrations of other trace atmospheric gases which absorb longwave radiation are also increasing (Ramanathan et al., 1985). Some of these have natural as well as human-generated sources, but the cycles of most are still poorly understood. Many have fundamental absorption bands located in the 8–12 micron window. Examples of these gases include: methane (formed during the anaerobic fermentation of organic matter by bacteria in waterlogged soils, and in the guts of mammals and termites as well as from mining and industrial processes), nitrous oxide (a product of the combustion of fossil fuels and the bacterial oxidation of nitrogen fertilizers), and the chlorofluoromethanes. There are no known natural sources of the chlorofluoromethanes, industrial compounds which are used as refrigerants, solvents and propellants for aerosol cans.

The recent large number of scientific studies still leave significant uncertainties about the future of climatic warming by the greenhouse effect, but a consensus has been reached on the following points: (1) the global carbon dioxide concentration has already increased by roughly 25% in the last 100 years; (2) other trace gases which may have a combined effect as large as carbon dioxide are also increasing; (3) the atmospheric concentrations of carbon dioxide and other trace gases will, in all likelihood, continue to increase; and (4) increases in the concentration of carbon dioxide and other trace gases will result in warming by a few degrees during the next century. The ecological consequences of a global warming of this magnitude are becoming clearer. For the most part, there won't be a clear crisis, just a slow, cumulative, and in some cases, irreversible change in the ecosystems of the earth. The aggregate of local human actions can thus modify the environment on a global scale. The capability of modifying the environment at that scale necessitates thinking at that scale, to think holistically in earth systems terms. Otherwise, the systems that support us, whether natural or human-created or modified, cannot be sustained.

SUSTAINABLE DEVELOPMENT OF THE BUILT ENVIRONMENT

The way people view their place on Earth is changed forever by recognition of the fact that the globe functions as an ecological whole. Virtually every aspect of our activities in the human modified or built environment is linked in some way to the globe as a whole. Trace the linkages of any artifacts of the built environment; can you identify any which are not? For that reason, the global context has become basic to any understanding of the built environment. The built environment at any level can only be sustained if the integrity of the Earth's living system is maintained.

Humanity—closer and closer to a world civilization—is now beginning to recognize the significance of this for the first time. Indeed, if **sustainable development** had been achieved by any civilization in the past, history would have to be drastically rewritten. Historians have repeatedly observed that rapid degradation of the environment has been a significant factor in the decline of civilizations.

> How did civilized [societies] despoil this favorable environment? [They] did it mainly by depleting or destroying the natural resources. [They] cut down or burned most of the usable timber from forested hillsides and valleys. [They] overgrazed and denuded the grasslands that feed [their] livestock. [They] killed most of the wildlife and much of the fish and other water life. [They] permitted erosion to rob [their] farm land of its productive topsoil. [They] allowed eroded soil to clog the streams and fill [the] reservoirs, irrigation canals, and harbors with silt. In many cases, [they] used and wasted most of the easily mined metals or other needed minerals. Then [their] civilization declined admidst the despoliation of [their] own creation or . . . moved to new land. There have been from ten to thirty different civilizations that have followed this road to ruin (the number depending on who classifies the civilizations) (Carter and Dale, 1955).

The goal of sustainable development is "a development strategy that manages all assets, natural resources, and human resources, as well as financial and physical assets, for increasing long-term health and well-being. Sustainable development, as a goal, rejects policies and practices that support current living standards by depleting the productive base, including natural resources, and that leave future generations with poorer prospects and greater risks than our own" (Repetto, 1986).

The **World Conservation Strategy** (IUCN, 1980) is a blueprint for sustainable development through the conservation of living systems. The following three requirements are presented as necessary for achieving the objectives of living systems conservation:

1. the maintenance of essential ecological processes and life-support systems primarily requires careful planning and allocation of uses and high quality management of those uses;
2. the preservation of genetic diversity primarily requires the timely collection of genetic material and its protection in banks, plantation, and so on, in the case of off-site preservation; and ecosystem protection in the case of on-site preservation;
3. the sustainable utilization of ecosystems and species requires knowledge of the productive capacities of those resources and measures to ensure that utilization does not exceed those capacities.

Both of the last two objectives require achievement of the first.

For effective implementation of sustainable development, human individuals and societies must be able to link their understanding of the global system to built environment activities. That means they must be able to qualify and characterize their ability to inhibit or promote local and regional development in relationship to elements of global environmental change. Implementation must also include institutional and organizational changes toward more effective international (i.e., global) research, policy-making, and management (Clark and Munn, 1986).

One of the main obstacles to implementation is a "lack of environmental planning and of rational use allocation" (IUCN, 1980). Since rational planning is the first requirement for achieving the objectives of living systems conservation, this obstacle must be overcome. The World Conservation Strategy identifies ecosystem evaluation and environmental assessment as the best means of implementing environmental planning.

POLICIES FOR ENVIRONMENTAL ASSESSMENT

In the United States, a number of tentative steps toward rational environmental planning have been taken in the twentieth century (several were noted by other authors in this text). The latest, and perhaps most profound of these, was taken in 1969 with the passage of the **National Environmental Policy Act** (U.S. Congress, 1969). NEPA, as the Act is called, expresses an appreciation for the Earth which goes beyond strictly linear thinking:

> The Congress, recognizing the profound impact of [human] activity on the interrelations of all components of the natural environment, particularly the profound influences of population growth, high density urbanization, industrial expansion, resource exploitation, and new and expanding technological advances and recognizing further the critical importance of restoring and maintaining environmental quality to overall [human] welfare and development . . . declares that it is the continuing policy of the Federal Government, in cooperation with state and local governments, and other concerned public and private organizations, to use all practicable means and measures, including financial and technical assistance, in a manner calculated to foster and promote the general welfare, to create and maintain conditions under which [humans] and nature can exist in productive harmony, and fulfill the social, economic, and other requirements of present and future generations.

NEPA also requires that an environmental impact statement be written to "accompany every recommendation or report on proposals for legislation and other major Federal actions significantly affecting the quality of the human environment." In the United States, twenty-seven states also require environmental assessment of local and regional projects through an environmental impact statement process.

Environmental assessment has been a consistent theme throughout this text. Consistent application of a holistic "fitness test," examined across the entire range of scales—from creating the smallest product to comprehension of processes at a whole-earth level—is necessary if humans are to live in quality built environments. That grasp of connections—from pencil to planet—will go a long way toward achieving the goal of sustainable development.

REFERENCES

Bazzaz, F. A. and Fajer, E. D. 1992. "Plant Life in a CO_2-Rich World." *Scientific American*.

Bolin, B. and Cook R. B. 1983. *The Major Biogeochemical Cycles and Their Interactions*. Wiley.

Carter, V. G. and Dale, T. 1974. Topsoil and Civilization. University of Oklahoma Press.

Catton, W. R. 1987. "The World's Most Polymorphic Species." *Bioscience*.

Clark, W. C. and Munn, R. E. (Eds.). 1986. *Sustainable Development of the Biosphere*. Cambridge University Press.

Cortright, E. M. 1975. *Apollo Expedition to the Moon*. NASA.

Earth System Sciences Committee. 1986. *Earth System Science: A Program for Global Change*. NASA Advisory Council.

Earth System Sciences Committee. 1988. *Earth System Science: A Closer View*. NASA Advisory Council.

Eliot, T. S. 1943. "Little Gidding," *The Four Quartets*. Harcourt, Brace, & Jovanovich.

Ehrlich, P. R. and Wilson, E. O. 1991. "Biodiversity Studies: Science and Policy," *Science*.

Franz, E. H. 1981. "A General Formulation of Stress Phenomena in Ecological Systems," *Stress Effects on Natural Ecosystems*. Wiley.

International Council of Scientific Unions. 1966. *The International Geosphere Biosphere Programme: A Study of Global Change*. ICSU.

IUCN/UNEP/WWF. 1980. *World Conservation Strategy. Living Resource Conservation for Sustainable Development*. Gland.

IUCN/UNEP/WWF. 1991. *Caring for the Earth: A Strategy for Sustainable Living*. Gland.

Keeling, C. D. 1990. *Atmospheric CO_2 Concentrations—Mauna Loa Observatory, Hawaii, 1958–1990*. Oak Ridge National Laboratory.

Kerr, R. A. 1983. "The Carbon Cycle and Climate Warming," *Science*.

Laszlo, E. 1972. *Introduction to Systems Philosophy*. Gordon & Breach.

Likens, G. E. 1981. *Some Perspectives of the Major Biogeochemical Cycles*. Wiley.

Lovelock, . E. 1972. "Gaia as Seen Through the Atmosphere," *Atmospheric Environment*.

Lovelock, J. E. 1979. *Gaia: A New Look at Life on Earth*. Oxford University Press.

Lovelock, J. E. 1986. "Geophysiology: A New Look at Earth Science," *Bulletin American Meteorological Society*.

Malone, T. F. and Roederer, J. G. (Eds.). 1984. *Global Change*. Cambridge University Press.

Marsh, G. P. 1864. *Man and Nature; or, Physical Geography as Modified by Human Action*. Scribner.

Odum, E. P. and Franz, E. H. 1980. "Whither the Life Support System?" *Growth Without Ecodisasters?* Wiley.

Ramanathan, V., Cicerone, R. J., Singh, H. B., and Kiehl, J. T. 1985. "Trace Gas Trends and Their Potential Role in Climate Change," *Journal of Geophysical Research*.

Repetto, R. 1986. *World Enough and Time: Successful Strategies for Resource Management*. Yale University Press.

Rubin, E. S., Cooper, R. N., Frosch, R. A., Lee, T. H., Marland, G., Rosenfeld, A. H., and Stine, D.D. "Realistic Mitigation Options for Global Warming," *Science*.

U. S. Committee for an International Geosphere-Biosphere Program. 1986. *Global Change in the Geosphere-Biosphere: Initial Priorities for an IGBP*. National Academy Press.

U. S. Congress. 1969. *The National Environmental Policy Act of 1969*. Public Law 91-190.

Vitousek, P. M., Ehrlich, P. R., Ehrlich, A. H., and Matson, P. A. 1986." Human Appropriation of the Products of Photosynthesis," *Bioscience*.

Washington State Legislature. 1973. *State Environmental Policy Act*. Revised Code of Washington.

Woodwell, G. M. 1974. "Ecosystems and World Politics," *Ecological Society of America*.

CHAPTER

31

Taking Action in the Built Environment: A Global Agenda

Diane Armpriest

Some experts, including scientists from all over the world, predict that at existing rates of consumption there are from 15–40 years left of the resources that are necessary to sustain human and societal needs (Gonzalez, 1990). Industrial societies have been very creative in originating and developing many new ideas that have substantially improved material standards of living. This development has been based on the intensive and extensive consumption of nonrenewable natural resources, and it has now become evident that the ways of thinking which brought all these changes have not been equally successful in addressing the extensive environmental degradation that has resulted. Now we are all challenged to find new ways of conceptualizing development in order to find "solutions" that restore or preserve healthy environments and improve the quality of life essential to the survival of humans and many other living beings.

Recent evidence of concern on the international political scene by scientists, economists, politicians and spiritual leaders provides some cause for optimism. According to Jessica Tuchman Matthews (1989) of the World Resources Institute, "there has been a wholesale shift in the public's attitude toward global environmental issues" during the past two years. She attributes this shift to several factors, including an increased flow of information worldwide and changes in the international political and economic scene. Matthews writes that "the 1990's will demand a redefinition of what constitutes national security," predicting that "national security in the future will shift from defending against other nations to defending against environmental degradation."

It is indeed important to address environmental policies at the global scale and to connect these to effective design strategies and political solutions at the regional and local scales. Environmental designers have not traditionally been educated or trained to consider or implement global policy. They are best at providing specific local responses to environmental problems within the realm of their expertise. It is now critical, however, that environmental designers as well as society begin to consider the global as well as local implications of daily lifestyles and design decisions. Rene Dubos (1981) put this simply and elegantly when he said "think globally, but act locally."

It can be overwhelming to consider the profound environmental problems humanity is now facing. It is important, however, to develop an attitude which allows us to maintain a sense of hope and enables us to be committed enough to take positive action. This is not an easy task as we tend to hear much more about problems than solutions from the media, political leaders, educators and design practitioners. In order to find solutions, however, we must first identify and increase our understanding of the problems themselves, as well as recognize and continue to develop design and action strategies to help resolve these problems.

What follows is an attempt to begin to identify opportunities available, particularly in the realm of environmental design, for taking action in response to global environmental concerns. This discussion begins with a brief introduction to critical environmental issues, followed by strategies for finding resolutions. It will become obvious that all these issues are intricately interwoven and that action is required by the general public, by government and business, as well as by the design professions.

ENVIRONMENTAL ISSUES

The U.S. Council on Environmental Quality and Department of State reported in the *Global 2000 Report to the President of the United States* (1980) that every aspect of the earth's ecosystems and resource base will be affected by the worldwide growth in population, redistribution of income, and depletion or degradation of resources. The report describes the following as primary issues or challenges which need to be addressed:

1. An accelerating loss of the resources essential for agriculture;
2. The decline in quality of the earth's water resources;
3. Rapid and widespread loss of tropical forests;
4. The emerging environmental stresses that affect the chemical and physical nature of the atmosphere;
5. The impacts of nuclear energy and the loss of nonrenewable energy sources;
6. The loss of plant and animal genetic resources.

These issues have not changed in the intervening years; however, they have become more widely recognized and acknowledged, not only among "environmentalists," but among other citizens and leaders from the general population. This awareness has come about by disasters such as the catastrophic accidents at the Chernobyl nuclear plant in the Soviet Union, the explosion at the U.S. owned Union Carbide chemical manufacturing plant in Bhopal, India, the spill caused by the wreck of the Exxon Valdez oil tanker in the Gulf of Alaska, and the ongoing conflicts in the Persian Gulf. In addition, scientific documentation and personal experiences of the air pollution in cities, the changing climate and the trend toward global warming have brought issues of atmospheric changes to the attention of millions.

At this time, and no doubt due in part to the incidents and discoveries of the 1980s, discussions have begun on an international scale aimed at finding solutions to these serious problems. One example that environmental issues are being taken much more seriously is the outcome of the July 1989 economic summit of seven leading industrial powers (United States, Japan, West Germany, France, Britain, Italy and Canada). The leaders agreed that "protecting the environment calls for a determined and concerted international response [to pollution of air, land and water] and for early adoption, worldwide, of policies based on sustainable development." In fact, over one-third of the summit communique addressed the environment, with issues of atmospheric pollution taking precedence. Environmentalists are concerned that the agreement lacks a specific action agenda; however, it is a clear indication that these issues are being recognized by international political leaders, setting challenges for action into the twenty-first century.

The key to resolving environmental problems is that they must be addressed at all levels by committed individuals, small groups and organizations as well as local, state, national and international governments. Numerous opportunities already exist for getting involved and many potential "solutions" await action implementation. This section discusses each of the environmental issues from the Global 2000 Report and presents opportunities for action and examples of solutions being developed at this time.

Destruction and Degradation of Agricultural Resources

"Agricultural systems are [human-made] communities of plants and animals, interacting with soils and climate" (Hough, 1981). These systems are at risk for two major reasons: The systems are typically out of balance in an ecological sense and the land resources upon which they are based are being lost to urban development, soil erosion, and nutrient depletion. In addition, people over the years have become greatly removed from the processes and systems that go into the production of the food they consume.

Agricultural productivity has greatly increased in recent years due to improved technology, to improved strains of plants, and to oil-based fertilizers, herbicides and pesticides. In order to be economically efficient, these practices require large areas of land and are extremely energy intensive. Eighty percent of worldwide production relies on only 11 species of plants (Hough, 1984). The consequences of this system of agriculture are that soil life is being destroyed; lakes, rivers and groundwater are being polluted by the use of chemicals; the lives of agricultural workers are being endangered by the use of pesticides and herbicides; and soil quality is being reduced by erosion and compaction from cultivation practices. Intensive farming on marginal lands leads to desertification.

More sustainable agricultural practices—which in some ways are a return to methods developed centuries ago—are gaining momentum. This approach involves taking a long-term view of the land and soil resources, seeking to establish a self-sustaining system of food production. These practices involve crop rotation, the use of organically derived fertilizers and natural systems of pest and disease control, minimal tillage and the production of a diversity of crops and animals. In addition, these farmers, in most cases, seek out local or regional markets, reducing transportation costs (and saving additional resources).

For many centuries, farmers utilized household wastes generated in cities, known as night soil, for fertilizing their crops. A contemporary application of this idea is the processing of by-products of the sewage treatment facilities for use as organic fertilizers. Many cities are now working to market this product (and at the same time reduce the volume of waste to be disposed of in landfills).

It requires far more land and resources to raise cattle than crops. Much of the grain and soy beans raised today go to feed cattle being raised for beef. Reducing (if not eliminating) consumption of beef can help conserve land as well as the petroleum based resources which currently fuel agricultural production. In addition, eating organically grown food products will increase the demand for these products, providing economic incentives for farmers to change their production methods.

Individuals might also consider taking new approaches to developing and maintaining their yards and gardens. People can begin to envision such land not only as a place to provide aesthetic pleasure, but as an agricultural resource and as a system that can become self-sustaining if its development and management are based on the principles of ecology.

In 1971, 8.6% of Massachusetts was in farmland compared with 60% about 60 years before (Hough, 1984). In the United States, as well as many other nations, agricultural land is gradually being lost to urban development and wasteful suburban sprawl. The loss of this land, along with the changes in agricultural practices, contributes to the fact that the majority of the food a city consumes can no longer be produced locally, or even within the region.

This does not have to be the case, however. In China, cities such as Shanghai and Beijing produce the majority of their vegetable supply within the urban boundaries of the city (Hough, 1984). Many larger cities are also encouraging urban farmers through the development of neighborhood and allotment gardens established on vacant land within the city. These gardens not only provide the garden-farmer with fresh fruits and vegetables, they provide productive green spaces on land that once lay derelict. In many cases, the gardeners are low-income families with no previous experience with gardening or community involvement and these programs have given them many new skills (gardening, garden design, group interaction techniques and community politics) as well as a new sense of self esteem.

In cases where agricultural land is rededicated (or rezoned) for housing, a new approach to site selection and design is required. Designing sites where land use is determined by the inherent capabilities and suitabilities of the land is an approach that was eloquently described by landscape architect/ecologist Ian McHarg in *Design with Nature*. Using this system, relatively flat, fertile land would be used for agricultural purposes, ecologically sensitive land (such as wetlands) would be protected, and less productive land would be used for

1. Children enjoying their work in one of 19 neighborhood gardens in Cincinnati, Ohio (*courtesy of Civic Garden Center of Greater Cincinnati*).

more intensive urban development. In some places, such as the state of Oregon, this approach to local and regional planning has been used to guide new development. At the Woodlands New Town Development near Houston, Texas, designed by Ian McHarg, these principles have not only been used to develop the ecological based community plan, but provided design alternatives that have saved millions of dollars in development.

Quality and Quantity of Water Resources

Water, according to tradition, is the sustainer of life, yet we are now faced with serious problems related to the supply and demand for water as well as the quality of this precious resource. Urban areas have developed in landscapes that are not necessarily capable of supplying the water and other natural resource needs of residents. Phoenix, Arizona, Los Angeles, California, and urban developments in desert areas throughout the world are prime examples of cities where water shortages already exist. In the United States, these shortages are exacerbated by the public taste for water-intensive landscapes, such as the green lawn, and water consumptive lifestyles: frequent showers, use of dishwashers, swimming pools, etc. All these habits of water use result in much larger scale environmental, political and economic issues.

One key issue in water conservation is that society has always considered water to be a "free" commodity and the prices paid for household and municipal uses of water are greatly discounted. It takes a vast amount of energy in terms of the development of dams, transportation facilities, and treatment systems to provide water for individual and industrial use even in areas with apparent surpluses. If citizens are required to pay more accurate prices for water, perhaps conservation would happen more easily. If conservation becomes the norm, then fewer resources will be spent on the production of clean water.

Designers and consumers can also make an effort to reduce consumption without greatly altering lifestyles. Development of water conservation devices and systems in the areas now experiencing shortages has been a priority, in addition to educational efforts to change lifestyles. "Save water, shower with a friend" is a well known slogan in California which has now imposed legal restrictions on the use of water.

An acre of lawn requires 27,000 gallons of water per week (Earthworks Group, 1989). The concept of the "Xeriscape," based on the use of native, drought tolerant plants in landscape design, addresses this problem directly by providing alternative approaches to develop gardens, yards and parks that rely on less water, yet still provide users with the amenities they desire. These gardens, yards, and urban and regional parks may not always be dominated by the "traditional" green, suggesting that the public will need to develop a new landscape aesthetic.

Use of rain water and recycling greywater (water previously used but not contaminated with toxics) for secondary use can be implemented at many scales: watering residential yards, public parks, and rights-of-way, even supplying water for fountains.

At a larger scale, planners have been active in developing policy related to the "rights of ownership" of water. By the time it reaches the ocean, the Colorado River is nearly drained by intensive use for agriculture, urban development, and the production of hydro-electric power. This creates serious conflicts among the inhabitants of all the states through which it flows, and with Mexico; any successful efforts to resolve this situation will require new ways of conceptualizing the problem and the development of a cross-boundary (bioregional) policy based on sustainability.

At the other end of the spectrum, many cities and communities are faced with problems of extensive flooding. This has been caused by intensive development in flood plains, by increases in the percentage of land now covered with impermeable materials, and by the clear-cutting of forest lands. "Paving" not only prevents rainwater from penetrating the soil, it intensifies the volume and speed of runoff during periods of heavy rainfall. New methods for managing stormwater are being developed, including systems for detaining it on site and releasing it slowly into the system and for capturing it on site and allowing it to infiltrate back into the soil.

Water resources are also subject to pollution. In 1977, the Environmental Protection Agency identified 129 organic and inorganic toxic pollutants that entered waterways via urban run-off, industrial discharge, fallout, leaching from landfills

2. Earthworks Park in Kent, Washington, was designed by Herbert Bayer, winner of a public art competition. It is not only internationally recognized as a work of environmental art, it serves as a stormwater detention system, preventing flooding to the residents and businesses downstream.

and other disposal sites and chemical spills (Spirn, 1984). Reducing pollutants at the source is perhaps the most effective strategy and has met with success in many communities. In many cases in the United States, manufacturers and municipalities alike are required by law to treat liquid effluents before discharging them into waterways. These regulations have already accounted for major improvements in the quality of water in many rivers throughout the industrialized world.

When toxics enter water systems through indirect means (non-point sources), they are much more difficult to control or regulate. Urban runoff could all be collected and treated before being released to waterways. The problem could also be approached at a more grass roots level through education and individual effort. One community is painting warnings on stormwater grates, letting people know how damaging it is to dump toxics in this way. Many filling stations and auto repair shops are collecting and recycling oil products rather than disposing of them as wastes. One mechanic actually takes home waste oil and uses it to fuel his furnace.

Many examples can also be cited of the destruction of coastal ecosystems as a result of water pollution and siltation due to land development, degrading habitat for wildlife and fish. Environmental planners are skilled in assessing the value of these sensitive lands and are learning to work with developers to come up with creative solutions. In Arcata, California, for example, treated effluent from the wastewater treatment system is discharged into the coastal wetland, enhancing and restoring the ecosystem while meeting community needs.

The Permanent Loss of Forest Resources

The permanent loss of forest resources is occurring as a result of urban development, agriculture and cattle ranching, the production of building materials and paper products, the creation of developments such as hydroelectric projects and related dams, power plants, reservoirs, roads, etc., and for use as fuel. In tropical rain forests, for example, about 50 acres per minute are being lost (Earthworks Group, 1989), but the same kind of destruction is also occurring in other rural and urban forests throughout the world.

Although forest resources are technically renewable, logging and other methods of clearing, such as burning, often leave soil resources eroded or completely stripped of nutrients and no longer productive for growing trees. This may also result in the loss of water recharge and retention potential, the loss of wildlife habitat, and the extinction of plant and animal species that thrive in a forest ecosystem. Another significant loss is the decrease in the amount of oxygen being produced as a result of the process of photosynthesis. A land area the size of Ohio is being deforested each year in the tropical rain forests which produce 40% of the Earth's supply of oxygen (Earthworks Group, 1989).

Several general approaches can be taken to the problem: reduce the consumption of wood products and their derivatives and of products that result in deforestation; be selective about the source of wood products used or specified for use in construction; and consider reforestation and forest (or tree) preservation and health to be a priority in all personal or professional projects.

In developing nations, where wood is the primary source of fuel, experimentation with solar and fuel-efficient ovens, pumps and other devices is now underway. On a larger scale, leading institutions such as the World Bank, and regulatory bodies such as the International Monetary Fund, are beginning to take action to place strict environmental controls on projects they fund or support in developing areas.

Site development and design can address some of these problems by careful analysis and evaluation of existing forest and plant resources, by judicious cutting and development practices which assure continued health of trees, and by maximum revegetation of all sites. It is also important to consider the overall health of the site ecosystem, preserving or restoring conditions that support healthy development of plant and animal life. This might involve clustering rather than dispersing buildings; minimizing impermeable surfaces and utilizing semi-permeable paving wherever possible; designing structures that require minimal use of manufactured wood products (and other materials as well, for that matter); and more widespread use of recycled wood fibers (e.g., for paper products).

Planting need not be seen as a purely aesthetic decision: planting strategies can effectively moderate climates; reduce heating and cooling loads in buildings; cool and shade roadways, sidewalks and parking lots; control and enhance winter winds and summer breezes; filter particulates from the air; block or filter noises or create positive sounds; provide habitat for birds and other wildlife; and increase the supply of oxygen (Robinnette, 1972).

Sound timber management policy is an obvious key: forests should be managed and maintained for sustainability and long-range goals. An issue in the public eye at this time is the preservation of the few remaining old growth stands of Redwood trees in northern California and southern Oregon. These are very old, slow-growing trees, and highly valued for timber. Citizens are concerned about the management strategy now in place and are becoming involved in stopping logging operations by direct intervention. Protestors occupy the canopies of trees many feet above the forest floor so loggers will not cut the trees down, and groups of people lie on the ground to halt the progress of bulldozers to stop the construction of logging roads in order to prevent the destruction of what they consider to be an irreplaceable resource.

Atmospheric Pollution and Degradation

A great deal of discussion has surrounded problems related to atmospheric pollution and degradation in recent years and again there are a number of factors to consider. The greenhouse effect which is leading to global warming is caused when industrial gases (such as carbon dioxide, nitrous oxides, methane and ozone) thicken the blanket of atmosphere surrounding the earth, trapping heat and raising the average temperature of the earth. This has the potential of not only greatly altering ecosystems, but of melting icecaps and raising the level of the oceans. Atmospheric pollution, which renders air unsafe to breath (for humans as well as other animal and plant life), is caused by many of the same gases that encourage the greenhouse effect. Ozone, which is primarily created through atmospheric reactions with auto emissions, not only creates blankets of smog, but causes major health problems for people and plants, eventually affecting health, crop yields and fish populations. Chloroflourocarbons (CFC's) are gases—used in aerosol cans, some refrigerants, and in the production of many foam materials commonly used in construction—which ultimately make their way into the upper atmosphere and deplete the ozone layer. This in turn increases the penetration of ultra violet light to the earth's surface, contributing to the global warming trend and increasing the likelihood of cancer and other health problems for all inhabitants of the earth. Each of the areas of concern is extremely complex and all are inextricably linked.

Reliance on the automobile is perhaps the biggest contributor to these problems, and changing the driving habits of people in the industrialized nations, especially the United States, is required. This will entail not only a change in attitude about the car, but the development of reliable and easily accessible mass transit alternatives. In the meantime, a number of states are adopting emission control standards and testing procedures which are beginning to address some of the problems. It is also necessary to improve fuel efficiency, and to explore alternative fuel sources (ideally renewable resources). One man in the U.S. midwest has converted his old Volkswagen bug to run on cooking oil, relying on fast food restaurants to supply his fuel.

Climate-based architectural design minimizes heating and cooling loads and is another essential starting point. Air conditioning systems are particularly energy consumptive and frequently involve the use of refrigerants that produce CFC's. Specification of efficient mechanical systems and working to develop better cooling systems as well as the technology for solar and other forms of renewable energy supplies should also be a high priority. Many materials used in building interiors are known to release toxic substances and these should be carefully studied and understood before they are used.

Increasing the emphasis on use of plants in landscape and urban design as well as engineering for highways and hillside stability will increase opportunities for purification and reoxygenation of the atmosphere. Planners can work to develop local and regional zoning and to pass building ordinances which encourage energy conservation and they can work to regulate the consumption and production of energy on the larger scales.

Several major political actions, with great potential to affect change, have been realized in recent years. For example, an international agreement to control the release of CFC's, now referred to as the Montreal Protocol, was signed in 1987 by 24 nations. The Protocol, which was later strengthened and signed by 100 nations, calls for completely phasing out all CFC's by the year 2000. In the United States, Congress and the President, after many years of debate, have approved new legislation, the Clean Air Act of 1990, which will begin to readdress the issue of air quality after a long lapse in attention. This legislation, following in the footsteps of the original Clean Air Act, is a good beginning; however, many experts believe that much more stringent requirements need to be developed to adequately address this problem.

Soils are similarly degraded as a result of both atmospheric pollution and the disposal of toxic substances on or below the surface of the earth. Gasworks Park in Seattle, Washington, was built on the site of an old gas plant where tons of toxic materials had leached into the soil. Instead of all the structures and soils being removed when the site was deeded to the city for a park, the structures remained to provide a rich and striking reminder of the past, and soils were treated through natural means to restore natural balance to the site. This park, designed by Richard Haag, has become a model for many other cities faced with the task of reclaiming abandoned industrial sites.

3. Industrial relics provide the centerpiece for Gasworks Park, viewed from between mounds created with waste and debris and planted with highly tolerant grasses.

Impacts of Nuclear Energy and the Development of Renewable Energy Sources

Nuclear energy was once seen as the panacea to solve the problem created by the approaching depletion of nonrenewable energy resources. Some experts now believe that, while there may be great potential in nuclear power, the potential for widespread and immediate loss of other human and environmental resources as a result of a nuclear accident is greater. Cautious development of this technology as well as strictly enforced site planning, design and operations standards for such facilities are essential, including dealing effectively with the extremely toxic waste by-products of nuclear energy production. Most energy today is derived from burning nonrenewable fuels such as oil, coal and natural gas, and from the generation of hydroelectric power. Aside from the fact of a limited supply of these resources, the environmental impacts resulting from their extraction, transportation, combustion and transmission, have been devastating. In addition, the economic cost of these fuels is skyrocketing, especially if they have to be imported.

Again, the reduction of overall consumption of energy and nonrenewable resources is essential. This has already been demonstrated as effective by the first conservation measures introduced in the U.S. in the 1970s. The early focus was on things such as home insulation and lighting, heating and ventilation systems. Since that time, citizens of the U.S. "have enjoyed a 35 percent rise in the gross national product without increasing their energy consumption" (Rosenfeld & Hafemeister, 1988). This is not to say that everything has been done that could be done, but a significant start has been made. Environmental designers can assist in this process in a number of ways. Industrial and product designers can eliminate the concept of "disposability" from their vocabulary, develop products and processes which require minimum inputs of energy and/or utilize energy produced by renewable sources. Architects, interior designers, landscape architects and engineers can specify building materials which are the least energy consumptive to produce or least damaging to the environment. For example, materials such as aluminum and concrete are both extremely energy and resource consumptive to produce and better alternatives can probably be found.

Energy derived from renewable resources using systems such as passive and active solar, wind generation, and methane and alcohol fuels derived from agricultural production are in the very early stages. These resources can and are being developed at the building unit scale or for mass production.

The high winds that blow over the Altamont Pass in California are now harnessed by thousands of wind generators that cover the hillsides while cattle graze on the land below. Large-scale solar collection systems are also under development in many sunny climates throughout the world.

These renewable resources can also be developed as an integral part of the building process and although significant work has been done in this area, there is still much left to do. A number of examples of creative and holistic thinking can be cited. Michael Reynolds, an architect practicing in New Mexico, has developed an earth-sheltered, passive solar housing type based on the use of old tires crammed with earth as foundations, discarded aluminum cans as building infill walls, and discarded bottles for greenhouse planter walls. The roof structure utilizes downed logs salvaged from forest lands (Reynolds, 1990). In another example, a dairy farmer in Pennsylvania has devised a two-tiered barn that allows him to house and milk the cows, collecting their wastes and urine and converting them to methane. He generates enough methane to heat the barn and fuel all the farm vehicles. Part of the by-products of the process are also used for bedding for the animals. By putting the entire herd on line, he will probably have enough surplus methane to sell, in addition to the milk (Gonzalez, 1990).

Earth Connection is a new environmental learning center designed by students and faculty at the University of Cincinnati and sponsored by the Sisters of Charity of Cincinnati. It utilizes passive and active solar as the primary energy source, is tapped into the natural processes of the site through the use of water, solar energy and breezes, is being constructed with materials that are as resource efficient as possible, is being built by volunteers from donated materials and services, and is intended to provide meeting spaces and resources for learning about 'living lightly' on the Earth.

4. South elevation of the EarthConnection structure features south-facing glass to collect heat from the sun (passively), solar hot water collectors (on lower roof) that heat water that is then circulated through tubes embedded in the floor, heating the concrete and radiating heat to the interior spaces, and photovoltaic panels (mounted on the tower) which generate electricity for selected functions in the building.

Reduction of Genetic Resources

Species diversity is important to maintain in order to keep ecosystems balanced. From an agricultural point of view, maintaining gene pools is also important to continue development of strains of plants that are resistant to pests and disease. The Nature Conservancy estimates that as many as three species are being lost per day, in most cases because of loss or degradation of habitat and ecosystems. In other cases, extinction results from hunting animals for trophies, for fur, for ivory, or for other fashionable commodities.

Loss of habitat frequently results from development related to resource extraction (strip mining, logging, farming, etc.) or urbanization. Preservation and restoration efforts described in the section on forest resources apply here. In urban and suburban conditions, a number of possible actions can be taken. At the level of the backyard or park, plantings are being designed to attract specific wildlife species—particularly birds and butterflies. Plantings can also be designed to support other kinds of organisms as well. In fact, creating diverse habitat

Table 1

ENVIRONMENTAL ISSUE	BUILT ENVIRONMENT DESIGN STRATEGIES		
	Products/Interiors	**Structures/Landscape**	**City/Region/Earth**
Agricultural Resources	Organic farming/gardening techniques Tools and methods to eliminate erosion, increase productivity	Site design for erosion control and to avoid compaction Reduce suburban sprawl	Avoid development on agricultural land
Water Resources	Water use reduction devices for building and landscape Low water planting design Develop non-toxic materials	Greywater recycling On-site stormwater management Eliminate toxics from garden	Wetland preservation Sewage and water treatment systems
Forest Resources	Minimize materials in products Eliminate need for packaging Develop new building materials Reduce, reuse, recycle	Utilize wood products that are easily regenerated Eliminate rare/endangered hardwoods	Develop urban forestry programs Guidelines/zoning for forest management
Atmosphere	Energy conservation Develop pollution control devices Non-toxic materials/methods in home/workplace	Energy-efficient buildings and landscapes reduce use of fossil fuel Increase volume of trees planted and use of air cleansing varieties Energy efficiency	Reduce suburban sprawl Design cities to maximize air circulation Pollution control ordinances and incentives
Energy	Passive and active solar technology Develop materials with low embodied energy	Design with climate Superinsulated buildings Energy efficient site planning and landscape design Reduce reliance on chemicals in garden	Reduce/Reuse/Recycling programs Energy conservation incentives Reduce suburban sprawl Increase public transit, reduce use of auto
Genetic Resources	Avoid use of products from endangered species (fur, ivory, feathers, etc.)	Planting design for diversity Prairie or other ecosystem restoration	Increase diversity for wildlife habitat Strengthen/enforce legislation to preserve rare and endangered species

for desirable wildlife will often help control less desirable pests such as rodents or starlings (Spirn, 1984). An even more effective measure is to consolidate and link large collections of open space and develop this land as wildlife habitat. Such linkages can provide much more diversity than small individual efforts (Forman and Godron, 1986).

Because wetlands provide a habitat that supports particularly diverse collections of living things, special efforts are being taken to preserve these areas. Legislation has been passed and regulations developed to ensure that appropriate sites are either preserved or replaced when large-scale developments are built, such as federally subsidized highways or sewage treatment plants.

To diminish the taking and supply of products, trophies or souvenirs made of the fur or other parts of endangered species, the most obvious action is to not purchase these items. Organized boycotts have actually resulted in department stores closing their fur salons and have caused major tuna companies to change their fishing practices to stop the killing of dolphins.

TAKING ACTION

It is clear that many opportunities are available for thoughtful and well-prepared individuals to develop environmentally sound lifestyles and to contribute substantially to the solution of the problems presented in this chapter. At this point in time, working in these areas or developing an environmentally based design practice may not be an easy undertaking. However, a number of things might make these challenges more manageable. First of all, it is important to become well informed and educated. Many mistakes are made by well-intentioned, but ill-informed people—concerned public and environmental designers alike. This may involve establishing a network of informed and committed colleagues working together, the exchange of information, or simply the offer of moral support. In Cincinnati, Ohio, a citizens group, the Alternate Energy Association, emerged from this kind of thinking and networking. This can happen locally, nationally and internationally, utilizing meetings, professional and scientific publications and journals, and computer-based communications.

One strategy for implementation of change involves the "infiltration" of professional organizations by "environmentalists" or like-minded designers, making use of institutional power and resources. Once in leadership positions, such thinkers and doers can institute change from the top down. The opposite extreme, employed by organizations such as Earth First and Greenpeace, involves direct confrontation by nonviolent means to force change. Recent decisions by major tuna manufacturers to change fishing practices, thus saving the lives of thousands of dolphins, is witness to this method.

As this book has repeatedly emphasized, solutions will often involve working at several levels: from developing new products or manufacturing processes, to getting them approved, accepted and demanded for use by the larger population, to making mass production or implementation economically feasible. Living in an area where environmental quality is poor provides opportunities for the development and implementation of innovative solutions. Finally, it is important to identify individuals, groups or organizations to serve as sources of inspiration, ideas and support for your own endeavors.

While problems may sometimes seem insurmountable, it is also important to recognize that the present is one of the most exciting times to be practicing environmental design. There are opportunities for radical innovation and environmental change that have never before existed, and designers are well equipped to make a difference. It is also important to keep in mind that progress is being made in all areas—only a few of which are recounted here. It seems that now, as never before, an international ground-swell of interest in these issues is taking place—and the time seems right for meaningful, sustainable action.

REFERENCES

Dubos, Re. 1981. *Celebrations of Life*. McGraw-Hill.

Earthworks Group. 1989. *50 Simple Things You Can Do To Save the Planet*. Earthworks Press.

Forman, R. T. T. and Godron, M. 1986. *Landscape Ecology*. Wiley.

Gonzalez, P. 1990. "Earth Consciousness Lectures," *Julie Penrose Center*.

Hough, M. 1984. *City Form and Natural Process*. Routledge.

Mathews, J. T. 1989. "Interview by Rushworth M. Kidder," *Christian Science Monitor*.

Reynolds, M. 1990. *Earthship, Vol. 1*. Solar Survival Press.

Robinnette, G. 1972. *Plants, People and Environmental Quality*. Landscape Architecture Foundation and National Park Service.

Rosenfeld, A. H. and Hafemeister, D. 1988. "Energy Efficient Buildings," *Scientific American*.

Spirn, A, W. 1984. *The Granite Garden*. Basic Books.

U. S. Council on Environmental Quality and Department of State. 1980. *Global 2000 Report to the President of the United States, Vol. 1*. Pergamon Press.

Wann, D. 1990. *Biologic: Environmental Protection by Design*. Johnson Books.

CHAPTER

32

Earth: World-As-Presence

Gerald L. Young

A pressing need exists in contemporary industrialized societies to respond to widespread fragmentation. A decline in shared values has occurred, resulting in a complex and compounded fracture between what humans feel and what they think, between what they think and what they can do. People are confused by the conflict between reason and emotion that they think separates science and art. Even the private inner and public outer selves of individuals must respond in different ways to different environments. The need to deal with fragmentation—to reconnect part and whole (individual and environment, individual and society)—is widely recognized. In Albert Gore's acceptance of the nomination for vice-president in 1992, he emphasized this belief that

> There is a fundamental link between our current relationship to the earth and the attitudes that stand in the way of human progress. For generations, we have believed that we could abuse the earth because we were somehow not really connected to it . . . just as the false assumption that we are not connected to the Earth has led to the ecological crisis, so the equally false assumption that we are not connected to each other has led to our social crisis. . . .

The poet T. S. Eliot described the creative process as doing things separately and then perceiving possibilities for focusing them together, for alteration, and then for creating a whole from the parts. The process is incomplete at the separation stage; for closure, it must be taken to that holistic culmination, the putting of parts together. A lot of that creativity produces artifacts and objects in the built environment, indeed, the built environment itself. Bricks, for example, are formed separately, often far from building sites, then brought together in all kinds of places, in all kinds of creative ways. A truly creative process acknowledges the parts and the wholes, that they are connected, and that the linkage can result in integrated rather than fragmented components in the built environment.

NEEDED CONNECTIONS BETWEEN UNIT AND WHOLE

Each and every individual person needs increased awareness, needs their consciousness raised enough to be able to agree that "I am truth since I am part of what is real"—but only part! Each individual needs to take care, however, that they do not magnify that part, whether in themselves or in their work, inflating it to ridiculous proportions, hoping in the process that no one will notice that the tiny thing is only a part and not a whole. The built environment already has too many isolated, out-of-context artifacts that are ill-fitted to their surroundings. A holistic perspective requires everyone—designers and public alike—to regain humility and that sense of connection, a sense so essential in all human lives. Shakespeare, who understood this concordance, the creative conjunction between unit and whole, provided an imaginative and unexpected gestalt perspective:

> If the true concord of well-tuned sounds, by unions married, do offend thine ear, They do but sweetly

> chide thee, who confounds in singleness the parts that thou shouldst bear. Mark how one string, sweet husband to another, Strikes each in each by mutual ordering, Resembling sire and child and happy mother Who all in one, one pleasing note do sing: Whose speechless song, being many, seeming one, Sings this to thee: 'thou single wilt prove none.'

Over half a century ago, Lewis Mumford (1931), a long-time critic of the way the built environment has been put together, blamed "specialists" as a chronic malady of contemporary intellectual life, as servile, dismissing all such as "ignorant of any thought or discipline other than their own, and therefore fundamentally ignorant of essential relationships even within a limited field." He died without changing his mind: all people—individually and collectively—have an obligation to change their minds, and to help accomplish the primary purpose of this book.

Preoccupation with the relationship of parts and wholes is an ancient dialectic, more respectable now in metaphysics than in science (though gaining in the latter). Francois Molnar (1966), a painter, has suggested that the relationship between what he calls the "unit and the whole" is the "fundamental problem of the plastic arts": how materials relate to objects, objects to rooms, rooms to structures, and structures to their context are all essential part-whole relationships to be solved in the plastic arts that create the built environment. One of the reasons for the endurance of this ancient interest is because people are intrigued by how things fit; another is that they like to know how things work and a systemic whole can function only if the parts are smoothly meshed and properly connected. The functional integration of parts into wholes has been summarized as a law: "all things fuse that can fuse, and nothing separates except what must."

THE WHOLE AS AN ORGANIZED, INTEGRATED UNIT

All life, of course, is a matter of such "fusing," of organization, of the use of energy to at least temporarily counter the tendency toward entropy. Many scientists have described biology, the study of life, as a science of organization; ecology, as an offshoot of biology, can be similarly described as a science that studies the organization of the interrelationships between life and its environment. Some writers claim that the most recognizable pattern in evolution is a progressive one towards ever higher levels of organization and ever tighter integration. A healthy built environment could be described in similar terms—and good ones are. A conception of any organized, functional whole is one of integration, of integrity.

An increase in organization, however, immediately engages a conflict between the interests of the individual (private interest, the part) and that of the group (public interest, the whole). Note the ever-recurring conflicts between private designs and public reactions to those designs. The built environment demands an understanding of the **axiom of organization**: organization inevitably demands further organization; organization is inescapable! The emergence of life forms on earth required a wholly new mode or principle of structural integration. Humans, a product of that emergence, and a complex result of such integration, should learn from it—use their intelligence to fashion a world, a built environment, that connects and integrates human activities into a coherent whole.

Organization is, of course, related to form and structure. Organization is in essence disposition of the parts as **means** toward functioning of the whole (the brick and the wall). The functioning of any whole will inevitably require ever closer integration and finer tuning of the interaction of the parts.

LEVELS-OF-INTEGRATION

A convenient way to express this axiom, this challenging dialectic between parts and whole, is in terms of increasing organization leading to higher **levels-of-integration**. The problem of relating parts and wholes within a coherent scheme—and levels-of-integration theory as a solution to that problem—were examined in some detail in Chapters 4 and 5. The reader will remember that ordering nature (or the built environment, as well as other parts and wholes) in a hierarchical continuum provides at least four immediate and apparent advantages: (1) it clearly organizes the content of complex entities and objects; (2) it places each entity in context, making its place in the whole as well as its place as a whole readily apparent; (3) it allows easier discrimination and subsequent analysis of each individual part without losing sight of that part's place in context, in the whole; and (4) it connects the two extremes of organization—of holism and reductionism, of analysis and synthesis, of parts and whole—along an organizational continuum.

Higher levels of integration imply synthesis as well as analysis, a greater synthesis becomes necessary for a constant melding of parts into wholes. Analysis focuses on ever smaller, isolated samples of the universe; analysis pares away the context. Such information needs to be restored when the concern is with the other end of the spectrum, or the linkages between the two ends. Consideration of higher levels provides context, implies interdependence. Connectivity is implicit in notions of interdependence and that in turn implies communication of information, the essence of the interaction process. All of this connotes order, which once more leads naturally to an idea of an integrated system. Order and system are fundamental to each person, each community and society, and to the creation and then study of the built environment. Levels-of-integration is a simple but significant means of coming to grips with complexity, with the fundamental problem of the plastic arts (Young, 1992).

WORLD AND WORLD VIEW: THE ECUMENICAL EYE

The term **world** can be used in a holistic sense as a **region that contains all regions**. Contrast the words universe and world: if everything absolutely, then universe should be used; if everything concerning humans, then world (or earth) is the word. Differentiate further by understanding that a word is needed, not only for specific and imaginable objects, but for whatever the totality may be; universe is such a word. A simple distinguishing feature of the two words then, is their holistic connotations: **world** is the totality as we know it, the bounded earth, and **universe** the totality "as it may be." In the third volume of his fictional *Dune* trilogy, Frank Herbert peers into the future and invents a group that might just be appropriate now, a body called the Commission of Ecumenical Translators. In the C.E.T. 'Commentaries' can be found a declaration that: "The Universe . . . is one thing, a wholeness against which all separations may be identified." Such translations are needed in the here and now—translations that view both universe and world as whole entities, but that use the infinite and incomprehensible whole of the universe to play off against, to see the world as an accessible whole, one that can be comprehended and cared for—and sustained as a life-support system.

1. One world seen by the twentieth century ecumenical eye.

One indication that we have begun can be found in what has been labeled **world view** (Sahtouris, 1989, Harman, 1991). This phrase has been used to designate the environment viewed ecumenically, as image really, a singular image developed separately by the people of each particular culture and even by different individuals within a culture. This can be described as each particular culture's image of itself in relation to an idealized pattern of self and surroundings. Even more appropriate ecologically is **world-as-presence**, a conception that emphasizes that a person's (or a group's) interpretation of the world around is not founded on a visual sense alone, but grounded in all of the senses simultaneously. It circumscribes the world to the extent to which humans are ecumenically aware, an awareness based on the information received by all the senses, mediated by culture and past experience and interpreted by mind.

Noted naturalist and anthropologist Loren Eiseley (1946, 1970) has argued that a sense of world presence was much better developed in pre-industrial humans, who were more intimately engaged with the total natural environment than is true for contemporary, technological, and economic humans, for whom technology and its vocabulary is the primary world. However, people today (should) have a much better grasp of the **global** totality. The pre-industrial world view may have been more integrated, but was often limited to the horizon. Each person's view today is wider, more diffuse and less tied to the immediate environment. Eiseley adds the observation that these two world views need to be reconciled if humanity is to survive; people need to build integratively and to reconcile conditions off-site—increasingly way off site, even around the world (see Boulding, 1991).

World-as-presence is an ecumenical world, where people inhabit the **ecumene**—dwell there knowingly and in sustainable ways. Sustaining lives and sustaining environments in their richness and productivity means sustaining connections, getting involved with, getting to know the world around at all levels, not just the local one, the most simple, the most comfortable.

World-as-presence then is always a holistic conception, since it is a conception of that which exists: this is true whether it is the pre-industrial image of a natural and bounded totality or the technosphere of industrialized civilizations. In contemporary times, "that which exists" is now truly global, ecumenical in its essence, whether perceived as such or not by any particular individual or group. That which exists, world-as-presence, must increasingly be comprehended as world in the whole-earth sense. And, in an age of accelerated interaction, it has become a humanized whole. For the first time in human history the earth is close to totally covered with people, all of whom, at least in a larger sense, are in contact with one another. The contacts may appear superficial and many human conceptions of the globe as superficial, but that is an argument for greater attention to a holistic perspective, an argument for the more incorporative ecumenical eye.

A WIDER AWARENESS: THE EYE OF OSIRIS

Ruth Nanda Anshen described the Eye of Osiris as the inner eye, claiming that humans see in two ways, with their

> physical eyes, in an empirical sensing or seeing by direct observation, and also by an indirect envisaging. [They possess in addition to the two sensing eyes] a single, image-making spiritual and intellectual eye. And it is the in-sight of this inner Eye that purifies and makes sacred our understanding of the nature of things; for that which was shut fast has been opened by the command of the inner Eye. And we become aware that to believe is to see.

It is this inner eye that symbolizes human access to, and understanding of, the larger totalities not easily apprehended by sense data, either personal or from instrumental extension. People must be able to see, not only the brick in their hand, but to visualize all the design potential that brick contains as well as all the possible impacts and consequences, reaching as far in space and time as necessary. The symbolism that impressed Anshen is buttressed further, for the purposes of a holistic view, by the suggestion that the name Osiris might have originally meant "the Seat of the Eye" and also because there exists in the Osirian cycle of legends as well an image of the celestial Eye. If humans are to understand and accept their place in the universe, it will be at least in part by allowing a wider opening of the inner eye: "it is not wisdom to be only wise—and on the inward vision close the eyes."

Universe in such a context is an interesting and varied conception: it can be presented definitively as all absolutely, whatever, wherever. Bucky Fuller (1975)

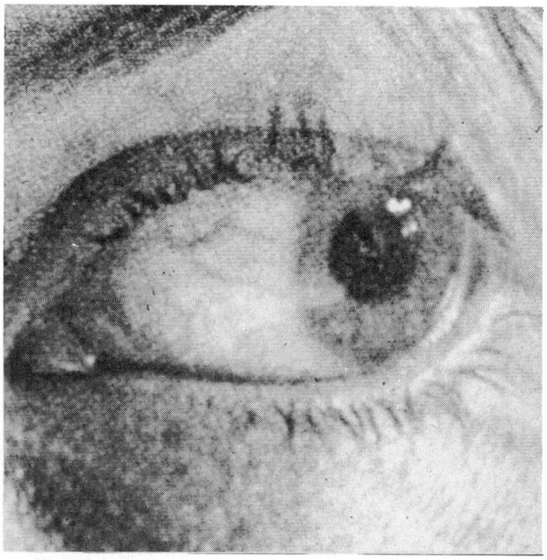

2. The inner eye sees what cannot be seen by the actual physical eye.

noted that the word universe comes from the Latin **vertere**, meaning "to turn" plus the prefix **uni-**,meaning one, then presents a literal meaning: "to turn into one system, into one whole." This interpretation has been widely adopted. With such understanding, no artifact can be viewed in isolation, but each is seen as a microcosmos, and then fitted as one with the macrocosmos, the universe.

THE MEANING OF EVERYTHING

People still have to accept Henry David Thoreau's statement that the universe may be wider than their view of it because it will probably remain so. But, the word osiris has also been defined as meaning many-eyed, which implies that each one of the 5 billion plus humans create within a personal view of the without. In individually created world views, then, if people can't actually prefer the inner to the outer eye, they can at least take that first step by trying to temper their concepts with awareness, by trying to incorporate the image and the meaning filtering through that Osirian eye. This should be a powerful incentive for unification, an incentive that the painter Molnar found in the eye itself, recognizing with the poet Yeats that the individual, solitary imagination may yet make and unmake humankind "and even the world itself, for does not the 'eye alter all' "?

Many students, scholars, philosophers, scientists, people of every persuasion, of the present time and of other times, have strived to view the world and the universe through the Eye of ecumene and that of Osiris. Yet Eiseley (1970) could still say that something is wrong with the human sense of the world presence, claiming that it is still self-centered. In a world of accelerated change, however, the luxury of such limitation is no longer affordable. Twentieth-century humans must grapple with greater complexities and ever-expanding vistas. The brick is no longer just a simple, singular artifact to be objectified with the outer eye, or even to be locally integrated with other bricks by the artist's eye. Humans must also ask: Where was the mud dug? What was disturbed in the process? What was the energy source for the kiln that baked the brick? Did the kiln create a pollution problem? Does the wall, or the house, or other artifact created by organizing the bricks, fit into its context locally and regionally? How fit is the final product? How healthy—or unhealthy—and how far-reaching are the impacts and consequences? Can the whole process be sustained?

The human organism reaches its greatest strength in integrity, in the fullest possible connections to its environment, both natural and built. Certainly, beginnings have been made; the quests for meaning in the greater world, for expansions of awareness, the attempts to connect and integrate parts with wholes, to establish the earth as presence, are extraordinary in terms of the paths that have been followed: the paths to peace followed by Quakers (and others) such as Elise and Kenneth Boulding (Boulding, 1991); the recalling of GAIA as both a hypothesis and a world view (Sagan, 1990); the resurgence of metaphysics as a way of "feeling" the world where disciplines fall short (Smith, 1986); attempts to blend spirituality into the sciences (Harman, 1991), unified perspectives on sociocultural evolution (Laszlo, 1992), repeated efforts to conceive a world community (Holsti, 1985; Eban, 1990; Cetron and Davies, 1991; Meadows, 1991; Clarke, 1992; Piel, 1992; Robertson, 1992), and, of course, ecology as a base for an integrated, contemporary world view (Goldsmith, 1988; Oates, 1989, Sterling, 1990).

We cannot deny these extensions for, as Deikman (1974) has suggested, **consciousness is everything**: humans can be conscious of the existence of wholes without being able to comprehend them precisely through sight or touch or smell or feel. Don't sell the species short; humans are capable of comprehending the entire universe. Consciousness is the reason for trying to apprehend such a whole, including humanity's part in relation to it, and it is the result of so trying.

The time is right for a new philosophy for the conduct of life, one that will consider every facet of human existence as a constituent of an interrelated and progressively integrating whole. It is no accident that consciousness, which gives meaning to everything, can be defined in terms of organization, an axiom (as noted) of all life. The more aware a person is, the more that person is conscious of being an integrate, a part of the whole, rather than an isolate, apart from the whole. The more aware the creators of the built environment are, the more likely it is that such environments will be composed of integrated objects, part of the whole, rather than isolated objects, apart from the whole. Such awareness may be painful, may limit the degrees of freedom of individuals and nations, may indeed be overwhelming in its complexity and even its ultimate understanding.

However, decisions based on greater awareness can be, must be, made now, in the everyday of all human lives. Ecologists, designers, scientists, and lay-people, anyone seriously interested in building environments (and aren't all humans), need to first construct an integrative and inclusive understanding of the environment itself—built and natural—as one. They need to understand, as described in this book, that each component builds on the others, is interdependent with them and the same with the next and the next, creating a sophisticated awareness of every part and every whole—from brick to buildings, from atom to earth.

REFERENCES

Anshen, R, N. 1962. See the prologue written by Anshen to any of the books in the Eye of Osiris series. Simon & Schuster.

Boulding, E. 1991. "The Old and New Transnationalism: An Evolutionary Perspective," *Human Relations*.

Cetron, M. and Davies, O. 1991. "Ceding Sovereignty for the Global Good," *Crystal Globe: The Haves and the Have-Nots of the New World Order*. St. Martin's.

Clarke, A. C. 1992. *How the World Was One: Beyond the Global Village*. Bantam.

Deikman, A. J. 1974. "The Meaning of Everything," *The Nature of Human Consciousness*. Viking Press.

Eban, A. 1990. "Toward a World Community," *Living Philosophies*. Doubleday.

Eiseley, L. 1946. *The Immense Journey*. Random House.

Eiseley, L. 1970. *The Invisible Pyramid*. Scribners.

Fuller, R. B. 1975. *Synergetics: Explorations in the Geometry of Thinking*. Macmillan.

Goldsmith, E. 1988. "The Way: An Ecological World-View," *The Ecologist*.

Harman, W. 1991. "A New World View," *At the Leading Edge: New Visions of Science, Spirituality and Society*. Larson Publications.

Holsti, K. J. 1985. "A City Common to All: Theories of Global Society," *The Dividing Discipline: Hegemony and Diversity in International Theory*. Allen & Unwin.

Laszlo, E. 1992. "Unitary Trends in Sociocultural Evolution," *World Futures*.

Meadows, D. H. 1991. *The Global Citizen*. Island Press.

Molnar, F. 1966. "The Unit and the Whole: Fundamental Problem of the Plastic Arts," *Module Proportion, Symmetry, Rhythm*. Braziller.

Mumford, L. 1931. *The Brown Decades: A Study of the Arts in America, 1865–1895*. Harcourt, Brace.

Oates, D. 1989. *Earth Rising: Ecological Belief in an Age of Science*. Oregon State University Press.

Piel, G. 1992. *Only One World: Our Own to Make and to Keep*. W. H. Freeman.

Robertson, R. 1992. *Globalization*. Sage Publications.

Sagan, D. 1990. "The Living Earth: Hypothesis or World View?" *Biospheres: Metamorphosis of Planet Earth*. McGraw-Hill.

Sahtouris, E. 1989. "Worldviews From Plato to the Present," *GAIA: The Human Journey from Chaos to Cosmos*. Pocket Books.

Smith, Q. 1986. *The Felt Meanings of the World: A Metaphysics of Feeling*. Purdue University Press.

Sterling, S. 1990. "Towards an Ecological World View," *Ethics of Environment and Development: Global Challenges and International Response*. University of Arizona Press.

Young, G. L. 1992. "Between the Atom and the Void: Hierarchy in Human Ecology," *Advances in Human Ecology*.

PART IV

Conspectus

CHAPTER 33

Conspectus on the Built Environment

"Conspectus" is an interesting word. It challenges both author and reader to formulate some "conclusions-in-perspective" about the subject of this book—this evasive and pervasive subject, the built environment.

The previous pages have built—one-by-one, level-by-level—a unique story about a seven-level world. The built environment has been unraveled and restored, layer-by-layer, discussing the **concepts** and **components** which give it substance and meaning.

For each of the seven levels, the uniqueness and definitions of component parts have been analyzed and explored, revealing each part's historical precedents and contemporary issues and challenges. Each section individually, and all collectively, have attempted to increase awareness, interest and participation in the content and contributions people can make, also individually and collectively, in the building of this humanly created world.

Besides analyzing the parts of the built environment, the authors have tried to synthesize or integrate the parts into a meaningful whole. This is a more difficult, but equally important task. Like the pages, chapters and sections of this book need to be integrated one to another, and to all the others, so must also the levels of the built environment. Various concepts were introduced and integrated throughout the text to foster this synthesis. **Levels-of-integration** is a fundamental concept which should help the reader achieve this desirable goal.

The levels of integration concept is represented in the book's graphic logo—the 7 levels within a unified sphere. These levels await the reader's synthesis, the reader's integration. Fulfilling this premise requires both thought and action. Readers, by adding add one symbolic vertical line to the diagram—linking the person at the top to the bottom layer—may begin to fulfill this quest. The line represents the reader's "lifeline." Each lifeline repeatedly penetrates into and through the layers of this interwoven fabric in both time and space.

The concept of **Human-Environmental (H-E) relationships (H-E-R)** was another important unifying theme throughout the book. This theme is reflected in the initial definition and in its graphic representation. It is also part of the words "built environment" or, more explicitly, humanly built-environment. This construction has evolved through time as it will continue to develop into the future. Further evidence of these implied H-E-R relationships can be found in the initials B-E created by the two words built environment. Each letter of the alphabet is an artifact and many are derived from common objects found in the built environment. For example, the letter "B" originally represented a crude place to dwell, a shelter typified by a roof form and entrance; the letter E derives from the representation of a window (reference the two symbols in Figure 1). Putting the two symbols together, the reader ends where the story began—sitting in a room, looking out a window, observing the environment. B-E symbolizes our creative efforts, reminding us of ourselves, our home and the environment. The symbol fosters an inner-view and an outer-view, an introspection and outward-inspection . . . as a conspectus.

Inner and outer suggest a dialectic, which was also implicitly intended as a theme in this book: the

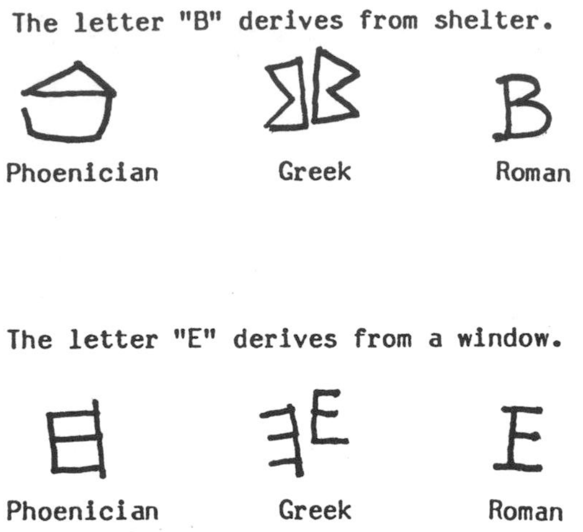

1. Original symbols of the letters B and E.

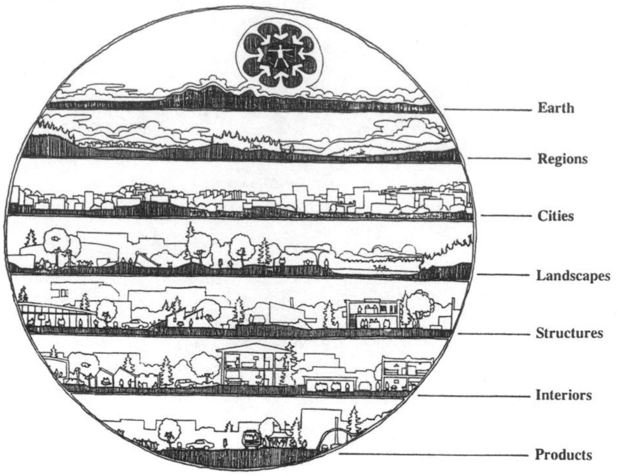

2. Integrative symbol of this study of the built environment.

pairing of contrasting ideas and their ultimate integration: each level with the one below and the one above; parts and wholes; individuals and society; individuals or individual groups and the built environment. A sense of achieved integration leads to questions of health, fitness, and creativity, questions raised repeatedly throughout the book.

A concluding step may be necessary. Each reader might want to look back and/or look forward, or both in a dialectic fashion. Many of the chapters in this text did that, building on the past to integrate the present into the future. Whatever your perspective, we hope these integrative essays on the built environment have opened your eyes to look more carefully through the window provided by this series of dialectic, integrated frames: products—interiors—structures—landscapes—cities—regions—earth.

The built environment is a delicate fabric. The nature of the built environment, like human nature, is delicate and responsive. Most authors tried to insert a sense of the need for professional responsibility by designers and an equal sense of civic responsibility by the public, especially achieved through personal and collaborative involvement in active creation of a better built environment for all.

We hope this creative inquiry into the built environment has also fostered some new awareness, a renewed interest in a topic close to us all, some grounds for optimism . . . and a measure of enjoyment.

Contributing Authors

DIANE ARMPRIEST, Associate Professor of Architecture, University of Cincinnati

TOM J. BARTUSKA, Professor of Architecture, Washington State University

ROBERT M. BARON, Professor of Architecture, University of Idaho

BETSY BOEHM-HSU, Landscape Architect and Planner, Stillwater, Oklahoma

CATHERINE BICKNELL, Associate Professor of Interior Design, Washington State University

KENNETH R. BROOKS, Professor of Landscape Architecture, Kansas State University

WILLIAM BUDD, Associate Professor of Environmental Science and Regional Planning, Washington State University

KENNETH L. CARPER, Professor of Architecture, Washington State University

ELDON H. FRANZ, Associate Professor of Environmental Science and Regional Planning, Washington State University

CARL W. HALL, Deputy Assistant Director for Engineering, National Science Foundation (ret.), Washington, D.C.

BASHIR KAZIMEE, Assistant Professor of Architecture, Washington State University

VICTORIA KOLMODIN, Graphic and Interior Designer, Seattle, Washington

HENRY MATTHEWS, Associate Professor of Architecture, Washington State University

IAN MCHARG, Professor and Chair of Landscape Architecture and Regional Planning (ret.), University of Pennsylvania

NOEL MOFFETT, FRIBA, Architect and Planner, London, England

MICHAEL S. OWEN, Associate Professor of Architecture, Washington State University

ROBERT J. PATTON, Professor and Chair of Architecture, Washington State University (Ret.), Architect, Orcas Island, Washington

LORINDA SILVERSTEIN, Interior Designer, Spokane, Washington

FREDERICK STEINER, Professor and Chair, Department of Planning, Arizona State University

KENNETH STRUCKMEYER, Associate Professor of Landscape Architecture, Washington State University

JO ANN THOMPSON, Professor and Chair of Apparel, Merchandising, and Interior Design, Washington State University

GERALD L. YOUNG, Professor of Biology and Environmental Science/Regional Planning, Washington State University

Index